The**Green**Guide

Auvergne
Rhone Valley

Auzon, Haute-Loire © Christian Guy/imageBROKER/age fotostock

 MICHELIN

THE GREEN GUIDE **AUVERGNE RHONE VALLEY**

Editorial Director	Cynthia Clayton Ochterbeck
Editor	Sophie Friedman
Principal Writer	Terry Marsh
Production Manager	Natasha George
Cartography	Stéphane Anton, Thierry Lemasson
Picture Editor	Yoshimi Kanazawa
Interior Design	Chris Bell
Layout	Natasha George
Cover Design	Chris Bell, Christelle Le Déan
Contact Us	Michelin Travel and Lifestyle North America One Parkway South Greenville, SC 29615 USA travel.lifestyle@us.michelin.com
	Michelin Travel Partner Hannay House 39 Clarendon Road Watford, Herts WD17 1JA UK ✆01923 205240 travelpubsales@uk.michelin.com www.viamichelin.co.uk
Special Sales	For information regarding bulk sales, customized editions and premium sales, please contact us at: travel.lifestyle@us.michelin.com

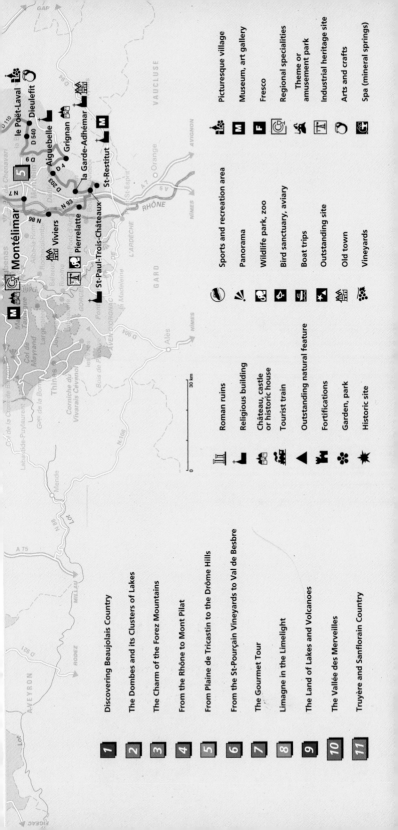

Roman ruins · **Religious building** · **Château, castle or historic house** · **Tourist train** · **Outstanding natural feature** · **Fortifications** · **Garden, park** · **Historic site**

30 km

Sports and recreation area · **Panorama** · **Wildlife park, zoo** · **Bird sanctuary, aviary** · **Boat trips** · **Outstanding site** · **Old town** · **Vineyards**

Picturesque village · **Museum, art gallery** · **Fresco** · **Regional specialities** · **Theme or amusement park** · **Industrial heritage site** · **Arts and crafts** · **Spa (mineral springs)**

1. Discovering Beaujolais Country
2. The Dombes and its Clusters of Lakes
3. The Charm of the Forez Mountains
4. From the Rhône to Mont Pilat
5. From Plaine de Tricastin to the Drôme Hills
6. From the St-Pourçain Vineyards to Val de Besbre
7. The Gourmet Tour
8. Limagne in the Limelight
9. The Land of Lakes and Volcanoes
10. The Vallée des Merveilles
11. Truyère and Sanflorain Country

HOW TO USE THIS GUIDE

PLANNING YOUR TRIP

The blue-tabbed PLANNING YOUR TRIP section gives you **ideas for your trip** and **practical information** to help you organise it. You'll find tours, practical information, a host of outdoor activities, a calendar of events, information on shopping, sightseeing, kids' activities and more.

INTRODUCTION

The orange-tabbed INTRODUCTION section starts by exploring **The Region Today**. The **History** section spans from prehistory to the present day, including information about famous local figures. **Architecture** covers everything from religious and military buildings to traditional rural housing, while the **Literature** section examines writers from the Auvergne. The final section delves into **Nature**.

DISCOVERING

The green-tabbed DISCOVERING section features Principal Sights by region, featuring the most interesting local **Sights**, **Walking Tours**, nearby **Excursions**, and detailed **Driving Tours**. Admission prices shown are normally for a single adult.

ADDRESSES

We've selected from the best hotels, restaurants, cafés, shops, nightlife and entertainment to fit all budgets. See the Legend on the cover flap for an explanation of the price categories. See the back of the guide for an index of hotels and restaurants.

Sidebars

Throughout the guide you will find blue, orange and green-coloured text boxes with lively anecdotes, detailed history and background information.

😋 A Bit of Advice 😋

Green advice boxes found in this guide contain practical tips and handy information relevant to your visit or a sight in the Discovering section.

STAR RATINGS★★★

Michelin has given star ratings for more than 100 years. If you're pressed for time, we recommend you visit the ★★★ or ★★ sights first:

★★★   **Highly recommended**
★★   **Recommended**
★   **Interesting**

MAPS

- 🅖 Regional Driving Tours map.
- 🅖 Region maps.
- 🅖 Maps for major cities and towns.
- 🅖 Local tour maps.

All maps in this guide are oriented north, unless otherwise indicated by a directional arrow. The term "Local Map" refers to a map within the chapter or Tourism Region. A complete list of the maps found in the guide appears at the back of this book.

© Christian Guy/hemis.fr

INTRODUCTION TO AUVERGNE RHÔNE VALLEY

PLANNING YOUR TRIP

DISCOVERING AUVERGNE RHÔNE VALLEY

CONTENTS

Welcome to Auvergne Rhône Valley

Very much at the heart of France, the Auvergne is a largely rural landscape, with 25 percent woodland, 45 percent grassland, 20 percent put to arable use, and only 10 percent given to urbanisation, mainly centred on the city of Clermont-Ferrand. The Rhône valley is long and wide and an important through route for transport. The valley boasts a host of different cultures and is dominated by Lyon, the second city of France.

AUVERGNE

CLERMONT-FERRAND AND MONTS DÔME *(pp94–125)*

Backed by the impressive volcanic uplift of the Monts Dôme, Clermont-Ferrand is the natural capital of the Auvergne. The city has a bright and bustling atmosphere.

MONT-DORE, ARTENSE AND CÉZALLIER *(pp126–158)*

In a magnificent setting below the Puy de Sancy, the spa resort of Mont-Dore lies in the upper reaches of the Dordogne. Artense is a granite plateau bordered by the foothills of the Mont-Dore. Straddling Puy-de-Dôme and Cantal, Cézallier is a characterful region of plateaux and mountains.

AURILLAC, CHÂTAIGNERAIE AND MONTS DU CANTAL *(pp159–187)*

Aurillac is the business and tourist capital of Upper Auvergne, a modern town built around a network of ancient streets and alleys. The verdant Monts du Cantal feature the most beautiful landscapes in the Auvergne, and cover a vast region formed by the largest volcano in France.

ST-FLOUR, SANFLORAIN AND MARGERIDE DU CANTAL *(pp188–197)*

St-Flour, isolated from the rest of the Auvergne by high mountains, is very much immune to external influence, although Sanflorain and Margeride embrace Languedoc-infuenced cultures and traditions.

VELAY AND BRIVADOIS *(pp198–219)*

Surrounded by the iconic volcanic forms of the region, Velay is often considered to be a sub-province of old Languedoc; its most striking attraction is Puy's cathedral. Centred around Brioude, the rurality continues in Brivadois, a place of small plains bordering Puy-de-Dôme and Cantal.

THIERS AND THE LIVRADOIS-FOREZ *(pp220–235)*

The Pay de Thiers – the eponymous town famed for its cutlery – and Livradois-Forez form one of the largest regional parks in France, varied in beauty and natural environment.

VAL D'ALLIER AND ALAGNON *(pp236–247)*

The valleys of Allier and Alagnon boast an exceptional historic and architectural heritage. The lively rivers and magnificent countryside beg to be explored by boat and on foot.

LIMAGNE, PAYS DES COMBRAILLES AND GORGES DE LA SIOULE *(pp248–260)*

Given largely to cereal production, the Limagne lies at the edge of the Massif Central. The Sioule is a tributary of the Allier renowned for the deep-cut gorges in its upper reaches. Combrailles covers almost 100 communities, representing an economic, cultural and social balance.

BOURBONNAIS *(pp261–296)*

Set amid high mountains, the Bourbonnais once performed a defensive role. Today it is a popular centre for golf, walking, cycling, horse riding and other adventure sports.

DRÔME ARDÈCHE

LYON *(pp297–337)*

The "City of Light" is magnificent at every level, from its architectural and cultural heritage, to its contemporary wealth and renown. Situated at the confluence of the Rhône and the Saône, Lyon is a World Heritage Site.

BRESSE AND THE DOMBES *(pp338–351)*

Bresse, famed for its chickens, extends north from the Dombes, into a region where heath and coppice alternate with farmland and marshes. The undulating plateau of La Dombes is characterised by an impervious surface of clay creating over a thousand lakes offering carp, pike and tench fishing opportunities.

BEAUJOLAIS AND THE MONTS DU LYONNAIS *(pp352–365)*

The attractive mountainous region of the Monts du Lyonnais is famed for chestnut groves, with vineyards and orchards in the low-lying valleys. The renown of the Beaujolais wines, extends far beyond the borders of France.

ROANNAIS AND LE FOREZ *(pp366–385)*

The character of the Roanne region is heavily influenced by a long tradition of textile activity and crafts, but, like the Monts du Forez, offers a wide range of scenery and eerie landscapes.

ST-ÉTIENNE AND LE PILAT *(pp386–400)*

Le Pilat has an especially rich and diverse heritage, and has been a regional park since 1974; St-Étienne by contrast thrived for many years on coal mining, before developing as a bicycle manufacturing city.

THE UPPER VIVARAIS AND LE VELAY *(pp401–416)*

Rising to an altitude of 1 754m, the Monts du Vivarais lie to the east of Massif Central, and are bordered to the west by the Monts du Velay, a region of plateaux networked by deep valleys.

THE LOWER VIVARAIS *(pp417–444)*

The limestone landscapes of Bas-Vivarais enjoy a mild, dry climate, and form a region of great contrasts.

DRÔME PROVENÇALE AND THE PRÉALPES DRÔMOISES *(pp446–455)*

Everything here is characteristic of Provence, to which this is the gateway. It belongs to the Rhône-Alpes, but its leanings are very much to the south and everything from olives to nougat evoke the atmosphere of Provence.

VALENTINOIS AND THE LOWER DAUPHINÉ *(pp456–483)*

The Valentinois is a small alluvial plain along the banks of the Rhône, progressively having more affinity with the landscapes to the south the further you go. The same is true of le Bas-Dauphiné, a setting of hilly outcrops and basalt plateaux.

Snowshoeing in Col de Serres, Impradine valley,
Puy Mary in the background,
Parc Naturel Régional des Volcans d'Auvergne
© Christian Guy/hemis.fr

Michelin Driving Tours

LOCAL DRIVES

The following is a selection of the Driving Tours in the Discovering section:

- **A mini tour of the volcanoes**
  See CLERMONT-FERRAND. A half-day tour of the volcanoes around Clermont-Ferrand. 35km/21mi. Visit the Plateau de Chanturgue and the spectacular Puy de Dôme.

- **Northern slopes of the Sancy Range**
  See MASSIF DU SANCY. From Le Mont-Dore. 85km/53mi, round trip – allow a full day. One of the most picturesque areas in the Auvergne.

- **Alpine Pastures of Le Cézallier**
  See CONDAT. From the Rhue Gorge to gentiane country. 80km/50mi – allow one day. Waterfalls, gorges and wildflowers.

- **Monts du Cantal**
  See MONTS DU CANTAL. The Route du Lioran from Aurillac. 55km/34mi – half a day. This agreeable drive makes the most of the Cère and Alagnon valleys.

- **The Puy Mountain range**
  See MONTS DÔME. 120km/75mi – allow a full day. Visit the volcanoes and byways of the Monts Dôme.

- **The Monts de Forez**
  *See THIERS. A full day tour in the Parc Naturel Régional Livradois-Forez. From Thiers via the Col de Béal – vineyards, chateaux and rugged scenery.

- **Approaching the Livradois**
  See ISSOIRE. 45km/28mi round trip – 2h. Issoire, the Château de Parentignat and beyond.

- **The Dauphiné d'Auvergne**
  See ISSOIRE. 60km/37mi – half a day. SW of Issoire between the Cézallier and the Allier valleys.

- **Discover Les Combrailles**
  See RIOM. From Riom, a round trip of 75km/47mi – allow half a day. Gorges, lakes and chateaux.

- **Limagne Bourbonnaise**
  See ST POURÇAIN-SUR-SIOULE. 75km/47mi – allow half a day. Visit medieval villages, manor houses and Romanesque churches.

- **La Bresse**
  See BOURG-EN-BRESSE. A round trip of 104km/65mi – a full day. Explore the small towns surrounding Bourg-en-Bresse and sample the best chicken you are ever likely to taste.

- **The Dombes lakes**
  See LA DOMBES. A round trip of 99km/61mi from Villars-les-Dombes – a full day. Myriad lakes and waterways.

- **Beaujolais vineyards**
  See BEAUJOLAIS. Villefranche-sur-Saône to St-Amour-Bellevue. 98km/61mi – half a day+. The road climbs through the vineyards of Beaujolais and crosses a granite escarpment before descending to the Saône.

- **Monts du Lyonnais**
  See MONTS DU LYONNAIS. From Lyon to St Étienne. 128km/80mi – allow a full day. Explore the hills to the southwest of Lyon.

- **Explore Le Pilat**
  See LE PILAT. From St Étienne to Condrieu. 89km/56mi – half a day. An agreeable way to discover the delights of the Parc Naturel Régional du Pilat.

- **Discover Lauze country**
  See LE MONASTIER-SUR-GAZELLE. Lac d'Issarlès to the Loire's source, and rural architecture.

- **Ardeche Gorge Panoramic Route**
  See GORGES DE L'ARDECHE. 38km/24mi starting from Vallon-Pont-d'Arc – half a day.

- **The Hills of Drôme**
  See CREST. 82km/52mi – 3hrs. Explore the gently sloping hills and discover pretty views and "perched" villages.

- **The Land of Stone Roofs**
  See CRÉMIEU. A tour of the Île Crémieu. 70km/43.5mi – half a day+. Cliffs, lakes, standing stones and country houses.

REGIONAL DRIVES

See the Driving Tours map on the inside back cover.

1 BEAUJOLAIS COUNTRY

Round tour of 129km/80mi leaving from Villefranche-sur-Saône.

This tour of the sun-drenched slopes of Beaujolais naturally starts from Villefranche-sur-Saône, seen by many as the capital of the famous Beaujolais *appellation*.

The former walled city of Belleville is now an important wine-making centre, but it has kept many vestiges of its 12C church. Corcelles Château boasts a fine 17C vat whose aromas will make your head spin! The "Hameau du Vin" and its "station" set up in Romanèche-Thorins form a small museum that pays tribute to the noble traditions that have governed the art of wine-making throughout the centuries, and the adjoining safari park will delight young children.

In Beaujolais each vineyard has developed its own peculiarities: the Fleurie grapes yield a young, lively wine, whereas the Villié-Morgon bottles are usually for laying down. A great many *crus* can be found in Beaujeu, a town wholly devoted to the commerce of wine. After pausing to admire the stunning panorama stretching from Mont Brouilly to the Saône plain, pay a visit to the Salles-Arbuissonnas-en-Beaujolais Priory, dating back to the 10C.

The two châteaux of Montmelas-St-Sorlin and Jarnioux are your next stops, leading to the quaint village of Oingt, perched on a hillside and crowned by a tower.

Driving through the Bagnols vineyards, you reach Châtillon and its 12C stronghold. In St-Jean-des-Vignes, the Museum of Geology explains the origins of the topography which characterises the Beaujolais region and which has produced its unique *terroir*. The tour ends with the village of Chazay-d'Arzergues, from where you can return to Villefranche via Anse.

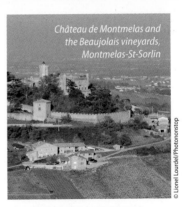

Château de Montmelas and the Beaujolais vineyards, Montmelas-St-Sorlin

© Lionel Lourdel/Photononstop

2 THE DOMBES AND ITS CLUSTERS OF LAKES

Round tour of 155km/96.5mi leaving from Lyon.

Leaving from Lyon, a city that has successfully taken up the challenges of modern life while preserving its historical legacy, this tour is a charming nature trail dotted with ancient monuments. Stop to admire the medieval towers of Rochetaillée Château and then press on to Ars, famous for its bishop who was canonised in 1925 and who is the patron saint of all parish bishops. After visiting Ambérieux-en-Dombes, another town with religious associations awaits you: Châtillon-sur-Chalaronne, where St Vincent de Paul founded the first brotherhood of charity and where you can visit the Apothicairerie. The tour then takes you to the Romanesque church in St-Paul-de-Varax and the 19C Notre-Dame-des-Dombes abbey, which was instrumental in draining the surrounding plains.

The bird sanctuary in Villars-les-Dombes is the perfect spot for a family outing, and the brick castle in Le Montellier is an impressive sight indeed.

The hilltop village of Pérouges, circled by ancient ramparts and crossed by winding streets, is often used as a backdrop for historical films. Finally, after a halt in Montluel, you can return to the city of Lyon and its many attractions.

③ THE CHARM OF THE FOREZ MOUNTAINS

Round tour of 200km/124mi leaving from Roanne.

The region, generally referred to as Forez, comprises a range of mountains, a series of plains, a natural park and a web of meandering roads. This tour begins in Roanne, a Roman city today known for its textile and food-processing industries. After a short drive through vineyards that produce a lively rosé wine, you reach pretty Ambierle with its old Cluniac priory, Flamboyant Gothic church and museum devoted to traditional costumes and lore. The fortified village of St-Haon-le-Châtel features some interesting Renaissance houses and the nearby Tache Dam, which dominates the local vineyards, and is the starting point for charming country walks across the Monts de la Madeleine. Driving down the Gorges Roannaises de la Loire, you come to St-Maurice-sur-Loire, where the church apse boasts remarkable 13C frescoes and the keep commands a fine panorama of the gorges. Also steeped in history are the two towns of St-Germain-Laval and Pommiers and their intricate network of cobbled alleys. After visiting the Château de la Vigne et du Vin in Boën, drop by the fortress in Sail-sous-Couzan and feast your eyes on the Forez plain. Château de la Bastie-d'Urfé was once the residence of the famed writer Honoré d'Urfé, whose romantic novel *L'Astrée* set a new literary trend in early-17C France. A more austere atmosphere permeates the 14C church in Champdieu and the old convent of Montbrison, dominated by its 18C dome and circled by stone ramparts. Although the living quarters within the castle were destroyed by a fire in the 18C, Montrond-les-Bains is a pleasant fortified city whose spa is ideal for treating diabetes and other disorders. After a breath of fresh air, strolling through the bird sanctuary at the Écopôle du Forez, resume your history lesson by exploring the ancient city of Feurs and visiting its Gallo-Roman Museum of Archaeology. The medieval hamlet of Villerest has a curious museum retracing the history of fire and its domestic uses through the ages. The Loire gorges cutting across the rocky plains lead you back to Roanne, where the tour can be nicely concluded with a boat ride.

④ FROM THE RHÔNE TO MONT PILAT

Round tour of 170km/105.6mi leaving from St-Étienne.

The tour begins in St-Étienne, a city with deep-rooted traditions that has kept abreast of the times, and houses an admirable Museum of Modern Art. Your journey then takes you to St-Chamond, the site of a factory producing armoured vehicles, Rive-de-Gier and St-Genis-Laval. You approach Lyon via the antique city of Oullins. As for the modern metropolis, frequently dubbed France's second capital, it offers a host of museums, cafés, restaurants and historical monuments. Further on, you reach Vienne, yet another Roman city, whose Jazz Festival enjoys a prestigious reputation. At your next stop, Condrieu, take a seat on the sunny quays and sip a glass of *viognier*, the local white wine, as you watch boats gliding into port. After visiting Pélussin and its museum, do not miss the stunning vista afforded by the Crêt de l'Œillon, extending over the Rhône valley and Crêt de la Perdrix. For a sweeping panorama, try the viewing table on the Pics du Mézenc. If weather conditions are favourable, why not tackle one of the skiing slopes at Le Bessat or venture down the formidable gully appropriately named "Chasm of Hell"? Round off the tour with a pleasant drive back to St-Étienne and a visit to the famous confectioner Weiss, whose chocolates will literally melt in your mouth.

5 FROM PLAINE DE TRICASTIN TO THE DRÔME HILLS

Round tour of 210km/130mi leaving from Montélimar.

The starting point of this tour is Montélimar, world famous for its delicious nougat topped with chopped hazelnuts and almonds! But the city is also a popular tourist destination, and has many attractions, including the Miniature Museum. The former episcopal town of Viviers leads to the Plaine du Tricastin, where Pierrelatte, encircled by three mountainous ranges, is home to a nuclear power plant, not to mention a crocodile farm. In St-Paul-Trois-Châteaux, make a point of visiting the cathedral and the Maison de la Truffe. For a change of scene, after admiring the church in St-Restitut, take time to check out the wine cellars at Le Cellier des Dauphins. History lovers will appreciate the White Penitents' Chapel in La Garde-Adhémar and the abbey church at Notre-Dame-d'Aiguebelle. You drive through a series of charming villages, including La Bégude-de-Mézenc, Le Poët-Laval, a medieval gem housing a former commandery, and Dieulefit, a bustling city dedicated to local arts and crafts. After leaving Soyons, you head for the Saoû forest at the foot of a sheer cliff face and offering pleasantly shaded walks. Or you may prefer to seek refuge in the keep at Crest. Finally, your drive back to nougat country introduces you to the pretty towns of Marsanne and Mirmande.

6 ST-POURÇAIN VINEYARDS TO VAL DE BESBRE

Round tour of 160km/99.5mi leaving from St-Pourçain.

The vineyards around St-Pourçain yield a lively, fragrant white wine, which it is your duty to taste...in moderation! More academic visitors will enjoy studying the numerous medieval frescoes that enliven the tiny churches dotted around St-Pourçain; the murals at Le Saulcet deserve special mention. After your exertions at the sports and leisure park in Le Pal, follow the course of the River Besbre, which guides you to Thoury and its pink-sandstone castle, to Jaligny and its Renaissance château, and finally to Lapalisse, a popular place among anglers for its waters teeming with trout and carp.

7 THE GOURMET TOUR

Round tour of 250km/155mi leaving from Ambert.

This tour pays tribute to Fourme d'Ambert, a deliciously smooth blue cheese made with cow's milk that is typical of the region. Made around Ambert and on the Forez heights, this delicacy is presented in the shape of a large circular slab speckled with blue and is lesser known but more subtle than the traditional Roquefort cheese. The nearby town of Thiers is the country's leading knife manufacturer and you will be ideally equipped to carve a generous slice of Fourme d'Ambert and savour it along the banks of the River Dore.

8 LIMAGNE IN THE LIMELIGHT

Round tour of 250km/155mi leaving from Clermont-Ferrand.

After leaving Clermont-Ferrand, the bustling yet discreet capital of the Auvergne, you will encounter the

Thiers

© Christian Guy/imageBROKER/age fotostock

15

curious lava flows of Volvic stone where the famous mineral water has its source. Your next stop is Billom, where a pleasant climate combines with a fine morning mist and a soft light reminiscent of the great Impressionist works. This stunning landscape is enhanced by the golden sunflower fields contrasting with the brown earthy plains, overshadowed by the volcanic range looming above the horizon.

Billom
© Christian Guy/imageBROKER/age fotostock

9 THE LAND OF LAKES AND VOLCANOES

Round tour of 415km/258mi leaving from Le Mont-Dore.

Whatever your reasons for visiting the Auvergne, you can but succumb to the charm of Puy de Sancy, the highest peak towering above central France. The Dore mountain range and Pays des Couzes form a natural setting of outstanding beauty, enclosing a cluster of deep blue lakes with shimmering waters (Guéry, Servière, Aydat, Godivelle, Chambon). The surrounding villages too are worthy of note: Montpeyroux and its colony of artists and craftsmen; St-Nectaire, where the local cow's milk cheese is matured on a bed of rye; Besse and its Alpine skiing resort; and lastly Orcival, graced with a fine Romanesque basilica.

10 THE VALLÉE DES MERVEILLES

Round tour of 335km/208mi leaving from Brioude.

Before setting out on this tour, pay a visit to the Basilique St-Julien in Brioude and admire the intricate carvings adorning the Romanesque east end. Following the peaceful, lazy meanderings of the Sénouire, you discover the abbeys of Lavaudieu and La Chaise-Dieu, where the chancel houses early splendid 16C tapestries from Brussels and Arras.

The Allier, on the other hand, is an impetuous river whose waters swell between Monistrol and Lavoûte-Chilhac. While the more adventurous tourists engage in a spot of canoeing or rafting, ramblers and cyclists can pause to admire the Romanesque church of Chanteuges and the flower-decked streets in St-Arcons.

The pretty painted churches dotted around the Haut-Allier region have earned it the name of "Vallée des Merveilles" (Valley of Wonders).

As you continue on the tour, you come upon Le Puy-en-Velay, one of the most extraordinary and unforgettable sites in France, sitting like a crown atop the landscape it dominates.

11 TRUYÈRE AND SANFLORAIN COUNTRY

Round tour of 270km/168mi leaving from St-Flour.

St-Flour, the starting-point of the tour, is perched on a basaltic plateau that faces south. You will be charmed by the landscapes around Les Margerides and by the chaotic course of the Truyère, which has carved sharp chasms between the Cantal and Aveyron rivers. After reaching Pierrefort and tucking into a tasty *aligot* consisting of mashed potatoes seasoned with garlic and Cantal cheese, you can pay a visit to the spa resort of Chaudes-Aigues. From the fine medieval castle of Pesteils, perched on its rocky outcrop, drive up to Plomb du Cantal, the highest summit of the range, where you will be greeted by a calm, soothing atmosphere and a sweeping expanse of lush countryside.

When and Where To Go

WHEN TO GO

The region covered by this guide presents a great variety of climatic conditions in all seasons. Spring weather is unpredictable: there may be heavy snowfall at higher altitudes while at the same time the valleys are fragrant with fruit blossom. In late spring, the Auvergne is outstandingly beautiful, as melting snow swells the rivers. The summer months are generally sunny and warm. The Ardèche gorges are especially popular in July and August, when many small craft take to the water.

Along the Rhône, the weather in autumn is usually mild, but in other regions (like the Cévennes) heavy rain is likely. The colours in the Puys, Livradois and Dombes regions are especially vibrant at this time of year. Winter brings snow to the high peaks, where it can cover the ground for several months, closing off mountain passes to traffic. The wind in the region of the volcanoes of Auvergne can be intense. But south of Valence and in the southern part of the Cantal region, the climate is milder, and winter skies are usually clear thanks to winds blowing up from the Mediterranean.

The city of Lyon seems to have a climate all its own: summers are hot and sticky, with thick morning mists, and in the winter a mist seems to hang overhead all day. Spring and autumn are the best times to visit the city, as the weather is usually clearer then.

WEATHER FORECAST

For **Météo-France** (national weather bureau, www.meteo.fr) reports in French, dial 3250, then select from the recorded choices (€2.99 per call + network provider's charge). Information about the weather can be downloaded to mobile phones from http://mobile.meteofrance.com.

For **departmental forecasts** dial ℘08 92 68 02… followed by the number of the *département*: Ain 01; Allier 03; Ardèche 04; Cantal 15; Drôme 26; Haute-Loire 43; Isère 38; Loire 42; Puy-de-Dôme 63; Rhône 69.

Mountain weather forecast: ℘3250 (select 4); for information about snow cover and avalanche risk, ℘08 92 68 10 20.

Weather forecast for microlights and light aircraft ℘08 92 68 10 14. Information is also available on www.meteo.fr.

THEMED TOURS
HISTORY

Routes Historiques are signposted local itineraries following an architectural and historical theme, accompanied by an explanatory booklet available from local tourist offices.

The **Route Historique des Châteaux d'Auvergne** takes in a selection of the best castles in the region: imposing ruined fortresses as well as elegant manor houses; some of these house exhibitions, organise concerts and sports events; others offer bed-and-breakfast accommodation or are open late in the evening to enable visitors to appreciate their fascinating atmosphere. There are six itineraries: Bourbonnais, Limagnes, Volcans, Livradois-Forez, Montagnes Cantaliennes and Haute-Loire.
🛈 Association de la Route Historique des Châteaux d'Auvergne: Comité Régional de Développement Touristique d'Auvergne, 7 allée Pierre de Fermat, 63178 Aubière. ℘04 73 29 29 84; www.route-chateaux-auvergne.org.

On the way to Santiago de Compostela – Pilgrims on their way to pay homage to the relics of St James have come through the Auvergne since the Middle Ages. Two itineraries converge on Le Puy-en-Velay: one from Lyon via

St-Ferréol and Monistrol-sur-Loire, the other from Cluny via Pommiers and Montbrison. Beyond Le Puy, the *via podiensis* (GR 65) leads to Roncevaux and the Spanish border (28 days on foot).

ARCHITECTURAL HERITAGE

Viaducts – The introduction of railways in this mountainous region meant the construction of several impressive viaducts spanning the Truyère, the Sioule, the Allier and the Besbre rivers. Six of these are now listed among the region's historic monuments: Garabit and Barajol (Cantal), La Récoumène (Haute-Loire), Les Fades (Puy-de-Dôme) and Neuvial and Rouzat (Allier).

TRADITIONS AND NATURE

The **Route des Jardins du Massif Central** links 27 botanical gardens dedicated to the preservation and promotion of the Massif Central's vegetation.
🛈 Association des Jardins du Massif central, Le Jardin pour la Terre, Terre Neyre, 63220 Arlanc. ℘04 73 65 00 71; www.jardinsmassifcentral.com.

The **Route des Métiers en Livradois-Forez** winds its way across the Parc naturel regional du Livradois-Forez, linking authentic workshops where ancient crafts are perpetuated: Maison des Couteliers (cutlers' workshop) in Thiers, Maison du Verre (glass workshop) in Puy-Guillaume, Moulin Richard-de-Bas (traditional mill) and Musée de la Fourme (cheese museum) in Ambert.
🛈 Parc naturel regional du Livradois-Forez, Maison du Parc, 63880 Saint-Gervais-sous-Meymont ℘04 73 95 57 57; www.parc-livradois-forez.org.

The **Route des Villes d'Eaux** links the region's numerous spas.
🛈 La Route des Villes d'Eaux, 8 avenue Anatole-France, 63130 Royat ℘04 73 34 72 80; www.villesdeaux.com.

The **Route des Fromages** is a gourmet tour of the main farming areas producing the best cheeses the Auvergne has to offer: Saint-Nectaire, Fourme d'Ambert, Bleu d'Auvergne, Cantal and Salers.
🛈 Association des fromages AOP d'Auvergne, 9 allée Pierre de Fermat, 63170 Aubière. ℘04 71 48 66 15; www.fromages-aop-auvergne.com.

WINE-TASTING

Côtes d'Auvergne (Puy-de-Dôme) – Some 1 240ha produce five different wines: Madargue, Châteaugay and Chanturgue north of Clermont-Ferrand, Corent and Boudes south of Clermont- Ferrand.
The Fédération Viticole du Puy-de-Dôme, place de la Mairie, 63340 Boudes ℘04 73 96 49 00, proposes a **Route des Vins** divided into three itineraries exploring the Riomois, Clermontois and Lembronnais areas.

Saint-Pourçain (Allier) – This is one of the oldest wine-growing areas in France; destroyed by phylloxera at the end of the 19C, the vines have been gradually replanted and the vineyards now cover 600ha.
🛈 Office de Tourisme, 29 Rue Marcelin Berthelot, 03500 Saint-Pourcain-sur-Sioule. ℘04 70 45 32 73; www.payssaintpourcinois.fr.

The following centres provide information about wine-growing in the Rhône valley:
♦ **Beaujolais** – Le Pays Beaujolais (bookings of tours and accommodation, guides/interpreters), contact – Maison du Tourisme, 96 rue de la Sous-Préfecture, 69400 Villefranche-sur-Saône. ℘04 74 07 27 40; www.villefranche-beaujolais.fr.
♦ **Côtes-du-Rhône** – You can browse at www.vins-rhone.com, or to obtain a list of cellars, wine-tour itineraries etc. contact the – Maison des Vins de Tournon, 16 avenue du Maréchal-Foch, 07300

Tournon-sur-Rhône.
℘04 75 07 91 59
– Maison des Vins d'Avignon, 6 rue des Trois-Faucons, 84024 Avignon. ℘04 90 27 24 00.

TOURIST TRAINS

These offer the opportunity of discovering some spectacular scenery, away from busy modern communications routes. Contacts include:

Chemin de Fer du Vivarais
Gare de Tournon St-Jean, Route du Grand Pont, 07 300 St-Jean de Muzols. ℘04 75 06 07 00; http://trainardeche. fr. Three viaducts, two tunnels and spectacular views.

Chemin de Fer Touristique du Haut-Rhône Montalieu Vercieu. ℘04 78 81 84 30; www.cft-hr.com. 50min steam-train journey between Montalieu and the Pont de Sault-Brenaz.

Les Voies Ferrées du Velay contact relevant Office de Tourisme – see https://velay-express.fr. Several daily trips between Tence and Ste-Agrève along the Lignon valley (mid July-August).

Chemin de Fer Touristique d'Anse
560 route de Saint Bernard, BP 10046, 69480 Anse. ℘04 74 60 26 16 (tourist office); www.cftanse.fr – runs from Easter to the last Sunday in October on Sundays, holidays (also Saturdays from June to September) in the afternoon.

Train Touristique des Monts du Lyonnais 5 place de la Gare, 69610 Sainte Foy l'Argentière. ℘06 07 27 88 42; http://train-touristique-monts-lyonnais.com. Exhibition of railway stock in Ste-Foy-l'Argentière station (end of the line). In addition, a steam train runs on Sundays from June to September.

Train Touristique de l'Ardèche Méridionale Viaduc 07, Gare de Vogüé, 07200 Vogüé. ℘04 75 37 03 52. Picturesque 14km/8.7mi journey from Vogüé to St-Jean-le-Centenier.

Train de la Découverte du Livradois-Forez – Several possibilities along the Dore valley between Courpière and La Chaise-Dieu via Ambert. AGRIVAP "train touristique", La Gare, Place Jean-Berne, 63600 Ambert ℘04 73 82 43 88; www.agrivap.fr.

Train Touristique des Gorges de l'Allier – Magnificent unspoilt landscapes unfold on this journey between Langeac and Langogne. The train runs through 53 tunnels and negotiates steep slopes and tricky bends. ℘04 71 77 70 17; www.langogne.com/train.htm.

Le Train Touristique Garabit – Guided tour from Aurillac via Le Lioran, Murat and the Garabit viaduct where the train stops for a while. Office de Tourisme du Pays de Saint-Flour, 17 bis, place Armes 15100 Saint Flour. ℘04 71 60 22 50; www.pays-saint-flour.fr.

Autorail Touristique Gentiane Express – A fine journey through the summer pastures of the famous Salers cattle, from Bort-les-Orgues to Lugarde via Riom-ès-Montagne and the Barajol viaduct. Daily in July and August, Sundays and holidays from mid April to September. Office du Tourisme de Bort-les-Orgues (℘05 55 96 02 49), or Office du tourisme du Pays Gentiane, Riom-ès-Montagnes. (℘04 71 78 07 37).

RIVER AND CANAL CRUISING
SELF-SKIPPERED HOLIDAYS

Boats can be hired in Port-sur-Saône, Gray, St-Jean-de-Losne and Roanne to explore the Saône and the Rhône from Corre to Port-St-Louis-du-Rhône. The main harbours on the way are Lyon, Les Roches-de-Condrieu and Valence l'Épervière; a basic service is available in St-Germain-au-Mont-d'Or, Tournon-sur-Rhône, Viviers and Avignon. In

the Lyon region, a series of mooring places along the Saône enables visitors to enjoy the surrounding area. Information is available from **Bureau de la Plaisance**, 2 rue de la Quarantaine, 69321 Lyon Cedex 05 ℘04 72 56 59 28.
The stretch of canal between Roanne and Briennon offers a pleasant journey with several locks along the way; contact **Marins d'Eau Douce**, Port de Plaisance, 42720 Briennon. ℘04 77 69 92 92. www.lesmarinsdeaudouce.fr.

CRUISES

Lyon City Boat offer cruises and boat trips along the Rhône and Saône rivers; information and bookings, 13 bis quai Rambaud, 69002 Lyon ℘04 78 42 96 81; www.lyoncityboat.com.

Information can also be obtained from Avignon Tourist Office (℘04 32 74 32 74; www.avignon-tourisme.com).

NATURE PARKS AND RESERVES

PARKS

The region described in this guide includes four regional nature parks:

♦ **Parc Naturel Régional des Volcans d'Auvergne** (&see Parc Naturel Régional des VOLCANS D'AUVERGNE). Château Montlosier 63970 Aydat. ℘04 73 65 64 00; www.parcdesvolcans.fr.

♦ **Parc Naturel Régional Livradois-Forez** (&see Monts du FOREZ). For information, contact the Maison du Parc, 63880 St-Gervais-sous-Meymont. ℘04 73 95 57 57; www.parc-livradois-forez.org.

♦ **Parc Naturel Regional du Pilat** (&see Le PILAT). For information, contact the Maison du Parc, Moulin de Virieu, 2 rue Benaÿ, 42410 Pélussin. ℘04 74 87 52 01; www.parc-naturel-pilat.fr.

♦ **Parc Naturel Régional des Monts d'Ardèche** (&see AUBENAS). This is the most recently created of the four parks. Domaine de Rochemure, 07380 Jaujac ℘04 75 36 38 60; www.parc-monts-ardeche.fr.

NATURE RESERVES AND NATURE-DISCOVERY CENTRES

The following organise activities on the theme of nature:

♦ **Vallée de Chaudefour**, Maison de la Réserve Naturelle de la Vallée de Chaudefour, Parc Naturel Regional des Volcans d'Auvergne, 63790 Chambon-sur-Lac. ℘04 73 88 68 80; www.parcdesvolcans.fr – guided tours (🐕 dogs are not allowed, even on a lead).

♦ **Sagnes de la Godivelle**, Montlosier, 63970 Aydat. ℘04 73 65 64 26, or 04 73 71 78 12 (during Jul-Aug, last two weekends in Jun and first two weekends in Sept).

♦ **Val d'Allier**, Outings are organised by the Ligue pour la Protection des Oiseaux. Espace Nature du Val d'Allier, 8 boulevard de Nomazy, 03000 Moulins ℘04 73 36 39 79; www.lpo-auvergne.org.

♦ **Centre permanent d'Initiatives pour l'Environnement d'Auvergne**, Château Saint-Étienne, 15000, Aurillac. ℘04 71 48 49 09; www.cpie15.com.

♦ **Office National des Forêts**, Direction territoriale Auvergne-Rhône-Alpes, 143, rue Pierre Corneille, 69406 Lyon. ℘04 72 60 11 90; www.onf.fr/auvrhal. Rambles through Tronçais forest.

♦ **Espace Nature du Val d'Allier**, &see address above.

What to See and Do

OUTDOOR FUN
AERIAL VIEWS
Hot-air balloons
Contact local tourist offices, or:

- **France Montgolfières**, 4 bis rue du Saussis, 21140 Semur-en-Auxois. ✆03 80 97 38 61; www.franceballoons.com.

- **Objectif: Vols en Montgolfière**, 12, rue des Blés, 37150 Bléré. ✆02 47 57 19 77; www.objectif-ciel-montgolfiere.com.

- **Quatre Vents**, rue du Commerce, 63230 Pontgibaud. ✆04 73 62 29 30; www.vol-montgolfiere-auvergne.fr.

- **Montgolfière Club du Velay**, Pouzols, 43200 St-Jeures. ✆04 71 65 47 89; www.montgolfiere-club-velay.com.

- **Les Montgolfières d'Annonay**, 23 Rue Saint-Michel, 07102 Annonay. ✆04 75 67 57 56; www.lesmontgolfieresdannonay.fr.

- **Centre Aérostatique de l'Ardèche**, 07430 St Clair. ✆04 75 33 71 30.

- **Montgolfière en Velay**, 55 avenue des Champs-Élysées, 43770 Chadrac. ✆06 06 83 43 43; www.montgolfiere-en-velay.fr.

Light aircraft and gliders
- **Aéroclub d'Auvergne**, Avenue Youri Gagarine, 63100 Clermont-Ferrand. ✆04 73 92 00 56; www.aeroclubauvergne.fr.

- **Aéro-club Pierre-Herbaud**, Aérodrome d'Issoire, 63500 Issoire. ✆04 73 89 16 62; www.aeroclub-issoire.fr.

- **Aéro-club du Livradois**, Le Poyet, 63600 Ambert. ✆04 73 82 01 64; http://aeroclub-ambert.fr.

Helicopters
- **Héli Volcan**, Aéroport de Clermont-Ferrand, 63510 Aulnat. ✆04 73 55 03 60; www.helivolcan.com.

Microlights
- **Aéro-club Combrailles**, École de pilotage, 63640 St-Priest-des-Champs. ✆04 73 86 84 52.

- **Air Libre**, Vallée Verte, place de l'Office de tourisme, 63710 St-Nectaire. ✆04 73 88 57 95; flights over the Massif du Sancy.

Hang-gliding and paragliding
The Auvergne mountains and the Massif du Mézenc in the Ardèche offer exceptional opportunities to practise hang-gliding and paragliding.

Ligue Auvergne de Vol Libre, 4 chemin des Garennes, 63960 Veyre-Monton. ✆04 73 69 72 00.

École Ailes Libres Auvergne Limousin, 63730 Les Martres de Veyre. ✆04 73 39 72 72 or 06 87 79 42 74. Departures are from the Camping de La Font Bleix.

Archipel Volcans, 19 route de Clermont, Laschamps, 63122 St-Genes-Champanelle. ✆04 73 62 15 15; www.archipel-volcans.com; other facilities include hot-air ballooning, rambling, snowshoeing, mountain biking, etc.

Espace Volcan, Route du Col de Moreno, Laschamps, 63122 St-Genès-Champanelle. ✆04 73 62 26 00. www.espacevolcan.fr.

Action Parapente, 1 Sommet du Puy de Dôme, 63870 Orcines. ✆06 75 94 61 06; www.action-parapente.fr.

Cycling in Aubenas

© Jon Arnold Images/hemis.fr

Delta Auvergne, La Fougedoire, 63600 Ambert. ℘04 73 82 91 41 or 06 80 40 07 00. www.deltaplane.net.

Barbule, École Ardéchoise de Parapente, 07140 Les Vans ℘04 75 39 36 67. www.parapente-fr.com/barbule.

CYCLING AND MOUNTAIN BIKING

Tourist offices should be able to provide lists of local firms that hire bicycles and mountain bikes (*vélos tout terrain,* or VTT). Some SNCF railway stations organise bike rentals, and mountain bikes can be hired in season from information points within the Pilat park. A leaflet giving details is available from railway stations. Local tourist offices also have details of suggested cycle and mountain bike routes.

Useful Addresses
* **Fédération Française de Cyclotourisme**, 12 rue Louis-Bertrand, 94200 Ivry-sur-Seine ℘01 56 20 88 88. www.ffct.org.
* **Fédération Française de Cyclisme,** Vélodrome National de Saint-Quentin-en-Yvelines, 1 rue Laurent Fignon, 78 180 Montigny le Bretonneux. ℘08 11 04 05 55. www.ffc.fr.

CAVING

Comité Départemental de Spéléologie, route d'Enval, 63200 Malauzat. ℘0890 719 223 (€2.99 per call + network provider's charge).

FISHING

The abundance of rivers, streams and lakes provides anglers with many opportunities to catch salmon, trout, perch, tench or carp; whatever the site, however, it is necessary to be affiliated to a fishing association and to abide by fishing regulations. Daily fishing permits are available in certain areas. Contact the local tourist office or apply to the local fishing federations or fishing tackle stores.

Useful Addresses
Fédération Nationale de la Pêche en France et de la protection du milieu aquatique, 17 rue Bergère, 75009 Paris. ℘01 48 24 96 00; www.federationpeche.fr.
* **Allier** – 47 boulevard Ledru Rollin, 03500 St-Pourçain-sur-Sioule. ℘04 70 47 51 55; www.federation-peche-allier.fr.
* **Cantal** – 14 allée du Vialenc, 15000 Aurillac. ℘04 71 48 19 25; www.cantal-peche.com.
* **Haute-Loire** – 32 rue Henri-Chas, Le Val-Vert, 43000 Le Puy-en-Velay. ℘04 71 09 09 44; www.pechehauteloire.fr.
* **Loire** – 6 allée de l'Europe, 42480 La Fouillouse. ℘04 77 02 20 00; www.federationpeche42.fr.
* **Puy-de-Dôme** – 14, allée des Eaux et Forêts, Site de Marmilhat Sud, 63370 Lempdes. ℘04 73 92 56 29; www.peche63.com. The federation's annual publication, *Le Pêcheur du Puy-de-Dôme,* includes a map of rivers and lakes.
* **Rhône** – 1 Allée du Levant, 69890 La Tour de Salvagny. ℘04 72 18 01 80. www.federation-peche-rhone.fr.

Forêt de Saoû near Crest, Drôme

GOLF

For locations, addresses and telephone numbers of golf courses in France, consult the map *Golfs, Les Parcours Français* published by Éditions Plein-Sud based on *Michelin map 989*.

Fédération Française de Golf, 68 rue Anatole-France, 92309 Levallois-Perret Cedex ✆01 41 49 77 00. www.ffgolf.org.

WALKING

Exploring the region on foot is an enchanting way of discovering the landscape and the life of the countryside. Many long-distance footpaths *(Sentiers de Grande Randonnée* or "GR")* cover the area described in this guide. Short-distance paths *(Sentiers de Petite Randonnée* or "PR")* and medium-distance paths offer walks ranging from a few hours to a couple of days.

Useful Addresses
Fédération Française de la Randonnée Pédestre (*64 rue du Dessous des Berges, 75013 Paris . ✆01 44 89 93 90; www.ffrandonnee.fr*)
A collection of *Topo-Guides* showing the routes and the time needed, details of access points, accommodation and places of interest en route for footpaths throughout France is published by the federation; some of the guides have

been translated into English and are available in bookshops in the region. You can also order the catalogue of publications online – see above.

- **Comité Départemental de Randonnée Pédestre de l'Allier**, Centre Éric Tabarly, 03300 Cusset ✆04 70 96 00 26; http://ffrandonnee-allier.fr.
- **Comité Départemental de Randonnée Pédestre du Cantal**, Maison des Sports, 15000 Aurillac. ✆04 71 63 75 29; http://rando.cantal.fr.
- **Comité Départemental de Randonnée Pédestre de Haute-Loire**, 21, rue Collège, 43000 Le Puy-en-Velay. ✆04 71 04 15 95; www.rando-hauteloire.fr.
- **Comité Départemental de Randonnée Pédestre du Puy-de-Dôme**, Centre d'Affaires Auvergne 15 Bis Rue du Pré La Reine, 63000 Clermont-Ferrand. ✆04 73 91 94 01; www. ffrandonnee-puy-de-dome.fr.

Chamina, 5 rue Pierre-le-Vénérable, 63057 Clermont-Ferrand Cedex 1 ✆04 73 92 81 44; www.chamina.com. This association promotes walking and mountain biking throughout the Massif Central region and the western slopes of the Rhône valley.
Cicerone Press in the UK (*www. cicerone.co.uk*) produce a number of walking guides to areas in and around the Auvergne.

Donkeys and Horse-drawn Caravans

How about a **walk with a donkey** for company and to amuse the children? Contact the **Fédération Nationale Ânes et Randonnées** (FNAR): www.ane-et-rando.com, or the **Comité Départemental du Tourisme** in Privas at ✆04 75 64 04 66, for the list of places where donkeys may be hired.

Horse-drawn caravans, complete with bunk beds and kitchen facilities, may be hired in some areas to follow a planned itinerary; contact the Parc naturel régional du Pilat ✆04 74 87 52 00 or local tourist offices.

Play It Safe

Safety first is the rule for everyone when it comes to exploring the mountains as a climber, skier or walker. The risks associated with avalanches, mudslides, falling rocks, bad weather, fog, glacially cold waters, the dangers of becoming lost or miscalculating distances, should not be underestimated.

Avalanches occur naturally when the upper layer of snow is unstable, in particular after heavy snowfalls, and may be set off by the passage of numerous skiers or walkers over a precise spot. A scale of risk, from 1 to 5, has been developed and is posted daily at resorts and the base of walking trails. It is important to consult this *Bulletin Neige et Avalanche* (BNA) before setting off on any expeditions cross-country or *hors-piste*.

Lightning storms are often preceded by sudden gusts of wind, and put climbers and walkers in danger. In the event, avoid high ground, and do not move along a ridge top; do not seek shelter under overhanging rocks, isolated trees in otherwise open areas, at the entrance to caves or other openings in the rocks, or in the proximity of metal fences or gates. A car is a good refuge.

KARTING

- **Speed2Max,** 160 av. Jean Mermoz, 63100 Clermont-Ferrand. ✆04 73 14 14 28; www.speed-2-max.fr.
- **Kartingliss,** 11 rue Louis-Blériot, 63800 Cournon-d'Auvergne. ✆04 73 84 27 41.
- **Concept Kart Indoor,** 98 avenue de Chazeuil, 03150 Varennes-sur-Allier. ✆04 70 45 61 61.

RIDING TOURS

For information about riding holidays, contact the **Comité National de Tourisme Équestre,** 9 boulevard Macdonald, 75019 Paris ✆01 53 26 15 50, which publishes the annual handbook *Cheval Nature, l'Officiel du tourisme équestre en France,* giving details of selected riding stables and equestrian establishments throughout France.

At regional level, contact:

- **Comité Régionale de Tourisme Équestre d'Auvergne**, 9, allée Pierre de Fermat, 63170 Aubière. ✆04 73 34 86 06; www.equitation-auvergne.com.

Via ferrata du Pont du diable, Thueyts, Parc Naturel Régional des Monts d'Ardèche

© Bertrand Rieger/hemis.fr

Super Besse ski resort, Parc Naturel Régional des Volcans d'Auvergne

- ◆ **Comité Régionale de Tourisme Équestre Rhône-Alpes**, Parc du Cheval, Bât. Equipôle, Le Luizard, 01150 Chazey sur Ain. ☎04 37 90 53 29; www.tourismequestre-rhonealpes.com.

ROCK-CLIMBING

There are numerous opportunities to tackle cliff faces in the Auvergne region. Information can be obtained from the following:

- ◆ **Club Alpin Français** (section Auvergne), 21 Rue Jean Richepin, 63000 Clermont-Ferrand. ☎04 73 90 81 62; www.clubalpin-clermontauvergne.fr.
- ◆ **Comité Départemental de la Fédération Française de la Montagne et de l'Escalade**, 22 ter, impasse Bonnabaud, 63000 Clermont-Ferrand. ☎04 73 29 24 71; www.ffme.fr..

In January and February, some winter sports resorts offer an introduction to ice climbing on frozen waterfalls:

- ◆ **Club Alpin Français du Haut-Cantal**, 1 ave. Fernand Brun, 15400 Riom-ès-Montagnes ☎04 71 78 14 63.
- ◆ **Le Mont-Dore**, Contact the Peloton de Gendarmerie de Montagne (mountain squad of the Gendarmerie Nationale), rue des Chasseurs Alpins, 63240 Le Mont-Dore. ☎04 73 65 04 06.

SKIING

The Auvergne region is well equipped for the practice of Alpine skiing with three important resorts: Mont-Dore (*see MONT-DORE*), Super-Besse (*see BESSE-EN-CHANDESSE*) and Super-Lioran (*see LE LIORAN*), where the **Ski Pass Massif Central** can be used. It is also ideal for those who prefer cross-country skiing as there is an extensive network of tracks spread over 12 main ski areas.

The Massif du Pilat and the high plateaux of the Ardèche are also suitable for cross-country skiing and ski touring. In addition, **summer skiing** and **sledging** are popular summer activities in Le Mont-Dore, Super-Besse and Picherande; information is available from tourist offices.

Useful Addresses

- ◆ **Club Nordique des Crêtes du Forez**, 3, rue de Goye 63600 Ambert. ☎04 73 95 20 61; www.cretesduforez.fr.
- ◆ **Domaine Lioran-Haute Planèze**, Col de Prat de Bouc, 15300 Albepierre-Bredons. ☎04 71 73 32 13; www.nordique-pratdebouc.com.
- ◆ **École de ski français de Super-Besse**, 1 ronde de Vassivière, 63610 Super-Besse. ☎04 73 79 61 75; www.esfsuperbesse.com.

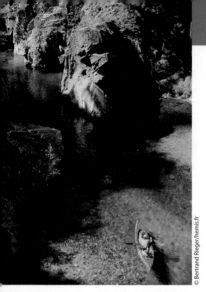

Kayaking in the Upper Ardèche valley, Thueyts

© Bertrand Rieger/hemis.fr

Snow-cover information –
The following provide up-to-date information about snow conditions in the various ski areas.

- **Club Nordique des Crêtes du Forez:** ✆04 73 95 20 61.
- **Super-Besse:** ✆04 73 79 62 92.
- **Zone Nordique du Mézenc:** ✆04 71 08 34 33.
- **Stations du Massif du Pilat:** ✆04 77 20 43 43.
- **Stations des Monts du Forez:** ✆04 77 24 83 11.

Useful Websites

The regional tourist office site **www.auvergne-tourisme.info** – has information on ski resorts and conditions. Another site for information and reservations is **www.france-montagnes.com**, including all the latest updates on snow conditions in French resorts (some sites also list available accommodation).
www.super-besse.com offers the possibility of visualising the resort's weather conditions in real time via several webcams.

WATERSPORTS

Natural and artificial lakes offer a wide choice of possibilities for the practice of various water sports: rowing, windsurfing, waterskiing, canoeing, kayaking, rafting and canyoning.

Canoeing and Kayaking

Discover the region from the swirling waters of the Ardèche, the Sornin or the Allier: information on suitable spots for canoeing from:

- **Fédération Française de Canoë-Kayak**, 87 Quai de la Marne, 94340 Joinville-le-Pont.
  ✆01 45 11 08 50; www.ffck.org. Map of French waterways available.

Rafting and Canyoning

Rafting is the easiest of these freshwater sports, since it involves going down rivers in inflatable craft steered by an instructor; special equipment is provided.

Canyoning is a technique for body-surfing down narrow gorges and over falls, as though on a giant waterslide. This sport requires protection: wear a wetsuit and a helmet.

Rowing

Club Aviron Vichy, 3 avenue de la Croix-St-Martin, 03200 Vichy. ✆04 70 32 36 52; http://clubavironvichy.e-monsite.com – leisure activities and competitions.

ACTIVITIES FOR KIDS 👫

Sights of particular interest to children are indicated with a KIDS symbol (👫). The Auvergne region of France has a lot to offer children, from having fun with water in amusement parks such as the Parc Aquatique d'Ambert (✆04 73 82 14 23), the Centre aquatique de Chamalières (✆04 73 29 78 78) or Iloa in Thiers (✆04 73 80 14 90 or 04 73 80 88 80), to visiting zoos, châteaux, museums and sights of special interest. 👣*see also Tourist Trains and Eco-tourism.*
Children are welcome everywhere in France; the French are very much family-oriented. It is quite commonplace to see well-behaved children dining in restaurants in the

early evening. Moreover, France is a wonderful destination to bring babies, toddlers, in fact, children of all ages. Most attractions, parks, museums and buildings offer reduced rates for children, with very young children often going free.

Useful Websites

Useful sources of ideas are **France for Families** (*www.franceforfamilies.com*), and **Tots to Travel** (*www.totstotravel. co.uk*), which contain a wealth of general information and tips. There are also other useful websites, like **Take the Family** (*www.takethefamily. com*), which has tips and destination guides, and **Baby Goes Too** (*www. babygoes2.com*), which contains pages of information to help parents travelling with small children. **Tiny Tot Travellers** (*www.tinytottravellers. co.uk*) does much the same thing.

When you get there

Many of the local tourist office websites have pages dedicated to what children can do, and it is useful to consult those for your destination. But, when you are in France, don't be afraid of visiting the tourist office to see if there is anything happening during your stay, like a local festival, concert or celebration.

SPAS AND MINERAL SPRINGS

SPAS OF THE AUVERGNE

There are dozens of spas in France, ranging from upmarket spa resort hotels to charming small spa villages that have relaxed visitors since the days of the Romans. The Auvergne and Rhône valley are no exception. The thalassotherapy, balneotherapy and thermal spring centres of the Auvergne are renowned for their professional treatments and warm welcome. Thermal spa waters from the volcanoes have therapeutic virtues that were appreciated by the Romans. Nowadays, spas offer care adapted to various ailments. Water cures exploit the riches of water from natural springs. You drink it and bathe in it, and each spring has its own peculiar properties that might help slimming, ease breathing problems or soothe physical or psychological ailments. Throughout the region, spas combine the benefits of fresh water with very fashionable and sometimes bizarre treatments: a chocolate body wrap, a body rub with black soap, a hot stone massage…

Flowing out of the immense natural filter formed by the volcanoes of Auvergne, mineral springs swell out of the ground at locations whose names have become famous brands of mineral or spring waters: Volvic, Châteauneuf, Sainte-Marguerite, Mont-Dore, Vichy, Saint-Yorre and Arvie will all find a place at your table or in a restaurant, not to mention less well-known brands like La Cantaline, La Tessièroise, Renlaigue, Chateldon or Hydroxydase.

RESORTS

The region has many spa resorts:

Bourbon-l'Archambault‡
  🕭*see BOURBON-L'ARCHAMBAULT*
La Bourboule‡
  🕭*see LA BOURBOULE*
Châteauneuf-les-Bains
  🕭*see GORGES DE LA SIOULE*
Châtel-Guyon
  🕭*see RIOM*
Chaudes-Aigues
  🕭*see GORGES DE LA TRUYÈRE*
Le Mont-Dore
  🕭*see LE MONT-DORE*
Montrond-les-Bains
  🕭*see MONTBRISON*
Néris-les-Bains‡
  🕭*see MONTLUÇON*
Neyrac-les-Bains
  🕭*see VALS-LES-BAINS*
Chamalières
  🕭*see CLERMONT-FERRAND*
St-Nectaire‡
  🕭*see ST-NECTAIRE*
Vals-les-Bains
  🕭*see VALS-LES-BAINS*
Vichy‡
  🕭*see VICHY*

Saturday market on Place François Mitterand, Vienne

INFORMATION

You can obtain brochures and information by contacting the following:

- **Chaîne Thermale du Soleil**, 32 avenue de l'Opéra, 75002 Paris. ℘0 800 05 05 32; www.chainethermale.fr.
- **La Medecine Thermale**, www.medecinethermale.fr.
- **Auvergne thermale**, 8 avenue Anatole-France, 63130 Royat. ℘04 73 34 72 80; www.auvergne-thermale.com.

SHOPPING
FAIRS AND MARKETS

Traditional fairs – These offer visitors an opportunity to witness long-standing local customs; the most colourful ones are listed below.

- **Tournon-sur-Rhône:** 29 August: onion fair
- **St-Sorlin-en-Valloire:** 1st Sat in September: foal fair
- **Claveyson**: 11 November: truffle fair
- **Chénelette**: 11 November: goat and cattle fair
- **Romans-sur-Isère**: from the last Sat in September to the 1st Sun in October: Dauphiné Fair

Markets – The market is an integral part of the French way of life, and a vital component of the country's rich heritage. It's almost unthinkable to visit France, and not spend some time in one of its thousands of markets. The most important fruit and vegetable market in the Rhône valley takes place in **Pont-de-l'Isère** daily except Sundays from May to September, on Mondays, Wednesdays and Fridays the rest of the year. Other markets in the Rhône valley:

- **Bourg-de-Péage:** Thu morning
- **Hauterives:** Tue morning
- **Romans-sur-Isère:** Tue, Fri and Sun mornings
- **Ruoms:** Fri morning
- **St-Donat-sur-l'Herbasse:** Mon morning
- **St-Rambert-d'Albon:** Fri morning
- **Tain-l'Hermitage:** Sat
- **Les Vans:** Sat morning; a traditional handicraft market livens up the town's historic centre between 6 and 10pm on Tue in July and August.
- **Villeneuve-de-Berg:** Wed morning; activities are organised on Tue evenings throughout July and during the first fortnight of August.

The excellent website – www.jours-de-marche.fr – lists more than 7 500, and admits to there being a great many more.

LOCAL SPECIALITIES

Beaujolais and **Côtes-du-Rhône** wines go well with local cheeses such as **Picodon**, made from goat's milk, or **St-Marcellin**, made from a subtle mixture of goat's and cow's milk. You may be tempted by a pair of fine **shoes** from Romans-sur-Isère, once the capital of the shoe industry (visit the interesting local museum), or by a hand-painted silk scarf or tie from Lyon, or even by **woollen clothes** from the local manufacture in St-Pierreville (Eyrieux valley). If you are looking for ideas, visit the **Marché de la Création** (painting, sculpture, pottery…) which takes place in Lyon along quai Romain

Rolland on Sunday mornings or the **Marché de l'Artisanat** (handicrafts) which takes place along quai Fulchiron, also on Sunday mornings.

BOOKS

Portrait of the Auvergne – *Peter Gorham (Robert Hale, 1975)*. There are few places in France where past and present mingle so naturally. Yet the true wealth of the Auvergne remains in its countryside…

Summer Days in Auvergne – *Herbert de Kantzow (Adamant Media Corporation, 2004)*. A descriptive account of the author's travels in France and the Auvergne, originally published in 1875.

Mourjou: The Life and Food of an Auvergne Village – *Peter Graham, (Prospect Books, 2003)*. The author explores the traditions, folklore and gastronomy of the Auvergne, discovering the rhythms of its rustic life, the warmth of its people and their passion for food.

Auvergne and its People – *Frances Marion Gosling (Elibron Classics, 2004)*. An idiosyncratic and antique look at the lives of the people of the Auvergne; this reproduction issue is full of atmosphere and detail.

Speak the Culture – *(Andrew Whittaker, Thorogood Publishing, 2008)*. A general guidebook that shows you where to go in France and what to say when you get there, reasoning that through exploring the people and their lifestyles you will achieve an intimate under-standing of France and its people.

The Grand Traverse of the Massif Central – *Alan Castle (Cicerone Press, 2010)*. A guide to biking or walking the 700km/435mi-long route that departs from Clermont-Ferrand. The guide is suitable for novices or experts, as some of the more challenging routes can be avoided.

Walking in the Auvergne: 42 Walks in Volcano Country – *Rachel Crolla and Carl McKeating (Cicerone Press, 2013)*. Essential walker's guidebook

that explores the tranquil Auvergne region.

FILMS

The **Auvergne Film Commission** is a collaboration of directors who make films in the beautiful landscapes of the Auvergne. Among these are:

7 years – *(Bruno Todeschini, Valérie Donzelli and Cyril Troley, 2005)*. Maïté is married to Vincent who has just been sentenced to seven years in prison. The only intimacy left to them lies in the prison's visiting rooms. Twice a week, she picks up his laundry, washes it, irons it, and brings it back to him…

The Singer – *(Cecile de France, Gérard Depardieu, Mathieu Amalric, 2005)*. Alain is a 50-year-old singer at popular balls who also performs before factory committees and at inaugurations. He has dyed hair and is famous throughout Clermont-Ferrand. Singing was his whole life until he became acquainted with Marion, a young woman…

To be and to have – *(Directed by Nicolas Philibert, 2002)*. There are still, almost everywhere in France, single-classroom schools that bring together under the same schoolteacher all the children from the same village, from nursery age to their last year of primary education. Whether their individual members are withdrawn or outgoing, these assorted little groups share everyday life, for better and for worse. It was in one of these schools, somewhere in the heart of the Auvergne, that this film was shot.

Bon Voyage – *(Isabelle Adjani, Virginie Ledoyen, Yvan Attal, Gregori Derangère, 2002)*. At the start of World War II, the fate of the free world hangs in the balance at the Hotel Splendide in Bordeaux. Cabinet members, journalists, physicists, and spies of all persuasions gather to escape the Nazi occupation of Paris.

Calendar of Events

JANUARY
La Bourboule
La Sancy Blanche. ✆04 73 81 31 04
www.sancy.com.

Villefranche-sur-Saône
Fêtes des Conscrits "La Vague".
www.loisirs-beaujolais.fr.

FEBRUARY
Le Mont Dore
Sancy Snow Jazz. ✆04 73 65 21 96
www.sancy-snowjazz.com.

Clermont-Ferrand
International Short-Film Festival.
✆04 73 91 65 73;
www.clermont-filmfest.com.

MARCH
Clermont-Ferrand
"Vidéoformes": International
digital arts festival.
✆04 73 17 02 17.
www.videoformes.com.

Clermont-Ferrand
Poetry week. ✆04 73 31 72 87;
www.auvergne.iufm.fr/poesie.htm.

Lyon
International Fair. ✆04 72 22 33 37;
www.foiredelyon.com.

Le Puy-en-Velay
Torchlight procession of the White
Penitents in hooded robes.

FEBRUARY: International Short-Film Festival, Clermont-Ferrand .

© Sauve qui peut le court métrage, Baptiste Chanat

APRIL
Yssingeaux
Carnival.

Cournon-d'Auvergne
Festival for young people: theatre,
puppets, dance, music.
✆04 73 69 90 40.

MAY
Vichy
Une Saison en Eté: theatre,
classical music, opera, variety
shows at the Vichy Opera House
from May to October. ✆04 70 30
50 30. www.ville-vichy.fr.

Allanche
Fete de l'Estive. ✆04 71 20 48 43;
www.cezallier.org.

Orcival
Torchlight procession and
midnight mass. ✆04 73 65 81 49.

Clermont-Ferrand
Feast of Our Lady of the Port
ending with a procession through
the old town. ✆04 73 91 32 94.

JUNE
Clermont-Ferrand
Medieval Festival in Montferrand.
✆04 73 23 19 29/06 66 26 62 54.
www.montferrandmedieval.org.

Vic-le-Comte
Celtrad: Celtic music festival.
✆04 73 69 02 12.

Villefranche-sur-Saône
Midsummer Night: bonfires,
singers, illuminations.
✆04 74 65 04 48.

JULY
Forez
Concerts of classical music in
churches and castles of the Forez
region. ✆04 73 51 55 67.

Auvergne
Thermathlon du Sancy: fun trek
along the Route des Villes d'Eaux
of the Massif Central (mountain
biking, walking, canoeing,
archery…). ✆04 73 31 20 32.

Orcines
Open Golf des Volcans:
International golf championship
(last week of the month).

04 73 62 15 51.
www.golfdesvolcans.com.

Issoire
International Dance and Music
Festival. 04 73 89 92 85.
www.festival-issoire.fr.

Ambert
Festival de Folklore. 04 73 82 66
34. www.livradoue-dansaire.com.

Royat
VOLCADIVA – song festival,
concerts and recitals.
04 73 29 74 70;
www.volcadiva.com.

Vollore
Concerts de Vollore: – classical
music, jazz and "musique tzigane".
04 73 51 55 67.
www.concertsdevollore.fr.

Gannat
World Cultures Festival.
04 70 90 12 67. www.cultures-
traditions.org.

AUGUST
La Chaise-Dieu
Classic and Sacred Music Festival.
04 71 00 01 16.
www.chaise-dieu.com.

Aurillac
International Street Theatre
Festival: 04 71 45 47 45.
www.aurillac.net.

Allanche
Secondhand market: the most
important in the Auvergne.
04 71 20 48 43.

St-Pourçain-sur-Sioule
Wine and Food Festival.
04 70 45 32 73.
www.payssaintpourcinois.fr.

Mont Brouilly
Wine producers' pilgrimage to
Brouilly Chapel. 04 74 66 82 19.

SEPTEMBER
Ravel
Pottery market. 04 73 68 44 74.

Le Puy-en-Velay
Les Fêtes du Roi de l'Oiseau: all
the splendour of a city in the
period of Francis I; 6 000 people
in costume. 04 71 09 38 41.
www.roideloiseau.com.

*SEPTEMBER: Fêtes du Roi de l'Oiseau,
Le Puy-en-Velay*

© Office de Tourisme de la communauté d'agglomération du Puy-en-Velay

SEPTEMBER–DECEMBER
**Beaujolais, Coteaux du
Rhône and du Forez**
Grape Harvest and Wine Festivals
in the wine-growing regions.

Puy-de-Dôme
Les Automnales: theatre and music
throughout the region.
04 73 42 23 29.
www.puydedome.com.

OCTOBER
Montbrison
Fourme Cheese Festival:
procession of flower-decked floats.
04 77 96 18 18.

Mourjou
Chestnut Festival. 04 71 49 69 34
www.mourjou.com.

Clermont-Ferrand
International Jazz Festival.
09 82 47 01 97.

NOVEMBER
Le Puy-en-Velay
International Hot-Air Balloon Rally.
04 71 09 38 41.
www.ot-lepuyenvelay.fr.

Lyon
Festival of Baroque Music.
www.lesgrandsconcerts.com.

DECEMBER
Lyon
Festival of Light. 04 72 10 30 30.

Know Before You Go

USEFUL WEBSITES

http://uk.france.fr

The French Government Tourist Office site has practical information and links to more specific guidance, for American or Canadian travellers, for example. The site includes information on everything you need to know about visiting France.

www.ViaMichelin.com

This site has maps, tourist information, travel features, suggestions on hotels and restaurants, and a route planner for numerous locations in Europe. In addition, you can look up weather forecasts, traffic reports and service station location, particularly useful if you will be driving in France.

www.ambafrance-uk.org
www.ambafrance-us.org

The websites for the French Embassy in the UK and the USA provide a wealth of information and links to other French sites (regions, cities, ministries).

www.france-travel-guide.net

A practical and developing website for the traveller, written by a Francophile travel writer. Includes essential information, as well as a wide range of regional and local content.

www.francethisway.com

A well-designed and informative website containing a wide range of useful information about France and travelling in France.

http://drive-france.com

Keep up-to-date with the rules and regulations governing driving in France, including all the things you need to know about legal changes and the motoring laws. You can also purchase travel essentials for the motorist, too.

TOURIST OFFICES ABROAD

For information and assistance in planning a trip to France travellers should apply to the official French Tourist Office in their own country:

Australia

French Tourist Bureau, 25 Bligh Street, Sydney, NSW 2000, Australia
℘(0)292 31 62 77;
http://au.france.fr.

Canada

Maison de la France, 1800 av. McGill College, Bureau 1010, Montreal, Quebec H3A 3J6, Canada
℘(514) 288 20 26; http://ca.france.fr.

South Africa

Block C, Morningside Close
222 Rivonia Road, MORNINGSIDE 2196 – JOHANNESBURG
℘00 27 (0)10 205 0201.

UK and Ireland

Lincoln House, 300 High Holborn, London WC1V 7JH. ℘0207 061 66 00;
http://uk.france.fr.

USA

825 Third Avenue, New York, NY 10022, USA ℘(212) 838 78 00;
http://us.france.fr.

IN THE AUVERGNE

Visitors will find more extensive information through the network of tourist offices. The details of local tourist offices, sometimes also called *syndicats d'initiative* in smaller towns, are listed after the symbol 🛈 in the introductions to individual sights.

REGIONAL TOURIST OFFICES:
Comité Régional du Tourisme (CRT)

♦ **Comité Régional de Développement Touristique d'Auvergne (CRT)** – Parc Technologique Clermont-Ferrand/La Pardieu, 7 allée Pierre de Fermat, 63178 Aubière.
℘04 73 29 49 99.
www.auvergne-tourisme.info.

- **Comité Régional du Tourisme Rhône-Alpes (CRT)** – 8 rue Paul Montrochet, 69002 Lyon. ☏04 26 73 31 59. http://en.auvergnerhonealpes-tourisme.com.

DEPARTMENTAL TOURIST OFFICES: Comité Départemental du Tourisme (CDT)

- **Ain (CDT)** – 34 rue du Général-Delestraint, CS90078, 01002 Bourg-en-Bresse. ☏04 74 32 31 30. www.ain-tourisme.com.

- **Ardèche (CDT)** – 4 cours du Palais, 07002 Privas. ☏04 75 64 04 66. www.ardeche-guide.com.

- **Drôme (CDT)** – 8 rue Baudin, 26005 Valence. ☏04 75 82 19 26. www.ladrometourisme.com.

- **Isère (CDT)** – 14 rue de la République, 38019 Grenoble. ☏04 76 54 34 36. www.isere-tourisme.com.

- **Loire (CDT)** – 22 rue Balay, 42021 St-Étienne. ☏04 77 43 59 14. www.loiretourisme.com.

- **Rhône (CDT)** – 142 bis, avenue Maréchal de Saxe, 69003 Lyon. ☏04 72 56 70 40. www.rhonetourisme.com.

- **Allier (CDT)** – Pavillon des Marronniers, Parc de Bellevue, 03402 Yzeure. ☏04 70 46 81 50. www.allier-auvergne-tourisme.com.

- **Cantal (CDT)** – 12, rue Marie Maurel, CS 80 007, 15013 Aurillac. ☏04 71 63 85 00. www.cantal-destination.com.

- **Haute-Loire (CDT)** – 1 place Monseignuer de Galard, 43000 Le Puy-en-Velay. ☏04 71 07 41 65. www.auvergnevacances.com.

Montverdun, fortified priory of the Pic de Montverdun in the background, Loire

© Franck Guiziou/hemis.fr

- **Puy-de-Dôme** – Contact Auvergne Rhône-Alpes Tourisme, 7 allée Pierre de Fermat, 63178 Aubière. ☏04 73 29 49 33. www.auvergnerhonealpes-tourisme.com.

Numerous towns and areas, labelled **Villes et Pays d'Art et d'Histoire** by the Ministry of Culture, are mentioned in this guide (Clermont-Ferrand, the Dauphiné d'Auvergne, the Forez, the Haut-Allier, Lyon, Montluçon, Moulins, Paladru-Les-Trois-Vals Lake, Le Puy-en-Velay, Riom, Saint-Étienne, Valence and Vienne). They are particularly active in promoting their architectural and cultural heritage and offer tours by qualified guides as well as activities for 6- to 12-year-olds. More information is available from local tourist offices and from www.vpah.culture.fr.

INTERNATIONAL VISITORS
FOREIGN EMBASSIES AND CONSULATES

Embassies provide diplomatic help to their citizens abroad, while consulates are a local base in Paris and in other large cities for adminstrative formalities.

EMBASSIES AND CONSULATES IN FRANCE

Australia	Embassy	4 rue Jean-Rey, 75015 Paris ☎ 01 40 59 33 00. www.france.embassy.gov.au
Canada	Embassy	37 avenue Montaigne, 75008 Paris ☎ 01 44 43 29 00. www.international.gc.ca
Ireland	Embassy	12 ave. Foch, 75116 Paris ☎ 01 44 17 67 00. www.embassyofireland.fr
New Zealand	Embassy	103, rue de Grenelle, 75007 Paris ☎ 01 45 01 43 43. www.mfat.govt.nz
South Africa	Embassy	59 quai d'Orsay, 75343 Paris ☎ 01 53 59 23 23. www.afriquesud.net
UK	Embassy	35 rue du Faubourg St-Honoré, 75383 Paris ☎ 01 44 51 31 00. www.gov.uk/world/france
	Consulate	16 rue d'Anjou, 75008 Paris ☎ 01 44 51 31 01 (visas). www.gov.uk/world/france.
USA	Embassy	2 avenue Gabriel, 75008 Paris ☎ 01 43 12 22 22. http://fr.usembassy.gov
	Consulate	2 rue St-Florentin, 75001 Paris ☎ 01 42 96 14 88. https://fr.usembassy.gov

ENTRY REQUIREMENTS

Passport – Nationals of countries within the European Union entering France need only a national identity card; in the case of the UK, this means your passport. Nationals of other countries must be in possession of a valid national **passport.**

☺ *In case of loss or theft, report to your embassy or consulate and the local police.*

☺ *You must carry your documents with you at all times; they can be checked anywhere.*

Visa – No **entry visa** is required for Canadian, US or Australian citizens travelling as tourists and staying less than 90 days, except for students planning to study in France. If you think you may need a visa, apply to your local French Consulate.

US citizens – General passport information is available by phone toll-free from the Federal Information Center (item 5 on the automated menu), ☎ 800-688-9889. US passport forms can be downloaded from http://travel.state.gov.

CUSTOMS

In Britain, go to the Customs Office (UK) website (*www.hmrc.gov.uk*) for information on allowances, travel safety tips, and to consult and download documents and guides. There are no limits on the amount of duty and/or tax paid alcohol and tobacco that you can bring back into the UK as long as they are for your own use or gifts and are transported by you. If you are bringing in alcohol or tobacco goods and UK Customs have reason to suspect they may be for a commercial purpose, an officer may ask you questions and make checks.

Australians will find customs information at www.border.gov.au/Trav; for **New Zealanders** Advice for Travellers is at www.customs.govt.nz.

HEALTH

First aid, medical advice and chemists' night service rota are available from chemists/drugstores *(pharmacies)* identified by the green cross sign.

It is advisable to take out comprehensive travel insurance cover, as tourists receiving medical treatment in French hospitals or clinics have to pay for it themselves. **Nationals of non-EU countries** should check with their insurance companies about policy limitations. Remember to keep all receipts.

British and Irish citizens, if not already in possession of an EHIC (European Health Insurance Card), should apply for one before travelling. The card entitles UK residents to reduced-cost medical treatment. Apply at UK post offices, call ☏ 0845 606 2030, or visit www.ehic.org.uk. Details of the healthcare available in France and how to claim reimbursement are published in the leaflet Health Advice for Travellers, available from post offices. All prescription drugs taken into France should be clearly labelled; it is recommended to carry a copy of prescriptions.

US and Canadian citizens can contact the International Association for Medical Assistance to Travellers (*www.iamat.org*).

Lift at Lyon-St-Exupéry airport station

© Brice Robert/Lyon Tourisme et Congrès

ACCESSIBILITY ♿

The sights described in this guide that are easily accessible to people of reduced mobility are indicated by the ♿ symbol. However, this does not necessarily mean that there is full access across the whole sight; check websites for any restrictions.

On French TGV and Corail trains there are wheelchair spaces in 1st-class carriages available to holders of 2nd-class tickets. On Eurostar and Thalys special rates are available for accompanying adults. All airports are equipped to receive physically disabled passengers. Disabled drivers may use the EU blue card for parking entitlements.

Many of France's historic buildings, including museums and hotels, have limited or no wheelchair access. Older hotels tend not to have lifts.

Tourism for All UK (*Pixel Mill, 44 Appleby Road, Kendal, Cumbria LA9 6ES. ☏ 0845 124 9971; www.tourismforall. org.uk*) publishes overseas information guides listing accommodation that they believe to be accessible but haven't inspected in person. Information about accessibility is available from French disability organisations such as **Association des Paralysés de France** (*17 bd. Auguste-Blanqui, 75013 Paris; ☏ 01 40 78 69 00; www.apf.asso.fr*). Useful information on transportation, holidaymaking, and sports associations for the disabled is available on *www.disabilityrightsuk. org* is a good source of info and support.

PETS

Recent regulations make it much easier to travel with pets between the UK and mainland Europe. Full details are available from the website of the **Department for Environment, Food and Rural Affairs** (*www.gov.uk/take-pet-abroad*).

Getting There and Getting Around

BY PLANE

It is very easy to arrange air travel to either of Paris' two airports (Roissy-Charles-de-Gaulle to the north, and Orly to the south). There are also regular flights from the UK to **Lyon-Saint-Exupéry** airport, which is linked to the city centre by a regular shuttle service. Contact airline companies and travel agents for details of package tour flights with a rail link-up or Fly-Drive schemes.

You can get from CDG airport into the centre of Paris by using the Roissybus, Airport Shuttle, or by using a taxi, which is much more convenient, but expensive. There is an extra charge (posted in the taxi) for baggage; the extra charge for airport pick-up is on the meter; drivers are usually given a tip of 10–15%.

BY SHIP

There are competing **cross-Channel services** (passenger and car ferries) from the United Kingdom and Ireland. To choose the most suitable route between your port of arrival and your destination use the Michelin Tourist and Motoring Atlas France, Michelin map 726 (which gives travel times and mileages) or Michelin maps from the 1:200 000 series (with the orange cover). For details apply to travel agencies or to:

♦ **Brittany Ferries** ℘0330 159 7000 (UK). www.brittanyferries.com. Services from Portsmouth, Poole and Plymouth to Caen (Ouistre-ham).
♦ **Condor Ferries** ℘0345 609 1024. www.condorferries.co.uk. Services from Weymouth, Poole and Ports-mouth.
♦ **DFDS Seaways** operate routes between Dover and Calais, Dover-Dunkerque Portsmouth-Le Havre and Newhaven-Dieppe.
℘(UK) 0871 574 7235 and ℘0800 917 1201. www.dfdsseaways.co.uk.
♦ **P&O Ferries** ℘0800 130 0030 (UK). www.poferries.com. Service between Dover and Calais.

BY TRAIN

Eurotunnel operates a 35-minute rail trip for passengers with a car through the Channel Tunnel between Folkestone and Calais ℘08705 35 35 35 (in the UK) or ℘08 10 63 03 04 (in France); www.eurotunnel.com.
Eurostar runs from **London** (St Pancras) to **Paris** (Gare du Nord) in under 3h (up to 20 times daily). In Paris it links to the high-speed rail network (TGV) which covers most of France. From Paris (Gare de l'Est), the French national railways **SNCF** (www.sncf.fr) operates an extensive service to the region.

Bookings and information

Oui.sncf (formerly Voyages-SNCF) is SNCF's online travel distributor in France (https://en.oui.sncf).
Citizens of non-European Economic Area countries must complete a landing card before arriving at Eurostar check-in. These cards can be found at dedicated desks in front of the check-in area and from Eurostar staff. Once you have filled in the card, please hand it to UK immigration staff.
France Rail Pass and **Eurail Pass** are travel passes which may be purchased by residents of countries outside the European Union (&See www.raileurope-world.com and www.eurail.com).
If you are a **European resident,** you can buy an individual country pass, if you are not a resident of the country where you plan to use it.
At the SNCF (French railways) site, **www.sncf.fr,** you can book ahead, pay with a credit card, and receive your ticket in the mail at home.
There are numerous **discounts** available when you purchase your tickets in France, from 25–50 percent below the regular rate. They include discounts for using senior cards and

Train Panoramique des Dômes,
Puy de Dôme

youth cards, and seasonal promotions. There are a limited number of discount seats available during peak travel times, and the best discounts are available for travel during off-peak periods.

Tickets for rail travel in France must be validated *(composter)* by using the (usually) automatic date-stamping machines at the platform entrance *(failure to do so may result in a fine)*.

The French railway company SNCF operates a **telephone information, reservation and prepayment service in English** from 7am to 10pm (French time) 📞08 36 35 35 39.

BY COACH/BUS

Eurolines – www.eurolines.com has information about travelling by coach in Europe.

BY CAR
DRIVING IN FRANCE

The area covered in this guide is easily reached by main motorways and national routes. **Michelin map 726** indicates the main itineraries as well as alternate routes for avoiding heavy traffic during busy holiday periods, and gives estimated travel times. **Michelin map 723** is a detailed atlas of French motorways, indicating tolls, rest areas and services along the route; it includes a table for calculating distances and times. The latest Michelin route-planning service is available on the Internet at **www.ViaMichelin.com.** Travellers can calculate a precise route using

such options as "shortest route", "route avoiding toll roads", "Michelin-recommended route" and also gain access to tourist information (hotels, restaurants, attractions). The service is available on a pay-per-route basis or by subscription.

The roads are very busy during holiday periods and, to avoid traffic congestion, it is worth considering taking to the secondary routes (signposted as *Bison Futé – itinéraires bis).* The motorway network includes rest areas *(aires de repos)* and petrol stations *(stations-service),* usually with restaurant and shopping complexes attached, about every 40km/25mi.

DOCUMENTS

Driving Licence
Travellers from other European Union countries and North America can drive in France with a valid national or home-state **driving licence**.

An **international driving licence** is useful because the information on it appears in nine languages.

Registration papers
For the vehicle, it is necessary to have the registration papers (logbook) and an approved nationality plate.

Insurance
Many motoring organisations offer accident insurance and breakdown service schemes for members. Check with your insurance company with regard to coverage while abroad. Because French autoroutes are privately owned, European Breakdown

Cover service does not extend to breakdowns on the autoroute or its service areas – you must use the emergency telephones, or drive off the autoroute, if you can, before calling your breakdown service.

ROAD REGULATIONS

The minimum driving age is 18. Traffic drives on the right. All passengers must wear **seat belts**. Children under the age of 10 must ride in the back seat. Headlights must be switched on in poor visibility or at night; dipped headlights should be used at all times outside built-up areas. Use sidelights only when the vehicle is stationary. In the case of a breakdown, a **red warning triangle** or hazard warning lights are obligatory, as are **reflective safety jackets**, one for each passenger, and carried within the car. it is now compulsory to carry an in-car **breathalyser kit**, too; you can be fined if you do not. UK right-hand drive cars must use headlight adaptors.

In the absence of stop signs at intersections, cars must **give way to the right**. Traffic on main roads outside built-up areas (priority indicated by a yellow diamond sign) and on roundabouts has right of way. Vehicles must stop when the lights turn red at road junctions and may filter to the right only when indicated by an amber arrow.

The regulations on **drinking and driving** (limited to 0.50g/l) and **speeding** are strictly enforced – usually by an on-the-spot fine and/or confiscation of the vehicle.

Further regulations – It is obligatory to carry spare lightbulbs; yellow fluorescent jackets in case of breakdown, one for each passenger, and accessible from within the car; in-car breathalyser kit. UK right-hand drive cars must use headlight adaptors.

Speed limits

Although subject to changes, speed limits are as follows:

- Toll motorways (autoroutes) **130kph/80mph** (110kph/68mph when raining);
- Dual carriageways and motor ways without tolls **110kph/68mph** (100kph/62mph when raining);
- Other roads **90kph/56mph** (80kph/50mph when raining) and in towns **50kph/31mph**;
- Outside lane on motorways during daylight, on level ground and with good visibility – minimum speed limit of 80kph/50mph.

Parking Regulations

In urban areas there are zones where parking is either restricted or subject to a fee; tickets should be obtained from the ticket machines (horo-dateurs – small change necessary) and displayed inside the windscreen on the driver's side; failure to display may result in a fine or towing. Other parking areas in town may require you to take a ticket when passing through a barrier. To exit, you must pay the parking fee (usually there is a machine located by the exit – sortie) and insert the paid-up card in another machine which will lift the exit gate.

Tolls

In France, most motorway sections are subject to a **toll** (péage). You can pay in cash or with a credit card.

Fuel

French service stations dispense:

- *sans plomb98* (super unleaded 98)
- *sans plomb95* (super unleaded 95)
- *diesel/gazole* (diesel, including premium diesel)
- *GPL* (LPG)

Prices are listed on signboards on the motorways, although it is usually cheaper to fill up before joining or after leaving the motorway.

The website www.prix-carburants.

gouv.fr collects information on current fuel prices around the country.

CAR RENTAL

There are car rental agencies at airports, railway stations and in all large towns throughout France. European cars have manual transmissions; automatic cars are available in larger cities only if an advance reservation is made. Drivers must be over 21; between ages 21–25, drivers are required to pay an extra daily fee; some companies allow drivers under 23 only if the reservation has been made through a travel agent.

Car hire and holders of UK driving licences

In 2015, changes to the UK Driving License came into force which mean

RENTAL CARS – RESERVATIONS	
Avis	www.avis.co.uk www.avis.fr
Europcar	www.europcar.com
Budget France	www.budget.com
Hertz	www.hertz.com
SIXT	www.sixt.com

that because details of fines, penalty points and restrictions are now only held electronically you are going to have to enable a car hire company to access your online driving record by means of a DVLA-issued pass code. Full details are available at www.gov.uk/view-driving-licence.

Where to Stay and Eat

WHERE TO STAY

FINDING A HOTEL

Turn to the **Addresses** within individual Sight descriptions for a selection and prices of typical places to stay (**Stay**) and eat (**Eat**). The key at the back of the guide explains the symbols and abbreviations used in these sections. Use the map of **Places to stay** (*overleaf*) to identify recommended places for overnight stops. To enhance your stay, hotel selections have been chosen for their location, comfort, value for the money, and in many cases, their charm, but it is not a comprehensive listing. Prices indicate the cost of a standard double room for two people in peak season. For an even greater selection, use the red-cover **Michelin Guide France**, with its well-known star-rating system and hundreds of establishments throughout France.

The **Michelin Charming Places to Stay** guide contains a selection of 1 000 hotels and guest houses at reasonable prices. Always be sure to book ahead, especially for stays during the high season.

A guide to good-value, family-run hotels, **Logis et Auberges de France**, is available from the French Tourist Office (www.tourisme.fr). The website gives a list of accommodation for each *département*, as well as links for making reservations, and a list of tourist offices all over France. Another resource, which publishes a catalogue listing holiday villas, apartments or chalets in each *département* is the **French national family tourism network Clévacances** (*www.clevacances.com*). For good-value, family-run accommodation, the **Logis** network, is one of the best organisations to contact (*www.logishotels.com*). **Relais & Châteaux** (*www.relaischateaux.com*) provides information on booking in luxury hotels with character:
UK: ✆0203 519 1967

France: ✆01 76 49 39 39
Australia: ✆1300 121 341
New Zealand: ✆0800 540 008
USA: ✆1 800 735 2478
www.viamichelin.com covers hotels in France, including famous selections from the Michelin Guide as well as lower-priced chains.

Economy Chain Hotels

If you need a place to stop en route, these can be useful, as they are inexpensive and generally located near the main road. Breakfast is available, but there may not be a restaurant; rooms are small, with a TV and bathroom.
Central reservation numbers and websites (online booking is usually available):

+ **Akena:** ✆0810 220 280; www.hotels-akena.com
+ **B&B:** ✆02 98 33 75 29; www.hotel-bb.com
+ **Best Hôtel:** www.besthotel.fr
+ **Campanile**, UK ✆0207 519 50 45; France ✆0892 23 48 12; www.campanile.com
+ **Kyriad**: UK ✆0207 519 50 45; France ✆0892 23 48 13; www.kyriad.com
+ **Première Classe**: UK ✆0207 519 5045; France ✆0892 23 48 14; www.premiereclasse.com
+ **International Hotels Group:** ✆0871 423 4896; www.ihg.com
+ **Best Western Hotels:** www.bestwestern.fr.
+ **Ibis and Accor Hotels:** UK ✆0871 663 0628; France ✆0825 88 22 22; www.ibis.com

COTTAGES, BED AND BREAKFAST

The **Maison des Gîtes de France** lists self-catering cottages or apartments, or bed and breakfast accommodation *(chambres d'hôtes)* at a reasonable price *(✆0826 10 44 44; www.gites-de-france.com).*

La Fédération des Stations Vertes *(BP 71698, 21016 Dijon ✆03 80 54 10 50; www.stationsvertes.com)* lists some

600 country and mountain sites ideal for families.
There is also **Bed and Breakfast France** *(12 rue des Tulipes, 85100 Les Sables d'Olonne; www.bedbreak.com).*
The **Fédération des Logis de France** offers hotel-restaurant packages geared to walking, fishing, biking, skiing, wine-tasting and enjoying nature (*✆01 45 84 83 84 (English spoken); www.logishotels.com).*
The adventurous can consult **www.gites-refuges.com**, where you can download a guidebook, *Gîtes d'étapes et refuges*, listing some 4 000 shelters for walkers, mountaineers, rock-climbers, skiers, canoe/kayakers, etc.: 74 rue A. Perdreaux, 78140 Vélizy ✆01 34 65 11 89.

HOSTELS, CAMPING

To obtain an International Youth Hostel Federation card (no age requirement; senior card also available) contact the IYHF in your own country. An online booking service *(www.hihostels.com)*, lets you reserve rooms up to six months ahead.
The two main youth hostel associations *(auberges de jeunesse)* in France are:

+ **Ligue Française pour les Auberges de la Jeunesse** 67 r. Vergniaud, Bâtiment K, 75013 Paris. ✆01 44 16 78 78. www.auberges-de-jeunesse.com/en.
+ **Fédération Unie des Auberges de Jeunesse** 27 r. Pajol, 75018 Paris. ✆01 44 89 87 27. www.fuaj.org.

There are numerous officially graded **campsites** with varying standards of facilities throughout the Rhône valley. The **Michelin Camping France** guide lists a selection of campsites. The area is very popular with campers in the summer months, so it is wise to reserve in advance.

WHERE TO EAT

Turn to the Addresses throughout the *Discovering* section for descriptions and prices of selected places to eat in the different locations covered in this guide. The Legend on the cover flap explains the symbols and abbreviations used in these sections. Use **The Michelin Guide France**, with its hundreds of establishments all over France, for an even greater choice. If you would like to experience a meal in a highly rated restaurant from the Red Guide, be sure to book ahead! In the countryside, restaurants usually serve lunch between noon and 2pm and dinner between 7.30pm and 10pm. It is not always easy to find something in between those two meal times, as the "non-stop" restaurant is a rarity in the provinces. However, a hungry traveller can usually get a sandwich in a café, and ordinary hot dishes may be available in a *brasserie*.

Among places in the Auvergne region that have been awarded the special distinction of *site remarquable du goût* are Billom – for its particularly fine pink garlic; St-Nectaire – for its soft cheese made from cow's milk; Salers – for its firm cheese similar to Cantal (*www.sitesremarquablesdugout.com*).

A TYPICAL FRENCH MENU

La Carte

The Menu

Entrées

Starters

Crudités — Raw vegetables
Terrine de lapin — Rabbit terrine (pâté)
Frisée aux lardons — Curly lettuce with diced bacon
Escargots — Snails
Salade au crottin de Chavignol — Goat's cheese salad
Potage — Soup, broth

Plats (Viandes)

Main Courses (Meat)

Bavette à l'échalote — Sirloin with shallots
Faux filet au poivre — Steak in a pepper sauce
Pavé de rumsteck — Thick rump steak
Côtelettes d'agneau — Lamb cutlets
Filet mignon de porc — Pork fillet
Blanquette de veau — Veal stew in a cream sauce

Plats (Poissons, Volaille)

Main Courses (Fish, Fowl)

Filets de sole — Sole fillets
Dorade aux herbes — Sea bream with herbs
Saumon grillé — Grilled salmon
Truite meunière — Trout fried in butter
Magret de canard — Breast fillet of duck
Poulet rôti — Roast chicken

Fromage

Cheese

Fromage de chèvre — Goat's cheese
Fromage maigre — Low-fat cheese
Fromage à pâte dure — Hard cheese
Fromage à pâte molle — Soft cheese
Fromage râpé — Grated cheese

Desserts

Tarte aux pommes
Crème caramel
Mousse au chocolat
Sorbet: trois parfums

Desserts

Apple tart
Warm baked custard with caramel sauce
Chocolate mousse
Sorbet: choose three flavours

Boissons

Bière
Eau minérale (gazeuse)
Une carafe d'eau
Vin rouge, vin blanc, rosé
Jus de fruit

Beverages

Beer
(Sparkling) mineral water
Tap water (no charge)
Red wine, white wine, rosé
Fruit juice

Menu Enfant

Jambon
Steak haché
Frites
Purée

Children's Menu

Ham
Minced beef
French fries
Mashed potatoes

Note: *Nos viandes sont garnies* translates as "meat dishes are served with vegetables".
Well-done, medium, rare, "blue" = **bien cuit**, **à point**, **saignant**, **"bleu"**.

Useful Words and Phrases

Here are some French words you may see on local maps or road signs

Sights

	Translation
Abbey	Abbaye
Belfry	Beffroi
Chapel	Chapelle
Castle	Château
Cemetery	Cimetière
Cloisters	Cloître
Courtyard	Cour
Convent	Couvent
Lock (Canal)	Écluse
Church	Église
Fountain	Fontaine
Covered Market	Halle
Garden	Jardin
Town Hall	Mairie
House	Maison
Market	Marché
Monastery	Monastère

Windmill	Moulin
Museum	Musée
Park	Parc
Square	Place
Bridge	Pont
Port/Harbour	Port
Gateway	Porte
Quay	Quai
Ramparts	Remparts
Street	Rue
Statue	Statue
Tower	Tour

Natural Sites

	Translation
Chasm	Abîme
Swallow-Hole	Aven
Dam	Barrage
Viewpoint	Belvédère
Waterfall	Cascade
Pass	Col
Ledge	Corniche
Coast, Hillside	Côte
Forest	Forêt

Cave	Grotte
Lake	Lac
Beach	Plage
River	Rivière
Stream	Ruisseau
Beacon	Signal
Spring	Source
Valley	Vallée

Shopping

	Translation
Bank	la banque
Baker's	la boulangerie
Big	grand
Butcher's	la boucherie
Chemist's	la pharmacie
Closed	fermé
Cough syrup	du sirop pour la toux
Throat lozenges	des pastilles pour la gorge
Entrance	l'entrée
Exit	la sortie
Fishmonger's	la poissonnerie
Grocer's	l'épicerie
Newsagent, bookshop	la librairie
Open	ouvert
Post office	la poste
Shop	le magasin
Small	petit
Stamps	des timbres

On the Road

	Translation
Car park	le parking
Driving licence	le permis de conduire
(To the) east	(à l') est
Garage (for repairs)	le garage
(To the) left	(à) gauche
Motorway	l'autoroute
(To the) north	(au) nord
Petrol	l'essence
Petrol station	la station essence
(To the) right	(à) droite
(To the) south	(au) sud
Straight ahead	tout droit
Toll	le péage
Traffic lights	le feu tricolore
Tyre	le pneu
(To the) west	(à l') ouest

Travel

	Translation
Travel	Voyager
Airport	Aéroport
Credit Card	Carte de crédit
Customs	Douane
Passport	Passeport
Platform	Voie
Railway Station	Gare
Shuttle	Navette
Suitcase	Valise
Train Ticket	Billet de train
Plane Ticket	Billet d'avion
Wallet	Portefeuille

Time

	Translation
Today	Aujourd'hui
Tomorrow	Demain
Yesterday	Hier
Winter	Hiver
Spring	Printemps
Summer	Été
Autumn	Automne
Week	Semaine
Monday	Lundi
Tuesday	Mardi
Wednesday	Mercredi
Thursday	Jeudi
Friday	Vendredi
Saturday	Samedi
Sunday	Dimanche

Numbers

	Translation
0	zéro
1	un(e)
2	deux
3	trois
4	quatre
5	cinq
6	six
7	sept
8	huit
9	neuf
10	dix
11	onze
12	douze
13	treize

14	quatorze
15	quinze
16	seize
17	dix-sept
18	dix-huit
19	dix-neuf
20	vingt
30	trente
40	quarante
50	cinquante
60	soixante
70	soixante-dix
80	quatre-vingts
90	quatre-vingt-dix
100	cent
1000	mille

Here are a few French translations for things you might need to say:

USEFUL PHRASES
Hello/good morning Bonjour
Goodbye Au revoir
Thank you Merci
Excuse me Excusez-moi
Yes/no Oui/non
Sorry! Pardon!
Why? Pourquoi?
When? Quand?
Please S'il vous plaît
Do you speak English?
    Parlez-vous anglais?

I don't understand
    Je ne comprends pas
Please talk more slowly
    Parlez plus lentement, s'il vous plaît
Where is …?   Où est…?
When does the … leave?
    À quelle heure part…?
When does the … arrive?
    À quelle heure arrive…?
When does the museum open?
    À quelle heure ouvre le musée?
When does the film/show start?
    À quelle heure commence le film/
    le spectacle?
When is breakfast served?
    À quelle heure sert-on le petit-
    déjeuner?
How much does it cost?
    Combien est-ce que celà coûte?
Where can I buy an English paper?
    Où puis-je acheter un journal
    en anglais?
**Where is the nearest petrol
station?**
    Où se trouve la station essence la
    plus proche?
**Where can I change travellers'
cheques?**
    Où puis-je échanger des cheques
    de voyages?
Where are the toilets?
    Où sont les toilettes?
Can I pay with a credit card?
    Est-ce que je peux payer avec ma
    carte bancaire?

Quai des Célestins, Lyon

© Camille Moirenc/hemis.fr

Basic Information

BUSINESS HOURS

Most of the larger **shops** are open Mondays to Saturdays from 9am to 6.30 or 7.30pm. Smaller, individual shops may close during the lunch hour. Food shops – grocers, wine merchants and bakeries – are generally open from 7am to 6.30 or 7.30pm; some open on Sunday mornings. Many food shops close between noon and 2pm and on Mondays. Bakery and pastry shops sometimes close on Wednesdays. Hypermarkets usually stay open without a break from 9am until 9pm, or even later. Although business hours vary from branch to branch, **banks** are usually open from 9am to noon and 2pm to 5pm and are closed either on Mondays or Saturdays. Banks close early on the day before a bank holiday. **Post offices** open Mondays to Fridays, 8am to 7pm, Saturdays, 8am to noon. National **museums and art galleries** are closed on Tuesdays; municipal museums are generally closed on Mondays.

COMMUNICATIONS
PUBLIC TELEPHONES

Due to the widespread use of mobile phones, the number of **public telephones** in France is decreasing. Those that remain accept pre-paid phone cards (*télécartes*), rather than coins. Some telephone booths accept credit cards (Visa, Mastercard/ Eurocard). *Télécartes* (50 or 120 units) can be bought in post offices, branches of France Télécom, *bureaux de tabac* (cafés that sell cigarettes) and newsagents and can be used to make calls in France and abroad. Calls can be received at phone boxes where the blue bell sign is shown; the phone will not ring, so keep your eye on the little message screen.

National calls

French telephone numbers have ten digits. Paris and Paris region numbers begin with 01; 02 in northwest France; 03 in northeast France; 04 in southeast France and Corsica; 05 in southwest France.

International calls

To call France from abroad, dial the country code (+33) + 9-digit number (omit the initial 0). When calling abroad from France, dial 00, then dial the country code followed by the area code and number of your correspondent.

International Dialling Codes

Dial 00 before the country code (*see box*) minus the first 0, then the full number.

Australia	61
New Zealand	64
Canada	1
United Kingdom	44
Eire	353
United States	1

MOBILE PHONES

While in France, all visitors from other European countries should be able to use their mobile phone as normal. Visitors from other countries need to ensure before departure that their phone and service contract are compatible with the European system (GSM).

The three main mobile phone operators in France are SFR, Orange and Bouygues:

Orange www.orange.fr
Bouygues www.bouyguestelecom.fr
SFR www.sfr.fr

The EU abolished roaming charges in June 2017, as a result EU citizens won't be charged extra for calls. But for the foreseeable future the application of this decision in practice remains unclear. If necessary, consult your own provider.

La Ruche-Trianon, Clermont-Ferrand

© Christian Guy/hemis.fr

INTERNET

The internet is widely available throughout France, and most hotels and many smaller establishments offer a free WiFi service...but not all of them.

ELECTRICITY

In France the electric current is 220 volts. Circular two-pin plugs are the rule. Adapters and converters (for hairdryers, for example) should be bought before you leave home; they are on sale in most airports. If you have a rechargeable device (video camera, portable computer, battery recharger), read the instructions carefully or contact the manufacturer or retailer. Sometimes these items only require a plug adapter, in other cases you must use a voltage converter as well or risk ruining your device.

EMERGENCIES

European Emergency Call: ✆**112**
Fire *(Pompiers)*: ✆**18**
Paramedics (SAMU): ✆**15**
Police: ✆**17**

POST

Main post offices open Monday to Friday 9am to 7pm, Saturday 9am to noon. However, many post offices, especially smaller ones, close at lunchtime between noon and 2pm, and some may close early in the afternoon; in short, opening hours vary widely. Stamps are also available from newsagents and tobacconists *(tabacs)*. Stamp collectors should ask for *timbres de collection* in any post office.

Postage via air mail:
UK: letter (20g) €1.10.
North America: letter (20g) €1.30
Australia and NZ: letter (20g) €1.30
Stamps are also available from newsagents and *bureaux de tabac*. Stamp collectors should ask for *timbres de collection* in any post office. A useful website for mailing information and prices is www.tarifs-de-la-poste.fr.

MONEY

The euro is the only currency accepted as a means of payment in France, as in the other European countries participating in the monetary union. It is divided into 100 cents or centimes. There are no restrictions on the amount of currency visitors can take into France. Visitors carrying a lot of cash are advised to complete a currency declaration form on arrival, because there are restrictions on currency export: if you are leaving the country with more than €10 000, you must declare the amount to customs.

BANKS

Bank hours vary from branch to branch, but for typical hours 🕐 *see BUSINESS HOURS above*.

One of the most economical ways to obtain money in France is by using **ATM machines** to get cash directly from your bank account (with a debit card), or to use your credit card to get a cash advance. Be sure to remember your PIN number; you will need it to use cash dispensers and to pay with your card in shops, restaurants, etc. Code pads are numeric; use a telephone pad to translate a letter code into numbers. PIN numbers have 4 digits in France; enquire with the issuing company or bank if the code you usually use is longer.

CREDIT AND DEBIT CARDS

Visa is the most widely accepted credit card, followed by MasterCard; other cards, credit and debit (Diners Club, Plus, Cirrus, etc.) are also accepted in some cash machines. American Express is accepted primarily in premium establishments. Most places post signs indicating which cards they accept; if you don't see such a sign, and want to pay with a card, ask before ordering or making a selection. Cards are widely accepted in shops, hypermarkets, hotels and restaurants, at tollbooths and in petrol stations. Before you leave home, check with the bank that issued your card for emergency replacement procedures. At the same time, inform the bank that you will be using your credit card abroad – it may prevent refusal of your card at cash desks. Carry your card number and its emergency phone numbers separately from your wallet and handbag; leave a copy of this information with someone you can easily reach.

🕐 *If your card is lost or stolen* call the appropriate 24h hotlines listed on *www.totallymoney.com/guides/lost-stolen-credit-card*.

Better still: always carry with you the correct number to call for your particular credit cards. You must report any loss or theft of credit cards or traveller's cheques to the local police who will issue you with a certificate (useful proof to show the issuing company).

PRICES AND TIPPING

Since a service charge is automatically included in the price of meals and accommodation in France, any additional tipping is up to the visitor, generally small change, and usually not more than 5 percent. Taxi drivers and hairdressers are normally tipped 10–15 percent.

Tour guides and tour drivers should be tipped according to the amount of service given: from €2–5 would not be unusual.

Restaurants usually charge for meals in two ways: a menu that is a fixed-price with two or three courses and sometimes a small jug *(pichet)* of wine, or *à la carte*, the more expensive way, with each course ordered separately.

Cafés have very different prices, depending on where they are located. The price of a drink or a coffee is cheaper if you stand at the counter *(comptoir)* than if you sit down *(salle)*, and sometimes it is even more expensive if you sit outdoors *(terrasse)*.

VALUE ADDED TAX

There is a Value Added Tax in France *(TVA)* of 19.6% on almost every purchase (some foods and books are subject to a lower rate). However, non-European visitors who spend more than €175 (including VAT) in a single shop on the same day can get the VAT amount refunded. Usually, you fill out a form at the store, showing your passport. Upon leaving the country, you submit all forms to customs for approval (they may want to see the goods), so do not pack them in checked luggage). The refund is usually paid directly into your bank or credit card account, or it can be sent by mail. Big department stores that cater to tourists offer special services to help you; be sure to mention that you plan to seek a refund *(remboursement)* before you pay for goods (there is no refund for tax on services). If you are visiting two or more countries within the European Union, you submit the forms only on departure from the last EU country. The refund is worthwhile for those visitors who would like to buy fashionwear, furniture or other fairly expensive items, but remember, the minimum amount must be spent in a single shop (though not necessarily on the same day). See www.douane.gouv.fr.

PUBLIC HOLIDAYS

Public services, museums and other monuments may be closed or may vary their hours of admission on public holidays (&see box). National museums and art galleries are closed on Tuesdays; municipal museums are generally closed on Mondays. In addition to the usual school holidays at Christmas and in the spring and summer, there are long mid-term breaks in February and early November.

1 January	New Year's Day (Jour de l'An)
24 April (2011) 8 April (2012)	Easter Day (Pâques)
1 May	May Day (Fête du Travail)
8 May	VE Day (Anniversaire 1945)
Thurs 40 days after Easter	Ascension Day (Ascension)
7th Sun-Mon after Easter	Whit Sunday and Monday (Pentecôte)
14 July	France's National Day (Fête Nationale)
15 August	Assumption (Assomption)
1 November	All Saints' Day (Toussaint)
11 November	Armistice Day (Armistice 1918)
25 December	Christmas Day (Noël)

DISCOUNTS

Almost all attractions offer discounted admission prices for children, seniors, students and (sometimes) family groups; many also offer discounts for advance booking online.

The ages that children's discounts apply to vary, but where these relate to Sights that are noted as specific attractions for children with the 👥 symbol, the price and age range for children are shown. Student discounts tend as a rule to be for French students only, on presentation of a student ID card.

TIME

France is 1hr ahead of Greenwich Mean Time (GMT). France goes on daylight-saving time from the last Sunday in March to the last Sunday in October. In France "am" and "pm" are not used, but the 24-hour clock is widely applied.

WHEN IT IS **NOON IN FRANCE**, IT IS	
3am	in Los Angeles
6am	in New York
11am	in Dublin
11am	in London
7pm	in Perth (6pm in summer)
9pm	in Sydney (8pm in summer)
11pm	in Auckland (10pm in summer)

SMOKING

In France smoking is banned in public places such as offices, universities railway stations, restaurants, cafés, bars, nightclubs and casinos. In 2013 the ban was extended to e-cigarettes.

CONVERSION TABLES

Weights and Measures

1 kilogram (kg) 6.35 kilograms 0.45 kilograms **1 metric ton (tn)**	**2.2 pounds (lb)** 14 pounds 16 ounces (oz) **1.1 tons**	**2.2 pounds** 1 stone (st) 16 ounces **1.1 tons**	*To convert kilograms to pounds, multiply by 2.2*
1 litre (l) 3.79 litres 4.55 litres	**2.11 pints (pt)** 1 gallon (gal) 1.20 gallon	**1.76 pints** 0.83 gallon 1 gallon	*To convert litres to gallons, multiply by 0.26 (US) or 0.22 (UK)*
1 hectare (ha) **1 sq kilometre (km²)**	**2.47 acres** 0.38 sq. miles (sq mi)	**2.47 acres** 0.38 sq. miles	*To convert hectares to acres, multiply by 2.4*
1 centimetre (cm) **1 metre (m)** **1 kilometre (km)**	**0.39 inches (in)** 3.28 feet (ft) or 39.37 inches or 1.09 yards (yd) **0.62 miles (mi)**	**0.39 inches** **0.62 miles**	*To convert metres to feet, multiply by 3.28; for kilometres to miles, multiply by 0.6*

Clothing

Women					Men			
	35	4	2½			40	7½	7
	36	5	3½			41	8½	8
	37	6	4½			42	9½	9
Shoes	38	7	5½		**Shoes**	43	10½	10
	39	8	6½			44	11½	11
	40	9	7½			45	12½	12
	41	10	8½			46	13½	13
	36	6	8			46	36	36
	38	8	10			48	38	38
Dresses	40	10	12		**Suits**	50	40	40
& suits	42	12	14			52	42	42
	44	14	16			54	44	44
	46	16	18			56	46	48
	36	6	30			37	14½	14½
	38	8	32			38	15	15
Blouses &	40	10	34		**Shirts**	39	15½	15½
sweaters	42	12	36			40	15¾	15¾
	44	14	38			41	16	16
	46	16	40			42	16½	16½

Sizes often vary depending on the designer. These equivalents are given for guidance only.

Speed

KPH	10	30	50	70	80	90	100	110	120	130
MPH	6	19	31	43	50	56	62	68	75	81

Temperature

Celsius (°C)	0°	5°	10°	15°	20°	25°	30°	40°	60°	80°	100°
Fahrenheit (°F)	32°	41°	50°	59°	68°	77°	86°	104°	140°	176°	212°

To convert Celsius into Fahrenheit, multiply °C by 9, divide by 5, and add 32.
To convert Fahrenheit into Celsius, subtract 32 from °F, multiply by 5, and divide by 9.
NB: Conversion factors on this page are approximate.

The Region Today

21C AUVERGNE AND THE RHÔNE VALLEY
POPULATION AND PEOPLE

The Auvergne enjoys one of the lowest population densities in France; indeed, the *département* of Cantal would be virtually uninhabited were it not for the town of Aurillac.

The total population of the Auvergne is around 1.35 million, with a population density of just 50 per square kilometre. Moreover, the population of the Auvergne is declining, with more deaths annually than births. By contrast the wider urban area population around Lyon alone, around 2 million, exceeds the whole of the Auvergne, of which Lyon hosts just under half a million.

LANGUAGE

Like all the regions in France the Auvergne has its own language, which has undergone continual development since the days of Antiquity. This means that the borders of the area in which the dialect of the Auvergne is spoken do not correspond to the historical and administrative borders of the province. *Auvergnat*, the dialect of the Auvergne, which is considered to be similar to North Occitan, is said to have developed from a Medio-Roman language used in the part of central France occupied by the Romans and which gradually died out in the face of competition from *oïl*, the language of northern France. The dialect spoken in and around Aurillac is closer to the Guyennais dialect spoken in the south-west of France (Aquitaine), which was under English domination for a considerable time, but it has nevertheless been influenced by *Auvergnat*.

RELIGION

France enjoys freedom of religion as a constitutional right. However, a long history of conflict led the state to break its ties to the Catholic church in the 20C. No statistics are kept of religious leanings, but while many believe France to be staunchly Roman Catholic, there is contrary evidence suggesting that more than 50 percent of its people are either atheist or agnostic, with only 25 percent adhering to the Roman Catholic faith.

SPORT
Outdoor Adventure

It would be easy to believe that with so much uninhabited countryside, the Auvergne was specifically designed for those who enjoy their adventure in the outdoors.

Walking and mountain biking prevail almost anywhere in the region, while kayaking and a wide range of water sports are provided for on the Allier and Loire rivers. Those who like to fling themselves from hillsides in the fond belief that a few metres of thread and a silk curtain will bring them safely to earth will find that hang-gliding is a major sporting activity among the volcanic landscapes of the Auvergne, especially around the Puy-de-Dôme.

In winter the transformation is spectacular, and there are fully equipped downhill skiing resorts on the Puy de Sancy and the Plomb du Cantal.

On your Bike

As well as the almost pathological love affair with all things cycling, the Auvergne is also proving hugely popular with motorcyclists, who have long had a soft spot for the Auvergne.

A problem in many parts of France, motorcyclists find the openness of the Auvergne a perfect treat. All-terrain motorcycles have a dedicated track at Clermont-Ferrand.

MEDIA
The Connexion

English language newspapers in France, other than imported UK newspapers, are virtually unheard of.

The Connexion is a monthly production targeting the expatriate community. Founded in 2002, *The Connexion* reports news stories of events in France and provides advice for expatriates living there. A free trial copy is available at www.connexionfrance.com.

Traditions in the Auvergne

Because of the isolated nature of much of the Auvergne countryside, many ancient traditions have survived; today, the utmost is being done to preserve the special character of this region and the cultural heritage.

Fêtes and Festivals

Many of the old customs are upheld on the most important occasions. Bonfires are still lit on the mountain tops to celebrate the summer solstice (Feast of St John), and local fêtes have kept up the tradition of the music and songs played to young girls by the young men of the village. There has also been a revival of country festivals to celebrate haymaking, cheesemaking, harvesting, grape harvests, etc.

Costume

Today every folk group has its own interpretation of traditional costume. The men wear the *biaude*, a voluminous dark blue smock over a pair of coarse black trousers, with a brightly coloured scarf, a wide-brimmed, black felt hat and the clogs or hob-nailed boots that are so vital when tapping out the dance rhythm. The women are dressed in long, waisted, multicoloured dresses with an embroidered apron and a headdress that varies depending on the region.

The Bourrée

This dance dates back a long time but it has been synonymous with the Auvergne since the 18C. The *bourrée* enacts the chasing of a coquettish young girl by an enterprising young man, whom she alternately runs away from and then beckons to.

Processions and Pilgrimages

Worship of the Virgin Mary has long been important in the Auvergne. Countless churches and chapels have been dedicated to her. Indeed, the statues of the Virgin Mary in the Auvergne are among the oldest in France.

Processions and pilgrimages in honour of the Blessed Virgin remain very much alive and are quite spectacular. The processions to Notre-Dame-du-Port (Clermont-Ferrand) or Orcival, and the pilgrimages to Mauriac and Thiézac in Cantal and to Marsat and Monton in Puy-de-Dôme are the most popular.

La Bourrée

© S. Sauvignier/MICHELIN

GOVERNMENT

Decision-making in France was once highly centralised, each *département* headed by a government-appointed prefect, in addition to a locally elected general council *(conseil général)*. But in 1982, the national government decided to decentralise authority by devolving a range of administrative and fiscal powers to local level. Regional councils were elected for the first time in 1986.

Administrative units with a local government consist of 36 779 communes, headed by a municipal council and a mayor, grouped in 96 *départements*, headed by a *conseil général* and its president. The centre of administration of a *département* is called a *préfecture* (prefecture) or *chef-lieu de département*, which is usually geographically central to the *départment*.

The *conseil général* discusses and passes laws on matters that concern the department; it is administratively responsible for departmental employees and land, manages subsidised housing, public transport, and school subsidies, and contributes to public facilities. The council meets at least three times a year and elects its president for a term of three years, who presides over its "permanent commission", usually up to 10 other departmental councillors. The *conseil général* has accrued new powers in the course of the political decentralisation that has occurred in France during the past 30 years.

Different levels of administration have different duties, and shared responsibility is common; for instance, in the field of education, *communes* run public elementary schools, while *départements* run public junior high schools and regions run public high schools, but only for the building and upkeep of buildings; curricula and teaching personnel are supplied by the national Ministry of Education.

New French regions

In 2014, the French Parliament (the National Assembly and the Senate) passed a law that reduced the number of regions in Metropolitan France from 22 to 13. The new regions took effect on 1 January 2016. In the Auvergne, the *départements* are Allier, Cantal, Haute Loire and Puy-de-Dôme. These are now combined with Ain, Ardèche, Drôme, Isère, Loire, Rhône, Savoie, Haute-Savoie into the new region of Auvergne-Rhône-Alpes, the third largest region in metropolitan France.

ECONOMY

INDUSTRY

Industry came into being in the 16C with the introduction of silk-working around Lyon, paid for by the capital earned from fairs. Later, the coalfields in the area were a major factor leading to the expansion of industry. Once the seams had been worked out, the energy supply was provided by the hydroelectric plants and, since the 1970s and 1980s, by the nuclear power plants along the Rhône valley. Around Clermont-Ferrand the major industry is tyre-making.

Metal-Working

After the gradual shut-down of the coal mines in the area around St-Étienne, the metal-working sector began to specialise in the production of steels, rare metals, fissile products for use in the nuclear industry, and smelting, a sector that benefits from the high demand for moulded components (boiler-making, pipes). The region along the Rhône ranks second to the Paris basin in the field of mechanical engineering (machine tools, precision engineering, car manufacture). Electrical and electronic engineering are well represented with companies producing high-voltage equipment, communications equipment and domestic appliances. Until the 19C, tin and copper were the materials used in the Auvergne.

Textiles

After the silk workers' revolts in 1831 and 1834 in the streets and alleyways of Lyon, the textile industry relocated to villages and manufacturers distributed the jobs (weaving and dyeing) to a rural workforce. This was the so-called outworker system which still functions today. The importance of silk has decreased greatly in the face of

Cattle in Les sucs de Meygal near Saint-Julien-Chapteui, Velay

competition from man-made fibres but the weaving of silky fabrics made of a combination of fibres and threads of all types has remained famous. The new products have remained faithful to the innovation and tasteful designs which won Lyon its reputation for silks.

The production and weaving of man-made textiles is carried out in Valence (nylon and polyester) and Roanne (viscose). The industry has many offshoots like dyeing and dressing, and clothing (ready-to-wear, sportswear, lingerie, hosiery, curtains, net curtains, ribbons, elastic, lace).

Chemicals

A major chemical industry developed in Lyon in order to meet the needs of the textile industry. It was here that one of Europe's petrochemical centres was established.

In Feyzin, there is a large oil refinery and the Institut Français du Pétrole has set up its largest research centre here. The region currently leads the field in certain areas of the chemical industry, notably fungicides, paint, varnish and, especially, pharmaceuticals.

Additional Industries

Other industrial activities in the region include tyre-making, food processing (dairy products, pork meat products, health foods), shoe-making, cabinet-making, quarrying (Volvic) and mineral-water bottling (Vichy, Volvic) as well as the production of building materials,

glass, wires, cables, leather, paper, jewellery, tobacco and enamelled lava (signposts, viewing tables). Thiers is one of France's major cutlery-making centres. Traditionally, industry in the Auvergne has centred around specialist crafts, production frequently operating on a cottage-industry scale, such as coppersmithing (Cantal), lace-making (Velay) and paper-making (Livradois).

Administration offices (local authority and government offices, etc) and tourism also play an important part in the local economy; traditional industries (eg cheese-making) no longer do any more than "top it up".

Harnessing the Rhône

Important works upstream and downstream of Lyon, completed during the second half of the 20C, have offered this highly industrialised region the possibility of tapping the power resources of the mighty Rhône (16 billion kWh are produced yearly). At the same time, a series of canals provide a total of 330km/205mi of navigable waterways between Lyon and the sea.

AGRICULTURE

The Auvergne is first and foremost a rural area, in marked contrast to the Rhône valley, where industry predominates. Life on farms experienced profound change during the 20C: the introduction of motor vehicles, and the destruction of hedgerows which ended the subdivision of properties into small fields.

In many places, the traditional landscape of fields and narrow lanes lined with walnut trees has given way to one of wide, open fields.

Farmers, who are decreasing in number, have also had to comply with the milk quotas imposed on them by the EU; despite these difficulties, animal breeding and crop farming remain an important part of the economy of the region.

Stock Breeding

The high plateaux and mountains are popular with cattle breeders and, to a lesser extent, sheep farmers. The pastures on the slopes of the Dômes and Dore mountain ranges provide grazing land for the **Salers** breed of cattle (of which it is said that its fiery red coat turns pale if it leaves the basalt areas of Cantal), the French black-and-white Friesian, and the Montbéliarde.

Towards the middle of May the animals leave their byres and, for the five months of summer, live on the mountain pastures which are now fenced so that there is no need for a herdsman to be in attendance. In days gone by, cowherds had a squat, low summer hut called a *buron,* built to withstand the wind.

The **fairs** give visitors an opportunity to enjoy the busiest moments of rural life. They are held in most of the centrally situated localities and in other places that lie in the heart of the stock-breeding areas. The largest fairs are held in late summer and in autumn.

Crops

In the Auvergne, wheat, barley and oats have traditionally been grown on the fertile black soil of the Limagnes, and now also sugar beet, tobacco, sunflowers and fodder or maize crops from selected strains of seeds.

At the southern end of the Rhône valley the dampness and cold of maritime or continental climates gives way to the heat and radiant skies of the south of France – almond and olive trees and a few mulberry bushes can be seen in the countryside. The natural environment here is both crop- and farmer-friendly.

The land is fertile and easy to irrigate; the soil is light and siliceous; well-sheltered corries and dales benefit from the spring sunshine.

Orchards

It was in 1880 that fruit production took over from wine, after the vineyards had been blighted by phylloxera. The long, fruit-producing season, made possible by careful selection of varieties and the differences in exposure or altitude, enable the orchards in the Rhône valley to produce one-third of all French fruit. Every type of fruit can be found here – raspberries, redcurrants and blackcurrants in Isère, sweet chestnuts in Ardèche, cherries, apricots, apples and pears and, in particular, peaches, the fruit that has made the Eyrieux valley famous.

Vineyards

The vineyards in the Rhône valley, which were already popular in Roman times, underwent massive expansion after the crisis in the silkworm-breeding industry in the mid-19C. Today, the vineyards, one-third of which produces high-quality wines, cover in excess of 150 000ha. The best are the **Côtes du Rhône**. Châteauneuf-du-Pape, St-Joseph, Crozes-Hermitage, Hermitage, Côte-Rôtie, Château-Grillet and Condrieu are wines that age well, and have brought the area its reputation for excellence. With an annual output of 3.5 million hectolitres of *appellations contrôlées,* the Rhône valley vineyards account for 15 percent of the total French production of fine wines.

The vineyards stretch for 200km/124mi producing a variety of wines thanks to the **types of vines** selected: Marsanne and Viognier for the whites, Syrah and Grenache for the reds. The wines also vary depending on the different types of soil on which the vines are planted – the crumbly granite of the gorges, and the sands, pebbles or marl that predominate in alluvial plains. There are climatic differences in the basins and, finally, the terraces that climb the hillsides between this area and the Alps face in different directions.

Further north, the vineyards of the **Beaujolais** – which are usually grouped with those of neighbouring Burgundy in wine guides – produce wines which go very well indeed with the traditional cuisine of Lyon, where they are to be found in every local brasserie or *bouchon*. The third Thursday in November is a "red letter" day locally (and further afield, now that the reputation of Beaujolais wines has spread abroad!) as it marks *l'arrivée du beaujolais nouveau,* or the release for sale to the public of the latest Beaujolais vintage *(vin primeur). For further details on Beaujolais wines,* 🌐*see BEAUJOLAIS.* The limestone hillsides to each side of the Limagnes used to be covered with vineyards. Nowadays, some of the wines fall within the all-enveloping name Côtes d'Auvergne, among them Châtaugay, Corent, Boudes and St-Pourçain.

FOOD AND DRINK
RHÔNE VALLEY

The Rhône valley abounds in good food because it is situated at the heart of various regions containing an outstanding wealth of local produce. Bresse is famous for its poultry, the Charolais area produces beef, the Dombes region abounds in game, the lakes of Savoy teem with fish and the Forez and Rhône valleys specialise in fruit.

In the 19C silk workers ate, like their employers, in small family-run restaurants. The dishes served were based on cheap cuts of meat and offal, but the food was plentiful and tasty. Diners could eat sausages, potted pork, black sausage, pigs' trotters, knuckle of veal and other stewed meats.

The tradition of good food remains unchanged. Today, local **specialities** include spicy saveloy sausage with truffles and pistachio nuts, pigs' trotters and tails, artichoke with marrow bone jelly, pork brawn in vinaigrette, and gently stewed tripe. Other dishes include braised, stuffed trout, fish in Burgundy wine and poultry cooked in stock with thin slivers of truffle inserted between the skin and the meat.

Forez

Hunting, shooting, fishing and stock-breeding provide the basic ingredients for a delicate, tasty type of cooking. Among the local dishes are crayfish and trout from the River Lignon, or poultry and meat of outstanding quality. Also on offer may be a local form of pork pie, a dish of duck, a delicious local ham, Feurs sausage or, in the autumn, game pâté; sometimes even woodcock.

Vivarais

Food here is rustic; this is the land of chestnuts and wild mushrooms such as St George's agaric and boletus. Among the filling, tasty specialities are partridge with cabbage, thrush with grapes, chicken cooked in a bladder, chicken with crayfish, goose and turkey with chestnuts, hare with *poivrade* (a highly seasoned sauce), and pork meat products from Ardèche. During the summer, the cherries, apricots, peaches, pears, plums and apples are among the finest such fruits found anywhere in France.

Lower Dauphiné

The Rhône valley area of Lower Dauphiné marks the transition between the Lyonnais area and Provence. This is the land of *gratin dauphinois*, veal with leeks, *pognes* (brioches, a sort of sweet bread) in Romans and Valence, cheese from St-Marcellin, Grignan-style braised beef and the inimitable Montélimar nougat.

Making Montélimar nougat

© Jean-Daniel Sudres/hemis.fr

AUVERGNE

The Auvergne, a rugged area of countryside, is not the place for complex, sophisticated cuisine; it specialises in family cooking – and plenty of it.

The food in the Auvergne has traditionally been farm cooking, and as a result it has been accused of lacking any appreciable local specialities; this criticism is, happily, totally unfounded. The people of the Auvergne have taken great national specialities and adapted them to suit local taste so that, in the Auvergne, food is rich and sometimes heavy, but it is always extremely good.

Meat and Fish

The *coq au vin* (chicken stew) is delicious, especially when flavoured with a good wine. The *tripoux* from Aurillac, St-Flour and Chaudes-Aigues are wonderful, too. There is ham from Maurs, local sausages, trout from mountain streams, eels from the Dore and salmon from the Allier.

Vegetables

The *truffade* from Aurillac is a smooth blend of fresh Tomme cheese and mashed potatoes; seasoned with garlic in Chaudes-Aigues and Aubrac, it is called *aligot*. Potato paté, a light pastry browned in the oven with a lot of fresh cream and potatoes, is one of the specialities of the Montluçon and Gannat area. Morel mushrooms are cooked with cream and used to fill omelettes and stuff poultry. Peas from the Planèze

and green lentils from Le Puy are well-known to gourmets.

Cheeses

This is one of the region's main specialities. The round, flat St-Nectaire is a delight when well matured. There is also Fourme d'Ambert and Fourme de Montbrison, a blue cheese with an orange-tinted rind, Bleu d'Auvergne and Cantal. These are the best-known of the local cheeses but there is in addition Murol, a variant of St-Nectaire, or the garlic-flavoured Gaperon, made on the plains and shaped like a rounded cone.

Locally, the cheese usually known as Cantal is called Fourme, named after the wooden mould (or form) used to hold it together. This word gave the French language the word *formage* (forming) which later became *fromage* (cheese).

Wines

The Auvergne still boasts a few wines like the famous St-Pourçain that can be left to age for up to four years, or Côtes d'Auvergne wines known since Roman times. But the best wine-growing areas are to be found in the Rhône valley, where Beaujolais and Côtes du Rhône are produced.

The vineyards on the Côtes du Rhône are thought to be the oldest in France, founded on vine stock introduced by the Greeks. They stretch along both banks of the river like a narrow ribbon, producing wines whose quality and balance are guaranteed by a skilful blend of varieties of grape. The reds should be consumed slightly cool, the whites well chilled. Château-Condrieu and Château-Grillet are among the greatest of all French white wines. If drunk young, they are a marvellous accompaniment to a crayfish gratin. Cornas was much appreciated by Charlemagne.

Further south, where the valley enters Provence, the vineyards produce the warm, friendly Châteauneuf-du-Pape, Gigondas, the sweet, suave and flavoursome Muscat from Beaumes-de-Venise and, on the other bank of the Rhône, the rosés from Tavel and the reds and rosés from Lirac and Chusclan.

St-Nectaire

© Chris Dave/age fotostock

History

TIMELINE
BCE PREHISTORY

7500-2800   **Neolithic Era: Stone Age.** Volcanoes in the Puys range cease to erupt. Farmer stock-breeders settle in the Rhône valley and the Massif Central, leaving some 50 dolmens and 20 or more menhirs.

c.180-700   **Bronze Age.** Human settlements become denser and the Rhône valley is the major amber and tin route. The Celts settle in Gaul. The Helvians settle on the right bank of the Rhône, the Allobroges on the left and the Arverni in the Auvergne.

Arverni domination of the Auvergne – The main expansion of the Celtic people occurred during the 5C BCE, probably as a result of the push southwards by Germanic tribes fleeing the rigorous climate of Northern Europe. Little is known about them; they had no written literature and were divided into different peoples in accordance with criteria that have remained mysterious. What *is* known is that the Celts in Gaul, like the **Allobroges** in Lugdunum (Lyon), were subject to the authority of the **Arverni** in the Massif Central. They traded with their own coinage. In order to ensure the submission of other peoples, their sovereigns acted as demagogues. King Luern, who reigned in the 2C, was famous for his gifts of gold. Rome, worried by his power, launched a campaign against his son, Bituit, who died in battle with Roman forces near Bollène in 121 BCE. The Roman legions settled in Vienne, the capital of the Allobroges.

The Arverni monarchy was no more. The great Celtic families took power and, thereafter, were forced to share it with the Aedui of Burgundy who were allied to Rome.

Prehistoric painting, Grotte Chauvet-Pont-d'Arc

© Clément Philippe/age fotostock

43   Lyon founded soon after Caesar's conquest of Gaul by one of his lieutenants, Munatius Plancus. Roman settlers arrive and build houses on the hillsides above the banks of the Saône.

27   Lyon, capital of the Gauls (Aquitaine, Lyon area, Belgium); the Rome and Augustus Altar is built on the hill at La Croix-Rousse.

CE

1C   Preachers come to spread the gospel in the Auvergne and the Rhône valley.

177   Marcus Aurelius instigates persecution. Christians are martyred in Lyon.

280   Emperor Probus removes the monopoly on sales of wine in Gaul previously enjoyed by the people of Lyon. This marks the start of Lyon's decline and, during the reign of Diocletian (284-305), the city is nothing more than the capital of the Lyon province.

406   After the invasion of the Vandals, the emperor introduces a federation of barbarian states in Gaul with the Visigoths in the Auvergne and the Burgundians on the left bank of the Rhône.

Sidonius Apollinaris stands up to the Visigoths – Sidonius Apollinaris was born in Lyon in AD 432 to a wealthy family of senators; later, his father-in-law, Avitus, was one of the last emperors of the Western world. Sidonius remained in Rome after the death of Avitus in AD 456 and wrote tributes to the emperors. His poetry pleased them and when he returned to the Auvergne, he was elected Bishop of Clermont.

Euric, King of the Visigoths, who already owned a large part of Aquitaine, threatened the Auvergne. Sidonius headed the resistance and withstood a siege lasting several years in the walled town of Clermont. Eventually the province was transferred to the barbarians in exchange for Provence, and Sidonius went into exile. Twenty years later, the province passed into the hands of the Franks after the Battle of Vouillé.

5C-9C Founding of the first abbeys – in Lyon, Vienne, Romans, in the Vivarais, the Lyonnais and the Velay.

761-767 Pepin the Short attempts to gain power over the noblemen of the Auvergne by means of military expeditions.

800 Charlemagne is crowned.

843 Treaty of Verdun. Charlemagne's empire is divided into three kingdoms (West, Central and East). The Auvergne is ruled by Charles the Bald (West Francia); the Rhône Valley by Lothair I (Lotharingia).

9C-10C Power is actually held by the many castle owners, all of them difficult to control. Safe on their feudal mottes, they war against their neighbours, devastate the countryside, attack churches and pillage monasteries.

951 The first pilgrimage to Santiago de Compostela starts from Le Puy-en-Velay.

999 Gerbert, a former monk from Aurillac, is elected to the papacy as Sylvester II. He is the first French Pope and he occupies the papal throne at the end of the first millennium.

1095 Pope Urban II preaches the First Crusade in Clermont. The wave of popular faith aroused by his call arrives just at the right time to channel the warring energies of the turbulent feudal lords.

The Pope has a chance to gauge the vitality of the church in the Auvergne. The Gregorian Reform purges the parishes by removing the power of the layman. The influence of a few of the great monasteries begins to spread. The Counts of Albon, who come from Vienne, extend their territory; their lands, stretching from the Rhône to the Alps, become known as Dauphiné.

Royal intervention in the Auvergne – Divided between their position as vassals to the King of France and their allegiance to the Duke of Aquitaine, the great lords of the Auvergne failed to come to an agreement that would enable them to set up their own state. These feuding lords of mixed loyalties governed large estates with no clearly defined borders, which eventually enabled the sovereign to annex sections of the region little by little over the 12C and 13C; first Riom and the Limagne, then Montferrand and the area subsequently known as Dauphiné and finally Lower Auvergne.

13C-14C The development of towns leads to the granting of numerous municipal charters. Royal authority gains a foothold and is strengthened in Auvergne and the Rhône valley:

1210 Philip Augustus annexes the Auvergne to his kingdom.

1292 Nomination of a royal "guardian" in Lyon.

1307 The so-called "Philippine" conventions strengthen Philip the Fair's hold on Lyon.

1308 The Bishop of Viviers recognises royal sovereignty.

1349 Dauphiné is annexed to France as the States of Dauphiné.

1229 The Treaty of Paris ends the Albigensian Crusade and the influence of the counts of Toulouse in the Vivarais area.

1241-71 The Auvergne is part of the appanage with which Alphonse of Poitiers, St Louis' brother, is endowed. He dies childless and the region is returned to the royal estate.

1262 Marriage of St Louis' son, Philip, to Isabella of Aragon in Clermont.

1337-1453 Hundred Years War.

1348 The Black Death ravages France.

1360 The Auvergne becomes a duchy and is given to John the Good's son, Jean, Duc de Berry.

15C The first firearms are made in St-Étienne.

1416-25 The Auvergne and the Bourbonnais region are united for 100 years under the authority of the House of Bourbon.

1419 The first fairs in Lyon, instituted by the heir to the throne, the future Charles VII, make the town one of the largest warehouses in the world.

1450 Charles VII grants Lyon a monopoly on the sale of silk throughout the kingdom.

Auvergne, held in appanage by Jean de Berry – The sovereign's hold on the Auvergne took it out of the sphere of influence of Southern France. It was divided in two with the creation of a bailiwick in the mountainous region corresponding to Upper Auvergne.

While the Bourbons continued to increase their power, with a barony that was raised to a duchy in 1327 (the Bourbonnais area), the Auvergne was granted in appanage to Jean, Duc de Berry in 1360.

War and epidemics combined with the heavy fiscal pressures imposed by a spendthrift lord. In order to circumvent the rules on land held in appanage, Jean de Berry transferred the Duchy of Auvergne to his son-in-law, the Duke of Bourbon, an action which the monarchy, by then in a weakened position, was obliged to accept formally in 1425. The Bourbons were then at the head of a huge feudal state which continued to exist until the Constable of Bourbon's treachery in 1527.

1473 The first book is printed in Lyon by Barthélemy Buyer.

1494 The start of the Italian Campaign. Charles VIII brings his court to Lyon.

1527 After the Constable of Bourbon's treachery, the Auvergne and the Bourbonnais region are confiscated by François I.

1528 The Reformation is preached in Annonay.

1536 A silk-making factory is opened in Lyon.

1562 Protestants led by Baron des Adrets ransack the Rhône valley and Forez area.

1572 After the St Bartholomew's Day Massacre, the Auvergne enters a period of chaos. Bloody battles are won in turn by the Huguenots, the royal army and members of the Catholic League.

1598 Promulgation of the Edict of Nantes which grants freedom of conscience to the Protestants along with limited rights to hold church services, and gives them political equality.

The Reformation and the Wars of Religion – In 1525, the Reformation spread right across the Cévennes and the Rhône valley, through the Vivarais area and along the Durance valley. The Auvergne, perhaps partially because of the mountainous lie of the land, was little concerned by the reformed religion, except in Issoire and the paper-making areas of Ambert and Aurillac.

The local people were attracted to Calvinist ideas, which allied with their taste for independence. The concepts were spread by craftsmen in the villages, carders and silk merchants travelling to Montpellier via Le Puy-en-Velay and Alès. The ideas were also spread by shoe-makers whose shops, like the tanneries, served as centres of propaganda. By 1550–60, the reformed religion had conquered the locality. Property belonging to the Catholic Church was sold and, by the end of the century, Mass was no longer being celebrated.

However, Catholics and Protestants were soon to engage in conflict. Eight wars, fought over a period of almost three decades, coincided with a time of political instability. Interspersed with ceasefires and edicts aimed at pacifying both sides, they never totally appeased the people's passion. In 1562 the murder of a group of Protestants in Champagne led to the Huguenot uprising, and Catholic resistance was led by the Parliament of Toulouse. The conflict was particularly bitter in the Dauphiné and Vivarais regions where the warring factions laid waste to entire towns and committed massacres.

The Baron des Adrets captured the main towns in Dauphiné, where he was the leader of the Huguenot movement, before moving on to decimate the Rhône valley with his troops and marching to the Forez area where he took Montbrison. After the tragic St Bartholomew's Day massacre (24th August 1572), the conflict took on a more political character and, paradoxically, led to forms of cooperation between Huguenots and Catholics in the face of royal authority and power.

Peace was not re-established until the Edict of Nantes was signed.

1629 Siege and destruction of Privas by the king's troops. Richelieu orders the dismantling of fortresses.

17C Counter-Reformation: founding of many convents.

1643 Accession of Louis XIV.

1685 Revocation of the Edict of Nantes. The dragoons sweep through the Vivarais area, ill-treating and killing people.

1783 First public ascent by the Montgolfier brothers in a hot-air balloon.

Auvergne's finest hours – Although the aristocracy in the Auvergne was careful not to become involved in the Fronde Revolt against the monarchy, the king brought the hand of royal justice to bear on the region in order to ensure its submission for all time.

In September 1665, Louis XIV sent commissioners to the Auvergne, to provide a display of royal authority. The return to law and order included the repression of often tyrannical behaviour and excessive violence used by the local nobility to stamp out revolt among the country people. In the Auvergne as elsewhere, rural uprisings had resulted from the constraints imposed by a central authority that had not yet acquired its finality. The Court heard 1 360 cases and passed 692 sentences, of which 450 were handed down by default for the suspects had fled as soon as the first of the 23 executions was carried out. Thereafter, offenders were sentenced in their absence and effigies were hung in their place. This simulation of justice "without any spilling of blood" (**Esprit Fléchier**) nevertheless allowed for the return of a large amount of property and

the destruction of castles that had been spared by Richelieu 40 years earlier.
The authority of the State and royal justice could be felt by all throughout France. The magistrates tried to remedy abuses of the system by drawing up regulations on statute labour, weights and measures.

The **Intendants** began to check the titles held by the nobility and laid the foundations for a fiscal reform in order to share the burden of taxation more fairly.

1789	Start of the French Revolution. 14th July: capture of the Bastille Prison. France is subdivided into *départements*.
1790	The first town council is set up in Lyon.
1793	A Resistance movement is set up in Lyon to fight the Convention: the town is subject to vicious reprisals as a result. In the Auvergne, **Georges Couthon**, a member of the Committee of Public Salvation, orders the demolition of bell-towers in the Auvergne on grounds of equality.
Early 19C	Mining begins in the coalfields around St-Étienne.
1804	The Jacquard loom is invented.
1820	Silk production becomes a boom industry in the Vivarais area.
1825	The Seguin brothers build the first suspension bridge over the Rhône.
1832	The St-Étienne to Lyon railway line is inaugurated. Barbier and Daubrée open a factory in Clermont and begin working with rubber; this is the pioneer of the future Michelin group.
1831-34	Silk workers revolt in Lyon.
1850	Pebrine, a disease that attacks silkworms, causes a crisis in the silk industry.
1855	The railway is extended as far as Clermont.
1870-71	The Fall of the Second Empire; the Third Republic is founded.
1880	Phylloxera destroys half of the vineyards in Ardèche. Orchards are planted in the Rhône and Eyrieux valleys.
1889	Phylloxera devastates the vineyards in the Limagne.
Late 19C	The chemical industry is set up in Lyon and metal-working sees a period of expansion.
1895	The cinematograph is invented by the Lumière brothers in Lyon.

The birth of the cinematograph – In 1882 a photographer from Besançon named Antoine Lumière opened a workshop in a shed in Lyon and began to produce dry silver bromine plates to a formula that he had invented himself. Within four years he had sold over one million plates under the brand name *Étiquette bleue*.

The former photographer's two sons, Louis and Auguste **Lumière**, worked with their father on a new device; the equipment, invented in 1895 and exhibited in Lyon in June 1896, was to be known as the cinematograph.

The general public, after initial indifference, rushed to see the first 10 films – short farces whose humour has withstood the test of time.

The first film, *Workers Leaving the Lumière Factory* was followed by *The Arrival of a Train in the Station*, *The Gardener* (including the famous scene of the gardener being doused with water from the garden hose) and *Baby Food*.

1940	Vichy becomes the capital of occupied France.

The Vichy government – The armistice signed in Compiègne on 22 June 1940 marked the defeat of France, which was divided into two zones – the North was occupied by Nazi Germany and the South was declared a free zone. Parliament, tolling the death knell of the Third

Famous Local Figures

Few regions in France have given the country so many scientists and engineers – the engineer Marc Seguin (steam boiler), the physicist André-Marie Ampère (electrodynamics), the physiologist Claude Bernard and cinematographers the Lumière brothers.

The Montgolfier brothers and the first flight – In the years before the French Revolution, the brothers Joseph and Étienne de Montgolfier became famous by achieving the first flights in a hot-air balloon.

Tirelessly continuing research into a gas that was lighter than air, Joseph completed his first experiment with a taffeta envelope filled with hot air. His brother joined him in his research and they launched their first aerostat on place des Cordeliers in Annonay on 4 June 1783. It was so successful that Louis XVI asked them to repeat it in his presence, and so it was that, on 19 September of that same year, the first "manned" flight took place in Versailles, under the control of Étienne and in the presence of the amazed royal family and Court. Attached beneath the balloon was a latticework cage containing the first passengers – a cockerel, a duck and a sheep. In just a few minutes, the **Réveillon** bearing the king's cipher on a blue background rose into the air and then came to rest in Vaucresson woods.

Lumière brothers

© Institut Lumière – OT/Lyon Tourisme et Congrès

One month later, at the Château de la Muette in Paris, Marquis d'Arlandes and Pilâtre de Rozier completed the first human flight in a hot-air balloon.

Jacquard and the weaving loom – Jacquard was born in Lyon in 1752. His father, a small-time material manufacturer, employed his son to work the cords that operated the complicated machinery used to form the pattern in silk.

After his father's death, Jacquard tried to set up a fabric factory, but his lack of commercial experience and the experiments he undertook to try and perfect the weaving of the fabric left him financially ruined. He continued to work nights on the design of a new loom and on a machine to manufacture fishing nets. He registered his first patent in 1801. The officers of the Republic were looking for inventors and so Jacquard was brought to Paris where he earned a salary of 3 000 francs.

At the newly created **Conservatoire**, he perfected a machine invented by a man from Grenoble named Vaucanson. In 1804 Jacquard returned to Lyon

Jacquard loom, Soierie Saint-Georges, Lyon

© Bertrand Rieger/hemis.fr

to complete work on the loom with which his name has remained linked ever since. In place of the ropes and pedals that required the work of six people, Jacquard substituted a simple mechanism based on perforated cards laid on the loom to define the pattern. A single worker, in place of five in earlier times, could make the most complicated fabrics as easily as plain cloth. By decreasing the production costs, it would be possible to withstand foreign competition and increase sales. Manufacturers set an example and, in 1812, several Jacquard looms were brought into service in Lyon. The experiment worked so well that the name is still in use today.

Thimonnier, the unfortunate inventor of the sewing machine – Unlike Jacquard, Thimonnier did not have the good fortune to see his invention being used in his native country. His father was a dyer from Lyon who had fled the town and its upheavals during the French Revolution. In 1795 the family settled in Amplepuis where Thimonnier was apprenticed to a tailor. In 1822 he left the region to set up in business as a tailor near St-Étienne. Haunted by the idea of sewing clothes mechanically, and taking inspiration from the hooks used by embroiderers in the Lyonnais mountain range, he built a wooden and metal device that would produce chain stitch – the first sewing machine. To register a patent, the inventor entered a partnership with Auguste Ferrand, a teacher at the Miners' School in St-Étienne. An application was filed on 13 April 1830 in the names of both partners. Thimonnier then left St-Étienne for Paris where the first mechanical sewing shop soon saw the light of day.

There, 80 sewing machines produced goods six times quicker than manual workers, arousing the hatred of Parisian tailors who feared that their profession was on the point of ruin.

On the night of 20 to 21 January 1831, 200 workers employed in the sewing and tailoring business ransacked the Parisian workshop. Thimonnier was ruined and he returned to Amplepuis where, in order to feed his large family, he again began work as a tailor. Thimonnier died at the age of 64 – without seeing the huge success enjoyed by the sewing machine.

Timeline

538-594 – Gregory of Tours (born in Clermont-Ferrand), churchman and historian.

938-1003 – Gerbert d'Aurillac, theologian and scholar who went on to become Pope Sylvester II.

1555-1623 – Henri de La Tour d'Auvergne, Marshal of France under Henri IV and Calvinist leader.

1623-1662 – Blaise Pascal (Clermont-Ferrand), academic, writer and philosopher (⌖ see LITERATURE).

1652-1719 – Michel Rolle (Ambert), mathematician and author of a treaty of algebra.

1757-1834 – Marquis de La Fayette (Chavaniac), general and politician

1851-1914 – Fernand Forest (Clermont-Ferrand), inventor (four-stroke engine).

1853-1929 – André Messager (Montluçon), composer.

1853-1931 and 1859-1940 – André and **Édouard Michelin** (Clermont-Ferrand), industrialists (rubber tyres and tourist publications).

1884-1932 – Albert Londres (Vichy), journalist and writer.

1911-1974 – Georges Pompidou, politician and President of the French Republic (1969–74).

b.1926 – Valéry Giscard d'Estaing, politician and President of the French Republic (1974–81).

Republic, vested all power in **Maréchal Pétain**, the victor of Verdun in 1916. The choice of a seat for the new government fell on the prosperous spa town of Vichy (🔗see VICHY).

1942–44 Lyon is the centre of the French Resistance Movement.

1944 Battles are fought in the Rhône valley and in the Cantal (Mont Mouchet) as part of the liberation of France. The Germans blow up the bridges over the Rhône.

Lyon, a centre of the Resistance Movement – Lyon, a city in the southern zone, found itself near the demarcation line after the signing of the armistice in 1940. Countless Parisians sought refuge here and initially it became the intellectual and patriotic heart of France. The city was one of the major centres for the printing of literature, posters and journals, many more popular with readers than the press that supported Vichy. Important Resistance actions were carried out in Lyon, but they were badly organised until the arrival of **Jean Moulin**, sent by General de Gaulle; the various groups then joined together in 1943 to form the *Mouvements Unis de la Résistance* (Unified Resistance Movements). Moulin set up an administrative structure for the Resistance, organising services that were common to all the networks and a secret army operating in the south of France and the Rhône valley.

1946 Start of the Fourth Republic.

1957 The Treaty of Rome leads to the setting up of the EEC.

1958 Birth of the Fifth Republic.

1969 Georges Pompidou, born in Cantal, is elected President of the Republic.

1972 The Auvergne and Rhône-Alpes regions are created.

1974 Valéry Giscard d'Estaing, Mayor of Chamalières (Puy-de-Dôme), elected President of the Republic.

1981 The first high-speed train service (TGV) runs between Paris and Lyon.

1986 **Superphénix**, Europe's first fast-breeder reactor to operate on an industrial scale, is brought into service in Creys-et-Pusignieu (Isère).

1989 Completion of the motorway link (A 71) between Clermont-Ferrand and Paris (Orléans).

1993 The EU introduces the Single Market.

1996 Lyon's hosting of the G7 summit confirms the city's international role.

2000 Clermont-Auvergne International Airport is inaugurated.

2002 Opening of **VULCANIA**. Located in the heart of the Puy range, Vulcania, the European Volcano Park, plunges you deep into the world of volcanoes and the Earth sciences.

2006 The 40th anniversary of La Chaise Dieu music festival, founded by Georges Cziffra in 1966.

2009 Olypique Lyonnais become French football ligue 1's most consecutive winners (2003-2009).

2012 François Hollande, who was born in Rouen, is elected President of France.

2014 Lyon's newest museum, the Musée des Confluences opens to wide acclaim.

2016 The Auvergne and Rhône-Alpes regions are combined into one new region.

2017 Emmanuel Macron is elected President of France, representing his "La République En Marche!" centrist political party. He beat the far-right National Front's Marine Le Pen. He appointed Le Havre mayor Édouard Philippe to be Prime Minister. His party wins an overall majority in parliamentary elections.

Architecture

ROMAN ARCHITECTURE IN THE RHÔNE VALLEY

By the 1C, the region had become the starting point for the conquest of Germany and Lyon was the capital of Gaul. In the 2C, major road building and town planning work was undertaken in Vienne and Lyon, then at the height of their power. However, the fires, pillaging and devastations by the Barbarians, coupled with the later destruction during the Middle Ages, destroyed the remains of the old civilisation.

From 1922 in Vienne and 1933 in Lyon, archaeologists began to uncover groups of buildings, in particular small theatres adjacent to smaller buildings or *odeons*. Some of the buildings are still being unearthed and large areas remain to be explored, in particular in St-Romain-en-Gal on the right bank of the Rhône where part of a residential district has been uncovered.

© Sime/Photononstop

Théâtre Romain, Vienne

THEATRES

These consisted of tiers of seats ending in a colonnade known as the **cavea**, an orchestra pit, a dais used by dignitaries and a raised stage *(scena)*. The actors performed in front of a wall with doors in it through which they made their entrances. Behind the wall at the back of the stage were the richly decorated actors' dressing rooms and the stores. Beyond that was a portico opening onto gardens where the actors walked before entering the stage. Spectators could stroll there during intervals or take shelter from the rain.

TEMPLES

A closed sanctuary contained the effigy of a god or the emperor, and an open vestibule. They were partially or totally surrounded by a colonnade. The Temple of Augustus and Livia in Vienne is one of the best preserved anywhere.

ROMAN BATHS

Roman baths were public and free of charge. They were not only public baths but also fitness centres, meeting places and a place for games and entertainment. Romans had acquired extensive knowledge concerning water supplies and heating. Water was brought to the baths by an aqueduct, stored in tanks then piped through a system of lead and mortar ducts. Waste water was carried away through a sewage system. The water and rooms were heated by a system of hearths and hypocausts in the basement. The hot air obtained by the burning of coal and wood circulated through a conduit built into the walls. The buildings were vast, sumptuous and luxurious. There were columns and capitals decorated with vivid colours, mosaic facing on the walls, marble floors and wall coverings, richly coffered ceilings, and frescoes and statues like those found in the remains of the Roman baths in Ste-Colombe near Vienne.

AMPHITHEATRES

Shows were staged in the arena, usually oval in shape. There were fights between wild beasts or gladiators, and people sentenced to death were executed. Around the arena were tiers of seats for the audience. Lyon, the official centre for the worship of Rome in Gaul, had its own amphitheatre.

CIRCUS

The circus attracted crowds of people who enjoyed watching chariot racing. In the middle of the track was a long rectangular construction – the **spina** – marked at each end by huge, semicircular stones. The horses and drivers wore the colours of the rival factions organising the competitions. Built partly of timber, the circus was, despite its impressive size, particularly vulnerable to destruction.

AQUEDUCTS

On the plateau to the south-west of Lyon stand well-preserved sections of aqueduct (Arches de Chaponost, *see LYON: Monts du Lyonnais*). Aqueducts were one of the essential features of any town. The tall arches built to maintain the level of the pipes were monuments in their own right. Indeed, the aqueduct, more than any other construction, is a striking illustration of the building skills of the Romans who attached very great importance to the quality of the water supplied to their towns and cities.

DECORATIVE ARTS

The large, delicately coloured mosaics found in Lyon (circus games, Bacchus etc.) prove that mosaic-makers were particularly active in Lyon. The medallions that decorated the sides of vases were made by potters from Lyon and Vienne who excelled in illustrations of scenes from mythology or everyday life.

RELIGIOUS ARCHITECTURE
THE ROMANESQUE PERIOD

There is no Romanesque School inherent to the Rhône valley since the region, situated as it is at the junction of countless roads, was influenced by artists from Italy, Burgundy, Provence – and the Auvergne. In the Auvergne a Romanesque School developed which is considered one of the most unusual in the history of the architecture of the Western world, giving the churches an air of similarity that is immediately apparent. It originated in the 11C. After the great invasions and the establishment of the Capetian kingdom, the Auvergne enjoyed a period of prosperity. The local people undertook land clearance, acquiring new areas of land and instigating new building projects. In

the 11C this movement was amplified by the Gregorian Reform and the desire on the part of men of the Church for independence from lay authorities. Gradually, countless churches and chapels were built across the countryside and, even today, they reveal something of the soul of the Auvergne and its people, for they are all built with an economic use of resources and an immense simplicity. This is what gives the architecture its strength.

The churches in Clermont-Ferrand (Notre-Dame-du-Port), Issoire, Orcival, St-Nectaire and St-Saturnin are just some of the finest examples of this Romanesque style in which the beauty is both austere and logical.

An Unusual School

It developed in the 11C and 12C within the large diocese of Clermont. The churches, often small but always beautifully proportioned, give an impression of being much bigger than they actually are. Paul Bourget describes the appearance of these churches, powerful and rugged as those who created them: "Seen from the east end, especially with the tight semicircle of chapels huddled up against the mass of the main building, these churches give a striking impression of aplomb and unity."

Volcanic Building Materials

In Limagne, arkose, a yellowish metamorphic sandstone, was used until the 13C. Volcanic lava stone was first used for bonding beneath load-bearing arches, in the upper sections of buildings which did not support the weight of the vaulting and to which they added a touch of colour. In the 13C improvements to the quality of tools made it possible to cut the hard blocks of lava stone and developments in stone-cutting techniques made it the commonest building material available.

GREAT CHURCHES IN LOWER AUVERGNE

The layout of the churches slowly changed to meet new needs arising out of pilgrimages. The basic layout is the one seen in Clermont Cathedral, which was consecrated in 946 and was the first one to have an ambulatory and radiating chapels. Today, all that remains is the crypt. Yet it took a period of trial and error (churches in Ennezat, Glaine-Montaigut) to achieve the perfection of the 12C buildings.

Exterior Features

West Front – Exposed to the weather and almost devoid of decoration, the west front – which includes a porch – forms a stark contrast to the east end because of its austerity. In some cases, it is topped by a central bell-tower and two side towers.

Bell-towers – Two-storey, traceried, octagonal bell-towers were a source of light, emerging from the mass of the building around the dome. They stood high above the chancel and ambulatory. In Auvergne, there are a large number of bell-cotes *(clocher à peigne)* – gable walls with openings in which the bells are hung in one or two tiers.

Side walls – The windows in the side aisles are built inside enormous load-bearing arches that support the walls. Beneath these arches, the stone often has a decorative role through its colour or layout. Above them is the line of the clerestory in which the windows are linked by arcading.

East end – The magnificent layout of the various levels at the east end is the most beautiful and most characteristic part of the Auvergne churches. This masterpiece of austerity counterbalances the thrust from the octagonal bell-tower. It stands like a carefully combined pyramid, giving an impression of harmony and security through the perfection of each of its elements and the regularity of the design.

Interior

The nave is often stark; the only decorative features are the capitals and they are not immediately apparent because most of these buildings are very dark.

Huge arches support the gallery and the weight of the bell-tower if it has been built above the west front.

Nave and vaulting – The wide naves lined with side aisles providing extra support were designed to cater for large numbers of pilgrims. Heavy Romanesque barrel vaulting replaced roof rafters which were too susceptible to fire and which, between the 5C and 11C, led to the loss of many churches.

Chancel – This part of the church was reserved for the clergy and the celebration of Mass. By raising it up a few steps and lowering the vaulting, perspective made it appear larger than it actually was. It was here that sculptors gave free rein to their talent and the beautifully designed carved capitals in the chancel are often the finest in the church.

In large churches, the chancel included a straight bay. Behind it was a semicircle around which tall columns, set out in such a way as to avoid blocking the light, extended into small raised arches forming a sort of crown.

Ambulatory – In large churches, an ambulatory extended beyond the side aisles and skirted the chancel. An even number of radiating chapels formed a crown around the ambulatory so that, on major feast days, several Masses could be celebrated simultaneously. The chapels were separated from each other by windows.

Transept and dome – The construction of the transept posed a difficult problem for architects; they had to design large ribbed vaulting capable of supporting the entire weight of the central bell-tower and which was formed by the interpenetration of the vaulting in the nave and the arms of the transept.

Crypt – Beneath the chancel in large churches, there is often a crypt laid out like the church above it. The chancel in the crypt, like the one in the upper church, is flanked by an ambulatory decorated with radiating chapels. The

Religious Architecture

ORCIVAL – Notre-Dame Basilica (12C)

Most of the churches in Auvergne are in the Romanesque style, and belong to a school of design which developed in the 11C and 12C, which has a number of unique characteristics.

Relieving or **discharging arch:** an arch built over a lintel to distribute the weight of the load-bearing walls

Two-storey, **octagonal bell-tower**

Geminated bays: occur in pairs

Bays: occurring in groups of two, three, four, etc

Transept

Rounded hip roof covering the chevet

Gable-wall

Semicircular bay

Sloping hip roof

Apsidal chapel or **radiating chapel**

Modillion: a horizontal bracket or console; here the decorative scrolling recalls wood shavings

Cornice with checkerboard pattern

Buttress: masonry structure bonded to and projecting from the wall, which gives stability

Chevet: the graceful fall of tiered roofs is the most distinctive and attractive feature of churches in Auvergne

R. Cortel/MICHELIN

CLERMONT-FERRAND – Notre-Dame-du-Port Basilica (11C and 12C)

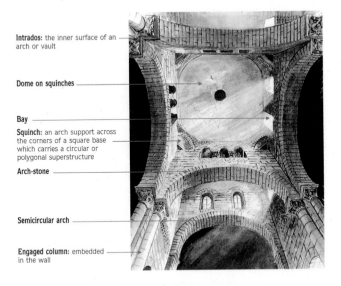

Intrados: the inner surface of an arch or vault

Dome on squinches

Bay

Squinch: an arch support across the corners of a square base which carries a circular or polygonal superstructure

Arch-stone

Semicircular arch

Engaged column: embedded in the wall

ISSOIRE – St-Austremoine Abbey (12C)

Abacus: the uppermost section of the capital

Foliated capital

Band

Bevelled edge

Historiated capital: decorated with scenes and characters

Astragal

Capital: the uppermost member of a column or pilaster crowning the shaft and taking the weight of the vaulting or the entablature

Column: a supporting pillar usually consisting of a cylindrical **shaft**, a **base** and topped by a **capital**

Painted motifs dating from the second half of the 19C

Chancel railing

R. Corbel/MICHELIN

LE PUY-EN-VELAY – Doorway of St-Michel Chapel (12C)

Seeming to rise out of the rock below it, this chapel has been called the "eighth wonder of the world". Eastern influences are apparent in the polychrome motifs and geometric designs.

Oculus: round opening

Cornice

Foliage scrolls: sculpted or painted decoration in the form of a leafy stem or vine defining a frieze

Bas-relief sculpture: projects slightly from the surrounding surface

Abacus

Capital: the uppermost member of a column or pilaster crowning the shaft and taking the weight of the vaulting or the entablature

Free-standing column: separated from the wall by a slight interstice

Masonry course: geometric design formed by the masonry

Archivolt

Trefoil arch

Tympanum

Lintel: sculpted with sirens facing each other

CRUAS – Former Abbey (11C to 13C)

This beautiful abbey, typical of the Vivarais region, has managed to withstand the ravages of time. As research continues, new discoveries have brought to light architectural marvels from the Carolingian and Romanesque periods.

Lantern

Denticles

Dome on squinches

Engaged colonettes

Drum: supporting a cupola

Modillion: a horizontal bracket or console; here the decorative scrolling recalls wood shavings

Blind arcading in a **frieze**

Apse

Transept chapel

Recessed bay: the sides splay so that the opening is wider on one side than on the other

Flamboyant window tracery: the interlacing ribs here represent flames, which explains why the term Flamboyant was applied to Late Gothic architecture

Lombardy banding or **pilaster strips:** slightly projecting vertical bands, linked by a frieze of small arches on top crypt never extends westwards beyond the transept.

Decorative Features

Capitals – The capitals are magnificently carved with fanciful scenes. Most of them are to be found around the chancel. Many artists introduced an entire portrait gallery of figures: figures from Antiquity rub shoulders with eagles, mermaids, centaurs, minotaurs, telamones, snakes, genies, figures from the Orient, griffons and birds drinking out of a chalice. Beside them are the heroes of medieval epics, the founders of the church, knights in armour dating from the period of the First Crusade and local saints.

Statues of the Virgin Mary in Majesty and statue-reliquaries – Worship of the Blessed Virgin Mary has always been an important part of religion in the Auvergne for, in Celtic countries, the Christian religion was grafted onto worship of a mother-goddess.

The Gothic Period

Gothic architecture came from the north and took some time to spread further south. It reached Lyon in the early 13C but the Rhône valley has none of the great churches of which Northern France is so proud and it continued to be subject to the influence of the south as is evident in the width of the buildings and the horizontal line of the roofs.

The Auvergne, strong in its own Romanesque School, resisted change for a long time. Not until the language of Northern France, *langue d'oïl,* was introduced in place of the Southern French *langue d'oc,* after the province had been conquered by Philip Augustus, did the Rayonnant Gothic style gain a foothold on the rebellious region, to the detriment of the sources of inspiration from further south which had been predominant until that time. This change of style marked the seizure of the province by the Capetians. There were, though, two main currents in the architectural style – Northern French Gothic and Languedoc Gothic.

Northern French Gothic

Clermont Cathedral, dating from the 13C and 14C, is only very vaguely reminiscent of the great buildings of the Paris basin and not until the 19C was Gothic architecture introduced into its west front and spires designed by the architect Viollet-le-Duc. Lava stone from Volvic, a building material that was too hard to be carved but which architects liked for its strength, resistance and permanence, gave the cathedral an austerity that even the sun cannot brighten up. The roofs on the chapels and side aisles consist of stone slabs forming a terrace beneath the flying buttresses, a very unusual design that was totally unknown in the north of France.

The same stylistic movement can be seen in the Ste-Chapelle in Riom.

Languedoc Gothic

Characterised by a wide nave devoid of side aisles, side chapels inserted between the piers and the absence of flying buttresses, this was the commonest style in the area. The abbey church at La Chaise-Dieu, a masterpiece of monastic architecture, is a fine example, as are other churches commissioned by the mendicant orders such as the Marthuret Church in Riom or Notre-Dame-des-Neiges in Aurillac.

Painting

A vast selection of medieval painting has been preserved within the Auvergne. The frescoes in the church of St-Julien in Brioude, for instance, date from the 12C; there is the 13C representation of the legend of St George in one of the ambulatory chapels in Clermont Cathedral, and the 14C Assumption and Coronation of the Virgin Mary in Billom. From the 15C are the Last Judgement in Issoire, St George Slaying the Dragon in Ébreuil, the Dance of Death in La Chaise-Dieu, and the frescoes in Ennezat. The triptych painted on wood by the Maître de Moulins is one of the last masterpieces of Gothic painting in France.

MILITARY AND CIVIL ARCHITECTURE

Defensive Castles

During the days of the feudal system, the country was dotted with castles; by building fortresses, lords, viscounts and barons could display their power and authority compared to that of the king. This is why there are so many castles, with outlines that adapt to the shape of the rock beneath them. From the 13C, they were subject to successive attacks by the troops under Philip Augustus, who conquered 120 of them from 1210 onwards, to destruction during the Hundred Years War and, at the end of the conflict, to destruction by villagers who, at enormous cost, succeeded in routing the mercenaries and captains who were using them as a source of building material for their own houses.

The Gentler Architecture of the Renaissance

The influence of the Italian Renaissance travelled to Northern France via the Rhône corridor and in the 15C it slowly penetrated the Auvergne where a certain taste for well-being made itself apparent after the end of the war. The fortresses were turned into charming residences in which ornamentation supplanted systems of defence, even

Eugenie Fountain at Royat

© Yann Guichaoua/age fotostock

if, in the Auvergne, the austerity of the building in lava stone remained intact. Numerous castles were bought up by gentlemen of the robe or members of the middle classes who had recently acquired wealth through trade.

Town Planning During the Classical Period

In Lyon this manifested itself in a new form of town planning, which can be seen mainly in the 17C Terreaux district around the town hall. In the 18C, a new concept of urban layout was introduced, based on speculation. The main feature of these areas is place Bellecour, laid out during the reign of Louis XIV and flanked by Louis XVI residences.

The 19C and the Architecture of the Auvergne Spas: a Fantasy World

In the spa towns of the 19C, "taking the waters" was not a new idea, but it was during this period that it became fashionable. On the pretext of taking the waters and enjoying a rest, members of high society, and those with power or money, flocked to spa towns. Their visits were an opportunity to lead an active social life and it was this that governed the architectural style. In the centre of the town were the pump rooms, a veritable palace to which the architects paid particular attention; around them were the parks and springs built to resemble Ancient Greek or Roman temples. The casinos and the luxury hotels were decorated with an exuberance that was almost Baroque. In the streets of the town, troubadour-style castles stood next to Venetian palaces, and Henri IV residences rubbed shoulders with Art Nouveau mansions.

The history of this architecture, designed for enjoyment and pleasure, is a history of intermingling. The eclectic mix was the result of ideas by the most fashionable urban architects of the day combined with those of the architects of the Auvergne who were inspired by a long tradition based on Early Romanesque architecture and the volcanic and granite rocks available locally; these

Military Architecture

TOURNEMIRE – Château d'Anjony (15C)

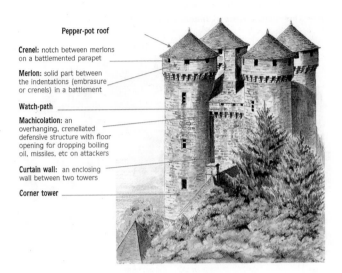

Pepper-pot roof

Crenel: notch between merlons on a battlemented parapet

Merlon: solid part between the indentations (embrasure or crenels) in a battlement

Watch-path

Machicolation: an overhanging, crenellated defensive structure with floor opening for dropping boiling oil, missiles, etc on attackers

Curtain wall: an enclosing wall between two towers

Corner tower

ST-POURÇAIN-SUR-BESBRE
Fortified gate of Thoury Château (15C)

Bartizan: a small overhanging turret with lookout holes

Machicolation

Main building

Fortified gatehouse controlling the entrance

Dormer window

Loophole

Mullioned window: the mullions are the vertical parts of the tracery, separating and supporting the window

Curtain wall

Slots for **swipe beams** (wooden beams to which the chains raising the drawbridge were attached)

Moat: wide ditch filled with water, protecting the curtain wall and towers

Entrance gate

R. Corbel/MICHELIN

Civil Architecture

MARCY-L'ÉTOILE – Château de Lacroix-Laval (17C – 18C)

Renovated under the guidance of Soufflot in the 18C, this château was ransacked from cellar to attic during the French Revolution. It has since been restored several times, but has kept the classic façade typical of family manor houses in the 18C.

Imperial roof

Dormer window

Triangular pediment

Ironwork balcony

Chain course masonry: the stones are laid in a pattern alternating length, width and depth, for a stronger bond

Bracket with **scroll** motif

Pavilion set forward of the main façade

Terrace

Fore part projecting from the rest of the façade for its entire height

Transom or **fan light:** upper segment of a door or window bay

Rustic Brace: also called **bossage,** this refers to stones which project beyond the mortar joint

Industrial Architecture

LYON – Halle Tony-Garnier (1914)

The covered market is a display of technical prowess: the 18000m^2/193 750sq ft area stands without interior pillars. Designed by local architect Tony Garnier, it now serves for cultural events and trade fairs, and remains a landmark of contemporary architecture.

Corbiestep façade: a derivative of 14C-17C design, where the edge of the gable was shaped into steps along the pitch of the roof.

Stringcourse

Blind bay

Segmented bay window

Rising keystone

Basin

Inside, **metal framework** with **ball-and-socket joints**

Obelisk

Buttress

R. Corbel/MICHELIN

Spa Resort Architecture

LE MONT-DORE – Caesar's spring gallery (1890 and 1935-38)

The design expresses the architectural eclecticism typical of spa towns. The inspiration can be traced to the Roman baths of Antiquity; the high ceilings and ornate decoration lend grandeur. The distinctive Romanesque style of Auvergne creates an atmosphere reminiscent of an opulent temple.

Transverse arch: semicircular, with **arch-stones** in an alternating white (limestone) and grey (andesite) pattern, typical of the Romanesque style in Auvergne

Cabochons in yellow glass

Entablature and **capitals** stucco moulding

Tympanum with **fresco** (Roman baths of Mont-Dore)

Coffered barrel vault

Colonnade of **engaged columns**

Claustra: a slab of stone or terracotta pierced in a geometric pattern, forming a bay

Grand arcade with false transom (fan light)

Floor laid with **tile** and **glass bricks**

Aedicula: a niche in the form of a **tabernacle**, from which Caesar's spring flows

R. Corbel/MICHELIN

ideas were also influenced by the mixture of water and a natural environment with a town of stone, including its culture and its social events. Even the railway stations were not forgotten, since they provided the first impression for visitors who had just arrived. The result was a luxurious style of architecture full of exuberance and voluptuousness in the dream world constituted by the resorts in the heart of the Auvergne.

The New Opera House in Lyon, a Fine Example of 20C Architecture

Throughout the 19C and 20C Lyon was considered an ideal place for architectural experiments. In 1825 iron suspension bridges were built over the Rhône, using new techniques. In 1896 the basilica on Fourvière hill was completed in a Byzantine-cum-medieval style.

In the 1970s, with a view to the launch of the high-speed train service which would bring Lyon to within 2hrs of Paris, a major development was begun in the La Part-Dieu district: a new business centre that was to take the city to the forefront of Europe's business world. In 1993 the latest architectural feat was completed; the old opera house designed in 1831 had to be renovated and it was **Jean Nouvel** who took up the gauntlet. All that remains of the old building are the four walls and an old foyer decorated with gold leaf and stucco-work.

TRADITIONAL RURAL HOUSING

Over the centuries, changes in rural housing have kept pace with changes in agricultural work. Housing has also been subject to the influence of neighbouring regions and new building techniques.

AUVERGNE

Roofs

Owing to its geographical situation the Auvergne is in contact with two civilisations, "the Northern French one in which roofs are built with a 45-degree slope and flat tiles, and that of the Mediterranean basin in which the roofs have a slope of 30 degrees and rounded tiles" (Max Derruau). In the mountains, thatch

is replaced by slate or corrugated iron. The most attractive roofs are those made of stone slabs called *lauzes* that look like gigantic tortoise shells. They can only be mounted on a steeply sloping roof with a very strong set of rafters. On the plains, the old round tiles and rows of guttering once common in the countryside are beginning to lose ground in the face of competition from more stable mass-produced tiles.

Housing in the Limagne

The houses with upper storeys, which belong to wine-growers or farmers specialising in mixed agriculture, are commonplace in the old villages huddling on the hillsides. The ground floor is used for work (stables, cellars) and the upper floor is the house, reached by an outside flight of steps leading to a balcony sheltered by a porch roof.

Housing in the Mountains

These houses are sturdy buildings, constructed from large blocks of basalt. The heavy roofs extend below the top of the walls. The single building contains both dwelling and byre side by side. They always face south, and are sheltered from bad weather by the haybarn. Doors and windows are narrow and the roof drops down to the ground at the rear of the building.

Housing in the Velay Area

Houses in this area are unusual as their walls are made of ashlar, with a predominance of grey or dark-red lava stone in volcanic areas, light-coloured granite in areas of older soil, and yellow arkose in areas of sedimentary rock. The blocks of stone are cemented together using a mortar that is often mixed with pozzolana, a reddish volcanic gravel. In the villages, a bell turret indicates the village hall *(assemblée)* or *"maison de la béate"*.

Shepherds' and Cowherds' Huts

A *buron* is a squat, stone-roofed temporary dwelling high up in the mountains, used by cowherds during periods of trans-humance. This was where the cheese and butter was made which the

From Beaujolais to Lower Vavarais

House in the Beaujolais region

Farm and dovecote on Dombes plateau

Jasserie: summer farmstead in the Forez mountains

House in Lower Dauphiné

Farm in the Mézenc range

House in Lower Vivarais

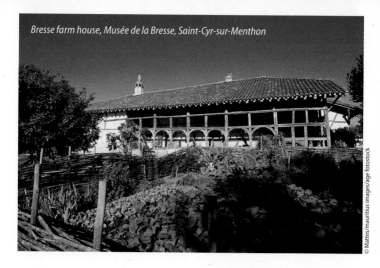

Bresse farm house, Musée de la Bresse, Saint-Cyr-sur-Menthon

© Mattes/mauritius images/age fotostock

cantalès, or master of the *buron*, then sent down to the valleys from time to time. A small number of these huts are still in use. In the Livradois and Forez areas, and on the slopes of Mont Pilat, there are "**jasseries**" or "mountain farms" used during the summer months. Solidly built of stone with thatched roofs, they consist of a living room, a byre and a cheese cellar below.

RHÔNE VALLEY

Housing in the Forez and Lyonnais Areas

Houses in the Forez area are farmsteads enclosed by high walls around a central courtyard. The walls are often made of rows of stones set at a slant.

In the Dombes area, the farmhouses are elongated and have an upper storey. External pebbledash protects the walls made of terracotta bricks or cob.

Housing in the Rhône Valley

On the **Valence and Montélimar plains**, the walls often have no doors or windows on the north side since this is where the mistral wind blows. Additional protection is often provided by a row of thuyas, cypress and plane trees. Large, isolated farmsteads consist of a group of buildings around a walled courtyard, and their external walls, devoid of doors or windows, make them look like fortresses.

Housing in Lower Dauphiné

Between Bourbe and Isère, pebbles or "**rolled stones**" were often used as a building material because they were commonplace in this area of moraine and alluvial deposits. The stones are assembled end on, on a bed of mortar, and the angle changes from one level to the next. In some areas (eg Morestel and Creys) there is a style of roofing that has been imported from the Préalpes: **crowstepped** or **corbie-stepped gabling.**

Housing in the Upper Vivarais

On the edges of the Velay area, along the Mézenc range and on the high plateaux above the upper reaches of the Ardèche and Eyrieux, the houses are low and squat with stone-slabbed roofs, seeming almost weighed down by this shell designed to withstand bad weather.

On the St-Agrève plateau, the granite farmhouses have an upper storey and bedrooms next to the hayloft.

Housing in the Lower Vivarais

Houses here have an upper storey and are built in a square, like southern French houses. The gently sloping roofs have half-round tiles. At the top of the wall, between wall and roof, there is typically a double or triple row of guttering made with fragments of tiles mounted in mortar. The south-facing wall is often decorated with a trellis.

Literature

A FEW GREAT WRITERS FROM THE AUVERGNE

Local writers have brought fame to a few of the Auvergne's prelates, among them Sidonius Apollinaris, Gerbert (10C) and Massillon who gave Louis XIV's funeral oration in the 18C. The Auvergne also had poets such as Théodore de Banville (1823–91) who founded the Parnassian School of Poetry and philosophers such as Pierre Teilhard de Chardin (1881–1955). In the 20C, Henri Pourrat and the chronicler Alexandre Vialatte have both described their native land, each in his own style. Of all the Auvergne authors, the best-known is Blaise Pascal, though Gregory of Tours, the medieval chronicler, is almost equally important.

Blaise Pascal

© Oxford Science Archiv/age fotostock

GREGORY OF TOURS

He was born c. 583 in Clermont-Ferrand into a rich family of Senators. He spent most of his life in Tours, to which he was appointed Bishop in 573, yet he never forgot the place of his birth. His *History of the Franks* which retraces the reigns of the Merovingian kings and their ancestors is one of the main sources of historical information about the Auvergne during the Dark Ages.

BLAISE PASCAL

It was in 1623 that Pascal, undoubtedly the most famous native of the Auvergne, was born in Clermont-Ferrand. His mother died when he was three years old and it was his father, President of the Court of Aids (forerunner of the Customs & Excise) in Clermont, who brought him up.

He retired to Port-Royal, which he was never again to leave, and continued his writings. It was because his memory played tricks on him that he began noting his *Thoughts,* with a view to writing an *Apology of the Christian Religion.* Pascal died in 1662, at the age of 39.

EUGÈNE IONESCO

Eugen Ionescu (1909–94), playwright and dramatist, was born in Romania but grew up in France, and came to be one of the foremost playwrights of the Theatre of the Absurd. As well as satirising the most banal situations, Ionesco depicts the loneliness of humans and the insignificance of our existence. Ionesco came to the theatre late, not writing his first play until 1948 (*La Cantatrice Chauve*, first performed in 1950 with the English title The Bald Soprano).

CONTEMPORARY WRITERS

Among the contemporary writers from the Auvergne, François Graveline rates highly. He is a journalist in Puy-de-Dôme where he was born in 1959. He has written a number of titles on the countryside and the mountains, notably *Allier Simple* (2004), *La Profondeur des Sommets* (2003), *Couleur Massif Central* (2002) and *L'Invention du Massif Central* (1997). Patrick Cloux (born 1952 in the Auvergne) has written several books on the region and the pleasure of walking: *Un Cheval deuz Traits* (2006) and *Marcher à l'Estime* (1993). Local history books, as well as historical novels, are written by Anne Courtillé, including *Les Messieurs de Clermont.*

Some worthwhile titles have been written by visitors or scholars. Peter Graham's sensitive depiction of of *Mourjou: The Life and Food of an Auvergne village*, ranks among the best, alongside Peter Gorham's *Portrait of the Auvergne* in Robert Hale's "Portrait" series.

Nature

The name **Auvergne** conjures up visions of a superb natural environment of outstanding beauty, a rugged landscape of mountain ranges and volcanoes, and lakes and springs in the heart of France. The area has been less accessible from the rest of France since time immemorial because of a lack of roads or railways. The **Rhône valley** is long and wide; its fast flowing river weaves its way through hills and mountains, plateaus and valleys, carving spectacular gorges, sinkholes and caves along its way. The valley separates the Massif Central and the Rhône-Alpes and much of the fertile land is given over to vineyards and agriculture.

RHÔNE VALLEY
THE RHÔNE CORRIDOR

La Dombes – This is a clay plateau dotted with lakes which ends in the fairly sheer "**côtières**" of the Saône to the west and the Rhône to the south. In the north, the plateau runs into Bresse. The waters of the melting glacier in the Rhône valley dug shallow dips into the surface of the land and left moraines, accumulations of debris swept along by the glacier, on the edge of the dips. It is on these **poypes** or slight rises that the villages were built.

The **Dombes** is now a charming area of tranquil countryside, with lines of trees, countless birds and calm lakes reflecting the sky above.

Lower Dauphiné

The countryside in Lower Dauphiné is a succession of stony plateaux, plains and hills. The **Île Crémieu** is a limestone plateau separated from the Jura to the north by the Rhône and to the west by an unusual cliff. The water that infiltrated the soil created a series of caves, the best-known of which are the Grottes de la Balme.

The **Balmes area** west of Vienne is partially covered in vineyards. It consists of granite and shale hills separated from Mont Pilat by the Rhône. It extends into the **Terres Froides plateau** which is slashed into strips by narrow valleys filled with fields of vegetables.

The **Bonnevaux and Chambaran plateaux** are vast expanses of woodland stretching south from Vienne and almost totally devoid of human habitation. The wide fertile **Bièvre and Valloire plains** specialise in cereal crops. They indicate the course once followed by the Isère, but abandoned after the ice receded.

The **Isère valley** itself opens out onto the Valence plateau; its well-cultivated terraces covered with walnut groves.

The Valence and Tricastin Areas

From Tain to the Donzère gorge, the Rhône valley widens to the east of the river, forming a patchwork of plains until it reaches the foothills of the Préalpes.

The **Valence plain** consists of a series of alluvial terraces built in steps. Its irrigated fields and its climate are a foretaste of the south of France and the Mediterranean. It was here that the "Tree of Gold", the mulberry, was first planted in the 17C and provided the local inhabitants with a reasonable living from the cultivation of silkworms. Nowadays, the many orchards have maintained the old-fashioned appearance of the countryside in which hedgerows abound.

The **Montélimar basin**, south of the Cruas gorge, is similar to but narrower than the Valence plain; olive trees grow on the south-facing slopes.

The **Tricastin area**, crossed by the Lauzon and the Lez, is a succession of arid hills covered with vineyards and olive trees. Its old villages perched on defensive sites form remarkable lookout posts.

THE EDGE OF THE MASSIF CENTRAL

The Massif Central ends to the east in a scarp slope high above the Rhône valley. It is a formidable precipice consisting of a mountain range that was broken down, raised up then overturned by the after-effects of Alpine folding. It has been severely eroded by the rivers, forming narrow gorges.

The Beaujolais Region

To the north, the upper Beaujolais is a mountainous zone of mainly granite soil. Tributaries of the Saône run down its steep slopes from west to east. The Lower Beaujolais, to the south, is formed of sedimentary soils. These soil types include a limestone that is almost ochre in colour and has earned the area the nickname 'Land of Golden Stone'. Economically, there is a clear demarcation of this region east to west, between the escarpment (La Côte) overlooking the Saône valley in the east, the wine-producing region, and the hills (La Montagne) or hinterland to the west, in which forests, crop-farming and industry predominate.

The Lyonnais Area

Set between the St-Étienne basin and the city of Lyon, the plateau is dotted with high grassy hills, pine forests, beech woods and orchards. The Mont-d'Or is a rugged area (highest peak: Mont Verdun, altitude 625m). The Lyonnais area owes its uniform appearance to the industries that have existed here for centuries. It ends in the Fourvière hill, the superb promontory that stands high above the confluence of the Saône and Rhône and the vast city of Lyon.

Forez and Roannais

In the **Forez mountains**, fields and meadows cover the slopes up to an altitude of 1 000m. Above them are oases of beech and pine forest, providing raw material for sawmills. In summer, animals are taken up to graze on the scrubby mountain tops (on the land called the Hautes Chaumes) rising to the Pierre-sur-Haute moors. At the foot of the mountains is the water-logged Forez plain crossed by the River Loire. This is dotted with volcanic hillocks where castle and church ruins are found.

The **Roanne basin** is a fertile rural area specialising in animal husbandry and is overlooked, to the west, by the vine-covered slopes of the Madeleine mountain range.

Mont Pilat and the St-Étienne Basin

Mont Pilat is a forest-clad pyramid with something of a mountainous air, rising above the surrounding dales. Its peaks are topped with granite boulders known as *chirats*, which form splendid observation platforms. The St-Étienne basin at the foot of the mountain follows the outline of the coalfield that stretches from the Loire to the Rhône, and contains a string of factories, in stark contrast to the pastures on the slopes of Mont Pilat and the Lyonnais mountain range.

The Vivarais Area

This forms the largest part of the eastern edge of the Massif Central. Huge basalt-lava flows running down from the Velay area, shale ridges and widespread erosion make this a bizarre landscape of strange natural features.

The **Upper Vivarais** reaches from Mont Pilat and the Velay area to the Rhône valley. People here earn a living from cattle farming and cutting timber in the pine forests. Nearer the banks of the Rhône, there are fruit trees and vineyards. The **Vivarais Cévenol** (lying within the Cévennes range) runs from the Upper Allier valley to the Aubenas basin. To the west, the "uplands" are strongly characterised by volcanoes. They are covered in pine, beech and meadow. From Lablachère and Privas to the Rhône valley, the **Lower Vivarais** is a limestone area with a succession of basins and plateaux in which scrub, olive trees, almond trees, blackberry bushes and vines provide a foretaste of a more southerly environment. To the north it is separated from the **Upper Vivarais** by the Coiron plateau and its black basalt cliffs. The unusual features of the vast plains (*planèzes*) grazed by flocks of sheep are the **dikes** and **necks** (pinnacles), the most famous of which is the one in Rochemaure. The limestone Gras plateau forms a stretch of whitish stone, with swallowholes, deep narrow gullies and rocks shaped like ruined buildings.

Mont Mézenc and conifer forest

© Ph. Bousseaud/Biosphoto

AUVERGNE
GRANITE AND VOLCANIC MOUNTAINS

In the region to the east, the climate is hard and the landscape rugged. From north to south, the **Madeleine** mountain range, and the **Forez and Livradois areas** consist of valleys, rounded hilltops, forest plateaux and pastures on which flocks of sheep graze. The area is covered with forests that provide timber.

Further south, the **Velay area** is a succession of vast basalt plateaux lying at altitudes of more than 1 000m beneath skies that are a foretaste of the Riviera. Dotted across the countryside are **outcrops of rock** formed by lava. Crops are generally so rare that the basin around Le Puy, which is irrigated by the Loire, looks almost like an oasis. The mountains in the **Devès area** form one vast plateau where lava flows are covered with pasture and fields of barley or lentils. Along the watershed between the Loire and Allier basins are deep lakes in volcanic craters.

The *planèze* (sloping plateau) is dotted with cinder cones consisting of black or reddish ash often capped with pine trees. The **Margeride plateau** is gashed by deep valleys and its climate and vegetation are reminiscent of the Forez mountains.

Limagnes

The *limagnes* are low-lying, fertile, sunny plains drained by the Dore and, more particularly, by the Allier and its tributaries. The plains consist almost entirely of arable land. To the east are the "poor Limagnes" or "Varennes," a hilly area of marshes, woodland, fields of crops and lush pastures where alluvium has been washed down from the crystalline mountains of the Forez area. To the west, the soil in the so-called fertile Limagnes region is dark brown, almost black. It has been enriched by the mixture of decomposed lava and volcanic ash. This is very rich land, producing tobacco, wheat, sugar beet, vegetable and seed crops and fruit.

Volcanic Uplands

To the west of the region, the **Dômes** and **Dore** mountain ranges and the mountains in the **Cézallier** and **Cantal** areas form a striking landscape of extinct volcanoes rising to an altitude of 1 885m at the highest peak, the Puy de Sancy. Around the Puy de Dôme, Puy Mary, Puy de Sancy, La Bourboule and St-Nectaire, forests, woods and pastures alternate with lakes and waterfalls. The **Artense,** which backs onto the Dore mountain range, is a rocky plateau worn away by glaciers; it now provides grazing land for sheep and cattle. The cultivated areas represent land that has been clawed back from the moors by the few people living there.

The Bourbonnais area – The scenery is like the people who live there – calm and temperate. It marks the northern edge of the Massif Central, and the gently rolling countryside is covered with a patchwork of fields hemmed in by hedges that give the landscape a wooded appearance.

The Besbre, Cher and Aumance valleys are wide and well drained, forming open, fertile areas crossed by major road and rail links. It is here that the main towns are to be found. The St-Pourçain vineyards, the impressive Tronçais Forest and the conifers on the mountainsides in the Bourbonnais area add a touch of variety to a landscape that is otherwise dominated by grassland.

AUVERGNE'S MINERAL SPRINGS

Whether naturally carbonated or still, water is one of the main sources of wealth in the Auvergne and it has been exploited here since antiquity. Puy-de-Dôme and the Vichy basin alone account for a third of French mineral springs. Volvic, the world-famous mineral water is bottled at source in the Auvergne. Ordinary springs are created by water that seeps into permeable land and eventually meets an impermeable layer down which it runs. When the impermeable layer rises to the surface, the water follows suit.

MINERAL SPRINGS

Either springs of infiltrated water or springs rising from the depths of the Earth's crust. In this case, substances or gases that have therapeutic properties are added naturally to the water as it flows underground. The adjective "**thermal**" is used more accurately to describe springs with water at a temperature of at least 35°C when it comes out of the ground: Vichy water, for instance has a temperature of 66°C and the water in Chaudes-Aigues rises to as much as 82°C.

RESURGENT SPRINGS

The water in these springs only flows at intervals, for example every eight hours. The column of water rising from the depths of the Earth is subjected, at some point along its course, to a very high increase in temperature. The steam produced at this point acquires sufficient pressure to project the upper part of the column of water above the surface of the ground. The projection is interrupted for as long as it takes to heat a second column, then the whole process begins again. This type of spring can be found in Bellerive, near Vichy.

© S. Sauvignier/MICHELIN

Mineral spring (iron), Vallée de Chaudefour

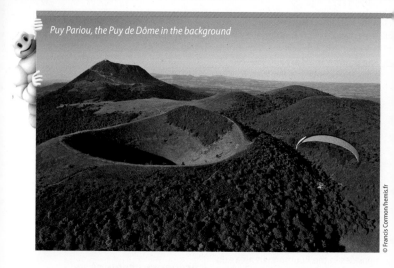

Puy Pariou, the Puy de Dôme in the background

© Francis Cormon/hemis.fr

The Volcanoes of the Auvergne

What makes the Auvergne so unusual is the presence of a large number of volcanoes which, although extinct, are a major feature of the landscape. They vary in appearance depending on their formation, type and age.

Inverse composite volcanoes (Stromboli-type)

In the depths of the earth, magma is subjected to enormous pressure and infiltrates through cracks in the Earth's crust. When the pressure becomes too great, there is an explosion accompanied by a sudden eruption of incandescent matter. A huge column of gas, smoke and vapour rises into the sky, spreading out like a parasol, while the matter in fusion (spindle-shaped volcanic bombs, gas-swollen pozzolana looking like a very lightweight, dark reddish-coloured stone) falls back to earth and accumulates around the mouth of the volcano, gradually building up a **cinder cone.** At the top is a **crater.** The most typical of all can be seen on the Puy des Goules and the Pariou.

When the pressure inside the Earth's crust decreases and the matter thrown up by the eruption is more fluid, lava flows are created, running from the crater or down the mountainsides. Depending on the type of rock, these **lava flows** (*cheires*) may cool to form a fairly smooth surface or, alternatively, be rough and full of boulders. When the mass of lava is very thick, it contracts as it cools, breaking into prisms or columns (very much like organ pipes, hence their French name *orgues*) such as those in Bort-les-Orgues or Murat.

Sometimes a lava flow or an explosion carries away a piece of the volcanic cone, as it did in the Puy de Louchardière or the Puy de la Vache; in this case, the crater is described as **breached** and is shaped like a half-funnel. In the Pariou and the Puy de Dôme, a new cinder cone was formed inside the crater of an older volcano. This led to the formation of a **multiple volcanic complex.**

Volcanic domes (Mount Pelée-type composite volcano)

Sometimes, the volcanic eruption throws up a lava paste which solidifies upon contact with the ground. It then forms a dome with steep sides but has no crater at the summit. The Puy de Dôme is a good example of this type of volcano.

Volcanoes with planèzes

When the Cantal volcano was active more than 9 million years ago, it would have been a formidable sight: it had a circumference of 60km/37mi and rose to an altitude of 3 000m. Formed by a succession of layers of lava and ash, it was dissected by erosion, which cut its sides into **planèzes** (sloping plateaux) with a tip pointing towards the centre of the volcano. The Dore mountain range, which is younger than the Cantal volcano (2–3.5 million years), also consists of successions of layers of lava and ash but the *planèzes* are less well developed.

Necks and dikes

Scattered across the Limagne in total disorder are volcanic systems which penetrated, and were consolidated within, a mass of sedimentary rock that has since been worn away. All that remain are a few spurs of rock called necks or ridges known as dikes, which no longer have their covering of soil. The Puy de Monton near Veyre, and Montrognon near Ceyrat, are typical necks. Montaudoux to the south of Royat is a good example of a dike.

Tables

Ancient lava flows originally spread out across the valleys, protecting the underlying soil from the erosion that cleared the area between rivers and caused an inversion relief. These lava flows now jut out above the surrounding countryside, forming tables like the Gergovie and Polignac plateaux.

Lahars

Volcanic eruptions are often accompanied by torrential rain and enormous emissions of water vapour. They then cause *lahars* (an Indonesian word) or flows of mud and boulders that move at astonishing speed, destroying everything in their path. The Pardines plateau near Issoire owes its existence to this type of phenomenon. South of Clermont-Ferrand, some of the small plateaux and hillocks in the Limagne area consist of rock formations created by underwater volcanic eruptions. Their "peppery" appearance is due to the mixing of lava and sediment from the bed of the lake.

Lakes of volcanic origin

The volcanoes have given the landscape of the Auvergne a very particular relief and magnificent stretches of water that reflect the surrounding countryside. In some places, a lava flow closed off a valley, holding back the waters of a river; examples of this are the Aydat and Guéry lakes (the latter was also formed by the action of glaciers). In other places, a volcano erupted in the middle of a valley, blocking it with its cone, as was the case in Chambon and Montcineyre. Still elsewhere, subsidence caused by underground volcanic activity was filled with run-off water (Lake Chauvet). *Maars* are lakes which were formed in craters (Lake Servière).

The volcanoes of the Auvergne at present

The volcanoes are now well preserved depending on their age and the hardness of their rocks. The **Dômes** mountain range, with its 80 volcanoes that became extinct around 7 000 years ago, has a strikingly fresh-looking relief. The **Dore** mountain range is older and has a more fragmented appearance. The lava flows on Sancy, Aiguiller and Banne d'Ordanche are heaped up to a height of more than 1 000m, but water, snow and glaciers have worn away the sides. With its 60km/37mi circumference and altitude of 3 000m, the **Cantal volcano** was even more impressive in its day. The landscapes today are only a fraction of the original; it is difficult to imagine the initial size of the range.

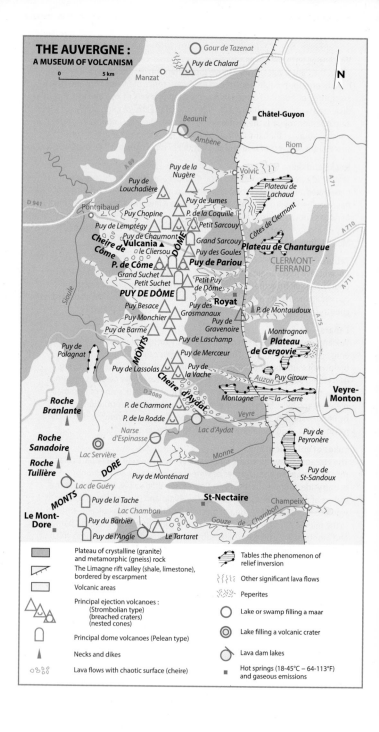

THE AUVERGNE :
A MUSEUM OF VOLCANISM

0   5 km

N

Legend:

Plateau of crystalline (granite) and metamorphic (gneiss) rock

The Limagne rift valley (shale, limestone), bordered by escarpment

Volcanic areas

Principal ejection volcanoes :
(Strombolian type)
(breached craters)
(nested cones)

Principal dome volcanoes (Pelean type)

Necks and dikes

Lava flows with chaotic surface (cheire)

Tables :the phenomenon of relief inversion

Other significant lava flows

Peperites

Lake or swamp filling a maar

Lake filling a volcanic crater

Lava dam lakes

Hot springs (18-45°C – 64-113°F) and gaseous emissions

PROPERTIES OF
THERMAL SPRINGS

When thermal water rises to the surface, it gives off a very low level of radioactivity which stimulates the human organism. However, the water is very unstable and deteriorates as soon as it comes out of the ground. This is why it is important to take the water where it rises to the surface and why spa towns were built. The composition of water varies depending on the type of rocks through which it passes.

People visit Vichy to treat disorders of the digestive system, Royat for heart and arterial diseases, Châtelguyon for intestinal problems, Le Mont-Dore for asthma, La Bourboule for respiratory diseases, St-Nectaire for liver complaints, and so on. Spa towns declined in popularity after World War II, but are enjoying a revival. The medical aspect of "taking the waters" has been maintained, but people also come to keep fit, enjoy a round of golf, a day at the races, or a night at the opera.

MINERAL WATER,
A BOOM INDUSTRY

The French drink more mineral water than any other nationality. This is why the Auvergne is so popular – it has everything they could ask for. Bottling has required the development of modern techniques, for water is one of the most difficult commodities to package.

It is, though, a source of employment for small towns such as Volvic which has become famous not only in France but far beyond its borders.

FLORA AND FAUNA
RHÔNE VALLEY

The Rhône valley is not only a major road and rail route and intersection of geographical areas, it also combines differing natural environments which have resulted in a variety of flora and fauna. Almost 3 000 species of plant, some 60 wild mammals and more than 200 birds have been observed in the forests, plains and lakes.

The Pilat Regional Nature Park alone boasts some 90 species of bird.

Flora

In addition to the plants ordinarily found in the centre of France, the area also has mountain plants which have come down from the Alps and the Jura, and Mediterranean plants that have spread from the south. Because of this, it is possible to find, in the mountains in the Forez area for example, gentians, monkshood, or the superb martagon (or Turk's Cap) lily. This is a very rare plant, a hardy annual growing to a height of 30–80cm or even, on occasions, to more than 1.10m, with clusters of reddish-orange flowers spotted with black growing on a tall stem. Nor is it unusual, on the lower plateaux and hillsides in the Saône and Rhône valleys, to see evergreen oak, Montpellier aphyllantes, lavender, purple orchid or other varieties of orchid growing in the month of April on dry grasslands.

Fauna

Just like flora, Mediterranean species of fauna are found in the Rhône valley as the northernmost habitats are sited in the Rhône basin. Among them is the Provençal field mouse, a tiny rodent, and the mouse-eared bat. Deer are adaptable creatures and occur throughout the region in forested areas. The Rhône valley is a major point along migratory routes followed by **birds** between Northern Europe and the Mediter-

Armeria maritima, Cantal mountains

© ANP PHOTO/age fotostock

89

ranean. The banks of the Saône and Rhône are full of larks, buntings, quail, plovers and curlews. But it is the lakes of the **Dombes** that boast the largest numbers of birds. Birds from all over the world can be seen at the bird sanctuary in Villars-les-Dombes where toucans and parrots rub shoulders with rare species such as the black-tailed godwit, or the corncrake, an endangered species.

The wels, the largest freshwater fish

Before it was introduced into France in the second half of the 19C by fish farmers, this species of large catfish was found mainly in the waters of the Caspian Sea and the River Danube. Those living in the Rhône and Saône can, in rare cases, grow to a length of 3m and weigh some 100kg. It feeds on bream, moorhens, ducks and rats; to kill its prey, it grabs their paws and drags them down to the river-bed until they drown. This little aquatic monster is, however, short-sighted and dislikes the light, so it waits until nightfall before seeking to catch its food; it is therefore unlikely to be seen, except perhaps on a dinner plate as it is becoming increasingly popular with fishermen.

Beavers of the Île du Beurre

The beaver is a hard-working animal, cutting, felling and nibbling branches of trees in order to build dams and dikes. These days, though, lodges are no longer built because beavers have changed their habits and they now live in burrows dug into the river banks. They are particularly fond of the banks of the Île du Beurre (in old French, *beurre* meant beaver). This island to the south of Lyon is the last place in France in which beavers live in the wild and, because of this, it has been covered by a preservation order since 1988.

AUVERGNE

The Auvergne has a diverse landscape, with extensive forest and peat bog, each area with a particular flora and fauna.

Vegetation at Different Altitudes

Forests in the Auvergne grow in specific tiers. The hillsides are covered with pedunculate oak on clay soil and sessile oak on better-drained ground. On the mountains there are beech and pine although conifer predominates in cold, damp areas. The beech is the most common tree in the Auvergne and grows to a height of 30-40m after 150 to 300 years. It is easily recognisable for its smooth, grey bark and leaf colouring – red in winter and soft green in spring. Natural pine groves cover the driest hillsides like those in Upper Loire.

The **moors** of the Margeride area often mark the abandonment of pastures or farmland. In fact, moorland precedes the stage at which land is overrun by forest. Ferns, calluna, gorse, myrtle and redcurrants grow here. Gradually, however, the forest takes over, with birch, hazelnut and pine being the first trees to appear.

The **mountain pastures** above 1 000m provide a natural environment for species that have been observed here for centuries, such as the three-coloured violet, the scented wild pansy, the redpurple saw-wort (used to produce a yellow dye), and globe flower. The gentian, a delightful yellow flower, is used to make the liqueur that bears its name; other species of gentian produce blue flowers.

The **subalpine stage** of vegetation begins at altitudes over 1 400m; plant life varies depending on the exposure of the slopes. Calluna and myrtle grow on moorland, and ground-cover plants on grassland, rocks and scree. It is here, from May to July, that the spring anemone blooms, a rare plant with delicately indented leaves and flowers with huge white petals tinged with purple. Mountain arnica, a downy plant with yellow flowers, is used to make creams that prevent bruising.

The blue carnation, which is actually a very unusual bluish green in colour, can be seen in tufts only a few inches high on the peaks in the Dore and Cantal mountain ranges.

The Alps viewed from Crêt de l'Œillon, Parc Naturel Régional du Pilat

Peat Bogs

Peat bogs are natural environments created by an accumulation of organic matter in damp areas. There are a number of features which lead to the formation of peat bogs, such as a break in a slope along the course of streams, or cold springs as in the mountains of Cantal. They also tend to form on valley floors, along meanders and streams like those in the Upper Forez area, in the bases of volcanic craters, or over-deepening caused by glacial erosion as in the Margeride, Forez and Artense regions. *Maars* (lakes in the bottom of craters) can also be overrun by vegetation, as can be seen in the Devès range and the Velay.

Peat is formed from a range of spongy mosses, which ensure photosynthesis and store water. These mosses retain up to 30 times their dry weight of water. The bogs are exceptional because some have survived for more than 5 000 years and have developed a unique form of plant and animal life.

Carnivorous plants like the sundew and drosera, which suffer from nitrogen deficiency, have adapted to this environment. They capture small insects by secreting a sticky substance. The animals are also extraordinary.

The Odyssey of the Salmon

Born in a river, the salmon stays in the area where it was born for two years before letting the river carry it down to the sea tail-first, during the period known as downstream migra-tion. At this stage its scales turn white. Certain salmon travel as far as Greenland. Here, they grow and acquire their more familiar appearance – it is the shrimps on which they feed that give them their "salmon pink" colouring.

Two years later the salmon swims up the Loire to return to its spawning grounds in Allier or Upper Loire, in particular around Brioude which is famous as the "salmon's paradise", a trip that can take several months. When the fish arrives, it is exhausted and very thin, because it has had to overcome a number of obstacles, quite apart from the fact that it does not feed in rivers.

The female burrows into the gravel on the river bed with her tail and lays the eggs that the male covers with his milt. The salmon then usually die, although sometimes a salmon survives to make the journey twice.

In the Auvergne, the salmon is the subject of many anecdotal tales. One recounts how, at the turn of the 19C when the railway line was being built through the Allier gorge, the workmen went on strike because they had nothing to eat – nothing, that is, but salmon!

REGIONAL NATURE PARKS

The Auvergne-Rhône Valley area includes four regional nature parks, described in the *Discovering* section of this guide (&see AUBENAS, Monts du FOREZ, Le PILAT and Parc naturel regional des VOLCANS D'AUVERGNE).

Grignan, Drôme Provençale
© Franck Guiziou/hemis.fr

Pushing gently at the gates of "outdoor heaven", the bright and busy city of Clermont-Ferrand enjoys a privileged position. The presence of such magnificent countryside, inspiring, energising and relaxing, at the very edge of town is a quality few French cities can boast. Nowhere does it seem that work, play and well-being so readily interplay as in the shadow of the Monts Dôme, and the opportunity to make the most of this explosive landscape is one that can be enjoyed by visitors and locals alike.

Highlights

1 Checking out the quaint streets of **Old Clermont** (p99)

2 Driving across the vast **Gergovie plateau** (p110)

3 Driving or walking to the summit of **Puy de Dôme** to enjoy the stunning view at sunset (p116)

4 For adults and children alike; **Vulcania** theme park (p122)

5 Enjoying a leisurely half-day at tranquil **Lac d'Aydat** (p123)

Up in the Air

It would almost be a travesty to visit this endearing region and not somehow get to the top of the Puy de Dôme. But whether you get there by car or on foot, it is worth taking a parapente flight with one of the local experts, if you have the courage. The entire range is magnificent to view any time, but from the air it really is something quite special.

Volcanic Landscape

So much is written about the volcanic origins of the region to the west of Clermont-Ferrand it is easy to become blasé about them. But once you leave the city behind and start exploring the rolling green hills and valleys, you find yourself lost for words. Even taking a picture runs the risk of trying to create an image that will never be as good as the one in your mind. Landscapes are remarkably rejuvenating and inspirational places; this is especially so, and in many ways more satisfying than, say, the Alps or the Pyrenees.

Taking the Water

Volvic is a mineral water drawn from springs issuing from the volcanic landscape. The springs were first tapped in 1922, but another 16 years were to pass before the first bottled water appeared on the market. Today, more than 1 billion bottles of water are produced annually, and exported to over 60 countries. This massive industry is the principal employer in its local commune.

Vulcania, the Puy de Côme and the Puy Dôme in the background

© Francis Cormon/hemis.fr/Getty Images

CLERMONT-FERRAND AND MONTS DÔME

Mozac ★★ Recommended
Royat ★ Interesting
Volvic Other sight described in this guide
⇒ Point of departure for tour
→ Volcanoes around Clermont
→ The country south of Clermont
→ Plateau de Gergovie
→ Monts Dôme

MONTMARAULT   MOULINS

Combronde

Davayat

Vée des Prades

Chazeron

Châtel-Guyon

Gorges d'Enval   Mozac   Riom

Château de Tournoël

Volvic   Marsat

Châteaugay

PUY-DE-DÔME

PARC

NATUREL

Volcan de Lemptégy   Puy Chopine
1018   1181

Vulcania

Plateau de Chanturgue
553

Puy de Pariou   1209

PUY DE DÔME   1465

Bois de Villars

Chamalières

Clermont-Ferrand

RÉGIONAL

Bois de la Pauze   Royat   Puy de Montaudoux

Arboretum   904   592   Beaumont

MONT DÔME   Puy de Charade   Aubière

Circuit automobile de Clermont-Ferrand - Charade   Ceyrat

DES   VOLCANS   Plateau de Gergovie
717

Puy de la Vache   1167   Gorges de Ceyrat

Montlosier   Opme

D'AUVERGNE   La Batisse   Le Crest   Monton

Randanne

Corent

Aydat   Lac d'Aydat   St-Saturnin

THE LAVA TRAIL   La Sauvetat

Montagne de la Serre

N

0   4 km

ST-NECTAIRE

95

Clermont-Ferrand★★

Clermont-Ferrand is the natural capital of the Auvergne. The city centre is built on a slight rise, all that remains of a volcanic cone. The old houses built of volcanic rock in the "Black Town" huddle in the shade of the cathedral. Over the past 30 years or so, Clermont's urban landscape has undergone major changes. New developments include the **Jaude** (a vast shopping complex), the **St-Pierre** district (covered market), the **Fontgiève** district (law courts, residential buildings), and place du 1er-Mai (sculpture by Étienne Martin), all of which combine contemporary architecture with an older urban environment. In 2006, an urban tramway was inaugurated, the first phase in a transport revival of the city, and the first tram system in France to use bi-directional pneumatic tyres.

For visitors arriving from the Pontgibaud direction, there is a good general **view★★** of the town from a **bend** on D 941A. From left to right, the nearby heights of the Côtes de Clermont and Chanturgue plateau give an indication of the original level of the Limagne plain prior to the major period of erosion. Opposite the platform lies the city itself, dominated by its black cathedral. In the distance, beyond the Allier valley, are the mountains of the Livradois area. To the right are the Comté volcanoes, Gergovie plateau and Montrognon rock. Avenue Thermale runs along a hilltop north of Royat. From it there are more superb **views★** over the town of Clermont and the surrounding area.

A BIT OF HISTORY

From Nemessos to Clermont-Ferrand – The Arverni oppidum (settlement) of Nemessos was built on the site of the rise now occupied by the cathedral. Its

▶ **Population:** 145 497.
⚫ **Michelin Map:** 326: F-8.
ℹ **Info:** Tourist office, Pl. de la Victoire, 63000 Clermont-Ferrand. ✆04 73 98 65 00. www.clermontferrand tourism.com. Ask about the **Clermont Pass** (€18.50 for 72 hours), at the tourist office.
▶ **Location:** Most of the bars, brasseries, theatres, pubs and restaurants are in the centre of the city, mainly around the place de Jaude.
🅿 **Parking:** Parking (charged) is available at a number of locations around the edge of the city centre. It is often better to park around the edge of the centre and walk in.
😊 **Don't Miss:** The place de Jaude; this is the focal point for everything that's 'happening' in Clermont-Ferrand.
🕐 **Timing:** The place de Jaude is a good place to start, to get a feel for the city, before going on to explore more widely.
👪 **Kids:** Visit the Espace Massif Central, or Vulcania.

name, meaning "wooded rise" or "sacred wood", is a reminder that the spot was used by the Druids as a place of worship. Gradually, over the course of the 1C, Druidic rites were abandoned.

A new settlement slowly grew up at the junction of several roads below the original town and, in honour of Caesar Augustus, its name was added on to that of the Roman Emperor. Augustonemetum had several major public buildings and a large number of private residences. An aqueduct brought water from the Villars valley to the summit of the rise where it was distributed to the various districts from a water tower.

Place de Jaude

© Lionel Montico/hemis.fr

At its height, in the 2C, the town underwent fairly large-scale expansion and its population rose to between 15 000 and 30 000 inhabitants. An ancient description indicates that it was "well-planted with vineyards, full of people, busy with traffic and trade and much given to pomp".

During the early Middle Ages the town sank into decline. It suffered a number of destructive sieges at the hands of the Franks, the Saracens and the Vikings. It was in the 8C that the name "Clermont" was first applied to the fortress destroyed by Pepin the Short in 761.

In the 10C the town entered a period of economic revival. Bishop Étienne II had a new cathedral built, the population increased, the town grew beyond the old town walls and there were no less than 34 churches and chapels inside and outside the walls.

For centuries the episcopal town of Clermont was rivalled by Montferrand, the count's stronghold, and later by Riom, the seat of the Court of Appeal. Clermont finally won the day and, in 1630, Montferrand merged with its neighbour to form the conurbation known as Clermont-Ferrand.

Blaise Pascal, a man of genius – A few years earlier, the great writer and philosopher **Blaise Pascal** (1623–62) was born in the town. Pascal was not only very gifted in the arts, he was also a brilliant scientist with an enormous talent for mathematics and physics. When he was 12, it became obvious that he had outstanding natural ability in geometry. At the age of 16, he amazed the philosopher Descartes with an essay on conic sections. Two years later, he invented a calculator. The "wheelbarrow" or "vinaigrette", a two-wheeled sedan chair, was also one of his inventions. It was Pascal, too, who had the idea of the "five *sous* coach service" travelling a fixed route and leaving at regular intervals. The coaches were an immediate success and they paved the way for the Parisian omnibus service. It was Pascal again, with his brother-in-law Périer, who proved the weight of air following an experiment at Le Puy-en-Velay.

Tyre town – It is perhaps surprising that Clermont, situated in the heart of the Auvergne far from the harbours through which rubber and cotton were imported and well away from the major wire-mills, became the leading centre of tyre production in France and, indeed, one of the industry's leading operators worldwide. The story behind this, however, is one of quite humble origins.

In the heyday of Romanticism, c. 1830, a former solicitor named Aristide Barbier, who had lost three-quarters of his personal fortune as a result of the difficult financial climate, set up in partnership with his cousin, Edouard Daubrée, a captain in the King's Light Cavalry who had resigned his commission in order

WHERE TO STAY

Dav'Hôtel Jaude..................................... (1)

WHERE TO EAT

Chardonnay (Le)..................................... (1)
Comptoir des Saveurs (Le)..................... (2)
Danièle Bath (Basserie)........................... (3)
Pile-Poêle (Le)... (4)

to open a small farm machinery factory on the banks of the River Tiretaine. In order to amuse her children, Madame Daubrée, niece of the Scottish chemist **Charles Macintosh** (1766–1843) who had discovered that rubber dissolves in petroleum, made a few rubber balls as she had seen her uncle do. The balls proved so popular that Barbier and Daubrée began mass-producing them. Soon, the factory diversified its output to include other items made of rubber, such as hoses and belts. However, after a period of prosperity, it fell into decline.

PARIS-BORDEAUX 1895

1ʳᵉ VOITURE sur PNEUS MICHELIN

© MICHELIN

In 1886 Barbier's grandsons, the **Michelin brothers** (André and, later, Édouard), took over the works. These two creative geniuses were the first people to apply scientific methods to industrial production. By meeting clients' real needs, carefully observing reality and constantly revising the knowledge and experience they had already acquired, they were able to create the first detachable bicycle tyre (1891). This development was followed by tyres for automobiles in 1895 and the low-pressure "Confort" tyre in 1923. In 1937 the "Métalic" tyre was introduced, with a steel carcass that made lorries a viable proposition as a method of transport, and in 1946 the radial-ply tyre (marketed under the name "X" in 1949) which combined a radial carcass that overcame the problem of overheating and a triangular steel belt to ensure good road-holding. In 2006, pneumatic, bi-directional tyres were used, for the first time in France, on the city's new urban tramway system.

OLD CLERMONT★★

A leisurely stroll in the old district will take you through the narrow alleys laid out around the cathedral and place de la Victoire, featuring quaint, old-fashioned fountains and houses with lava stone courtyards.

Place de Jaude

The ancient origins of the name of this square remain a subject of controversy. Two Renaissance documents use the name *platea galli* – "rooster square", since in local dialect the word for cockerel is *jô* or *jau*. The square is therefore thought to have been a poultry market. Another explanation links the origin of the word *jaude* to the name of a suburb of Clermont, known in the Gallic language as *Vasso Galate*. While *wasso* or *vasso* is said to be the name of a Gallic divinity, *galate* is merely a local name which has evolved over the years into *galde* or *gialde* (10C), *jalde* (12C) and, finally, *jaude*.

Place de Jaude is the centre of life in Clermont. It is bordered by trees and sur-rounded by department stores, cinemas and, on the south side, by the **Centre Jaude**, a vast shopping complex.

Église St-Pierre-les-Minimes

This vast domed church building in the Classical style has fine wood panelling in the chancel.

▷ Walk down avenue des États-Unis then turn right onto rue des Gras.

Rue des Gras

A flight of steps used to lead from here right up to the cathedral. At No. 28, note the straight flight of steps, gallery and balcony dating from the 17C. No. 22 has two entrances opening onto small inner courtyards. One of them, dating from the 15C, is carved with a man's head; the other is topped by a lintel on which angel musicians are shown surrounding a young woman.

▷ Take the second street on the left.

Marché St-Pierre

This market is situated at the heart of an old district that has been renovated, and stands on the site of a Romanesque church. It is a bustling centre on which narrow, picturesque shopping streets such as rue de la Boucherie converge.

▷ Return to rue des Gras then, at place de la Bourse, turn left onto rue Ph.-Marcombes (north of the cathedral) which leads to place de la Poterne.

Fontaine d'Amboise★

This fountain erected in 1515 by Jacques d'Amboise, Bishop of Clermont, is a very fine piece of Renaissance architecture, carved in lava stone from Volvic. The basin is decorated with charming foliage in the Italian style. The central pyramid is adorned with small, naked figures with water pouring from their mouths.

Rue du Port

No. 21 *(right)* is a narrow old house with machicolations; on the right, at the corner of Rue Barnier, stands a 16C

WHERE TO STAY

Albert-Élisabeth (Hôtel)...................................... ①

Holiday Inn Garden Court (Hôtel)........................ ②

Lafayette (Hôtel).. ③

Lune Étoile La Pardieu (Hôtel)........................... ④

Radio (Hôtel)... ⑤

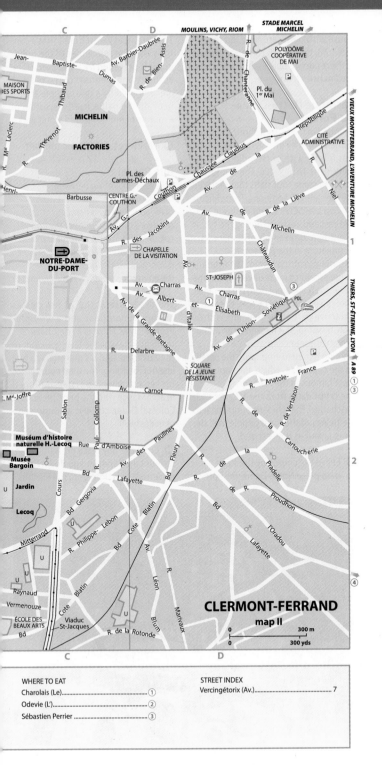

MOULINS, VICHY, RIOM

STADE MARCEL MICHELIN

Jean-Baptiste-Dumas

Av. Barbier-Daubrée

R. de Bien-Assis

POLYDÔME COOPÉRATIVE DE MAI

R. de Chanteranne

Pl. du 1er Mai

VIEUX MONTFERRAND, L'AVENTURE MICHELIN

MAISON DES SPORTS

Thibaud

MICHELIN

FACTORIES

CITÉ ADMINISTRATIVE

R. Mal Leclerc

Thévenot

R.

Chaussée Claudius

de

la

R. de la Liève

Niel

Henri-

Barbusse

Pl. des Carmes-Déchaux

CENTRE G.-COUTHON

Couthon

Av. G.-

Av. des Jacobins

Av. E.

de

Michelin

1

NOTRE-DAME-DU-PORT

R.

CHAPELLE DE LA VISITATION

Châteaudun

Av. Charras

Av. Albert-

Av. et-d'Italie

Charras

ST-JOSEPH

Élisabeth

Soviétique

POL.

3

Av. de la Grande-Bretagne

Av. de l'Union-

R. Delarbre

SQUARE DE LA JEUNE RÉSISTANCE

Anatole- France

R. de Vertaizon

THIERS, ST-ÉTIENNE, LYON   A 89

1
3

R. Mal-Joffre

Av. Carnot

R. de la Pradelle

Cartoucherie

2

Sablon

Paul-Collomp

U

Muséum d'histoire naturelle H.-Lecoq

Rue Paul d'Amboise

Av. des Paulines

Bd Fleury

R.

R.

la

de

R.

Proudhon

Musée Bargoin

Bd

R.

Lafayette

Bd

l'Oradou

Lafayette

Jardin

Cours

Bd Gergovia

Blatin

Côte

Av.

Bd

Lecoq

Mitterrand

R. Philippe-Lebon

Bd

Av. Léon

R.

Marvaux

4

U

Raynaud

Côte

Blatin

U

Blum

Vermenouze

ÉCOLE DES BEAUX ARTS

Bd

Viaduc St-Jacques

R. de la Rotonde

CLERMONT-FERRAND
map II

0   300 m
0   300 yds

C   D

house with barbican. Note, on the left at No. 38, the superb carriage entrance of the residence built in the early 18C for the financier Montlosier.

Basilique Notre-Dame-du-Port★★

Founded in the 6C by Bishop St Avit and burned down by the Vikings, the church was rebuilt with outstanding stylistic unity in the 11C and 12C. The bell-towers and lava stone roof slabs that replaced the tiles are 19C additions. The edifice is now on UNESCO's World Heritage List. The east end, restored during the 19C, is a consummate example of Romanesque architecture in the Auvergne.

The plain, robust design of Romanesque architecture as developed in the Auvergne is apparent from the entrance. The raised **chancel★★★**, the most attractive part of the building, is strikingly beautiful. It is flanked by an ambulatory with four chapels.

Lighting is used to emphasize the details on the **capitals★**, which are among the most famous in the Auvergne.

The **crypt** dates from the 11C. Beneath the chancel, the "Underground", dear to the hearts of the local people, has the same layout as the east end.

▷ Leave the church by the steps down to place Notre-Dame-du-Port.

The bare, heavy west front forms a contrast with the remainder of the building; it is preceded by a 16C porch. The austerity and bareness of the old wall are tempered by a row of triple arches beneath the gable, itself consisting of a mosaic of multicoloured stonework.

▷ Follow rue du Port and turn left.

Rue Pascal

"The streets climb up between careworn façades where gateways open, yawning, onto damp courtyards. In the depths of the iron-coloured shadow is the turret of a spiral staircase, a decorated gallery, a doorway with a lintel shaped like the point of a shield." (Henri Pourrat)

The old house at No. 22 has bosses on the ground floor and a wrought-iron balcony. No. 4 is M de Chazerat's residence; he was the last Intendant of the Auvergne and his mansion is a fine late-18C building. The **oval courtyard,** broken up by Ionic pilasters designed in accordance with the principles of the Colossal Order, conveys an impression of majesty.

▷ Cross the tiny place du Terrail with its fountain (1664) and go down rue du Terrail. Turn right onto rue Fléchier,

Basilique Notre-Dame-du-Port

© A. De Valroger/Michelin

leading to rue des Grands-Jours which skirts the east end of the cathedral.

Place de la Victoire

In the centre is a monument commemorating the Crusades, and a fountain with a statue of Pope Urban II. From this now pedestrian square, there is a general view of the cathedral.

Rue des Chaussetiers

Furniture and carpet shops fill the vaulted ground floors of old houses, and there is an abundance of doors and arches. At No. 3, at the corner of rue Terrasse, is the **Maison de Savaron,** a mansion built in 1513. The **courtyard★** contains a staircase turret linked to the main building by three floors of overhanging landings. The turret includes a superb carved doorway known as the "Door of the Wild Men", At No. 10 there is a Gothic doorway and mullioned windows. At the corner of rue des Petits-Gras are Romanesque arches (12C, the oldest examples of this style to be seen in vernacular buildings in Clermont).

Rue des Petits-Gras

At Nos. 4–6 (windows with grotesque masks), in the second of the two buildings beyond the courtyard, there is a monumental three-storey **staircase★** supported by corbels and oblique basket-handled arches. The straight flights of steps and landings are a particularly fine example of 18C architecture.

Cathédrale Notre-Dame-de-l'Assomption★★

○*Mon–Sat 7.30am-noon, 2-6pm (7pm Jun–mid-Sept), Sun and public holidays 9am–noon, 3–8pm).* **Bayette Tower:** *Mon–Sat 9–11am, 2–5.15pm, Sun 3–5.30pm.* ✆€2. *Guided tours: mid-Jul–Aug Tue and Fri 11pm; ask at tourist office for further details.* ℘*04 73 98 65 00; www.cathedrale-catholique-clermont.fr.*

This is a lovely Gothic church with a design based on cathedrals in the Île de France. Its sombre colour is due to the lava used in its construction; it is the only major cathedral built of this

Place de la Victoire and the cathedral

© Luc Olivier/Photononstop

particular type of stone. The church standing today was begun in 1248; a Romanesque church previously stood here, itself replacing one or two earlier churches.

Enter by the north door into the transept, beneath the Bayette Tower. Adjacent to the tower is the Guette Turret, once topped by a look-out post. The impression of lightness in the nave and, in particular, around the chancel shows the technical skills inherent in the Rayonnant Gothic style. The use of lava stone made it possible to reduce the width of the pillars, the arches of the vaulting, and the various sections of the openings. The scattering of the French fleur-de-lis motif and the towers of Castile visible on some of the windows would seem to suggest that they date from the days of St Louis; the King may have given them to the cathedral on the occasion of the marriage of his son (the future Philippe III) in the cathedral in 1262. Set in the gallery of the north transept arm is a clock with a **Jack o' the clock** that strikes the hours (**1**) dating from the 16C (the mechanism is 17C and 18C). Walk round the ambulatory.

Note, above the doorway flanked by foliage into the vestry (**2**), three paintings from 13C–15C.

(**3**) **Chapelle St-Georges** – Stained-glass window illustrating the life and martyrdom of the saint.

CATHÉDRALE N.-D.-DE-L'ASSOMPTION

(4) Chapelle St-Austremoine – To the right, Austremoine's arrival in the Auvergne where he was the first bishop. In the centre is an illustration of his martyrdom; to the left, the miracles accomplished after his death.

(5) Mary Magdalene windows – Stained glass illustrating the end of her life. 17C and 18C altar and Pietà. Statues of the Bishops of Clermont, St Arthème and St Alyre.

(6) Apsidal chapel – To the left is the life of John the Baptist; in the centre, the childhood of Christ and to the right the miracle worked by Theophilus.

(7) St Bonnet windows – St Bonnet was Bishop of Clermont in the 7C.

(8) Funeral chapel of the bishops – In the centre are 12C stained-glass windows from the former cathedral which illustrate the Life of Christ.

(9) Chapelle Ste-Marguerite – Altarpiece and Adoration of the Shepherds (17C).

(10) St Agatha windows.

(11) Chapelle St-Arthème – Endowed with an altarpiece which was rebuilt in 1840 using 17C statues. The **chancel★★** is closed off by large but light arches. Above the triforium, the long 13C and 14C stained-glass windows **(12)** have a grisaille background and only one large figure per lancet. Set against the pillars in the transept are two statues of the

Virgin Mary and St John (**13**); they were originally part of the rood screen which was demolished during the Revolution. At the west end of the inner north aisle note the 14C statue of Christ of the Last Judgement (**14**), once set against the tympanum of the north doorway. At the west end of the inner south aisle is a stained-glass window (1982) by Makaraviez illustrating the Apocalypse of St John (**15**).

OLD MONTFERRAND★★

Montferrand was founded by the counts of Auvergne who built a fortress on a rise that is now the site of place Marcel-Sembat, in order to counter the authority of the bishop, who was also Lord of Clermont. In the early 13C the town was rebuilt on the orders of a powerful woman named Countess Brayère and was turned into a bastide, a fortified hilltop town laid out to a strictly symmetrical geometric pattern. Montferrand was a commercial centre at the junction of several roads and, in the 15C, the wealthy middle classes began to commission townhouses. The narrow plots of land made available by Countess Brayère's town plan, however, forced the architects to design houses that were deep rather than wide. Most of the houses were built with lava stone. Montferrand was so commercially successful that, in the 16C, the king set up law courts – known as the Cour des Aides – to try fiscal and criminal cases. The proximity of Clermont caused rivalry and jealousy between the two towns. Montferrand eventually went into decline. In 1962, work was undertaken to renovate the old town of Montferrand, a project which involved some 80 old townhouses and mansions that have retrieved their original façades, decorated with carved heads, balustrades, staircase turrets, cornerstones and lava stone arches contrasting with the honey-coloured "Montferrand roughcast".

▶ Park in place de la Rodade.

Place de la Rodade

This square was once known as place de Belregard because of the view over the Puys range. In the centre stands the Four Seasons fountain made of lava stone.

▶ Enter the old town of Montferrand via rue de la Rodade.

Hôtel Regin
At No. 36.
This 15C and 16C town house belonged to a family of magistrates and is typical of the mansions built in Montferrand.

Hôtel Doyac
At No. 29.
Late-15C mansion built for Jean de Doyac, Royal Bailiff of Montferrand and Minister to Louis XI. Huge, imposing Gothic doorway.

Hôtel du Bailliage
At No. 20.
Bailiwick House is the former Consuls' Residence. Its gargoyles and vaulted rooms are of interest.
After rue de la Rodade widens, a set of timbered houses with corbelling comes into view on the left in the renovated district. Their rounded doorways are set out on high landings that show the original level of the roadway.

▶ Turn back; right on rue Marmillat.

Hôtel de la Porte
At No. 5.
In the courtyard of this mansion, also known as the Architect's House, there is a staircase turret decorated with a Renaissance sculpture from 1577.

▶ Turn right onto rue de la Cerisière.

Hôtel de la Faye des Forges
At No. 2.
A glass door protects a delightful inner door with a carved tympanum decorated with lions holding a phylactery. The house opposite has a double timber gallery, an unusual feature in Montferrand.

▶ Turn left along rue des Cordeliers onto rue Waldeck-Rousseau.

Rue Waldeck-Rousseau runs along the inside of the old ramparts, high above the road laid out along the moat which was once liable to flooding by the Tiretaine.

▶ Turn right onto Rue du Temple, back to Rue des Cordeliers.

Rue des Cordeliers
At No. 11.
Note the Renaissance ground floor flanked by pilasters and the delightful little inner courtyard.

Carrefour des Taules
This is the central junction in the old town. Its name is a reminder that this was a butchers' market.

Maison de l'Apothicaire
At No. 1 rue des Cordeliers.
The old Apothecary's House dates from the 15C and has two timbered upper storeys. At the top of the house, the

brackets on either side of the gable are decorated with an apothecary and the patient awaiting his operation.

▶ Turn left onto rue du Séminaire.

Halle aux Toiles
At No. 3.
The old cloth market, there is a long balcony supporting a fine row of four basket-handled arches and corresponding side doors.

Hôtel d'Étienne Pradal
At No. 22.
The ground floor of this mansion has superb semicircular and basket-handled arches. Its "Montferrand roughcast" and cornerstones made of lava stone are typical of the town's architecture.

Musée d'Art Roger-Quilliot★★
&⏱*Tue–Fri 10am-6pm, Sat–Sun and public holidays 10am-noon, 1-6pm).*
⏱*1 Jan, 1 May, 1 Nov, 25 Dec.* ⬤*€5, no charge 1st Sunday in the month.*
☎*04 43 76 25 25.*

www.clermontmetropole.eu.

A change of use – The history of these premises reflects the history of Montferrand and Clermont, each in turn the seat of official bodies. The museum stands on the site of the Palais Vieux above the town walls. It was the seat of the royal bailiwick of the Cour des Aides of the Auvergne, the Limousin and the Marches; the monumental gateway built in the early 17C in front of the courtyard that precedes the chapel is all that remains of this building.

When Montferrand and Clermont were combined, the Cour des Aides moved to Clermont and the Ursuline Order of nuns took over and reconstructed the buildings. The site was turned into a seminary after the Revolution, then into a military hospital from 1914 to 1918, and into barracks for riot police and *gendarmerie*, before being transformed into a museum.

The buildings and their surroundings are a reflection of Montferrand. They constitute the old "Gateway of the Rising Sun" and open the historic centre of the town to its suburbs.

Église Notre-Dame-de-Prospérité

The west front still has its north tower which was used as a watchtower. It is topped by a 16C lantern.

▷ Continue along rue Kléber.

Maison d'Adam et d'Eve

At No 4. In the courtyard on a balustrade is a 15C **bas-relief★** of Adam and Eve.

▷ Continue on rue Kléber.

Maison de l'Éléphant★

At No. 12.
A 13C Romanesque house. The great arches on the ground floor support the twin bay windows on the first floor.

Maison de l'Ange

At No. 14.
In the courtyard is a small, triangular tympanum above a doorway representing an angel carrying a coat of arms.

Maison de l'Apothicaire

© Luc Olivier/Photononstop

Fontaine du Lion

The fountain comes from a square to which it had given its name. On the gable is a lion carrying the blazoned coat of arms of Montferrand.

▷ Turn right twice onto rue Jules-Guesde.

Hôtel de Fontfreyde

At No. 28.
In the courtyard of this mansion is a Madonna and Child on the Gothic doorway into the staircase turret.

The balustrade on the gallery bears three fine Italianate medallions depicting Lucretia stabbing herself, torn between her husband and her seducer.

Hôtel Gaschier

At No. 20.
Three rows of galleries, one above the other, open onto the courtyard (15C–16C). The first floor is supported by superb pillars.

Hôtel de Lignat★

At No. 18.
This, the Lawyer's House, dates from the 16C. Gracious mullioned windows open onto the street. It opens onto Grande-Rue-du-Languedoc through an elegant door decorated with a garland of roses in the Italian Renaissance style.

Hôtel de Fontenilhes★

At No. 13.

The house, a fine residence dating from the late 16C, was built of lava stone from Volvic.

▶ Start walking along rue Notre-Dame.

Hôtel Mallet-de-Vandègre

At No. 2.

This building, with its austere courtyard, is said to have been the women's prison.

▶ Cross carrefour des Taules, walk along rue de la Rodade and turn left onto rue du Dr-Balme.

At No. 5 is a Romanesque house with colonnettes and capitals on the front. At No. 11 there is a second **Hôtel d'Albiat** dating from the 16C.

ADDITIONAL SIGHTS

Musée Bargoin★

45 r. Ballainvilliers. Ⓞ*Tue–Sat 10am–noon, 1-5pm, Sun, 2–7pm.* Ⓞ*1 Jan, 1 May, 1 Nov, 25 Dec.* ⊛€5, *no charge 1st Sunday in the month.* ℘*04 43 76 25 50. www.clermontmetropole.eu.*

This museum houses a sizeable **prehistoric and Gallo-Roman archaeological collection★** on the ground and basement floors, comprising artefacts discovered locally, particularly during recent excavations in the city of Clermont itself.

The Gallo-Roman period is the best represented, with a marvellous collection of statuettes of animals, men, women and children in white terracotta, pottery from Lezoux with fine examples dating from the 2C and vestiges of the great temple of Mercury built on the summit of the Puy-de-Dôme at the beginning of the Imperial era.

The **Carpet Museum** includes over 80 carpets from the Middle and Far East: Turkey, the Caucasus, Iran, Afghanistan, Turkestan, Tibet, China etc.

Hôtel de Fonfreyde Centre Photographique

34 r. des Gras. Ⓞ*Tue–Sat 2–7pm.* Ⓞ*1 Jan, 1 May, 1 Nov, 25 Dec. For each*

exhibition, a guided tour is arranged (no charge) on the 1st Sat of the month at 4pm. ℘*04 73 42 31 80.*

This Renaissance mansion houses temporary photographic exhibitions.

Muséum d'Histoire Naturelle Henri-Lecoq

Ⓞ*Oct–Apr Mon–Sat 10am–noon, 2–5pm, Sun 2–5pm; May–Sept Tue–Sat 10am–noon, 2–6pm, Sun 2–6pm.* Ⓞ*Public holidays.* ⊛€5, *no charge 1st Sunday in the month.* ℘*04 73 42 32 00.*

This museum is named after the naturalist Henri Lecoq (1802–71) whose wide-ranging collections of stuffed animals, rocks and regional flora make this a natural history museum very much centred on the Auvergne.

Parks

The attractive **Jardin Lecoq** stretches right in the town centre. Near the lake is a 14C entrance brought over from the Château de Bien-Assis, built for the Duc de Berry and owned, in the 17C, by Florin Périer, Blaise Pascal's brother-in-law.

L'Aventure Michelin

32 rue du Clos-Four. Ⓞ*Sept–Jun daily except Mon 10am–6pm; Jul–Aug daily 10am–7pm;* Ⓞ*2 wks in Jan.* ⊛€9.50 *(children 7–18, €5.50).* ℘*04 73 98 60 60. www.laventuremichelin.com.*

Tracing the history of the development of the eponymous company, the Michelin museum is a dream visit for any car fan, and is about so much more than the tyres for which it is famed. This is a history of the family, the evolution of transportation, tyres, modern media, marketing and much more, and all under the famed Michelin brand logo.

🚗 DRIVING TOURS

① VOLCANOES AROUND CLERMONT

35km/21mi. Allow half a day.

▶ Leave Clermont via place des Carmes-Déchaux and head N on boulevard J.-B. Dumas towards

AROUND CLERMONT-FERRAND

0 ———— 5 km

Limoges, then take rue de Blanzat on the right.

The road rises along the ravine separating the Côtes de Clermont from the Chanturgue plateau.

▶ 1.2km/0.8mi after the intersection with boulevard Charcot, turn right and drive on for 300m until you reach a junction.

🚶 A gravel path wends its way up towards the site, running along the edge of the ravine to the left *(1hr return)*.

Plateau de Chanturgue★

The Chanturgue plateau constitutes the remains of a vast volcanic table that erosion has worn down into several sections. In the bases of drystone walls, covered with stubble or concealed by the undergrowth, archaeologists have found the remains of what may have been Caesar's lesser encampment.

L'Oppidum des Côtes de Clermont

Follow the road to the start of a lane on the left, level with a right-hand turn and walk to the ridge of the Côtes de Clermont plateau (1h return).

🚶 History lovers will enjoy these ruins, the vestiges of a former stronghold.

▶ Go back towards Clermont and turn right onto boulevard Charcot, heading for Durtol. Go to avenue du Puy-de-Dôme (D 941A) via avenue de la Paix (D 941), then take côte de la Baraque.

Puy de Dôme★★★
🕮*see Monts DÔME.*

▶ In La Font-de-l'Arbre, take D 68.

Royat – 🕮*see Excursions.*

Chamalières

Lying south-west of Clermont, Chamalières is an important residential and business centre and the headquarters for some of the tourist and spa amenities in Royat.

Église Notre-Dame
Of the five churches that once stood in Chamalières, only one remains. Its nave embraces an early building, dating from before 1000.

Moulin de la Saigne

Beyond the church take rue de la Coifferie and rue du Languedoc.
The swift currents of the River Tiretaine have always favoured the installation of water-wheels: there have been flour mills along the river since the 10C and papermills from the 15C.

Musée de la Résistance

7 pl. de Beaulieu. ○*Mon–Sat 9am–noon, 2–5.30pm.* ○*Sun.* ☞€3. ☎*04 73 31 28 42.*
A collection of over 300 documents, reproductions, photographs and miscellaneous objects that bear witness to events during World War II.

▷ Cross place de Geretsried to no. 3 avenue de Fontmaure, within the Carrefour-Europe residential and shopping complex.

Galerie d'Art Contemporain

○*Tue–Sun 2–6pm.* ♿. ☎*04 73 30 97 22. www.amac-chamalieres.com.*
Space is fairly limited in this Modern Art Gallery, but the exhibitions are interesting and they attract all the latest names in modern painting and sculpture.

▷ Take avenue de Royat, then rue Blatin to return to the town centre (place de Jaude).

Parc Bargoin – ♿*see Excursions.*

② THE COUNTRY SOUTH OF CLERMONT

45km/28mi. Allow half a day.

▷ Leave Clermont starting from place de Jaude and take rue Gonod to the S. Then take avenue de la Libération, which leads to N 89.

Église de Beaumont

The former wine-growing village of Beaumont developed round the **Église St-Pierre**. Founded in the 7C, the church was attached to a Benedictine convent until 1792.

Ceyrat

At the junction with the road to Boisséjour, on the left, you will notice the curious remains of a volcano.

▷ Continue heading S.

Gorges de Ceyrat

These high granite cliffs have been deeply eroded by the river.

▷ Go back to N 89 and turn right. After 250m, turn left onto D 120. Follow signs for Château d'Opme.

Château d'Opme

♿○*Easter–Oct, Sun and public holidays 2.30–6pm (mid-Jul–mid-Sept, daily except Tue, 2–7pm).* ○*Nov–Easter.* ☎*04 73 87 59 35.*
This old fortress (11C) stands high above a mountain pass which was once the route taken by the Roman road from Clermont to Le Puy-en-Velay. It originally belonged to the counts of Auvergne and was converted into an elegant Renaissance château by Antoine de Ribeyre, Treasurer of France under Louis XIII. The upper terrace is laid out as a formal **French garden★** around an ornamental basin with a fountain, the entire area shaded by two avenues of lime trees.

▷ Return to the intersection of D 3 and D 120 and turn right.

The road climbs up to the Gergovie plateau, offering pretty views of Clermont, the Puys mountain range and the Monts Dore in the distance.

Plateau de Gergovie★

♿*see Excursions, below.*

▷ Drive along D 120 to La Roche-Blanche then head for Clermont along D 978. Drive 2km/1.2mi along N 9 and turn left onto D 777 (avenue R.-Maerte); 1.5km/0.9mi further on, turn right onto D 69 (avenue J.-Noellet) to Aubière.

The Battle of Gergovia

In the year 52 BCE, Caesar was carrying out his seventh military campaign in Gaul; he had just defeated the Gallic army in Bourges and the Gauls had retreated to the mountains of the Massif Central, pursued by six Roman legions. **Vercingétorix**, the leader of the Gallic coalition, had retreated to the Arverni's hillfort in Gergovia, which was defended by a drystone wall. Caesar captured the Roche-Blanche hill and set up a lesser encampment there, linking it to the main camp by a ditch along which he could move his troops. Caesar then ordered his troops to implement a diversionary movement by night, along the Bédat valley that skirted the Arverni's hillfort, to give Vercingétorix the idea that his army might be attacked from the rear.

The next day, three Roman legions moved from the main camp up to the lesser camp and, shortly after midday, launched an attack. Vercingétorix, however, was a good strategist and had concealed troops behind the Puy de la Mouchette who put up fierce resistance against the Romans. Furthermore, the Gauls on the plateau ran quickly back to the scene of the real battle and routed the Roman legions. The Gauls' success was short-lived, however: their chieftain was besieged in Alésia and finally surrendered to Caesar at the end of the summer.

◗ Continue along D 69, then turn left onto boulevard Louis-Loucheur. A little further on, boulevard C.-Bernard will take you back to place de Jaude.

EXCURSIONS

PLATEAU DE GERGOVIE★
14km/8.6mi S of Clermont-Ferrand.
The Clermont landscape is dominated by this vast plateau, whose vaguely trapezoid shape stands out clearly from the Limagne plain and Allier valley. From here, the view encompasses the entire Limagne de Clermont plain, the horizon enclosed by the Forez and Livradois mountains, and across the Allier valley, beyond which lie the Puys de la Comté.

Maison de Gergovie
🕙*Closed for refurbishment until 2019. Check website for details.* ✆*04 73 79 42 98. www.ot-gergovie.fr.*
The Information Centre on the plateau houses exhibitions on geology and local flora, archaeology.

Château de la Batisse★
12km/7.5mi. Allow 2h. Leave the plateau de Gergovie and head for Opme, then drive towards Chanonat. At the entrance to the village, turn right for La Batisse.
This **château** (👁guided visits: Apr–Jun and mid-Sept–Oct by reservation; Jul– *Aug Mon and Sun 3pm, 4.45pm, Tue–Fri 10.30am, 1/30pm, 3pm, 4.45pm.* ⏤€8.50. ✆*06 24 54 52 23. www.chateaudela batisse.com)* built of pale stone exudes an atmosphere of tranquillity and gracious living which forms a stark contrast to the feudal fortresses of Auvergne. It is flanked by a pepper-pot tower and two corner towers crowned with red-tiled domes and lantern turrets, all that remain of the original 15C castle.

◗ Return to Chanonat and turn right onto D 3 for Le Crest.

Le Crest
This wine-growers' village at the very tip of the Serre mountain range has a 13C church. There is a fine **view**★ from the old tower over the Gergovie and Limagne plateaux around Clermont.

◗ Go back down towards D 213 and A75, pass beneath them, and then take the small narrow road that climbs up around the Butte de Monton.

Monton
This village has its houses spread out over the southern slopes of a mound. Not far from Monton are a series of **troglodyte caves**, affording views of the surrounding countryside.

▶ Go back to Gergovie via La Roche-Blanche.

ROYAT

1km W of Clermont-Ferrand.
🏛 *1 av. Auguste-Rouzaud, 63130 Royat.*
📞 *04 73 29 74 70. www.ot-royat.com.*
Royat is a large, elegant thermal spa terraced on the slopes of the Tiretaine valley. The Tiretaine flows from the granite plateau at the base of the Dômes mountain range; until it leaves Royat, it is a torrent. The bottom of its bed was filled with lava from the Petit Puy de Dôme, the waters then cut gorges in it.
The **waters** of Royat were exploited by the Romans, who built public baths here. Although the baths met with mixed success until the mid-19C, they have enjoyed popularity and fame ever since. A hydropathic establishment was built and the visit here by Empress Eugénie in 1862 launched Royat as a spa.

Parc Thermal

This spa garden, completed by the new English-style park through which flows the Tiretaine, contains the hydropathic establishment and the casino. The remains of the **Gallo-Roman public baths**, can be seen. One of the pools had mosaic-covered arches and marble-covered walls. Terracotta pipes brought the water into the pool in small, semicircular cascades.

▶ At the end of the park.

Grotte des Laveuses

The "Washerwomen's Cave" is on the banks of the Tiretaine. Several springs gush from the volcanic walls before flowing into the Tiretaine.

Église St-Léger★

Built in the 11C, this fortified building deviates significantly from the churches of the Auvergne, it more resembles the churches of Provence. The bell tower is 19C.

Parc Bargoin

From Église St-Léger, follow avenue Jean-Jaurès then avenue Anatole-France.
This is a well laid out park on hilly land, and a botanical garden. It is home to the largest maple in France (250 years old).

🥾 Walks

A map of the area on place Allard indicates a number of signposted trails for walkers leaving from Royat, including the **Bois de Villars**, **Puy de Montaudoux**, **Arboretum de Royat** and **Bois de la Pauze**, **Puy de Charade** and **Vallée de la Tiretaine**, and **Chemin des Crêtes**.

ADDRESSES

🛏 STAY

⊖ **Hôtel Lune Étoile La Pardieu** – *89 bd Gustave-Flaubert.* 📞*04 73 98 68 68. www.hotel-lune-etoile.com. 45 rooms.* Close to La Pardieu, and cubic in design; modern and functional.

⊖⊖ **Dav'Hôtel Jaude** – *10 r. des Minimes.* 📞*04 73 93 31 49. www.davhotel.fr. 28 rooms.* This modern hotel within walking distance of the cathedral is located in a tranquil side street a few steps from the old quarter.

⊖⊖ **Hôtel Albert-Élisabeth** – *37 av. Albert et Élisabeth.* 📞*04 73 92 47 41. www.hotel-albertelisabeth.com. 38 rooms.* A small hotel near the station.

⊖⊖ **Hôtel Radio** – *43 av. P. et M. Curie. 63400 Chamalières.* 📞*04 73 30 87 83. www.hotel-radio.fr. Closed Jan and early Nov. 26 rooms. Restaurant⊖⊖ – Closed Sat lunch, all day Sun, and Mon lunch).* Drawing its inspiration from the very beginnings of the radio era, this hotel has a 1930s decoration scheme.

⊖⊖ **Hôtel Lafayette** – *53 av. de l'Union-Soviétique.* 📞*04 73 91 82 27. www.hotel-le-lafayette.com. Closed 24 Dec–4 Jan. 48 rooms.* Best Western hotel next to the station.

⊖⊖⊖ **Holiday Inn Garden Court** – *59 bd F.-Mitterrand.* 📞*04 73 17 48 48. www.ihg.com. 94 rooms. Restaurant⊖⊖.* Modern hotel close by the botanic garden, with easy access to the town centre.

🍴 **Mercure** – *1 Avenue Julien.* 📞 *04 63 66 21 00. www.mercure-clermint-ferrand-centre.com. 125 rooms.* Central chain hotel with good transport links; panoramic bar and fitness centre.

🍴/EAT

🍴 **Le Chardonnay** – *1 pl. Philippe-Marcombes.* 📞 *04 73 26 79 95. www.lechardonnay.fr. Closed Sat lunch and Sun.* The generous bistro style and the easy-going ambience make for a very enjoyable meal.

🍴 **Le Charolais** – *77 r. Pré-la-Reine.* 📞 *04 73 91 65 35. www.lecharolais.fr. Closed weekends and weekday evenings.* A favourite with meat-lovers; generous dishes at reasonable prices.

🍴 **L'Odevie** – *1 r. Eugène-Gilbert.* 📞 *04 73 93 90 00. www.restaurantodevie.com. Closed Sun.* A few steps from the Place de Jaude; serves brasserie-style cuisine.

🍴 **Le Comptoir des Saveurs** – *5 r. Ste-Claire.* 📞 *04 73 37 10 31. www.le-comptoir-des-saveurs.fr. Closed Tue–Wed evenings, all day Sun–Mon.* A kind of pick "n" mix approach to dining, chosing whatever takes your fancy.

🍴 **Restaurant l'Ostal** – *16 rue Claussmann, 63000 Clermont-Ferrand.* 📞 *04 73 27 77 86. www.lostal-restaurant.fr. Closed Sat lunch, and all day Sun–Mon.* A new gastronomic restaurant in the centre of Clermont. Modern setting, and relaxing if volcanic-influenced atmosphere. Well worth locating; everything is 'Fait Maison', i.e. prepared on the premises.

🍴 **Bath's Restaurant** – *pl. Marché St-Pierre, 63000 Clermont-Ferrand.* 📞 *04 73 31 23 22. Closed Sun, Mon and public holidays.* Opulent dining brightened by contemporary art; good selection of wines by the glass.

TAKING A BREAK

Garden ici Café – *48 pl. de Jaude.* 📞 *04 73 17 03 04. Daily 7.30am–1.30am.* Natives in the know frequent this large, chic and cosy café (formerly Le Suffren).

Les Goûters de Justine – *11 bis r. Pascal.* 📞 *04 73 92 26 53. Mon–Fri noon–7pm, Sat 2.30–7pm.* This unique tea room reminds you of a charmingly chaotic antique shop.

The Salvation Jane Pub – *14 rue Terrasse.* 📞 *04 73 25 39 50. www.pub-restaurant-clermontferrand.fr. Tue–Wed 6pm–1am; Thu–Fri 6pm–2am; Sat 5pm–2am.* The latest 'In' place, and a great hang-out for beer lovers; the range is exceptional and constantly being added to. The kitchen is open Tue–Sat from 7–10.30pm; everything is home-cooked (Fait Maison), and uses the best local produce. If you like quizzes, come along on Thu when you'll find one in English (and French).

ON THE TOWN

Bars, brasseries, cinemas, *crêperies*, pubs, restaurants and tea rooms are where you'll find most of the lively goings-on in neighbourhoods downtown. Many of these are concentrated around the place de Jaude, near the cathedral, and at place Sugny, rue Fontgiève and place Gaillard.

International Jazz Festival – held in October, Jazz en Tête is a well established event for jazz enthusiasts. 📞 *09 82 47 01 97; www.jazzentete.com.*

THEATRE AND ENTERTAINMENT

Contemporary music concerts are held in the Maison des Sports (Place des Bughes).

Classical music is generally performed in the Maison des Congrès.

Plays are regularly staged at the Opéra Municipal or at the Maison des Congrès. La Maison du Tourisme houses a Massif Central wing and a Romanesque Art exhibit.

Le Zénith – *Plaine de la Sarliève 63800 Cournon d'Auvergne. Reservations on-line at www.fnac.com, or contact the Tourist office in Clermont.* The hall seats 8 500, and features pop stars and big entertainment spectaculars.

SHOPPING

Marché couvert-espace St-Pierre – *Pl. St-Pierre.* 📞 *04 73 31 27 88. Mon-Sat 7am-7.30pm.* This covered food market features a few stands selling regional products… and chocolate!

LEISURE ACTIVITIES

Espace Massif Central – *place de la Victoire, Maison du Tourisme.* This place is the Massif Central's showcase, where the different areas, cultures and traditions are represented; it is also a lively meeting place.

Volvic

Volvic is built on the edge of the solidified lava flow from Nugère volcano. The village is not only famous for the extremely pure water of its spring, filtered through thick layers of volcanic rock and now exported throughout the world, but also for the quarrying and processing of its lava.

A BIT OF HISTORY

Volvic lava – Andesite, extracted from open quarries, is both solid and light; this pale-grey rock has been used as building stone since the 13C and the fact that many buildings in the Auvergne are black is due to atmospheric pollution and not to the stone's original colour. Volvic cemetery is full of extraordinary monuments cut from this stone.

The hardness of the lava and the fact that it can be enamelled at high temperatures have made it popular, for more than a century, for signs and plaques that have to stand up to the weather: clock faces, street signs, level gauges etc. As a result of its exceptional qualities, this rock was chosen by Michelin's road sign department to make enamelled lava corner-posts, signposts, wall plaques etc from 1920 to 1970. Andesite is also used to make apparatus used in the chemical industry, because of its excellent resistance to acids.

SIGHTS
Church

This was part of the old priory of Mozat; its nave and façade were rebuilt during the 19C. The vast 12C chancel is surrounded by an ambulatory opening onto three radiating chapels; a beautiful wrought-iron grille, from the Romanesque period, closes the axial chapel. There are interesting historiated capitals. At the entrance to the chancel, on the left, note the 14C Virgin with a Bird.

Musée Municipal Marcel-Sahut

2 r. des Écoles. ⊙*mid-May–Jun and Sept–early Nov Wed–Fri 2–6pm, Sat–Sun 10am–12.30pm, 2–6pm; Jul–Aug*

- ▸ **Population:** 4 573.
- ⚲ **Michelin Map:** 326: F-7 – 14km/8.7mi N of Clermont-Ferand.
- 🛈 **Info:** Pl. de l'Eglise, 63530 Volvic. ℘04 73 33 58 73. www.volvic-tourisme.com.
- ▶ **Location:** Volvic is 14km/9mi N of Clermont Ferrand and 10km/6mi from Riom; it is reached using the D 986.
- ⏱ **Timing:** Allow 2 hours.

Wed–Sun 10am–noon, 2–6pm. ♿. ⚌€3. ℘04 73 33 57 33.

The museum displays many works by Sahut, a native of this region, including charcoals, watercolours and paintings *(View of Nantes, The Tumbler)*.

Maison de la Pierre de Volvic

2 rte du Pont-Jany. ⊙*early Feb–Mar Tue–Thu 11am–1pm, 2–5pm; Apr–May daily 11am–6pm; Jul–Aug 10am–7pm; Sept daily except Sat 11am–1pm, 2–6pm; Oct daily except Sat 2–6pm.* ⊙*Nov–early Feb.* ⚌€7.50. ℘04 73 33 56 92. www.maisondelapierre-volvic.com.

A former underground quarry has been used to create the House of Stone, a centre focusing on lava and lava quarrying. Visitors travel to the heart of a **lava flow★** from the Puy de la Nugère, while a soundtrack reproduces the noises during different phases of an eruption.

Volvic Springs

⊙*Apr–Jun and Sept Mon–Fri 10am–12.15pm, 2–6pm, Sat–Sun and public holidays 2.30–6pm; Jul–Aug Mon–Fri 10am–6.45pm, Sat–Sun and public holidays 2–6.30pm; Oct Mon–Fri 2–6pm.* ⊙*Nov–Mar, 1 May.* ⚌*No charge.* ℘04 73 64 51 24. www.volvic.fr.

In the **Information Centre** there is a presentation of the hydrological characteristics of the Volvic area and of the bottling of its mineral water; there are also audiovisual shows about the Auvergne

Château de Tournoël

and its volcanoes. A network of foot-paths provides visitors with walking opportunities *(15min to 1h45)*.

🚗 DRIVING TOUR

MONTS DÔME
25km/15.5mi. Allow half a day.

▶ Leave Volvic N on D 15 towards Châtel-Guyon; left before the cemetery.

Château de Tournoël★
🔹Guided tours only: Jul-Aug 10.30am–12.30pm, 2–6pm. ❧€8. ℘04 73 33 53 06. www.tournoel.com.
Tournoël Castle, on the crest of a rocky spur overlooking the whole of the Limagne, was owned by the counts of Auvergne, captured and almost entirely destroyed it in 1213. In the 14C, however, it was rebuilt by Hugues de la Roche, who widened the bases of the towers.

▶ Rejoin D 15; continue towards Enval.

Châtel-Guyon✚
&see CHÂTELGUYON.

▶ Leave Châtel-Guyon SW on D 227.

Mozac★★ – &see RIOM.

Riom★★ – &see RIOM.

▶ Leave Riom to the SW on D 83.

Église de Marsat
Built in the 11C and 12C, the church consists of two heavily restored naves.

▶ Leave Marsat on D 446, heading for Riom. It joins up with N 9 at the entrance to the town. Drive for 3km/1.9mi towards Clermont-Ferrand, then turn right onto D 402.

Châteaugay
The town is overlooked by the squat out-line of its castle. Châteaugay was built in the 14C by Pierre de Giac, Chancellor of France, and its history is a tragic one. It was in the keep that the grandson of the Chancellor poisoned his wife, Jeanne de Giac, who had won over the heart of John the Fearless, Duke of Burgundy, before becoming one of his murderers' accomplices.

Keep★
🕐For details, apply to the town hall.
The square keep built in lava stone is the most interesting part of the castle; it is almost the only one in the Auvergne to have remained intact. Richelieu did not include it in his demolition orders, and during the French Revolution, Couthon, a member of the National Convention, was unable to raze it to the ground.

Monts Dôme ★★★

The range of volcanic cones known as the *Chaîne des Puys* or Dôme mountain range rises to the west of Clermont-Ferrand and stands high above the Limagne plain. Some 80 extinct volcanoes stretch in a line over a distance of some 40km/25mi *(see INTRODUCTION: Volcanoes of the Auvergne)*. From the summit of the Puy de Dôme, the highest of the "cones" with an altitude of 1 465m, the view extends right across the range, over this extraordinary and magnificent landscape.

- **Michelin Map:** 326: D-8 to E-9.
- **Location:** The most splendid way of getting an idea of the landscape is to take the Apr–Sept shuttle service from Clermont-Ferrand railway station to the Puy de Dôme, or you can simply take the Panoramique des Dômes rack railway (*see below*).
- **Kids:** Vulcania theme park.

A BIT OF GEOLOGY

The Dôme mountain range has the youngest volcanoes in the Auvergne. They came into being in the Quaternary Era and the earliest human settlers may have witnessed their eruptions. The cones, which rise up from the plain in a long string, stand on a plateau of crystalline rocks 900–1 000m high. Most of the volcanoes rise by only 200–300m above this plateau, with the exception of the Puy de Dôme which rises to 500m above it.

These extinct volcanoes are not all the same shape. Several, such as the Puy de Dôme, are shaped like bells or domes; others contain a single or double crater, whereas a few have a breached crater. Areas of forest grew naturally, but much of it has been planted since the Count of Montlosier set the first example in the early 19C, showing that forests could be grown on land thought of as barren – he was initially taken for a fool. Long black lava flows known as *cheires* form heaps of rocks dotted with juniper and pines; they are scattered all across the plateau. One of these flows, created by the Puy de Lassolas and the Puy de la Vache, closed off the Veyre valley and created **Lac d'Aydat**.

VOLCANO WALK

1 LE PUY DE DÔME★★★

11km/7mi from Royat (see CLERMONT-FERRAND).

PANORAMIQUE DES DÔMES

This rack railway with panoramic windows that provide 360°views of the volcanoes of the Auvergne is by far the easiest way of reaching the summit. Trains leave every 40 minutes (*9am–7pm*) during the season, and every hour otherwise. €12.30–€13.50 (return). *www.panoramiquedesdomes.fr.*

The ascent of the Puy de Dôme and the extraordinary panorama visible from the summit, best seen at sunset, are quite unforgettable.

The Toll Road

In 1926 this road replaced the tracks used by the miniature steam train which had operated for about 20 years. The road, which is well designed, has a constant slope of 12 percent for about 4km/2.5mi. As it spirals around the Dôme it offers a wonderful variety of views, becoming more extensive higher up. The first ascent on bicycle took place in 1891 in 28min; in 1913 a high-powered car reached the summit for the first time, in just 11min.

Today, it is no longer possible to drive the toll road. From April to September, a shuttle operates from the centre of Clermont-Ferrand to the train station. For timetables, visit www.t2c.fr.

© Francis Cormon/hemis.fr

Puy de Dôme

Le Puy de Dôme★★★

This former volcano is the oldest, highest and most famous of the Dôme mountain range, of which it is the centre. It was only in 1751 that the volcanic origin of these mountains was recognised; until then, it was believed that they were part of gigantic fortifications built by the Romans.

Sacred Mountain – From the earliest times, the solitude of this Puy, which is so difficult to get to, has been awe-inspiring. The Gauls made it a sanctuary for their god Lug. The Romans replaced it with the cult of "Mercury of the Dome". They built a magnificent temple to him, the foundations of which were discovered in 1872 during construction of the first observatory. This temple and all its treasures were destroyed by the Barbarian invasions.

According to popular superstition, all the sorcerers of the Auvergne meet on the deserted mountaintop for blood-curdling midnight revels.

The weight of air – It was on the Puy de Dôme that **Blaise Pascal** carried out an experiment in 1648 that proved the theory about the weight of air. It had already been noted that mercury rises to about 76cm/30in in a tube in which a vacuum has been created. To explain this phenomenon, it was said that "nature hates vacuums". This axiom however did not satisfy Torricelli; he put forward the hypothesis that it is the weight of the air that pushes the mercury up.

Captivated by this idea, Pascal thought that, if this were the case, the weight of the air should be less at the top of a mountain. As Pascal was in Paris, he asked his brother-in-law to help. The latter chose a fine day, left a mercury barometer in Clermont and went with the Minimes Fathers to the top of the Puy de Dôme. He was overjoyed to see that the mercury rose 8.4cm/3.40in less than it did in Clermont. The theory about the weight of the air had been proven.

Puy-de-Dôme rather than Mont-Dore – In 1790, following the Revolution, administrative *départements* replaced the former provinces in France. There was talk of giving the name Mont-d'Or (Golden Mountain) – as Mont-Dore was then spelt – to the Lower Auvergne constituency, but the deputy for Clermont, Gaultier de Beauzat, was alarmed that such a wealthy sounding name would give the wrong impression to outsiders. He asked for the less compromising name of Puy-de-Dôme, and it was accepted.

The Michelin Grand Prix

In 1908, when Henri Farman was making the first circular flight (1km/0.6mi) in the world, the Michelin brothers offered a Grand Prix of 100,000 francs to any aviator who could fly from Paris, with a 75kg passenger on board, to the top of the Puy de Dôme in less than 6 hours, skirting the cathedral of Clermont by 1 500m on their right.

Only three years later, on 7 March 1911, despite predictions that this feat could not possibly be achieved within less than a half a century, the aviator **Eugène Renaux**, with his passenger Senouque, successfully met the prescribed conditions in just 5hrs 11min.

Ascent on Foot
via the Chemin des Muletiers
Allow 45min for the ascent.

🅿 Park at the Ceyssat Pass in a forest of fir trees. It was up this winding path (35–40 percent slopes) that chariots pulled by five to eight tandem-driven horses transported materials needed to build the Roman temple and subsequently, in the 19C, the observatory.

The Summit
Reception and Information Centre
www.planetepuydedome.com.

This houses a display on volcanoes and exhibitions specifically on the Puy de Dôme and on various other sites of interest to be explored in the locality.

The summit offers several dining options. At the main train station, a take-away stand offers sandwiches and drinks. At the summit, the 1911 (🕑mid-Mar–Dec; 📞04 73 87 43 02) is a fine dining restaurant serving refined seasonal food and using local ingredients, and the Bousset is a bar and café with self-service facilities for lunch. A covered picnic area is also available with drink and snack machines.

Panorama★★★

To the north and south, over a distance of about 30km/19mi, can be seen the 100 or so extinct volcanoes forming the Dôme mountain range; a marvellous museum of volcanic shapes, a lunar landscape unique in France and perhaps in the world.

To the north can be clearly distinguished volcanoes of the same origin as the Puy de Dôme which resemble enormous craterless molehills: Petit Suchet, Clierzou and Sarcouy. The others are all cones of debris topped with craters: Petit Puy de Dôme or Nid de la Poule ("Hen's Nest"), Grand Suchet, Puy de Côme, Pariou and Louchadière.

The view extends over 11 *départements*, one-eighth of the total surface area of France. Visibility varies almost from one minute to the next. The puys may be covered with grass or heath, with fir-groves or hazel copses. The chain itself is uninhabited as any rain which falls soaks into the volcanic rocks.

It is at sunset that the view is most spectacular. Fiery trails weave through the volcanic cones. The mountain throws its shadow to the east, covering first the Orcines plateau then suddenly reaching Clermont before gradually invading the plain: the extreme tip of its shadow goes right to Thiers.

Temple of Mercury
⊶No access.

This Temple to the God Mercury (now a ruin) was built by the Romans. Originally it was twice the size of the famous Maison Carrée (1C) in Nîmes; 50 sorts of marble were used to decorate it. The television transmitter stands on the original site of a monumental bronze statue of Mercury by the Greek sculptor Zenodorus. It was, according to Pliny the Elder, one of the marvels of the ancient world.

The path winds around the ruins and passes in front of the monument recalling Renaux's exploit.

MONTS DÔME

DRIVING TOUR

② **PUYS MOUNTAINS★★★**
120km/75mi round trip. Allow one day.

Royat★★
♨ *see CLERMONT-FERRAND.*

▶ Leave Royat on D 941C SE then turn right onto D 5.

The road climbs above the plain until it reaches the granite base from which the volcanic cones rise.

Puy de Gravenoire
There are pozzolana quarries here. This old volcano, now clothed in pine forests, juts out from above the great Limagne fault. Its lava flowed down through the fault towards Royat and Beaumont, then the cone was formed from the materials thrown up during the eruption: ash, scoria and volcanic bombs.

At the top of the rise is the village of **Charade** at the foot of its own extinct volcano, the **Puy de Charade**.

The road then runs along the southern section of the **Clermont-Ferrand-Charade Racing Circuit**.

Follow the road through Thèdes and St-Genès-Champanelle and, in Theix, take N 89 which crosses the lava flow at Aydat.

Cheire d'Aydat

This is a lava flow 6km/4mi long and 1 200m wide. It was thrown up by the Lassolas and La Vache volcanoes, and cooled to form a heap of blackened scoria. The desolation of this volcanic landscape is softened to some extent by juniper bushes, broom, birch trees and, on the shores of Lake Aydat for which the lava flow forms a dam, a forest of pines and spruces planted in the second half of the 19C.

▶ Just beyond Col de la Ventouse, turn right onto D 5 towards Murol and right again along D 788.
At the junction turn right towards Randanne.

On the way to Randanne the road skirts the Puy de Combegrasse where the first gliding competition to be staged in France was held in 1922.

▶ From Randanne, D 5 leads to the Puy de la Vache.

Puy de la Vache

3km/1.9mi from Randanne (situated along N 89 between Clermont-Ferrand and Le Mont-Dore) on D 5.
🚶 *1h on foot there and back.*
This well-shaped volcano (alt 1 167m) offers, along with its neighbour, Puy de Lassolas, one of the most characteristic views of the Dôme chain.

Montlosier castle

The **Comte de Montlosier,** a returned émigré in the early 19C, wanted to demonstrate that it was possible to make a forest grow in places which had previously been considered barren; the experiment was carried out on his property. Initially considered to be a madman, he eventually gained recognition when the results of his efforts became tangible. His work was taken up and extended by the Forestry Department.

The castle now houses the offices of the Parc Naturel Regional des Volcans d'Auvergne and organises exhibitions devoted to the region.
🚶 *The path leading to the breached crater of the Puy de la Vache (1hr on foot there and back) runs to the left off D 5. It follows the Cheire d'Aydat, a mass of solidified lava with a rough surface.*

The Volcano

The crater first spewed ash and slag, which formed the cone, then the lava mounted, filling the crater.
Under such enormous pressure the southern flank of the crater gave way, the volcano opened up and a real torrent of molten material poured out over the plateau, forming the present Cheire d'Aydat, 6km/3.7mi long which, by blocking off the Veyre valley, formed Lac d'Aydat.

▶ Return to Randanne and turn right on N 89.

Near the village of Recoleine, the road crosses a landscape dotted with volcanic rocks just breaking the surface of the ground. At the crossroads of Les Quatre-Routes, D 941A on the right runs up towards the Puys until it reaches Col de la Moreno between the Puy de Laschamp (south) and the Puy de Monchier (north), both of which are covered in forest.
From Col de la Moreno the route runs along D 52 northwards to Ceyssat and Champille, providing interesting views of the numerous volcanic cones above the road.
The narrow D 559 (right) crosses the lava flow from the Puy de Côme, swathed in beech and conifer, then meets D 941B; turn right towards Col des Goules and La Fontaine du Berger.
This area is the site for the theme park **Vulcania★★**, which is devoted to volcanic activity in Auvergne (👉*see below*).

Le Grand Sarcouy

🚶 *1h30 on foot there and back along a well-marked footpath leading off D 941B just after Col des Goules.*

The Grand Sarcouy is still known as a "cauldron" because of its shape. In the south side of this gigantic mass of domite is a vast cavern.

Puy de Pariou★

Take D 941B W of Clermont; beyond Orcines, 500m after the Shepherd's Fountain (Fontaine du Berger), park beside the road. Take a path off to the left (1h30 on foot there and back).
Visitors should know that the Puy de Pariou was used for military training. So it is forbidden to cross the firing range and the trenches. Visitors are advised not to pick up any projectile or suspect device lying on the ground.

Puy de Pariou is one of the most beautiful crater volcanoes in the Puys chain. It consists of two volcanoes, one inside the other. Step over the side wall of the first crater, which produced the still visible lava stretching across the road near Orcines. From here it is possible to climb to the second, far more impressive crater, a regular funnel with a depth of 96m. From the edge of this crater there are views of the Dôme mountain range, in particular, to the west, beyond the Clierzou and the Puy de Côme with its two craters that fit perfectly inside one another; to the north, over the Puy Chopine, the Puy de Chaumont and, behind the Puy des Goules, the Sarcouy; to the south, over the Puy de Dôme.

Ternant

Just before reaching Ternant, when on a level with the great cross in the village, the road (*D 773*) provides superb views over Clermont and the Limagne plain.

▷ Take the path on the right, 300m before the junction with D 941B.

Puy Chopine

2h on foot return.
In dry weather the path provides access to the volcanic cone's summit.

▷ Carry on along D 559 to the junction with D 941B and turn right towards Pontgibaud.

Volcan de Lemptégy
© Christian Guy/hemis.fr

Volcan de Lemptégy★

04 73 62 23 25.
www.auvergne-volcan.com.
This **open-topped volcano** is an old quarry hollowed out of a volcanic cone. The site is impressive, as visitors can go down into the very centre and see evidence of three successive phases of volcanic activity from 60,000 years ago.

▷ Carry on along D 941B.

Pontgibaud

This large peaceful village on the river was known in Gallo-Roman times for its silver-bearing lead mines. **Château Dauphin** (*guided tours: Easter–Oct Sun and public holidays 2–6pm; Jul-Aug daily except Mon 2–7pm. €6. 04 73 88 73 39; www.chateaudauphin.com*) is a lava stone fort which was built in the 12C.

Gorges and Site de Montfermy★

Leave Pontgibaud to the N on D 418 running alongside the Sioule gorges. In Montfermy, leave the car next to the bridge spanning the River Sioule.
Take the path skirting the left bank of the river, leading to a waterfall and the ruins of an old mill.
On leaving Pontgibaud, D 941 begins to climb the west side of the mountain

range. Beyond St-Ours and Le Vauriat the road provides stunning views of the **Puy de Louchadière**, one of the main extinct volcanoes in the range, and has a breached crater 150m deep.

Further on, to the left, is the easily recognisable outline of the **Puy de la Nugère**. Beyond Col de La Nugère and Le Cratère the road winds down to the Limagne plain.

👥 PARC EUROPÉEN DU VOLCANISME VULCANIA★★

This gigantic theme park is devoted to the history of Auvergne and more specifically to its geological formation. Designed after plans by the architects **Hans Hollein** and **Philippe Tixier**, the park aims to spread knowledge about volcanoes and other Earth sciences, while contributing towards the protection of natural sites in Auvergne.

VISIT

15km/9.3mi W of Clermont-Ferrand along D 941B. ⏱*Late Mar–early-Nov from 10am: check website for details.* 🎫*From €24.50.* 📞*04 73 19 70 00. www.vulcania.com.*

The range of attractions is constantly evolving, as new ideas surface. Here is a sample of attractions both current and in recent times: **Allée de la Grande Coulée**, an imposing 165m-long wall, leads to the **Caldera**, a circular area where the **Great Cone** is situated. The glowing crater marks the start of a fascinating journey to the centre of the Earth. You are invited to walk through a succession of wide spaces and galleries showing more or less spectacular aspects of volcanic activity, such as the **Rumbling Gallery**, which re-creates the conditions of an erupting volcano, complete with incandescent projections and formidable sound effects! You can either follow the suggested itinerary or travel as you please in a highly interactive way **"From the Cosmos to the Centre of the Earth"** then **"In the heart of a volcano"**; you can learn about the meaning of volcanoes in different cultures in **"Of volcanoes and men"** and end your visit with the **Volcanic Garden**,

a huge, brightly lit greenhouse where a wide variety of plant species thrive on volcanic soil, or in the **Showroom**, where a giant screen projects impressive images of volcanic eruptions in countries all over the world.

ADDRESSES

🛏 STAY

🛏 **Chambre d'Hôte Chez Mme Gauthier Jocelyne** – *Recoleine, 63210 Riom. 3km/1.8mi NW of Randanne via N 89.* 📞*04 73 87 10 34. Closed from 15 Nov-Jan. Reservations required off-season. 3 rooms.* A warm reception awaits you in this former barn neighbouring the Puy de Dôme mountain range and set in a tranquil and natural environment.

🛏 **Chambre d'Hôte Chez M. Bony** – *Bravant, 63210 Olby. 2km/1.2mi N of Les Quatre-Routes dir. Ussel and secondary road.* 📞*04 73 87 12 28. Closed mid Nov-mid Feb. 5 rooms.* This tastefully renovated farm is located in the heart of a charming village.

🍽 EAT

🍽 **La Fourniale** – *Allée du Château, Recoleine, 63210 Nebouzat. 3km/ 1.8mi NW of Randanne via N 89.* 📞*04 73 87 16 63. http://lafourniale.com. Closed Mon–Tue Sept–Jun. Reservations required off-season.* Aficionados of authentic Auvergnat cuisine frequent this inn housed in an ex-sheepfold. The setting is as rustic as can be, with wood tables and a stone trough protruding from the wall.

🍽 **Le Village Auvergnat** – *La Font-de-l'Arbre, at the base of the Puy de Dôme, 63870 Orcines.* 📞*04 73 62 25 34. www. levillageauvergnat.fr. Closed Mon–Thu evenings off-season. Reservations required.* Located at the foot of the Puy de Dôme, this restaurant serves regional specialities.

🍽🍽 **Auberge de la Moreno** – *Col de la Moreno, 63122 St-Genès-Champanelle. At the intersection of D 941 and D 52, on the peak.* 📞*04 73 87 16 46. Closed first 2 wks of Jan and last 2 wks of Nov.* This small inn appeals to diners in search of authenticity, offering satisfying "100% regional" dishes.

Lac d'Aydat ★

This lake, situated at an altitude of 825m, is a perfect example of a volcanic reservoir; its waters were retained by the Aydat lava flow (♿ *see INTRODUCTION: Volcanoes of the Auvergne*). This tranquil stretch of water, reaching a maximum depth of 15m, is ideal for boating and angling. It lies in a wooded setting and is a delightful destination for an outing. Near the north bank is a small island called St-Sidoine in memory of the country house that Sidonius Apollinaris, Bishop of Clermont in the 5C, is said to have had built for himself on the shores of the lake.

🚗 **DRIVING TOUR**

THE LAVA TRAIL
40km/37mi round trip. Allow 2h.

This round tour gives you the opportunity to admire Aydat Lake from several different viewpoints and to discover a variety of landscapes.

Aydat
The church has unusual buttresses in the shape of adjacent turrets.

▶ Leave Aydat on D 90 towards Sauteyras. Turn right towards Rouillas-Bas then left onto D 145. There are numerous views of the Serre mountain range (♿ see below).

Nadaillat
A fine example of a village built of black lava stone.

▶ Leave Nadaillat to the E on D 96.

Montagne de la Serre
The long backbone of the Serre juts out like a promontory into the Limagne plain. It is a typical example of "inversion relief".

▶ Continue N to St-Amant on D 96.

- ♿ **Michelin Map:** 326: E-9.
- **Info:** Sauteyras, 63970 Lac d'Aydat. ℘04 73 79 37 69. www.tourisme-lescheires.com.
- ▶ **Location:** The most scenic approach is by the D 788, from Veyreras to Fohet.
- **Kids:** Swimming, pedaloes.
- ⏱ **Timing:** Half a day should be enough even for the most enthusiastic kids.

St-Amant-Tallende
This village and its shops form an attractive sight seen from the medieval bridge. Note the fortified house in the old town.

▶ Continue along D 8.

St-Saturnin ★
This village in the Monne valley was the home of the barons of La Tour d'Auvergne who later became the counts of Auvergne. This is the family that produced Catherine de' Medici – daughter of Lorenzo de' Medici and Madeleine de La Tour d'Auvergne – who became Queen of France after marrying Henri II. St-Saturnin attracted a colony of painters and several writers, including novelist and critic **Paul Bourget** (1852–1935). The location of St-Saturnin near the Monts Dômes and the Couzes and Comté valleys, its picturesque streets, its castle and its little square with a charming 16C fountain, make this an attractive tourist destination.

Church ★★
The church was built in the 12C and is very simple. Despite the lack of apsidal chapels, the **east end** is nonetheless quite attractive. The radiating transept chapels, the wide ambulatory around the semicircular chancel, and the powerful mass of the transept, which has the best-preserved octagonal bell-tower in the Auvergne, form a remarkable architectural whole. The external

Map showing:

CLERMONT-FD | PLATEAU DE GERGOVIE | CLERMONT-FD

Puy de la Vache ★ 1167

Cheire d'Aydat

1006 Puy de Vichatel

Nadaillat

PARC

La Roche-Blanche

Chanonat

La Batisse

Le Crest

Montagne de la Serre

Rouillas-Bas

NATUREL

Chadrat

Sauteyras

Veyre

St-Amant-Tallende

Aydat

Lac d'Aydat ★

St-Saturnin ★

RÉGIONAL DES VOLCANS

Fohet

Cournols

D'AUVERGNE ★★★

Gorges de la Monne

Monne

Olloix

LAVA ROUTE

0   2 km

Plauzat

CHAMPEIX

decoration is elaborate, with its strings of billet-moulding, its modillions and its set of arches, some of them remarkable just for the alternate colouring of their basalt and arkose archstones. In contrast to this lavish decoration, the side buttresses and simple end-wall of the west front are striking in their lack of ornamentation.

Inside, note the high barrel-vault of the nave, the galleries above the side aisles with their groined vaulting, the eleva-tion of the transept crossing with its sup-porting diaphragm arches and the crypt resting on powerful pillars. Next to the church is the small 11C **Ste-Madeleine Chapel** fortified in the 14C.

Château Royal

Guided tours (50min): May–Sept 10am–7pm. €7. 04 73 39 39 64. www.chateaudesaintsaturnin.com.
This imposing fortress, which has under-gone extensive restoration, is typical of

Chaîne des Puys, Puy Pariou in the foreground, Parc Naturel Régional des Volcans d'Auvergne

© Francis Cormon/hemis.fr

the military architecture of the Middle Ages: triple curtain wall, ramparts, towers with machicolations and crenellations. The main part of the building, with a massive, late-15C roof, is flanked by two wings (14C and 15C). The keep, the watch-path (views of the village and its surroundings) and formal gardens are open to visitors.

▶ D 28 and D 119 go through an austere landscape of cropped grass dotted with rocks, but they provide some extensive views before reaching Olloix. Stop near the multilobed cross on the roadside to enjoy the panoramic view.

Olloix

This village consists of a string of old houses stretching out along the road. It was once the seat of a commandery of the Knights of St John of Jerusalem (Order of Malta) and one of its daughter-houses was the Knights Hospitallers' commandery in La Sauvetat. The **church** contains the tomb of Odon of Montaigu. The road down into the Monne gorge (D 794) provides a number of delightful views.

▶ Beyond Fohet, D 788 to the right of the calvary leads back to Aydat.

EXCURSION

Parc Naturel Régional des Volcans d'Auvergne★★★

This park is the largest of all France's regional nature parks; it encompasses 153 localities in the *départements* of Puy-de-Dôme and Cantal and has a resident population of 88 000. Five main natural regions make up the park: the **Dôme** mountain range of volcanic hills *(puys)*; the **Dore** massif, the vast grass-covered basalt plains of **Cézallier**; the **Artense** with its granite hills, moorland and valleys dotted with lakes and peat bogs; and the **Cantal** mountains.

The main aim of the park is to protect the region's exceptional natural and architectural heritage, which it does by running nature reserves and making

good any sites that have fallen into disrepair. It is also involved in boosting the local rural economy – based largely on agriculture and handicrafts – and developing tourism in the region (information centres, lodging for ramblers, marked footpaths and itineraries, cross-country skiing).

Maisons du Parc

There are eight excellent Maisons du Parc dotted around, to inform visitors about activities within the park and present the local flora and fauna as well as typical local products: Maison des Fromages, Égliseneuve d'Entraigues; Maison du Buronnier, Belles-Aigues near Laveissière; Maison de la Pierre, Volvic; Maison de l'Eau et de la Pêche, Besse-en-Chandesse; Maison de la Faune, Murat; Maison des Fleurs d'Auvergne, Lac de Guéry; Maison des Tourbières, St-Alyre-ès-Montagne; La Chaumière de Granier, Thiézac.

Fauna and Flora

The region's varied flora includes 2 000 different species, including gentian, Alpine anemone, bilberry valerian. The mountainous areas are the natural habitat of moufflon, chamois and marmot. Wild boar, roe deer, fox, marten and genet (rarer) live in forests. There are numerous birds of prey including eagle owl, short-toed eagle, kite and goshawk.

🚗 Camping Chadelas

63970 Aydat – *2km/1.2mi NE of Aydat, take D 90 then road on right (near the lake).* ℘*04 73 79 38 09. www.camping-lac-aydat.com.* ⏰*Apr–early Nov. Reservation recommended. 150 sites; food service.* A pleasant, hilly pine forest is where you will find this campsite by the lake. Shaded sites, children's playground and a variety of activities and pastimes nearby.

MONTS DORE ARTENSE AND CEZALLIER

The Dore mountains rank among the country's oldest winter sports resorts, forming a magnificent landscape dominated by the Puy de Sancy. This is a magical area, winter or summer. When the snows have gone, the region is a delight to explore at a leisurely pace, bright of face, loud with birdsong and endlessly enticing. Like much else hereabouts, the Dore and Cézallier ranges have volcanic origins and this makes for exciting, convoluted scenery where the valleys are as distinctive as the peaks. Bounded by the Dordogne, and abutting the volcanic masses of the Dore, the Artense is a granite plateau once covered by huge glaciers that gave the region its unusual appearance.

Highlights

1 Learning how **St-Nectaire** cheese is made and matured, and sampling some (p129)

2 The panorama from the summit of the **Puy de Sancy** (p131)

3 Exploring the troglodytic houses in **Farges** (p142)

4 Joining a costumed visit to the **Château de Murol** (p142)

5 Driving the windswept volcanic plateaux of the **Monts du Cézallier** (p153)

Made in France

A dearth of good soil meant that in spite of charming woodland copses, little could be commercially produced in the Artense. But as the marshes that predominated were drained, so the land became suitable for rearing the distinctive red Salers cattle alongside more familiar black and white Friesians; together these breeds produce the milk that goes into the lovely Cantal cheese and the tangy Bleu d'Auvergne.

The delectable **Saint-Nectaire cheese** has also been made in the Auvergne since the 17C. It is said to be named after the Marshall of Sennect-erre who served it to Louis XIV. It is a pressed cheese, uncooked and made from cow's milk, with Holstein, Mont-béliarde and Salers being the preferred breeds. Saint-Nectaire is one of a select group of cheeses produced in France to have its own AOC status, awarded in 1979; it even has its own website: www.fromage-aoc-st-nectaire.com.

The plant gentian grows healthily on the hills slopes of Cantal and the Monts du Cézallier, where, since 1929 they have been producing Gentiane Avèze using roots handpicked by locals as a way of supplementing their income. The drink is slightly bitter, quite strong and an acquired taste to be consumed in moderation. Elsewhere they use verbena along with over 30 other plants to make the soothing but still distinctive Verveine du Velay.

Volcanoes and Glaciers

Today at the centre of the Auvergne Volcanoes Natural Park, the Massif du Sancy and Le Mont-Dore was fashioned by fire and ice more than 20 million years ago. The range is a spectacular destination for walkers, offering a mixture of gentle slopes, rugged crags and deep gorges. There are three peaks in excess of 1 800m, all with breathtaking views. The massif boasts over 650km/400mi of walking trails at all levels. This huge green area has numerous lakes, peat bogs, gorges and craters and endless peaceful ways.

Romanesque Legacy

The end of the 10C into the 11C, the Romanesque period, was a time of extensive building throughout the Auvergne, more so than elsewhere in France. The region has over 250 Romanesque buildings, among the highest incidence in Europe. It is a unique heritage of considerable purity and unity. The so-called Auvergne School developed around Clermont-Ferrand in the late 10C, by which time it had already achieved a level of maturity in Germany and the northern parts of France.

Map legend:

Symbol	Meaning
★★★	Highly recommended
★★	Recommended
★	Interesting
Tauves	Other sight described
→	Departure point for tour

PUY DE SANCY

Murol

Le Mont-Dore

0   8 km

MONTS DORE, ARTENSE AND CÉZALLIER

Map labels (clockwise/by region):

PONTGIBAUD · CLERMONT-FERRAND · Cordès · Basilique d'Orcival · Roches Tuilière et Sanadoire · Lac Servière · Lac de Guéry · Puy de Mazeyres · Bourg-Lastic · St-Sauve-d'Auvergne · Avèze · La Banne d'Ordanche · Col de la Cr°-Morand · St-Nectaire · Farges · Messeix · Murat-le-Quaire · Gorges d'Avèze · La Bourboule · Le Mont-Dore · Murol · Plat. de Charlannes · Tauves · Roche Vendeix · Lac Chambon · Puy de Bessolles · Saurier · Singles · St-Pardoux · Rocher de l'Aigle · Vée de Chaudefour · La Tour-d'Auvergne · PUY DE SANCY · Bagnols · Super-Besse · Lac Pavin · Besse-et-St-Anastaise · Chastreix · N.-D. de Vassivière · Puy de Montchal · plateau de l'Artense · Lac Chauvet · PARC NATUREL RÉGIONAL DES VOLCANS D'AUVERGNE · Lac de Montcineyre · PUY-DE-DÔME · Tarentaine · Col de la Chaumoune · Val · Lac de la Landie · St-Alyre-ès-Montagne · Bort-les-Orgues · Barrage et lac de Lastioulles · Égliseneuve-d'Entraigues · La Godivelle · Champs-sur-T.-Marchal · Orgues · Cascade de Cornillou · Belvédère du Veysset · Monts du Cézallier · Parrot · Artout · Saignes · Gorges de la Rhue · Forêt de Maubert · Condat · Abbaye de Féniers · Signal du Luguet · Cascade d'Apcher · Chastel-Merlhac · Rhue de Cheylade · Marcenat · Cascade de la Vazèze · Auzers · CANTAL · Cascade de la Terrisse · Les Prades · Cascade des Veyrines · Gorges de la Sianne · Allanche · MURAT

Family Time

The family has always been a strong unit in French culture, but things are growing when it comes to holidays. Increasingly, especially in the Auvergne, resorts are catering for mass family invasion, when mum, dad, children, brothers and sisters, aunts and uncles, cousins and grandparents come together for what may prove to be a great opportunity for an annual reunion among the "blended" family. The wide open spaces of the Auvergne readily lend themselves to such gatherings, and there is a growing opportunity for visiting families and friends to share the same "togetherly" experience… and the pets can often come, too.

St-Nectaire★

Two villages are grouped together under this name: the thermal spa of St-Nectaire-le-Bas (Lower St-Nectaire), which spreads out over 2km/1mi in a green valley, and the old village of St-Nectaire-le-Haut (Upper St-Nectaire) dominated by its church. In the Middle Ages a Benedictine priory was established as an offshoot of La Chaise-Dieu Abbey; a castle, no trace of which remains, was also built on the hill. It was inhabited by the glorious St-Nectaire family whose most famous member was **Madeleine de St-Nectaire** – young, beautiful and virtuous, widowed early, always followed by 60 men on horseback; she sided with the Protestants in the Wars of Religion, defeated the king's lieutenant in Upper Auvergne and ended up killing him by her own hand. The name "St-Nectaire" is also given to a well-known cheese, made with pasteurised or unpasteurised milk, which has been produced for centuries in a well-defined area within the Cantal and Puy-de-Dôme *départements*.

▶ **Population:** 733.
🕭 **Michelin Map:** 326: E-9 25km/15.5mi W of Issoire.
🖹 **Info:** Les Grands Thermes, 63710 St-Nectaire.
  📞 04 73 88 50 86.
  www.stnectaire.com.
▶ **Location:** St-Nectaire lies 25km/15.5mi to the west of Issoire, on the D 996.
🕓 **Timing:** A splendid and relaxing area; allow one or two days.

ST-NECTAIRE-LE-HAUT
Église St-Nectaire★

This church, constructed around 1160, is typical of Romanesque architecture in the Auvergne; it occupies a very beautiful site near the Dore mountain range. It was built in honour of St Nectaire, the companion of St Austremoine and monks from La Chaise-Dieu were the first priests in charge of it.

Grottes du Mont Cornadore

🕓 *Feb–May and Oct 11am–noon, 2–6pm; Jun 10am–noon, 2–7pm; Jul–Aug 10am–7pm; Sept 10am–noon,*

Église St-Nectaire

© Ivan Vdovin/age fotostock/Robert Harding

2–6pm; Christmas–early Jan 11am–noon, 2–5pm. ⊗€6.50. ☏04 73 88 57 97. *www.grottes-du-cornadore.com.*
The Romans built public baths in these caves, where today visitors can discover the source of the spa water, its medical uses and petrifying properties.

Maison du Saint-Nectaire

🕐*Feb–Jun and Sept–Oct 10am–noon, 2–7pm; Jul–Aug 9am–7pm (except noon–2pm on some days); Christmas–early Jan 10am–noon, 2–6pm.*
🕐*Nov–Christmas, and Jan.* ⊗€5.50.
☏04 73 88 57 96.
www.maison-du-fromage.com.
A video show *(in French)* explains the origin of farmhouse St-Nectaire cheese, how it is made and matured. There is a demonstration cellar and a sampling at the end of the visit.

THE SPA RESORT⚜

The thermal spa, with smart shops lining D 996, has more than 40 springs. Their waters issues at temperatures ranging from 8˚C–56˚C. Its treatment installations are grouped together in the modern Gravières spa establishment; the waters are used to treat kidney and metabolic complaints.

Fontaines Pétrifiantes

🕐*All year from 9.30am, except mid-Nov–mid-Dec; consult website for current variable times.* 🕐*25 Dec, 1 Jan.* ⊗€6. ☏04 73 88 50 80.
www.fontaines-petrifiantes.fr.
The water gushes forth at more than 50˚C from volcanic faults.
Since 1821, seven generations of the same family have developed the technique of petrification, turning it into a real art form.

🚶‍♂️WALKING TOURS

Puy de Châteauneuf

🚶 *30min on foot there and back. Fairly steep climb. Follow the street climbing up from the north-east end of the church, then take a rocky path on the left.*

The path leads to the top of the Puy (934m) from where there is an attractive view of the Dore mountain range. The side of the mountain is hollowed out by nine caves which, like the Jonas caves (👆*see BESSE),* were probably inhabited in prehistoric times, then used again in the Middle Ages.

Puy d'Éraigne

🚶 *30min on foot there and back. Follow a rocky and very difficult path branching off to the left from the road to Sapchat, D 150.*
From the summit there is a stunning vista of the Dore mountain range.

Cascade de Saillant

2km/1.2mi E of St-Nectaire-le-Bas.
👆*see BESSE-ET-SAINT-ANASTAISE, The Couze valleys.*

ADDRESSES

🛏STAY

⊜⊜ **Régina** – *43 Avenue du docteur Roux 63710 Saint Nectaire.* ☏04 73 88 56 06. *www.hotel-regina-saint-nectaire.com. Closed Nov–Jan. 17 rooms. Restaurant⊜⊜.* You can't miss the little tower that marks a corner of this hotel built in 1904. 🏊Swimming pool.

⊜⊜⊜ **Chambre d'Hôte Le Chastel Montaigu** – *63320 Montaigut-le-Blanc. 10km/6mi E of St-Nectaire via D 996.* ☏04 73 96 28 49. *www.lechastelmontaigu. com. 5 rooms.* A fortified medieval castle; you'll sleep in the turret, in one of the delightful, beautifully furnished rooms.

🍴EAT

⊜ **Auberge de l'Âne** – *Les Arnats. 8km/4.8mi N of St-Nectaire via D 150 and D 643.* ☏04 73 88 50 39. *www.auberge-de-lane.com. Closed Oct and Mon–Tue except Jul–Aug. Reservations. required.* This country inn has been serving typical Auvergnat fare for 40 years. Plain and simple dining.

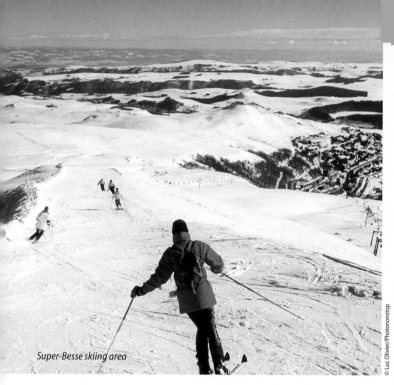

Super-Besse skiing area

© Luc Olivier/Photononstop

Massif du Sancy★★★

The Massif du Sancy, which forms part of the Dore mountain range, consists of a set of extinct volcanoes. It is one of the most attractive and appealing areas in the Auvergne thanks to the dramatic power of some of the peaks, the depth of its valleys, its waterfalls and its lakes. The highest peak in the range, Puy de Sancy, rises to an altitude of 1 885m and is the highest summit in central France.

A BIT OF HISTORY

Three huge volcanoes – The mighty system of volcanoes, of which the last remains form the Dore mountain range, evolved at the end of the Tertiary era. At its zenith, it covered an area three times larger than that of Vesuvius and consisted of three large cones in jux-taposition (Sancy, Banne d'Ordanche and Aiguiller) whose craters opened at

- 🕐 **Michelin Map:** 326: D-9.
- 🛈 **Info:** Office du Tourisme du Mont-Dore, Av. de la Libération, 63240 Le Mont-Dore. ✆04 73 65 20 21. www.sancy.com.
- ▶ **Location:** Just 50km/30mi SW of Clermont Ferrand, within the Parc Naturel Régional Volcans d'Auvergne.
- 👁 **Don't Miss:** The Puy de Sancy panorama.
- 🕐 **Timing:** Allow a full day for a driving tour of the area, and much longer to explore on foot.

an altitude of almost 2 500m. Volcanic lakes add a touch of beauty to the landscape, which is covered with forests of pine, spruce and beech. Lower down the slopes are valleys with meadows and hedgerows.

Rhinoceros in the Auvergne –
Between the periods when the volcanoes were active, life returned to the
Dore area. Footprints and bones found
among the volcanic ash prove that laurel, bamboo and other plants, which are
now found only in hotter climes, once
grew on the slopes of the volcanoes,
while rhinoceros, elephants and sabre-
toothed tigers roamed the countryside.

Former glaciers –The great period of
glaciation which spread across Europe
at the beginning of the Quaternary Era
covered the Dore mountain range with
an ice cap more than 100m thick.
This considerable mass dug out corries
and deep valleys, created the scarp
slopes down which the waterfalls cascade, and threw into relief the most
resistant sections of mountain, the
peaks and enormous rocks that add
to the picturesque beauty of the Dore
mountain range.

Final throes – Decapitated and dismantled by the glaciers and by the surging
meltwaters that accompanied the fusion
of the ice flows, the central area of the
range looked very much as it does today
when the first human settlers arrived. It
was then that a new volcanic upthrust
occurred along the edges: secondary
volcanoes erupted, closing off valleys
with their cones and lava flows, goug-
ing out craters and creating a number
of lakes.

🚗 DRIVING TOURS

1 PUY DE SANCY★★★

Le Mont-Dore⛄⛄
🖈 *see Le MONT-DORE.*
🚶 *From Le Mont-Dore, drive to the
upper part of the winter resort (4km/
2.5mi) in order to reach the* **cable-car
station**. *After a 3min ride, allow 45min
on foot to the summit.*

Panorama★★★
Rising to an altitude of 1 885m, Puy de
Sancy in the Dore mountain range is the
highest peak in central France.

2 NORTHERN SLOPES ★★★
*A round trip of 85km/53mi. It is also
possible to start this trip from
La BOURBOULE.*

Le Mont-Dore⛄⛄
🖈 *see Le MONT-DORE.*

▶ Leave Le Mont-Dore N along
D 983; 3km/1.9mi further on, turn right
onto D 996.

Col de la Croix-Morand
Alt. 1 404m.
This pass is also known as **Col de Diane**,
although the real pass of this name is set
away from the road. It used to have a
bad reputation, for according to a local
saying: "The Col de la Croix-Morand
claims one man every year."

▶ Return to D 983 and turn right
(beware: in winter, this road is
sometimes blocked by snow).

After driving through the forest then
through a valley with hillsides covered
with basalt rock falls, the road reaches
Lake Guéry (view of the Sancy massif).

Lac de Guéry★
The lake was formed by a basalt flow
that closed off the end of the valley. The
pastures are studded with black rocks
and the surrounding pine forests create
a rather austere environment lightened
in the springtime by great expanses
of snow.

Centre Montagnard Cap Guéry
Col du Guéry, 63210 Orcival. 🕐 *Jun and
Sept Wed–Fri noon–6pm, Sat–Sun
10am–6pm; Jul–Aug daily 10am–6pm;
Christmas–Mar Sat–Sun 11am–4.30pm.*
✆ *€5.50– €8.50.* 📞 *04 73 65 20 09.*
www.capguery.com.
Located at Col de Guéry, this centre
belonging to the Parc Naturel Régional
des Volcans d'Auvergne, provides an

Orcival with Basilique Notre-Dame

N

Rochefort-Montagne

A 89

USSEL

A 25

D 2089

D 2089

D 922

Dordogne

D 922

AURILLAC

D 203

La Barquette

★ Cordès

✝ Basilique
d'Orcival ★★

Sioule

PARC   NATUREL

D 216

D 27

D 983

★ Roche
Sanadoire ▲

★ Roche Tuilière ▲

Col de Guéry
1264

RÉGIONAL

★★ La Banne
d'Ordanche ▲ 1512

★ Lac
de Guéry

Lac Servière ★

Col de la
Croix-Morand
1401

Puy de la
Tache
1627

D 5

D 996

ISSOIRE

Murat-
le-Quaire

D 609

D 130

D 996

★ La Bourboule

Plateau de
Charlannes △

★ Roche Vendeix

DES

D 203

St-Pardoux

La Tour-
d'Auvergne

D 645

D 645

Chastreix

D 88

D 615

→→→ Le Mont-Dore

Le Capucin
1465 △

VOLCANS

Chastreix-
Sancy

Roc Courlande ▲

Réserve naturelle
de Chastreix-Sancy

★★★ Puy de
Sancy
1885

Col de la Croix
St-Robert
1426

D 983

Plateau de
Durbise
Vallée de

Chaudefour ★★

Puy
Ferrand
1846

★ Lac
Chambon

D 36

Rocher
de l'Aigle ★

D 36

ISSOIRE

★ Besse-et-
St-Anastaise

Super-Besse

D 149

D 149

Tarentaine

Vassivière ✝

Lac Pavin ★★

Puy de
Montchal ★★

Plateau   de   l'Artense

D'AUVERGNE ★★★

D 978

D 203

D 978

MASSIF DU SANCY

0   4 km

Lac Chauvet

Lac de
Montcineyre

© Gerard LABRIET/Getty Images

CLERMONT-FERRAND

introduction to the local flora. The Sentier nature Terra Alta is a unique, educational and unusual attraction for young and old alike.

Roches Tuilière et Sanadoire★

From Col de Guéry there is a fine **view**★★ over the deep, wooded Chausse corrie from which the rocks of Tuilière and Sanadoire stand out.

To the left is **Tuilière rock**★, once the chimney of a ruined volcano. **Sanadoire rock**★ to the right is all that remains of a volcanic cone. Near the junction of D27 and D983, a path off D983 leads to a rocky promontory.

▷ Continue along D 983.

Lac Servière★

This lake is a former crater with gently sloping sides, except to the south where it cuts into the Puy de Combe-Perret. A round lake as unruffled as a mirror, its shores are lined with pines, firs, and meadows.

▷ Turn back and follow D 27 on the right.

Orcival★★

Orcival, a small town in a cool valley watered by the River Sioulet, has a superb Romanesque church founded by monks from La Chaise-Dieu.

Basilique Notre-Dame★★

This grey mass of volcanic andesite was probably erected during the first half of the 12C and, judging by its remarkable stylistic unity, was the result of uninterrupted construction.

The very beautiful, although sparsely decorated, east end has four radiating apsidal chapels; one of these, on the south side, encompasses the crypt.

The panels of the three doors still have their Romanesque hinges and ironwork; the most elaborate, with ornamental foliage and human heads, are on the south door (known as St John's door). In thanksgiving for released prisoners, chains have been hung from the blind arcades in the southern part of the transept, next to the entrance. A high gable wall forms the west façade.

The most striking features of the interior are the slender pillars and the way the light disperses through the church, through an increasing number of windows from the nave to the transept, culminating in the chancel where most of the light is concentrated.

▷ Leave Orcival N along D 27.

Château de Cordès

2.5km/1.5mi N along D 27.
Jun, Sun 2–6pm; Jul–Aug 10am–noon, 2–6pm (Guided tours of the chateau at 11am, 2.30pm and 4pm).
€4 (€8 for garden and chateau in Jul and Aug only). 04 73 21 15 89.
www.chateau-cordes-orcival.com.

An avenue lined with hedgerows enclosing two beautiful formal flowerbeds designed by André Le Nôtre (17C) leads up to this charming 13C–15C manor house, restored in the 17C.

▷ In La Baraquette turn left towards Rochefort-Montagne and Murat-le-Quaire. Turn left onto D 609.

La Banne d'Ordanche★★

see La BOURBOULE.

▷ Beyond Murat-le-Quaire, return either to La Bourboule on D 609 or to Le Mont-Dore on D 996.

As well as the long-distance footpaths, marked with red and white stripes, and the local paths (Pays Balisé), marked in red and yellow, there are many other interesting footpaths.

③ THE SANCY RANGE★★
85km/53mi. Allow one day.

Some of the roads may be blocked by snow from November to April. The trip can also start from La BOURBOULE.

Le Mont-Dore‡‡

see Le MONT-DORE.

> Leave Le Mont-Dore E on D 983 and turn left onto D 36.

Col de la Croix-St-Robert

From the pass there is a superb **panoramic view★★** to the west over the Millevaches plateau, to the east over Lake Chambon, Murol plateau and castle and, in the distance, the mountains in the Forez and Livradois areas.

The road runs down beyond the pass towards Besse-et-Saint-Anastaise across the **Durbise plateau** with its vast expanse of pasture where the winter sports resort of **Chambon-des-Neiges** has been built.

> Continue along D 36 and leave the car in the parking area at the entrance of the site.

Vallée de Chaudefour★★

This interesting valley was gouged out of the granite and lava by the glaciers of the Quaternary Era, which covered the slopes of the Dore mountain range, and by the River Couze which flowed through the area after the glaciers had melted.

The valley floor and lower slopes boast abundant plant life. Some of the upper slopes and peaks are gashed by ravines, others bristle with rocks which have been laid bare and carved into strange shapes by erosion.

Geology enthusiasts will discover many examples of volcanic rock, and there are numerous good climbs for those interested in mountaineering.

Viewpoint

From a small bridge spanning the Couze, a spring can be seen and there is a picturesque view over the valley floor forming a majestic amphitheatre. When facing Puy Ferrand, with the Roc de la Perdrix to the left and, opposite, the sharp pointed pyramid of the Aiguille standing out against its slopes.

To the right of Puy Ferrand stand some interesting rock formations, the Crête de Coq and the Dent de la Rancune.

> Return to the car park and continue along D 36.

Rocher de l'Aigle★

From "Eagle's Rock" there is a striking view of the Chaudefour valley and the Dore mountain range.

> Keep driving along D 36.

Besse-et-St-Anastaise★

see BESSE-ET-ST-ANASTAISE.

> Leave Besse SW along D 149.

Lac Pavin★★

see BESSE-ET-ST-ANASTAISE.

Vallée de Chaudefour

© Hervé Lenain/hemis.fr

▶ Return to D 978 and turn left.

Chapelle de Vassivière

During the summer, this 16C pilgramage chapel, standing in a beautiful rural setting, houses the statue of Our Lady of Vassivière.

▶ Turn round and then turn right onto D 978 towards La Tour-d'Auvergne.

Lac Chauvet

Lake Chauvet was formed by a series of volcanic eruptions that caused soil subsidence.

▶ Return to D 203 and turn left; 12km/7.5mi further on, turn right onto D 88.

Chastreix

Chastreix-Sancy is known for winter sports. The church is a fine building with a nave but no side aisles.

▶ Leave Chastreix N on D 615.

Roc Courlande

The road leads to the winter sports resort of Chastreix-Sancy then to Courlande rock on the west side of the Puy de Sancy.

▶ Turn back to rejoin D 203 and turn right.

La Tour-d'Auvergne

This is a small town in a delightful, rustic setting crisscrossed by streams forming waterfalls. It lies on a basalt plateau ending in prismatic columnar basalt rock that can be seen near the church. The market place laid out on the top of these prisms seems to be made of gigantic cobblestones.

▶ Continue NW along D 203.

Église de St-Pardoux

Interesting Gothic church which still has 13C strap hinges on its doors and a fine gilt-wood altarpiece.

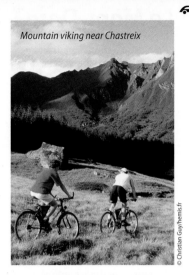

Mountain viking near Chastreix

© Christian Guy/hemis.fr

▶ Return to La Tour-d'Auvergne and drive NE on D 645.

Roche Vendeix★

♿ *see La BOURBOULE.*

▶ Return either to La Bourboule by continuing along D 88 beyond Vendeix rock, or to Le Mont-Dore by turning right onto D 645.

ADDRESSES

🛏 STAY

🛏 **Central Hôtel** – *63113 Picherande. 5km/3mi W of Lac Chauvet via D 203.* ☎*04 73 22 30 79. www.picherande-centralhotel. fr. Restaurant for hotel guests only. 16 rooms.* Set right in the village, this family home built in 1930 has a rather outdated decor, but it is impeccably run. Simple, inexpensive meals. Bathrooms are shared, but at these prices a little inconvenience is to be expected. Family atmosphere.

🛏 **Chambre d'Hôte Château de Voissieux** – *63210 St-Bonnet-près-Orcival. 4km/2.4mi NE of Orcival via D 27 and D 556.* ☎*04 73 65 81 02. 3 rooms.* Nestling in a park in the heart of the Auvergne countryside, a B&B in a 13C château built of volcanic stone.

Le Mont-Dore††

Le Mont-Dore stretches out along the banks of the upper reaches of the Dordogne in a magnificent corrie in the shadow of the Puy de Sancy; it is a spa town (the season lasts from mid May-early October) and a remarkably well-equipped winter sports resort.

The ski area (see below) covers the north face of the Puy de Sancy and the slopes of Le Capucin. Paths that are waymarked in winter provide an opportunity to discover the unexpected beauty of the volcanic landscape under snow. In summer the resort offers a wide range of leisure facilities and is an ideal base for ramblers or those touring by car.

▸ **Population:** 1 381.
♿ **Michelin Map:** 326: D-9 – 45km/28mi SW of Clermont-Ferrand.
🛈 **Info:** Av. de la Libération, 63240 Le MONT-DORE ℘04 73 65 20 21. www.sancy.com.
▶ **Location:** Le Mont Dore lies 45km/28mi to the south-west of Clermont-Ferrand.
👁 **Don't Miss:** A ride in the ancient funicular.
🕐 **Timing:** Half a day is sufficient to look around the spa town.

THE SPA TOWN

The waters were used by the Gauls in swimming pools, the remains of which have been discovered beneath the Roman baths. The latter were a splendid sight and much larger than the present establishment.

It was not until Louis XIV's reign that the "Mont d'Or", as Mme de Sévigné wrote, regained its clientele – in spite of the fact that there was no road to the resort. The road was not built until the 18C, and the fashion for "taking the waters" emerged in the 19C.

Établissement Thermal

The pump rooms were built between 1817 and 1823 and later extended and modernised. The most remarkable rooms are the **Hall des Sources**, the **Salle des Gaz Thermaux**, the **Galerie César★** and the main foyer (**Salle des Pas Perdus★**) the arches of which bear delightful frescoes up to first floor level: note the low height of the stairs constructed to ease the suffering of those with asthma.

Funiculaire du Capucin

© Hervé Lenain/hemis.fr

HIKES AROUND MONT-DORE

THE RESORT

Le Mont-Dore was one of the earliest winter resorts in France, dating from 1907. Situated south of the town, it takes advantage of the elaborate equipment and activities designed for visitors taking the waters (accommodation, skating rink, swimming pool, entertainment). During the winter season there is alpine skiing, monoskiing, snowboarding, cross-country skiing, snowshoeing and climbing frozen waterfalls.

Restaurants take second place to the pursuit of outdoor pleasure in Le Mont-Dore, but there are several places where you can enjoy regional dishes like *truffade* – potatoes with melted cheese – and the distinctive creamy *aligot*.

Ski Area

Alpine ski runs are on the north slopes of the Puy de Sancy, which enjoy good snow cover. In winter, a free shuttle service operates between the town and the slopes. The **ski pass**, which can be bought in Le Mont-Dore, entitles holders to ski on the Super-Besse skiing area (*see BESSE-ET-SAINT-ANASTAISE*).

For **cross-country skiing**, there are marked tracks starting west of Le Mont-Dore (below Le Capucin).

NEAR THE RESORT
Chemin de Melchi-Roze

About 1h on foot.

This flat path overlooking the town is a delightful place for a stroll in the late afternoon or in cool weather.

Chemin des Artistes★

About 1h on foot along the path running down to the tennis courts.

This walk leads through the woods and offers attractive views of the resort. It is also possible to reach this path by taking the funicular to Le Capucin (*see below*).

Funiculaire du Capucin★

May–Jun and Sept Wed–Sun 10am–12.10pm, 2–5.40pm; Jul–Aug daily 10am–12.10pm, 2–6.40pm. €6.20 (adult return; child 5–11, €4.70) – combined ticket with téléphérique €10/€7. 04 73 65 01 25.

When this elegant 100 year-old funicular was inaugurated in 1898, it was electrically powered, although the resort itself was not yet enjoying the benefits of electricity. The funicular has two beautiful wooden carriages, which shuttle to the Salon du Capucin (*10min by funicular then 8min on foot*).

Pic du Capucin★

🚶 *1h walk from Salon du Capucin.*
The path runs for some distance through woodland. From the summit of Le Capucin there is a particularly fine view of the Massif du Sancy.

TOWARDS COL DE LA CROIX-MORAND
Waterfalls

🚶 *3km/2mi NE via Le Queureuilh and Prends-toi-Garde hamlets. About 3h on foot.*
The most outstanding of the three cascades (Saut du Loup, Queureuilh and Rossignolet) is the **Queureuilh★** which drops down in a very attractive natural setting.

Puy de la Tache

🚶 *5km/3mi E. 1h30 on foot there and back.*
The road rises in a series of hairpin bends up to **Col de la Croix-Morand** where the landscape becomes increasingly rugged and bare. From here it is possible to walk to the summit of the Puy de la Tache.

TOWARDS PUY DE SANCY
Grande Cascade★

🚶 *3.5km/2.2mi SE along D 36. About 1h30 on foot. Beware: the access path can be slippery.*
At the waterfall's foot, a footbridge leads to steps to the Plateau de Durbise.

Puy de Sancy★★★

🚶 *Sancy station situated 4km/2.5mi along D 983. Cable-car ride (3min) then 20min on foot to the summit (🐾see Massif du SANCY).*
Rising to an altitude of 1 885m, Puy de Sancy is the highest peak in central France. It is part of an ancient strato-volcano that has now been dormant for over 220 000 years.
The valley to the north is the source of two streams, the *Dore* and the *Dogne*, which later combine to form the *Dordogne*.

ADDRESSES

🏠 STAY

🍽🍽🍽 **Chambre d'Hôte La Closerie de Manou** – *Le Genestoux. 3km/1.8mi W of Mont-Dore via D 996, towards Murat-le-Quaire.* 📞*04 73 65 26 81. www.lacloseriedemanou.com. 5 rooms.* Nestling in verdure, this 18C Auvergnat house is enchanting! Its cosy bedrooms are harmoniously and tastefully decorated.

🍴 EAT

🍽 **Mon Clocher** – *5 Rue Maurice Sauvagnat.* 📞*04 73 65 05 41.* Mon Clocher is ideally located in the heart of Mont-Dore's pedestrian and shopping zone between the church, the casino and the spa. The dining room's decor is countrified: old farming implements and shining copper pots.

🍽 **Le Bougnat** – *23 Avenue Georges Clemenceau.* 📞*04 73 65 28 19. Closed mid-Nov–mid-Dec.* Reservations required. The furnishings chosen to decorate this old restored *buron* are faithful to tradition.

RECREATION

Given its altitude and location at the heart of all things mountainous and wintry, there is a strong temptation to look on Le Mont-Dore as just another playground for the ski-bound. But there's real focus on the pursuit of well-being at a more leisurely, less hazardous pace, whether it is a simple self-indulgent spa session or treatment for allergies, asthma, rheumatism and respiratory issues *(Thermes du Mont-Dore, 1 pl. du Panthéon; 📞04 73 65 05 10).* A little more demanding, just, is the nine-hole golf course (2 162m) at Le Mont-Dore, with a 10-station driving range. In such a splendid location, it is impossible not to be distracted by the magnificent views of the Puy de Sancy *(Golf-Club du Mont-Dore, Rte de la Tour-d'Auvergne; 📞04 73 65 00 79; www.golfdumontdore.org; closed Dec–Mar).* But where Le Mont-Dore scores heavily is in its various opportunities for walking. The town is surrounded by the most exquisite landscapes, across which paths and tracks offer a network of escape routes, and the chance to appreciate the natural beauty of the region in a healthy way.

Besse-et-Saint-Anastaise★

With its old houses and fortifications, Besse is a picturesque and charming town, and the beauty of its surroundings makes it a popular place to stay. The town is the setting for a biological research centre specialising in the study of regional flora and fauna, which was set up by the Faculty of Science of Clermont-Ferrand University.

▶ **Population:** 1 560.
○ **Michelin Map:** 326: E-9.
▯ **Info:** 13 Rue Notre Dame, 63610 Besse-et-Saint-Anastaise. ℘04 73 79 52 84. www.sancy.com.
◐ **Location:** Besse lies midway between Aurillac and Mauriac, in the south-west of Cantal.
◉ **Don't Miss:** A tour of the Old Town.
○ **Timing:** Allow half a day.

OLD TOWN
Houses with picturesque corbelled turrets line the narrow streets of the old town.

Rue des Boucheries★
This is a quaint street with black houses made of lava stone. Note the 15C shops and **Queen Margot's House** (15C), on the corner with rue Mercière. According to local legend, Marguerite de Valois lived in this house. Its Gothic doorway, surmounted by a coat of arms, opens onto a beautiful spiral staircase.

Town Gate★
Corner of rue de l'Abbé and Le Petit Mèze.
In the 16C this gate, which is protected by a barbican, was adapted to the use of fire arms. The belfry was added at a later date.

Château du Bailli
These remains of the outer town wall are visible from the road *(northwest)* behind the church.

ADDITIONAL SIGHTS
Musée du Ski
11 Rue de la Boucherie. ○*During school holidays 9am–noon, 2–6pm; at other times by arrangement.* ⊚€4.50. ℘04 73 79 57 30. www.sancy.com.
This skiing museum is the first of its kind in France. Among the displays are 30 different pairs of skis, a 1925 bobsleigh, ski boots and shoes and a pair of 1910 skates. Prints and photographs show Besse at the turn of the 20C.

Maison de l'Eau et de la Pêche
Rue de la Boucherie. ○*Mid-Jun–mid-Sept, daily except Sat 10am–noon, 2–7pm.* ○*1 Jan, 25 Dec.* ♿ ⊚€5. ℘04 73 79 55 52.
Located on the banks of the Couze de Pavin, this house contains an exhibition centre displaying local aquatic species, equipped with video, microscopes, models and computer terminals.

EXCURSIONS
Super-Besse❋
6km/3.7mi W.
Super-Besse is first and foremost promoted as a winter sports resort, but it is also popular in summer because of its quiet, peaceful surroundings.
There are a variety of chalets and holiday residences available. The vast, south-facing ski slopes are reached by ski lift; additional facilities include a skating rink and a swimming pool.

Ski Area 🎿
This resort, developed at the foot of Puy de la Perdrix, has south-facing ski slopes, drag-lifts, chair-lifts, and a gondola leading to 27 Alpine-ski runs (seven green, six blue, eleven red and three black runs). The ski pass sold on location gives access to the Mont-Dore skiing area *(see Le MONT-DORE).* In summer, the nearby lake can be used for swimming, canoeing and wind-surfing.
🚶 The area is ideal for walking.

Puy Ferrand

15min by cable-car, then 45min on foot there and back from Super-Besse.

🚶 The cable-car for Perdrix leaves from the Biche corrie and ends at the peak of Puy de la Perdrix. Follow the crest to the summit of Puy Ferrand, which offers a **view**★★ of the Dore mountain range, the lakes and Chaudefour valley.

Lac Pavin★★

4.5km/3mi SW of Besse. via D 149, which is a one-way road, joining up with D 978 from Besse to Condat, or via the "Fraux road" S of Besse which connects Besse to Pavin via a pasture-covered mountain.

The Fraux parking area offers a lovely **view**★ of the lake. This lake, surrounded by forests and superb rocks, is one of the most beautiful in the Auvergne.

In the past, it was said that the old town of Besse was swallowed up by the lake as a divine punishment, and that throwing a stone into it would unleash terrific storms; this is why it is called Pavin, from the Latin *pavens* meaning dreadful.

🚶 A gentle path offers a very pleasant stroll around the lake (about 45min on foot).

Puy de Montchal★★

🚶 The summit overlooking Lac Pavin offers a magnificent **panorama**★★ – to the northwest, the Dore mountain range; to the north, the Dômes mountain range clustered around Puy de Dôme; further to the east, the Couzes and Comté valleys; to the northeast and east, the Livradois and Forez mountains and to the southeast, in the far distance, the Chaise-Dieu plateau and Velay mountains.

Chapelle de Vassivière

8km/5mi SW on D 36 (see map p132) in the direction of La Tour-d'Auvergne. 3km/1.5mi after the crossroads separating lac Pavin from Super-Besse, take a minor road to the right.

This lovely 16C pilgrimage chapel stands amid a splendid pastoral setting southeast of Puy de Sancy.

Lac de Montcineyre

8km/5mi SW along D 36. Skirt Lac de Bourdouze and, 1km/0.6mi further on, follow a path on the right (1km/0.6mi).

Crescent-shaped Montcineyre lake owes its existence to the wooded Puy Montcineyre, which dams the valley.

Follow the lake shore for a stunning view of the Sancy massif (*Massif de SANCY*).

🚗 DRIVING TOUR

THE COUZE VALLEYS
65km/40mi. Allow 1–2 days.

▶ Leaving from Besse, take D 633, a charming corniche road offering interesting views of the Couze de Pavin valley and the Courgoul gorges. It becomes D619 after crossing Trossagne. Turn right onto the narrow road running above the Grottes de Jonas.

Grottes de Jonas

🕐*Daily Feb–early Nov at varying hours; call or check website for details.* 🕐*Dec–Jan.* ⊛€7 (child 5–12 years, €5.50). ✆ 04 73 96 31 69.
www.grottedejonas.fr.

The most rudimentary of these man-made caves carved out of the volcanic tufa in a cliff were doubtless inhabited in prehistoric times. Over the centuries their descendants also made use of them; in the Middle Ages a chapel – its vaulting still bears traces of **frescoes** dating from 1100 – and a fortress were built in the caves. The tower of the fortress contains a spiral staircase with 80 or so steps carved into the rock; it leads up to apartments laid out over several floors.

▶ Return to Le Cheix and turn right onto D 978 then right again onto D 621.

Cheminée de Fée de Cotteuges

Before reaching the hamlet, turn right onto the Bedeaux track.

St-Floret

© Gérard Labriet/Photononstop

This path leads through a wood to an earth pillar standing among excavations. This interesting geological formation, known as the "**Fairy's Chimney**" is a clay column topped by a block of hard rock.

Beyond Cotteuges the road crosses one of the *cheires* (lava flows) that are a characteristic feature of this area. Further on, high above to the left of the road, stand a number of superb sheer-sided rocks.

▶ Continue along D 621.

Saurier

This is an old fortified village. Left of the road crossing the River Couze there is an attractive view of the old bridge and its chapel. The valley narrows again and basalt rocks can be seen on the hillsides.

▶ Take D 26 towards Issoire.

St-Floret★

First of all, take a look at Chastel plateau, probably the original site of the village. The **Église du Chastel** is built on a promontory overlooking the Couze de Pavin. Near the church are the remains of a Merovingian graveyard (tombs dug into the rock, ossuary).

The **château**, located in the village of St-Floret itself, was built in the 13C and modified a century later. Large 14C **frescoes★** depicting episodes from a tale of chivalry (Tristan) decorate the walls in the lower chamber.

▶ After the church, turn left onto D 28, which will take you to Champeix.

Champeix

This village stands between hillsides once carpeted with vineyards. The ruins of the old medieval castle, the "Marchidial", stand high above the village on a sheer-sided spur of rock.

Site du Marchidial

Can be reached on foot starting from the bridge; access by car: follow D 28 towards St-Floret; after 1km/0.6mi, turn right towards the college.

🏃 In the upper part of Champeix, this district owes its name to the markets and fairs which used to take place on the plateau during the Middle Ages. A narrow lane running east leads to the ruins of the former medieval fortress offering a fine view.

▶ Leave Champeix heading W towards St-Nectaire on D 996.

Montaigut-le-Blanc

The village lies in the shadow of its ruined castle. Its somewhat Mediterranean appearance – houses with flat roofs and rounded tiles, terraced vineyards, and fruit trees at the head of the valley – heralds the Limagne plateau.

▶ Carry on along D 996 for another mile or so. Turn right onto D 640. Just after Treizanches, turn left onto D 150.

Farges

This hamlet is home to an interesting group of **troglodytic houses** *(Les Mystères de Farges: ↝guided visits (1h), every 20 min: May–Jun, Sept and school holidays 10am–noon, 2–5pm (Jul–Aug 10am–6pm); rest of year by appointment; ☞€6.60. ℘04 73 88 52 25. www. st-nectaire.com)*, hollowed out of the white tufa that date from the Middle Ages. Visitors may also like to discover more about the maturing process of St-Nectaire cheese, in a cellar where this takes place.

A little further on from Farges, a quarry comes into sight to the right of the road. The powdery white rock extracted here is pumice stone, evidence of the tremendous volcanic eruptions that shook this region millions of years ago.

▶ Carry on along D 150, then turn left.

Puy de Mazeyres★

From the hilltop, there is a beautiful **panorama** of the Dore mountain range.

▶ Rejoin D 150.

St-Nectaire★★

♿*see ST-NECTAIRE.*

▶ From St-Nectaire-le-Bas, take D 996 for Champeix, as far as Saillant.

Cascade de Saillant

In this village the river tumbles over a basalt outcrop, forming a waterfall.

▶ Return to St-Nectaire and take D 996 towards Le Mont-Dore.

🏛♿ Château de Murol★

🕐*Daily: Feb–Mar and Oct–mid-Nov 10am–6pm; Apr–Jun and Sept 10am–7pm; Jul–Aug 10am–8pm; mid-Nov–Jan 2–5pm (Christmas period 10am–5pm. 🕐8–31 Jan, 14 Jul. ☞€9 (child 10–17, €4.50); tariff varies according to type of visit. ℘04 73 88 82 50. www.murolchateau.com.*

It was a descendant of the lords of Murol, Guillaume de Sam, an erudite baron and patron of the arts, who completed the original, inner fortress by building the keep, the second chapel and the eastern buildings. The castle, after passing into the hands of the powerful D'Estaing family in the 15C, was lavishly ornamented and, at the beginning of the following century, encircled by a huge curtain wall flanked with towers.

Murol emerged victorious from a siege during the time of the Catholic League. Peril having been averted, Jean d'Estaing foresook his vast abode and built the charming pavilion at the foot of the inner castle. Abandoned some time afterwards, Murol was spared by Richelieu because of the D'Estaing family's influence at court. After being used as a prison for some time, it became a robbers' hideout during the Revolution. During the 19C it fell into ruin and the inhabitants of the region came here looking for building stone.

Château de Murol in autumn, Puy de Sancy in the background

© Francis Cormon/hemis.fr

In recent years, extensive alterations have been made to the castle. Guided tours and colourful evening shows are organised by the *Compagnons de Gabriel* to provide an authentic medieval atmosphere. Visitors pass through the outer curtain wall through a fortified gatehouse on the southside, passing the Murol tower on the right.

The Renaissance Pavilion (**1**) stands in the outer courtyard (the windows provide an attractive view of the Capitaine tower).

To the north is the inner castle (Château Central), its walls rising above a thick basalt base. Next to the keep, connected to a tower of smaller dimensions by a curtain wall, are the chapels. The first (**2**)

CHÂTEAU DE MUROL

0   40 m

Keep

3

Chapels

2

Watchpath

7

7

1

7

Main building

Ramp

Inner Courtyard

6

5

4

Kitchen

Bakery

N

Watchpath

was built in the 13C; the second (**3**) in the 15C, and though of greater proportions is less graceful. A stepped ramp leads up to an elegant door (**4**) decorated with the Murol and Gaspard d'Estaing coats of arms. In the inner courtyard, note the gallery once surmounted by the Knights' Hall followed by the guard-room.

Take the spiral stairway of the Chautignat tower up to the terrace from which there is a very beautiful **panorama**★ of Murol, the Couze valley, Lake Chambon, the Dore mountain range and the Tartaret volcano. The watch-path leads to the Châtelaine tower (note the 16C door, **5**). Next come the kitchen, the bakery and its outbuildings (**6**). The adjacent rooms (**7**) were living quarters.

▶ On leaving the castle, walk down to the village, cross the road and walk through a gate leading into the Parc Municipal.

Parc Municipal du Prélong

Once part of a private estate (the house now contains the Musée des Peintres de l'École de Murols), the park boasts a beautiful collection of azaleas, rhododendrons and camellias. The French-style garden has alleyways lined with box trees leading to the rose-garden, offering a striking contrast to the English-style park.

At the entrance stands the **Chaumière** (○*daily 3–6pm*) which houses a small archaeological collection.

Musée des Peintres de l'École de Murols

○*Jun–Oct daily 10am–noon, 2.30–6.30pm; Nov–May daily except Mon–Tue 10am–noon, 2.30–6.30pm.* ○*1 Jan, 1 May, 14 Jul, 25 Dec.* ⊜€4. ℘*04 73 88 60 06. www.musee-murol.fr.*

At the turn of the 20C, some 50 landscape painters found inspiration in and around the village. Gathered round Abbé Boudal, who was the initiator of this artistic movement, and Charenton who was its leader, this group of artists was close to two contemporary trends, Impressionism and Fauvism. The permanent collection is displayed in several rooms, with another room reserved for temporary exhibitions.

▶ Leave Murol on D 996, then turn left at the junction with D 5.

The road runs along the slopes of the Tartaret volcano.

Lac Chambon★★

The lake was formed by the Tartaret volcano, which erupted in the middle of the Couze valley and stemmed the flow of water. It is a vast but fairly shallow lake lying in a very attractive setting. It is dotted with tiny islands and has an extremely jagged shoreline, except on the north, and to the south-east where there is a large beach.

To the north of the lake is a slender rocky peak known as the **Saut de la Pucelle** (Maiden's Leap) which is all that remains of the ancient **Dent du Marais** volcano. The village of Chambon-sur-Lac lies at the end of the Couze de Chaudefour, in a mountainous area to the west of the lake, and consists of a group of houses huddling round the church.

The tiny skiing resort of **Chambon-des-Neiges**✳ (Chambon 1200 and Chambon 1400) lies high above the Chaudefour Valley (℮*see Massif du SANCY*). The resort is equipped with snow-making facilities; it has a number of pistes designed for both Alpine and cross-country skiing.

▶ Return to Murol and turn right onto D 5 towards Besse. After 2km/1.2mi turn right onto D 619, then after about 100m turn left.

Puy de Bessolles★

This peak is one of the best look-out points in the Couzes region, giving an impressive view of the Dore mountain range and Lake Chambon.

🔼 *Follow the footpath signposted Plateau de Bessolles-Panorama. Allow 45min on foot there and back, and 2h to follow the footpath right round the plateau (signposted in yellow).*

▶ Go back to Besse via D 5.

Lac Chambon

© Bernard Jaubert/Getty Images

ADDRESSES

🏠 STAY AND 🍴 EAT

⊜⊜ **Le Levant** – *20 r. de l'Abbé-Blot, 63610 Besse-et-St-Anastaise. ℰ04 73 79 50 17. www.lelevant-besse.fr. Closed Sun eve and all day Mon.* How do you like your trout? With cabbage, wild mushrooms or lentils? Or would you prefer a different regional dish? There's plenty of choice here, served in a decor that seems to be firmly grounded in the 1970s.

⊜⊜ **Le Lac Pavin (Hotel-Restuarant)** – *Au Lac Pavin. 4km/2.4mi W of Besse via D 149. ℰ04 73 79 62 79. www.lac-pavin. com.* The fish – char, among others – served in this restaurant once lived in the alpine lake that you see from the dining room. The owner, who is also the chef, prepares simple dishes from fresh ingredients. A few modest rooms have views of the lake.

⊜⊜ **Hostellerie du Beffroy** – *26 rue Abbé Blot, 63610 Besse-et-Saint-Anastaise. ℰ04 73 79 50 08. www.lebeffroy.com. Closed Mon and Tue (except in Jul–Aug), Wed lunch in Jul–Aug. Reservations required Sun. Restaurant⊜⊜.* This handsome 15C building in the village centre used to be the guardhouse. The gourmet fare is served in a charming dining room with white-draped tables and old wooden beams.

⊜⊜ **Ferme-Auberge La Voûte** – *8 rue de la Mastre, 63320 Clémensat. 5km/3mi S of Champeix via D 28. ℰ04 73 71 10 82. Open Sun lunch and Sat, evenings Jul–Aug except Sun and Mon. Reservations required.* A very popular farm-inn nestling in a small village. The vaulted dining room is often crowded with savvy diners enjoying fare from the farm, local recipes or savoury Auvergnat specialities (to be ordered ahead). Spacious, refurbished bedrooms.

⊜⊜ **Chambres d'hôtes 'Plus belle la vue'** – *Trossange, 63610 St-Pierre-Colamine. 7km/4.2mi NW of Besse via D 978 and D 619. ℰ04 73 55 05 86. Closed Jan, Mon, Tue evening and Wed evening except school holidays. Reservations recommended.* The view from the terrace of this aptly named inn is breathtaking. Whether you dine al fresco in the summer or by the fireplace in the winter, local cuisine is the mainstay here, chosen à la carte or from one of the hearty fixed-price menus.

La Bourboule ‡‡

La Bourboule, located at an altitude of 852m in the lush valley of the Upper Dordogne, enjoys a climate with few seasonal variations. This well-known spa and rest resort offers many facilities for children. The town is situated at the confluence of the Dordogne which, at this point, is no more than a mountain stream 12km/7.5mi from its source, and the Vendeix, a tributary that also has its source in the Sancy range. The resort's pump rooms, casino, town hall and gardens line the banks of the two rivers, which are crossed by a dozen or so bridges and footbridges.

THE SPA RESORT

La Bourboule's first spa was opened in 1821. At the time its cabins were closed off with serge curtains, revealing the bathers at the whim of the wind. The bathing water was used by several patients in turn, and water for the showers was pumped manually by an elderly peasant.

In 1854, Thénard the chemist discovered arsenic in the waters of La Bourboule, perfect, apparently, for the treatment of respiratory disorders. When the news spread, every house-owner in the town promptly began exploring his property in the hope of finding his own spring and each person did his utmost to excavate faster and pump harder than his neighbour.

Today, the town's springs are managed by the Société Thermale de La Bourboule and the Compagnie des Eaux Minérales. There are two springs in La Bourboule – a hot spring at Choussy-Perrière (60°C/140°F), and a cold spring at Fenêstre (19°C/66°F). Their waters contain metalloid arsenic and are used to treat respiratory diseases and dermatoses using techniques such as inhalations, sprays and electro-sprays, baths and showers. Treatment is available in two spa centres: **Choussy** and **Grands Thermes**.

▶ **Population:** 1 894

⏱ **Michelin Map:** 326: D-9.

ℹ **Info:** 15 pl. de la République, 63150 La Bourboule. ℘04 73 65 57 71. www.sancy.com.

◖ **Location:** La Bourboule isn't especially large and the best way to get a feel for the place is on foot (◖see Walking Tour). The more energetic can walk up to La Banne d'Ordanche (1h return) for a splendid view over the valley and the town.

🅿 **Parking:** Opposite the Parc Fenestre, on Ave. Agis Ledru.

🕐 **Timing:** Take a ride in the little tourist train, and then explore the town on foot before wandering off up the valley sides.

👪 **Kids:** Parc Fenestre, a splendid wooded park with children's play area.

The resort has all the facilities of a major spa town including tennis courts, stables, a swimming pool, an amusement park etc.

WALKING TOUR

A pleasant walk round the town will give you an opportunity to admire the Victorian-style architecture of the hotels and to understand how the city developed at the foot of the Roche des Fées. Near the church, a convincing pastiche of Romanesque art, you can see the **Maison Rozier** and its imposing balcony (Boulevard Georges-Clemenceau), the Grands Thermes, the former town hall, now a chocolate factory called the Marquise de Sévigné, and the casino, a listed, entirely renovated building.

⚇ Parc Fenestre★

🕓*Apr–late Sept, but times vary; please check the website for details.* ✆*04 73 81 06 04. www.parcfenestre.com.*

This splendid wooded park – partly planted with sequoias – is a charming place for outings and relaxation. The children's play area consists of wide expanses of lawn and outdoor games. An additional attraction is the cable-car linking the park with the **Charlannes plateau**.

Roche des Fées

🚶*1h on foot there and back. Take the footpath from place G.-Lacoste.*

This granite "Fairy Rock" rises some 50m above the spa and provides an attractive view of the town and its surroundings.

🚶 WALKING

① TALES OF TOINETTE

10km/7mi N of La Bourboule.

▶ Leave the town on D 88.

Murat-le-Quaire

A rocky spur, once the site of a castle, marks the entrance to this village. There is a look-out point on the spur with a pretty view of the upper section of the Dordogne valley. Besides its role as a rural holiday destination, Murat-le-Quaire hosts a Bread Festival every other year (odd numbers) as part of its campaign to preserve local tradition.

▶ From the church, take D 609 towards La Banne d'Ordanche, as far as the school.

Scénomusée La Toinette et Julien★

♿🕓*Daily: Jan–Mar and Oct–Nov 2–6pm; Apr–Jun and Sept 10am–noon, 2–6pm; Jul–Aug daily 10am–noon, 2–7pm.* 🕓*Mid Nov–20 Dec.*

👓*Toinette: €7.20; Julien: €5.50; combined ticket: €9.60.* ✆*04 73 81 12 28. www.toinette.com.*

A gateway opens into a large courtyard in which the town hall and the museum are to be found.

The museum contains an account of rural life through the seasons in the Dore mountain range region of the Auvergne during the 19C, presented through the eyes of a local woman of that period, Toinette Chaumard.

Beyond the belvedere lies the **Grange de Julien**, a barn where Toinette's young son returns from his travels and reflects on the future prospects of rural life in the area.

▶ Carry on along D 609 past a lake, then follow it uphill round a series of hairpin bends with pleasant views, to the end of the road.

La Banne d'Ordanche★★

🚶 From the car park a steep footpath leads uphill to a viewing table (*1h*). La Banne d'Ordanche (in the dialect of the Auvergne *banne* means "horn") rises from a grassy hillock. From the top of this basalt outcrop – the remains of the central chimney of an old volcano – there is a **wide view★★** of the Dordogne valley, the Puy de Sancy range, Puy de l'Angle, the Dômes mountain range and the Limousin.

© Hervé Lenain/hemis.fr

② TOUR OF WATERFALLS
3km/2mi. Allow 4h.

▷ Leave La Bourboule on D 130 along the Dordogne towards Le Mont-Dore. 1.5km/0.9mi after the swimming pool a track leads off opposite the Mont-Dore water company building (left of the road). Leave the car.

🚶 Take the GR 30 footpath to the right. Go past a farm and uphill into the forest. After a 15min walk, take a path to the right that cuts downhill.

Cascade de la Vernière★
The Vernière waterfall is formed by a large volcanic rock which obstructs the bed of the Cliergue.

▷ Return to the path and turn onto the track leading to the Plat à Barbe refreshment kiosk. Here it is possible to go down a stepped path (potentially dangerous) to a platform constructed opposite the Plat à Barbe waterfall.

Cascade du Plat à Barbe★
This waterfall owes its name (literally "shaving dish") to the dip worn in the rock by its waters.

③ THE BRIGAND'S DEN
4km/2.5mi trip. Allow 4h.

▷ Leave La Bourboule to the S on D 88 towards La Tour-d'Auvergne. 3.5km/2.3mi on past Parc Fenêstre, turn right and leave the car at Vendeix-Haut.

Roche Vendeix★
Access along a footpath off D 88 by an inn. 30min on foot there and back.
This rock of basalt carries the ruins of a castle which was re-fortified in the 14C by Aimerigot Marcheix, an infamous local brigand eventually caught by the king's men in 1390; he was taken to Paris and beheaded and quartered.

④ WOODLAND TO VALLEY
7km/4.5mi trip. Allow 1h.

▷ Leave La Bourboule to the W on D 129 towards La Tour-d'Auvergne via Col de la Sœur. About 500m after crossing the Dordogne, beyond a crossroads, leave the car and take a footpath branching off to the right.

Lac de Barrage
🚶 *30min on foot there and back.*
This delightful path runs through Charlet woods to the dam whose reservoir stretches for 1km/0.6mi along the Dordogne valley.

▶ Continue along D 129 and, 3km/ 1.9mi further on, turn left onto D 610.

Plateau de Charlannes

The beautiful Charlannes plateau is popular with spa patients for its restful scenery; it offers views of the Dore and Cantal mountains.

EXCURSIONS

St-Sauves-d'Auvergne

4km/2.5mi NW along D 996.
This village, situated on the north bank of the Dordogne, houses an interesting museum for children of all ages.

▲▲ Le Monde Merveilleux du Train et de la Miniature

🕐*Jul–Aug daily 10am–noon, 2–6.30pm; mid–end-Jun and 1–mid-Sept daily 2.30–5.30pm.* 🕐*Oct–Mar.* ✆€5.50 (children €3.50). 📞04 73 65 54 61.
This museum on three levels contains collections of toys and models (cars and lorries). There is a train diorama as well as the reconstruction of a typical village from the Auvergne, with miniatures picturing ancient crafts.

Le Mont-Dore ‡‡

🐾*See Le MONT-DORE.*

Tauves

A small village surrounded by lush pastures studded with houses roofed in the typical *lauze* tiles.

THE GORGES D'AVÈZE ★

60km/38mi round tour from Tauves. Allow 3h.

▶ Drive W out of Tauves along D 29.

Singles

This former miners' village has a pleasantly located church that overlooks the Burande and the Dordogne gorges.

▶ Return to "La Guinguette" (the paradise of anglers) and continue on D 73 until you reach Messeix.

Messeix

This little town was once famous for its coalmines. The Romanesque church here was altered in the Gothic period but has retained its attractive 13C entrance.

▶ Follow D 987 towards Tauves.

Gorges d'Avèze★

This rocky gorge, situated on the border of the Puy-de-Dôme and of the Corrèze regions, offers breathtaking views of the upper section of the River Dordogne which has its source at the Puy de Sancy, some 30km/18.5mi east of the gorge.

Avèze

The church presents interesting furnishings (altarpieces, statues of St Roch and St Blaise). Nice panorama of the nearby gorges.

▶ Return to Tauves on D 987.
You can make a detour via St-Sauves (🐾see above) to admire its superb setting, a result of the glacial period.

ADDRESSES

🏨 STAY

🛏🛏 **Hotel de l'Aviation** – *32 R. de Metz.* 📞*04 73 81 32 32. www.hotel-aviation.net. 41 rooms and 8 furnished apartrments.* Parc Fenêstre, a few steps from this 1900s gable-ended dwelling, is a nice place for your morning jog. The hotel's practical rooms may be a bit outmoded, but are neat and tidy. Simple cuisine. Indoor pool and fitness room.

RECREATION

In summer, the **La-Bourboule-Charlannes** complex organises guided mountain-bike excursions (110km/68mi of marked tracks). Those who prefer rambling have a wide choice of itineraries crisscrossing the Massif du Sancy along some 670km/416mi of waymarked paths. In winter the Charlannes plateau becomes a cross-country skiing area (58km/36mi of tracks); the École du Ski Français (ESF) organises ski tours.

Bort-les-Orgues and L'Artense

Set in the Dordogne valley, Bort owes its fame to the celebrated basalt columns which overlook it, and to its enormous dam. The town is an excellent starting point for exploring the granite plateau of the Artense, an area with much to commend a leisurely tour.

▶ **Population:** 2 967.
◉ **Michelin Map:** 330: Q-3.
🛈 **Info:** Pl. Marmontel, 19110 Bort-les-Orgues. ☎05 55 96 02 49. www.tourisme-hautecorreze.fr.
◉ **Location:** Bort lies SW of Clermont-Ferrand along the A89.
🅿 **Parking:** Limited parking areas in the centre of town.
◉ **Don't Miss:** The famous Orgues de Bort.

SIGHTS
Barrage de Bort★★
The dam's sheer size makes it a showcase of hydroelectric production. Its reservoir is partly filled by water from the Rhue, a tributary of the Dordogne. The road running along the top of the dam (390m long) overlooks the reservoir upstream dotted with **cruisers** (🕒*May–Sept: boat trip (1h) Château de Val/Dordogne valley; Jul–mid-Sept: boat trip (1h) Bort Dam/Château de Val 11am, 2–5pm).*
A tourist itinerary *(apply to the Tourist office:* ☎*05 55 96 02 49)* can be followed, starting from the foot of the dam on the west bank between the hamlet of Les Granges and Bort's tanning and leather works.

Church
The extremely simple architecture of Bort's church (12C and 15C) highlights a few fine works of art including modern stained-glass windows. A 17C priory stands by the church.

Cascade du Saut de la Saule
Leave Bort on D 922 towards Mauriac and turn left onto the road running up to the clinic. Follow the path across the Rhue, then turn left and follow the river.
🚶 The path soon reaches a little gorge where pebbles caught by the waters have formed so-called "giant's cauldrons". Walk on to the outcrop beyond, which overlooks the Saut de la Saule; here the Rhue crosses a threshold of rock 5–6m high.

🚗 DRIVING TOURS

ORGUES DE BORT★
Round trip of 15km/9mi. Allow 2h.

A Convoluted Landscape

The Artense, a granite plateau south-west of the Dore mountain range, is cut across by the Tarentaine, a tributary of the Rhue which rises from Puy de Sancy. The plateau was once covered with vast glaciers that gave this region its highly unusual appearance of varied relief with peaks separated by small basins that are now lakes, peat bogs or marshy grasslands.

In a landscape typical of the Auvergne, the Artense is graced by charming copses, but the region was long known for the poverty of its soil. The marshes are gradually being drained, making it possible to breed red Salers cattle, more and more frequently sharing their pastures with black-and-white Friesians. Most of the milk produced by these cattle is used to make Cantal cheese and particularly the local blue cheese, **Bleu d'Auvergne**.

This tour explores the volcanic valleys and granite plateaus along the boundaries of Cantal and Puy-de-Dôme.

▶ Leave Bort on D 979 towards Limoges; then turn uphill on D 127.

As the road climbs, there is a beautiful view of the Rhue valley on the left.

▶ Just after the last houses in Chantery, park and turn right onto steps leading directly to the foot of the "Grottes des Orgues". These impressive columns extend for 2km/1mi and vary in height from 80–100m.

▶ Return to D 127 and, 2km/1.2mi further on, turn right onto a road that leads towards a television transmitter. Park and walk to a viewing table.

🚶 The vast **panorama**★★ extends over the Dordogne valley, the Artense and Cantal regions and the Dore mountains. To the south-west lies Lake Madic, relic of an earlier course of the Dordogne.

▶ Return to the car and follow D 127 for another 500m: here a path on the left leads to a rocky outcrop.

From here there is a panoramic view over Puy de Sancy, the mountains of Cantal, the Dordogne and its tributaries, the Monédières range and the Millevaches plateau.

L'ARTENSE
85km/53mi.

Between the Cantal and Puy-de-Dôme departments, the Artense is bounded on the west by the Dordogne, to the south and east by the Rhue, and to the north by the foothills of the Dore mountains.

▶ Leave Bort to the E on D 979. As it climbs the hillside, the road provides wonderful views of the columnar basalt around Bort.

Champs-sur-Tarentaine-Marchal
This holiday resort is huddled in a wooded valley near the confluence of the Rhue and Tarentaine.

▶ Leave Champs-sur-Tarentaine-Marchal N along D 49 towards Lanobre and turn immediately right onto D 22, a pretty road winding across the plateau.

Barrage and Lac de Lastioulles

An outdoor leisure park has been laid out in pleasant **surroundings★★**, on the north side of the reservoir.

▶ Drive though St-Genès-Champespe and follow D 614 towards Issoire. As you come out of the village, take D 30 on the right.

Lac de la Landie

This lake is surrounded by peaceful meadows and woodlands.

▶ Rejoin D 614 then take D 203 on the right to Lac Chauvet.

Lac Chauvet

See Massif du SANCY.

La Tour-d'Auvergne

See Massif du SANCY.

▶ Drive SW out of La Tour-d'Auvergne along D 47.

The road to Bagnols passes the foot of the Pont de la Pierre waterfall.

Bagnols

This village lies in the undulating Tialle valley, a place of meadows and copses.

▶ Shortly after entering the Cantal département, turn left onto D 922.

Château de Val★

Apr–Jun and Sept–mid-Oct daily except Tue 10am–noon, 2–6pm;Jul–Aug daily 10am–12.30pm, 2–7pm; mid-Oct–early Nov and Feb–early Mar daily 2–6pm. €6. *04 71 40 30 20. www.chateau-de-val.com.*

Since the reservoir at Bort became functional, the **setting★★** in which the 15C Château de Val stands is very picturesque.

▶ Turn back. At the crossroads take D 922 on the right to get back to Bort.

ADDRESSES

STAY

Camping Municipal de la Siauve – *15270 Lanobre, 3.5km/2.2mi N of Bort-les-Orgues via D 922 and secondary road. t04 71 40 31 85. www.camping-lac-siauve. fr. Open mid-Apr–mid-Sept. Reservations recommended. 220 sites.* Located on the edge of the lake in a beautiful natural environment, this is the perfect campsite for beach activities, fishing and sightseeing. Chalets and cabins for rent.

Le Rider – *Av. de la Gare.* *05 55 96 00 47. www.lerider.fr. 17 rooms. Restaurant.* Meals are taken in a dining room-veranda with wrought-iron furniture and an original trompe-l'œil fresco of a country landscape.

Château de Val

Village near La Godiville in winter

Monts du Cézallier★

The Cézallier range is situated between the Dore mountain range and the mountains of Cantal; it consists of a succession of granite plateaux lying at an altitude of more than 1 200m, which were covered with a layer of basalt during the Tertiary Era.

> 🖱 **Michelin Map:**
> 326: E-10 to G-11.
> ▶ **Location:** Lying south of Clermont-Ferrand, accessible by the A 75.
> 🕐 **Timing:** This is a region for leisurely exploration; allow as much time as you can, certainly a day to enjoy the tours.

A BIT OF HISTORY

The volcanoes, from which the flows spread out all over the area, have neither cones nor craters. Indeed, they scarcely even jut out from above the surrounding countryside because the lava produced by the eruptions was very fluid and did not build up around the vents of the volcano. On the eastern side in particular the plateaux are gashed by impressive valleys.

The Cézallier range is one vast area of pasture dotted with former shepherd's huts (*burons*) and a few villages with huge barns and byres, and fountains made out of old drinking troughs. Here, in the summer months, thousands of heads of cattle graze on the plateaux. The local people supplement their income by digging up gentian roots, used in the production of an alcoholic drink.

Despite its lack of hotels and places to stay, the Cézallier area is popular with those who enjoy wide open spaces, solitude and fresh air, and also with winter sports enthusiasts, especially cross-country skiers, since the lie of the land is ideal for this sport. Downhill skiing is also catered for, although facilities are, as yet, limited. The area is part of a regional park, the Parc Naturel Régional des Volcans d'Auvergne.

EXCURSION

Ardes-sur-Couze

41km/25mi E of Condat.

This old fortified town, once capital of the Duchy of Mercœur, has a 15C **church** in front of which there is a cross dating from the same period. Inside the church, the gilt-wood high altar (17C) features eight sculpture groups depicting the Passion. Near the chancel a strange carved wooden bas-relief adorns the shrine of St Hubert. Opposite the pulpit, there is a 16C stone **Pietà,** and the chapel at the back of the church contains a 15C lectern.

The **Musée des Vieux Métiers** (○open Jun–mid Sept 10am–noon, 2-7pm. ☞€3. ℘04 73 71 81 41) shows exhibits relating to traditional crafts in the area, mainly used during the 19C.

≗≗ The Parc Animalier d'Auvergne (○Apr–early Jul 10am–6pm; early Jul–early Sept 9.30am–7.30pm; rest of year times vary, check website for details. ○Dec–Jan. ☞€15 (child 3–9, €11). ℘04 73 71 82 86; www.parcanimalier-dauvergne.fr), is a cross between a traditional zoo and a safari park. A great many animals of all types can be seen in relative freedom.

🚗 DRIVING TOURS

Two trips are described below; the first leads through the "mountains" and the second follows the valley which plunges down to the River Alagnon to the east of the range.

1 ALPINE PASTURES
90km/56mi. About 5h.

Condat – ◖see CONDAT.

▷ Leave Condat S on D 679 towards Allanche.

The road skirts a stretch of water that is a recent reconstruction of a lake originally built in the 12C by monks.

Abbaye de Féniers
The Cistercian abbey founded in the late 12C was rebuilt in 1686 and closed during the French Revolution. The buildings were partially destroyed by fire in 1872; only a few vestiges of the abbey, cloisters and church have survived.

▷ Turn right onto D 16.

The road to St-Bonnet-de-Condat runs down into the Santoire valley and through a wooded gorge.

▷ In St-Bonnet-de-Condat; left on D 36.

Marcenat
This is a modest winter sports resort which has also specialised in the production and selling of local cheese.
Beyond Marcenat there are some superb views to the left of the road, over the Cézallier range.

Les Prades
Columnar basalt. From the summit, there is a delightful view of Landeyrat and the upper Allanche valley cutting into the planèze.

Abbaye de Féniers

© Hervé Lenain/hemis.fr

La Godivelle with Aubrac cattle

© Francis Cormon/hemis.fr

◐ Turn left off D 679 onto D 39 then D 23. Both roads cross the plateau.

Apcher

A short distance to the west of this village, an attractive waterfall drops down from the edge of the plateau.

◐ On leaving Anzat-le-Luguet, leave D 23 and turn left onto D 271.

Parrot

Small winter sports resort.

Signal du Luguet★

🚶 1h30 on foot there and back from Parrot. Climb up to the summit across the meadows slightly to the left of the ski lift.

The wooded summit scarcely stands out above the plateaux. From it there is a vast **panoramic view★** over the Dore mountain range and the mountains of Cantal.

◐ Continue along D 721 to Boutaresse then turn right onto D 724.

The road twists and turns through picturesque scenery.

St-Alyre-ès-Montagne

On a rise near the small village is the south-facing church overlooking superb countryside nestled in the shadow of Mount Gamet.

○ Leave St-Alyre W along D 36; 3km/1.9mi further on, turn left onto D 32.

La Godivelle

This is a typical Cézallier hamlet with sturdy granite houses and a large, round fountain. Its other main feature is its geographical location, between a crater lake, the Lac d'En Haut (Upper Lake), and another, peaty lake, the Lac d'En Bas (Lower Lake), the haunt of countless migratory birds.

Ramble

⚑ 3hr30 there and back, starting from La Godivelle; follow the yellow markings; keep dogs on a leash.
Walk across the peat bogs and high pastures as far as Jassy and return to La Godivelle via the lakes of Saint-Alyre and En-Bas.

○ Drive N out of La Godivelle along D 32, then 3km/1.9mi further on, turn right onto D 26.

Col de la Chaumoune

Near this mountain pass are several conifer plantations.

○ Turn left onto D 30 and, 6km/3.7mi further on, turn left again onto D 978.

Égliseneuve-d'Entraigues

This small resort has a Romanesque church, but do not miss the regional Cheese Museum housed inside a barn. The **Maison des Fromages** explains the history and production of St-Nectaire, Cantal, Bleu d'Auvergne and Fourme d'Ambert.

○ D 678 leads back to Condat along the lovely Rhue valley.

② VALLÉE DE LA SIANNE
50km/31mi. About 1h30.

Allanche

Winter resort. The west end of the town still has remnants of its ramparts.

Rail-biking

Pedal away along disused tracks between Allanche and Lugarde.

○ Head E from Allanche on D 9 towards Chavanon.

Between Allanche and Vèze, the road crosses the Cézallier's great alpine meadows and then, at the top of the rise, the mountains of Cantal come into view. The cliff road subsequently runs down to the **Gorges de la Sianne★**, providing some fine views of the ravine on the way. Beyond several gorges where huge boulders jut out from above both banks of the river, the valley widens out, becoming less sombre, and fruit trees appear.

Auriac-l'Église

This village is attractively situated to the right of the road.

○ Turn right onto D 8.

Blesle★
♨ *See ST-FLOUR.*

○ Return to Allanche via the Bellan Valley, Anzat-le-Luguet and D 23, which will take you back to Vèze.

You can also pursue your route towards Massiac and the Alagnon gorges (♨see ST-FLOUR).

Countryside near Condat, Massif de Sancy in the background

Condat

This pleasant resort lies in the centre of a fertile basin into which flow the Rhue d'Égliseneuve, Bonjon and Santoire rivers.
Its numerous slate-roofed villas standing on the sunlit slopes of the Rhue valley were almost all built by local people who went elsewhere to seek their fortune, many of them as linen-drapers.

▶ **Population:** 1 062.
◉ **Michelin Map:** 330: E-2, 32km/20mi SE of Bort-les-Orgues.
▯ **Info:** Place de la Mairie, 15190 Condat. ℰ04 71 78 66 63.
◐ **Location:** At the heart of the Massif Central, SW of Clermont Ferrand.
◐ **Timing:** Take a leisurely half-day.

🚗 DRIVING TOUR

1 RHUE GORGE TO GENTIANE COUNTRY
80km/50mi. Allow one day.

◐ Leave Condat to the W.

The D 679 road follows the right bank of the Rhue. The road offers fine views of the gorge and Les Essarts lake-reservoir, then enters the lovely Maubert Forest planted with pine and beech. In the middle of the forest, the Gabacut, having dug numerous cauldrons into the rock, drops down in two small waterfalls.

Cascade de Cornillou
30min on foot return. 50m before the exit from the hamlet of Cornillou, turn left on a cart track.
🚶 Just before reaching a deserted barn, turn right onto an uphill track that soon

runs along the shores of a small lake-cum-reservoir. Turn left across a small bridge; further on, an overgrown path leads to the top of the waterfall.

Gorges de la Rhue★★
Upstream from Embort, the river flows through a gorge with sides covered in greenery. The ravine widens out at the confluence of the two Rhues. Between Sarran and Champs, the road follows a dry valley where the Rhue flowed.

Champs-sur-Tarentaine-Marchal
👁see BORT-LES-ORGUES.

◐ Leave Champs E along D 679.

Bort-les-Orgues
👁see BORT-LES-ORGUES.

RHUE GORGE TO
GENTIANE COUNTRY

Leave Bort on D 922 in the
direction of Mauriac and after
5km/3mi turn left onto D 3 to Riom ès
Montagnes. The D 678 takes you back
to Condat, following the opposite side
of the Rhue.

② CHEYLADE VALLEYS AND
GENTIANE COUNTRY★★
see RIOM-ÈS-MONTAGNES.

③ BELVÉDÈRE DE VEYSSET
AND FORÊT DE MAUBERT
20km/12.5mi. About 45min.

Leave Condat via the steep,
winding D 62 N.

Belvédère de Veysset
The road leads to Montboudif, birthplace of Georges Pompidou (1911-74),
President of the French Republic from
1969 to 1974. A **museum** (*daily mid
Jun–mid Sept 10am–noon, 2–6pm; Apr–
mid-Jun and mid-Sept–Oct Sat, Sun and*

public holidays 2–6pm. €4. *04 71 78
68 68; www.montboudif.fr)* is dedicated
to his memory.

Turn left before the church onto
D 622 and, a short distance further on,
left again onto D 722.

Forêt de Maubert
The beautiful state-owned Maubert
et Gaulis forest consists of landscaped
woodland with a predominance of pines
but also beech, lime and a few oaks.
Many of the trees reach remarkable
heights, and provide quality timber. In
the heart of the forest, one beech tree
reaches a height of 43m, with a girth
of 3.1 metres. It is believed to be more
than 200 years old, and is nicknamed
the 'King of Maubert', a title previously
enjoyed by a huge fir tree, which disappeared in 1930.

At the junction with D 679 follow it
back to Condat.

The Rhues

A number of streams and rivers on the north side of Cantal bear the name
Rhue. The largest of them, the Grande Rhue, flows into the Dordogne below
Bort-les-Orgues after crossing a bar of rock known as the Saut de la Saule
(*see BORT-LES-ORGUES*), but an underground drainage channel takes some
of its water into the Bort reservoir. The Grande Rhue rises in the south of the
Dore mountain range near the Biche corrie. Once its waters have been swollen
by the Rhue de Cheylade that flows down from the mountains of Cantal, the
Grande Rhue flows through very picturesque wooded gorges.

AURILLAC CHÂTAIGNERAIE AND MONTS DU CANTAL

From simple stone cottages roofed with huge slate slabs they call *lauze*, to fine châteaux, rambling *maisons bourgeoises*, and isolated farmsteads, the architectural heritage of Cantal is evident everywhere you go. It typifies a way of life played out against a landscape of intense natural beauty, for Cantal, the southernmost of the *départements* that comprise the region of Auvergne, is dominated by the voluptuous Monts du Cantal and high-level plateaux of impermeable rock.

A Capital Place

Aurillac is a bright and modern place tacked on to an old town of narrow, twisting streets crammed with shops and cafés. In the district known as Carmes, south of the old town, the park on the place du Square is a shady niche of peace and quiet, its tiny pond populated by numerous carp and the odd terrapin. From here it is a real pleasure to wander the adjacent streets of the old quarter wherein timber-framed houses topped with heavy *lauzes* gaze on a street scene that will have changed little over the years. Were it not for Aurillac, Cantal would be virtually uninhabited.

Highlights

1 A leisurely stroll around the Old Town *and Carmes District of* **Aurillac** (p163, p164)

2 A driving tour of the stunning **Monts du Cantal** (p168)

3 Walking the paved path from **Pas de Peyrol** to the summit of **Puy Mary** (p170)

4 Spending a day in the charming village of **Salers** (p178)

5 The **Château d'Anjony** and the village of **Tournemire** (p187)

Peaks and Pastureland

Lying within the Parc Naturel Régional des Volcans d'Auvergne, the green and wooded hills of the Monts du Cantal were formed as part of a vast volcano – the largest extinct volcano in France – later moulded by glaciers into a central core with 12 radiating valleys. Highest of the peaks is Plomb Cantal (1 855m), part of a ring of summits that delimit the volcanic boundaries. Rivers are also a defining feature here: the west and northwest of the *département* is bounded by the upper reaches of the Dordogne, the south by the Lot and the gorges of Truyère. Elsewhere, the river valleys of the Cère and the Rhue, the one rising on the slopes of the Plomb du Cantal, the other on Puy Mary, fashion dramatic and fecund landscapes that ripple into the hazy distance, supporting numerous small settlements of antiquity and agrarian rusticity.

The entire region was once covered by trees, but they were gradually cleared by shepherds and have today disappeared from large tracts of countryside. The underlying strata support excellent pastureland where the landscape is dotted with *burons*, small, stone-built huts, originally used to produce cheese. Today, you encounter herds of the russet-coated Salers cattle everywhere, a sure sign that this is one of France's foremost dairy regions.

Timeless Beauty

Two of the "Most Beautiful Villages in France" are in the Cantal département. One is Tournemire, with its huddle of cottages and be-towered Château d'Anjony; the other is Salers, above the Maronne, a settlement with the tang of Scottish Lowland towns about it.

Salers is a compact and architecturally well-preserved town, and of some considerable antiquity. The narrow streets are a joy to wander, leading by towers, through doorways, emblazoned archways and courtyards, and with occasional views of the hills on the other side of the Maronne valley. There are fine bourgeois houses here, the former homes of lawyers in the employ of the regional government.

AURILLAC, CHÂTAIGNERAIE AND MONTS DU CANTAL

MONTS DU CANTAL

MONTS DU CANTAL
Plomb du Cantal
Le Lioran
Chanterelle

★★★ Highly recommended
★★ Recommended
★ Interesting
● Other sight described

↑ Point of departure

Chestnut grove country
Pas de Peyrol
Churches of the Northern Plateaux
Vallée de la Jordanne
Route de Lioran
Route des crêtes
Les gorges de la Maronne
Cheylade Valleys & Gentiane Country
Upper Goul Valley and Carladès

Gorges du Pas de Cère
Rocher des Pendus
Jou-sous-Monjou
Messilhac
Grotte des Anglais
Vic-sur-Cère
Pesteils
Polminhac
Rocher de Carlat
Rocher de Ronesque
Sédaiges
Route des Crêtes
Arpajon-sur-Cère
La Plantelière
AVEYRON
Cropières
Vixouze
Jordanne
Cère
Puy de l'Arbre
RODEZ
Montsalvy
Aurillac
Conros
Châtaigneraie cantalienne
Sansac-de-Marmiesse
Marcolès
Calvinet
Mourjou
VALLÉE DU LOT-VIELLEVIE
Nieudan
St-Étienne-Cantalès
Viescamp
Entraygues
Laroquebrou
Maurs

TULLE
SIRAN

161

Aurillac by the Jordanne

© Bernard Jaubert/Getty Images

Aurillac★

Aurillac, the business and tourist capital of Upper Auvergne, is a modern town that has sprung up around an old neighbourhood with narrow, winding streets.

A BIT OF HISTORY

Gerbert, the first French Pope (10C–11C) – Aurillac's Gallo-Roman origins were brought to light by the discovery of a 1C temple (rue Jacques-Prévert, reached from avenue Milhaud). In the 9C St Gerald, Count of Auvergne, built an abbey, laying the foundations for the city's future prosperity; this abbey gave Christianity its first French Pope. Gerbert, a shepherd from the Aurillac area, attracted the attention of the monks of St-Géraud, who quickly taught this unusually bright student everything they knew. After completing his studies at the abbey, Gerbert left for Spain where he studied medicine and mathematics at the Moorish universities. He built the first pendulum clock, invented an astrolabe for sailors and improved the church organ. In AD 999 he became Pope under the name Sylvester II. He was the "Pope of the Millennium", who managed to impose the "Truce of God" – whereby hostilities were suspended on certain days and during certain seasons – on the feudal classes.

▶ **Population:** 28 285.
⛓ **Michelin Map:** 330: C-5 – Local map see Monts du CANTAL.
🛈 **Info:** 7 due des Carmes, 15000 Aurillac.
📞 04 71 48 46 58.
www.iaurillac.com.
▶ **Location:** At the southern edge of Cantal, Aurillac is 156km/97mi SW of Clermont-Ferrand.
🅿 **Parking:** There are numerous parking places in the centre of town.
☺ **Don't Miss:** A tour of the old town; plan from tourist office.
🕐 **Timing:** Allow half a day for a tour of the old town, or a full day if you want the bigger picture.

Gold-washers – According to Gerbert's contemporaries, his knowledge smacked of witchcraft. The gold flakes found in the River Jordanne were popularly ascribed to his spells.

The gold industry was born, but remained fairly primitive: flakes of gold were collected by holding fleeces in the water to trap them.

Baron des Adrets (16C) – The people of Aurillac remained at odds with their lord, the abbot, but eventually managed to obtain administrative autonomy, as the consuls' residence (Maison Consulaire) proves.

The town was flourishing when it became involved in the Wars of Religion. In 1561, the governor ordered the slaughter of the large local Protestant population. They were avenged eight years later by the Baron des Adrets, a Protestant leader notorious for his brutality. His men began by swooping down on the monasteries on the outskirts of the town, burning or flaying the monks alive. On the night of 6 September 1569 the Huguenots blew up the town gate and burst their way in on the slumbering citizens, who were caught unawares and so put up minimal resistance.

From lace to umbrellas – Aubenas was struggling to recover from these events for many years until Colbert founded a laceworks that doubled as a gold and silver smithy. This entrepreneur also encouraged other industries, such as boiler-making and tanning, which have since declined.

Modern Aurillac's economy is based on agriculture and the manufacture of furniture, cheese, plastics and umbrellas.

WALKING TOUR

OLD TOWN
Place St-Géraud
The Romanesque façade with arcades and colonettes opposite the church entrance probably belonged to a pilgrims' hospice. The colonial house on the left dates from the late 15C.

Église St-Géraud
This old abbey church was founded in the late 9C by Count Gerald and became a stopover for pilgrims on their way to Santiago de Compostela.

▶ Walk down rue du Monastère and rue des Forgerons and turn right onto rue Victor-Hugo.

On reaching the 19C Hôtel de Ville, follow rue Vermenouze to place d'Aurinques. The **Chapelle d'Aurinques,** built at the end of the 16C in a tower in the city wall, was completed in the 19C.

▶ Follow rue de la Coste.

No. 7 in rue de Noailles, on the right, has a **Renaissance courtyard** (access through cours de Noailles).

▶ Return to rue de la Coste.

No. 4 rue du Consulat is notable for its staircase tower.

Maison Consulaire
This Renaissance building has been restored and turned into an exhibition hall. Note the sculptures adorning the door on rue de la Coste.

▶ Continue to place Gerbert and the *Musée de Cire* (history of Aurillac).

View of the Jordanne
The old houses along the River Jordanne can be seen from a spot near Pont Rouge (Red Bridge) and Cours d'Angoulême.

VOLCANIC LANDSCAPE
Château St-Étienne
The castle keep dates from the 13C; the rest of the buildings date mostly from the late 19C. The upper terrace offers a magnificent view of the Jordanne valley and the Cantal mountains.

🖐🖐 Musée des Volcans★
🕐 Jul–Aug daily except Sat 10am–6pm; school holidays Mon–Fri 10am–noon, 2–6pm; rest of year Tue–Fri 2–6pm.
🕐 1 Jan, 1 May, 1 Nov, 25 Dec.
🎟 €4 (under 18, no charge).
📞 04 7148 07 00. www.aurillac.fr.
A double staircase enclosing a banner 13m high, leads into the Volcano Museum, which includes four large, well-appointed rooms offering interactive models, multimedia terminals and video films to explain volcanic phenomena. There is plenty for children to see and do in this innovative setting.

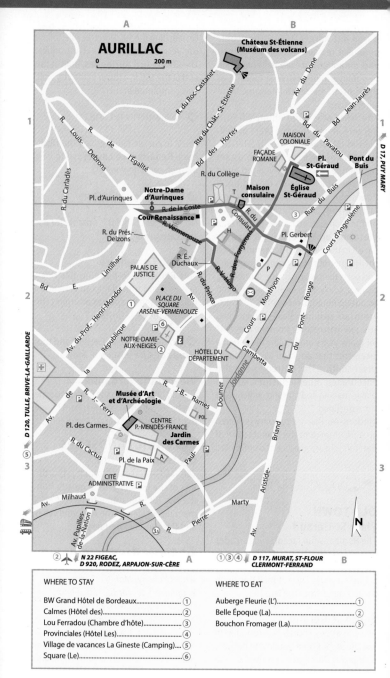

AURILLAC

0   200 m

WHERE TO STAY

BW Grand Hôtel de Bordeaux	①
Calmes (Hôtel des)	②
Lou Ferradou (Chambre d'hôte)	③
Provinciales (Hôtel Les)	④
Village de vacances La Gineste (Camping)	⑤
Square (Le)	⑥

WHERE TO EAT

Auberge Fleurie (L')	①
Belle Époque (La)	②
Bouchon Fromager (La)	③

CARMES DISTRICT
Jardin des Carmes
Once part of a monastery, this pleasant garden gives access to an arts centre.

Musée d'Art et d'Archéologie
Centre Pierre Mendès France, 37 rue des Carmes. ⊙*Tue–Sat 10am–noon, 2–6pm (Jul–Aug also Sun 2–6pm).* ⊙*1 Jan,*

1 May, 1 Nov, 25 Dec. ♿ ⊜€2.50.
📞*04 71 45 46 10. www.aurillac.fr.*
The Art and Archaeology Museum is housed in the former Visitandines Convent (17C) which, after the Revolution, was used as a stud farm before being recently turned into an arts centre.

Les Écuries – (♿◷*during exhibitions, daily except Sun and public holidays 1.30-6.30pm;* 📞*04 71 45 46 08)*, a museum annexe in the former stables, houses contemporary art exhibitions (painting, sculpture and photography).

🚗 DRIVING TOURS

THE CÈRE TO THE MARONNE
100km/62mi. Allow one day.

Nearby dams, rivers and gorges; refreshing undulating countryside.

▷ Leave Aurillac on N 122 heading towards Figeac.

Sansac-de-Marmiesse
A restored barn on the outskirts of the village houses the town hall and the **Maison du Bâti** (♿◷*Tue-Fri 9am-noon, 2–5pm, Sat 9am-noon;* ◷*Sun, Mon and public holidays;* ⊜*no charge;* 📞*04 71 47 74 75. www.sansacde-marmiesse.fr)*, a local museum illustrating the 13 different areas which make up the Cantal region with their specific types of rural housing and traditions.

▷ Continue along N 122 then turn right onto D 64 to Viescamp and on to the dam on the River Cère.

Barrage de St-Étienne-Cantalès★
An imposing dam resembling a vault contains the waters of the River Cère. The view is enhanced by the charming sight of small islets, peninsulas and jagged coastlines.

▷ D 207, then D 7 lead to Laroquebrou, a pretty village on the banks of the Cère.

Laroquebrou
Small municipality located at the entrance to the Cère gorges, dominated by an isolated outcrop and the ruins of the **castle** (◷*Jul–Aug only; call for opening hours.* ◷*Sept–Jun.* 📞*04 71 46 00 48)*, once home to the Lords of Montal.

▷ Follow D 653 that cuts across D 120 at Pont d'Orgon, then take D 2 for 15km/9mi. Turn right onto D 302 and continue until you reach the Enchanet dam spanning the Maronne, a tributary of the Dordogne.

Barrage d'Enchanet★
Its elegant silhouette is set against the backdrop of the Maronne gorges. D 61 offers a good overall view of the dam.

▷ D 442 leads to St-Santin-Cantalès. Continue on D 52 and go back to Aurillac via St-Victor.

CHESTNUT GROVE COUNTRY
100km/62mi. Allow one day.
This round tour through "La Châtaigneraie Cantalienne" offers an interesting insight into local chestnut land, with long plateaus, luxuriant valleys and typical architecture.

▷ South of Aurillac, drive through Arpajon-sur-Cère and onto D 6 (2km/1.2mi).

🏛🏛 Arpajon-sur-Cère – La Plantelière (Arboretum)
◷*Dawn to dusk.* 📞*04 71 43 27 72. www.caba.fr.*
Enjoy a pleasant stroll through gardens of different styles including the Devil's garden, the pond, the maple grove and the oak grove.

▷ Return to Arpajon-sur-Cère, turn right onto D 58, which leads to Conros.

Château de Conros
🎧*Guided visits: Jul–mid-Sept, daily except Sat, 2–6pm.* ⊜€6. 📞*04 71 63 50 27. www.chateau-conros.com.*
On a spur of rock high above a meander of the River Cère stands the massive

Marcolès

© Hervé Lenain/hemis.fr

medieval keep that once belonged to the Astorgs, lords of Aurillac.

▶ Continue along D 58 to the intersection with D 217, turn left and drive 12km/7.5mi; D 66 leads to Marcolès (3km/1.9mi).

Marcolès

In this restored medieval city, characteristic narrow lanes stem from rue Longue closed off by an elegant 15C **porch**. West of the village, the D 64 leads to the **Rochers de Faulat** (1.5km/0.9mi) where several megaliths stand on a mound planted with oak trees.

▶ Take D 64, then D 217 and follow the banks of the River Rance.

Entraygues

Small village featuring a château typical of the area with its pepper-pot roofs.

▶ Go on driving until you reach Maurs.

Maurs

Maurs is situated to the south-west of the mountains in Cantal on a hill beside the River Rance, and is the main town in the **La Châtaigneraie** area. The granite plateau is almost entirely covered with undulating moorland and gashed by green valleys where most of the local population lives.

In Maurs, which still has the circular layout dating to the days when it was a fortress, there is a definite air of Southern France; this is the start of the "Cantal Riviera" with its flowers and vineyards, explaining why Maurs has been dubbed the "Nice of Cantal".

By the late Middle Ages, Maurs had become one of the six "good towns" in Upper Auvergne and the seat of a provostship. It suffered during the Wars of Religion: captured and recaptured by the Huguenots in 1568 and 1583, it was pillaged and ransacked; in 1643 peasant rebels from the Rouergue sought refuge here and the King's troops were forced to intervene.

▶ Follow D 663 towards Decazeville then D 28 to Mourjou.

Mourjou

The pleasing **Maison de la Châtaigne** (👥👤♿🕐*Apr–mid-Nov daily except Mon, 2–6pm (Jul–Aug daily 1.30–6.30pm); Oct during festival Sat–Sun 10am–6pm. ⊜€5 (child 6–12, €2.50). ℘04 71 49 98 00. www.maisondelachataigne.com*) traces the use of chestnuts through the ages in an imaginative and interesting display.

▶ Follow D 28 to Calvinet, then take D 19 and drive 15km/9mi to Montsalvy.

Montsalvy

Nestling on the Plateau de la Châtaigne-eraie, this once fortified town has kept several of its original gates. Near the church stand the **ruins** of the former abbey: the cloisters, the chapter-house, and the restored 14C refectory.

▶ Return to Aurillac on D 920.

ADDRESSES

🛌 STAY

☺ **Camping Village Vacances La Gineste** – La Gineste 15150 Arnac – 3km/2mi NW via D 61. ℘04 71 62 91 90. www.village-vacances-cantal.com. At the end of a road, surrounded by nature, this camping site enjoys a prime location on a peninsula on the Enchanet lake.

☺ **Chambre d'Hôte Lou Ferradou** – At Caizac, 15130 St-Étienne-de-Carlat. ℘04 71 62 42 37. www.louferradou.com. 5 rooms. Close to the Monts du Cantal, this old stone farmhouse offers smartly decorated rooms, and a cuisine that uses produce from the garden.

☺☺ **Hotel des Calmes** – 20 r. Carmes, Aurillac. ℘04 71 48 01 69. www.hoteldescarmes.fr. Closed one week in April, two weeks in July and 20 Dec-3 Jan. 23 rooms. Simple rooms, some with exposed beams, and one displaying the work of Danish painter Gorm Hansen. Traditional cuisine served without fuss.

☺☺ **Le Square** – 15 pl. du Square, Aurillac. ℘04 71 48 24 72. http://hotel-le-square.com. 18 rooms. Restaurant☺☺. Modern building near the old chapel. The rooms at the back are quieter.

☺☺ **Hôtel les Provinciales** – Pl. du Foirail, 15130 Arpajon-sur-Cère. ℘04 71 64 29 50. www.hotel-provinciales.com. 20 rooms. Restaurant☺ (closed Sat lunch and all day Sun). At the gateway of Aurillac, this hotel features 20 cosy, functional rooms. The Restaurant "Félix Café" has a warm atmosphere and designer décor, and offers inventive, traditional cuisine prepared from fresh ingredients grown locally.

☺☺☺ **Best Western Grand Hotel de Bordeaux** – 2 ave de la République. ℘04 71 48 01 84. www.hotel-de-bordeaux.fr. 36 rooms. The best hotel in Aurillac, housed in a beautiful building dating from around 1850. Elegance, refinement and a warm welcome, and just a short distance from the centre of the town.

🍴 EAT

☺ **Le Bouchon Fromager** – 3 pl. du Buis. ℘04 71 48 07 80. Mon–Sat noon–2pm, 7–11pm. Both wine bar and cheese restaurant, this inviting, rustic eatery is often packed with patrons enjoying a fine wine, served by the glass, and the delicious cuisine of the Cantal.

☺☺ **La Belle Époque** – 50, chemin de Lasfargues, 15130 Sansac-de-Marmiesse. 7km/4.2mi W of Aurillac via N 122 and D 153. ℘04 71 62 87 87. www.labelleepoque-cantal.fr. 5 suite/apartments also available, minimum stay of 2 nights (☺☺). Closed Oct–Mar. A restaurant set in an old, secluded house in the countryside. The smart interior design features murals depicting the 1920s.

☺☺ **L'Auberge Fleurie** – Pl. du Barry, 15120 Montsalvy. 30km/20mi S of Aurillac. ℘04 71 49 20 02. www.auberge-fleurie.com. Closed Sun evenings and all day Mon except Jul–Aug. A charming inn of some antiquity, where the chef serves up tasty cuisine. Superb cellar, and if you want somewhere to stay, the inn has beautiful **colonial-style rooms** (☺☺☺).

SHOPPING

Distillerie Louis-Couderc – 14 r. Victor-Hugo. ℘04 71 48 01 50. www.distillerie-couderc.com. Tue–Sat 9am–noon, 2–7pm. Closed public holidays. Founded in 1908, the Couderc distillery sells a wide variety of regional products made from gentian root, chestnut cream and berries.

Boutique Piganiol – 28 r. des Forgerons. ℘04 71 63 42 60. www.piganiol.fr. Closed public holidays. Piganiol have been manufacturing umbrellas in Aurillac since 1884.

La Vitrine du Don – 10, Rue des Frères 15000 Aurillac. ℘04 71 43 08 51. www.ledondufel.com. Apr–Sept Mon–Fri 10am–6.30pm, Sat–Sun 10am–noon, 2–6.30pm; Oct–Mar daily 10am–6pm, except Sat morning and Sun morning. Nigel and Suzy Atkins, potters who specialise in salt-glazed stoneware, create utilitarian and decorative pieces that are all the rage.

Les Monts du Cantal★★★

The mountains of Cantal, formed by the largest extinct volcano in France, embrace the most magnificent scenery in the Auvergne. Several of the peaks rise to more than 1 700m. Some, like the Puy Griou, are jagged; others, such as Puy Mary, are pyramid-shaped. The highest summit, Plomb du Cantal, is rounded and soars to a height of 1 855m. From the mountain heartlands, deep, picturesque valleys fan out, providing easy access for visitors.

A BIT OF GEOGRAPHY

The Etna of the Auvergne – The volcano in Cantal reached an altitude of 3 000m, and included a number of vents from which flowed viscous lava that solidified into needles, or the more fluid lava that spread out all round the volcano over an area 70km/44mi in diameter.

Effects of erosion – Glaciers formed in Cantal during the Quaternary Era. Their slow but powerful action wore down the summit of the mountain, uncovering the lava plugs that filled the vents, digging out corries that later became the valleys, and giving the mountain range the appearance it has today.

Dairy industry – The entire range was once covered with forest. Gradually, land was cleared and today it has disappeared in all but the entrance to a few valleys. Thanks to the basalt content of the lava, which produces a better quality pasture, Cantal has become best-known as a pastoral region.

⌘ DRIVING TOURS

1 ROUTE DU LIORAN★★
55km/34mi. About 4h.

This itinerary follows the Cère and Alagnon valleys.

- ⌘ **Michelin Map:**
  330 : D-3 to E-5.
- ▷ **Location:** This is very much walking country without any clearly defined centres of habitation.
- ⌘ **Don't Miss:** The Puy Mary; not the highest, but a superb vantage point.
- ⌘ **Timing:** Realistically, you will need to spend a few days here.

Aurillac★ –
see AURILLAC.

▷ Leave Aurillac E along D 117, then the N 122.

The villages along the road have picturesque houses with hipped roofs that are typical of this area. The road then runs into the wide, attractive Cère valley.

Polminhac
The houses in the village huddle round the foot of Pesteils Castle.

Château de Pesteils –
see VIC-SUR-CÈRE.

Vic-sur-Cère★ –
see VIC-SUR-CÈRE.

Pas de Cère★★
🚶 *45min on foot there and back.*
The footpath leads off N 122, 3km/2mi upstream from Vic-sur-Cère.
The path crosses a small meadow, then runs down through the woods to the Cère, which flows between high, narrow walls of rock.

Cascade de la Roucolle
From here, there is a wonderful view of the Roucolle waterfall and the Cère gorge.

Thiézac –
see VIC-SUR-CÈRE.

Pas de Compaing★

High above the road on the left are tall cliffs from which, in rainy weather or when the snow melts, drops the superb **Malbec waterfall** (*it is inadvisable to park immediately below the cliffs because of the risk of a rockfall*).

A short distance further on, the valley narrows and the road runs along the hilltop high above the deep gorge known as Pas de Compaing. Further on, the road enters the St-Jacques-des-Blats basin and the view extends to the end of the Cère valley, with the conical outline of Puy Griou to the left.

St-Jacques-des-Blats

This is an ideal centre for walking.

Col de Cère★

The D 67 skirting the Lioran road tunnel crosses the watershed separating the Dordogne basin into which flows the Cère, and the Loire basin into which flows the Alagnon. Just below the pass, the impressive pyramidal outline of Puy Griou can be seen to the left, in the distance. Beyond the wide Cère valley is the narrow Alagnon valley made darker by the pine forests lining it.

Le Lioran★

The winter and summer holiday resort of Le Lioran is encircled by the magnificent pine forests that cover the slopes of the Alagnon valley above meadows dotted with old shepherds' huts (*burons*, used for cheese-making).

Super-Lioran★

Accessible via Le Lioran (N side of tunnel). With the emphasis almost exclusively on winter sports, Super-Lioran, at a higher altitude than Le Lioran, is situated opposite the high grassy Font-d'Alagnon corrie and closed off by pine woods. This modern winter sports resort stands in highly attractive surroundings. The resort is comprised of three separate sites: Font d'Alagnon, Font de Cère and Prairie des Sagnes.

Most of the ski runs are on the north and east-facing slopes of Plomb du Cantal.

On Top of the World

Plomb du Cantal *(45 min there and back by cable-car and on foot from Super-Lioran)* is the highest peak in the Cantal range. From the summit there is a vast panoramic **view★★**. To the west, beyond the Cère valley, extend Cantal's great volcanic cones – Griou, Peyre-Arse, Mary, Violent and Chavaroche. A number of footpaths lead from the summit to the Puy Gros (view of the Cère valley at Thiézac) or to the Prat de Bouc via the Tombe du Père pass.

Gorges de l'Alagnon★

3.5km/2.3mi NE towards Murat, then turn right (signpost) and follow a path 500m long down to the upper reaches of the river.

When the water level is low, it is possible to follow the river bed to the left over a distance of almost 200m. At the head of this very attractive ravine are piles of huge boulders.

② PAS DE PEYROL★★

80km/50mi. Allow 6h.

This itinerary runs through "Puys" country along the Impradine, Mars and Maronne valleys. *D 680 which crosses the Peyrol pass is often blocked by snow from November to as late as June.*

Puy Griou★★★

🚶 A strenuous walk. Begin by heading for the pastures in La Font d'Alagnon, then turn left through the woods to a holiday camp; there, bear right.

A clear path rises towards the alpine pastures of Col de Rombière (superb **view★** over the Jordanne valley and the great volcanic cones in Cantal) then turns left. For the summit, there is a strenuous climb over basalt rocks. From the top there is an exceptional **view★★★** of the Puy Mary, the Puy de Peyre-Arse, and Plomb du Cantal barring the horizon to the north.

Gorges de l'Alagnon★

Beyond the **Pierre-Taillade bridge** which carries N 122 across a narrow stream fanning out in its course, the valley widens but the scenery is more sombre than in the Cère valley.

A few miles beyond Laveissière, the road runs along the foot of the handsome **Château d'Anterroches**, then the basalt rocks above Murat come into view.

Murat★ –

See MURAT.

▶ Leave Murat NW on D 3.

As the road begins to climb, Plomb du Cantal, Puy de Peyre-Arse and Puy Griou come into view, one after the other, to the left. The road then skirts the foot of Chastel rock and runs down from Entremont pass offering views of the Dore mountain range in the distance and Puy Mary on the left.

After **Dienne** you turn into the Impradine valley, as the road climbs up towards the Pas de Peyrol. Here, it clings to the sheer sides of Puy Mary and provides **views★★** over the Impradine and Rhue de Cheylade valleys, the Dore mountain range and the Cézallier area.

Pas de Peyrol★★

This is the highest mountain pass in the Massif Central. In the foreground, there is a view of the wooded Falgoux corrie overlooked by the Roc d'Auzière.

Puy Mary★★★

A steep footpath follows the northwest ridge of the mountain. From the summit there is a breathtaking view of Cantal's gigantic extinct volcano and a superb view over the crystalline plateaux that form the base of the volcanic area of the Auvergne.

In the foreground is a striking view of the gigantic fan formed by the valleys radiating out from the centre of this natural water tower, separated by massive ridges with altitudes that decrease in the distance.

Rural life varies with the altitude across this countryside divided by deep corries. In the depths of the valleys near the villages are fields of crops and meadows. In the lesser exposed areas are birch woods followed by beeches halfway up the slopes, and then conifers. At higher altitudes alpine pastures are dotted with burons (the huts once lived in by shepherds during the summer) surrounded by ash trees. The drive down from Pas de Peyrol affords splendid views over the Mars valley.

THE CANTAL MOUNTAINS

0   5 km

Cirque du Falgoux★★
The Mars valley starts here, as the river gouges out a course for itself along the foot of Puy Mary.

▶ Head NW along D 12.

Vallée du Mars★
The road follows the valley, in which there is a striking contrast between the shaded slopes, covered in woodland but devoid of houses, and the sunny slopes carpeted with meadows and trees, and dotted with houses. In the **Gorge de St-Vincent★** the valley narrows. To the left of the road beyond the gorge is the Château de Chanterelle, a fortified residence dating from the 17C.

▶ Return to D 680 (or drive to Salers on D 212 – follow signs to Anglards – and D 22).

At the pass known as Col de Néronne, the road moves to the other side of the hill and overlooks the wide, glacial Maronne valley far below.

Puy Violent★

Walkers will enjoy Puy Violent, leaving from St-Paul-de-Salers.

▶ Go to Vielmur and turn left. Follow a narrow shepherd's lane which leads beyond the Croix des Vachers.

🚶 The walk to the top of the mountain (2h30 return) affords a lovely panorama, namely of the Maronne valley.

③ CREST ROAD★★
60km/38mi.

This itinerary takes over from the previous one and runs along the Aspre and Doire valleys. *The road up to Col de Legal is blocked by snow during the winter months, often until as late as April.*

Salers★★ – *see SALERS.*

▶ Leave Salers on D 35 E.

Running along the western slopes of Cantal's ancient volcano, the road crosses a few of the valleys which fan out from the heart of the range. It hairpins down into the Maronne valley then crosses the river and enters the Aspre valley. The traces left by the ancient glaciers that formed these valleys are obvious, even today. On the hillsides, are huge boulders, erratics, carried there by the ice and now left lying scattered.

Fontanges

To the right, at the entrance to the village, is a chapel dug into a mass of volcanic rock; entry is through a wrought-iron door set between colonnettes and archivolts. The castle, which now lies in ruins, once belonged to the family of Louis XIV's mistress.

▶ Continue on D 35 along the Aspre.

Col de Legal

From this pass there is a view into the distance over the Limousin plateau.

▶ At Col de Bruel turn right onto D 60 to Tournemire.

Tournemire – *see TOURNEMIRE.*

Château d'Anjony★ – *see TOURNEMIRE.*

▶ Turn back and take D 35 to the right.

Beyond the Croix de Cheules, the D 35, which is called the **Route des Crêtes★★**, follows the long ridge that separates the Authre and Jordanne valleys, and the journey provides some very attractive views of them.

▶ After 6km/4mi, turn right onto D 58 to Marmanhac.

Château de Sédaiges

Sédaiges, rebuilt in the 15C and modified in the 18C and 19C, is neo-Gothic. The furnishings and decor reflect the lifestyle of a 19C aristocratic family.

▶ Return to the Route des Crêtes, D 35.

As the road slopes down towards Aurillac, the broad plain at the edge of the town can be seen stretching away, whereas to the left there is a magnificent view of the Jordanne valley.

Aurillac★ – *see AURILLAC.*

④ VALLÉE DE LA JORDANNE★★
25km/15mi

Pas de Peyrol★★ – *see above.*

▶ Leave the pass on D 17 S.

The cliffroad overlooks the superb Falgoux corrie, where the River Mars rises. Beyond Redondet pass there is a view of Plomb du Cantal before the road runs into the Jordanne valley.

Rudez

Huddled together, the village houses cling to the mountain slopes in order to leave the valley floor free for pasture.

© Franck Guiziou/hemis.fr

Jordanne valley and the Cantal mountains

Vallée de la Jordanne★★

The slopes that flank this picturesque valley are lush and green, carpeted with meadows screened by clumps of trees. Here and there are a few rocky escarpments dotted with caves.

Cascade de Liadouze

🏃 The waterfall drops over a threshold of rock into a narrow gorge.

Mandailles

This village, lying in picturesque surroundings, is the starting point of numerous rambles.

▶ Turn right onto D 59.

The road crosses the Jordanne then wends its way up the hillside.

Croix de Cheules

The crossroads marks the start of the Crest Road.

Vic-sur-Cère★

The old town of Vic in the Cère valley, with its picturesque houses clustered around the church, is a spa town with a mineral spring (pump room).

A BIT OF HISTORY

The "mad monk" – In the 12C Pierre de Vic, the youngest son of a local family who had been forced to enter the church despite not having a religious vocation, was put in charge of a rich priory when he was still very young; he turned it into a pleasure-dome, composing drinking songs and love ballads there. He gradually wearied of his sedentary life and began to travel and sing ballads at the courts of Philippe Auguste, Richard the Lionheart and the King of Aragon. The "mad monk", as he called himself, carried off first prize at the Courts of

▸ **Population:** 2 003.
⌖ **Michelin Map:** 330: D-5. 20km/12.4mi NE of Aurillac – Local map see Monts du Cantal.
🛈 **Info:** Av. André-Mercier, 15800 Vic-sur-Cère. ☎04 71 47 50 68. www.carlades.fr.
▶ **Location:** Vic-sur-Cère lies along the Aurillac–Murat road.
👁 **Don't Miss:** The Château de Pesteils.
🕑 **Timing:** Allow half a day.

Love Literary Tournament and won the Golden Hawk at a contest at Le Puy.
Winning barrels (16C) – During the Wars of Religion **Captain Merle** was escorting a convoy of supplies for the

Huguenots when the Roman Catholics ambushed him in a gorge. Merle ordered the men to cut the mules' traces and flee. After they had gone some distance, he stopped the stampeding men, having calculated that the Catholics would fall upon the casks of wine instead of pursuing his men. He proved to be right; after rallying his men, he counter-attacked, wiping out his drunken adversaries.

OLD TOWN

Turreted houses still grace the town centre, testifying to the city's former prosperity.

▶ For a tour of the old city, allow 20–30min. Leave from place de l'Hôtel-de-Ville. Turn left towards place de Monaco.

Note the elegant turreted house at No. 4 passage du Chevalier-des-Huttes.

▶ Turn left towards place de Monaco.

Maison des Princes de Monaco

South of the church, off rue Coffinhal. This 15C house (*No. 4*) served as a residence on several occasions for the princes of Monaco, to whom Louis XIII had given the Carladez region in 1642, the capital of which was Vic, and which remained in their possession until the Revolution. The house has a turret with a mullioned window and a door surmounted by a badly damaged bas-relief depicting the Annunciation.

▶ Continue on rue Coffinhal.

Maison Dejou

At No. 5, there is a small *hôtel particulier* from the late 17C with a semicircular pediment.
Retrace your steps. On the left, note the tower adjoining the façade of the École St-Antoine on rue du Moine-de-Montaudon.

▶ Walk down to place de l'Église, pass behind the east end and follow the path to the waterfall.

Lou Cap Del Liou
Pretty old mill spanning the Iraliot.

▶ Walk up to the church.

Église St-Pierre
This partly Romanesque building has undergone many alterations. Note the graceful apse and the curious modillions on the south façade. Opposite the church, the former bailiwick is now private property. Walk up to the calvary along rue du Dr-Civiale. From the chapel there is a fine panoramic view of the town.

☙WALKS

Cascade du Trou de la Conche and Rocher de Maisonne
Behind the church, take the street leading to a footbridge over the Iraliot. On the other side of the torrent, walk up a very steep path.
🚶 At the top of the rise the road divides: *(left)* to Trou de la Conche cascade; *(right)* to the top of Maisonne rock, giving a fine view of Vic and the valley below.

Grotte des Anglais
Leave Vic on N 122 towards Murat and immediately turn onto the road to La Prade. Park on the platform.
🚶 A small knoll commands a nice view of the spa, with Curebourse plateau and wood in the background.

▶ Go to Fournol village (vestiges of a Roman bridge down below). Bear left to rejoin and cross N 122.

Opposite, slightly to the right, a signposted trail leads to the **Grotte des Anglais**, a cave that gave shelter to bandits and highway robbers during the Hundred Years War (1337-1453).

EXCURSIONS

Thiézac

▶ 9km.5.6mi NE along N 122.

This is a sunny summer resort with a Gothic church (Église St-Martin) and a

Stairs of the Rocher de Carlat

© Hervé Lenain/hemis.fr

chapel (Chapelle Notre-Dame-de-Consolation) which overlooks the village – it was after undertaking a pilgrimage here that Anne of Austria conceived, after 22 childless years of marriage, the future Louis XIV.

Cascade de Faillitoux

5km/3.1mi to the W. Leave Thiézac on the road to Vic and, soon after the graveyard, turn right onto D 59.
Around 3km/2.1mi further on, the road goes through Lasmolineries village, offering views of the Faillitoux waterfall flowing from its basalt ledge.

🚗 DRIVING TOUR

UPPER GOUL VALLEY AND CARLADÈS

80km/50mi. Allow one day.

◻ Leave Vic to the SE on D 54, heading for Raulhac and Mur-de-Barrez.

Rocher des Pendus

Leave the car near Col de Curebourse and take the path on the right, opposite Auberge des Monts.
🔲 From this rock there is an extensive **panorama★★** over the Cère valley, the Cantal mountain range, Carladès rock, the Châtaigneraie and the Aurillac basin.

◻ Continue along D 54.

Église de Jou-sous-Monjou

Interesting Romanesque church with a fine belfry and a porch resting on a slender column.

◻ Take D 59, then D 600 until you reach Raulhac.

On the way, note the Château de Cropières (⊶ *not open to the public)*, a typical manor from the Cantal region.

◻ Continue along D 600 towards Mur-de-Barrez.

Château de Messilhac

⏱ *Guided tours (45min) mid-Jun–Aug 2.30–6.30pm.* ⊚€6. ℘*04 71 49 57 86. www.messilhac.com.*
At the end of a track, this former fortress stands proudly in a delightful bucolic setting. The Renaissance façade, flanked by two square towers crowned by pointed roofs, is pierced with mullioned windows.

◻ On leaving Mur-de-Barrez, D 990 and D 459 (right) lead to Ronesque rock.

Rocher de Ronesque★★

This basalt rock forms a plateau dominating the entire countryside. It was formed in the same way as Carlat rock; first covered by volcano activity then deeply gashed by large valleys. The picturesque hamlet at the foot of the rock is typical of the Cantal where the houses often have roofs of stone slabs called *lauzes*.

Rocher de Carlat★

The scenery here is typical of the Carlat area. The region was covered with basalt by lava flows from the volcanoes of Cantal; erosion fragmented the coating of rock, isolating a few flows which now stand, sheer-sided, at the top of steep hillsides. With its delightful valleys and its houses with steeply sloping hipped roofs of stone slabs surrounded by gardens and orchards, the Carlat region is a pleasant place to stay or travel around.

▶ Cross the breach and skirt, to the left, the north side of the rock.

Climb the Escalier de la Reine carved out of the rock to reach the northern edge of the plateau; there is a wonderful **view★** of the mountains of Cantal. Then climb Murgat rock, topped by a statue: the view stretches southwards beyond the village, to the Carlat region.

▶ Continue on D 990 to Vézac. D 208 on the right leads to Polminhac.

Château de Pesteils★

May–Jun and Sept 2–6.30pm (Jul–late Aug 10am–7pm). €8.50. 04 71 47 40 03. www.chateau-pesteils-cantal.com. Visits by candlelight and "medieval festivals" are organised in the summer.

This beautiful medieval castle, built on a rocky promontory on the north bank of the Cère overlooking the town of Polminhac, was one of the strongholds designed to defend the valley. The imposing 13C square keep is crowned with a machicolated watch-path.

Murat★

Murat lies in the pleasant Alagnon valley, in a scenic **setting★★**. Its grey houses with stone-slabbed roofs rise picturesquely on terraces up the slopes of the basaltic Bonnevie hill. Two other steep peaks overlook the small town: Chastel rock to the north-west and Bredons rock to the south-east topped by an interesting Romanesque church. Murat is an ideal centre from which to tour the volcanoes of Cantal and enjoy rambling in the surrounding state-owned forest. In August there is a large influx of music lovers who come to enjoy the International Festival of World Music and Dance.

A BIT OF HISTORY

Nothing is impregnable to the French – The **Count of Anterroches**, who was born near Murat, is remembered for his reply to the proposal by the English, at Fontenoy, to fire first: "Gentlemen, we never fire first. Fire yourselves." This was not simply a gesture of courtesy

▶ **Population:** 1 991.

Michelin Map: 330: F-4. 25km/15.5mi NW of St-Flour – Local map see Monts du CANTAL.

Info: pl de l'Hôtel de Ville, 15300 MURAT. 04 71 20 09 47. www.murat.fr.

▶ **Location:** Murat lies in the Alagnon valley, west of St-Flour, along the road to Aurillac.

Parking: In the centre.

Don't Miss: Stroll around the streets and stop for a coffee.

Timing: Murat is not large; a couple of hours will suffice.

but rather an application of the tactic by which troops would come under fire first and then march on the enemy while the latter were reloading their muskets. Anterroches is also credited with another famous saying: as he stood

Murat

before Maastricht, someone declared that the town was impregnable. "Nothing," replied Anterroches, "is impregnable to the French."

THE TOWN

A brochure about this town of steep, narrow streets is available from the tourist office.

Église Notre-Dame-des-Oliviers

The church dates from the late Gothic period but has a modern west front.

Halle

This covered market is a fine example of 19C ironwork architecture.

Former Bailiff's Court

The building dates from the 16C and opens onto rue de l'Argenterie through a doorway decorated with moulding.

Maison Rodier

This elegant Renaissance-style building has some attractive bonding in trachyte (a type of volcanic rock) and a corbelled watch-tower.

Consul's Residence

Faubourg Notre-Dame.

The late-15C stone façade has two storeys with narrow windows topped by an ornament. Note the two carved angels above the door, part of which consists of linenfold panels.

Rocher de Bonnevie

The sides of this hill feature strange basalt columns which are remarkable for the uniformity and length of their prisms. A castle once stood on the hill but it was razed to the ground on the orders of Richelieu; it did, however, take six months and six hundredweight of gunpowder to complete the task.

There is a fine view over Murat, the Alagnon valley, the mountains of Cantal and the Chevade valley.

Maison de la Faune

🕐 *Jul–Aug 10am–noon, 2–7pm (Sun, 2–7pm); school holidays 10am–noon, 2–6pm (Sun, 2–6pm); rest of the year by appointment.* ✆€5 (child 8–15, €3.50). ✆04 71 20 00 52. www.murat.fr.

This former mansion has retained a late-15C turret. Inside, a large collection of beetles and butterflies, stuffed birds and animals are displayed in reconstructions of their natural environment.

EXCURSIONS

Église de Bredons★

SE along D 926. 🚹 *Contact the town hall for information.* ✆04 71 20 02 80.

The small fortified 11C church is all that remains of the Benedictine priory. The doorway on the south side has billet moulding. Inside, note the monumental giltwood altarpiece completed in 1710 for the High Altar; the intricate detail and abundance of gold and polychrome make this a grandiose piece of decoration. The Resurrection is depicted in the centre. Other giltwood altar screens decorate the chapels.

Albepierre-Bredons★
5km/3mi SW on D 39.
This tiny village built on a volcanic hill overlooks the Alagnon valley. Underground houses were once built into the caves in the rock. From the top of the village, there is an interesting view of Murat below and of the Rocher de Bonnevie in the distance.

ADDRESSES

🛌STAY

🛏 **Chambre d'Hôte La Gaspardine** – *Gaspard, 15300 La Chapelle d'Alagnon.* 📞*04 71 20 01 91. www.cantal-hote.com. 4 rooms.* Isolated in a peaceful place, this former farm, just 2km/1mi from the town, opens onto a beautiful flowery terrace with a most agreeable view over the Alagnon valley. The rooms are decorated with good taste, and the dinner menus favour the specialities of the region.

🍴/EAT

🍴🍴 **Le Jarrousset** – *3km/1.8mi E of Murat via N 122 dir. Clermont-Ferrand.* 📞*04 71 20 10 69. www.restaurant-le-jarrousset.com. Closed Tue except Jul–Aug and Mon.* This rural restaurant in a pavilion set back from the road has a contemporary-style dining room with a veranda giving onto the garden and a terrace in summer. Fine dining without the pretensions of haute cuisine; a peaceful place for a relaxing evening.

Salers★★

Salers is one of the prettiest little towns in Upper Auvergne and has a very distinctive character. It stands at an altitude of 951m and has retained from its military and judicial past a rare set of ramparts and old houses, grouped together on a pinnacle giving a magnificent view of the confluence of the River Aspre and River Maronne. Salers is also a tasty farmhouse cheese made from unpasteurised full-cream milk.

A BIT OF HISTORY
Arms and the gown (15C–16C) – The twofold character of the buildings in Salers can be explained by the town's history. Initially unwalled, it suffered cruelly at the hands of the English and the mercenaries or "free companions", who roamed the highways; as a result the ramparts were built, and still stand

▸ **Population:** 357.
🏅 **Michelin Map:** 330: C-4. 20km/12.4mi SE of Mauriac – Local map see Monts du CANTAL.
ℹ **Info:** Pl. Tyssandier-d'Escous, 15140 Salers. 📞04 71 40 70 68. www.salers-tourisme.fr.
▶ **Location:** Salers lies 20km/12.5mi SE of Mauriac, and 45km/28mi from Aurillac, via the D 680.
🅿 **Parking:** There is generous parking around the centre.
🌀 **Don't Miss:** A gentle stroll through the old streets is needed to fully appreciate the timeless beauty of the village.
🕐 **Timing:** Allow half a day, and enjoy a relaxing lunch.

Salers

© Christian Guy/imageBROKER/age fotostock

today. In the 16C Salers became the seat of the bailiwick of the Upper Mountains of the Auvergne and the established *bourgeois* families, from which the judges were selected, started building their impressive turreted houses.

⭐ WALKING TOUR

Eglise St-Mathieu★
A 12C porch still remains from the Romanesque church which pre-dated the present church, begun in the 15C. The bell-tower, which was struck by lightning, was rebuilt in the 19C.

◗ On leaving the church, pass a fountain on the left and follow rue du Beffroi uphill.

Go under the Tour de l'Horloge (clock-tower, also known as Belfry Gate), flanked by a round tower with machicolations. Just beyond the gate, on the right, is the house of Pierre Lizet with its Gothic window and Renaissance portal.

Place Tyssandier-d'Escous
The old houses of dark lava stone with their clean, sober lines, flanked by corbelled round or polygonal turrets, and their pepper-pot or many-sided roofs, look like a stage-set; the scene is completed by a fountain in the centre.

On the main square a monument has been raised to Tyssandier d'Escous who improved the region's breed of cattle in the 19C and made it famous.

Ancien Baillage
This Renaissance building, the former Bailiff's Court, stands at the corner of rue du Beffroi. It is a vast residence of fine architectural design, flanked by two corner towers. Inside are several rooms open to view, one of which has a beautiful Renaissance fireplace.

Maison de Flojeac
Opposite the tourist office. The house has a turret with canted corners.

Maison de la Ronade
This building has a tower rising five storeys high. It has been converted into a guesthouse and tearoom.

◗ At the entrance to rue du Couvent, on the right, a wooden door leads to a large courtyard.

Maison des Templiers – Musée de Salers
Rue des Templiers. ◷ *Mon–Thu and Sun 10am–12.30pm, 2–5.30pm, Sat 2–5.30pm.* ⊛ €5. ℘ *04 71 40 75 97. www.salers-tourisme.fr.*
The 15C building houses an exhibition on the town's folklore and past: recon-

179

struction of Auvergne interiors, cheese-making, chemist's shop dating from 1890, religious objects and garments.

▷ Turn left onto avenue de Barrouze.

Esplanade de Barrouze

The small, shaded park here offers an impressive view★ of the Maronne, Rat and Aspre valleys and also of the Puy Violent massif.

▷ Retrace your steps.

Maison Bertrandy

The house has a round tower and an attractive door.

▷ Return to Grande-Place, then take rue du Beffroi back to the church.

EXCURSIONS
Les Burons de Salers ★
4km/2.5mi from Salers on the road to Puy Mary.
🕐*Apr–Sept 10am–7pm. ⊗€5. ℘04 71 40 70 71. www.buronsdesalers.fr.*

Appropriately located in a restored *buron* (shepherd's hut), this "cheese house" retraces the history of the Salers breed of cattle and of the local cheese-making tradition; fine collection of tools. Another *buron* presents the history of the "Salers", a liqueur made from the gentian plant.

Anglards-de-Salers
10km/6.2mi N on D 22.
The Auvergne-style church with its octagonal belfry is quite purist in its architectural style.
Below it stands the 15C **Château de la Trémolière** (🕐*Jun–Sept. ⊗€5. ℘04 71 40 05 72*) which houses a collection of 16C Aubusson tapestries.

▷ You can extend your tour by pressing on to Mauriac (☝see MAURIAC).

Pleaux
Pleaux enjoys a modest workaday atmosphere, a mutually supportive community and a smattering of sturdy

bourgeois houses in the Renaissance style along the narrow streets that ripple from the Grand Place and the broad square where the market is held.

ADDRESSES

⌂ STAY

⊖ **Chambre d'Hôte M. et Mme Prudent** – R. des Nobles. ☎04 71 40 75 36. 6 rooms. In the heart of Salers, this stunning 17C house has a charm all its own. The simple rooms are comfortable, the pretty garden looks out towards the volcanoes, and breakfast is served either outdoors or in a handsome room typical of the region, unless you'd rather be served in bed.

⊖ **Hôtel Les Voyageurs** – 15380 Le Falgoux. ☎04 71 69 51 59. 14 rooms. Auberge in the true Auvergnat tradition with an inglenook fireplace lined with benches in the bar. The rooms have been refurnished and are soberly rustic but well kept. Regional dishes in the restaurant.

⊖⊖ **Chambre d'Hôte La Michie** – Au Bourg, 15380 Le Falgoux. ☎04 71 69 54 36.http://guy.supersac.pagesperso-orange.fr. Closed Nov–Easter. 5 rooms. Restaurant ⊖⊖. This building was completely restored by the owner. There is a nice common lounge with seating around the fireplace, and a dining room decorated with antique furniture. The restaurant menus provide regional dishes using local produce. The rooms are bright, spacious and welcoming.

⊖⊖ **Hôtel Le Gerfaut** – rte de Puy Mary – 1km/0.5mi NE via the D 680. ☎04 71 40 75 75. www.salers-hotel-gerfaut.com. Open from Mar-Oct. 23 rooms. Above the town, a modern and functional place to sleep peacefully. The rooms have all been refurbished and some are equipped with balconies or terraces with views over the valley.

⋔ EAT

⊖⊖ **La Diligence** – R. du Beffroi. ☎04 71 40 75 39. www.ladiligence-salers.com. Closed mid Nov–Mar. Don't be fooled by the modern look of this establishment – the dishes served here are traditional local fare. If the *crêpes* won't satisfy your appetite, the *truffade*, *tripoux*, *pounti* or *potée auvergnate* will, especially when washed down with a native wine.

⊖⊖ **Le Bailliage** – R. Notre-Dame. ☎04 71 40 71 95. www.salers-hotel-bailliage.com. Closed mid-Nov–Jan. An inviting dining room and lovely terrace on which to enjoy the mouth watering cuisine of the Auvergne. The hotel element has large rooms overlooking the garden or the surrounding countryside. An agreeable retreat.

Riom-ès-Montagnes★

Situated in the western part of the Parc Régional des Volcans, Riom-ès-Montagnes is a small town linking the Rhue valley to the Cantal mountain range and a thriving commercial centre with an important cheese industry. The production of an aperitif based on the gentian plant contributes to the prosperity of the town which is the ideal starting point for excursions through gentian country, its high pastures and Romanesque churches.

▸ **Population:** 2 798.
⌕ **Michelin Map:** 330: E-2
▤ **Info:** 1 av. Fernand-Brun 15400 Riom-ès-Montagnes. ☎04 71 78 07 37. www.tourisme-gentiane.com.
▶ **Location:** 24km/15mi from Bort-les-Orgues via the D 922.
☺ **Don't Miss:** Visit the beautiful valley of the Cheylade.
👪 **Kids:** Exploring the countryside.

SIGHTS
Église St-Georges★
The only remaining parts of the original 11C are the chancel, the apse, the dome and the transept.

Espace Avèze
🕐 *Mid-Jun–mid-Sept 10am–noon, 3–7pm; the rest of the year by appointment.* ♿ ⊕ *No charge.* 📞 *04 71 78 03 04. www.aveze.com.*
This firm, founded in 1929, produces an aperitif based on the gentian plant picked in the surrounding mountains. An exhibition space, offering a view of the bottling hall, is devoted to the gentian and its use in the production of the aperitive. Avèze is the only gentian-based drink extracted by soaking the plant for nine months in a mixture of water and alcohol.

Gentiane Express
🕐 *Departures Apr–Oct at 3pm (mid-Jul–Aug 10am). 2½h round trip. Booking essential; check website for details.* ⊕ *€16 (child 4–12, €9).* 📞 *04 73 39 72 21. www.gentiane-express.com.*
This tourist train takes passengers across high pastures where the famous Salers cattle graze in summer. The itinerary links Bort-les-Orgues and Lugarde via Riom-ès-Montagnes and the Barajol viaduct.

Brasserie de l'Ecir
This brewery produces the *Pastourela*, made with the pure water of the Cantal area. The quality of the water is such that there is no need to filter or pasteurise the beer brewed here. The visit ends with beer tasting… naturally.

EXCURSIONS
St-Étienne-de-Choimeil
14km/8.7mi NW along D 3 then D 205. Turn right before the Romanesque church.

Botanical trail
3.5km/2.2mi round tour. Allow 1h.
🚶 This pleasant ramble through woodland offers the opportunity of discovering the local flora in its natural environment.

🚗 DRIVING TOUR

② CHEYLADE VALLEYS AND GENTIANE COUNTRY★★
90km/56mi. About one day.
♿ *see map p158.*

After crossing the dry Sapchat valley, and the Rhue de Cheylade valley, the road overlooks the wooded Véronne valley and runs along its hillside. Riom-ès-Montagnes appears in the midst of a fresh pastoral setting.

▶ Head S from Riom along D 3.

Soon a superb **panoramic view** unfolds to the left over the Dore mountain range and the upper plateaux of the Cézallier area. Beyond lie the ruins of the Château d'Apchon and the mountains of Cantal.

Apchon
This is a typical Cantal village with its sturdy houses. 🚶 A footpath leads off from rue de la Porte-du-Barre to a viewing table and the **castle ruins** *(30min on foot there and back; access to the ruins could be dangerous for children).*

▶ Leave Apchon S (D 249) then turn right onto D 63.

Collandres
The Romanesque church of this tiny village stands on the site of a former look-out post over the Véronne valley. The road, which goes past the church, runs across high pastures where cattle graze in summer. In the Cantal region, these pastures extend over an area of some 80 000ha.
Turn left at the first junction towards La Chatonnière. The road runs through woodland and pastureland dotted with burons (shepherds' huts) and farms. Besides cattle grazing in the fields, you are likely to see birds of prey and herons.

▶ Return to Collandres and leave the village S along D 263.

Cascade du Pont d'Aptier
This waterfall in its unspoilt setting is the ideal place for a picnic.

▶ Beyond the bridge, turn left onto D 249.

Chapelle de la Font-Sainte
This 19C place of pilgrimage, can be seen in the middle of the fields.
The road (D 49) runs through St-Hippolyte and down to the Rhue de Cheylade. After crossing the river, the Puy Mary is visible to the right of a long ridge starting at the Puy de Peyre-Arse.

Cheylade
This resort above the Rhue is popular with anglers and is a good starting point for rambles.

▶ 2.5km/1.5mi S of Cheylade, turn right on D 262. Park near a bridge and walk a further 100m to the right.

Cascade du Sartre★
The waterfall is formed by the Rhue which flows down a drop of 30m.
Continue along D 262 and, beyond another bridge, turn right on a path offering an attractive view of the **Cascade de la Roche**, a waterfall formed by a tributary of the Rhue which drops down over the rocks in a series of mini-cascades.

▶ Turn back and continue along D 62.

Le Claux
This small resort is ideal for a variety of outdoor activities: cross-country skiing and snowshoeing in winter (**Maison de Montagne** – ☎04 71 78 93 88), paragliding, climbing, riding and rambling in summer.
Beyond Le Claux, the view of the Puy Mary and the Cheylade valley with its forested floor becomes increasingly impressive. The road rises in a series of hairpin bends and continues through woods until it reaches the alpine pastures. It then crosses Col de Serres and arrives at the Impradine valley, hollowed into a bowl shape by ancient glaciers.

During the final climb up to Pas de Peyrol, the road crosses the Eylac pass, clings to the sheer sides of the Puy Mary and provides a number of splendid **views★** over the Impradine and Rhue de Cheylade valleys, the Dore mountain range, and the Cézallier area.

Pas de Peyrol★★ –
See Monts du CANTAL.

▶ Go back 3km/1.9mi along D 62, then turn right onto D 23, heading for Dienne.

The road hugs the steep Impradine and Santoire valleys.

Puy Mary★★★ –
See Monts du CANTAL.

▶ Leave Puy Mary along D 680 then turn right onto D 12 towards Le Falgoux. Beyond Col d'Aulac, turn left as you enter the Marihou woods.

Site de Cotteughes et Preydefont
The remains of drystone huts abandoned during the Middle Ages testify to the area's long-standing cattle breeding tradition.

Trizac
This large village is renowned for its cattle markets.

▶ Turn right onto D 205.

Menet
As the road runs down towards the village, it affords views of its harmonious white buildings. The nearby lake offers relaxing activities (angling, pedalo, etc).

▶ Leave Menet E; D 36 runs through woodland back to Riom.

Mauriac★

Situated between the Dordogne and Puy Mary, this small town, which is an important agricultural trading centre, consists of black, lava stone houses on the edge of a vast basalt plateau.

SIGHTS
Basilique Notre-Dame-des-Miracles★

This is the most important Romanesque building in Upper Auvergne, erected between the 12C and the 14C. The vast main doorway at the west front is the best piece of Romanesque carving in the area. Around place Georges-Pompidou are a few old houses including one with double Romanesque bays. Note the old houses with twinned Romanesque openings surrounding place Georges-Pompidou.

Monastère St-Pierre

Mid-Jun–mid-Sept 10am–noon, 2.30–6.30pm. Sun am and Tue mid-end Jun and 1–mid-Sept, and Sun am in Jul–Aug. €3. *04 71 68 07 24.*
This monastery was once a daughter-house of Église St-Pierre-le-Vif in Sens. It is possible to see a few Gallo-Roman remains, some of the foundations of the Carolingian church (early 9C), the 11C chapter house (columns made with local marble) and part of the cloisters (14C–15C).

▶ Follow rue du Collège.

Hôtel d'Orcet

Currently the Sous-Préfecture. This 16C–18C building incorporates the 12C tympanum that decorated the doorway into the monastery refectory.

▶ Continue along rue du Dr-E.-Chavialle; the first left leads to the museum.

Musée des Arts et Traditions Populaires

Mon–Fri mid-Jun–mid-Sept 2–6pm. 04 71 68 07 24. €3.

- ▶ **Population:** 3 977.
- **Michelin Map:** 330: B-3 – 19km/11.8mi NW of Salers.
- **Info:** 1 r. Chappe-d'Auteroche, 15200 Mauriac. 04 71 68 19 87. www.tourisme.paysdemauriac.fr.
- **Location:** 20km/12mi NW from Salers, 50km/31mi north of Aurillac.
- **Timing:** 2–3 hours to wander.

Housed in a former prison, this museum has a range of collections: Gallo-Roman ceramics, religious artefacts etc. There are temporary exhibitions of regional arts and crafts.

EXCURSIONS
Puy St-Mary

Climb up to the chapel at the top of the grassy hill known as Puy St-Mary. From here there is a panoramic view of Mauriac, the mountains of Cantal and the plateaux bordering the Auvergne and the Limousin.

Château de la Vigne

04 71 69 00 20.
www.chateaudelavigne.com.
This 15C castle is flanked by two round towers topped by pepper-pot roofs, and a square tower that served as a keep and to which, in the 18C, a second building was attached. Inside, there are 16C frescoes on the walls and ceiling of the Salle de Justice.

🚗 DRIVING TOUR

CHURCHES OF THE NORTHERN PLATEAUX
Round trip of 70km/44mi. Allow a day.

▶ Head NE from Mauriac on D 922 and turn right onto D 678.

Église du Vigean

In the small church is a **reliquary★** made of 13C Limousin enamelwork.

Château d'Auzers

▶ Follow D 678. About 2km/1mi before reaching Moussages, take D 12.

Moussages

Overlooking a square decorated with an old fountain and surrounded by old houses is the church, whose Romanesque east end has carved modillions.

▶ Leave N on D 22 then turn right.

Château d'Auzers★

☛ *Guided visits Apr–Oct 2–6.30pm.* ℘*04 71 78 62 59. www.auzers.com.* This 14C and 16C castle comprises a central building flanked by two high turrets crowned by pepper-pot roofs.

▶ 2km/1mi after leaving Auzers, turn right onto D 22, heading to Saignes.

Saignes

This small but appealing summer resort perched above the Sumène valley has a Romanesque church and several quaint 15C houses.

▶ Turn right towards Le Monteil then left onto D 36.

Chastel-Merlhac

Its circular shape makes this eroded lava flow look like a basalt fortress.

▶ Return to Saignes and turn NE onto D 236 towards Riom; turn right onto D 15 then right again onto D 3.

Antignac

The **Jardins ethnobotaniques** (ⓒ*daily except Sat at 3pm.* ⓒ*1 Jan and 25 Dec.* ⚭€*5, no charge 1 May.* ℘*04 71 40 21 16)* grow plants of medieval origin found on archaeological sites.

▶ Leave Antignac on D 3 to Bort-les-Orgues; turn left on D 15, then D 315.

Ydes-Bourg

The exhibition called ♣♣ **Insectes du Monde** (♿ⓒ*Jul–Aug 2–7pm.* ⚭€*3.* ℘*04 71 40 59 81)* is mainly devoted to butterflies and moths, many of which come from Hungary, Mexico and Pakistan.

▶ Rejoin D 922; right to Bassignac.

Bassignac

The ♣♣**Jardin Délirant** (ⓒ*10am–8pm;* ⚭€*4 (children, €2.50).* ℘*04 71 67 32 50)* is devoted to textiles and weaving. The garden grows more than 150 species of textile plants as well as plants used in dyeing.

▶ Rejoin D 922 to return to Mauriac.

Saint-Cernin

This small town is a pleasant base from which to explore the western Cantal mountain range.

One of the most striking features of the surrounding countryside is the castle of Anjony. Strategically located on the tip of the Tournemire promontory, it dominates the lush landscape of the Doire valley with its four tall towers.

▶ **Population:** 1 155.
⚙ **Michelin Map:** 330: c-4
ℹ **Info:** Le Bourg, 15140 St-Martin-Valmeroux. ℘04 71 69 44 41.
▶ **Location:** 20km/13mi N of Aurillac via the D 922.
👪 **Kids:** Château d'Anjony.
🕐 **Timing:** Allow half a day and enjoy a leisurely stroll and maybe a coffee.

ST-LOUIS CHURCH

The 12C **Église St-Louis**, dominated by its bell-tower, was altered in the 15C and boasts some fine **woodwork★** (note in particular the misericords on the 14 choir stalls, from the chapter-house at St-Chamant), a handsome Louis XIV lectern near the pulpit and lovely **corbels** carved into the basalt of the church's east end.

🚗 DRIVING TOUR

GORGES DE LA MARONNE★
55km/34.2mi round tour. Allow 2hrs.

▶ Leave St-Cernin to the N towards D 922; head for Mauriac and turn onto the first road on the right.

Château du Cambon
🚶 *Guided visits Jul–Aug 2.30–6.30pm; Jun and Sept by arrangement.* ∞€6. ℘04 71 47 60 48.
This fine 18C castle, built of dark basalt stone, has been whitewashed. The owner takes visitors on a guided tour, from the chapel and the first-floor bedrooms to the ground-floor reception rooms.

▶ Rejoin D 922 towards Mauriac.

St-Chamant
The **church** contains eight choir stalls decorated with **painted panels★**. The **château** (🚶 *guided visits Jul–Aug 2.30–6.30pm. ∞€5 (park and interior).* ℘04 71 69 26 85. http://saintchamant. free.fr) is 17C with a 15C square machic-

olated keep; inside are wonderful **tapestries★**, in very good condition, decorated with themes including spring, mythological events and the crusades. The castle chapel houses a lovely gilded wooden altarpiece (18C) depicting the Holy Family.

▶ Leave St-Chamant to the W on D 42. Rejoin D 922.

St-Martin-Valmeroux
A small glove-making centre with a Gothic church, an old fountain and the ruins of château de Crèvecœur.

▶ Leave St-Martin to the W on D 37.

The winding road to Loupiac dominates the Maronne valley, flanked by luxuriant slopes. Beyond Loupiac stands the ruins of Branzac castle.

Château de Branzac
This massive keep with corner towers representative of Cantal fortified architecture is now just a picturesque ruin on the end of a promontory.

▶ Return to D 37.

🚶 Opposite the last house in St-Christophe-les-Gorges, on the road to St-Martin-Cantalès, take the path *(45min on foot there and back)*, cross the railway tracks and go to the chapel Notre-Dame-du-Château.

Notre-Dame-du-Château

The chapel is an attractive building roofed with *lauzes*, sitting in a lovely **setting★** overlooking a double meander of the river.

▶ Leave St-Christophe-les-Gorges to the south on D 6.

Gorges de la Maronne★

The valley narrows and enters a canyon bordered by lush vegetation.

▶ Continue along D 6, entering the Gorges de la Bertrande.

Église de St-Illide

This Romanesque church (☜ *closed to the public*) was enlarged in the 15C.

▶ Leave St-Illide E and follow D 43 back to St-Cernin.

EXCURSIONS

Tournemire★
6.5km/4mi to the E of Saint-Cernin via the D 160.

This lovely village in the heart of the Cantal mountains has been recognised as one of the most beautiful villages in France. The lava-stone houses are covered with slate roofs. The small, Romanesque church is built of coloured volcanic tufa.

Château d'Anjony★

☜ *Guided tours daily Feb–Mar and Oct–Nov 2–5pm; Apr–Jun and Sept 2–6pm; Jul–Aug daily 11am and 11.30am except Sun, 2–6.30pm.* ☞€8. ℘04 71 47 61 67; www.anjony.fr.

This castle of reddish basalt is one of the most remarkable in Auvergne. Strategically located on the tip of the Tournemire promontory, it dominates the lush landscape of the Doire valley with its four tall towers.

The castle was built in the 15C by Louis II of Anjony, the companion of Dunois and Joan of Arc, near the towers of Tournemire which had been held in joint fief by his family and the Tournemires since 1351. This dual ownership led to three centuries of bloody rivalry between the families, one of old feudal stock, the other having prospered through business and service to the royal family. The feud ended around 1650.

The main hall on the first floor boasts a coffered ceiling with three tiers of beams, and throughout the castle there are some fine furnishings and furniture: a vast fireplace, tapestries from Aubusson and Flanders, a tester bed and a reclining seat. The Knights' Hall on the second floor has **frescoes★** of Michel of Anjony and his wife Germaine of Foix in late-16C dress, and scenes illustrating the legend of the Nine Valiant Knights from a medieval poem.

The lush, volcanic landscape of green hills and glacial valleys that surrounds St-Flour and its villages delivers the sort of subtle pleasure that comes from a soothing massage. It is such a joy to explore, like being enveloped in a cosy world of endless relaxation, a place where the metronome of life is set at *andante* rather than *allegro*, and the harmonies between man and the land combine to make a pastoral symphony worthy of the greatest composers. It is all such a complete contrast to St-Flour itself, a place at once both charming and dynamic.

Highlights

1 Exploring the upper town of **St-Flour** and buying local produce at the Saturday market (p190)

2 Walking the path to the tiny **Sailhant waterfall** (p193)

3 Admiring the **Garabit viaduct**, built by Gustave Eiffel before he created the Eiffel Tower (p194)

4 Exploring the rugged **Gorges de la Truyère** (p194)

5 Stepping back in time at the **Château d'Alleuze** (p195)

Dark Rocks

The local rock around St-Flour, as else-where in Cantal, is the dark and sombre basalt, with the result that many of the buildings have a gloomy façade. But that belies the attractions of the place, not least the Gothic cathedral with its twin towers, which rather dominate the countryside for some distance. Of this elevated town the saying goes: "None ever took you by force except the wind!" And this is true, for no-one ever did.

What's in a Name?

Originally, the name of "Margeride" applied only to a lordship, in this case one whose castle was ruined in the 15C, and to a forest area. The original location is near Saint-Loup Védrines on the road from Saint-Flour Langeac. It gradually became the generic name for all the surrounding mountains. This in turn became the National Forest that formalised the name in the 19C. Geographers later extended the name to the entire granite plateau in the 20C.

Flora

The vegetation across the region largely consists of pine and beech forests (in the damp areas), with man-made forests of spruce and extensive areas of broom heath and heather. There are also bogs in which you can still find relics of Ice Age plants (especially the rare dwarf birch and willow of Lapland).

Gorges de la Truyère at Laussac

© Christian Guy/hemis.fr

ST-FLOUR, SANFLORAIN AND MARGERIDE DU CANTAL

Sanflorain Lands

At the centre of Les Pays du Sanflorain, the Planèze is a vast area of basalt plateaus, virtually flat. Until quite recently the area hosted crops of rye, peas, lentils and other grains. With better sunshine and lower rainfall than the areas to the west, protected by the mountains, the Planèze was for many years regarded as the granary of the Upper Auvergne, over which St-Flour was the guardian. Planèze was very much at the heart of things, and from it different landscapes radiated, each with its own strong identity and culture.

Feeling Sheepish

In the 16C, Margeride adopted the agro-pastoral system of farming, similar to that used in Planèze. This was based on extensive use of rangelands for livestock in combination with cereal cultivation around the village (mainly rye).

Sheep farming was of great importance as it ensured the fertilisation and management of the land. The sheep were entrusted to a shepherd who brought the flock back into the village every night.

© Christian Guy/hemis.fr

St-Flour★★

St-Flour is perched on the end of the *planèze* which bears its name, at an altitude of 881m on a basaltic table 100m above the River Ander. The beauty of its **site★★** can be best appreciated from an eastern approach which reveals a line of houses dominated by the massive towers of the cathedral, looming above rocky escarpments. The town developed around the tomb of St Flour, one of the Evangelists preaching in the Auvergne in the 4C. During the Middle Ages, under the administration of three elected consuls, it had a population of 7 000 people. In 1317, the Pope made it a cathedral town.

A BIT OF HISTORY

Revolt of the Tuchins – During the Hundred Years War St-Flour was close to the battlefield. The Treaty of Brétigny (1360) made St-Flour a frontier town, "France's key to Guienne" (Aquitaine). Fear of the English grew, but it was the mercenaries, more than the English, who controlled the country from the fortresses of Saillant and Alleuze. The town was often attacked, its outlying districts burnt and pillaged. The consuls made pacts with the enemy who, in return for a fee, agreed to leave the people of St-Flour in peace. However, the truce was endangered by some of the inhabitants, nicknamed the *Tuchins,* who saw it as tantamount to capitulation, and who were seen as patriots by

▶ **Population:** 7 120.
⚐ **Michelin Map:** 330: G-4.
🛈 **Info:** 17 bis, pl. d'Armes, 15100 St-Flour.
  ℘04 71 60 22 50.
  www.saint-flour.com.
▶ **Location:** There are two towns: one, modern and busy, on the plain; the other, perched on a huge rocky upthrust overlooking the Ander and Lescure valleys, a network of old streets and cranky buildings, wherein lies all the interest.
🅿 **Parking:** There are ample parking areas in both the upper and lower town.
☺ **Don't Miss:** The view from the town walls, or the museum in the Hôtel de Ville.
🕐 **Timing:** Half a day to explore the upper town; beware the *priorité à droit.* On Saturday there is a lively market in the Old Town.

the lower classes. Formed secretly into a band, they waged implacable guerilla warfare on the occupant. After 1384 the *Tuchins* also attacked the rich and privileged orders, and became outright robbers. Having become dangerous to local authorities, they were overcome by the troops of the Duc de Berry.

CATHEDRAL DISTRICT
Cathedral★
🕓 *9am–6pm (Jul–Aug 8.30am–7pm).*
📞 *04 71 60 22 50.*

Built in late-Gothic style, it stands on the vast place des Armes and is a reminder of the town's vocation as a stronghold. Its construction, begun after the collapse in 1396 of the Romanesque basilica which preceded it.

The architect had previously worked for the Duc de Berry, which explains why the construction is not in the usual style of the region. On the west front, the right-hand tower is pierced with square mullioned windows letting daylight into two rooms once used as a prison.

Inside, the lines of the five aisles are strikingly sober. Under the organ loft, a 15C mural depicts **Purgatory and Hell**.

Old Streets
From place d'Armes, lined with arcades and old façades (particularly at the corner of rue de Belloy), walk to rue Sorel and the church of St-Vincent, a former Dominican convent.

Follow rue des Jacobins on the left, then rue de la Collégiale named after a disused 14C church: **Notre-Dame collegiate church** whose apse has Flamboyant windows. **Rue Marchande** has a few interesting old houses, including No. 31, the governor's house, a 15C mansion whose façade and courtyard can be seen, and at No. 15, Hôtel Brisson with a 16C courtyard, its original windows separated by columns with rope moulding. Other interesting streets include **rue du Breuil** (15C house at no. 8), and **rue des Tuiles-Haut** (old houses).

Ancienne Maison Consulaire
The façade of this former consul's residence dates from the 16C. The courtyard (enter through No. 17 bis), from which can be seen three houses successively bought by consuls in the 14C and 15C to serve as their consular establishment, has an old well, a 15C staircase turret and various painted inscriptions. It houses the Musée d'Art et d'Histoire Alfred-Douët (💰*see Museums below*).

Terrasse des Roches
Behind the east end of the cathedral.
From this square on the old ramparts there is a lovely view of the lower part of the town, the Ander valley and the Margeride mountains.

WHERE TO STAY	
L'Étape (Grand hôtel de)	①
Pagnoune (Chambre d'hôte La)	②
St-Jacques (Hôtel)	③

WHERE TO EAT	
Chez Geneviève	①

MUSEUMS

St-Flour prides itself on its rich cultural heritage and its many museums, which will enlighten you on local art and history.

Musée de la Haute-Auvergne

Place d'Armes. ○*Nov–Mar Thu–Fri 2–5pm; Oct and Apr–Jun Wed–Sat 2–6pm; Jul–Sept daily 10.30am–6.30pm.* ○*1 Jan, 1 May and 25 Dec.* ✆*€4 (free 1st Sun of month)* ✆*04 71 60 22 32.*

This museum is located in the former bishop's palace rebuilt in the 17C. Displays in the low 15C vaulted rooms explain how blue-veined Fourme cheese is made (including Cantal and Salers varieties) and the different facets of pastoral life, particularly the shepherd's huts or *burons* where the cheese is made. On the ground floor, in the former chapel, note a 12C polychrome wooden statue of St Peter from the church at Albepierre-Bredons, a 14C statue of St Flour, nine 16C carved wooden panels and a lovely set of Marian statues from the 12C to the 18C. The next room leads to the chapter-house, the only vestige of the Cluniac priory, where the treasure of the cathedral of St-Pierre and portraits of bishops are displayed.

The exhibits on the first floor concentrate on Auvergne folklore: popular music and its traditional instruments, hats and headdresses, a collection of regional carved-wood pieces, Cantal furniture (chests, cupboards, dressers, wooden bed panelling). The contents of the archaeological section mainly come from the digs at Mons and also from Laurie, near Massiac. A beautiful bronze **brassard★** consisting of six rings attached with a bar, and bracelets and swords, are the main items displayed.

Musée d'Art et d'Histoire Alfred-Douët

○*Nov–Mar Thu–Fri 2–5pm; Oct and Apr–Jun Tue–Sat 2–6pm; Jul–Sept daily 10.30am–6.30pm.* ○*24 Dec–2 Jan.* ✆*€4 (free 1st Sun of month, except Dec–Jan).* ✆*04 71 60 44 99.*

www.musee-douet.com.

Beyond the entrance hall with its collection of ancient weapons is the library which boasts Diderot's *Encyclopaedia*; the guard-room with its monumental fireplace and the Consul Room where fine tapestries hang, containing Renaissance furniture; the Louis XVI bedroom with painted wood panelling displays 18C furniture and the gallery is exclusively decorated with 17C paintings and furniture. In addition, you will see fine Limousin enamels and glassware as well as a collection of pewter and copper.

EXCURSIONS

Roffiac

2km/1.2mi W along D 40.

An old restored mill, **Moulin du Blaud** (♿○*Ring tourist office for information, or* ✆*04 71 60 75 75*), houses a trout information centre providing all you want to know about this freshwater fish which you can catch *(no licence required; fishing tackle hiring facilities)* in the lake. The museum, which illustrates fishing in the past, includes an observation laboratory, aquariums and a model of a dam. A nature-discovery trail runs round the lake.

Coltines

13.5km/8.4mi NW. Leave St-Flour on the D 679 then take the D 40. Turn right onto D 14 for Coltines.

👥 Musée de l'Agriculture★

○*Jul–Aug 10am–noon, 2–6.30pm; rest of the year 10am–noon daily except Sun, 2–5pm.* ○*1 Jan, 25 Dec.* ♿. ✆*€6 (children under 10, €3.50).* ✆*04 71 73 27 30.*

Located in a 17C house, this interactive museum is devoted to agriculture in the Auvergne region from the turn of the 20C to the 1950s.

Massiac

28km/17.3mi N of St-Flour on E 11.

This old village, in an excellent setting by the River Alagnon, is enlivened by a traditional weekly market (Tuesday mornings) and two picturesque annual fairs (Jun and Oct). The town's past is evidenced by the town hall, a fine 17C wooden house with a round stone tower belonging to the former ramparts.

Musée Municipal Élise-Rieuf

&🕐*May–Jun and 1st 2 weeks of Sept, Sun and public holidays 2.30–6pm; Jul–Aug daily except Mon 2.30–6.30pm.* ℰ*04 71 23 03 95.* *www.musee-elise-rieuf.org.*
The museum displays portraits of people from the Auvergne and China, Provençal and Scandinavian landscapes and Italian towns painted by Élise Rieuf, a native of Massiac (1897–1990).

🚗 DRIVING TOURS

VALLÉE DE L'ANDER
40km/25mi. Allow 4h.

▶ Leave St-Flour E onto D 990. After crossing the River Ander, turn right onto D 250.

Gorges de l'Ander
Continue along the edge of the river which runs between both rocky and wooded slopes. The path ends in a very picturesque meander, at the hamlet of Le Bout du Monde ("World's End").

▶ Turn around and at the crossroads take D 250 on the left, then left again onto a small road leading to Grizols. After the village, turn left onto D 40.

Site du Château d'Alleuze★★
&*see GORGES DE LA TRUYÈRE Driving Tour.*

▶ Leave Alleuze to the N on D 116.

Villedieu
The church, half-Romanesque, half-Gothic, has an attractive door with a wrought-iron knocker. In the chancel, notice the beautiful High Altar, the staffs and finely carved lectern.

▶ Continue along D 116. At the intersection turn right onto D 921, then onto D 926, heading for Murat.

Église de Roffiac
The church is a little Romanesque building from the beginning of the 12C.

▶ Leave Roffiac to the N on D 104. Park in the hamlet of Le Sailhant.

Cascade du Sailhant
15min on foot there and back.
🚶 The path to Le Sailhant (or Le Babory) waterfall weaves among the houses bordering the beautiful volcanic rocks on which Château du Sailhant is built.
The tiny cascade falls into a semicircle of tall cliffs; in the hollow lies a small lake. It is also possible to park at the entrance to the château and walk the short distance to the edge of the cliff, which offers a bird's-eye view of the cascade and the lake in its rocky surrounds.

▶ Leave Le Sailhant S along D 40. Further on, D 979 leads back to St-Flour.

ADDRESSES

🏨STAY

⬤ **Hôtel St-Jacques** – *8 pl. de la Liberté.* ℰ*04 71 60 09 20. www.hotel saintjacques.com. Closed Nov–Jan.* **28 rooms.** A former staging post on the way to Santiago de Compostela. Family rooms; city views.

⬤⬤ **Grand Hôtel de l'Étape** – *18 av. de la République par D 909.* ℰ*04 71 60 13 03. www.hotel-etape.com. 23 rooms. Restaurant⬤⬤.* 1970s building with large and practical rooms; ask for one with views of the mountains.

⬤⬤ **Chambre d'Hôte La Pagnoune** – *Valadour, 15320 Loubaresse.* ℰ*04 71 73 74 69. 7 rooms.* A 19C farmhouse with nicely decorated rooms and rustic dining room.

🍴EAT

⬤ **Chez Geneviève** – *25 r. des Lacs.* ℰ*04 71 60 17 97. Closed Sun and Mon except Jul–Aug.* A friendly ambiance and hearty regional cuisine using fresh, local produce make this small restaurant very popular. Reservations are advised.

Gorges de la Truyère★★

The River Truyère has carved narrow, deep and sinuous gorges, often wooded and rugged-looking, through the granite plateaus of Upper Auvergne. These are among the most attractive natural sites in central France. Dams, built to serve the needs of hydroelectric power stations, have transformed them into one long lake without affecting their picturesque aspect, except when the waters are low. There is no road alongside the river, though many cross it, offering lovely views.

- **Michelin Map:** 330: H-5 to I-6 – 4km/2.5mi N of Chaudes-Aigues.
- **Info:** Laval, 15320 Chaliers. ℘04 71 73 72 21.
- **Location:** The gorges lie a short distance to the south of St-Flour.
- **Don't Miss:** The Viaduc de Garabit.
- **Timing:** A visit to the gorges can be combined with a tour of St-Flour (*see St-FLOUR*). Allow at least a day to visit both.

🚗 DRIVING TOURS

1 ALONG THE GRANDVAL RESERVOIR★★
60km/37mi. About 2h.

▶ From the 165m long Garabit bridge there is a view of the viaduct.

Viaduc de Garabit★★
The Garabit viaduct is an elegant, and very bold, construction designed by an engineer named Léon Boyer and built (1882-84) by Gustave Eiffel. It has an over-all length of 564m and stretches across the River Truyère at a height of 123m. Its 448m superstructure is supported by a bold metal arch. Since the Grandval dam was built, the water below the viaduct has risen to the level of the support-ing piles of the bridge, which still stands 95m above the maximum level of the dam's waters. It was the experience gained in Garabit that enabled Eiffel to design and build his famous 300m tower in Paris for the 1889 World Fair.

▶ At the southern end of the bridge turn right to Faverolles.

The route crosses the rocky Arcomie ravine and the Arling stream and con-tinues to Faverolles where the Cantal, Margeride and Aubrac mountains come successively into view.

Château du Chassan
🕐 May–Oct by arrangement (except Jul–Aug daily 2–6.30pm). ⊚€6. ℘04 71 23 43 91.

GORGES OF THE TRUYÈRE

In a region where medieval fortresses abound, this château provides a more peaceful addition to the landscape. In the 18C Jean-François de Ponsonnaille demolished the feudal castle of Faverolles in order to build the present house, which has remained in the family ever since.

The main building, with its austere façade, is embellished by a carved balcony and flanked by two wings, one of which is still lived in, whereas the other has been turned into an exhibition hall. The hallway has a stone staircase topped with a basket-handled arch. A 15C horse-blanket on the wall bears the Ponsonnaille family coat of arms: three bells or cowbells flanked by two lions and topped with the count's coronet. In the dining room, the oak dresser still occupies the place for which it was made; its well-proportioned design distracts from any inherent heaviness.

Belvédère de Mallet★★

Park after a sharp left-hand bend and walk to the promontory (⚐ 10min there and back).

From here, there is a splendid view over Grandval reservoir. From D 13 turn right on D 40 through Fridefont, and down along a twisting route to the ridge of the dam itself.

Barrage de Grandval★

This "multiple-arch", concrete dam is supported by thick buttresses. The central arch of the dam houses a circular power station beneath a metal dome which produces 144 million kWh per year. The lake formed upstream of the dam is 28km/17mi long.

▷ After a very sharp left-hand bend the road drops into a wooded valley, offering splendid views of the ruins.

Château d'Alleuze★★

The castle ruins may be reached by car along D 48. Park the car near the grave-yard and follow the steep path for 5min.
The fortress was built in the 13C by the Constables of the Auvergne but belonged to the Bishops of Clermont when, during the Hundred Years War,

Bernard de Garlan – an adventurer who sided with the English – took it by storm and set up camp. For seven years he terrorised the region, pillaging a wide area and holding it to ransom.

The D 48 scenic road, west of Barry, skirts the narrow Alleuze valley, providing some breathtaking **views★★** of the castle and its ruins, a vast keep flanked by four round towers standing on a spur of barren rock. An even better view of the site may be had from the village of **La Barge**. Park beside the war memorial and turn left towards the church.

▷ In Alleuze turn back and take D 48 towards Lavastrie, then D 921 left to Chaudes-Aigues.

② THE PLANÈZE★
40km/25mi. About 2h.

At the foot of the Plomb du Cantal, the St-Flour planèze unfolds to the east and south-east; a vast plateau where fields of crops stretch as far as the eye can see, earning the region its reputation as the agricultural heart of Upper Auvergne.

Chaudes-Aigues
Chaudes-Aigues is ideally situated in the picturesque Remontalou gorge. As its name suggests, there are hot springs here, which have made it not only a spa resort, but also a town where hot running water has been piped to houses since ancient times.

Today, 32 of the springs are tapped (they are said to be the hottest in Europe). The springs were slow to find widespread popularity, largely because of the difficult access. However, they now seem to be on the verge of a massive boom, firstly due to the opening of the A 75 motorway and secondly thanks to the ongoing renovation work undertaken to develop the spa. Dominating the town on the south side is the Tour du Couffour, which still features its circular medieval keep.

The route briefly follows the west bank of the Remontalou valley then turns right onto the *planèze*, which offers extensive views of St-Flour plateau,

as well as the Cantal and Margeride mountain ranges.

Espinasse
From this small village there are plunging views down over the River Truyère. From Auzolles on, the road clings to the steep sides of the **Lévandes valley**.

A long, vertiginous descent into the valley follows, with breathtaking views of the wooded valley floor and southern slopes. After crossing the Lévandes, the road runs along the **Sarrans reservoir,** a particularly beautiful lake when water levels are high.

Pont de Tréboul★
This suspension bridge is a stunning piece of modern engineering. It replaced a Gothic bridge, built by the English in the 14C, which was submerged, together with the village of Tréboul, when the valley was flooded.

▷ Cross the bridge and turn left to Pierrefort. Park the car 600m after the overhead bridge, beyond a bend to the right.

Belvédère du Vézou★
🚶 *15min there and back.*
A path leads through broom and ferns up to a rocky height overlooking the confluence of the River Vézou and River Truyère. The **view** of the lake and the jagged **Turlande rocks** is very attractive. The scenic D 65 climbs the initially deep and wooded Vézou valley.

Beyond Le Meynial volcanic rocks can be seen on either side of the road.

After **Pierrefort** the road runs across a plateau and then returns to the Truyère Valley, dropping almost to the level of the water and offering splendid views over the lake.

Laussac
The village is built on a promontory that the flooding of the valley has turned into a peninsula. *The northern part of the gorge is described in this guide, whereas the south-western section is described in the Languedoc-Roussillon-Tarn Gorges guide (☞see ENTRAYGUES-SUR-TRUYÈRE).*

Ruynes-en-Margeride

La Margeride is a granite range lying parallel to the volcanic mountains of Velay. It stretches from the River Allier in the east to the high volcanic plateaus of the Aubrac in the west. The highest section consists of extensive plateaus covered with vast pastures interspersed with forests of pines, fir and birch. Below the Montagne lie "**Les Plaines**", undulating stretches of land broken by numerous spurs of rock.

- ⓖ **Michelin Map:** 330: H-4.
- ⓘ **Info:** Le Bourg, 15320 Ruynes-en-Margeride. ℘04 71 23 46 69.
- ⓛ **Location:** 13km/8mi SE of St-Flour via the D 4.
- ⓣ **Timing:** Allow a full day or more to drive around the plateau.

L'ECOMUSÉE DE LA MARGARIDE★

Since 1975 the open-air museum has specialised in a study of rural society in this region, it helps to preserve the natural and cultural heritage and gives visitors an insight into traditional lifestyles through the restoration of typical buildings, exhibitions, walks and regional discovery holidays.

The three sites here reveal different aspects of rural life in the Margeride region. The **Ruynes tower** at Ruynes-en-Margeride focuses on the aromatic and edible plants of yesteryear in the St Martin garden. At Loubaresse (17km/10.5mi to the south of Ruynes), **Pierre Allègre's farm★** portrays the life of a local family in the late 19C. At Signalauze (5km to the south of Ruynes), a reconstructed classroom from the **Clémence Fortille school** depicts school life in the first half of the 20C.

🚗 DRIVING TOUR

LE MONT MOUCHET
50km/31mi. Allow 3h.

Mont Mouchet (1 495m) is one of the peaks in the Margeride range and, in May 1944, it became one of the main centres of the Resistance in the Massif Central. On 2 June, 3 000 men from the French Maquis pushed enemy forces back beyond Paulhac. On 10 June, after occupying Ruynes-en-Margeride, where 27 civilians were massacred, a large German detachment pillaged and set fire to Clavières, but were halted by the Resistance Movement and had to withdraw to St-Flour. The following day the Germans again attacked Clavières, but the Maquis had time to organise its defences.

A national monument to the French Resistance Movement was erected here, and faces the Mont Mouchet Forestry Commission Centre that had been used by the Resistance in the Auvergne as its headquarters. A **museum** (ⓖⓞ*May–Jun and Sept daily except Mon 10am–12.30pm, 2–6pm; Jul–Aug daily 10am–1pm, 2–6pm). ⓐ€5. ℘04 71 74 11 91. www.resistance-mont-mouchet.com*) contains documents and photographs from the war.

The road now wends its way through **Auvers Forest**, known locally for its mushrooms and blueberries.

⊳ Go back to D 113, turn left, then 2km/1mi further on, turn left again onto D 41.

Auvers
Near the church, a granite base supports a monumental bronze statue depicting "**La Bête du Gévaudan**", a wild animal that devoured cattle and terrorised local farmers in the area; it was eventually hunted down and shot near Auvers by Jean Chastel on 19 June, 1767.

⊳ Continue along D 41, which skirts the east slope of the Mont Mouchet. After 5km/3mi, turn left onto D 412. D 4 will take you back to Ruynes.

VELAY AND BRIVADOS

When you think of Velay, three words spring instantly to mind: *dentelle* (lace), *lentilles* (lentils) and *verveine* (a green liquer flavoured with verbena, a herb). But more than this, Velay proves to be one of the most extraordinary regions in France. Likewise the Brivadois to the north-west, an area largely composed of small plains *(limagnes)* and the foothills of the Livradois and Margeride. Brivadois is mainly located on the Haute-Loire, but it overflows into Puy-de-Dôme and Cantal. Largely given to agriculture in one form or another; this is a peaceful and relaxing countryside.

Highlights

1 Trying any menu dish that includes **Puy lentils** (p198)

2 A leisurely exploration of **Puy-en-Velay** (p200)

3 Taking a driving tour around **Vallée de la Borne** (p207)

4 Wandering the old streets of **Brioude** (p210)

5 The largest Romanesque church in Auvergne; **St Julian's Basilica** (p210)

Verveine du Velay

The "formula" for Verveine liqueur was discovered in 1859 by a herbalist named Joseph Rumillet-Carter. It was initially marketed under his name. The plant, verbena in English, has been long considered to have magical properties; the Romans are known to have called it the "herb of Venus" because of its alleged aphrodisiac qualities.

Volcanic Plateaux

Many local villages throughout the region are built on or of volcanic stone. A tour of this region gives an excellent overview of the landscape. Such a tour might take in St-Paul-de-Tartas with its Romanesque church built of purplish volcanic rock; the attractive, once-for-tified village of Pradelles, with a local museum in one of the houses with Renaissance windows on the market square, and the Musée Vivant du Cheval de Trait (Draught-Horse Museum) housed in a 19C inn (including reconstructed workshops and a collection of carriages dating from the end of the 19C as well as various breeds of donkeys).

Puy Lentils

Lentils, which probably originated in the Near East where it was one of the first crops cultivated by Man, have been part of our diet since Neolithic times. They have the third-highest protein content of any plant-based food. Le Puy-en-Velay is renowned for its particular

Basilique St-Julien, Brioude

© Christian Guy/hemis.fr

VELAY AND BRIVADOIS

0   4 km

LE-PUY-EN-VELAY ★★★ Highly recommended

Lavaudieu ★★ Recommended

Paulhac ★ Interesting

Saugues If you have time

➡ Driving Tour showing point of departure

PARC NATUREL

Auzon

RÉGIONAL

DU

LIVRADOIS-

FOREZ

Paulhac
Brioude
Lespinasse
Vieille-Brioude
Lavaudieu
Château de Domeyrat
Mazerat-Aurouze
Plateau d'Ally
St-Ilpize
Allègre
Bellevue-la-Montagne
Chavaniac-Lafayette
Vorey
Blassac
Chilhac
Peyrusses
Lavoûte-Chilhac
St-Cirgues
Aubazat
La Rochelambert
St-Paulien
Arlet
Héraud
HAUTE-LOIRE
Langeac
St-Vidal
Polignac
Chanteuges
St-Arcons-d'Allier
Ste-Marie-des-Chazes
LE-PUY-EN-VELAY
Pinols
Forêt de Margeride
Pébrac
Prades
St-Privat-d'Allier
Monts
LA MARGERIDE
Mont Mouchet 1497
Solignac-sur-Loire
St-Didier-d'Allier
du
Devès
Saugues
Monistrol-d'Allier
Paulhac-en-Margeride
St-Préjet-d'Allier
Tour de la Clauze
Lac du Bouchet
Le Mazlieu-Ville
St-Christophe-d'Allier
St-Haon
Chapeauroux

N

ST-ÉTIENNE

variety of green lentils, grown on the thin soils of the region. They have a distinctive flavour, and are high in protein and low in carbohydrates, being widely used throughout France, but especially in the Auvergne, in soups and as an accompaniment to many rustic dishes. The lentils from Puy have their own appellation, in much the same way as wine and cheese; indeed it was the first vegetable in France to receive an AOC distinction.

The Beast of Gévaudan

La Bête du Gévaudan is said to have been a wolf-like animal that roamed the Auvergne in the 18C, killing about 100 people. Every effort to slay the beast failed and it ultimately achieved national notoriety. The King himself – Louis XV – took a personal interest, because of the unrest the killings caused in an area already burdened with religious and political tension. Many descriptions of the beast were put forward at the time and in the centuries that followed, from the fantastic to the prosaic, but none has ever been confirmed. Yet evidence remains to prove that the beast really did exist, and was not just a myth. Among all the popular monster stories La Bête du Gévaudan is unique: whatever it was, it left behind 100 corpses as proof of its presence.

Le Puy-en-Velay with St-Michel-d'Aiguilhe, Rocher Corneille and Cathédrale Notre-Dame

Le Puy-en-Velay★★★

The site of Le Puy-en-Velay is one of the most extraordinary in France. Out of a rich plain set in a depression rise enormous peaks of volcanic origin: the steepest, the St-Michel rock (or Mont d'Aiguilhe) is surmounted by a Romanesque chapel, making it even higher; the largest, Corneille rock (or Mont d'Anis) is crowned by a monumental statue of the Virgin Mary. This strange and splendid vision is complemented by a visit to the church of Notre-Dame du Puy, no less strange, almost oriental, which houses the Black Virgin still venerated by numerous pilgrims. On Saturday, market day, the town is a striking sight: place du Breuil and the old streets between the square and the market become incredibly busy. In autumn, the Festival of the Bird King (Fête du Roi de l'Oiseau) is held, in commemoration of an age-old local custom to discern the town's best archer, celebrated in a Renaissance atmosphere that pervades the upper end of the town during the festivities.

▶ **Population:** 19 712.
⚙ **Michelin Map:** 331: F-3.
🔢 **Info:** 2 pl. du Clauzel, 43000, Le Puy-en-Velay. ℘04 71 09 38 41. www.ot-lepuyenvelay.fr.
◖ **Location:** Le Puy-en-Velay is situated south-west of Lyon and St-Etienne, and is accessible from the A 75.
🅿 **Parking:** There are plenty of car parks around the southern ring road, but precious few within the town itself.
👁 **Don't Miss:** St Michel-d'Aiguilhe.
🕐 **Timing:** Head for the cathedral area first, and then wander the streets, or follow one of the Town Walks. Allow a full day to explore.

A BIT OF HISTORY

City of the Virgin Mary – The site of Le Puy seems to have been an ancient place of pagan worship (remains of a 1C sanctuary among the cathedral foundations), evangelised in the 3C. Apparitions

The Puy Basin

The Puy basin owes its formation to the collapse of the Vellave plateau, an after-effect of the alpine folding during the Tertiary period. Sediment stripped from the hills partly filled the basin, which was then cut by the River Loire. At the end of the Tertiary Era a series of volcanic eruptions convulsed the region; the bed of the Loire was shifted east.

During the Quaternary Era the erosion began again, forming spurs from the most resistant of the volcanic reefs, of various origins; these include basalt tables, the remains of lava flows (Polignac rock), volcanic chimneys (St-Michel rock, Espaly and Arbousset peaks) and parts of eruptive cones (Corneille and Ceyssac rocks, Denise volcano). As the lava flow cooled, combinations of prismatic columns were formed, such as those at Espaly. It is to these volcanic phenomena that the basin owes its highly original physiognomy.

of the Virgin Mary and miraculous cures near a dolmen capstone (since known as the "Fever Stone") encouraged the first bishops to come and settle here, probably at the end of the 5C. A basilica was erected, then a cathedral, around which a town soon developed.

In the Middle Ages, pilgrimages to Le Puy were popular since it was also a point of departure for the pilgrimage to Santiago de Compostela in Spain. Along with Chartres, Le Puy is the oldest site of Marian worship in France. Kings, princes and crowds of humble origin flocked here to invoke the mother of God.

In the 12C the havoc wrought by a group of privateers, known as **Les Cotereaux**, posed a serious threat to the pilgrimages and all they contributed to the town in terms of prosperity and renown. The **Black Virgin** brought even greater fame to Le Puy. The present statue, dating from 1856, replaces the original one mutilated and burnt during the French Revolution.

City of lace – In Le Puy and the Velay, as well as in the region of Arlanc, handmade lace was an important part of the local economy. It probably originated in the 17C and soon began to develop so that a special organisation was established. In all the villages, women worked at home for merchants in the neighbouring towns. "Collectors" who provided the lacemakers with thread and cartoons (patterns), served as intermediaries.

Originally reserved for the gentry, lace became so popular that, in 1640, the Toulouse Parliament outlawed its use as clothing. A Jesuit priest, moved by the distress of the lacemakers who suddenly found themselves out of work, managed to have the ban lifted.

Moreover, he invited his fellow missionaries to make Le Puy lace known throughout the world. This benefactor from Le Puy later became the patron saint of lacemakers. The lace trade retained its religious overtones for a long time: the art was passed on not only from mother to daughter but also by religious women known as "the beatified" who also taught catechism and cared for the sick.

WALKING TOURS

1 THE TREASURE TRAIL★★★

The cathedral dominates the upper part of the town, which is one large conservation area. Start from place des Tables with its graceful Chorister Fountain (15C) and walk up to the cathedral via the picturesque rue des Tables lined with stone steps bordered by several old houses.

Cathédrale Notre-Dame★★★

This marvellous Romanesque building, now a World Heritage Site, owes its unusual appearance to the influence of the Orient; Byzantine influence, a result of the crusades, can also be seen in the octagonal domes over the nave.

The original church corresponds to the present east end. When work was begun to extend it in the 12C, shortage of space quickly became a problem. The last bays of the nave (built two by two, in two stages), together with the west porch, were built virtually above a sheer drop, with the tall arcades serving as open piling. At the end of the 12C, the For Porch and St-Jean Porch were added. Extensive restoration was carried out on the cathedral in the 19C.

Route Under the Cathedral

Steps lead to the main door under the four bays built in the 12C. At the level of the second bay, two 12C **panelled doors★** close off two side chapels; their faint decoration in relief recounts the life of Christ. Go through the main door, framed by two red columns.

Straight ahead, the main staircase leads right into the cathedral, opposite the High Altar, which led to the saying that: "One enters Notre-Dame du Puy through the navel and leaves through the ears."

▷ Take the central staircase or, if it is closed, the right-hand one which leads to a door in the side aisle.

Interior

The most unusual feature of the church is the series of domes which cover the nave (that over the transept crossing is modern). Note the pulpit (**1**) and the beautiful high altar (**2**), which supports the wooden statue replacing the original Black Virgin burnt during the Revolution. The Baroque organ, recently

Cloisters, Cathédrale Notre-Dame

© Office de Tourisme de la communauté d'agglomération du Puy-en-Velay

restored, is located at the west end of the nave. Bishop Jean de Bourbon's 15C fleur-de-lis tapestry hangs at the end of the chancel.

In the north aisle hangs a large painting by Jean Solvain known as the "Vow of the Plague" (1630) (**3**) illustrating a thanksgiving procession held in place du For. In the north arm of the transept are beautiful Romanesque frescoes: the Holy Women at the tomb (**4**) and the Martyrdom of St Catherine of Alexandria (**5**).

A gallery on the left contains a **fresco of St Michael★** (late 11C-early 12C), the largest known painting in France depicting the Archangel Michael.

The famous stone known as the **"Pierre des fièvres"** (**12**) is in the chapel next to St-Jean Porch.

For Porch

This porch with highly elaborate capitals dates back to the late 12C. The smallest door is known as the "Papal Door" because of the inscription above it.

From the small place du For there is an attractive overall view of the site and a particularly good view of the belfry.

◘ Walk around the east end via rue de la Manécanterie.

St-Jean Porch

This porch preceded by a large flattened arcade was designed for sovereigns to pass through; it connects the cathedral to the 10C and 11C baptistery, whose entrance is flanked by two stone lions. The leather-covered doors have beautiful 12C strap hinges (wrought-iron brackets).

◘ Pass under the belfry to the small courtyard adjoining the east end of the cathedral.

On the way, note the tombs of abbots and canons, and in the courtyard (**6**), behind the Romanesque well, the Gallo-Roman low-relief sculptures incorporated into the base of the east end and the frieze above: they depict hunting scenes.

Cloisters★★

The beautiful cloisters abut the north face of the cathedral; each gallery is from a different period; the oldest, to the south, is Romanesque.

The **historiated** capitals in the west gallery include one (**7**) depicting a dispute about an abbot's crook, and another (**8**) showing a centaur.

A remarkable **Romanesque railing★** (**9**) closes the west gallery. From the south-west corner of the cloisters, a Romanesque chimney can be seen rising above the altar boys' house.

Around the cloisters, above the arcades, is a delicately decorated **cornice** illustrating a medieval bestiary. The polychrome arch stones and the quoins with their black, white, red and ochre

LE PUY-EN-VELAY

WHERE TO STAY	
Bilhac (Gîte de)	①
Domain de Bauzit (Chambre d'Hôte)	②
Dyke Hôtel	③
Gourmantine (Chambres d'hôte La)	④
Moulin de Barette (Hôtel Le)	⑤
Paravent (Chambres d'hôte La)	⑥

WHERE TO EAT	
Chamarlenc (Le)	①
Écu d'Or (L')	②
Lapierre	③
Poivrier (Le)	④

lozenges form a decor reminiscent of Islamic art.

Chapel of Relics

The Chapel of Relics or Winter Chapel derives its name from the beautiful gold altarpiece which, until the Revolution, housed relics brought to Notre-Dame du Puy.

Religious Art Treasury★★

The Treasury, displayed in the former Velay State Room above the Chapel of Relics, contains a large number of works of art, including an 11C silk cope, a 13C engraved enamel reliquary, a polychrome-stone 15C Nursing Virgin, a magnificent 16C embroidered cloak for the Black Virgin, and a piece of 15C parchment showing the Genesis of the World to the Resurrection.

Penitents' Chapel

The entrance is through a panelled wooden door carved in the Renaissance style and flanked by two groups of wreathed columns. Inside, the paintings decorating the gallery, the panelled walls of the nave and, in particular, the beautiful coffered ceiling, recount the Life of the Virgin Mary.

St-Jean Baptistery

This building, dating back to the 10C and 11C, and connected to the cathedral by the porch of the same name, served as a baptistery for all the parishes in the town during the Revolution.

Prior's Lodgings

🕐 *Jul–mid-Sept 10am–noon, 2–6pm.* 📞 *04 71 05 62 75.*
Adjoining the St-Jean Baptistery, the vaulted rooms of the former residence of the administrator of baptisms house a historical exhibition on Velay, and a remarkable collection of rural and craftsmen's tools.

Rocher Corneille

🕐 *Feb–mid-Mar and Oct–mid-Nov 10am–5pm; mid-Mar–Apr 9am–6pm; May–Sept 9am–7pm (Jul–Aug 7.30pm).* 🕐 *Mid Nov-Jan.* 📞 *04 71 04 11 33.*

This is the remainder of a cone, no doubt belonging to the volcano of which St-Michel rock is the chimney. The rock is surmounted by a monumental statue of Notre-Dame-de-France erected in 1860 by national subscription. This cast iron statue is 16m high and weighs 110t. An outstanding 213 cannon from among the trophies from the capture of Sebastopol given to contractors by Napoleon III were melted down to cast it.
It is possible to go up inside the statue to neck level.

▷ Return to place des Tables.

② THE OLD QUARTER★

The tall, red-roofed houses of the old town cluster around Corneille rock, while the circular boulevards mark the start of the lower, more modern town.

▷ Turn left onto Rue Raphaël.

Prominent citizens and members of the middle class once lived in this street. At No. 38 is the Lace Centre; No. 56 is a handsome 16C building on five levels, known as the Logis des Alix Selliers.

▷ At the end of this street turn left onto rue Saulnerie then left again onto rue Roche-Taillade.

On the corner with rue Cardinal de Polignac is the 15C Hôtel du Lac de Fugères and, further to the right at No. 8, the Hôtel de Polignac, the Polignac family mansion with its 15C polygonal tower. Back beyond rue Roche-Taillade, at No. 3 rue Vaneau, rises the Hôtel des Laval d'Arlempdes.

▷ Walk back down rue Roche-Taillade which runs onto rue Chênebouterie.

Note, at No. 8, the courtyard with a 15C turret, and opposite at No. 9, the birthplace (16C) of Marshal Payolle.
The road leads to place du Plot which, at the end of the week, bustles with a colourful market around La Bidoire fountain, dated 1246.

Nearby, at No. 8 rue Courrerie there remains an interesting 16C façade next to the Hôtel de Marminhac with arched windows bearing keystones carved with masks. Continue to place du Martouret – the site of many executions during the Revolution – where the Hôtel de Ville now stands.

▶ Return to place du Plot and follow rue Pannessac.

This part-pedestrianised street is bordered by elegant 16C and 17C Renaissance houses with overhanging fronts, sometimes flanked by a tower or watch-turret (Nos. 16, 18, 23).

To the right, some of the alleys – rue Philibert, rue du Chamarlenc – retain a medieval character.

The façade of No. 16 rue Chamarlenc, known as the Demeure des Cornards (the Cornards were companions whose prerogative it was to poke fun at the town's burghers) is adorned with two horned heads, one laughing, the other sticking out its tongue, surmounted by satirical inscriptions.

At No. 42 Rue Pannessac, the Logis des André, and at No. 46 the 17C Logis des Frères Michel decorated on the ground floor with masks and carved quoins, and on the upper storeys with masks, garlands and scrolls, both reveal the opulence of the wealthy merchant who lived in this district.

At the end of the street, the 14C **Pannessac Tower** retains a level of trefoiled machicolations. It is the last remaining trace of the original 18 fortified gateways, with twinned towers which allowed access through the town walls.

▶ Retrace your steps.

Église du Collège

At the beginning of the 17C, a Jesuit priest named Martellange built a building in the new Italian Baroque style for the order's newly founded college.

ADDITIONAL SIGHTS
St-Michel-d'Aiguilhe★★

🕐 *Feb–mid Mar and Christmas period (except 25 Dec) 2–5pm; mid-Mar–Apr and Oct–mid-Nov 9.30am–noon, 2–5.30pm (public holidays 9.30am–5.30pm); May–early Jul and Sept 9am–6.30pm; Jul–Aug 9am–7pm.* 🕐 *1 Jan, 25 Dec.* ∞€3.50. 𝄞 *04 71 09 50 03. www.rochersaintmichel.fr.*

St-Michel Chapel crowns St-Michel rock, a gigantic needle of lava which rises up in a single shaft to a height of 80m above ground level. Its slender belfry, in the form of a minaret, looks like a pointed finger of rock.

▶ Walk up montée de Gouteyron linking the Aiguilhe rock and the upper town. Alternatively, you can reach the foot of the rock by car and park nearby.

This chapel probably replaced a temple dedicated to Mercury. The building standing today, which dates from the 10C–12C, shows Oriental inspiration in its trefoil portal, its decoration of arabesques and its black, white, grey and red stone mosaics. Inside, the highly irregular ground plan follows the contours of the rock. The complexity of the vaulting testifies to the architects' ability to make the most of the site. The small columns, which form a sort of ambulatory around a short nave, are surmounted by carved capitals.

The vaulting above the small apse is decorated with 10C paintings. On the right, objets d'art found under the altar in 1955 are on display; note in particular a small 11C wooden reliquary Christ and a 13C Byzantine ivory cask.

A covered watch-path goes around the chapel, overlooking Vieux Pont, the old cusp bridge that spans the Borne.

Musée Crozatier

🕐 *Closed for renovation.* 𝄞 *04 71 06 62 40. www.lepuyenvelay.fr.*

The museum collections are housed in an imposing building (1865) erected at the bottom of the Henri Vinay garden, which includes, among other monuments, the beautiful portal from Vorey priory.

Église St-Laurent

The church of St-Laurent is a rare example of Gothic art in Velay; it dates from the 14C and was part of a Dominican convent.

🚗 DRIVING TOURS

VALLÉE DE LA BORNE

Round trip of 60km/37mi. Allow half a day.

▶ Leave Le Puy SW on D 590 to Espaly-St-Marcel.

Espaly-St-Marcel

Shortly before reaching the railway, turn right towards the car park.

Piton d'Espaly

This peak was formerly crowned with a castle which, after serving as a residence for the bishops of Le Puy (Charles VII, while dauphin then subsequently king of France, was given hospitality here during his frequent pilgrimages), was ruined during his battles involving the Catholic League *(private)*.

Rocher St-Joseph

🕐*Sanctuary: daily 10am–6pm.* 📞*04 71 09 16 71. www.josephbonespoir.org.* The upper terrace, built at the foot of the statue, offers a **view★** of the old town of Le Puy-en-Velay.

▶ Rejoin D 590 and continue towards Chaspuzac. Turn right onto D 113 then right again onto D 112.

Château de St-Vidal

🔒*Not open to the public.* This castle, its massive towers dominating the village which clusters below around a rise in the Borne valley, was the fief of Baron Antoine de la Tour, governor of Velay in the 16C. The castle has retained from its feudal days the vaulted cellars and Gothic kitchen with its immense fireplaces. Gothic and

Renaissance decorative elements from the alterations carried out in the 15C and 16C still remain, including the galleries with ribbed vaulting lining three sides of the inner courtyard, the beamed ceiling and carved stone doorway of the State Rooms, and the southern façade.

▶ Return to D 113, turn right towards Clazelle then left onto N 102 and right again onto D 25. When the castle appears in the distance, turn left.

Château de Rochelambert

🎫*Guided visits only (45mn): May–Oct daily 2pm, 3pm, 4pm, 5pm; Nov–Apr daily except Thu 2pm, 3pm, 4pm.* 🕐*1 Jan, 25 Dec.* 💶*€7 (children, 5–12, €5).* 📞*04 71 00 48 99. www.chateau-de-la-rochelambert.com.* Built on the banks of the River Borne, this 15C–16C castle set in pastoral surroundings was the setting of one of George Sand's novels, *Jean de la Roche*.

▶ Continue along the minor road for 2km/1.2mi then turn left onto D 13.

Allègre

This village nestles round the ruins of a feudal castle built on the southern edge of the Boury volcano. Once through the Porte de Monsieur, you see the Chapelle de Notre-Dame de l'Oratoire standing in the centre of the square.

Tourbière du Mont Bar

🚶 *2h there and back. The climb is rather steep, but shaded by fir trees.* This Stromboli-type volcano is the only one of its kind in France, for its crater is filled with a peat bog. A marked footpath leads to the bog and enables visitors to walk all the way round.

▶ Leave Allègre S along D 13.

St-Paulien

Once the capital of the Velay region, this village was a bishopric until the 6C. The church is a fine example of Romanesque style from Auvergne.

Château de Polignac

▶ Leave St-Paulien S along D 906 then follow D 102.

Polignac★

Rising on its basalt hillock, the fortress of Polignac still has imposing remains of its powerful martial past from both Antiquity and the Middle Ages. The view of the site, from D 102, is superb.

Church

This is a beautiful Romanesque building with a Gothic porch and a 12C Romanesque-Byzantine dome.

Château

🕑*Feb–Mar 1.30–5pm; Apr–Jun and Sept–Oct 10am–noon, 1.30–6pm; Jul–Aug 10am–7pm; 1st 2 wks in Nov 10am–noon, 1.30–5pm.* ✍€5. ℘*04 71 04 06 04. www.forteressedepolignac.fr.*
The building, which could house 800 soldiers as well as the family and servants, is perched on an enormous basalt platform, the remaining fragment of a lava flow; the platform sits on a softer strata of rock which has been protected from erosion as a consequence.

▶ Return to D 102 which leads back to Le Puy.

ADDRESSES

🍴STAY

🛏 **Dyke Hôtel** – *37 bd du Mar.-Fayolle.* ℘*04 71 09 05 30. www.dykehotel.fr. Closed Christmas week, 1 Jan. 15 rooms.* The contemporary rooms are small but tidy.

🛏 **Gite de Bilhac** – *Bilhac, 43000 Polignac.* ℘*04 71 09 72 41. www.gite-bilhac.com. 5 rooms.* This beautiful fully restored family farm has kept the rustic character of the hostel it was a few years ago. Accommodation is very simple, but well maintained.

🛏 **Chambre d'Hôte Domaine de Bauzit** – *43750 Vals-Près-le-Puy.* ℘*04 71 03 67 01. www.domainedebauzit.fr. 5 rooms.* Nestled in a vast area, this former monastery exudes serenity. The decor of the room pays tribute to four different countries in Asia, while the fifth and last, "Auvergne", is simpler but equally comfortable.

🛏 **Chambre d'hôte La Gourmantine** – *Chemin de Ridet, 43000 Polignac.* ℘*04 71 05 94 29. www.gourmantine.fr. 5 rooms.* Located at the foot of the castle, this fully restored 18C farmhouse enjoys a quiet corner of the village. Cosy rooms and home cooking.

🛏🛏 **Hôtel Le Moulin de Barette** – *43700 Blavozy.* ℘*04 71 03 00 88. www. lemoulindebarette.com. Closed mid-Jan–mid-Feb. 42 rooms.* In addition to the main ivy covered building, there are many "motel" rooms, simple and functional. Camping site adjacent; swimming pool; restaurant🍴🍴.

⊜⊜ **Chambre d'Hôte La Paravent** – *43700 Chaspinhac. 10km/6mi NE of Le Puy via D 103 dir. Retournac, then D 71. ☎04 71 03 54 75. www.la-paravent.com. 5 rooms. Restaurant⊜⊜.* The decor is authentic and the cosy bedrooms are very welcoming.

Puy laces

© Office de Tourisme de la communauté d'agglomération du Puy-en-Velay

♈/EAT

⊜⊜ **Le Chamarlenc** – *19 r. Raphaël. ☎04 71 02 17 72. http://lechamarlenc.free. fr. Mon–Wed lunch only; Thu–Sat lunch–dinner. Closed Sun.* This small restaurant in the historic centre serves a cuisine based on local produce and organic cereals.

⊜⊜ **L'Écu d'Or** – *59-61 r. Pannessac. ☎04 71 02 19 36. www.restaurantlecudor.com. Closed Sun evening.* In the pedestrianised part of town, this picturesque restaurant has an arched dining room decorated with murals. Regional cuisine.

⊜⊜ **Le Poivrier** – *69 r. Pannessac. ☎04 71 02 41 30. www.lepoivrier.fr. Closed all day Sun, all day Mon, Tue evening.* Sleek restaurant; specialities include beef from Haute-Loire.

⊜⊜ **Lapierre** – *6 r. des Capucins. ☎04 71 09 08 44. Closed weekends out of season, and public holidays.* A little family restaurant off the beaten path serving flavoursome traditional fare.

SHOPPING

Market – *Pl. du Plot. Sat morning.* On the public square with a water fountain, the country comes to pay its respects to the city in the form of baskets overflowing with the finest farm produce; berries and mushrooms in season.

Marché aux Puces (Flea Market) – *Pl. du Clauzel. Sat and fair days.* Bargain hunters, second-hand buffs and bric-a-brac enthusiasts should visit the Place du Clauzel.

Centre d'Enseignement de la Dentelle au Fuseau (lace-making centre) – *38/40 r. Raphaël. ☎04 71 02 01 68. www.ladentelledupuy.com. Closed public holidays.* We can thank St. François-Régis, patron saint of lace workers, for inspiring the creation of this establishment allowing us to discover lace in an original manner!

Maison de la Lentille Verte du Puy – *R. des Tables. ☎04 71 02 60 44. www. lalentillevertedupuy.com.* Emblem of the region, the Le Puy green lentil was the first vegetable in France to receive an AOC (Appellation d'Origine Contrôlée) label.

Distillerie de la Verveine du Velay-Pagès – *Z.I. de Blavozy, approx. 6km/3.6mi E of Le Puy via N 88, exit ZI de Blavozy, dir. St-Étienne, 43700 St-Germain-Laprade. ☎04 71 03 04 11. www.verveine.com. Jul–Aug Mon–Sat guided visits at 10.30am, 2.30pm, 3.30pm, 4.30pm; Jun and Sept by appointment only. €6.50.* The Pagès distillery takes visitors on a discovery tour of the production of Verveine du Velay liqueur.

Sabarot – *Z.A. Lacombe, 43320 Chaspuzac. ☎04 71 08 09 10. www.sabarot.com. Mon–Thu 9am–5pm, Fri 9am–4pm.* Founded in 1819, Sabarot was originally a flour mill. A century later, the company branched out into the Le Puy lentil. 20

ON THE TOWN

Le Michelet – *5 bis pl. Michelet. ☎04 71 09 02 74. Mon–Wed 7.30am–1am, Thu 7.30am–2am, Fri–Sat 9am–4am.* 1960s America and its symbols seem to attract the young people of Le Puy.

Le Bistrot – *7 pl. de la Halle. ☎04 71 02 27 08. Tue–Fri 5pm–1am; Sat 10am–12.30pm, 5pm–2am. Closed Sun–Mon and last 2 wks of Aug.* The terrace is calm despite its proximity to the old town.

The King's Head English Pub – *Pl. du Marché-couvert. ☎04 71 02 50 35. Mon–Fri 5pm–1am, Sat 10am–1am. Closed 1st week of Jul.* The decor is rustic, the choice of beers and whiskies inspired and the atmosphere as English as can be. Light meals include the Le Puy version of fish and chips.

Brioude★★

Built on a terrace overlooking the plain, Brioude is a beautiful and active city in the Val d'Allier with a pronounced southern style and rich heritage. Take time to stroll the streets and admire the beautifully restored façades of canonical houses. In the vicinity of Brioude, particularly along the banks of the Allier, many churches and castles wait to be discovered.

A BIT OF HISTORY

A saint, and a bandit from the Alps
– Legend has it that a tribune of the Roman Legion named Julian, who was born in the Vienne region and converted to Christianity, sought refuge in Brioude and was martyred in the year 304. Pilgrims flocked to Brioude to pray at St Julian's tomb, particularly during the time of St Gregory of Tours (6C).

From the 9C onwards, the God-fearing town was subject to the authority of the canon-counts of St-Julien and remained so until the French Revolution, which put an end to their aristocratic tyranny. Folk tales in Brioude still make reference to Mandrin, the notorious smuggler from Dauphiné. On 26 August 1754 he entered the town with a band of armed men, sought out the manager of the warehouse where tobacco was stored and taxed (the Farmers General held a monopoly on the sale of tobacco) and made the unfortunate man purchase a large batch of contraband Nicotine grass at an excessively high price. Mandrin then withdrew, while the people of Brioude turned a blind eye for they were delighted at the trick played on a system which they hated. The victim, however, never recovered from the shock; he died eight days later.

BASILIQUE ST-JULIEN★

St Julian's Basilica is the largest Romanesque church in the area, a "vast stone-built shrine standing over a famous tomb" (Bernard Craplet). It is typical of the Romanesque style seen in the Auvergne with its tiered east end and

▸ **Population:** 7 042.
◔ **Michelin Map:** 331: C-2.
▤ **Info:** Place Grégoire de Tours, 43100 Brioude.
ℰ 04 71 74 97 49.
www.ot-brioude.fr.
◖ **Location:** Brioude is southeast from Clermont Ferrand, and accessible via the A 75.
ℙ **Parking:** Limited parking in the town centre.
◈ **Don't Miss:** The town walk is especially agreeable.
◔ **Timing:** A relaxing half-day would be sufficient, including lunch.

varying colours of masonry, though it differs in other respects – the portals are topped with smooth or carved coving or zigzag moulding instead of the traditional string-course of billet moulding. The ornamentation at the east end is also noticeably Burgundian in style.

Exterior

Building began on the church as it stands today with the main entrance (the narthex) in 1060, and was completed in 1180 (chancel and east end). Its nave was raised and given rib vaulting in 1259, but the west front and square bell-tower above it were rebuilt in the 19C, as was the octagonal bell-tower above the transept crossing.

The fine concentric layout of the **east end★★** makes this the most remarkable part of the building. It is one of the last examples of Romanesque architecture in the Auvergne.

The side **porches★** with their groin vaulting constitute the oldest part of the church. They have an unusual appearance, the result of their use as chapels during the 16C and the inclusion of a gallery over the top.

Interior

The nave is particularly striking for its size and the warm hues of the red sandstone walls and pillars. The pebble pavement★ dating from the 16C in the nave and from the pre-Romanesque era in the fifth bay in the centre was uncovered, together with the small crypt beneath the chancel, following restoration and excavation.

The church contains a large number of **capitals★★** embellished with acanthus leaves, narrative scenes or themes commonplace in Auvergne churches.

The basilica contains a number of **altarpieces** and old **statues** that are worthy of note. The walls and pillars in the first bays, the ambulatory and the north gallery above the narthex still contain traces of 12C and 13C **paintings★**, which are surprising for their diversity, "modernism" and spirited representations of human figures. Turn to the right on entering the basilica to see:

(**1**) (south aisle) 14C statue of Christ the Leper (Crucifix), carved in wood with canvas backing, brought here from the former leper hospital in La Bajesse, near Brioude.

(**2**) (south aisle) 14C statue of Virgin Mary in childbirth in wood.

(**3**) (south aisle) 14C statue of Madonna with Bird carved in lava stone.

(**4**) (5th bay, south pillar) capital of Christ surrounded by the Evangelists.

(**5**) (first pillars of transept) carved corbels of heads of royal figures.

(**6**) (chancel) carved altarpiece (17C) behind the High Altar.

(**7**) (chancel, north pillar) capital depicting the Holy Women.

(**8**) (north aisle) 14C gilt wooden statue of the Madonna with Bird.

(**9**) (Chapel of the Cross) altarpiece attributed to 17C sculptor Vaneau.

(**10**) (3rd bay, north pillar) two capitals of groups of soldiers around a wounded soldier or prisoner.

(**11**) (south pillar in narthex) capital of the Punishment of the Moneylender; painting

of a woman in profile, with an enlarged eye.

(**12**) (St Michael's Chapel) – in the south gallery of the narthex *(access by a spiral staircase)* – 12C frescoes; capital depicting donkeys playing musical instruments.

TOWN WALK

Hôtel de Ville

This is built on the site of the former castle of the canon-counts of St-Julien. There is a fine view over the Brioude section of the Limagne plain and the Livradois range from the adjacent terrace.

Old Houses

In the district around the basilica is a network of narrow streets with old buildings and remarkable façades.

To the north, on the corner of rue Talairat: 17C mansion with turrets and carved door; rue du 4-Septembre: no. 29, Lace Centre *(see below)*; No. 25, 16C shop with arcades; No. 22, 15C building known as **Mandrin's House**; place St-Julien: 15C half-timbered house; south of the basilica: No. 21 rue de la Tour d'Auvergne, 18C mansion; place Eugène-Gilbert, Romanesque house with turret.

ST-JULIAN'S BASILICA

0   10 m

CHEVIOT ★★

Ambulatory

Pl. Grégoire
de Tours

Chancel

6

Crypt

7

5   5

TRANSEPT

3
2

Sacristy

4

8

1

9

Rue Notre-Dame

NAVE

★ Porche
Nord

R. du
Chapitre

10

Porche ★
Sud

11

Place
St-Julien

Narthex

12

N

Hôtel de la Dentelle

⏱*Apr–Oct Mon–Sat 10am–noon, 2–6pm, Sun 2.30–6pm.* ✆*€11.* ✆*04 71 74 80 02. www.hoteldeladentelle.com.*
The centre, housed in the 15C former residence of the counts of Brioude, contains collections of lacework and lace-making equipment as well as a workshop where lace-makers can be seen at work.

Maison du Saumon et de la Rivière

♿⏱*Apr–Jun and Sept Mon–Sat 10am–noon, 2–6pm (Sun, 2–6pm); Jul–Aug Mon–Sat 10am–12.30pm, 2–7pm, Sun 2–6pm; Oct and school holidays daily 2–6pm.* ✆*€6.50.* ✆*04 71 74 91 43.*
www.aquariummaisondusaumon.com.
The Atlantic salmon, which reaches the spawning grounds of the Upper Allier at the end of its 800km/500mi journey upstream, is part and parcel of Brioude's history. Before learning about the importance of salmon fishing in the Brioude area in bygone days, you can see over 30 local species of river wildlife. But the main attraction is the "salmon river", a curved length of glass where migratory fish swim in simulated currents.

EXCURSIONS

Château de Paulhac★

5km/3mi NW of Brioude via the D 20.
⏱*Closed for restoration following fire damage.* ✆*04 71 50 27 76.*
This magnificent fortress was first mentioned in documents in the 10C. The three towers and dungeon were built in 1160, and the castle itself rebuilt in the 15C and 19C.

Château de Lespinasse★

11km/7mi SW of Brioude via the D 588. After 10km/6mi turn left towards Lubilhac, then immediately turn left.
👥*Guided tours mid Jul–Aug at 3pm and 5pm.* ✆*€7.* ✆*04 71 76 82 12.*
www.chateaudelespinasse.fr.
Erected on the site of an ancient Gallo-Roman town, this medieval castle is one of the oldest buildings in Brivadois. Its square tower was built in the 12C. In the 15C, the advantageous

marriage of Louis, the son of the Lord of Lespinasse, to Jeanne, dauphine of Auvergne, allowed the construction of circular towers. From the castle you get a magnificent view of the mountains of the Livradois.

Plateau d'Ally★

22km/13.5mi SW of Brioude. Leave along the D 588, in the direction of Aurillac. After about 1km/0.5mi, turn left onto the D 12, then left again at the D 122, and then continue to Ally.
On the borders of Haute-Loire and Cantal, the small town of Ally lies on the edge of a plateau at around 1 000m. Until the last century, the people of Ally were mainly involved in farming along with craft production and mineral mining. This declined gradually, leading to a change of plan and a new emphasis on tourism; today its mines, windfarms and mills (✆*04 71 76 77 22)* all welcome visitors.

🚗 DRIVING TOUR

HAUT-ALLIER AND SÉNOUIRE VALLEY★★

120km/75mi. Allow one day.

▶ Leave Brioude to the E on N 102, heading for le Puy-en-Velay.

Vieille-Brioude

An impressive winepress dating from 1873 stands in place de la Croix, testifying to the town's important wine-growing activities in the past. A whole network of cellars and galleries was dug through the rocky spur on which Vieille-Brioude is perched.

Musée-jardin de la Vigne

⏱*Mid-Jun–mid-Sept 9am–7pm.* ✆*04 71 50 92 44.*
www.museejardindelavigne.fr.
Located at one end of the town, the Romanesque church stands in the middle of a garden where flowers grow next to herbs and medicinal plants.

CLERMONT-FERRAND

Parc

naturel   régional

Livradois-

Forez ★

Brioude ★★

Frugières-le-Pin

ST-FLOUR

Vieille-Brioude ★★ **Lavaudieu**

Château de Domeyrat

Paulhaguet

Mazerat-Aurouze

Chavaniac-Lafayette ★

★ **St-Ilpize**

Blassac

★ **Lavoûte-Chilhac** ○ **Chilhac**

St-Cirgues **Aubazat** ✝ **Peyrusse**

Reilhac   Héraud   Siaugues-Ste-Marie

✝ **Arlet**

Langeac

LE-PUY-EN-VELAY

Chanteuges   **St-Arcons-d'Allier**

ST-FLOUR

CHURCHES OF THE HAUT ALLIER

0   6 km

✕ **Pébrac**

SAUGUES

▶ In Vieille-Brioude, turn right onto D 585, which follows the upper valley of the Allier to Lavoûte-Chilhac.

St-Ilpize
This medieval town, clinging to a basalt rock and towering above the River Allier, is crowned by the ruins of a castle. The defensive walls enclose a 14C **chapel**.

▶ Rejoin D 585; turn right onto D 144.

Église de Blassac
The church is built on a flow of basalt. Its chancel contains a set of 14C frescoes.

▶ Rejoin D 585.

Lavoûte-Chilhac
This village stands on the banks of the Allier, which washes up against the walls of the houses. It has an elegant 11C

bridge, restored in the 15C, and a Gothic **church** and 18C Benedictine abbey.

Maison des Oiseaux du Haut-Allier
◷ Jul–Aug daily except Sat, 2.30–6.30pm. ℘04 71 77 43 52. www.lpo-auvergne.org.
This information centre of the Ligue pour la Protection des Oiseaux presents the bird population of the Gorges de l'Allier and organises nature trails.

▶ Rejoin D 585, which at this point hugs a meander in the Allier, giving a good view of the countryside.

Église de St-Cirgues
Inside, the two bays and the splays of the windows in the chancel are covered with interesting frescoes.

▶ Carry on along D585.

Église d'Aubazat

This village in a pleasant setting has a church with a Pietà and wooden statues representing an Entombment (15C).

▶ Rejoin D 585 for a further 500m, and at the crossroads turn right onto D 41, and then right again onto D 16.

Église d'Arlet

This hamlet at the bottom of the Cronce valley has a Romanesque church.

Chilhac

Small village built on a terrace of columnar basalt. Its **Musée Paléontologique** ♟♟ (◷*Easter–Oct Sat–Sun and public holidays – Jul–Aug daily 10am–noon, 2–6pm.* ⊛€5 (child 6–18, €3). ✆04 71 77 47 71/47 26. www.museechilhac.com) presents artefacts uncovered on local excavation sites since 1960.

Église de Peyrusses

This church contains a Virgin Mary in Majesty and splendid – if somewhat faded – frescoes.

▶ Follow D 585 through Reilhac.

Langeac

This busy little town lies in a cultivated "corridor" at the downstream end of the Allier gorge. One or two old houses are still to be seen along its streets.

▶ Leave Langeac S along D 585.

Église de Chanteuges

This attractive Romanesque church belonged to a local abbey which used to be the summer residence of the abbots of La Chaise-Dieu.

▶ Turn right under a bridge, onto D 30.

Pébrac

After running along the pretty little valley of the Desges between pine-covered slopes, the road brings you to this quiet hillside village with red-roofed houses and the ruins of an 11C **abbey**, which underwent extensive alteration in the 15C. Beautiful carved capitals have survived from the Romanesque era.

▶ Return to the intersection with D 585 and carry on along D 30, crossing to the opposite bank of the Allier.

St-Arcons-d'Allier

The **church** has a very classic Romanesque nave with basalt columns. Its arcades are roofed by sturdy relief arches. The **Musée du Fer Blanc** displays miscellaneous items made of tinplate: lamps, moulds etc.

▶ Cross the River Allier, drive through St-Arcons and take D 302 to Sauges. Turn left onto D 590, heading for Langeac. When you reach the locality called "Héraud", turn right.

Château de Chavaniac-Lafayette

🏛*Guided visits Jul–Aug 10am–6pm; Apr–Jun and Sept–Nov daily except Tue 10am–noon, 2–6pm.* ⊛€7. ✆04 71 77 50 32. www.chateau-lafayette.com.

The residence where Marie-Joseph-Gilbert, **Marquis de La Fayette**, was born on 6 September 1757, stands on one of the final outcrops of the Livradois area above the Allier valley; the history of Franco-American relations is more important here, however, than any archaeological feature.

A general biographical exhibition provides an introduction to the visit; next comes the kitchen where La Fayette's childhood is evoked, then the treasure room where personal objects and letters are displayed; this leads to the bedroom where he was born.

▶ Leave Chavaniac to the W on D 51; at the first crossroads, turn right onto D 21, then take D 4.

Mazerat-Aurouze

This village has a lovely church built in pink stone, with frescoes depicting the lives of monks and peasants.

Château de Chavaniac-Lafayette

© Luc Olivier/Photononstop

▶ Go back to Brioude via the Sénouire Valley, by taking D 4 to Paulhaguet, then D 56.

Domeyrat

The castle (🕐 *Jul–Aug daily except Sat 2–5pm.* 📞*04 71 76 82 95)* ruins dominating the Sénouire and its Romanesque bridge are a fine example of medieval military architecture. Dismantled in 1795, it still towers proudly above the River Sénouire spanned by the five arches of a Romanesque bridge.

▶ Continue along D 20, then D 203.

Lavaudieu★★

ᐸ *see LAVAUDIEU.*

▶ Return to Brioude on D 20.

ADDRESSES

🏨 STAY

🛏🛏 **Ermitage St-Vincent** – *Pl. de l'Église, 43100 Vieille-Brioude.* 📞*06 80 67 17 45. www.ermitage-saintvincent.fr. Closed Dec–Jan. 5 rooms. Restaurant* 🍽🍽*.* Comfortable roomsand a garden bursting with flowers.

🛏🛏 **Chambre d'Hôte Le Prieuré** – *43100 Lamothe.* 📞*04 71 76 44 61. 5 rooms.* Built on the heights above Brioude, this ancient priory offers a superb panoramic view.

🍴 EAT

🍽 **Pons** – *7 r. d'Assas, Brioude.* 📞*04 71 50 00 03. Closed Sun evening, Tue evening and Mon. Reservations recommended.* The local population patronises this restaurant for its friendly atmosphere and regional cooking.

🍽🍽 **Le Beffroi** – *R. du Vallat, Ardes-sur-Couze.* 📞*04 73 71 85 76. Closed Sat Sept-Easter.* Regional cuisine is served in two dining rooms whose vast bay windows look out on the garden.

SHOPPING

Cave Saint-Julien – *17 r. du Commerce.* 📞*04 71 74 90 18.* Wines from all corners of France line the shelves of this shop.

Gilles Guinet – *10 r. du Commerce.* 📞*04 71 50 12 47.* Vanilla *bavarois*, nougatine and caramelised pears *(le Manon)* vie for attention in the pastryshop.

Octagonal belfry, Lavaudieu

Lavaudieu★★

This hamlet, established on the banks of the Sénouire, still has the remains of an abbey founded in the 11C by St Robert, the first abbot of La Chaise-Dieu. The Benedictines continued to live here until the French Revolution.

SIGHTS
Abbey Church
The octagonal belfry has two storeys of semicircular bays. Inside, the nave is decorated with fine 14C **frescoes**★ in the Italianate style: they represent scenes from the Passion and such calamities as the Black Death.

Cloisters★★
◆▶Guided visits by arrangement, call or check website for details. ◌€6. ℘04 71 76 08 90.
www.abbayedelavaudieu.fr.
Little remains of the abbey buildings but there are particularly fine cloisters (restored), the only ones in the Auvergne to have escaped destruction.
They include charming single or double colonnettes, some of them twisted, some cylindrical or polygonal, with capitals decorated with carvings of foliage and animals.
The projecting upper storey is supported by oak posts. In the refectory is

- ▶ **Population:** 238.
- ◔ **Michelin Map:** 331: C-2.
- ▤ **Info:** Le Bourg, 43100 Lavaudieu. ℘04 71 76 46 00.
- ◖ **Location:** A peaceful setting midway between Clermont-Ferrand and Le Puy-en-Velay. 10km/6.2mi SE of Brioude.
- ◔ **Timing:** 2-3 hrs will suffice.

a 12C **mural** (restored) which covers the entire end wall.

Maison des Arts et Traditions Populaires
◔Same conditions and hours as the Cloisters. ℘04 71 76 08 90.
This Traditional Arts and Crafts Museum is housed in an old peasant baker's house dating from the late 19C. The oven, well, bread trough and counter are still visible. On the ground floor, the living room contains a collection of everyday domestic items. The byre houses tools from old crafts (clog-making, carpentry). Beside it is the *veillade*, the room where people gathered in the evening to chat, sing and tell stories. The cupboard contains an interesting collection of headdresses and nightcaps. On the first floor are three bedrooms.

© Stephane Debove/iStockphoto.com

The so-called Lacemaker's Room contains superb samples of pillow, crochet and bobbin lace and several lengths of trimmings.

EXCURSIONS
Frugières-le-Pin
3.5km/2.2mi E on D 20.
A museum devoted to the French Resistance and the deportation of many of its members was set up here as a tribute to Joseph Lhomenède, who was mayor of the municipality and who died in Buchenwald in 1944.

Musée de la Résistance, de la Déportation et de la Seconde Guerre Mondiale
⏱*Jun–Oct 10am–noon, 2–7pm; Nov–May 2–7pm.* €6. ℘*04 71 76 42 15.*
Located near the former station, the Second World War Museum contains numerous documents, posters, weapons and uniforms as well as moving photographs showing the sacrifices made by underground activists.

Vallée de la Sénouire
♿*see BRIOUDE.*

ADDRESSES

🍴STAY
THE ABBEY INN

🛏🛏 **Auberge de l'Abbaye** – ℘*04 71 76 44 44. Closed Sun evening except summer, and Mon.* A pleasant rustic atmosphere reigns in this village inn housed in an old stone residence. The tasty regional fare is served in a dining room with exposed beams and a hearth.

Saugues

This small town favoured by anglers is the site of a number of large markets. It is dominated by an ancient keep known as the "Englishmen's Tower". Between the Margeride and the Allier, which cuts an almost uniformly narrow valley forming magnificent gorges, lies Saugues country with its stone walls, mountain streams and harsh climate.

SIGHTS
👥 Musée Fantastique de la Bête du Gévaudan
👣 *Guided visits.* ⏱*Daily mid-Jun–mid Sept 2.30–6.30pm (Jul–Aug 10am–noon, 2.30–6.30pm).* €5.50 *(children €3.50).* ℘*04 71 77 64 22.* www.musee-bete-gevaudan.com.
This new museum is dedicated to the notorious creature that slayed and devoured countless sheep, goats and shepherds in the 18C, locally known as "La Bête du Gévaudan".

▸ **Population:** 1 933.
♿ **Michelin Map:** 330: D-4 – 44km/27mi SW of Le Puy-en-Velay.
ℹ **Info:** Cours St-Gervais, 43170 Saugues. ℘04 71 77 71 38. www.gorges-allier.com.
▸ **Location:** 44km/27.5mi SW of Puy-en-Velay.
⏱ **Timing:** Half a day. On Maundy Thursday, at nightfall, a long-standing traditional Procession of the Penitents is held.

Tour des Anglais
⏱*Daily Jul–Aug 10am–noon, 2.30–6.30pm.* €3. ℘*04 71 77 71 30.*
The name of this tower dates back to the Hundred Years War. The Treaty of Brétigny (8 May 1360) put an end to the contracts of the "mercenaries" enlisted in the English army. They became **free**

companions, dubbed "The Englishmen", living on pillage and robbery, and soon took over the town. The royal troops did not succeed in ousting them and it was only once they had been paid off in gold that they finally left.

Church
The church, surmounted by an octagonal bell-tower, houses a 12C Auvergne Virgin and a 15C Pietà as well as the shrine of St Bénilde.

Diorama sur St Bénilde
🔁 🕐 Jul–Aug 3–7pm.
✆ 04 71 77 82 53.
Thirteen set-pieces retrace the life of **Pierre Romançon** (1805-62), Brother Bénilde of the Christian Schools, the first state primary school teacher in Saugues, who was canonised in 1967. The exhibition is held in the actual school where he taught and was the principal.

EXCURSIONS
Tour de la Clauze
10km/6.2mi SW of Saugues on D 33.
This impressive-looking tower was originally built to keep watch over La Margeride. What remains of the formidable citadel is the *donjon*, once surrounded by fortified walls. The stronghold played a major role during the Wars of Religion but subsequently slipped into neglect.

🚗 DRIVING TOUR

FROM THE ALLIER GORGES TO THE DEVÈS
Round tour of 105km/65.2mi. Allow 4h.

▷ Leave Saugues to the N on D 585.

St-Arcons-d'Allier –
🔁 *See BRIOUDE.*

▷ Take D 48 which runs along the east bank of the Allier.

Chapelle Ste-Marie-des-Chazes
This isolated chapel on the east bank of the Allier stands on a peaceful spot

at the foot of a striking basalt rock. A monumental flight of 30 steps leads to a porch-belfry (rebuilt in the 19C) crowned by a conical lantern.

▷ Cross the Allier once more before going through St-Julien-des-Chazes and carrying on along D 48.

Prades
This small village is situated in a splendid **setting★** hemmed in by the valley sides. The sinuous D 301, half cut into the valley slopes, commands some beautiful views. After dropping downhill a little, it runs along the foot of the ruins of the **Château de Rochegude.**

Monistrol-d'Allier
This village lies in a very impressive **setting★** in the Allier valley.

▷ Leave Monistrol E on D 589, and turn right in St-Privat-d'Allier onto D 40.

St-Didier-d'Allier
This small village occupies a precarious site on a steep-sided rock.

▷ Take D 40 as far as Le Pont-d'Alleyras, then turn left onto D 33.

Lac du Bouchet★
A woodland footpath leads round the lake. Allow 45min.
🚶 This lake is 28m deep and at the bottom of an old crater, which explains its almost circular shape. The surrounding lake shore is covered with pine, spruce and fir trees planted between 1860 and 1900. No river or stream is known to feed the lake, nor any overflow channel, yet the clarity and freshness of the lake's waters show that they are being constantly renewed.

St-Haon
The village built on the edge of the plateau has a church with a remarkable late-12C apse.

▷ Follow D 31.

GORGES FROM THE ALLIER TO THE DEVÈS MOUNTAINS

Chapeauroux

This hamlet is built on the confluence of the Allier and the Chapeauroux in an attractive valley crossed by a sweeping railway viaduct with 28 arches.

▶ On leaving Chapeauroux, turn right onto D 321.

St-Christophe-d'Allier

From the road leading up the steep slope to this village there is a broad view of the Allier gorge.

▶ Follow D 32 and just before it crosses the Ance, turn right onto D 34.

St-Préjet-d'Allier

This village on the eastern flank of the Margeride has two dams spanning the Ance: La Valette and Pouzas.

▶ Take D 33 alongside the graveyard. It leads back to Saugues.

ADDRESSES

🛏 STAY

🍴🍴 **Chambre d'Hôte des Gabales** – *Rte du Puy-en-Velay.* ℘*04 71 77 86 92. www.lesgabales.com. Closed Dec–Jan except during Christmas school holidays. 5 rooms. Reservations required.* Skillful renovations have given this bourgeois house built in the 1930s a new appeal.

RECREATION

Sportival Haut-Allier – *43300 Langeac.* ℘*06 80 35 20 82. www.sportival.fr. Open all year.* This centre offers many outdoor activites: climbing, canoeing, kayaking, adventure trails, walking, off-road biking and more. The site is magnificent, in the heart of the Allier gorge.

The Livradois and Forez look out over a land of grass and trees, a land of long-established traditions. In the east of the Massif Central there is a marvellous, amorphous realm of wide, open spaces, a landscape that is hard to take in at first glance. Through the middle flows the River Dore, with its nourishing waters. On its right bank, the Monts du Forez, covered with pine, seem untouched since the dawn of time. On the left, the Livradois reigns, made up of a series of plateaux and granite outcrops, divided by hollows.

Highlights

1 Bird watching in the **Livradois-Forez national park** (p222)

2 Taking a walk around the old part of **Thiers** (p223)

3 Treating yourself to a fine piece of **Thiers** cutlery (p223)

4 Visiting the paper-making mill **Richard de Bas** in Ambert (p230)

5 Admiring exquisite 16C tapestries at the abbey of **La Chaise-Dieu** (p233)

Museums

The residents of the areas embraced by the park are proud of their history and the craftsmanship they have practised over the centuries, reflected in various local museums: cutlery-making (Thiers); lace-making (Arlanc); paper-making (Richard-de-Bas); agriculture and cheese-making (Ambert).

La Moule Perlière

Rediscovered in 1994, the cool and clear waters of the Livradois-Drill have yielded pearl-bearing mussels, although they are small and of little value. Annoyingly, you can neither eat them nor gather them: the so-called "pearl mussel" has protected status in Europe, which prohibits any interference either with the mussels themselves or their environment.

Water, Water Everywhere

The importance of water, the most discreet of elements, cannot be underestimated. Man has adopted it and put it to work, making the fortune of Thiers in particular. The combination of the Dore and the spirited Durolle enabled the town to become the capital of cutlery-making from the 16C. At Ambert, water has been used for the odyssey of paper-making. In the 16C, more than 300 paper mills operated in the area.

A special reminder of those pioneering times remains in Richard de Bas Mill in Ambert, which today houses an eco-museum that brings the history of the industry back to life.

Cloisters, Église Abbatiale St-Robert, La Chaise-Dieu

© Luc Olivier/Photononstop

THIERS AND LIVRADOIS-FOREZ

0   4 km

Map labels

Maringues

D 906   D 201

D 224   Dore   D 324

A 89   D 2089

D 2089   D 1089   A 89   ST-ÉTIENNE

Thiers

D 2089

Vallée des rouets

les Margerides

Lezoux   Noirétable   D 44

D 2089   D 212   D 7   D 53   D 1089

Ravel   D 229   D 223   D 44   **Vollore**   D 312   **Vollore-Montagne**

CLERMONT-FERRAND   D 212   D 906   D 223   **Courpière**   D 42   **LOIRE**

Aulteribe   D 223

PUY-DE-DÔME   D 42   D 97   D 37   *Monts du Forez*

Billom   D 997   **Sauviat**   D 906   **Olliergues**   D 102   D 6   LYON

St-Dier   D 58   *PARC*   D 225   ⚠ *Col du Béal*

d'Auvergne   D 997   D 40   1390   D 255

Les Martinanches   D 65   **Cunlhat**   D 37   **Job**   *Rocher de la Volpie*   D 496

NATUREL   D 996   D 67   *Col des Supeyres*   1366

D 225   **St-Amant-Roche-Savine**   *Cirque de Valcivières*   D 67   **Jasserie du Coq-Noir**

La Ferme des Bois Noires   St-Eloy-la-Glaciere   **Ambert**   D 906   **Moulin Richard de Bas**

Sauxillanges   D 105   D 37   **Musée de l'école 1900**

▲ *Butte d'Usson*   **Fournois**   **Livradois-Forez tourist train**

RÉGIONAL   D 999   **Marsac-en-Livradois**

ISSOIRE   D 214   **St-Germain-l'Herm**   D 906   La Chaulme

D 33   D 205   D 257

Brassac-les-Mines   D 999   **Novacelles**   D 205   D 104

Auzon   D 5   *DU LIVRADOIS-*   D 105   D 300   **Arlanc**   D 498

N 102   D 588   *FOREZ*   D 907   **Dore-l'Église**   D 9

ALLIER   D 906   Craponne-sur-Arzon

La Chaise-Dieu   D 498

D 13   **HAUTE-LOIRE**   D 906   D 9

Monts du Forez ★★ Recommended

Thiers ★ Interesting

Ambert If you have time

⬅ Driving Tour showing point of departure

Luxurious Peasant Dishes

The authentic recipes of Auvergne, which are still widely enjoyed today, as with all traditional or so-called "local" or "regional" dishes, were primarily cheap yet nourishing peasant dishes based on what was available: potatoes, pork and vegetables. The Auvergne speciality "Potée", for example, is a hotpot-type dish containing lard, ham hock, ribs, fresh local sausage, a few carrots, turnips, haricot beans, cabbage and potatoes, and clearly adheres to the underlying principles of peasant cooking. Saint-Pourçain *andouillette* (a type of sausage) and Mézenc beef (described as a "fin gras", this meat is marbled through with fat, which makes it melt in the mouth), served with green Puy lentils – the AOC designation differentiates Puy lentils from other pulses – are just some of the choice dishes you'll find at the Auvergne table, almost everywhere.

Parc Naturel Régional Livradois-Forez★

One of the largest protected areas in France, the Livradois-Forez National Park was set up in 1986 and covers an area of 297 000ha of woodlands and traditional farming. The park seeks to revitalise a declining rural environment and to present and promote local heritage, especially crafts and industry.

A haven for nature lovers, the landscape and its flora and fauna have been shaped by altitude, numerous waterways and a varied terrain.

VISIT

The Maison du Parc offers information about getting around, and can give details about the **Livradois (Agrivap) discovery trains** (*see p230*) that make exploring the vast area a bit easier. There are numerous waymarked paths crisscrossing the park, dedicated to walking and biking. Those fond of sports will appreciate the facilities for water sports and paragliding.

⚓ **Michelin Map:** 326: H/J 8/11 and 330 I/L 1/3.

ℹ **Info:** Maison du Parc 63880 Saint-Gervais-sous-Meymont. ☎04 73 95 57 57. www.parc-livradois-forez.org.

▶ **Location:** 65km/40mi SE of Clermont-Ferrand.

👓 **Don't Miss:** The music festivals of La Chaise-Dieu and Thiers.

👪 **Kids:** Explore the walking trails.

🕐 **Timing:** You can spend a whole day here; visit in spring or autumn to see migrating birds.

ADDRESSES

🏠 STAY

🍽🍽🍽 **Auberge de Chabanettes** – *Côtes de Chabanettes, 63590 Auzelles. 29km/18mi E of Issoire. ☎04 73 72 86 27. www.aubergedechabanettes.com. Closed Jan. 5 rooms.* This delightful family run boutique-hotel and spa in the heart of the Livradois-Forez National Park, offers a splendid and peaceful escape from the brouhaha of town and city life. Restaurant with good wine list, parking, WiFi, Whisky bar, spa, sauna and riverside terrace. Perfect for a touch of escapism.

Parc Naturel Régional Livradois-Forez near Ambert in winter

© Christian Guy/hemis.fr

Thiers★★

The town's **site★★** – on the side of a ravine through which the River Durolle flows – has a magnificent view over the Limagne and the Dômes mountain range. This, and the town's historic district, make Thiers an attractive tourist destination. It is the waters of the Durolle which made Thiers' fortune: paper and knives have been made here since the 15C and although paper-making has nearly disappeared, cutlery-making continues to contribute to the town's renown. The town was first founded on the south bank of the Durolle, around the original church of Le Moutier.

- ▶ **Population:** 11 685.
- **Michelin Map:** 326: I-7
- **Info:** Hôtel du Pirou, 63300 Thiers. ℘04 73 80 65 65. www.thiers-tourisme.fr.
- **Location:** Thiers lies within the Parc Naturel Régional du Livradois-Forez, just 40km/25mi east of Clermont-Ferrand.
- **P** **Parking:** Beside the Eglise St Genès, and at the northern end of town.
- **Don't Miss:** The view from the Terrasse du Rempart; Maison des Couteliers.
- **Timing:** Allow half a day to explore this lovely town.

WALKING TOURS

1 THE OLD CITY★

A number of 15C, 16C and 17C half-timbered houses have been restored in the centre of the old town (Vieux Thiers). These picturesque houses line narrow, winding streets known as *peddes*, many of them reserved for pedestrians.

▶ Start from place de la Mutualité and walk down rue Prosper-Marilhat leading onto rue Terrasse.

Terrasse du Rempart★
The terrace offers a beautiful **panorama★** of the Limagne, the Dore mountain range and the Dômes mountain range. The view of the sunset can be magnificent from here. The viewing table is made of enamelled lava stone.

▶ 50m further on, turn right onto rue du Bourg.

Rue du Bourg
At Nos. 10 and 14 note the 15C Volvic-stone doorways; No. 20 is a 16C house.

Place du Pirou
This square is dominated by the early-15C **Hôtel du Pirou★**. The house, with its pointed gables and timbered façade, is a handsome example of civil architecture of the Middle Ages.

Rue Grenette
No. 8 is a 16C and 17C house (Maison dite de Lauzun).

Rue de la Coutellerie
Note the unusual houses at Nos. 12 and 14, the latter with wooden corbels carved in a somewhat free and vigorous style. No. 21, the Maison de l'Homme des Bois (15C), is decorated with an enigmatic ape-like figure. This house and the ancient alderman's house at No. 58 contain the Cutlers' Centre and the Cutlery Museum.

Musée de la Coutellerie
23 and 58 rue de la Coutellerie.
Guided visits (1h30): Feb holidays–May, Oct and Christmas holidays daily except Mon 10am–noon, 2–6pm; Jun and Sept daily 10am–noon, 2–6pm; Jul–Aug daily 10am–12.30pm, 1.30–7pm. €7 (Jun–Sept; €5.80 otherwise). Jan, 1 May, 25 Dec. ℘04 73 80 58 86.
www.musee-coutellerie-thiers.com.

THIERS

0 _____ 200 m

LE VIEUX THIERS

Pl. de la Mutualité
Pl. Belfort
Pl. Duchasseint
R. des Grammonts
Pl. A. de St-Exupéry
R. Prosper-Marilhat
Av. Ph. Dufour
R. Conchette
Terrasse du Rempart
R. du Bourg
Hôtel du Pirou
Pl. et R. du Pirou
R. Grenette
Musée de la Coutellerie
St-Genès
R. de la Coutellerie
Musée de la Coutellerie
Pl. Lafayette
R. du Moutier
Logis abbatial
St-Jean
Pl. du Navire
Orangerie
St-Symphorien du Moutier
Creux de l'Enfer
Centre d'art contemporain
Pont des Ceychalles

At No. 21, five rooms are devoted to the history of the cutlery industry in Thiers: history and origins, crafts and techniques, working conditions, leisure, commercialisation and advertising etc. At No. 58 craftsmen may be watched working on the different phases of the manufacture of a knife. Workshops on the ground floor specialise in the polishing, shaping, mounting and carving of top-quality knives in limited numbers. In the basement a *son et lumière* show evokes the deafening world of the forge (power-hammer, furnace etc).

▶ Follow rue Chabot on the left and take the first street on the left leading to the steps; turn left then first right onto impasse Jean-Brugière.

Église St-Genès

This Romanesque church has undergone many alterations. The west front and the bell-tower have been rebuilt but the south transept retains the interesting decoration on its gable and graceful windows.

▶ Walk through the public gardens surrounding the east end of the church of St-Genès.

The north door, which gives onto place du Palais, is preceded by an 18C porch, in the wall of which an elegantly carved 14C recess has been incorporated.

▶ Turn right onto rue du Palais and leave place du Pirou to the right.

Thiers Cutlery Trade

For many centuries Thiers has been the largest French cutlery manufacturing centre. The origin of the town's specialisation dates back to the Middle Ages: legend has it that Auvergne knights from the first crusade (1096–99) brought back the secret of cutlery manufacture. In fact, the Thiers metallurgical industry dates back to the 14C. By the 16C, the town's cutlery trade had developed sufficiently for it to start exporting its products to Spain, the Netherlands and Lombardy.

Blades of all types were sharpened on grinding wheels powered by the waters of the Durolle. Cutlery production has subsequently been modernised, leaving the traditional figure of the knife-grinder lying face down over his grinding-wheel with his dog lying on his legs to keep him warm as but an image of the past. Developments in technology and electricity have led to enormous factories. Today Thiers still has nearly 300 manufacturers or craftsmen.

Rue du Pirou

At No. 11 stands the **Maison des Sept Péchés Capitaux**, named after the decorations (Seven Deadly Sins) on the seven beams supporting the first floor; at No. 9, note a corbelled construction. Further along is the "Coin des Hasards", an intersection dominated by the tower of Maître Raymond (15C), one of the ancient towers from Thiers castle.

▶ Continue along rue Alexandre-Dumas and place Antonin-Chastel. Take a few steps to the left and follow rue Conchette.

Rue Conchette

In the courtyard at No. 4 there is a 16C staircase; at No. 10, an inner façade on pillars. At No. 18, in the courtyard with its turret, two 16C medallions.

▶ Return to place de la Mutualité.

② THE OLD MANUFACTURING VALLEY

This tour starts from the Maison des Couteliers. The return journey is by local bus (TUT).

▶ Walk down rue du Quatre-Septembre, heading towards the Creux de l'Enfer (signposted itinerary). You will reach place St-Jean and its church.

Église St-Jean

This 15C church occupies a picturesque site overlooking the Durolle.

▶ A path to the right as you leave the church runs round the church and leads to Creux de l'Enfer.

Creux de l'Enfer, Centre d'Art Contemporain

&♿⏰*Daily except Tue 1–6pm.*
⏰*1 May and 25 Dec.* ☎*04 73 80 26 56.*
www.creuxdelenfer.net.

This contemporary arts centre is set up on the premises of a former factory facing the impressive Durolle waterfall. Exhibitions focus on unusual aspects of modern art that draw inspiration from the nearby landscape. The site is also used as an artists' workshop for experimental projects.

Creux de l'Enfer, Centre d'Art Contemporain

▷ Walk along avenue Joseph-Claussat.

Vallée de la Durolle

The route follows the Durolle. The river's many waterfalls once operated numerous cutlery works. There were at least 140 falls over a distance of 3km/2mi. The most picturesque are those known as the **Creux de l'Enfer** ("Hell-Hole") falls, just before St-Jean bridge, and the **Creux du Salien** falls, just after Seychalles bridge (15C).

Église du Moutier

The church was part of the powerful Benedictine abbey founded in the 7C. At the corner of avenue Joseph-Claussat stands the fortified **Logis Abbatial du Moutier**, the last remains of the abbey.

Orangerie

&. ⊙Wed only 2.30–5.30pm. ℘04 73 80 53 53. www.ville-thiers.fr.
Located in Moutier park, the orangery has been turned into an information centre on the environment. The large hothouse is landscaped: pool, walls made of plants and exotic species contrast with a desert environment.

▷ Continue along rue du Moutier to place du Navire (note the Pont du Navire, listed as a historic monument) then travel back to the town centre by public transport (from the church of Moutier).

EXCURSIONS
Château et Jardins de la Chassaigne

Leave Thiers N towards Vichy. Beyond the tunnel, turn left onto D 94C, and follow signposts to the castle. Visitors enter through the gardens. ♥ Guided tours of the interior. ⊙Jun–mid-Sept daily except Tue 2.30–6pm. ⊛€5. ℘04 73 80 59 08. http://lachassaigne. pagesperso-orange.fr.
The 15C manor, which had already suffered during the Revolution, was dismantled at the beginning of the 20C; its trees were also felled with the exception of the lime tree in the main courtyard.

Although the castle was still inhabited, its upkeep was neglected until acquired new owners in 1986.

⚤ ILOA "Les Rives de Thiers"

12km/7.5mi. At the large roundabout at the entrance to Thiers, head for Vichy. Take the fork at the toll-booth and at the next roundabout turn left.
This large leisure park offers facilities for a great many sports: rambling, cycling, riding, swimming, tennis and golf.

St-Rémy-sur-Durolle

9km/6mi N on N 89 and a small road on the left.
The scenic road winds through woodland before reaching St-Rémy. This cutlery-making centre is built on the southern flank of "Thiers mountain", an extension of the Bois Noirs massif.

▷ In St-Rémy, take a road uphill on the left to the wayside cross. Leave the car near the sports ground and walk to the top of the cliff (👣15min there and back).

From the wayside cross, the **panorama★** includes the Forez mountains, the Margerides, the Plomb du Cantal and the Dômes mountain range. Northeast of St-Rémy, on the right of D 201, a large lake offers various watersports such as swimming, sailing and rowing.

🚗 DRIVING TOURS

① LES MARGERIDES★
5km/9.5mi. Allow 3h.

A delightful drive across the plateaux and valleys of Les Margerides (⊛see RUYNES-EN-MARGERIDE).

▷ Leave Thiers NE along N 89 towards Lyon.

From the look-out point by the turn-off to St-Rémy, there is an attractive view over to the right of the Durolle gorge, Thiers and the Limagne.

THE FOREZ MOUNTAINS

0   4 km

N

In Château-Gaillard, take the first turning to the right.

Vallée des Rouets
Walking boots recommended.
Guided visits in the mill – €5, rest of the visit unguided. Jul–Aug noon–7pm; Jun noon–6pm; Sept 2–6pm. 04 73 80 81 95. www.ville-thiers.fr.

The various paths formerly used by craftsmen have been restored and are now clearly signposted, offering interesting views of both architectural features and natural sites. There used to be 27 cutlery workshops in the valley; the last one in operation was the Rouet Lyonnet (1816) which closed in 1976.

Beyond Château-Gaillard and Bellevue turn right on D 320.

The road crosses the river and winds through green and fertile countryside.

On leaving Vernières there is a view of the Durolle valley, and the village of St-Rémy on the mountainside; D 102 descends to Thiers and makes a right-hand bend near Borbes rock.

Rocher de Borbes

From the rock there is an extensive **view★** of the Limagne, the Dômes and the Dore mountain ranges, the Livradois and, in clear weather, the Cantal mountains.

▶ Continue on D 102 to return to Thiers.

② LA DORE TO MONTS FOREZ★★

130km/81mi. Allow one day.

This Dore is a tributary on the right bank of the Allier, rising in the mountains of the Livradois area. It flows down in a south-easterly direction into deep, granite gorges then turns northwards to cross, at a leisurely pace, the Ambert plateau.

▶ Leave Thiers to the W and drive up to Pont-de-Dore to cross the river. Follow D 906, then D 44 on the right.

Château d'Aulteribe★

5km/3mi NW along D223.
🕐*Jan–mid-May and mid-Sept–Dec daily except Mon 10am–noon, 2–5.30pm; mid-May–mid-Sept daily 10am–noon, 2–6.30pm.* 🕐*1 Jan, 1 May, 1 and 11 Nov, 25 Dec.* ✎€6.
🖉*04 73 53 14 55.*
www.chateau-aulteribe.fr.
This castle was rebuilt in the 19C in the Romantic style, on the site of an austere medieval construction. The estate was bequeathed to the National Historic Monuments Trust in the 19C.

▶ Take D 223 then turn right onto D 906.

Courpière

The town lies at the entrance to a gorge formed by the River Dore. In addition to its picturesque houses, Courpière boasts a number of interesting castles in the vicinity and is the ideal starting point

for excursions through Livradois country. During the summer season visitors can take the **Livradois-Forez Tourist Train** *(Livradois-Forez tourist railway –* 🔶*see AMBERT, p230)*, which runs along the Dore valley between Courpière and Ambert.

Church★

This Auvergne-style Romanesque building is topped by a Gothic bell-tower.

Château de la Barge

2km/1mi N on D 58 in the direction of Escoutoux. ♿*⌐Guided visits Jul–Aug Mon–Fri 2pm, 3.30pm, 5pm; May and Sept–Oct by appointment.*
🖉*04 73 53 14 51.*
This handsome residence is still circled by its moat. In the 16C the former citadel was converted into a Renaissance château. Two centuries later, it was graced with a terraced garden which its present owners are constantly refurbishing.

▶ Beyond Courpière, continue to Ambert on D 906; right onto D 316.

Sauviat

This village stands high above a meander of the River Dore as it flows through a narrow valley.

▶ Drive down on D 316 and rejoin D 906 on the right.

Olliergues

Situated on the north bank of the Dore, over which there is a 15C bridge, Olliergues has terraces of houses rising up the hillside and features a castle that once belonged to Marshal Turenne's family.

▶ Continue towards Ambert and 3km/2mi before reaching Ambert, turn right onto D 66 and right again onto a road leading to Volpie rock.

Rocher de la Volpie★

🔼 From the rocky Volpie peak the **view★** stretches over the Livradois mountains with the Ambert plain in the foreground. Those reluctant to tackle the climb can take a path to the right beyond the farm, which leads across the meadows to the foot of the rock (*20min there and back*).

▶ Rejoin D 66 and turn right.

Église de Job
Superb 15C church topped by a large square belfry.

▶ D 255 to the right then D 40 leads to Col du Béal.

Col du Béal★
From this pass there is a wide panoramic view over the mountains of the Auvergne and the Lyonnais area.

▶ Leave Col du Béal on D 102.

The road crosses vast expanses of pasture and soon provides a superb view of the mountains of the Livradois area.

▶ In Brugeron, take D 37 towards Olliergues and, when you reach the hamlet of Les Mines, turn right onto D 97.

The road follows the Faye valley.

▶ Shortly after crossing the River Faye, turn right onto D 42.

Vollore-Montagne
This mountain village is an ideal centre for walkers. The forests, the landscapes of woodland and meadow, and local beauty spots make this part of the journey most enjoyable.

▶ Drive W on D 312.

Château de Vollore
8km/5mi E along D 7. ✎✎*Guided visits Jul–Aug daily by reservation.* ◎◎€15 *(unaccompanied visits Jul–Aug €5).* ℘04 73 53 71 06. *www.chateauvollore.com.*
This 17C building of pale granite stands on a spur, and is flanked to the south by a large 12C keep and to the north by a 14C tower. It has been in the same family for over two centuries, and is today

lived in by the descendant of Geneeral de la Fayette.

▶ N along D 7; 7km/4mi beyond Ste-Agathe, the road begins its descent to Thiers via the Margerides route.

③ LE VAL LAGAT
✆*see AMBERT.*

ADDRESSES

🛏STAY
⊜⊜**Hôtel l'Aigle d'Or** – *8 r. de Lyon, 63300 Thiers.* ℘04 73 80 00 50. *Closed 2 wks in Apr; Oct–mid-Nov. 18 rooms.* Founded in 1836; comfortable lounge and cosy, soundproofed rooms.

⊜⊜⊜**Le Clos St Eloi** – *49 av. du Général-de-Gaulle.* ℘04 73 53 80 80. *31 rooms. Restaurant* ⊜⊜. Quiet rooms, spacious and colourful; a nice retreat between town and country, amid lush greenery that invites you to relax.

⊜⊜⊜ **Hotel Eliotel** – *51, rte de Maringues, Pont de Dore, 63920 Peschadoires. 6km/4.8mi W of Thiers via N 89.* ℘04 73 80 10 14. *www.eliotel. fr. 17 rooms. Restaurant* ⊜⊜. Only 3 minutes from the A89, this hotel offers comfy rooms and excellent cuisine, often combined as packages to encourage a little indulgence.

🍴EAT
⊜**La Belle Excuse** – *6 rue du Bourg, 63300 Thiers.* ℘04 82 79 52 08. *www. restaurant-la-belle-excuse.com.* A warm setting with beamed ceilings at the centre of town. The chef prepares simple and tasty traditional dishes from the region.

⊜⊜**L'Auberge des 4 Chemins** – *Rte de Clermont, Pont de Dore, 63920 Peschadoires.* ℘04 73 80 25 68. *www. aubergedesquatrechemins.com. Closed Mon and Tue.* Located at a crossroads, this unpretentious family-run inn welcomes gourmets to a small terrace in a courtyard or either of two dining rooms. Surrounded by flowers, you will find simple and traditional cuisine infused with strong flavours of the region.

Ambert

The small, seemingly-isolated town of Ambert lies in the middle of a low, wide plain between the Livradois and Forez mountains.
Ambert is a centre of diversified economic activity (including the manufacture of braiding) and the ideal starting point for excursions across the surrounding high pastures.

SIGHTS
Église St-Jean★
Place St-Jean.
The church of St-Jean is a typical example of flamboyant Gothic architecture.

Hôtel de Ville
Boulevard Henri IV.
An unusual rotunda made famous by Jules Romains' *Copains* novel.

Maison de la Fourme d'Ambert et des fromages d'Auvergne
Guided tours (45mn). Apr–early Nov daily except Sun and Mon 10am–12.30pm, 2–6.30pm; Jul–Aug, daily. €6. 04 73 82 49 23. www.maison-fourme-ambert.fr.
This museum devoted to cheese-making is housed in a 15C building. Guided tours describe the manufacture of Fourme d'Ambert, the delicious local blue cheese.

Mus'Energie
Apr–Nov daily except Mon 2–6pm (Jul–Aug daily 10.30am–1pm, 2–6.30pm. €7 (children, 6-12 years €5). 04 73 82 60 42. www.mus-energie.fr.
This museum installed in a former saw mill boasts a large collection of steam-powered machines from the early 20C.

EXCURSIONS
Livradois–Forez tourist train★
Leaves Ambert at 10.30am and 2.15pm; mainly ooperates in Jul–Aug and some out-of-season days; check website for

- **Population:** 7 206.
- **Michelin Map:** 326: J-9.
- **Info:** 4 pl. de l'Hôtel-de-Ville, 63600 Ambert. 04 73 82 61 90. www.vacances-livradois-forez.com.
- **Location:** At the heart of the Livradois-Forez, 77km/48mi from Clermont Ferrand and 79km/49mi from St-Étienne.
- **Timing:** Half a day to explore; market Thursday morning.

details. €12–€16 (children, €8–€12.50 return). 04 73 82 43 88. www.agrivap.fr.
In the summer, a panoramic tourist train travels along the Dore valley via Ambert, through typical landscapes of the Livradois-Forez Regional Park.

Moulin Richard de Bas★
5km/3mi E of Ambert via D 996, and then the D 57. Guided tours (1h) daily all year 9.30am–12.30pm, 2–6pm (mid-Jul–Aug 9.30am–7pm). 1 Jan and 25 Dec. €7.70 (child 6–17, €5.30). 04 73 82 03 11. www.richarddebas.fr.
Old houses and paper mills are evidence of the industrial importance of the Lagat valley which, for several centuries, was one of the main paper-making centres in France. Today, Richard-de-Bas is the only remaining mill in production.

🚗 DRIVING TOURS

LE VAL LAGAT
60km/37mi. Allow one day.
See THIERS for tour map (route 3).

▶ Leave Ambert E along D 966, heading towards Montbrison.

Musée de l'École 1900
In Saint-Martin-des-Olmes. Apr–Jun and Sept–Oct daily 2–7pm; Jul–Aug

Moulin Richard de Bas

daily 10am–7pm. ⊙1 Jan, 25 Dec.
≈€5.50 (child 6–12, €3.50). ℘04 73 72
66 80. www.ecole1900.fr.
The village school, dating from the
1880s and closed in 1989, houses this
interesting school museum which recre-
ates the atmosphere of a 20C classroom.

▶ Turn around and take the first road
on the right.

♟ Moulin Richard-de-Bas★
(♟see Excursions).

▶ At Valeyre, turn right onto D 67.

⚑ A discovery trail, Le Chemin des
Papetiers, starts from Valeyre and runs
along a steep mule track.

Cirque de Valcivières
This attractive *cirque* shelters several
hamlets on its stream-strewn slopes
and among the fields.

▶ Turn right onto D 106, and up to
the Col des Supeyres.

Col des Supeyres
Alt. 1 336m.
This pass on the eastern edge of the
Livradois-Forez Nature Park is sur-
rounded by a landscape of badly-
drained mountain pastures.

Un colporteur et des Jasseries
⚑ From Col des Supeyres, walk through
high pastures along a discovery trail, following in the footsteps of pedlars.

♟ Jasserie du Coq-Noir
⊙Noon–7pm: Jul–Aug daily; May–Jun
and Sept Sat–Sun and public holidays.
≈No charge. ℘04 73 95 31 33.
www.coq-noir.fr.
This former summer farm offers valuable insight into mountain farming, roof
thatching and cheese-making.

▶ Return to Col des Supeyres and
Valcivières.

After Valcivières the route follows a
rock-strewn ravine to emerge above
the Ambert plain and then descends
the lower slopes of the Forez mountains.

▶ D 66, then D 906 back to Ambert.

LIVRADOIS TO THE DORE★
*100km/62mi round tour. Allow one day.
(♟see region map).*

▶ Leave Ambert W along D 996,
for St-Amand-Roche-Savine. The
Le Monestier/St-Amand road takes
you past a small castle, the Domaine
Nobles des Escures.

St-Amand-Roche-Savine
Every summer, this charming hamlet
nestling amid the Livradois heights welcomes many visitors, especially during
the lively rock festival.

▶ Drive N; 1km/0.5mi after
St-Amand, turn right onto D 87,
then D 65.

Cunlhat

Pretty trading community formerly specialised in wool-making, surrounded by lush wooded vegetation.

�és) Leave Cunlhat to the S and drive along D 105 to St-Eloy-la-Glacière; turn left after entering the village.

La Ferme des Bois Noirs

Unaltered since it was built in 1763, this farmhouse illustrates the life and work of a peasant family in the Livradois region, a poor mountainous area where men had to take on seasonal work to supplement the meagre income the family derived from farming.

◉ Drive back to St-Eloy and turn left onto D 105 to Fournols.

Fournols

This small summer resort boasts several fine old mansions and a priory.

◉ D 37 will lead to St-Germain-l'Herm.

St-Germain-l'Herm

Summer holiday resort offering a wide range of activities.

◉ Follow D 999 and turn right onto D 999A; drive through St-Bonnet-le-Chastel, and continue to Novacelles.

Novacelles

You will enjoy visiting this small village tucked away in a valley watered by the Dollore.

◉ Take D 105 to St-Sauveur-la-Sagne, then D 38 along the Dore gorges. Turn right onto D 907.

La Chaise-Dieu★★

See La CHAISE-DIEU.

◉ Drive N out of La Chaise-Dieu along D 906 then turn right onto D 202.

Dore-l'Église

The village, situated at the confluence of the Dore and Dorette, has a 12C church that underwent alterations in the 15C. To the left of the church is a Gallo-Roman memorial.

◉ Take D 906 N.

Arlanc

The small market town is hemmed in between Forez and the Livradois mountains. The **Musée de la Dentelle** (℘04 73 95 00 03) is housed in the vaulted cellars of the town hall.

Jardin pour la Terre

Daily, Jun–Sept 2–7pm: €6; Jul–Aug daily 10.30am–7pm: €6.50. ℘04 73 95 00 71. www.arlanc.com/Jardin.html.
This garden retraces the history of small trees and shrubberies from all five continents and their adjustment to European climatic conditions.

Marsac-en-Livradois

On the square to the south of the church stands the old White Penitents' Chapel, which houses a museum bursting with memorabilia relating to this brotherhood.

◉ Go back to Ambert on D 906.

ADDRESSES

La Chaise-Dieu★★

Set amid lush green countryside with gently rolling hills, the vast buildings and ornate architectural style of the famous abbey of La Chaise-Dieu come as a magnificent surprise. The abbey derives its name from the Latin *Casa Dei*, meaning "the House of God".

A BIT OF HISTORY

Foundation of the abbey – In 1043 Robert de Turlande, a former canon from Brioude, withdrew with a few companions to this desolate plateau. He was soon joined by increasing numbers of followers and founded a monastery under the Benedictine Rule for which, in 1052, he obtained the Pope's protection. Its success continued to grow to the extent that, at Robert's death in 1067, the monastery had 300 monks and 49 priories.

Increasing numbers of priories continued to be founded, and this made La Chaise-Dieu the third most important French monastic order in the mid-12C. The abbot was all-powerful. He was accountable to no-one but the Pope. In the 12C and 13C the abbots maintained the Order's independence and kept alive the spirit in which the abbey had been founded, thereby avoiding the excesses which weakened the great abbey at Cluny.

Papacy of Clement VI – The situation suddenly deteriorated in the early 14C, when the abbot's authority was undermined and several priories broke away from the mother-house. The election, however, in Avignon, of Pope Clement VI – one of the abbey's former novices and monks – brought a halt to this decline. The Pope had the church rebuilt as it is today between 1344 and 1352 to designs by an architect from Southern France named Hugues Morel. The Pope's nephew, Gregory XI, completed the building (last three bays in the nave and the abbey buildings).

▶ **Population:** 723.
Michelin Map: 331: E-2 40km/25mi NE of Le Puy-en-Velay.
Info: Rue de la Gare, 43160 La Chaise-Dieu. &04 71 00 01 16. www.la-chaise-dieu.info.
Location: La Chaise-Dieu is all about its abbey, so the best way to orient yourself is to wander the maze of streets and see how the abbey would have dominated the original community here.
Don't Miss: The old houses in the narrow streets adjacent to the place de l'Église.
Timing: Explore first, and then spend some time in the abbey, especially the cloisters; allow at least half a day.

In the early years of the 16C, Jacques de St-Nectaire gave the abbey a dazzling set of tapestries.

Contemporary rebirth – After centuries of decline, the abbey finally attracted attention in the early years of the 20C; yet it was not completely restored until after World War II.

In 1965 the pianist **Georges Cziffra** fell in love with the abbey, and founded a festival of religious music in aid of the restoration project. The Festival de la Chaise-Dieu continues to make a name for itself as one of the main festivals of its type in France.

ABBEY
Église Abbatiale St-Robert★★

Guided visits only: daily during Jul–Aug, except during the festival in Aug. No charge. &04 71 00 05 55. www.abbaye-chaise-dieu.com.
Solidly built of granite, the church gives an impression of grandeur and austerity which seems to reflect the personality of its founder, Clement VI.

Aile de
l'Écho

Place   Lafayette

Ancienne Chapelle
Notre-Dame 3

★★**ABBEY CHURCH OF ST-ROBERT**

Sacristy

Place   de   l'Écho

Tour Clémentine

Waxwork
Museum

★★**CHANCEL**

1

l'Aumône

5   2   2

5

5   4

2

6

★**CLOISTER**

NAVE

Salles
casadéennes

de

Rue

7

Place de la Mairie

Place de l'Abbaye

N

0   20 m

West Front

The architecture of the west front is military in style. It overlooks a sloping square decorated with a 17C fountain and is flanked by two towers, neither of which is very high. The portal, including a pier embellished with a statue of St Robert, was damaged by the Huguenots in 1562. The small house concealing the base of the south tower is said to have been used by Cardinal de Rohan.

Nave and Side Aisles

The interior has a vast nave roofed with flattened vaulting and is flanked by side aisles of the same height.

A 15C **rood screen** (**1**) breaks up the perspective and seems to reduce the height of the nave. At the top of it is a fine statue of Christ (1603) with, at the foot of the Cross, two wooden stat-

ues representing the Virgin Mary and St John (15C). The superb **organ loft★** (**2**) facing it dates from the 17C.

Chancel★★

The chancel is surrounded by 144 oak **choir stalls★★** (**3**) dating from the 15C, decorated with particularly fine carvings depicting a wide range of subjects. Above the enclosure are exquisite **tapestries★★★** (**4**) from Arras and Brussels, made of wool, linen and silk, and dating from the early 16C. The subjects are drawn from the Old and New Testaments and illustrate the theme of Salvation copied from the Poor Man's Bible that was so commonplace in the Middle Ages. They are accompanied by legends written in Gothic script.

In the middle of the chancel is **Clement VI's tomb** (**5**). The Pope had it made dur-

Tapestries and the choir stalls in the chancel, Église Abbatiale St-Robert

ing his own lifetime and carved by Pierre Roye, Jean David and Jean de Sanholis. The north aisle features the famous fresco of the **Dance of Death**★ (**6**) (2m high and 26m long): the three panels juxtapose the great and famous of this world and the dead; the dead are shown inviting the living to dance with them, a reminder of what lies before them.

The fresco depicts the powerful to the left, the wealthy in the middle and the craftsmen to the right. This theme was frequently depicted in the 15C, yet never before has it been treated with such realism and such a sense of movement. In the south aisle lies the mutilated **tomb** of Abbot Renaud de Montclar (**7**) dating from the 14C; it still has its decoration of carved cherubs.

Cloisters★

The cloisters were built at the end of the 14C. Only two galleries have survived to the present day; one of them has an upper storey which was used as a library. Beyond the cloisters is a square: on the left-hand side, the second flight of steps into the hospice leads to the Echo Chamber where two people standing in opposite corners can speak to each other in whispers and hear each other perfectly.

Monks' Library

This sober, vaulted room follows the line of the north gallery of the cloisters upon which it is built. It contains the abbey **treasury**, in which there are magnificent Brussels tapestries on display, as well as a 17C ivory statue of Christ, Clement VI's broken ring and various valuable pieces of church plate.

⟪🏃⟫WALKS

Sentier du Serpent d'Or

2h there and back.

🥾 Starting from La Chaise-Dieu *(next to the village hall)*, is Serpent's Lane, named after the golden, meandering waters of the Sénouire. This will take you down to the banks of the river, passing through Breuil Forest.

Signal de St-Claude

1km/0.6mi E. 🥾 *Beyond the railway bridge, turn right onto the path that leads to the summit some 600m further on.*

Fine view of Pierre sur Haute, the mountains in the Forez and Lyon areas, Mont Pilat, the Cévennes, the mountains of Cantal and the Dore mountain range.

ADDRESSES

🛏STAY

⊜ **Chambre d'Hôte La Jacquerolle** – *R. Marchédial. ✆04 71 00 07 52. 4 rooms.* Set in the lower part of the village, this handsome house built of local stone has a dining room furnished in period pieces.

⊜⊜ **Écho et Abbaye** – *Pl. de l'Écho. ✆04 71 00 00 45. Closed mid-Nov–Mar and Wed except Jul–Aug. 10 rooms.* A tranquil hotel behind the abbey.

🍽EAT

⊜ **Le Lion d'Or** – *Av. de la Gare. ✆04 71 00 01 58. Closed Jan–Feb.* A restaurant in a traditional Auvergnat dwelling at the end of the town's main street.

Allier is the most prosperous of all the departments in the Auvergne, it is also in parts the flattest. Small, vibrant, market towns nestle amid countryside of meadows, forests, rivers, not least the eponymous Allier, and the Alagnon, and over 1 000 lakes (many with beaches and sporting activities). There are more than 500 châteaux in Allier, many open to the public. Not surprisingly, the economy tends to revolve around agriculture and tourism, with revenue from tourism increasing steadily each year.

Highlights

1   The view from the top of the clock tower in **Issoire** (p238)

2   Passing a few quiet hours in the sleepy hillside village of **Mareugheol** (p242)

3   Remarkable stained-glass windows in the gothic **Sainte-Chapelle** in Vic-le-Comte (p243)

4   Exploring narrow streets in the medieval district of **Billom** (p244)

5   A long and leisurely drive through the **Alagnon Gorge** (p247)

Auvergne AOC

Perhaps not instantly thought of as a wine-producing area, the Auvergne nevertheless has its own AOC distinction, an award that can be used by five distinct areas within the region: Madargue, Châteauguay, Chanturgue, Corent and Sulking. By all accounts the quality of the wines is improving all the time.

The Heady Scent of Garlic

Modern Billom plies a wide variety of economic activities: sawmills, wood veneering, car body workshops and industrial brush and ironware works. Cultivation of the regional speciality, garlic, is declining, but many companies continue to store and sort fresh garlic for consumption or to process it for pharmaceuticals, powders and garlic paste.

Along the Alagnon

The Alagnon river, a tributary of the Allier, flows for 86km/53mi through the centre of France. It rises near the village of Laveissière, not far from the Plomb du Cantal. The river takes a generally northeasterly direction, passing through Cantal (Murat and Massiac), Haute-Loire (Lempdes-sur-Allagnon – note the double "ll" used in Haute-Loire) and the Puy-de-Dôme (Beaulieu). Finally, the river joins the Allier at Auzat-la-Combelle.

A Bird in the Hand

Embedded in the meanders of the Allier river, the Allier Nature Reserve is home to many birds, not least the squacco heron, migrating osprey, whiskered terns and small passerines en route to the Limagne during the annual migration.

Gorges de l'Alagnon near Léotoïng

© Luc Olivier/Photononstop

VAL D'ALLIER AND ALAGNON

0   4 km

Issoire ★★ Recommended

Blesle ★ Interesting

Massiac Other sight in this guide

⇨ Point of departure

→ Approaching the Livradois

→ Dauphiné d'Auvergne

→ Castles and wine-growing villages

→ Val d'Allier

→ Livradois Châteaux

→ Gorges de l'Alagnon

RIOM

THIERS

THIERS

CLERMONT-FERRAND

Pont-du-Château

Chauriat

Chas

Billom

Glaine-Montaigut

Mauzun

St-Dier-d'Auvergne

Busséol

Montmorin

N.-D.-de-la-Roche

Corent

Puy de St-Romain

Chaux-Montgros

Les Martinanches

Vic-le-Comte

La Sauvetat

Montpeyroux

Yronde et Buron

PARC

Manglieu

Coudes

ALLIER

NATUREL

Couze de Chambon

RÉGIONAL

Grottes artificielles

Issoire

Parentignat

Sauxillanges

PUY-DE-DÔME

Tourzel-Ronzières

Perrier

Puy d'Ysson

Butte d'Usson

Ronzières

Bansat

Colamine-sous-Vodable

Mailhat

DU

Mareugheol

Nonette

LIVRADOIS - FOREZ

Villeneuve

Boudes

St-Germain-Lembron

Vallée des Saints

Jumeaux

St-Gervazy

Auzon

Gorges de l'Alagnon

LE PUY-EN-VELAY

Château de Léotoing

Blesle

Leyvaux

Ste-Madeleine

Massiac

CHAPELLE N.-D.-DE-VAUCLAIR

MILLAU

237

Issoire★★

Issoire is located on the Couze river, near its junction with the Allier, south of Clermont-Ferrand and on the fertile plain of Limagne. The town is said to have been founded by the Arverni, a powerful Gallic tribe that inhabited the present-day region of Lyon. They gave their name to this region – Auvergne. During the 17C religious wars of the Reformation, Issoire suffered severely, and most of the old town was destroyed.

A BIT OF HISTORY

Little Geneva – In 1540 a former Dominican monk arrived in Issoire from Germany and converted the Consuls to the Lutheran faith. He was burnt alive on the bailiff's orders but his death led, in fact, to numerous additional conversions. Issoire became a "Little Geneva", washed in the blood of the many martyrs to the new faith.

Architecturally, pride of place goes to the ornate 12C Abbatiale Saint-Austremoine, formerly the church of a Benedictine abbey, and one of the largest Romanesque churches in the Auvergne. But there is an agreeable, provincial ambiance about the place that rewards even the shortest break. Today, surrounded by boulevards, the town is bright, refreshing, and a delight to explore, not least its remarkable Renaissance **clock tower**, formerly the town belfry (&see Tour de l'Horloge).

🐾WALKING TOUR

The early-19C **corn-exchange**, situated next to the tourist office, has been turned into an entertainment centre. Follow rue Ponteil which starts opposite and leads to the **Tour de l'Horloge** (clock tower &see Sights).

On reaching place de la République (the former Grande Place), where a busy market takes place on Saturday mornings, note the 15C **Maison Charrier** with its Gothic doorway and the **fountain**

- ▶ **Population:** 14 729.
- 🕐 **Michelin Map:** 326: G-9.
- 🚩 **Info:** 9, place Saint Paul, 63500 Issoire. 𝒫04 73 89 15 90. www.issoire-tourisme.com.
- ⏹ **Location:** Most shops, restaurants and bars cluster around the clock tower.
- 🅿 **Parking:** Ample car parking in the centre of town.
- 👁 **Don't Miss:** The view from the top of the clock tower.

adorning the centre of the square, designed in 1823 by the architect Ledru. Beyond, to the left, is the **Maison aux Arcades**; turn left onto rue des Fours and admire the 15C–17C **Hôtel Bohier**, which houses a Renaissance staircase. Turn left at the end of the street to reach the **Centre Pomel** (&see Sights). Opposite, on the corner of square Cassin, the Maison de la Bascule (weights and measures building) houses the **Musée de la Pierre Philosophale** containing a collection of 1 000 minerals. Walk round the cathedral and back to place de la République. Turn right onto rue de la Berbiziale; on the corner, note the 15C **Maison du Chancelier Duprat** with its rectangular corbelled tower. Continue to place St-Avit; the 18C Maison Bartin on the left has fine wrought-iron balconies.

ABBATIALE ST-AUSTREMOINE★

St-Austremoine, once the church of a Benedictine abbey, was built in the 12C and dedicated to Austremoine, the first bishop of the Arverni people, martyred in the 3C; it is now the parish church, replacing the neighbouring Église St-Paul, which was destroyed shortly after the French Revolution.

Exterior

The **east end**★★ stands on a wide esplanade. This is the most perfect section of the building, a consummate example of Romanesque architecture as it developed in the Auvergne. No other church boasts such harmonious proportions, such purity of line and such restraint in its decoration. Its powerful, well-balanced design consists of various different elements; note the mosaics and sculptures representing signs of the Zodiac.

Interior

The two-storey **nave** is striking for its magnificent proportions; the painted decoration was added in the mid-19C. At the southern entrance to the ambulatory there is one of the finest, and most complete, views of the building as a whole. Walk round the chancel; it is particularly interesting for its superb narrative **capitals★**.

Crypt

This is one of the finest crypts in the Auvergne. The stocky columns supporting the vaulted roof give an impression of strength that is further emphasised by the total lack of decoration.

SIGHTS
Centre Pomel

This houses the **Centre d'Art Roman Georges-Duby** (&ᴑJul–Aug Tue–Sun 10am–12.30pm, 2–6pm; May–Jun and Sept–Oct Tue–Fri and Sun 2–6pm, Sat 10am–12.30pm, 2–6pm. ℘04 73 89 56 04. http://centre-artroman.issoire.fr), which displays the vestiges of the Monastère St-Austremoine.

Tour de l'Horloge

ᴑMar–Jun and Oct–Nov Tue–Sun 2–6pm (Sat 10am–12.30pm, 2–6pm); Jul–Aug Tue–Sun 10am–12.30pm, 2–6pm. ᴑDec–Feb, 1 May. &(except belfry). ⊚€3. ℘04 73 89 07 70. http://tour-horloge.issoire.fr.
The chimes of the Renaissance belfry (15C) can still be heard throughout town. A lively "**Scenovision**" presentation enlightens visitors to the rich and colourful past of Issoire and eight short documentary films retrace the impact of the Renaissance (printing and other

great discoveries). Temporary exhibitions are also organised. From the top of the tower there is a fine panoramic view over the town, the Limagne landscape, the Monts-Dore and Livradois mountains.

EXCURSION
Auzon★

28km/17mi SE of Issoire.
Auzon's dramatic **setting★** on a sheer-sided spur of rock overlooking the valley of the river that shares its name is best appreciated when seen from D 5, coming from the Allier valley. This old fortified town still has many traces of its ramparts and castle and boasts a fine collegiate church.

🚗 DRIVING TOUR

APPROACHING THE LIVRADOIS

45km/28mi round trip. Allow 2h.
(& see region map).

▷ Leave Issoire on D 996 to the SE.

Château de Parentignat★

◥◣Guided visits. ᴑJun and Sept Sat–Sun 2–6pm; Jul–Aug daily 10.30am–12.30pm, 2–6pm. ⊚€10. ℘04 73 89 51 10. www.parentignat.com.
The château was built towards the end of Louis XIV's reign (early 18C) and has remained in the same family since. The main courtyard has formal grass parterres, contrasting with the English-style landscape gardens bordered by orange trees and roses. The ancestral treasures include furniture as well as paintings by Nicolas de Largillière, Mme Vigée-Lebrun, Rigaud and Van Loo.

▷ Continue along D 996 towards Sauxillanges. After 6km/3.7mi, take D 709 on the right.

Butte d'Usson

The basaltic rock of Usson was once the site of a formidable castle, of which nothing remains but the memory of

Marguerite de Valois. "Usson is a town situated on a plain where there is a rock, and three towns one on top of the other in the shape of a Pope's mitre", says an ancient text. The castle was built by the Duc de Berry, and believed to be impregnable. On the door was written "Mind the traitor and the tooth!" meaning that only treason or famine could get the better of it.

View

From a viewing table off D 709 to the north of the town there is a beautiful view of the Limagne d'Issoire in the foreground and the Puys chain in the background.

Puy d'Usson

A gentle path leads to the summit on which a chapel has been built; it provides a good **panorama★** of the region. During the climb, a beautiful set of basalt columns can be seen in an old quarry.

Return to D 996.

Sauxillanges

The 11C church with 15C alterations contains a mural depicting the Deposition and a 15C statue of Our Lady of the Woods. The Prior's Chapel, now a heritage centre, **Maison du Patrimoine** (check website for details. ℰ04 73 96 85 10. www.musee-sauxillanges.com), is part of the remains of a priory founded in 927 and attached to the Cluniac Order. The Gothic vaulting is decorated with interesting hanging keystones bearing the coats of arms of the various priors. You can take the direct route (D 214) or choose to go the long way to St-Étienne-d'Usson on D 144 towards Sarpoil.

In Bansat, turn right onto D 24, then turn left in St-Martin-des-Plains, heading for Mailhat.

Église de Mailhat

The small Romanesque church has a square belfry with double openings, and a five-sided apse.

D 123 leads to Orsonnette, then to Nonette.

Nonette★

The village is built on a promontory overlooking the Allier. The half-Romanesque, half-Gothic **church**, once part of a priory, has a carved Romanesque doorway and, inside, a superb late-14C bust of Christ (north chapel). The ruins of the 14C **castle** (*45min on foot there and back via a steep path*) stand on a height offering a splendid **panorama★**.

DAUPHINÉ D'AUVERGNE★
60km/37mi. Allow half a day.

At the end of the 12C, the region to the southwest of Issoire between the Cézallier and the Allier valleys, comprising rugged countryside scored by the various Couzes flowing between hilly outcrops and basalt plateaux, formed the Dauphiné d'Auvergne, a sort of local royal fief whose lords and their entourage set up a glittering court in Champeix, Vodable and Mercœur successively.

Leave Issoire to the W on D 996, towards Champeix.

Perrier

The village of Perrier is overlooked by a plateau bristling with bizarre rocks, evidence of violent eruptions thousands of years ago in the Dore mountain region, which unleashed gigantic flows of mud mixed with boulders, or **lahars** (*see NATURE*). Erosion subsequently sculpted the fantastic rock formations known as "fairies' chimneys".

Artificial Caves

1h walk there and back. From the church in Perrier, take the footpath to the caves ("Chemin des Grottes").
These caves were hollowed out of the volcanic rock and used as troglodytic dwellings.

From the caves, follow the route indicated as "vue panoramique".

From the plateau there is a remarkable **view**★ of the surrounding rocks, the feudal keep, the village and the Couze de Pavin.

▶ On leaving Perrier, take D 26 left (2km/1.2mi), then left onto D 23.

Tourzel-Ronzières

Small wine-growers' houses in this village bear witness to a viticultural past, specifically during the 18C and 19C when Tourzel's main source of income was wine. One of these lava-walled houses is home to a small museum on the pork butcher's trade.

Further down, the **Maison de Pays** (◉ *May–mid Sept 10am-7pm.* ☎ *04 73 71 40 09*), another house typical of the region, contains a display evoking scenes from local history, as well as a wide variety of local farm produce.

▶ Follow D 23 for another 1km/0.6mi, then turn left onto D 124.

Ronzières

At the entrance to the village, a narrow track (⊶ *closed to traffic*) climbs up to a basalt plateau on which a pre-Romanesque church stands. In the graveyard, on the edge of the plateau, two viewing tables give information on the view of the surrounding countryside, which stretches over the Puy d'Ysson, the Couze de Pavin, Perrier plateau and Lembron plain.

Examples of the two volcanic features so characteristic of the Dauphiné d'Auvergne region are easy to pick out.

▶ Take D 124 as far as Vodable and turn left onto D 32 to Solignat.

Puy d'Ysson★

This cone was formed by the chimney of a volcano; the plug of lava was laid bare by erosion.

From the summit, there is a **panorama** of the Dore mountain range, the extinct volcanoes of the Comté region, the Limagne around Issoire, the Livradois mountains and the Cézallier.

▶ Drive back down to Solignat and take D 32 back to Vodable.

Église de Colamine-sous-Vodable

The church stands surrounded by its graveyard, on the side of a combe. It boasts a Romanesque chancel and a group of wooden statues.

▶ Rejoin D 32 and travel for 4km/3mi towards Dauzat-sur-Vodable, then turn left onto D 48.

Boudes

Neatly sheltered by a range of hills to the north and by the Avoiron pinnacle to the west, this village was the only one in the entire region to escape the ravages of phylloxera. Thanks to the good soil here, local vines produce fine quality wine, including a particularly well regarded white wine. The layout of the vineyards, on a single slope, well-exposed to the sun, and the brightly coloured houses form a striking sight. Note the fine dovecots.

▶ Leave Boudes to the S, crossing the Couzilloux, and take the track to the right which runs along the side of the graveyard.

Vallée des Saints★

🚶 *1h walk return.*

A waymarked path enables visitors to explore this area to the full, admiring the giant red and ochre pyramids with which it is populated. Their outlandish silhouettes, like gigantic statues, have earned the valley its name.

▶ Return to Boudes and turn right at the church to rejoin D 48.

St-Germain-Lembron

This small, once-fortified village in the midst of an agricultural region still boasts some 18C houses with double-gabled roofs.

▶ Take D 48 towards Boudes once again, then turn off to the right after 1km/0.6mi onto D 125.

The road climbs towards Châlus, from where there are beautiful views of the volcanic necks and tables rising above the Limagne.

Villeneuve

Narrow streets lined with old houses and wash-houses surround a 15C church.

Château de Villeneuve-Lembron★

Guided visits. Jan–mid-May and mid-Sept–Dec daily except Mon 10am–noon, 2–5.30pm; mid-May–mid-Sept daily 10am–noon, 2–6.30pm. 1 Jan, 1 May, 1 and 11 Nov, 25 Dec. €6. 04 73 96 41 64. www.chateau-villeneuve-lembron.fr. This seigneurial castle was built for the Aureille family, one of whose members was the diplomat Rigault, who served under Louis XI, Charles VIII, Louis XII and François I and fought alongside Charles VIII in the Italian campaigns.

▶ Follow D 125; left onto D 720.

Mareugheol

Mareugheol is a typical example of a fortified village built during the Middle Ages in order to protect the inhabitants from the marauding bands of robbers that plagued the region. Old stone houses stand along narrow streets within a rectangular fortified wall of which only a few stretches of wall and a stump of corner tower remain.

▶ Take the D 719, then turn right onto the D 32, back towards Issoire.

ADDRESSES

⊜ STAY

⊜⊜ **Chambre d'Hôte Paul Gebrillat** – 1, Chemin de Siorac, 63500 Perrier. 3km/1.8mi W of Issoire via D 996. 04 73 89 15 02. Closed Dec–Jan. 3 rooms. In a village right near the volcanoes, this pretty 18C house is inviting indeed. Charming rooms and reliable advice for adventurous tourists.

⊜⊜⊜ **Château de Grange Fort** – 63500 Les Pradeaux. 7km/4.2mi SE of Issoire, take A 75, exit 13, dir. Parentignat and D 34, rte d'Auzat-sur-Allier. 04 73 71 02 43. www.lagrangefort.com. 5 rooms. Restaurant⊜⊜⊜; camp site; chalets. A 17C château with superb crenellated towers set in the bosom of a park encircled by mountains. The rooms may feature a canopy bed, a sculpted door, a parquet floor or original mouldings.

⊜⊜ **Chambre d'Hôte Les Baudarts** – 63500 Varennes-sur-Usson. 6km/3.6mi E of Issoire via D 996 and D 123. 04 73 89 05 51. Closed Oct–Apr. 3 rooms. This Provençal-style house with pink walls and a Romanesque tiled roof is all elegance and sophistication. The bedrooms are spacious and the living room is superb.

⚑/EAT

⊜ **Le Boudes La Vigne** – 63340 Boudes. 15km/9mi S of Issoire via D 909 and D 48. 04 73 96 55 66. http://leboudeslavigne. franceserv.com. Set in the heart of a quaint wine-making village, this hotel-restaurant, part of which is in the cellar, has its regular patrons.

⊜⊜ **La Bergerie de Sarpoil** – 63490 St-Jean en Val. 10km/6mi E of Issoire via D 999. 04 73 71 02 54. http:// labergeriedesarpoil.com. Closed Sun evening, Mon evening (except Jul–Aug), all day Tue–Wed. Reservations required. A coaching inn and sheepfold in the olden days, this restaurant, featuring old stone walls in the dining room, has retained old-fashioned charm.

⊜⊜ **La Cour Carrée** – 17 Avenue du Tramot, 63500 Perrier. 5km/3mi W of Issoire via D 996. 04 73 55 15 55. www. cour-carree.com. Closed Sun evening, Wed evening, Sat lunch Sept-Jun and Mon. Reservations recommended. This former winemaker's abode is entered via the small square courtyard.

SHOPPING

Maison Chazal – 4 r. Gambetta. 04 73 89 20 11. The vaulted wine cellar boasts about 350 different vintages and 50-odd brands of whisky.

Pascale et Patrick Védrine – 8 r. du Ponteil. 04 73 55 28 18. The unique décor and warm atmosphere set this baker's shop apart.

Vic-le-Comte★

Vic-le-Comte lies in the middle of Comté, a region made up of a series of volcanoes that form a transition between the plain and the Livradois mountains.
Most of the volcanoes have been eroded and only their chimneys remain. There are more than 50 eruptive pinnacles, now covered in woodland; in the past, grapevines grew on the more exposed slopes. Today, Vic-le-Comte has a papermill owned by the Bank of France, which makes the watermarked paper used for bank notes printed in Chamalières.

▸ **Population:** 5 037.
- **Michelin Map:** 326: G-9 – 16km/10mi N of Issoire.
- **Info:** Les Pradets, 63114 Montpeyroux. ℰ 04 73 96 68 80. www.allier-comte-communaute.fr.
- **Location:** Vic-le-Comte is 25km/15.5mi from Clermont Ferrand, and 16km/10mi from Issoire, via the A 75 autoroute.
- **Parking:** There are a number of car parks both in the centre and just outside.
- **Don't Miss:** The fortified village of Montpeyroux.
- **Timing:** Allow half a day for a leisurely walking tour.

WALKING TOUR

Sainte-Chapelle★
A beautiful Gothic building heralding the Renaissance. The richly coloured **stained-glass windows★** depict scenes from the Old and New Testaments. The very fine stone **altarpiece★** (1520) is the work of Florentine artists.

Old Houses
Rue Porte-Robin has several buildings with 15C and 16C façades. The old town gate, **Porte Robin**, is all that remains of the fortified curtain wall.
Continue straight ahead towards rue du Palais, at the entrance to which are two corbelled houses.

▷ Take the covered passage on the right, rue des Farges, then rue de Coulogne beyond; turn back.

🚗 DRIVING TOUR

CASTLES AND WINE-GROWING VILLAGES
45km/28mi. Allow half a day.

▷ Drive S out of town along D 49. In Yronde, take D 136.

Yronde
This is where Le Bouchet abbey once stood. Note the lovely small church.

Buron
The road runs round the village, overlooked by the ruins of a castle.

▷ Cross the River Allier; take D 229 left.

Coudes
This ancient village at the confluence of the Allier and Couze de Chambon once thrived on a major river traffic in wine.

▷ Continue along D 229, across the A 75 motorway, then turn right on D 797.

Montpeyroux★
This fortified hillside village overlooks the Allier to the east. A medieval gateway gives access to narrow twisting lanes leading to the three-storey 13C **keep**. Some of the old houses in the village have been restored and their cellars are a reminder of the wine-growing past of the village, which now welcomes a colony of artists and craftsmen.

Montpeyroux

© Francis Cormon / hemis.fr/Getty Images

The road follows the east bank of the river, jotted with wine-growing villages such as Mirefleurs, La Roche-Noire and St-Georges-sur-Allier.

▷ On leaving St-Georges-sur-Allier, turn right on D 759.

Château de Busséol★

🚶Guided visits. ⏰mid-Jun–mid-Sept daily 10am–noon, 2.30–6pm; mid-Sept–mid-Nov and Mar–mid Jun Sat–Sun and public holidays 2.30-5.30pm. ⊜€7. ☎04 73 69 00 84.

The main façade collapsed in 1963 but has since been rebuilt with Romanesque-style windows.

▷ Leave Busséol S and follow D 4 then continue on D 229. In Benaud hamlet, turn right on D 116 then take D 81. Park at Saint-Maurice.

Puy Saint-Romain

🚶 90min on foot there and back.

The setting of the puy is striking; the summit, an ancient place of worship, offers a **panormama★** encompassing the *Comté Puys*, the Forez mountains, the Livradois mountains, the Dore and Dôme mountain ranges, Clermont-Ferrand and the Limagne.

▷ Go to Longues on D 758 and D 1, then follow the D 225 back to Vic-le-Comte.

▷ Continue along D 797. In Authezat, turn left on D 96.

La Sauvetat

Once fortified, the village has retained part of a commander's residence, belonging to the Order of St John.

▷ Leave La Sauvetat NE along D 630, cross the A 75 and rejoin D 96.

Corent

This village overlooking the River Allier clings to the north-eastern slopes of the Puy de Corent; it is known for its high-quality wine, one of the five vintages making up the Côtes d'Auvergne *appellation*.

▷ Follow the D 118 to cross the River Allier. Turn left to join the D 1.

Billom★

Billom is situated on the Limagne plain at the foot of the Livradois mountains. It flourished in the Middle Ages and had a university before Clermont-Ferrand. This university, transformed in the 16C, became the first Jesuit college and was well known in the Auvergne.

A BIT OF HISTORY

During the Reign of Terror in the wake of the French Revolution, Couthon, a member of the Convention, issued a famous edict ordering the demolition

▶ **Population:** 4 882.
🖮 **Michelin Map:** 326: H-8.
🛈 Info: 13 r. Carnot, 63160 Billom. ☎04 73 68 39 85. www.billom.com.
▷ **Location:** Billom lies 27km/17mi SE of Clermont-Ferrand.
🅿 **Parking:** Parking is limited in the centre of town.
◉ **Don't Miss:** A walk around the Medieval district.
◷ **Timing:** 2–3hrs would suffice, but stay for lunch.

of all belfries in the province on the basis that they were "contrary to equality"; this was how the church of St-Cerneuf lost its elegant little tower.

WALKING TOUR

MEDIEVAL DISTRICT

From the *Hôtel de Ville* follow quai de la Terraille to place du Creux-du-Marché, surrounded by old houses. Cross Pont du Marché-aux-Grains: three troughs and gutters hewn out of Volvic stone are visible on the parapet on the right – they were used to measure grain.

Walking up rue de l'Étézon, note the 16C belfry on the right and the 16C Maison du Bailli at the top of the street.

▶ Turn left, and walk past the former trade tribunal to place des Écoles.

Maison du Chapitre

This 15C mansion, known as the chapter-house, was part of the medieval university and was used as a prison during the Revolution.

Porte de l'Évêché

This gateway into the medieval town marked the first line of fortifications.

Église St-Cerneuf★

This Gothic church was erected over an old Romanesque church from which a **crypt★** remains.

▶ Turn right on leaving the church, and turn left onto rue Pertuybout.

Maison de l'Échevin

The entrance to this 16C alderman's house features an attractive staircase tower and a well with its wheel.

Rue des Boucheries

This narrow street paved with pointed stones is flanked by medieval houses including the Maison du Doyen which has a beautiful basket-handle arch over its window and a Renaissance staircase, and the 15C Maison du Boucher which has stone walls on one side, half-tim-

bered walls on the other and two overhanging upper floors.

DRIVING TOURS

VAL D'ALLIER
50km/31mi. Allow 3h.

▶ Leave Billom along D 997 for Pont-du-Château and turn left onto D 81.

Chas

This old fortified village has kept its gateway and turret and its Romanesque church, fronted by a Renaissance porch and a pretty fountain.

Chauriat

Located north of the Comté, this small wine-growing village stands out because of its two churches. The deconsecrated Église Ste-Marie was built in Merovingian times. The Église St-Julien is characteristic of the Auvergnat Romanesque style.

▶ Drive to Pont-du-Château along D 4.

Pont-du-Château

For a long time this strategically important town was fortified: it was the location of the only bridge spanning the Allier between Moulins and Brioude. During the 19C Pont-du-Château was a busy port loading up goods for Paris; this history is recalled in the **Musée Pierre-Mondanel** (*guided visits Jul–Aug 10am–noon, 3–6pm; rest of the year by appointment. ☏04 73 83 73 98*), housed in the kitchens of an old château.

▶ Leave Pont-du-Château to the S and take D 1 heading towards Vic-le-Comte.

The road meanders along the banks of the River Allier, offering pretty views of the mountain ranges.

▶ Turn left onto D 117, which crosses Mirefleurs. Follow a steep slope towards the road to Busséol.

Château de Busséol
See VIC-LE-COMTE.

▶ Continue along D 117, then D 301 towards St-Julien-de-Coppel.

Drive up through Notre-Dame-des-Roches, a small chapel perched on a rock, for a view of Billom country.

▶ Continue on D 118 to see the ruins of Coppel Tower; just before La Beauté, turn left. D 14 will take you back to Billom through the lush Angaud valley.

LIVRADOIS CHÂTEAUX
45km/28mi. Allow 3h.

This route provides lovely views of the first Livradois summits and gives access to the main strongholds in the Pays de St-Dier.

Château de Montmorin
Guided visits Jul–Aug, daily, 2–6pm. €6. 04 73 68 30 94. www.chateau-de-montmorin.fr.
This former citadel used to consist of a keep flanked by round towers; it now lies largely in ruins. Rooms in the main building have been turned into a museum.

▶ Take D 337, then D 338 towards St-Dier-d'Auvergne.

St-Dier-d'Auvergne
The 12C church here was fortified in the 15C; it has a buttressed west front with arcading.

▶ Drive 5km/3mi to the S on D 997.

Les Martinanches
Nestling at the bottom of a valley is a **castle** (*guided visits afternoons only mid-Jul–Aug. €6. 04 73 70 81 98; www.chateau-des-martinanches.com*), built originally in the 11C but altered in the 15C and the 19C. Inside there are beamed ceilings, fine porcelain and earthenware, and period furniture.

Château de Mauzun
The mighty fortress standing on a spur of basalt rock, once the property of the bishops of Clermont-Ferrand, offers a fine view of the Limagne plain. Although still in ruins, the castle retains its two defensive walls and 20 towers.

▶ Take D 20 to Neuville, then D 152 and D 229 back to Billom.

Massiac

The rocky headlands of St-Victor and St-Madeleine frame this ancient village, situated at the confluence of three rivers: the Alagnon, the Alagnonnette and the Arcueil.

SIGHTS
Église Saint-André
This church is notable for its 17C painting by Guy François, *L'Adoration des Bergers*.

Musée Municipal Élise-Rieuf
Jul–Aug daily except Mon 2.30–6.30pm; May–Jun and 1st–mid-Sept Sun and public holidays 2.30–6.30pm. Oct–Apr. 04 71 23 03 95. www.musee-elise-rieuf.org.

▶ **Population:** 1 875.
▶ **Michelin Map:** 331 H-3
▶ **Info:** pl. de la Gare, 15500 Massiac. 04 71 23 07 76. www.pays-saint-flour.fr.
▶ **Location:** 28km/17.3mi N of St-Flour on E 11.
▶ **Timing:** There is a traditional weekly market (Tue am) and two annual fairs (Jun and Oct).

The museum displays portraits of people from the Auvergne and China, Provençal and Scandinavian landscapes and Italian towns painted by Élise Rieuf, a native of Massiac (1897–1990).

🚗 DRIVING TOUR

GORGES DE L'ALAGNON
70km/43.5mi round tour. Allow half a day.

The road alongside the lower reaches of the River Alagnon between Le Babory-de-Blesle and Lempdes-sur-Allagnon makes a most appealing drive.

▶ Drive N out of Massiac towards Clermont-Ferrand; at the roundabout, take the small road which skirts the motorway slip road then passes under the motorway.

Site de la Chapelle Ste-Madeleine★
The small 11C chapel stands on top of a spur of basalt rock, at the south-eastern extremity of the Chalet plateau.
On the opposite bank of the river, another spur of basalt rock (735m), the Plateau de St-Victor, occupied by pre-historic Man, later served as a look-out to keep watch over the Alagnon valley and the river crossing.

▶ Return to the roundabout and follow D 909 N. In Le Babory, turn left onto D 8 which crosses the Alagnon.

Blesle★
This ancient village on the west bank of the Voireuze was founded around a Benedictine abbey. **Église St-Pierre★** (11C–12C) has some interesting furniture and statues in the treasury.
Other monuments of note include a great square **keep**, a 14C **bell-tower**, all that remains of the church of St-Martin (destroyed in the Revolution), 15C and 16C houses, and the turret and doorway (17C) of the old hospice.
Do not fail to visit the **Musée de la Coiffe** (🕐*Apr–Sept 10am–noon, 2.30–5.30pm. ⌨€4. ☎04 71 76 27 08*), set up in a former 16C hospital and presenting over 400 typical headdresses from the Auvergne and Velay areas.

▶ Return to the right bank of the Alagnon by taking D 8 in the opposite direction and turn left onto D 909.

Further north, the ruins of Léotoing Castle can be seen on high ground to the right (*Ⴆsee below*). The valley becomes narrower and wilder.

▶ In Lempdes head N on D 909, in the direction of St-Germain-Lembron. After 3km/2mi take D 35 on the left, then D 141 on the right.

St-Gervazy
The **castle** is the setting of visits presented by members of the association "La Vie de Château", which have been in charge of restoration work for the past 10 years. The Romanesque **church** houses a replica of the 12C Virgin Enthroned that was stolen a few years ago.

▶ Return to Lempdes; follow D 653 S over a distance of 4km/2.5mi then turn right onto D 655.

Léotoing★
The chapel located at the entrance to the village houses a model of the site and several panels providing information on local history, architecture and traditions. The fine view encompasses the Alagnon gorge, the Cézallier, the Brioude plain, the Livradois, the Plateau de la Chaise-Dieu and the Monts du Velay.

Castle
🐾*The tour of the ruins is undertaken at the visitor's own risk; it is not advisable for children or anyone suffering from vertigo; good walking shoes are recommended.*
Substantial remains of this 14C fortress overlooking the River Alagnon are still visible. To reach them, walk through the fortified gate. The Romanesque **church** contains traces of a fresco depicting the Deposition and carved capitals.

▶ At the foot of the hill, take D 909 on the left. On leaving Lanau, turn left onto D 19 which later meets up with D 653. Return to Massiac via Grenier-Montgon.

This largely low-lying area is pierced north to south by the spectacular gorges of the Sioule, a river that rises in the foothills of the Monts du Sancy, ultimately joining the Allier near St Pourçain sur Sioule. The Combrailles form a mosaic of tiny villages, châteaux, mills, churches and chapels around which a vast area of open space proves ideal for walking, mountain biking and horse riding. Elsewhere, an abundance of museums allow you to discover different aspects of life and culture in this beautiful region, not least its remarkable geology, history and prehistory.

The Limagnes

The Limagnes are low-lying, fertile, sunny plains drained by the Dore and the Allier. The plains are almost entirely arable. To the east, the "Varennes", is a hilly area of marshes, woodland, fields of crops and lush pastures where alluvium has been washed down from the mountains of the Forez. To the west, the soil in the so-called fertile Limagnes region is dark brown, almost black. This is very rich land, producing tobacco, wheat, vegetable and seed crops and fruit.

Lezoux

The fairs and markets that animated this ancient town in the 2C brought Lezoux considerable renown, and enhanced its reputation as a major centre for the production of ceramics distributed throughout much of the "Roman" empire. But little was known about this remote centre until the Middle Ages. On the eve of the Revolution it was owned by Chazerat Claude Charles, who built a castle (now destroyed) to the north of the town.

Ancient Combraille

The origins of the ancient lordship of Combraille date from Celtic times when the Gallic tribe, the Cambovices, formed a "fatherland". The original region was divided into three departments in 1790 – Allier, Creuse and Puy-de-Dôme. Today it embraces 10 cantons and 103 communes.

Méandre de Queuille, Gorges de la Sioule

© Francis Cormon/hemis.fr

LIMAGNE, PAYS DES COMBRAILLES AND GORGES DE LA SIOULE

0   4 km

★★ Recommended
★   Interesting
    Other sight described

Mozac   Point of departure
Ebreuil   Les Combrailles
Volvic   Discovering La Limagne
          Gorges and Castles
          Queuille Meander

Riom★

The old town of Riom perched on a small hill on the western edge of the Limagne region still reflects the splendour of bygone days within the ring of boulevards laid out on its now demolished walls.

It is a city of considerable elegance preserving a noble integrity that rests on its former position as the capital of the province of Auvergne until the Revolution. But it is also a festive city, skilfully blending music, heritage, gastronomy and *savoir-faire*. The city has no fewer than 16 classified historical monuments, earning it the appellation *Ville d'Art et d'Histoire*. A lively summer of events ends with a popular and animated jazz festival.

A BIT OF HISTORY

Capital city – At the beginning of the 13C Philippe Auguste's campaign was instrumental in making Riom's fortune as the monarchy decided to base its administration here.

In 1360 Duc **Jean de Berry**, the son of Jean le Bon (the Good), was given the Land of Auvergne, elevated to a duchy, as an apanage. The Duke, ostentatious and extravagant, was surrounded by a brilliant court of artists and chose Riom as one of his favourite places of residence. He ordered extensive work to be carried out on the old castle which he had converted by the architect Gui de Dammartin.

After the Duke's death, Riom and the Duchy of Auvergne passed to the Bourbon family. The town remained very much attached to the king; when Joan of Arc needed powder and arrows for the siege of La Charité-sur-Loire, she appealed to the people of Riom, who were reputed for their wealth. They pledged 60 gold écus but were slow to send them. In 1430 the townspeople received a letter of reminder; the priceless letter has been preserved at the town hall, though the saint's hair, caught in the wax seal on the letter, has now disappeared.

▶ **Population:** 19 487.

Michelin Map: 326: F-7 – 15km/9.5mi N of Clermont-Ferrand.

Info: 27 Pl de la Fédération, 63204 Riom. ℘04 73 38 59 45. www.tourisme-riomlimagne.fr.

Location: Riom is situated 15km/9mi north of Clermont-Ferrand, accessible from the A 71.

Parking: The centre of Riom is pedestrianised, but there are a number of car parks around the periphery.

Timing: Allow half a day.

WALKING TOUR

▶ Start from place des Martyrs-de-la-Résistance.

Sainte-Chapelle★

In the Palais de Justice. Jul–Aug Tue–Fri 10am–noon, 3–5pm; Jun and Sept Wed–Fri 3.30–5pm. Sat–Sun and public holidays. €2. ℘04 73 38 59 45. The chapel (14C), the only remainder of the Duke of Berry's castle, has some remarkable late-15C **stained-glass windows★** in the chancel.

Musée Régional d'Auvergne★

Mid-May–mid-Nov 2–5.30pm (Jul–Aug 2.30–6pm). 14 Jul, 1 and 11 Nov. €3. ℘04 73 38 17 31.

This Regional Museum of Arts, Crafts and Traditions, laid out on three floors, houses a remarkable collection of farming implements, rural and craft tools, furniture, games, domestic items and costumes which, with the reconstruction of typical Auvergne interiors, reflect the physiognomy of the province prior to the Industrial Revolution.

The collection of headdresses and the room of religious statuary (13C-18C) are particularly interesting.

● Walk along rue de l'Hôtel-de-Ville.

Musée Mandet★

🕐 Tue–Sun: Sept–Jun 10am–noon,
2–5.30pm; Jul–Aug 10am–noon,
2.30–6pm. 🕐 1 Jan, Easter Sun, 1 May,
14 Jul, 15 Aug, 1 and 11 Nov, 25 Dec.
€3, no charge on Wed, or for under 18.
📞 04 73 38 18 53.

This museum is arranged into two private mansions: one, Hôtel Dufraisse (built 1740), houses the painting collections; the other, Hôtel Desaix, houses the Richard Bequest. The first rooms display the **painting collection**.

On the first floor, rooms decorated with delicate woodwork present a series of paintings from the 17C Flemish and Dutch Schools and the 17C and 18C French Schools. The second floor is given over to 19C painting, particularly the works of Alphonse Cornet, an artist from Riom.

The **Richard Bequest** includes interesting collections of ornamental objets d'art.

Hôtel de Ville

🔊 Tours of the courtyard. ♿ 🕐 Mon–Fri 8am–5.30pm. 🕐 1 Jan, 25 Dec.
📞 04 73 33 79 00.

In the vestibule is an enamelled stone plaque reproducing the letter from Joan of Arc to the people of Riom. The lovely 16C **courtyard★** is enclosed by two buildings decorated with vaulted arcades; note the basket-handled arches and a staircase turret with a carved door. Beneath the arcades stand two bronze sculptures by Rodin, including *Gallia Victrix* (modelled on Camille Claudel) and a marble sculpture by Rivoire (the Kiss of Glory).

Maison des Consuls★

Fine 16C residence. The ground floor of the Consuls' House has five archways. The first-floor windows support an elegant frieze crowned by two busts of women and two busts of Roman emperors. The wooden house opposite dates from the 15C.

Carrefour des Taules★

Near this crossroads (*taule* is an old word for stall) which forms the intersection of the main streets of old Riom stand some of the town's most interesting old houses. There are façades with carved windows at the corner of rue de l'Hôtel-de-Ville and rue de l'Horloge.

Rue de l'Horloge

The street is lined with old mansions with remarkable courtyards (*see below*) and beautiful windows such as those of no. 4 and above all no. 12. The town's belfry, with its gilt clock face, stands at the beginning of the street.

251

Tour de l'Horloge

© Christian Guy/hemis.fr

Tour de l'Horloge★

⏱ Tue–Sun: 10am–noon, 2–5pm (Jul–Aug daily 10am–noon, 2–6pm).
⏱ 1 Jan, 25 Dec and days when the fair is held. ✆€1. ☎04 73 38 99 94.
www.riom-communaute.fr.
Surmounted by a 17C dome, this octagonal Renaissance tower rests on a square medieval base. It houses an exhibition retracing the history of the town.

Hôtel Arnoux-de-Maison-Rouge
7 rue de l'Horloge.
The corridor, lit with oval windows, leads to a delightful early-17C courtyard.

Cour de l'Hôtel Guimoneau★
12 rue de l'Horloge.
16C door. Go through the corridor into the attractive courtyard. The staircase is decorated with delicate carvings including an Annunciation. On the left, the gallery incorporates four statuettes representing, from left to right, Fortitude, Justice, Prudence and Temperance.

▷ Return to carrefour des Taules and turn right onto rue St-Amable.

Basilique St-Amable
Only the nave and part of the transept remain from the original 12C church. The chancel, from the early 13C, is a combination of Romanesque and Gothic (capitals with full-face figures and large crockets). The northern side chapels,

with their fine ribbing on carved figure bases, date from the 15C; the southern side chapels and the west front are 18C. The sacristy features fine wood panelling (1687) around the chapter's chancel, and an interesting collection of silks.

▷ Follow rue du Commerce, turn right onto rue Hyppolyte-Gomot and walk to the intersection with rue Sirmon.

The numerous fountains that were erected in Riom in the 17C and 18C make strolling through the town very pleasant. One of the most famous is the 17C Adam and Eve Fountain, decorated with caryatids, by the Riom sculptor Languille.

▷ Return to the crossroads and take rue du Commerce.

Rue du Commerce
The modern sculptures of lava stone contrast with older works of the same material. At No. 36, note the caryatids of the Hôtel Valette de Rochevert.

Église Notre-Dame-du-Marthuret★
This church was built in the Languedoc style; it dates from the 14C and 15C.
The west front was extensively damaged during the French Revolution; a copy of the Virgin with a Bird stands against the pier. On place J.-B.-Laurent, the fountain recalls the Hero of the Battle of Marengo,

General Desaix (1768–1800), who was born in Ayat-sur-Sioule.

🚗 DRIVING TOUR

LES COMBRAILLES
Round trip of 75km/46.6mi. Half a day.

The Combrailles is a crystalline plateau traversed north to south by the Sioule gorge which irrigates the area. The land is bordered to the west by the Combraille Limousine (Auzances region), to the east by the Riom plain and the Chaîne des Puys in the Bourbonnais bocage, and north and south by the Sancy (1 886m) and the upper valley of the Dordogne.

▶ Leave Riom W on D 986 towards Pontgibaud.

Mozac★★
This town lies at the gateway to Riom and is famous for the capitals and treasure in its church. An abbey was founded here by St Calmin in the 7C.

CHURCH★
The church was built in the 12C to a design inspired by the great churches of the Auvergne, but underwent major reconstruction in the 15C following an earthquake. During the French Revolution the cloisters and part of the abbey buildings were demolished.

Remains from the Romanesque period include a series of fine **capitals★★** in the nave and north side aisle which are renowned for their importance in the history of Romanesque sculpture.

At the end of the nave are two of these very beautiful 12C capitals; they were originally part of the ambulatory, which no longer exists.

On the approach to the chancel there is a rich Romanesque bestiary visible, with griffins, men astride goats, dragons, a corded monkey (third pillar on the left), centaurs, birds of paradise, masks etc.

On the floor of the chancel is a third capital depicting four angels closing the mouths of four other characters;

this is an illustration of a passage from St John's Book of Revelations. The chancel also contains 15C stalls. A 15C wood carving of the Madonna with a Bird stands near the baptistery.

TREASURY★★
The most priceless object is the enamel **reliquary of St Calmin★★**, said to date back to 1168. It is displayed in a glass case in the right arm of the transept.

▶ Rejoin D 986 and follow it towards Pontgibaud.

Volvic –
🕭*see VOLVIC.*

▶ N of Volvic, before the D 15-D 83 junction, turn left.

Château de Tournoël★★
🕭*See VOLVIC.*

▶ Return to Volvic and take D 15 left alongside the graveyard. At the D 15 exit to Enval, leave the car just before the bridge spanning the Ambène.

Gorges d'Enval★
🔲 Having crossed the bridge, take a path uphill to the left along the shaded banks of the river. After a few minutes of occasionally strenuous walking, cross the ford over the mountain stream, which forms a waterfall here that drops down into a picturesque gorge.

▶ Continue to Charbonnières-les-Varennes then turn left onto D 16 towards Paugnat.

Manoir de Veygoux
🕭🕐*Apr–Jun and Sept–early Nov 10am–6pm daily except Sun–Mon; Jul–Aug daily 10am–7pm.* ☞€8.50 (child 5–15, €5.50). ℘04 73 33 83 00. www.veygoux.com.
The manor, where General Desaix spent his childhood, is partly concealed by a building added in recent years. Walk round the building to see the restored façade. Inside, there is a modern illustra-

Gour de Tazenat

© Francis Cormon/hemis.fr

tion of the life of this general who won fame during the Revolution and later in Bonaparte's army.

▷ Return to Charbonnières-les-Varennes then drive to Châtel-Guyon.

Châtel-Guyon✝

Châtel-Guyon is situated on the edge of a regional park (Parc Naturel Régional des Volcans d'Auvergne).

The Calvary stands on a hilltop overlooking the centre of town, on the site once occupied by the castle of Count Guy II of Auvergne, after whom the town was named.

The spa resort enjoyed a massive boom in the 19C. Pipes bring water from 12 springs up to the park on the banks of the River Sardon. The main feature of the springs is their magnesium content, the highest in Europe; their temperature varies from 27.5°C to 38°C. The spa itself includes the **Grand Spa** (1st class) and the **Henry Spa** (2nd class) which was completely rebuilt in 1983.

The resort specialises in the treatment of digestive and gynaecological disorders. Today, life in the resort centres on the casino-theatre, the park at the foot of Mont Chalusset containing the Grands Thermes, and avenue Baraduc which is lined with cafés and souvenir gift shops.

ÉGLISE STE-ANNE

The church is decorated in a modern style. The stained-glass windows made of Baccarat crystal distil light onto **Byz-** antine-style frescoes painted by the Estonian artist Nicolas Greschny.

▷ Leave Châtel-Guyon on D 415 towards Manzat.

Château de Chazeron

🕾 *Guided visits (45mn) Jul–Aug, daily except Sun 2.30–6.30pm; May–Jun and Sept Wed, Sat–Sun 3–6pm.* 🕾€6. ✆*07 68 65 00 54.* *www.chateau-chazeron.com.*

This medieval castle was altered in the 17C by the architect Mansart. A staircase was built on the site of the former east tower, three of the outer walls were also demolished and the moat filled in, then two wings were built, one of them containing the servants' kitchen (south wing).

The tour provides a lively insight into the history of the castle. The château is now a cultural centre, with exhibitions of drawings and avant-garde furniture.

▷ Follow D 415 to the junction with D 227. Turn right at Pont de la Ganne on D 19 towards Combronde.

Gour de Tazenat★

🚶 A footpath leads around the lake: leave from the refreshment stand in an anticlockwise direction. The first part of the footpath is flat but becomes steep in places along the second part. The green waters of Lake Tazenat lie in a volcanic crater. The lake marks the northern boundary of the Puys range.

◉ In Charbonnières-les-Vieilles, take D 408 NE to Montcel then turn left to St-Hilaire-la-Croix.

Église St-Hilaire-la-Croix

This attractive building stands on the shores of the "Red Lake", whose waters once mingled with the blood of martyrs, or so says local tradition. The lofty late-12C church shows strong Limousin influence (capitals decorated with palmettes and foliage motifs).

◉ Take D 1244 to Combronde, then S of the village take D 412.

Sources Pétrifiantes de Gimeaux

◔*Not currently open to the public; call for updates.* ℰ*04 73 63 57 59.*
These natural thermal mineral springs are a geological phenomenon known locally as the "volcano". The industry of encrusting objects with lime dates back to the early 19C and uses tried and trusted techniques.

◉ Carry on along D 17 on the banks of the Danade.

Château de Davayat

🗣*Guided visits Jul–Sept daily except Sat 2.30–6pm.* ♿. ☞€5. ℰ*04 73 63 30 27.*
A fine avenue of chestnut trees leads to this Louis XIII manor built by Blaise Roze, a wealthy merchant from Riom.

Aigueperse

This charming town at the heart of the Limagne is circled by avenues that have replaced the former ramparts. The Hôtel de Ville (town hall) is housed in a 17C convent building; note the three Jack o' the clocks who chime the hours.

EXCURSIONS

Lezoux

15km/9mi to the W of Thiers.
In the 2C, Lezoux was a major centre of the ceramics industry, which was

The ambitious plans for the house and gardens were curtailed at Roze's death.

◉ Return to Riom via St-Bonnet along D 2144.

ADDRESSES

🛏STAY

◔◔ **Chambre d'Hôte la Rambaude** – *8 r. de la Limagne, 63460 Beauregard-Vendon.* ℰ*04 73 63 35 62. www.la-rambaude.com. 3 rooms. Closed Nov–Mar.* Out in the country, this hotel is surrounded by a beautiful garden. The décor of this former mansion does not lack charm; comfortable rooms and cosy lounge.

◔◔ **Chambre d'Hôte La Maison de la Treille** – *25 r. de l'Église, 63200 Davayat.* ℰ*04 73 63 58 20. http://honnorat.la.treille. free.fr. 4 rooms.* Beautiful mansion dating from 1810 inspired by Italian neo-Classicism. The rooms are cosy and are located in an orange grove in the garden.

🍴EAT

◔◔ **Le Flamboyant** – *21 bis r. de l'Horloge.* ℰ*04 73 63 07 97. www. restaurant-le-flamboyant.com. Closed Tue lunch and Mon.* Located in a historical edifice of the old town that used to be a girls' school, this restaurant welcomes diners in three small rooms and serves regional and traditional cuisine.

▸ **Population:** 2 700.
⚙ **Michelin Map:** 326: G-6.
ℹ **Info:** Office Culturel Nord Limagne, 158 Grande Rue, 63260 Aigueperse. ℰ04 73 63 72 70. www.aigueperse.net.
◉ **Location:** 34km/21mi NNE of Clermont Ferrand.

fuelled by the plastic clay quarried in the Limagne. Within a radius of 3km/2mi, the remains of more than 200 potters' kilns have been uncovered, and pottery made in Lezoux has been found as far away as England and Prussia. The town, in which there is now a large oil-making plant, still has a 15C belfry topped by a tower. It stands adjacent to one of the old town gates.

The **Musée de la Céramique** (ⓞApr–Sept Mon–Fri 10am–6pm, Sat–Sun 2–7pm; Oct–Mar Mon–Fri 10am–5pm, Sat–Sun 2–6pm; ⓞJan, 1 May, 1 and 11 Nov, 25 Dec. ⊛€5. ℰ04 73 73 42 42; http://musee-ceramique.puy-de-dome.fr) contains collections of sigillated pottery (marked with a seal) dating from the 1C to the 4C – vases, cups, dishes, goblets, bowls etc – brick-red in colour, with rough but varied decorations in relief (animals, figures, floral motifs).

Ravel

6km/3.7mi SE of Lezoux along D 223.
This village, set among the pasture and woodland of the Limagne, is easily identified by the **château★** (☛guided visits May–Aug Tue–Sun 10am–5pm; Sept–AprSat–Sun only 2–5pm, except public holidays. ⊛€7. ℰ04 73 62 95 15; www.chateauderavel.com) which overlooks its houses and its church. In 1294, the castle was given by Philip the Fair to his chancellor Pierre Flotte and passed by inheritance and marriage to the D'Estaing family, who had it renovated in the 17C. The most beautiful and best preserved part of its decoration dates from the 18C.

Church

The building has two 14C stained-glass windows in the nave and another (late 13C) in the sacristy.

🚗 DRIVING TOUR

DISCOVERING LA LIMAGNE
70km/43.5mi. Allow 3h.

This itinerary runs across the Limagne, a vast fertile plain extending north of Clermont-Ferrand towards the Bourbonnais region.

▶ Leave Aigueperse to the N. D 2019 and then D 2009 lead to the Butte de Montpensier, 4km/2.5mi further on.

Butte de Montpensier

Montpensier "Hill" is a typical volcanic neck. A fortress once stood on the hilltop and it was here that King Louis VIII, the father of St Louis, died in 1226 on his return from the Albigensian Crusade. The castle was razed to the ground on the orders of Richelieu in the 17C.

▶ Take the D 151.

Château d'Effiat★

6km/3.7mi NE of Aigueperse.
☛Guided tours Jul–Aug daily except Mon at 2.30pm, 4pm and 5.30pm. ♿(interior only). ⊛€8. ℰ04 73 63 63 16. www.chateau-effiat.com.
On the Vichy to Aigueperse road stands the Château d'Effiat, a fine Louis XIII building of considerable historic and architectural interest.

▶ Take D 93 and drive to Bas-et-Lezat, then take D 63.

Villeneuve-les-Cerfs

A picturesque **dovecote★** stands in a meadow at the entrance to the village.

▶ Continue along D 63 until you reach the intersection with D 1093 and turn right.

Maringues

This large village of Gallo-Roman origin, a busy agricultural trading centre, stands along the recently canalised Morge. Until the mid-19C, wool and leather-working were the traditional local activities: around 1850 there were 60 tanneries operating along the river.

▶ Leave to the SW and take D 224, heading for Riom.

Ennezat

Ennezat, a large farming village on the Limagne plain lies near marshes in a landscape of vast, geometrical fields separated by drainage ditches and rows of aspen trees and willows.

▷ Leave Ennezat and follow the diverted route to Vichy on D 210.

Thuret

A 13C keep dominates the village.

▷ Leave Thuret on D 211 and drive to Sardon. Enter Sardon on D 51, then, on leaving the town, turn left onto D 122 to the junction with D 985. Turn right onto D 985 to St-Myon.

St-Myon

There is a small Romanesque church here with a fine stone-slabbed roof.

▷ Continue along D 223 to the E.

Artonne

St Martin of Tours came here to pray at the tomb of St Vitaline.

A nature discovery trail "Coteau du Puy St-Jean" leads to a viewpoint overlooking the village.

▷ Drive NW out of Artonne and turn right onto D 22 towards St-Agoulin then follow D 12.

Château de la Roche

This medieval manor, slightly altered in the 16C, was the fief of the vassal families of the dukes of Bourbon. The illustrious **Michel de L'Hospital** was born at La Roche, which he was given as a dowry in 1537.

▷ Take the D 12 for Aigueperse, turn left, then take the D 439 towards Vensat.

Château de Villemont

🕐 *Apr–Sept.* 📞 *04 73 38 02 48. www.villemont.net.*
Michel de Veyny, nephew of Chancellor Duprat, built this chateau in the 16C on the site of the "Maison de Villemont".

▷ Take the D 439, then the D 2009 back to Aigueperse.

Gorges de la Sioule★★

The upper course of the River Sioule has a winding, undulating character as it flows down the Dômes mountain range, contrasting with the lower course, which is flat with numerous islands in the Limagne basin. As erosion brought down the level of this calcareous basin, the Sioule, flowing at an increasing speed, cut into the granitic plateau upstream, thereby hollowing out a gorge between the outlying areas of Ébreuil and Châteauneuf-les-Bains. An intricate network of footpaths and bridleways enable visitors to

- ♿ **Michelin Map:** 326: C-5 to E-7.
- ℹ **Info:** 63390 Châteauneuf-les-Bains.
- ▷ **Location:** 30km/18.6mi NW of Riom. Access to the gorges is effected to the NW of Riom, by the N 144 (direction Montluçon).
- 👁 **Don't Miss:** The gorges de Chouvigny, and the Méandre de Queuille.
- 🕐 **Timing:** You will need a whole day to do the gorges justice.
- 👥 **Kids:** Visit the Château de Chouvigny.

discover the attractions of the area, which is also ideal for fishing and canoeing.

🚗 DRIVING TOURS

1 GORGES AND CASTLES
40km/25mi. About 3h.

This delightful itinerary explores the gorges and visits an important château.

Ébreuil
The small town lies on the banks of the Sioule which, having crossed the famous gorge of the same name, flows through a wide, fertile valley. The **Église St-Léger★**, built in the 10C and 13C, was part of a Benedictine abbey whose buildings were replaced in the 18C by the present hospice (to the right of the west front) and by an abbot's palace (behind the east end) that is now a retirement home.

The belfry-porch, remarkable for the purity of its architectural design, was added to the 11C west front around 1125.

▶ Leave Ébreuil to the W on D 915.

The corniche road, 4km/2.5mi after Ébreuil, overlooks the Sioule. On the

Detail of a fresco, Église St-Léger, Ébreuil
© Hervé Lenain/hemis.fr

steeper and more rugged slope on the right, bare granite alternates with heather. Beyond Péraclos, the road descends down to the river's edge.

Château de Chouvigny
🚗 *Guided visits only (45mn): Jul–Aug daily except Mon 2–6pm.* ⊚€5. ℘04 70 59 81 77. www.chouvigny.net.
This Bourbonnais-style fortress is built on a spur of rock in a delightful **setting★** in a valley, its impressive crenellated silhouette towering high above the gorge of the Sioule flowing below.

Gorges de Chouvigny★★
At the entrance to the gorge the road cuts through a rocky headland, the left part of which, detached from the rest, is called **Roc Armand**. The summit can be reached by a staircase cut out of the rock.

Upstream, there is a beautiful view of the gorge – wooded slopes spiked with granite tips – whereas downstream, Chouvigny Castle can be seen. Beyond Armand rock, the gorge becomes very picturesque.

At the entrance to a tunnel there is a **viewpoint** on the left, over a bend in the Sioule dominated by high cliffs. Upstream, the Sioule flows silently and smoothly down.

Below the viewpoint, however, it flows quickly and noisily through a mass of pebbles; it is gradually wearing down a shelf which interrupts the natural slope. The picturesque valley unfolds a succession of wild-looking gorges and green narrow stretches.

Menat
This small village was once home to a 6C Benedictine monastery. Today there remain the 12C abbey church, vestiges of the 15C cloisters, along with the buildings housing the town hall and the Museum of Palaeontology.

MUSÉE DE PALÉONTOLOGIE: "LE GÎTE À FOSSILES"
🕐 *Apr–May Sat, Sun and public holidays 10.30am–noon, 2–6.30pm; Jun–*

GORGES OF THE SIOULE

Sept daily except Tue 10.30am–noon,
2–6.30pm. €5. ✆04 73 85 54 22.
The museum is chiefly devoted to the
small geological basin of Menat, dating
from the end of the Secondary Era. The
exhibition "La Marche vers l'Homme"
illustrates the evolution of life on earth
from the first cell up to modern Man.

PONT-DE-MENAT

This is an ideal point of departure for
canoeing and kayaking. Crossing the
river, there is an attractive view (right)
of the old humpback bridge.
Soon, on the edge of a cliff ahead, the
romantic ruins of **Château-Rocher** (13C)
loom into sight. Immediately below the
ruins is an attractive view of a bend in
the Sioule, a typical example of an
incised meander: the concave bank (this
side), excavated by the direct attack of
the current, is steep; the convex bank
(opposite), which receives the alluvial
deposits, is low and cultivated.

The road then rises, providing greater
views of the river; it reaches its culmi-
nation just before the intersection with
D 99 from St-Rémy-de-Blot. Forming a
ledge above a small, still-active mill, it
offers a fine view of the entire valley.

Lisseuil

Here the road reaches the bottom of the
valley. The village church has a beautiful
Romanesque Virgin (13C) in its restored
chancel.

Ayat-sur-Sioule

An attractive road leads to this village,
once the home of General Desaix (1768–
1800), one of Napoleon's officers.

Châteauneuf-les-Bains

This thermal spa actually consists of several hamlets. Twenty-two springs are
tapped here, providing cold water for
bottling and hot water (ranging from
28–36ºC) for the baths treating rheumatism and nervous disorders.

2 QUEUILLE MEANDER
60km/38mi. About 3h30.

This remarkable geographical feature is well worth a visit; the time will come when it is no longer there.

Châteauneuf-les-Bains
See above.

▶ Take D 227 W.

St-Gervais-d'Auvergne
The village is built on a knoll. Its Gothic church still has some Romanesque features. Beautiful lime trees shade the terrace by the church. The **Maison des Combrailles** (*Place R-Gauvin, 63390 St-Gervais d'Auvergne; ℘04 73 85 82 08*) provides information on the area.
South of St-Gervais the road winds through the middle of a wood, offering some lovely views of the Sioule before crossing the river. It then runs along the east bank, which follows numerous meanders and circumvents the seams of porphyry which lie in its path.

Viaduc des Fades★
This structure, built by the engineer Vidard at the beginning of the 20C, is one of Europe's highest rail viaducts.

BARRAGE DE BESSERVE
The dam, located upstream of the viaduct, is a gravity dam – its strength is provided by its sheer mass.

Méandre de Queuille★★
🚶 Walk behind the east end of the church and continue through undergrowth to a viewpoint at the end of the promontory overlooking the Queuille meander, formed by the Sioule after it was widened by a dam.
This side, the concave bank of the loop, is high and spiked with rocks; opposite, on the convex side, the river forms a tight circle around the Murat "peninsula", a long wooded headland.

BARRAGE DE QUEUILLE
Downstream from the meander is another gravity dam.

▶ Return to Les Ancizes-Comps and turn left on D 61.

The road provides a magnificent descent through the Sioule valley.

Chartreuse de Port-Ste-Marie
At the bottom of the valley, perched on a rock, are the ruins of a 13C Carthusian monastery.

Miremont
The Romanesque church here with its massive square bell-tower rises up on a peak dominating a loop in the river.

ADDRESSES

🛏 STAY

🍴🛏 **Montarlet** – *63390 St. Gervais d'Auvergne. 3km/1.8mi W of St-Gervais-d'Auvergne via D 532, dir. Espinasse then turn left. ℘04 73 85 87 10. www.montarlet-chambresdhotes.com. 3 rooms.* Located in a lovely, natural environment, this old farm is a pleasant stopover. The restored bedrooms are delightful, with their sponge-painted walls, antiques and carefully chosen fabrics.

🍴🛏 **Castel Hôtel 1904** – *63390 St-Gervais-d'Auvergne. ℘04 73 85 70 42. www.castel-hotel-1904.com. 17 rooms. Restaurant🍴🛏🍴.* This 17C manor became a hotel in 1904. The inviting interior is a reminder of centuries past with its period furniture, waxed parquets, grandfather clocks and statuettes. There is a formal restaurant, and a good value, more relaxed bistro.

RECREATION

Sioule Loisirs – *Pont de Menat, 63560 Menat. ℘04 73 85 52 87. www.val-de-sioule.com/loisire.html. May–Sept from 9am. Reservations required.* Canoe and kayak rentals for trips down the Sioule. All-day and half-day itineraries possible. Horse riding, mountain bikes, fishing, aerial sports.

Bourbonnais is an ancient province, one that corresponds roughly with the present-day department of Allier with a little bit of Cher thrown in; its capital was, and still is, Moulins. The region marks the northern edge of the Massif Central, and takes the form of gently rolling countryside covered with a delightful patchwork of fields edged by hedgerows, which tend to give the area a wooded appearance. The Besbre, the Cher and the Aumance are the principal valley through-routes.

Vichy Pastilles

At the end of the 19C, the Empress Eugénie discovered these little acidic sweets and encouraged her ladies-in-waiting to take them also.

The result was immediate: in 1885 an imperial decree recognised the originality of the pastilles of Vichy. Used as an aid to digestion, the original pastilles were pure bicarbonate of soda. Later they were made using salts extracted from Vichy water, and today are flavoured with mint, lemon and aniseed.

The Oldest Vineyards in France?

Tradition has it that grapevines first appeared on the hillsides of the Bouble and the Sioule valleys a little before the Christian era. The stony ground of this region is ideal for vine growing, which developed rapidly during Roman times, and later at the demand of the monasteries and local squires.

Highlights

1 The artworks and stained-glass windows of the **Notre-Dame Cathedral** in Moulins (p264)

2 A guided walk in the **Tronçais Forest** (p277)

3 "Taking the waters" at one of the **Vichy** springs (p285)

4 An evening of music at the Vichy **Opera House** (p288)

5 The world's largest rolling ball clock in **Lavoine** (p295)

Bocage

Throughout much of the Auvergne, you encounter a landscape that might be described as *bocage*. It is probably a Norman word referring to a small forest, or a terrain of mixed woodland and pasture with fields and winding country lanes.

Forêt de Tronçais

© Hervé Lenain/hemis.fr

BOURBONNAIS

NEVERS, BOURGES

BOURBONNAIS

0 ——— 8 km

FÔRET DE TRONÇAIS	★★★ Highly recommended
Moulins	★★ Recommended
Chareil	★ Interesting
Huriel	Other sight described

Musée rural de la
Sologne Bourbonnaise

NIÈVRE

Arboretum de Balaine

Le Riau

D 133

Avrilly

Augère

Agonges

St-Menoux

Autry-
ssards

Moulins

Souvigny

Yzeure

Bressolles

Toulon-s-Allier

Vieux
Bostz

Besson

Noyant-
d'Allier

Fourchaud

Châtel-de-Neuvre

ALLIER

Verneuil-en-
Bourbonnais

St-Pourçain-
sur-Sioule

hantelle

Chareil

Étroussat

Ussel-
d'Allier

Charroux

Jenzat

Cognat

Gannat

Biozat

Brugheas

St-Yorre

Vichy

Cusset

Site des
Hurlevents

Busset

PUY-DE-DÔME

Ris

Seganges

Sept-Fons

LOIRE

MÂCON

Le PAL

Thoury

Beauvoir

Châtelperron

Puy
St-Ambroise

442

Jaligny

Chavroches

La Palice

Lapalisse

Droiturier

Le Breuil

St-Étienne-
de-Vicq

Châtel-Montagne

Puy du Roc

Le Mayet-de-
Montagne

Arronnes

Montagne
bourbonnaise

Pierre
Charbonnière

644

1031

Forêt de
l'Assise

Lavoine

Vallée de la Credogne

NEUILLY-EN-DONJON

LYON, ROANNE

1

2

3

 CLERMONT-FERRAND

263

Moulins★

Moulins lies on the banks of the River Allier and is the quietly charming main town of the Bourbonnais area. It boasts a range of economic and industrial activities linked to the rich farmland of the Moulins region, with food industries, shoe factories and machine tool production. The wide avenues and streets of the old town are an ideal place for a stroll.

A BIT OF HISTORY

The Duchy of Bourbonnais – Bourbon lands first appeared in literature in the early 10C, but it took more than three centuries for the lords and counts of Bourbon to create a state capable of rivalling its neighbours, Berry and Burgundy. The Bourbons achieved their aim by taking advantage of their geographical location between the kingdom of France and the duchies of Auvergne and Aquitaine, placing their troops at the service of the crown. This alliance with royal authority, combined with a skilful policy of marriage (Béatrice de Bourbon married Robert, Count of Clermont, St Louis' sixth child, in 1265), facilitated the building of a vast State and led to eight Bourbons becoming King of France. In 1327 the Barony of Bourbon became a duchy and, in the following year, it was raised to the peerage by Philip VI.

Arts at the Court of Moulins – The duchy enjoyed its golden age during the 15C and, at the same time, the court in Moulins entered a period of splendour and brilliance, with artists summoned here by Charles I, Jean II, Pierre II and Anne of France. Pierre de Nesson recounted the misfortunes of Jean I; the Flemish musician Jean Ockeghem sang for Charles I before moving on to the king's chapel. Sculpture flourished under Jean II, firstly with Jacques Morel, then with Michel Colombe and his followers, Jean de Rouen and Jean de Chartres. It is, however, the painters who produced the finest works, notably the **Master of Moulins** who created the famous "Triptych" (&see opposite).

▶ **Population:** 20 103.
& **Michelin Map:** 326: H-3.
Info: 11 r. François-Péron, 03000 Moulins. &04 70 44 14 14. www.moulins-tourisme.com.
▷ **Location:** Moulins lies roughly midway between Nevers and Clermont-Ferrand, and is accessible from the A 71.
P **Parking:** Park around the edge of the town centre rather than in it.
& **Don't Miss:** Take a tour around the lovely streets of the cathedral district.
& **Timing:** The heritage here merits a three-day visit.
& **Kids:** Visit the Val d'Allier nature reserve.

CATHÉDRALE NOTRE-DAME

&*Daily 9am, noon, 2–6pm.* &*1 Jan, 1 May, 14 Jul, 15 Aug, 1 Nov and 25 Dec.* &*04 70 20 57 77. www.moulins-tourisme.com.*
Work began on a church in the 15C and it was made a cathedral in the 19C. Notre-Dame is particularly interesting for its works of art and **stained-glass windows★★**, which depict famous figures from the Bourbons' Court.

1) **St Catherine's or the Dukes' Window** – Late 15C. The window shows the Cardinal of Bourbon on the right and Pierre II and Anne of France on the left, worshipping St Catherine.
2) **Crucifixion Window** – Late 15C. The bottom of the window shows **The Entombment of Christ★**(16C).
3) **Window of the Virgin Mary Enthroned** – Late 15C.
4) **Tree of Jesse Window** – 16C.
5) **Elegant spiral staircase**.
6) **Window of the Suffering and Triumphant Church** – Early 16C.
7) **Window of the Church Militant** – 16C. The Crown of Thorns is

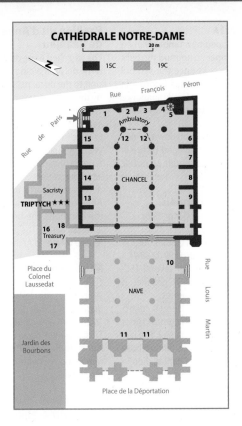

CATHÉDRALE NOTRE-DAME

handed over to the King.

8) **Chapel of the Black Virgin** – The Black Virgin, a replica of the one in Le Puy-en-Velay, serves as a reminder that Moulins was one of the stopovers used by pilgrims on their way to Le Puy-en-Velay and Santiago de Compostela.

9) **Chapter Chapel** – The centre of the stained-glass window depicts the martyrdom of St Barbara.

10) **Classical Painting** – Two Carthusian monks.

11) **The Annunciation** – 18C painting on each side of the doorway.

12) **Window depicting the life of the Virgin Mary.**

13) **St Mary Magdalene Window** – 16C.

14) **Window of Christ on the Cross** – Late 15C.

15) **St Elizabeth of Hungary's Window** – Early 16C.

The Salle du trésor displays **Triptych by the Master of Moulins★★★** (&see *INTRODUCTION, Architecture*). This splendid painting on wood, probably completed in 1498, is considered to be one of the last masterpieces of Gothic painting in France.

The room also contains a 17C ivory crucifix reliquary **(16)** mounted on an ebony stand, the Aubery Triptych **(17)** and the Bethlehem Triptych **(18)** attributed to 16C Flemish painter Joos van Cleve.

WALKING TOUR

CATHEDRAL DISTRICT
& See map p267.

▷ Leave the cathedral by the north door, walk round the east end of the church and go down rue Grenier, then rue des Orfèvres.

Jacquemart★

The belfry, topped by a timber-framed roof and a campanile housing the bells and automata, was once the symbol of the town's privileges as a borough. Today, the Jacquemart family announce the time of day for those working in, or visiting, the city.

The clock tower was burnt down in 1655 and was once again ravaged by fire in 1946. in 1947 it was rebuilt by public subscription.

Musée du Bourbonnais

6 pl. de l'Ancien-Palais. ○*Apr–Sept 10am–noon, 3–6.30pm; Oct–Mar 10am–noon, 3–5.30pm.* ○*Mon, Tue, 1 May, 25 Dec.* ⊛€6. ℘08 99 02 88 41.

The museum, housed in several 15C-17C buildings linked by 17C galleries, is devoted to four main themes:

Religious art – Abbé Déret's collections are displayed on the ground floor (statues, liturgical objects etc). The history of the Order of the Visitation whose founder, St Jeanne de Chantal, died in Moulins in 1641, is also evoked.

Salles ethnographiques – Several rooms contain reconstructions of workshops illustrating ancient crafts and a 19C farmhouse interior. Fine collections of headdresses, hats and regional costumes as well as musical instruments and objects of daily life.

Collection d'orfèvrerie Française et Européenne – This collection of French and European gold plate includes some unique items such as a 17C ewer in gilded silver.

Collection de jouets, poupées et fers à repasser – A fine collection of antique dolls gathered by the founder of the museum during the course of her various travels.

▶ Take rue de l'Ancien-Palais.

Donjon de la Mal Coiffée

All that remains of the old castle is a massive keep restored in the 15C and named "The Dishevelled" because of its roof. Used as a prison until 1986, its walls bear the inscriptions of past prisoners.

Pavillon dit d'Anne de Beaujeu

The so-called Anne de Beaujeu Pavilion is the only remaining part of the extension to the ducal palace commissioned by the princess around 1495.

This elegant construction is one of the earliest examples of Renaissance architecture in France and was used in later years by King Charles VIII.

A porch tower stands in front of the Italianate façade, which presents six arcades decorated with the initials of Peter and Anne of Beaujeu and the emblems of the Bourbons, the belt of hope, thistle and stag beetle. The pavilion houses the Musée d'Art et d'Archéologie.

Musée Anne de Beaujeu★★

○*Tue–Sat 10am–noon, 2–6pm, Sun 2–6pm.* ○*1 Jan, 1 May, 25 Dec.* ⊛€5 *during exhibitions,* €3 *otherwise.* ℘04 70 20 48 47. www.mab.allier.fr.

This museum occupies the so-called Anne de Beaujeu Pavilion, the only remaining part of the extension to the ducal palace.

Mausolée du duc de Montmorency★

The mausoleum, completed in 1653, is the work of Parisian artists, the Anguier Brothers, and was commissioned by the wife of Henri II of Montmorency after she was widowed by Richelieu in 1632 and sent to the Convent of the Visitation in Moulins (now the high school). It was transported in pieces by road from Paris to Montargis and then by waterway.

QUARTIER DES MARINIERS

While you are visiting the historical heart of Moulins, you can explore the neighbourhood formerly occupied by the town's community of bargemen, starting from the Église du Sacré-Cœur.

Musée du Bâtiment

18 rue du Pont-Guinguet. ○*Daily except Mon and Tue 2–6pm.* ○*1 Jan, 1 May, 1 Nov, 25 Dec.* ⊛€3.50. ℘04 70 34 23 69. http://musee-batiment.planet-allier.com.

Tools, building materials and techniques but also fixtures and fittings of bygone days are displayed in this unusual and interesting museum housed in a fine 18C building.

ESPACE NATURE DU VAL D'ALLIER

8 boulevard de Nomazy
Individual self-guided tours and group tours all year. Public holidays. No charge. 04 70 44 46 29.

The **Val d'Allier Nature Reserve** extends along both banks of the River Allier, between Moulins and St-Pourçain-sur-Sioule. Information about guided nature rambles organised by the Ligue pour la Protection des Oiseaux (LPO) is available from the Espace Nature.

Place d'Allier, Église du Sacré-Cœur in the background

© Hervé Lenain/hemis.fr

WHERE TO STAY		WHERE TO EAT	
Chalet (Hôtel le)............................①		Cours (Restaurant des)......................①	
Grande Poterie (Chambre d'hôte la)............③		Logis Henri IV......................③	
Parc (Hôtel le)............................⑥		Saint-Martin (Auberge)......................⑥	

🚗DRIVING TOUR

CHÂTEAUX IN THE BOURBONNAIS AREA
100km/62mi. Allow one day.

This itinerary is a good way of getting to know the Bourbonnais area.

▶ Leave Moulins to the NE heading towards N7 , then turn right onto D 12.

Yzeure
The village of Yzeure is older than Moulins, and was the seat of the parish until the Hundred Years War.

Château de Seganges
🔑*Closed to the public.*
Small château built at the same time as the Anne de Beaujeu Pavilion.

▶ Continue on D 29, turn right onto D 29.

The road wends its way through Munet Forest, offering pretty glimpses of both coniferous and broad-leaved trees.

▶ Leaving the forest, take D 133 on the left. At the entrance to Auroüer, continue along D 133 on the left.

Château du Riau
🔑*Guided tours Jul and Sept daily except Sat 2.30–6.30pm. ⌧€7. ✆04 70 43 34 47. www.chateau-du-riau.com.*
The Riau estate comprises several buildings dating from the 15C to the 18C which lie in a lovely green setting on the border of the Allier and Nièvre regions. The most remarkable building is the **tithe barn★** built in 1584, with its stables on the lower ground floor and grain storage on the three upper floors; the top floor, with its beautiful timber roof, provides an attractive view of the castle, moat, **fortified gatehouse** and dovecote. The gatehouse contains the chapel and the guard-room. In the square tower, a 15C staircase with a wooden balustrade leads to **bedrooms**

decorated in Louis XV, Louis XVI and Empire styles.

▶ Continue along D 133 until you reach Villeneuve-sur-Allier. On leaving the village, turn right onto D 433.

Arboretum de Balaine★
♿🕐*Daily Mar–Nov 9am–noon, 2–7pm. ⌧€10. ✆04 70 43 30 07. www.arboretum-balaine.com.*
This botanical garden founded in 1804 is landscaped in the English style and includes numerous species: various types of fir (Caucasian, Spanish, Douglas), giant sequoias, oaks, Cedar of Lebanon and locally grown varieties. The trees are pleasantly set amid beautiful shrubs of rhododendron, azalea, bamboo and dogwood.

▶ Return to Villeneuve-sur-Allier and take D 133 to Bourbon-l'Archambault on the right. After leaving Bagneux, D 133, then D 13 cut across the forest of Les Prieurés Bagnolet. Leave D 13 at the end of a straight section; right onto D 54.

St-Menoux★
🚶*see BOURBON-L'ARCHAMBAULT.*

▶ Leave St-Menoux to the S on D 253.

Souvigny★★ – 🚶*see SOUVIGNY.*

▶ Leave Souvigny to the E on D 945, heading for Moulins. On leaving the village, turn right onto D 34, which crosses the railway line.

Besson
This village has an interesting Romanesque church with a single nave. Note the Château de Rochefort, whose ruins overlook the Guèze valley.

▶ Leave Besson to the SW on D 34.

Château du Vieux Bostz
🕐*Visits by arrangement. ✆04 70 42 80 84.*
This castle, dating from the 15C and 16C, is curious because of its many square and round turrets with delicate belfries.

Continue along D 34. At the crossroads, turn left onto D 291, then take D 292 on the right.

Château de Fourchaud
Huge, imposing castle featuring two massive towers with pepper-pot roofs and a sturdy-looking keep. Originally erected in the 14C, the stronghold was heavily restored during the following century.

Continue along D 292. In Bresnay, take D 34 for 4km/2.5mi, then turn left onto D 33.

Châtel-de-Neuvre
Pretty village with a Romanesque church built on a promontory dominating the Allier valley. Enjoy the **view★** extending over the nearby river and landscape.

Leave Châtel-de-Neuvre to the E on D 32, crossing the Allier, then turn left onto D 300.

Toulon-sur-Allier
This hamlet used to be an important centre for the production of pottery back in Gallo-Roman times.

Leave Toulon-sur-Allier to the S on N 7, then take N 79 on the right. After crossing the Allier, take N 2009 to Moulins on the right.

Bressolles
Small village situated north-east of the charming Prieurés Moladier forest.

ADDRESSES

STAY

Le Parc – 31 av. du Gén.-Leclerc. ℘04 70 44 12 25. www.hotel-moulins.com. 28 rooms. Restaurant. A few steps from a verdant park and the train station. Modest bedrooms and two dining rooms, rustic and contemporary.

Chambre d'Hôte La Grande Poterie – 9 r. de la Grande-Poterie, 03000 Coulandon. ℘04 70 44 30 39. www.lagrandepoterie.com. 4 rooms. Open mid-Mar–Oct. Restaurant. Ancient farm at the centre of a woodland park.

Le Chalet Montégut – 26 rte du Chalet, 03000 Coulandon. ℘04 70 46 00 66. www.hotel-lechalet.fr. 28 rooms. Restaurant. In the centre of a park; quiet, delightful and provincial.

EAT

Auberge Saint-Martin – Place du Bourg, 03000 Coulandon. ℘04 70 46 06 10. Closed Sun, Mon and Tue evenings. Traditional dishes served in a rustic but homely dining room.

Restaurant des Cours – 36 cours Jean-Jaurès. ℘04 70 44 25 66. www.restaurant-des-cours-moulins.fr. Closed Wed. This fetching bourgeois house in the heart of the city is embellished by a lacework of Virginia creeper.

Logis Henri IV – 13 Rue du Quatorze Juillet, 03340 Neuilly-le-Réal. ℘04 70 43 87 64. Closed Sun evening and Mon. The logis was a hunting lodge back in the 16C. You'll enter the half-timbered dining room with its pretty tiled floor via the *perron*.

TAKING A BREAK
Le Grand Café – 49 pl. d'Allier. ℘04 70 44 00 05. Summer: daily 8am–1am; rest of the year: closed Sun, Tue, 1 Jan and 25 Dec. Built in 1899, this café is classified as a historic monument. An imposing fresco honouring Gambrinus, the god of ale, surrounds customers.

Le Vieux Moulins – 2 r. de l'Ancien-Palais. ℘04 70 20 67 81. This eminently agreeable establishment has always been a crêperie. Moreover, the bar has a terrace on the pedestrian street, the pavement of which is used by the owner to organise her concerts and other original goings-on.

Souvigny★★

Souvigny, which lies among wooded hills in the middle of a rich farming area, retains the most beautiful sanctuary in the Bourbonnais region, a reminder of the town's past splendour. It is renowned for its 11C church wherein lie the tombs of many of the most influential dukes of Bourbon. The town has the status of "Grand Site of the Auvergne" and is keenly promoting its important architectural heritage.

A BIT OF HISTORY

Resting place of the Dukes of Bourbon – In 916 Aymard, lieutenant of the Duke of Aquitaine, sold his land at Souvigny to the monks of Cluny; in doing so he bestowed an uncommon destiny upon the former Carolingian villa here. Two famous abbots from the powerful Burgundian abbey died in the monastery founded here: St Mayeul in 994 and St Odilon in 1049. The saintliness of the two men, soon united in the same tomb, drew numerous pilgrims to Souvigny, and the oldest of the Cluny priories, showered with gifts, developed dramatically. The lords of Bourbon, descendants of Aymard, created a state around Souvigny which was to become the Duchy of the Bourbonnais. In the 14C and 15C the monastery underwent further alterations when Duke Louis II and Duke Charles I decided to make the sanctuary their necropolis.

- ▶ **Population:** 1 961.
- 🚗 **Michelin Map:** 326: G-3 – 13km/8mi W of Moulins.
- 🛈 **Info:** Mairie de Souvigny, 03210 Souvigny. 𝒫04 70 43 60 38. www.ville-souvigny.com.
- ◐ **Location:** Lying 13km/8mi west of Moulins along the D 945, Souvigny is equally accessible from Bourbon-l'Archambault.
- ⊙ **Don't Miss:** A visit to the museum.
- ◔ **Timing:** To make the most of Souvigny and the surrounding area, allow a full day.

ABBEY
Église Prieurale St-Pierre-et-St-Paul★★

The west front of the original Romanesque edifice, of which only the left door remains, was preceded in the 15C by an avant-corps with a portal and a wide Flamboyant opening.

Two Romanesque bell-towers, connected since the 15C by a gable with a rose window, dominate the priory. The three Romanesque bays in the centre of the façade belonged to the original building consecrated in 1064. The north side shows the church's different stages of construction: the towers, the second aisle and the ambulatory are 12C whereas the upper part of the nave and the transept are 15C.

Nave and aisles – The interior has surprisingly large dimensions: 87m by 28m. The double side aisles flanking the nave, and the double transept are evidence of Cluniac influence. The inner aisles, built in the 11C, are very narrow with barrel vaulting whereas the outer aisles, which are later, have groined or pointed vaulting.

Chapelle Vieille★

The old chapel has a beautiful stone screen in Flamboyant Gothic style.

- ◆ Tomb of **Louis II of Bourbon,**

Église Prieurale St-Pierre-et-St-Paul

© Hervé Lenain/hemis.fr

known as Louis the Good, and his wife, Anne of Auvergne. The two marble recumbent figures are still extremely realistic, despite the defacements.

♦ 15C **Entombment**.

Chapelle Neuve★★
The new chapel is larger than the old chapel and has a very fine enclosure.

♦ Tomb of Charles I and his wife, Agnes of Burgundy by Jacques Morel. The figures, clothed in flowing cloaks, rest on a black marble slab.

♦ A graceful Mary Magdalene from the late 15C.

♦ The Virgin, Child and St John (16C).

♦ Small 15C Pietà.

Cloisters
Only one side of these 15C cloisters remains, with groined vaulting because of the arrangement of the pillars. French-style gardens have been laid out on the site of the priory buildings.

SIGHTS
Musée de Souvigny
Apr–May and Oct–Nov daily except Tue 9am–noon, 2–6pm; Jun and Sept daily 9am–noon, 2–6pm; Jul–Aug daily 9am–noon, 1–6pm. Sun mornings all year. 4€ *(museum and garden)* 04 70 43 99 75. www.ville-souvigny.com/Musee.

This museum to the right of the priory church houses local history collections, as well as a glass-working exhibition. Next to the sarcophagi, recumbent figures and capitals stands a 12C **calendar★★**, the most striking piece in the collection. This 1.8m octagonal pillar, weighing 840kg/1 848lb (over 0.75t), is carved on two sides with scenes showing the labours of the months and the corresponding signs of the Zodiac; symbols of strange peoples and fabulous animals adorn the other faces.

Local history is recalled in the Souvigny glassworks founded in 1755: the master glassmakers' tools and examples of glassware (carafe stoppers, pharmacy bottles, champagne glasses) on show are reminiscent of this ancient craft.

🚗 DRIVING TOUR

COMBRAILLE BOURBONNAISE
65km/40.5mi. Allow 4h.

This lush bocage countryside with its pretty churches will charm all visitors.

▶ Leave Souvigny to the SW on D 945, heading for Le Montet.

Noyant-d'Allier
The most striking feature of this former miners' town is its pagoda, surrounded by Buddha statues.

▶ Continue N on D 18.

Église de Meillers
See Bourbon-l'Archambault, Driving Tour.

▶ Leave Meillers to the S on D 18, then turn right onto D 106.

The Côtes-Matras command an enjoyable vista of the Allier plain.

▶ At Champs-Regneauds, take the D 945 right towards Le Montet.

Le Montet
The 12C Église St-Gervais-et-St-Protais was fortified in the 14C, but today only the nave and the side aisles have survived.

▶ Leave Le Montet to the W on D 22, heading towards Cosne-d'Allier. After 9km/5.6mi, turn right onto D 68.

Buxières-les-Mines
This locality features the very last open-air coal mine in the area.

Église St-Maurice
This church has a curious two-tier bell tower and a blind nave crowned by barrel vaulting.

▶ Return to Souvigny via D 289, then D 11, driving along the Gros-Bois and Messargesoak forests.

Montluçon

The economic capital of the Bourbonnais area, facing the first outcrops of the Combraille hills, mainly huddles round the castle that once belonged to the dukes of Bourbon, but its industrial suburbs stretch over a long distance northwards, up the Cher valley.

A BIT OF HISTORY

Successful rebirth – The completion of the Berry Canal in 1841 linked the iron seams of Berry and the coalfields of Commentry. Because of this, throughout the Second Empire when the steel industry began to develop, Montluçon enjoyed rapid expansion. It became the centre of a major railway network and its functions as a trading and administrative centre spilled over into the surrounding countryside. By the turn of the 20C, the iron and coal seams were exhausted.

Musical son – André Messager (1853-1929), the composer, first became known as a conductor in Covent Garden in London, then in the Opera House in Paris. But he quickly gained a reputation as a composer of operettas and ballets.

OLD TOWN★

▷ Start from avenue Marx-Dormoy and head for the castle.

Rue Grande, Montluçon

© Hervé Lenain/hemis.fr

- ▷ **Population:** 39 217.
- ⚙ **Michelin Map:** 326: C-4.
- 🛈 **Info:** 67 ter boulevard de Courtais, 03110 Montluçon. ℘04 70 05 11 44. www.montlucontourisme.com.
- ▷ **Location:** Montluçon lies north-west of Clermont-Ferrand and is easily accessed using the A 71 autoroute.
- 🅿 **Parking:** There are several car parks in the centre of town.
- ◉ **Don't Miss:** the Château des Ducs de Bourbon.
- 🕐 **Timing:** Montluçon is a bustling place; you may find it useful to allow a full day to explore.

Château des Ducs de Bourbon

The castle was built during the Hundred Years War (14C–15C) by Louis II de Bourbon and his successors, Jean I and Charles I. Banks of flowers climb the old walls, and the castle itself consists of a vast rectangular building flanked, on the town side, by a turret and a large rectangular tower with crenellations.

▷ Turn right onto rue des Serruriers and continue along Grand-Rue.

This old street is lined with 15C houses (Nos. 42, 39 and 27). Continue to place Notre-Dame with its 18C buildings. Stroll through **passage du Doyenné** which leads to place de la Comédie. On Saturday mornings this part of town is filled with colour by its flower market.

Musée des Musiques Populaires

🕐*Tue–Sun: Jun–Aug 10am–7pm; Sept–May 2–6pm. ⊛€7.50 (child 7–12, €2; 13–18, €4). ℘04 70 02 19 62. www.mupop.fr.*

This museum has seen extensive renovation in recent years in order to embrace contemporary trends in music. There are over 700 instruments in the collections and a number of workshops making and

MONTLUÇON

0   200 m

WHERE TO STAY	
Bourbons (Hôtel des)	①
Garden (Hôtel Le)	②
Mona Lisa (Hôtel)	③

WHERE TO EAT	
Eau à la Bouche (L')	①
Grenier à Sel (Le)	②
Safran d'Or	③
Vie en Rose (La)	④

repairing stringed instruments as well as hurdy-gurdies, bagpipes and brasses.

Église Notre-Dame

The church, never completed, was built on the orders of Louis II de Bourbon on the site of a Romanesque sanctuary.

◗ Turn left along rue du Petit Château.

Castle Esplanade

From here there is a **view★** over the entire town, the industrial estates beyond and, in the distance, the first outcrops of the Massif Central, the peaceful Cher valley and the Berry region.

◗ Return to place Notre-Dame and turn left onto rue de la Fontaine.

On the right, rue Pierre-Petit leads to the **Président-Wilson Gardens**; rue des Cinq-Piliers on the left leads to the picturesque place St-Pierre.

Église St-Pierre

The church of St-Pierre, built in the 12C and 13C, is hidden by houses, some of which date from the 15C.

◗ Rue St-Roch and rue des Serruriers lead back to the foot of the castle opposite the statue of Marx Dormoy, former Mayor of Montluçon.

EXCURSIONS

Hérisson

24km/14mi N of Montluçon.

Coiled in a loop of the Aumance river, this pretty medieval village was formerly the meeting place of artists influenced by the School of Barbizon. Among these, the artist **Henri-Joseph Harpignies** (1819–1916) often stayed in Hérisson and the region provided him with the inspiration for some of his finest landscapes. This quaintly attractive town has several old houses (15C–18C) and two 15C fortified gateways among its relics. Above the village stands the impressive ruined mass of a beautiful russet-coloured 13C castle.

🚗 DRIVING TOURS

CANAL DE BERRY

65km/40.5mi. Allow 3h.

This round trip, running west and north of Montluçon, offers an interesting insight into the local cultural heritage.

▶ Leave Montluçon to the NW on D 916, heading for Boussac.

Do, mérat

In one of the castle's outbuildings, the **Musée de la Vigne** (&☉*May–Sept Sun and public holidays 3–5pm. ✆04 70 64 20 01*) illustrates the techniques of wine-making in Allier.

Huriel

12C **Donjon de la Toque** (☉*Jul–Aug daily except Tue and Thu 9am–noon, 2–6pm; Jun and Sept Sat–Sun 3–6pm; ☞€4*).

▶ Leave Huriel to the N and take D 40 to La Chapelaude, then take D 943 on the left for 11km/6.8mi. At the locality called Goëlat, turn right.

Église de St-Désiré★

This remarkable Romanesque construction was once an 11C priory.

▶ Take D 479 N of St-Désiré.

Vallon-en-Sully

A charming village in local pink sandstone, set alongside the Berry canal.

▶ Return towards Montluçon on D 301, running along the River Cher and the Berry Canal. Stop at Magnette; from there cross the canal.

Musée du Canal de Berry

Port de Magnette, Audes. ☉*May–Jun and Sept Wed, Sat–Sun and public holidays 2–6.30pm; Jul–Aug Wed–Sun 10am–12.30pm, 2–6.30pm. ☞€5. ✆04 70 06 63 72. www.museecanaldeberry.fr.* The museum will enlighten visitors as to the history of the canal and the successive stages of its construction.

FORMER MINING COUNTRY

50km/31mi. Allow 3h.

▶ Leave Montluçon to the SE on D 2144 in the direction of Clermont-Ferrand.

Néris-les-Bains

This peaceful health resort was once a busy Gallo-Roman city. Visit the Merovingian necropolis, the ancient baths and the **Musée gallo-romain** (☉*Jul–mid-Sept Wed–Sat 2.30–6pm, and Sun mid-Jun–Aug; ✆04 70 03 42 11*), which displays Gallo-Roman artefacts discovered in Néris: ceramic pieces, coins, jewellery, and sculptures in bronze.

▶ Leave Néris to the E on D 998.

Commentry

Until the end of World War I, Commentry was at the heart of an area devoted to mining. Today this activity has been replaced by chemical, mechanical and other industries.

▶ Leave Commentry to the SE and continue along D 998.

Église de Colombier

Crowned by an elegant 12C belfry, the church and its nearby priory, defended by a citadel, form a harmonious architectural ensemble.

▶ Leave Colombier N on D 200.

Malicorne

Jardin-Verger is a dazzling garden-orchard bursting with colour: the rose garden alone boasts several hundred varieties.

▶ Leave Malicorne to the N on D 69. Turn left onto D 438, which will take you back to Montluçon.

ADDRESSES

🛏 STAY

😴🍽 **Hôtel Des Bourbons** – *47 av. Marx-Dormoy.* ☎*04 70 05 28 93. www.hotel-des-bourbons.com. 44 rooms. Restaurant*😴🍽. Opposite the station, a renovated 19C building with functional rooms, and traditional menus served in a modern setting.

😴🍽 **Hôtel Le Garden** – *12 av. Marx-Dormoy, 03310 Néris-les-Bains.* ☎*04 70 03 21 16. http://hotellegarden.monsite-orange.fr. Closed Nov–early Jan. 19 rooms. Restaurant*😴🍽*.* Near the station, this former villa has contemporary rooms. The restaurant serves simple cuisine in an attractive dining room.

😴🍽 **Hôtel Mona Lisa** – *40 r. Boisrot-Desserviers, 03310 Néris-les-Bains.* ☎*04 70 08 79 80. http://hotel-monalisaneris.monalisa.fr. 57 rooms. Restaurant*😴🍽*.*

The Belle Époque façade of this hotel opposite the casino conceals well-equipped and air-conditioned rooms.

🍴 EAT

🍽 **L'Eau à la Bouche** – *26 r. Grande.* ☎*04 70 03 82 92.* Very popular when the lunch-hour strikes, this establishment serves meals centred around sandwiches, fondues, grilled titbits and *tartiflette*, made from high quality local ingredients. Countrified decor with exposed beams, enjoyable atmosphere and friendly welcome.

🍽 **La Vie en Rose** – *7 r. de la Fontaine.* ☎*04 70 03 88 79. www.resto-lavieenrose03.com. Closed Sun lunch.* Outside, a pretty pink façade; inside, orange-toned walls, old photos and advertising posters round out this restaurant's bistro-style decor. The menu offers Bourbon specialities, featuring famous Charolais beef, served with soft jazz in the background.

😴🍽 **Le Grenier à Sel** – *Pl. des Toiles.* ☎*04 70 05 53 79. www.legrenierasel.com. Closed Sat lunch in winter, Mon lunch in Jul–Aug, Sun evening and Mon rest of year.* This attractive, ivy-covered manor in the old quarter of Montluçon is surrounded by a walled garden. The contemporary fare is flavoursome and the spacious, pleasantly furnished rooms are conducive to a good night's sleep.

😴🍽 **Safran d'Or** – *12 pl. des Toiles.* ☎*04 70 05 09 18. Closed Sun and Tue evenings, and Mon.* Small restaurant in bistro style, serving traditional cuisine.

Forêt de Tronçais★★

Tronçais forest is located at the junction of the Berry and Bourbonnais regions; it has a total surface area of over 10 000ha and contains a remarkable plantation of trees. Its many pools and beauty spots make it a popular recreational area.

EXCURSIONS

Ainay-le-Château
3km/1.9mi N of the forest on D 953.

- 🚶 **Michelin Map:** 326: D-3.
- 🛈 **Info:** Pl. du Champ-de-Foire, 03350 CÉRILLY. ☎04 70 67 55 89. www.pays-de-troncais.com.
- ▶ **Location:** 30km/19mi N of Montluçon, accessed by the D 2144, via Meaulne. From Moulins it is best to go via Cérilly and along the D 953.
- 👪 **Kids:** Take a ride in an electric boat.
- 🕐 **Timing:** At least half a day, more if possible.

The Largest Oak Forest in Europe

Trials and tribulations – Tronçais forest, after being administered by the dukes of Bourbon, was confiscated in 1527 together with the other lands owned by the High Constable. Poorly managed and neglected in the 16C and 17C, it slowly deteriorated. The devastation wrought by livestock, the improper use of certain parts of the forest by neighbouring parishes or lords, and the uncontrolled felling of trees meant that by 1670 nearly three-quarters of the forest was ruined.

To meet the country's requirements for ship timber, Colbert undertook to protect and replant the royal forest. The new plantations were not to be used until the trees were 200 years old. In 1788, the opening of the Tronçais Iron Foundry led to fresh destruction of the forest with two-thirds of its surface area reduced to coppice with standards in order to produce the charcoal needed for the manufacture of cast iron. In 1832 conservation measures were fortunately taken and the forest was replanted on the basis of a cutting cycle of 160 years. This was extended to 180, then to 225 years in 1928.

Cultivating the forest – Tronçais forest is divided into series, which in turn are divided into blocks. Oak trees account for 70 percent of its plantations, with beech and Scotch fir the second most densely planted species.

The main aim of the forest remains the production of high-quality timber. The most sought-after trees are therefore of exceptional dimensions, their trunks sometimes more than 20m high and 1m in diameter at a man's standing height. To achieve this, the area around the most promising oaks must be surrounded by other trees during the oaks' growth period, then gradually cleared by successive felling. Logs with a diameter of 50cm and more are sliced in specialised industrial yards far from the forest. Some are exported to other EU countries (particularly Germany). The veneers produced supply the cabinet-making industries and are eventually sent abroad – to Sweden, the USA, Belgium. Oaks that are 40–50cm in diameter provide wood for cooperage (split or made into staves to make barrels); Tronçais oak is particularly prized for the maturing of Cognac and claret. Oak trees of small diameter or lesser quality are converted into building timber or firewood.

Formerly part of Berry and old Aquitaine, Ainay became a Bourbonnais stronghold in the late 12C. Although the castle has not survived, there remain vestiges of the ramparts (towers, sections of wall). The 12C Porte de l'Horloge in the main street was once used as a guard-room and prison.

The **Église St-Étienne** was built in the 16C on the site of a former Romanesque church. The west doorway, giving onto a small square overlooking the Sologne, is adorned with a fine Virgin with Child from the 17C.

🚗 DRIVING TOURS

① EASTERN SOLOGNE REGION★★★

20km/12.5mi. About 2h. This itinerary takes a tour of the Pays de Tronçais.

Cérilly

This was the home of the writer Charles-Louis Philippe (1874-1909), the author of semi-autobiographical novels based on his memories. His birthplace (☉May–Oct Sat–Sun and public holidays 3–6pm. ☎04 70 67 52 00), at No. 5 in the street which bears his name, is open to the public.

Leave Cérilly to the N on D 111 which leads through the eastern part of the forest. Cross over Rond de Brot roundabout and D 978A, then take the first tarmacked road on the left, Ligne de Cros-Chaud.

Étang de Pirot★

Rond des Pêcheurs offers a lovely overall **view** of the vast Lake Pirot.

Take Ligne des Pêcheurs, then turn right on D 978A.

Fontaine Viljot

On the right-hand side of the road (170m). Park on the left verge.

Oaks and conifers form a charming border to the crystal clear water of this spring. Legend has it that, if a maiden wishes to marry, she must throw a pin into the spring; if the pin pricks the bottom, the maiden has "pricked a heart." South of the Rond Viljot, walk to the **Square Oak** (*Chêne Carré*). This 300-year-old tree has a total height of 26m and a circumference of 5.96m.

Émile-Guillaumin and Charles-Louis-Philippe Oak Trees

These two trees close to the roadside to the north commemorate two novelists from the region.

At Rond Gardien, turn sharp right onto the Planchegross forest road (one-way) up to the car park.

Rond de la Cave

30min on foot there and back.

This large, sheltered picnic area lies at the very heart of the forest. Return to **Rond Gardien** (*viewing table*) and continue to Tronçais. The factory here was built on the edge of Lake Tronçais.

Take D 250 on the right.

Étang de St-Bonnet★

The lake, to the left of the road, sits in a very attractive setting. The bathing area and path around it are popular destinations for a walk.

Futaie Colbert★
🚶 *30min on foot.*
There is a marked trail from Rond du Vieux-Morat. Beautiful plantation of 300-year-old oaks in a cool, undulating setting (protected area).

Stebbing Oak
1.5km/0.9mi from Rond du Vieux-Morat.
Isolated in the middle of a plantation of young trees is a typical 300-year-old oak (37m high and 3.95m in circumference).

Rond de Buffévent
🚶 *2km/1mi from Rond du Vieux-Morat.*
Short walks along the forest road lead to magnificent 300-year-old oaks: **Jacques-Chevalier**, **Jumeaux** (the Twins) and **Sentinelle** (the Sentry).

② WESTERN SOLOGNE REGION★
30km/19mi. About 1h.

St-Bonnet-Tronçais
A pleasant place to stay on the edge of the forest. Guided tours of the surrounding area are organised by the **Centre Permanent d'Initiatives Pour l'Environnement** (*CPIE – Avenue Nicolas-Rambourg, Tronçais 03360 St-Bonnet-Tronçais; ☎04 70 06 14 69*).

▶ From St-Bonnet-Tronçais take D 250 S. Beyond Tronçais factory turn right, at Rond du Chêne Aragon turn right on D 145.

Étang de Saloup★
The road bisects the lake.

▶ Turn left on D 39, then follow route Forestière des Lurons. From the car park, take the footpath (past a no-entry sign).

The path ends at **St-Mayeul Chapel** overlooking a ravine.

▶ From the car park turn right onto the narrow route Forestière des Vauves winding through the ravine and right to Rond de Meneser.

Rond de Meneser
Various paths provide pleasant walks *(minimum 30min on foot there and back).*

▶ Continue on the forest road; turn left on D 110; in Le Breton turn left on D 312.

The road runs through the forest to **Meaulne**, and to the Aumance valley.

ADDRESSES

🛏 STAY AND ¶/EAT

🍽 **Le Tronçais** – *12 Avenue Nicolas Rambourg, 03360 Tronçais. ☎04 70 06 11 95. Closed Sun evening, Mon and Tue off-season. 12 rooms. Restaurant🍽🛏.* Calm, spacious bedrooms. Bright dining room with bay windows opening out onto the countryside.

🛏🍽 **Chambre d'Hôte l'Ombre de Gazinière** – *03350 Theneuille. ☎04 70 67 59 17. Closed Oct–Easter. Reservations required. 3 rooms. Restaurant🍽🛏.* Formerly an outbuilding belonging to the neighbouring manor house, this attractive 17C edifice has been very nicely renovated. Gorgeous garret bedrooms where chequered fabrics, solid beams and rustic furniture create a very pleasant country atmosphere. Round swimming pool in the garden.

SIGHTSEEING

"Discovering the forest" – The forest offers walkers additional attractions besides the contemplation of its oak trees. Mushroom pickers will find boletus, hydnum, russula and chanterelles. There is also quite a large population of red deer, roe deer and wild boar. Great crested grebes can often be glimpsed on Pirot Lake.
In season, **guided tours** of the forest are organised *(for 1–2 months in summer, from the rond de Tronçais; contact for information ☎04 70 46 82 00; for information on tourist activities, call ☎04 70 67 55 89).*

Vichy ⚓

Vichy, a world-famous spa resort and holiday town, attracts numerous visitors because of its high-quality shopping facilities and the very wide range of entertainment it has to offer: casino-theatre, cabarets, festivals, concerts, exhibitions, lectures and horse races. The parks along the banks of the Allier add to the pleasure of staying here. The multi-purpose sports centre, situated north of the town, is one of the best designed sports complexes in Europe. The Sporting Club completes the complex with its 18-hole golf course, tennis courts and swimming pool. Lake Allier, created after the construction of a dam bridge on the river downstream from the town, is used for international competitions (rowing, regattas, water-skiing etc).

> ▸ **Population:** 25 756.
> 🕭 **Michelin Map:** 326: H-6.
> 🛈 **Info:** 19 Rue du Parc, 03200 Vichy. ☎0825 77 10 10. www.vichy-destinations.fr.
> ▶ **Location:** NE of Clermont-Ferrand, set on the River Allier.
> 🅿 **Parking:** There is ample parking in the town centre.
> 🕭 **Don't Miss:** The Spa district
> 🕐 **Timing:** You can comfortably explore the town in half a day, but a longer period will give you time to experience its spa facilities.

THE SPA RESORT

The healing properties of Vichy water were appreciated by the Romans, who built a small spa town here – Vicus Calidus. After a long period of relative obscurity, Vichy's vocation as a spa was resurrected in the 17C and since then countless celebrities have come to spend a pleasant holiday here while tending to their health.

THE SPA DISTRICT★

The "spa resort" architecture of the late 19C and early 20C, the period when Vichy, the "Queen of Spa Towns", was at its most popular, is well worth a closer look. The buildings of the Vichy spa complex have been carefully restored and listed as protected for some years now, and make up a rich and unique part of France's architectural heritage.

Parc des Sources★

This beautiful park planted with chestnut and plane trees was laid out on the orders of Napoleon I and links a number of springs.

The spa district effectively grew up around it, and it has remained the centre of the town's spa industry and leisure facilities.

In the mornings the district is permeated with the peculiar atmosphere of the spa, punctuated by the comings and goings of people taking the waters, gathering in clusters around the springs as they await their "glass of water".

In the afternoon, and on gala evenings, fashionable society comes to life, going for an evening stroll, having a drink on the terrace of the Grand Café or attending some glittering function.

Halle des Sources

Fed by the waters of Vichy's six thermal springs, the **Pump Room** is built of glass and metal, and its very transparency and the fluidity of its design bring to mind the element which is dispensed within.

Centre Thermal des Dômes

The luxury assembly rooms in a neo-Moorish style were designed by Charles Lecoeur, architect of the Grand Casino, and inaugurated in 1903. The central dome and corner cupolas are covered in gold enamelled roof tiles.

Grand Casino★

The Grand Casino, which opened in 1865, represents the influence of general good spirits on people's health. The

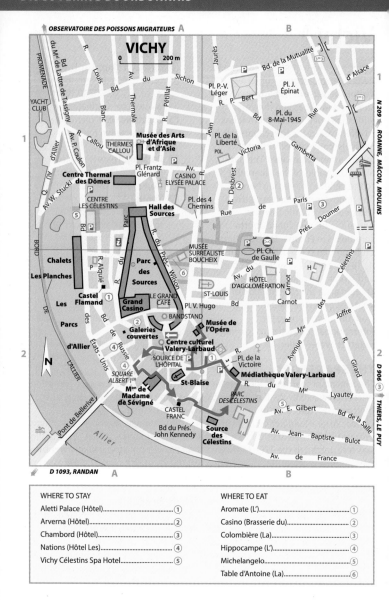

⛪ OBSERVATOIRE DES POISSONS MIGRATEURS

VICHY

0 _____ 200 m

WHERE TO STAY	
Aletti Palace (Hôtel)	①
Arverna (Hôtel)	②
Chambord (Hôtel)	③
Nations (Hôtel Les)	④
Vichy Célestins Spa Hotel	⑤

WHERE TO EAT	
Aromate (L')	①
Casino (Brasserie du)	②
Colombière (La)	③
Hippocampe (L')	④
Michelangelo	⑤
Table d'Antoine (La)	⑥

first of its kind in France, it housed various assembly rooms and gaming halls beneath a single roof. From 1900 to 1903, it was renovated and extended with the addition of an opera house under the direction of architect Charles Lecoeur. Inside, the superb Art Nouveau decor is the work of wrought-iron worker Émile Robert and master glass-artist François Chigot.

Covered Arcades

These are beautifully delicate Art Nouveau creations in wrought iron, crafted by Émile Robert for the 1889 World Exhibition in Paris and transferred to Vichy in 1900.

The balustrade of the bandstand, also the work of Robert, forms a garland of musical motifs *(concerts in season)*.

The Vichy Government

From early July 1940 until 20 August 1944, Vichy was the capital of the French State during Nazi German occupation of the north of France. Vichy, with a direct railway line to Paris (the "Thermal-Express"), relatively modern telephone links, and many hotels which could be requisitioned for government offices, was chosen in preference to cities such as Clermont-Ferrand, Marseille or Toulouse. It had the added advantage of being quite close to the line of demarcation between occupied and unoccupied France. Maréchal Pétain, hero of Verdun during World War II, was granted full executive powers by the French parliament.

The disproportionate centralisation of government power in this city was accompanied by a strictly monitored exercise of power and the laying aside of the fundamental principles of democracy. During the dark days of the Vichy regime, the city was subject to a permanent police presence, with the oppressive atmosphere further heightened by furtive and unexplained comings and goings, cowed public apathy and an overriding austerity totally at odds with the city's previous role as a health and leisure resort. On 20 August 1944, the representatives of the toppled regime who had remained in place were taken back to Germany by the Nazis as they retreated.

Hotels, Chalets and Villas

Despite the demolition of the prestigious Queen's Hotel, most of the grand hotels on which Vichy's reputation is based have survived intact. The Hôtel du Parc is among the most impressive neo-Baroque buildings in town. Walk along rue du Parc and turn onto rue Prunelle *(first on the right)* where the mansion at No. 8 is a pastiche of an English cottage. Take a glimpse along rue Alquié *(on the right)* which looks like an English street. The row of **chalets★** lining avenue des États-Unis (Nos. 101 to 109bis) was built from 1862 to house Napoleon III and his entourage, who used to come regularly to take the waters at Vichy. Turn onto rue de Belgique *(second on the left)* to admire the Venitian-style villa with St Mark's lions at No. 7 and the **Castel Flamand★** at Nos. 2–2bis. Retrace your steps and turn left onto rue Alquié leading to boulevard de Russie.

The Palais des Parcs (the old Ruhl) at No. 15 is another neo-Baroque hotel. It was after the fall of the Empire that architects unleashed the full power of their imagination to create truly eccentric buildings. There are some remarkable examples of florid design along boulevard de Russie (neo-Classical at Nos. 17, 19 and 21★, Art Deco at No. 29).

WALKING TOUR

OLD VICHY

▷ Start from the Source de l'Hôpital. Follow avenue A.-Briand to reach square Albert-1er (signposting).

Note the Ermitage du Pont-Neuf Hotel, which exemplifies Art Deco style. The **Maison de Madame de Sévigné**, constructed during the time of Louis XIII, has been extensively restored and converted into a hotel (Pavillon Sévigny). The Marquise of Sévigné would stay here when she came to spend the season at Vichy.

▷ Continue along rue de la Tour (on the right) then rue Verrier (on the right) and walk past the 16C Castel Franc, remodelled in the 19C when it became the town hall.

Source des Célestins

The water from this spring now flows as far as the Pump Room, but it is worth taking the short walk to have a look at the elegant Louis XV pavillion which houses the spring itself. The **Célestins Park** contains some magnificent evergreen trees, as well as traces of the old convent after which the spring and the park are named.

▷ Head for rue du Mar.-Lyautey.

Médiathèque Valéry-Larbaud★

&⚕🔊*Guided tours Tue 10am–noon, 2–6pm; Wed 10am–6pm; Thu–Fri 2–6pm; Sat 10am–5pm. ℰ04 70 58 42 50.*
The local multimedia library presents an exhibition on the author **Valéry Larbaud**, who was born in Vichy in 1881. Around 14 000 books, 180 manuscripts, 8 800 letters and many other documents are displayed on antique furniture.

▷ From place de la Victoire, turn left onto rue d'Allier. Look to your right along rue Besse; no. 2 was the birthplace of the famous reporter Albert Londres (1884–1932).

Église St-Blaise

The old church, altered many times over, has a highly venerated Black Virgin, known as Our Lady of the Sick and Suffering; only the statue's head is original (12C).

▷ On leaving the church, follow rue Hubert-Colombier lined with villas illustrating a variety of styles. Turn left onto rue du Mar.-Foch.

Musée Municipal de Vichy

&🕔*Daily except Sun and Mon 2–6pm, Sat 2–5pm.* 🕔*Public holidays. ℰ04 70 32 12 97. www.ville-vichy.fr/musees.*
Set up in the **Centre Culturel Valéry-Larbaud**, this small museum is devoted to local archaeology, contemporary painting, as well as postage stamps, coins and medals from Vichy. There is a collection of modern painting and sculpture with works by Gustave Moreau and Picasso.

▷ The Opera Museum is opposite.

Musée de l'Opéra de Vichy

🕔*Apr–mid-Dec daily except Mon and public holidays 2–6pm.* 🔊€4. *ℰ04 70 58 48 20. www.operavichy-musee.com.*
This museum presents in rotation the archives of the Grand Casino Theatre which were faithfully kept until the 1960s: costumes, accessories, posters, stage documents, programmes of all the operas performed from 1901 onwards, and 10,000 photographs of artists, of famous people who visited the town.

ADDITIONAL SIGHTS

Musée des Arts d'Afrique et d'Asie

16 avenue Thermale (opposite Thermes Callou). 🕔*May–Oct daily except Mon 2–6pm.* 🔊€4. *ℰ04 70 97 76 40. www.musee-aaa.com.*
The former Musée du Missionnaire contains exhibits collected by missionaries and private donations now entered in a catalogue for the first time since the foundation of the museum in 1923. A quarter of the collection is displayed in eight rooms, inside a 19C house.

Parcs d'Allier★

These beautiful landscape gardens created at the request of Emperor Napoleon III are built on land reclaimed from the river. They are graced with trees of various species, lakes with swans and ducks, rock gardens, rose gardens and flowerbeds, and are ideal for long, peaceful strolls. The Parc du Soleil provides all sorts of attractions for children.

EXCURSION

St-Pourçain-sur-Sioule★

29km/18mi NW of Vichy
This small market town, an important crossroads on the Sioule, is popular with anglers and walkers alike. It owes its name to St Pourçain, a former slave turned monk, who defended the Auvergne from the ravages of Thierry, son of Clovis, the king of the Franks.
🔲 From St-Pourçain-sur-Sioule's place Maréchal-Foch, with its attractive fountain dominated by the belfry of the ancient monastery, **walk★** through the covered passageway to the carefully

The Vichy Springs

Vichy's mineral and thermal springs contain mainly bicarbonate of soda and carbonic acid. The main springs belong to the State and are operated by a contracting company founded in 1853. The waters here are used to treat conditions of the liver, gall-bladder and stomach, diabetes, migraines, nutritional and digestive disorders, and also rheumatological complaints.

Waters from the Grande Grille, Hôpital and, in particular, Célestins springs, are bottled and exported the world over.

Hot springs – These are the basis of the Vichy drinking cures. The **Grande Grille** is named after the grille which used to protect it from thirsty animals. The bubbling water (temperature 40°C) comes up from a depth of 1 000–1 200m. The **Chomel** (temperature 41°C) is named after the doctor who captured the spring in 1750 and managed the waters. A third hot spring, the **Hôpital** (temperature 33°C), rises in a rotunda-shaped pavilion behind the Casino.

Cold springs – Part of the regimen includes drinking the water. The **Parc** (temperature 24°C) gushes forth in the Parc des Sources. The **Lucas** (temperature 24°C) is named after the doctor and inspector who bought the spring at the beginning of the 19C on behalf of the State. The **Célestins** has a temperature of 21.5°C.

Thermal establishments – The Centre Thermal des Dômes can provide up to 2 500 people with thermal and related treatments each morning. The Callou pump room, like that of the Célestins, boasts the latest technical innovations.

Hall des Sources

© Hervé Lenain/hemis.fr

© S. Sauvignier/MICHELIN

restored courtyard, cours des Bénédictins, which offers a beautiful view of the bell-tower and imposing roof of the **Church of Ste-Croix**. This vast, former abbey church was constructed in several stages from the 11C to the 15C. Whimsical, humorous carvings decorate the 15 stalls' misericords.

Musée de la Vigne et du Terroir★

May–Jun and Sept Wed–Sun 2–5pm (Jul–Aug Tue 2.30–6pm, Wed–Sun 10am–12.30pm, 2.30–6pm). €4. 04 70 45 62 07.

Great care has been taken in presenting the history of the region's main agricultural activity. A spiral staircase in the clock tower (15C) leads to rooms with attractive beams and stonework. Here a large number of items show the different aspects of vine-growing and wine-making.

Palais de la Miniature

Gare de St-Pourçain. *Apr–mid-Nov daily except Tue, 3–7pm (mid-Jun–mid Sept daily 10am–noon, 3–7pm).* €5. 04 70 45 99 01.

A railway network comprising trains and carriages on a scale of 1:87 runs through Bourbonnais landscapes.

🚗 DRIVING TOURS

AROUND VICHY
75km/46.6mi. Allow 2h30.

▶ Leave Vichy to the SE on D 906. Before entering Abrest turn left onto D 126, heading for Cusset, then right onto D 270 to Vernet. At the entrance to the village, on the right, a narrow road leads to a platform especially laid out as a site.

Site des Hurlevents

The view extends over the Vichy basin, the Allier valley, the Limagne, the Monts Dôme and Bois Noirs.

▶ Rejoin D 906 and continue until you reach the entrance to St-Yorre.

St-Yorre

This small town famed for its numerous springs of mineral water has become a major centre for glass-making.

▶ Leave St-Yorre to the E on D 121.

Château de Busset

Guided tours only at 3pm and 4.30pm: May–Jun and Sept–Oct Sat–Sun; Jul–Aug Wed–Sun daily. €6. 04 70 59 13 97. www.busset.com.

Erected on a granite promontory overlooking the Allier valley, this elegant castle has belonged to the same family for 14 generations. Although considerably remodelled since it was built in the 13C, the edifice has retained a drawbridge and four defensive towers including the fine Tour d'Orion.

▶ On leaving Busset, turn left onto D 121 running by the cemetery, then take D 995 on the left. D 995 crosses the River Sichon, offering pleasant views of the lower valley.

Cusset

This town on the outskirts of Vichy is circled by wide avenues lined with century-old trees. Place Victor-Hugo has several gabled houses, notably the Taverne Louis XI.

The door and window of the Maison Barathon are embellished with fine late-16C sculptures. Set up in the only vestiges of the 15C curtain wall, the **Musée de la Tour Prisonnière** (*guided tours of the underground passages May–Sept at 2.30pm, 3.30pm, 4.30pm and 5.30pm.* 04 70 96 29 17) presents an exhibition on local history through an extensive collection of documents, weapons, costumes, drawings, paintings and street plaques.

▶ Leave Cusset to the NE on D906B.

St-Étienne-de-Vicq

This hamlet has a Romanesque church with unusual architectural features.

▶ Rejoin D 906B. In Bost, turn right onto D 190. At the church crossroads,

AUTOUR DE VICHY

take D 558, then turn right onto D 907. In Les Gadons, take D 174 on the right.

Comptoir européen de la Confiserie

94 allée des Ailes. ⏱*Apr–mid-Nov, daily (except Sat–Sun) 9am–noon, 2–6pm (Fri 2–6pm).* ☎*04 70 30 94 79.*
A gangway overlooking the workshop will introduce visitors to the art of making and packaging **Pastilles de Vichy**, a type of boiled sweet made with Vichy water that became popular in the days of Empress Eugénie.

▶ Bear right towards St-Germain-des-Fossés, then turn left onto D 27. In Vendat, take the D 279.

Cognat

300m beyond the village, turn left onto a lane leading to the church.
This unusual 12C building stands on a knoll commanding a pretty **view** of the Limagne and Monts Dôme.

▶ Return to Cognat and turn right onto D 117.

The road cuts across Montpensier Forest (⏱*see AIGUEPERSE*).

Brugheas

🚶 Lying on the banks of the Sarmon, this village is an ideal starting-point for country walks and bicycle rides.

▶ Leave Brugheas to the SE on D 221, heading for Hauterive. Before reaching the area known as "La Tour", turn left onto the narrow lane bordered by meadows and small ponds.

Source du Dôme

This bubbling spring, the hottest in the Vichy basin, yields algae that are used in the preparation of mineral mud baths.

▶ The path runs through a small wood then across pastoral countryside. On reaching the surfaced road, turn left onto D 131 which leads back to Vichy via Bellerive bridge.

ADDRESSES

🖼️ STAY

Arverna Hôtel – *12 r. Desbrest.* ☎*04 70 31 31 19. www.arverna-hotels-vichy.com. 23 rooms.* A family hotel in a shady street between the train station and the spas. Bedrooms are small but functional.

Hôtel Chambord – *82-84 r. de Paris.* ☎*04 70 30 16 30. www.hotel-chambord-vichy.com. Closed Jan. 25 rooms.* Three generations of the same family welcome you to this hotel; sound-proofed rooms.

Les Nations – *13 bd Russie.* ☎*04 70 98 21 63. www.hotel-lesnations.com. Open Apr–Oct. 70 rooms.* Enjoys a central location, functional rooms and traditional food. Restaurant ☺☺.

Aletti Palace Hôtel – *3 pl. Joseph-Aletti.* ☎*04 70 30 20 20. www.hotel-aletti.fr. 126 rooms.* Belle Epoque architecture and ambience in this palatial former spa near the Parc d'Allier.

Vichy Célestins Spa Hotel – *111 bd des États-Unis.* ☎*04 70 30 82 00. www.vichy-spa-hotel.fr. 131 rooms.* A big, modern and very chic hotel on the banks of the Lac d'Allier. Bright, sizeable rooms. Restaurant ☺☺☺.

🍴 EAT

Brasserie du Casino – *4 r. du Casino.* ☎*04 70 98 23 06. www.brasserie-du-casino.fr. Closed Tue–Wed.* Experience an authentic brasserie from the 1930s! It's all here: the old-fashioned atmosphere, the ambient gaiety, and tables so close to one another that you can eavesdrop on your neighbour.

La Colombière – *136 Avenue de Thiers, 03200 Abrest. 5km/3mi SE of Vichy via D 906.* ☎*04 70 98 69 15. Closed Sun evening and Mon.* This 1950s villa with a dovecote by the side of the road is rather imposing. Bountiful cuisine with a good choice of fixed-price menus.

L'Aromate – *9 r. Besse.* ☎*04 70 32 13 22. Closed Sun and Tue evenings, and all day Wed.* Cuisine tastefully flavoured with herbs and spices.

Michelangelo – *44 av. Eugène-Gilbert.* ☎*04 70 32 85 15. Closed Sun–Tue evenings and Wed.* The chef, originally from Piedmont, prepares Italian recipes. Good choice of wine.

La Table d'Antoine – *8 r. Burnol.* ☎*04 70 98 99 71. www.latabledantoine.com. Closed Thu evening in winter; Sun evening and Mon (except public holidays).* Inventive, savoury cuisine.

L'Hippocampe – *3 bd de Russie.* ☎*04 70 97 68 37. www.restaurant-hippocampe.com. Closed Tue lunch, Sun evening and Mon.* A good place to enjoy seafood.

ON THE TOWN

L'Ascot Bar – *3 pl. Joseph-Aletti.* ☎*04 70 30 20 20. www.hotel-aletti.fr. From 11am.* With its Art Deco and posh interior, this Vichy bar is a classic. Drink here in a musical setting.

Le Blue Note – *Vichy Célestins Hôtel, 111 bd des États-Unis.* ☎*04 70 30 82 00. www.vichy-spa-hotel.fr. Noon–midnight.* An inviting piano-bar frequented by spa-goers and celebrities visiting Vichy. Live music from 7pm onwards Fri, Sat and Sun.

Le Grand Café – *7 r. du Casino.* ☎*04 70 97 16 45. www.casinovichygrandcafe.com.* Its location right in the middle of the thermal park makes this the most popular of the spa establishments.

Le Samoa – *13 sq. de la Source-de-l'Hôpital.* ☎*04 70 59 94 46. Opens at 8.30am. Closed Sun morning in winter.* Under the shady arcades lining the square, this Vichy institution is popular.

Casino de Vichy "Élysée Palace" – *Passage de la Comédie.* ☎*04 70 97 93 37. Mon–Fri 10am–3am, weekends until 4am.* Slot machines and traditional games (*boules*, blackjack, French and English roulette) vie for the favours of enthusiasts.

SHOWTIME

Palais des Congrès – *Opéra de Vichy, 5 r. du Casino.* ☎*04 70 30 50 50. www.congres-vichy.fr. Tickets: Tue–Sat 1.30–6.30pm; phone reservations: Tue–Fri 10am–12.30pm. Closed Sun–Mon except performance days.* A citadel of Vichy culture, this handsome Art Nouveau-style opera house has opted for an exacting programme alternating opera, theatre, dance and even pop music.

Château de La Palisse

© Hervé Lenain/hemis.fr

Lapalisse

Lapalisse lies on the banks of the River Besbre and is dominated by the outline of its castle. The is a good point to use as a base for exploring the Besbre valley, renowned for its many châteaux.

SIGHTS
Château de La Palice★★

Guided visits Apr–Oct daily 9am–noon, 2–6pm. ∞€6. *℘04 70 99 37 58.*
Little remains of the original medieval castle; the building standing today dates from 1527 and was designed by Florentines and is, as a result, an example of early Renaissance architecture.

The drawing room once had walls covered with leather from Cordoba; it contains the Chabannes family portraits.

The **Golden Salon★★** is decorated with a magnificent gilded coffered ceiling and two tapestries of knights, representing Godefroi de Bouillon and Hector. The tapestries, of 15C Flemish manufacture, come from a series of hangings 3.80m high and 4m wide, with a 30cm border. The chapel was rebuilt in the mid-15C but was pillaged during the Revolution. In the outbuildings (fine timber ceilings) there is a collection of standards and flags gathered by a priest from Doyet.

- ▸ **Population:** 3 247.
- ⚲ **Michelin Map:** 326: I-5 – 23km.14.3mi NE of Vichy.
- ▯ **Info:** 9 place Charles Bécaud, 03120 Lapalisse. ℘04 70 99 08 39. www.lapalisse-tourisme.com.
- ◖ **Location:** Lapalisse occupies a central position in France to the NE of the Auvergne and 90km/56mi from Clermont Ferrand.
- ◷ **Timing:** This is a complex area to explore, and to do so can take one or more days.

EXCURSION
Neuilly-en-Donjon
27km/17mi NE along D 994 then right onto D 989.
This small village is mostly known for the delightful **porch★** of its Romanesque church, characterised by painstaking detail and remarkable craftsmanship.

Monsieur de La Palice

15C–16C – Jacques II de Chabannes, Lord of La Palice, Marshal of France, won renown for his valour during the campaign to capture the Milan region. He was killed at the Battle of Pavia in 1525. The French expression *une verité de La Palice* – meaning something that is so obviously true that it hardly bears pointing out – has its sources in a poem his officers wrote in his honour.

> *M. de La Palice est mort,*
> *Mort devant Pavie.*
>
> *Un quart d'heure avant sa mort*
> *Il était encore en vie.*

Although they meant to express that he had fought bravely up to the last instant, the words "A quarter hour before his death, he was still alive" have lost their meaning of courage in the face of battle and come to imply naïvety bordering on dim-wittedness.

🚗 DRIVING TOUR

BESBRE VALLEY★
60km/37mi. Allow 4h.

▶ Leave Lapalisse to the NW on D 480, along the left bank of the Besbre.

The Besbre valley contains a surprising variety and number of castles. Only a few are open to visitors, but they are all worth a close look. This quiet little river, which rises in the Bois Noirs (Black Woods) at the foot of the Puy de Montoncel, flows into the Loire south of Bourbon-Lancy.

Chavroches
As it climbs towards the castle, the road gives a glimpse of the 15C main building. The gate and outer walls are 12C-13C.

▶ Drive along the one-way street then turn right and follow D163 then D205.

Jaligny
This little town is well known in France for being the adopted home of poet, journalist and novelist **René Fallet**. There is an **exhibition** (🕐*Wed–Fri 11am–noon. ℘04 70 34 91 13*) about him in the old town hall.

Jaligny is also an agricultural centre famed for its fair. The **Château**★ (⚬━*not open to the public*), visible from afar, consists of two sturdy towers with Renaissance windows.

▶ Leave Jaligny heading NE along D 21.

Châtelperron
Small, secluded village dominated by the rounded turrets of its château (⚬━*not open to the public*).

Préhistorama
🕐*Apr–Sept daily except Tue 10am–noon, 2–6pm (Sun and public holidays 2–6pm); Oct–Mar Wed–Sun 2–5pm.* ⌨€4. 🕐*Jan. ℘04 70 34 84 51. www.03web.fr/prehistorama.*
This museum is housed in the former railway station. It retraces the daily life of Neanderthal man.

▶ Continue to St-Léon then turn left.

Puy St-Ambroise
The **view**★ stretches over the entire Besbre Valley and, to the north and west, over the Sologne Bourbonnaise, a flat region studded with copses.

▶ Return to St-Léon; follow D 53 to Vaumas to rejoin the Besbre valley.

Château de Beauvoir★

🚻🕐*Gardens: open all year 9am–7pm (Nov–Apr 10am–5pm).* 🕐*Sat–Sun from May–mid-Oct.* 📞*04 70 42 00 44.*

This ancient 13C stronghold shows traces of the 15C renovations carried out by the La Fin family. It differs from the other castles in the region because of its layout: the buildings are set at right-angles to each other. The old watchtower is a typical example of Bourbonnais architecture.

▶ Continue along D 480, then turn left onto D 296.

Château de Thoury★

🕐*Gardens only: mid-Apr–mid-Oct 10am–noon, 2–6pm.* 📞*04 70 42 03 95.*

This attractive 11C, 12C and 15C stronghold is surrounded by a park. High curtain walls link the two main buildings and the machicolated entrance gate which has two turrets with pepper-pot roofs; it is reached via a drawbridge over a moat.

The tour takes in the inner courtyard (16C gallery), the guard-room, the dining room, the salon (fine Etruscan vase dating from 450 BCE), the watchtower (family mementoes) and the vaulted 11C cellar.

▶ On leaving the château, turn right.

👪 Parc le Pal★

🚻🕐*Open mid-Apr–Sept at variable hours and days; check website for current details.* 🎫*€29 (children under 10, €26).* 📞*04 70 42 03 60. www.lepal.com.*

The amusement park is laid out around place de la Gaîté, a copy of a Parisian square in the middle of the countryside. A dozen or so different attractions include a monorail, rafting, a water train, a caterpillar, a rollercoaster etc.

The zoo is home to more than 500 species of animals – including elephants, giraffes, big cats, monkeys, deer, waterfowl, parrots and birds of prey – which roam at semi-liberty in an environment reproducing their natural habitat.

▶ From the park, turn left onto the road back up to D 480. Drive through Dompierre-sur-Besbre, then turn N onto D 55.

Abbaye de Sept-Fons

This abbey is housed in 18C buildings; the church was rebuilt in 1955.

An audio-visual presentation describes monastic life. The monks make excellent organic food, including a wide range of delicious jams.

▶ Take the D 15 as far as Beaulon.

Musée rural de la Sologne Bourbonnaise

🕐*Open Jun–mid-Sept, Sun and public holidays 2.30-6.30pm.* 🎫*€4.* 📞*04 70 42 70 89.*

This museum contains one of the most comprehensive collections of rural life in Bourbonnais.

▶ Return to Lapalisse by the D 15, D 55, then D 480.

ADDRESSES

🛏**STAY**

🍴 **Chambre d'Hôte Les Vieux Chênes** – *Laprugne, 03120 Servilly. 6km/3.6mi W of Lapalisse via D 480 and D 32.* 📞*04 70 99 07 53. Closed Nov–mid-Mar. 5 rooms. Restaurant🍴.* In this impeccably run country home, the very spacious rooms are downright basic, but we like it anyway. It is surrounded by nature.

🍽**EAT**

🍴 **Auberge de l'Olive** – *Av. de la Gare, 03290 Dompierre-sur-Besbre.* 📞*04 70 34 51 87. www.auberge-olive.fr. Closed Sun evening (Dec-15 Apr) and Fri (except Jul-Aug).* This inn on a busy road is full of surprises. The light and airy veranda is a very inviting setting for a meal, as is the more rustic dining room with fine wooden beams and a lively blue theme.

Charroux★

Charroux is built on a hilltop and was one of the 19 castellanies of the Barony of Bourbon. The old houses, built of dressed stone and ornamented with carved mouldings, have been restored and make the village particularly attractive.

> ▶ **Population:** 390.
> ⏱ **Michelin Map:** 326: F-5 – 15km/9.3mi N of Gannat.
> ℹ **Info:** Maison de Tourisme ℘04 70 56 87 71. www.charroux.com.
> ▶ **Location:** Charroux en Bourbonnais (to be precise) is just 10min from the exit of the A 71, midway between Montluçon (N) and Clermont Ferrand (S).
> ◷ **Timing:** Leave plenty of time for the driving tour.

▰▰WALKING TOUR

Église St-Jean-Baptiste
This fortified 12C building was once part of the town walls. The belfry rises above the transept crossing but its pyramid-shaped spire has been truncated.

▶ Leave via the north aisle.

On the square there is a **medieval house** with an overhanging upper storey. On the left stands the belfry, a square tower once used as a watch-tower.

Rue de la Poulaillerie
An old stone well stands in the centre of this picturesque cobbled street.

Musée de Charroux
ⓞ*Mar–Jun and Sept Sat–Sun and public holidays 3–6.30pm; Jul–Aug daily 3–7pm.* ⊛€3. ℘04 70 56 81 71. www.musee-charroux.net.
This **Regional History Museum** is set up in a house decorated with carvings of animal heads, figures and nailhead moulding; objects and documents provide an insight into the history of the Charroux area.

Porte d'Orient
The East Gate was one of the bastions in the town wall. The defensive system is still visible today.

EXCURSIONS
Gannat
13km/8.5mi S on the D 42 and D2009.
This ancient town on the edge of the Limagne plain and the granite base below the mountains of the Auvergne,

on the threshold of the "Gateway to Occitania", the point of contact between two old forms of French language – *langue d'oc* and *langue d'oïl*. The area is important archaeologically, and digs have uncovered rhinoceros skeletons thought to be at least 23 million years old, together with the remains of crocodiles and fossilised birds.
Every summer the town is filled with the sounds of traditional folk dancers, musicians and singers for the colourful international 10-day **World Cultures Festival**.

Jenzat
6km/3.7mi SE on D 42.
The late-11C church here is decorated with 15C paintings in tempera which are known as "Frescoes by the Masters of Jenzat". The **Maison du Luthier** (&ⓞ*Jul–Aug Sat–Wed 2.30–6.30pm; Jun and Sept Sat–Sun 2.30–6.30pm.* ⊛€4. ℘04 70 56 81 78. www.maison-luthier-jenzat.fr) contains a museum on the craft of making musical instruments, in particular hurdy-gurdies.

Église de Biozat
18km/11.1mi SE.
This Romanesque church is typical of the Limagne area with its barrel-vaulted nave. From here you can drive 4km/2.5mi to Effiat and join up with the Limagne discovery trail (&*see AIGUEPERSE*).

Landscape of the Bourbonnais, the Bourbonnais mountains in the background

© Christian Guy/hemis.fr

🚗 DRIVING TOUR

BOURBON COUNTRYSIDE
60km/37mi. Allow 2h30.

▶ Leave Charroux W and follow D 35 for 2km/1mi, then turn right onto D 68. Cross the motorway and take D 183 left.

Veauce
Nestling in a large shaded park, the castle (9C–15C), is perched on top of a rocky outcrop overlooking the River Veauce.

▶ Leave Veauce N on D 118, then D 987. At Croix des Bois, take D 284 right.

Forêt des Colettes
This forest of beech, oak and pine is dominated by the Signal de la Bosse.

▶ At D 998/D 987, turn right, cross Coutansouze and take D 68 on the right.

Bellenaves
This village has a fine Romanesque church.

▶ Leave Bellenaves to the N on D 42.

Chantelle
On a steep promontory stands a Benedictine abbey, built on the ruins of a former castle and monastery.

▶ Take Grand-Rue (D 987) to rue Anne-de-Beaujeu, which leads to the Abbaye St-Vincent.

The church dates from the Romanesque era. Only the nave is open.

▶ Leave Chantelle to the E on D 987. After 6km/4mi, take D 115 on the right.

Château de Chareil-Cintrat ★
🕐 *Mid-Jun–mid-Sept daily except Mon and Sat 10am–noon, 2–6pm.* 🕐 *1 Jan, 1 May, 1 and 11 Nov, 25 Dec.* ⊘€3.50. 𝄞 *04 70 56 94 28.*
www.chareil-cintrat.fr.
This former stronghold, restored in the 16C, is owned by the State. Part of the exterior has recently been restored (the doorway, the terrace and the 19C well). The interior is notable for its two imposing Renaissance fireplaces and its 16C **mural paintings★** in shades of brown, representing mythological themes (Mars, Venus, Cupid, legend of Adonis).

▶ Go back to D 987, heading for Chantelle, then take D 115 on the left and proceed to Ussel-d'Allier.

Ussel-d'Allier
A dirt track to the left of the D 223 leads to a raised viewing table offering a panorama of the Bourbon countryside.

▶ Return to D 223.

Église d'Étroussat
The church boasts 14 modern **stained-glass windows★** attributed to Frédérique Duran.

▶ Leave Étroussat to the S on D 35 and drive back to Charroux.

Montagne Bourbonnaise

Comprising the Black Forest and the mountains of Madeleine, the Montagne Bourbonnaise is a place of gently sloping pastures backed by woodlands of beech, oak and spruce. It rarely exceeds 1 000m. Walking and fishing in summer, and skiing in winter are the main activities.

Vallée de la Credogne★

From a high rock at the side of the road, the Credogne river forms the **Cascade du Creux-Saillant**. A tributary of the Dore, la **Credogne** runs along a pretty valley, through which the D 114 tracks it for much of the way.

🚗 DRIVING TOURS

1 LA VALLÉE DU SICHON
50 km/30mi. Allow 3h.
See map opposite.

Le Mayet-de-Montagne
Musée de la Vannerie – l'Osarium
Open Jul–Aug 10am–noon, 2–7pm; Easter–Jun and Sept–Oct 2–6pm. €4. 04 70 59 75 24.

This small museum tells the story of the weavers and village life in the early 20C. There are over 700 exhibits including the picnic hamper belonging to Admiral Nelson.

Maison de la Montagne Bourbonnaise
Easter–Sept 10am–noon, 2–7pm; rest of the year 10am–noon, 2–6pm. 04 70 59 75 24.

On the other side of the church this house is an outlet for craftsmen and farmers; it also provides tourist information.

▶ Leave Le Mayet-de-Montagne on the rue de Vichy then the D 62 for 500m, then turn left onto the D 176 as far as Arronnes.

- **Michelin Map:** 326 F/H 5/7.
- **Info:** R. Roger-Dégoulange, 03250 Le Mayet-de-Montagne. 04 70 59 38 40. www.tourisme-montagne-bourbonnaise.com.
- **Location:** 27km/17mi SE of Vichy by the D25.
- **Kids:** The Ecomusée at Lavoine.
- **Timing:** Allow a full day or more to explore fully.

Arronnes
Ancient Cluniac site, the village was built around the only remaining priory church of the 11C St Leger. A waymarked trail explains the local history.

Maison de la Paysannerie
Jul–Aug Fri 2–6pm, Sat–Sun 10am–6pm. 04 70 41 80 81.
Two galleries are devoted to the life and times of farmers, bakers and blacksmiths; small farm shop.

▶ Take the D 995 heading SE in the direction of Ferrières-sur-Sichon.

Glozel
In the world of archaeology, Glozel was the subject of controversy during the 1920s about the authenticity of the so-called "Field of the Dead", when a young farmer discovered some votive tablets, the significance of which still occupies the minds of scientists.

An interesting **museum** (*Call or check website for opening hours: 04 70 41 12 96; www.museedeglozel.com*) contains many bones, ceramics, stones and engravings, some of which date to the Upper Paleolithic period.

▶ Follow the D 995 to Cheval-Rigond, and take the little lane on the left climbing to the château.

Château de Montgilbert
From the parking walk up to the remains of the château, but take care in doing so.

This imposing 13C fortress, flanked by four round towers and a square tower, is reinforced by an outer wall. **La Maison de la Vallée du Sichon** houses a small exhibition about the history of the castle.

▶ Return along the D 995 and head towards Ferrières-sur-Sichon where you turn right (D 122).

Grotte des Fées

⏱9am–noon, 2–7pm (torches supplied). ✆04 70 41 11 47.
From the hamlet of **Forest**, a road and then a path lead down into the Sichon valley to this cave.

▶ Return to Ferrières-sur-Sichon, head SE on the D 995. Keep an eye open for the Cascade du Sichon.

Rocher Saint-Vincent

🔥30min there and back. The access road begins on the left, 1km/0.5mi after the hamlet of Matichard.
A path leads to the top of the rock from which there is an extended panorama. The rock stills bears traces of the 11C Pyramont castle.

▶ Follow the D 995, and turn right on the D 422 towards Lavoine.

Lavoine

Don't miss the biggest **horloge à billes** (a rolling ball clock; 30sq m) in the world in the village square!

🔥🔥 Écomusée du Bois et Scierie à Eau

🔥Guided visits: May–Oct 2.30–6pm. ⏱€4. ✆04 70 59 35 69.
At the gateway to the Black Forest, this area is a natural wooded environment. The museum explains the flora and fauna of the area as well as the life and times of a forester.

▶ Return along the D 995 and take the road to Laprugne. From this village the D 7 leads back to Mayet-de-Montagne.

② LES MONTS DE LA MADELEINE★

The Monts de la Madeleine roughly parallel those of the Bois Noirs.

▶ Leave Le Mayet-de-Montagne heading SE and taking the D 7 for 2.5km/1.5mi, then turn left onto the D 120.

Saint-Clément

They still make wooden clogs in this small village on the Besbre. Following the reunification of Germany in 1990, Saint-Clément was the geographical centre of the member countries of the European Union.

▷ Leave Saint-Clément heading SE and take the D 177.

The route follows the heavily wooded valley of the Besbre and provides improving views as height is gained of the valley of Sapey on the left.

Forêt de l'Assise★

The route descends through the forest to reach the **Loge-des-Gardes** (a small winter sports station) or the **Maison Forestière de l'Assise**, at the centre of the massif forest.

▷ Follow the D 182.

Gué de la Chaux

🚶 *1h.*
On the plateau de la Verrerie, a flora and fauna trail has been created in the middle of a huge bog.

▷ Make a U-turn and take the D 177 on the right. At the crossroads at Grand-Borne, turn right on the D 47, for Les Noës. Just before les Forges, turn right towards les Robins.

La "Route magique"

😊 *About 50m before a junction, stop the car as it is descending and see what happens… With the car in neutral, the car rolls backwards, giving the impression of going up the slope. This strange optical illusion has no explanation, but draws the curious.*

▷ Return to the intersection with the D 177, and turn right onto the D 478.

The route passes close to the small winter sports station of **Font-Blanche**, and then provides lovely views of the Monts de la Madeleine, to the right.

▷ Follow the D 478 then, at the col de la Rivière, take the D 120 on the left. As you approach Saint-Nicolas-des-Biefs, take the D 477 on the right.

Pierre Charbonnière★

At Goutaudier, take a track climbing on the right; follow this for 500m.
🚶 *1h30 there and back.*
The trail climbs through the woods to an assembly of rocks from where you get a superb view to the east of Roanne and the Monts de la Madeleine.

▷ Follow the D 477 to Trapière, and then turn left onto the D 25.

Cascade de la Pisserotte

🚶 *1h30 there and back.*
The Barbenan falls in two stages into a very beautiful setting.

▷ Continue on the D 25.

Puy du Roc★

Beyond the crossroads, immediately after a tower house, turn left and, 200m further on, turn left onto a trail that climbs to the top of the rock.
🚶 *45min there and back.* A path leads to the summit, (644m), which provides a splendid **panorama**★ to the north of the Bourbonnais, to the west of the Monts Dôme and Monts Dore and to the south and east of the Bois Noirs and the Monts de la Madeleine.

▷ Follow the D 25.

👥 Châtel-Montagne★

In the village you can visit ten workshops belonging to artists and craftsmen, along with the Heritage House, dedicated to the Romanesque.

Église Notre-Dame

The remains of a former Benedictine priory, this 12C church is a fine example of Romanesque architecture in the Bourbonnais.

▷ Leave Châtel-Montagne heading SW and take the D 207 which leads back to Le Mayet-de-Montagne.

Twenty centuries of history and a superb geographical situation at the confluence of the Saône and the Rhône give Lyon an appearance quite unlike any other city and justify its inclusion on UNESCO's World Heritage List. Yet, too often it is bypassed by tourists in a hurry, when it is perfectly equipped to serve as a stopover for a few days, or a prime destination in itself.

Introducing Lyon

The rivers Rhône and Saône provide the magnificent sight of their very differing courses as they flow past the foot of the two famous hills, Fourvière and La Croix-Rousse, facing the low plain of Dauphiné. Flowing down from the north, the Saône skirts the small Mont-d'Or range and enters the Pierre-Scize gorge gouged out between Fourvière and La Croix-Rousse. The Rhône arrives from the Alps, a wide river that washes the lower slopes of La Croix-Rousse. During Roman times, the confluence lay at the foot of the hill. The alluvium built up by the Rhône gradually pushed the confluence further south and the resulting peninsula became the main centre of the city. The Fourvière and La Croix-Rousse hills have numerous terraces from which to admire the town; the views from some of these are famous, including the Fourvière Basilica viewing table, place Rouville and rue des Fantasques in La Croix-Rousse. Further away but no less outstanding are the panoramic views from the Esplanade de Ste-Foy and Mont Thou.

Lyon's current prosperity serves as a reminder of the fact that the city's finest hours, during the Roman Empire and the

Highlights

1 Taking a river tour on a unique **bateau-mouche** (p302)

2 The unusual architecture of the **Fourvière basilica** (p312)

3 The views from the various *montées* on **Fourvière Hill** (p312)

4 The bustling streets of **La Presqu'île** and its squares (p316)

5 The outstanding collections at **Musée des Beaux-Arts** (p318)

Renaissance, were times when trade was of major importance and the city succeeded in taking full advantage of its outstanding geographical situation. It is, after all, on the road to Italy, between Central and Eastern France, and midway between Northern France and the southern provinces.

Lyon is not only an industrial city specialising in metalworking, chemistry and building trades, and famous for its silk and synthetic fabrics; it is also a university town and a world-famous

Quai Général Sarrail along the Rhône and the passerelle du Collège

© Pierre Jacques/hemis.fr

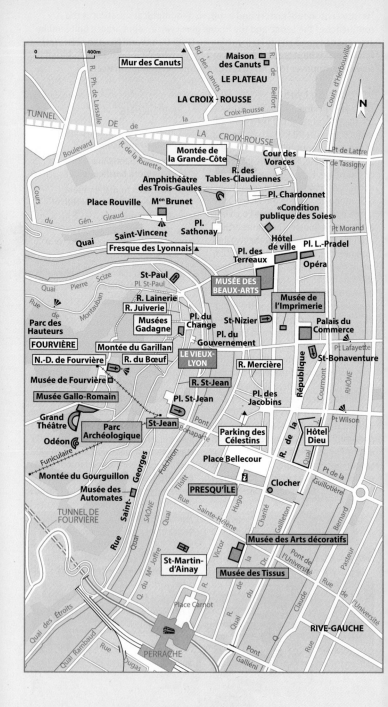

0   400m

Mur des Canuts

Maison des Canuts

LE PLATEAU

LA CROIX - ROUSSE

TUNNEL

Croix-Rousse

Pt de Lattre

LA

CROIX-ROUSSE

Montée de la Grande-Côte

Cour des Voraces

de Tassigny

Boulevard

R. des Tables-Claudiennes

Amphithéâtre des Trois-Gaules

Pl. Chardonnet

Place Rouville

M^on Brunet

«Condition publique des Soies»

Pt Morand

Quai   Saint-Vincent

Pl. Sathonay

Hôtel de ville

Pl. L.-Pradel

Quai   du   Gén. Giraud

Fresque des Lyonnais

Pl. des Terreaux

Opéra

Quai   Pierre   Scize

St-Paul

Pl. St-Paul

MUSÉE DES BEAUX-ARTS

Musée de l'Imprimerie

Rue   de   Montauban

R. Lainerie

R. Juiverie

Musées Gadagne

Pl. du Change

St-Nizier

Palais du Commerce

Parc des Hauteurs

Pl. du Gouvernement

Pt Lafayette

FOURVIÈRE

Montée du Garillan

LE VIEUX-LYON

St-Bonaventure

N.-D. de Fourvière

R. du Bœuf

R. Mercière

Musée de Fourvière

R. St-Jean

République

Musée Gallo-Romain

Pl. St-Jean

Pl. des Jacobins

Courmont

RHÔNE

Grand Théâtre

St-Jean

Pont

Pt Wilson

Odéon

Parc Archéologique

Bonaparte

Parking des Célestins

Hôtel Dieu

Funiculaire

Montée du Gourguillon

Place Bellecour

Pt de la Guillotière

Musée des Automates

PRESQU'ÎLE

Clocher

TUNNEL DE FOURVIÈRE

Musée des Arts décoratifs

St-Martin-d'Ainay

Musée des Tissus

RIVE-GAUCHE

Place Carnot

PERRACHE

Pont Galliéni

LYON'S MOST BEAUTIFUL AREAS AND MONUMENTS

MUSÉE DES BEAUX-ARTS	★★★	Highly recommended
Rue St-Jean	★★	Recommended
Musée Gadagne	★	Interesting
Opéra		Other site site described in this guide

MUSÉE DE L'AUTOMOBILE HENRI-MALARTRE

N

BD

PÉRIPHÉRIQUE

D 48

Quai du Commerce

SAÔNE

Quai Joseph Gillet

RHÔNE

Cité internationale (musée d'Art contemporain)

Ch. de Gaulle

Bd Laurent Bonnevay

Ateliers de soierie vivante

Quai

Jardin zoologique

Av. Roger Salengro

LA CROIX-ROUSSE

Bd des Belges

Parc de la Tête-d'Or

Grandes serres

VILLEURBANNE

Cours

Émile Zola

LES GRATTE-CIEL

FOURVIÈRE

Cours

Lafayette

Cours

Tolstoï

Aqueducs romains

LA PART-DIEU

LE VIEUX-LYON

Nouveau Musée (Institut d'Art contemporain)

PRESQU'ÎLE

Félix

Faure

Crs Gambetta

Av.

Av. Lacassagne

Musée africain

PERRACHE

Cours

A.

Musée Lumière

Avenue

Berthelot

Thomas

Quai Jean-Jacques Rousseau

SAÔNE

Centre d'histoire de la Résistance et de la Déportation

Route

Bd des

Av. Jean Mermoz

RHÔNE

Halle Tony-Garnier

de

États-Unis

Avenue

Paul

Santy

Musée des Confluences

GERLAND

Av. Tony Garnier

Vienne

Musée Urbain Tony-Garnier

0   1 km

Grand Aquarium de Lyon

299

- ▶ **Population:**
  City: 509 233; Conurbation:
  2 265 375.
- ♿ **Michelin Map:** 327: H/I-5
  – Local map see Monts du
  LYONNAIS.
- 🔲 **Info:** Pl. Bellecour, 69214
  Lyon. ℘04 72 77 69 69.
  www.lyon-france.com.
- ◗ **Location:** Lyon lies in a
  natural plain in the Rhône
  valley, 460km/287mi ESE
  from Paris.
- 🅿 **Parking:** Massive
  underground car park
  beneath place Bellecour,
  but be sure to make a note
  of exactly where you left
  the car – getting back
  to it can be confusing.
  Underground parking also
  at les Célestins, les Terreaux
  and la République.
- 😊 **Don't Miss:** The Fourvière
  district, but allow most
  of a day for a worthwhile
  exploration. A tour of
  Presqu'île and its squares is
  time well spent; check out
  the *traboules* (alleyways)
  in Vieux Lyon. La Part-
  Dieu district has a fine
  pedestrianised precinct.
- 🕐 **Timing:** Begin from place
  Bellecour, and wander the
  streets aimlessly; this is no
  place to be methodical!
  Organised tours covering
  1, 2 or 3 days are detailed
  below, but a longer stay
  will gain the most from this
  magnificent city, as will
  "free range" exploration;
  make a point of heading for
  the out-of-the-way places.
- 👫 **Kids:** Take a boat trip in a
  bateau-mouche, or visit
  the Musée de l'Automobile
  Henri-Malartre. A session
  with Guignol is popular;
  likewise visit the Parc de la
  Tête d'Or.

centre in the field of medicine. It has a
Court of Appeal and an Archbishopric
(the Archbishop of Lyon bears the
title "Primate of the Gauls"). The city
is a popular tourist venue, famous for
its cuisine: it is one of the best-known
gastronomic centres in France.

Twenty Centuries of History

Capital of the Gauls – According to a
Celtic legend two princes, Momoros and
Atepomaros, stopped here one day at
the confluence of the rivers and decided
to build a town. While they were digging the foundations, a flock of crows
flew down around them. Recognising
the event as evidence of divine intervention, they decided to call their city
Lugdunum (Crows' Hill).

Julius Caesar set up his base camp here
during his relentless campaign to con-
quer Gaul. After his death, one of his
lieutenants, Munatius Plancus, brought
Roman settlers here (43 BCE). Shortly
afterwards Agrippa, who had been
ordered by Caesar Augustus to organise Gaul, chose Lugdunum as his capital.
The network of imperial roads began
in Lyon and five major routes radiated
out from the city towards Aquitaine, the
Ocean, the Rhine, Arles and Italy. Caesar
Augustus stayed in the town; Emperor
Claudius was born here. In the 2C, aqueducts brought water to Fourvière from
the surrounding mountains.

The city, governed by its council, held a
monopoly in the trade of wine throughout Gaul. The mariners in its harbour
were powerful ship-owners; its potters were veritable industrialists. The
wealthiest of the city's traders lived in
a separate district, on the Île des Canabae, around where St-Martin-d'Ainay
stands today. On the slopes of La Croix-
Rousse was the Gallic town, Condate.
The Amphitheatre of the Three Gauls
(the votive inscription was uncovered
in 1958) and the Temple of Rome and
Caesar Augustus were the setting for
the noisy Assembly of Gauls once a year.

Christianity in Lyon – Lyon became the
meeting-place for businessmen from all
over the country. Soldiers, merchants

and missionaries arrived from Asia Minor and began spreading the new gospel. Soon, a small Christian community developed in the town.

In AD 177, a popular revolt broke out and led to the famous martyrdom of St Pothin, St Blandine and their companions. Twenty years later when **Septimus Severus**, having defeated his competitor Albin (who enjoyed popular support from the locals), decided to set fire to the town, he found that there were still 18 000 Christians in Lyon. He had them massacred; among them featured St Irénée, St Pothin's successor.

This faith has continued through the ages. On 8 December each year, the **Feast of the Immaculate Conception** is celebrated in Lyon with a great deal of pomp and enthusiasm. In the evening, thousands of multicoloured lanterns can be seen in the windows of the city.

The origins of this **"Festival of Lights"** date from the occasion of the consecration of the gilded Madonna of Fourvière in 1852. Floods had delayed the work of sculptor Fabish, who was not able to deliver the statue by the deadline of 8 September. Accordingly the ceremony was postponed until 8 December, the Feast of the Immaculate Conception. On the day itself, heavy rainfall resulted in cancellation of the evening festival. However, contrary to all expectations, the rain stopped at precisely the time the festivities had been scheduled to start. All over the city, thousands of balconies were lit up by tiny lights placed there in a spontaneous gesture by Lyon residents. This religious custom has become a traditional festival during which the city councillors and store owners inaugurate their Christmas displays.

Lyon in the Middle Ages – After Charlemagne's reign, Lyon passed from one family to another through legacies and dowries. Finally, the city was placed under the temporal authority of its archbishops. During this period a large number of major building projects were completed. Churches and abbeys sprang up in Lyon and the surrounding area. The Pont du Change (Exchange Bridge) was built over the Saône; the Pont de la Guillotière, designed by the Pontiff Brothers, provided access to the other bank of the Rhône.

In the early 14C, Lyon was annexed to royal authority and obtained the right to elect 12 consuls. A municipal charter was proclaimed at Île Barbe in 1312. The consuls, all of them members of the rich *bourgeoisie*, raised taxes and ensured that there was law and order. The people of the working classes, who were quick to rebel and who had not hesitated in besieging the archbishop in his palace, discovered to their cost that the consuls were even more heavy-handed than the clergy had been.

A cultural centre – At the end of the 15C the setting up of fairs and the development of banking attracted traders from all over Europe. Social, intellectual and artistic life blossomed, stimulated by a visit from François I and his sister, Marguerite, who held the most dazzling court.

Famous "booksellers" took the fame of Lyon's printers far and wide. There were 100 printers' workshops in the town in 1515, and more than 400 by 1548.

Painters, sculptors and potters, all of them steeped in Italian culture, prepared the way for the French Renaissance. Lyon boasted brilliant poets and storytellers such as **François Rabelais** (1494–1553). He was a doctor at the local hospital and, for the fairs in 1532 and 1534, published his works *Gargantua* and *Pantagruel*. It was, though, a woman, **Louise Labé**, who embodied the spirit of the day, not only for her grace and beauty but also for her skill in poetry. At the age of 20, Louise had developed comprehensive linguistic (Greek, Latin, Spanish and Italian) and musical talents.

After a stint at the siege of Perpignan (not for the faint-hearted!), she eventually married a gentleman-rope-maker (*cordier* in French) from Lyon and opened a salon for poets, artists and men of learning, just as Madame de Sévigné was to do a century later.

GETTING AROUND

Maps – In addition to the maps included in this guide, Michelin town plans 30 and 31 and Michelin map 110 (the surroundings of Lyon) will be useful.

Access – By road via motorways A 6, A 7, A 42 and A 43. The city also boasts a regular 2hr link with Paris by TGV. Perrache and La Part-Dieu stations are close to the town centre by métro. There are flights to and from most major cities via Lyon-St-Exupéry airport, linked to the town centre by a shuttle service.

Parking – There are several underground car parks strategically placed for easy access to the town centre. Some of these are architectural gems, the most spectacular being the Parc Célestins by Buren, whose columns adorn the Jardins du Palais-Royal in central Paris.

Public transport – The underground train/subway (métro) is the most convenient mode of public transport, and is especially well adapted to the needs of tourists. The best-value ticket to buy is the 1-day **ticket-liberté**, for unlimited travel on the Lyon urban transport network (métro, bus, funicular railway, trolley-bus). Details from TCL (Transports en Commun Lyonnais) kiosks or call ☎04 26 10 12 12, www.tcl.fr.

Cultural Pass: You can buy a 1–4-day **Lyon City Card: Pass Culturel et Touristique** which will gain you admission to museums, sights and transport, as well as reductions in theatres, on shopping, etc. Adult prices range between 1 day (€24), 2 days (€33), 3 days (€42), 4 days (€55). (*discount for online purchase at www.lyoncitycard.com*).

TOURING THE CITY

Planning your visit – If you have only **one day** to spend in Lyon, then you must devote the morning to Old Lyon (on foot), to the Fourvière terrace and the Roman theatres (use the funicular), but you will not have time to visit the museums; the afternoon should be spent touring the Presqu'île with its Fabric Museum and, either visiting the Fine Arts Museum or an enjoyable walk around the Gros Caillou, on the slopes of the Croix-Rousse.

Two days will enable you to get better acquainted with Fourvière and the various museums and to stroll along the River Saône on the first day. The second day should be devoted to touring the Presqu'île on foot and to visiting its museums (fabrics, printing and hospice museums); you should even have time to take a stroll in the Croix-Rousse district.

Organised tours – Lyon, which is listed as a "Town of Art and history", offers discovery tours conducted by guide-lecturers approved by the Ministry of Culture and Communication. Information at the tourist office or on www.vpah.culture.fr. The Lyon tourist office offers tours of the city on foot, or by bus, boat, taxi or even helicopter (*discount for online bookings*). **Lecture tours** are available around Old Lyon, Croix-Rousse and the Tony Garnier district.

Bateaux-mouches river trips – ☎04 78 42 96 81. www.lyoncityboat.com. From quai des Célestins. These unique long-boats enable visitors to discover a different face of Lyon, seen from its four river banks: one trip explores the confluence of the Saône and Rhône; the other follows the Saône up to and round the Île-Barbe.

"La Belle Cordière", as she was known, penned some pleasing verse herself, as well as encouraging others.

Scientific advances – Literature and the arts reigned in the Lyon of the 16C. Science became all the rage in the 18C, with the **Jussieu brothers**, famous botanists, and Bourgelat, who founded the first veterinary school in Europe in Lyon in 1762. In 1783 **Jouffroy** tested steam navigation on the Saône

See pp500-501

with his "Pyroscaphe", the first really viable steamboat; however, it brought him nothing but the ironic nickname of "Jouffroy the Pump". In 1784, **Joseph Montgolfier** and **Pilâtre de Rozier** succeeded, at Les Brotteaux, in rising into the air on board a hot-air balloon. This was one of the first flights. A few years later, **André-Marie Ampère**, the great physicist, and **Joseph-Marie Jacquard**, who invented a weaving loom, showed their own form of inventive genius.

"Lyon is no more" – During the French Revolution, the residents of Lyon resisted the Convention. Retribution was harsh: on 12 October 1793 the Committee of Public Safety declared that "Lyon waged war on liberty. Lyon is no more." Houses were destroyed, countless local people died, and Lyon was renamed a "Free Commune".

Lyon's "Mr Punch" – Guignol, the popular wooden puppet who is well-known throughout France, his dutiful wife Madelon, and his usual sparring partner, Gnafron, whose fine bass voice has coarsened somewhat through excessive consumption of Beaujolais, all embody the popular spirit of the local people in a way that provokes laughter without giving offence. **Laurent Mourguet** (1769–1844), who created Guignol, was a local weaver. The few neighbours for whom he first performed his comedy shows were enthusiastic. Soon, as his success grew, so did his public: he staged performances all over Lyon, in the Petit Tivoli, and in the main avenue in Les Brotteaux where, on Sundays, three rows of chairs were set out. After Mourguet's death his 16 children, all of whom had been trained by him, perpetuated his art form. Nowadays, comedies based on current affairs are played out on the stage of the Guignol de Lyon theatre.

Threads of History

Silk, the fibre from cocoons produced by the caterpillars of the Bombyx moth, otherwise known as silkworms, was discovered in China, and was brought to France by Louis XI in 1466. The French silk industry did not really begin to evolve until the 16C; at this time Lyon was chosen as the central silk depot, and cultivation of the mulberry bushes on which silkworms feed was begun on a large scale. The industry's expansion continued under Louis XIV, with notable innovators such as Philippe de Lassalle playing a major role in its development, but was brought to an abrupt end by the outbreak of the French Revolution. It received a new lease of life under Napoleon's Empire, finally reaching its apogee in c. 1850, shortly after which a devastating silkworm plague broke out, decimating French silkworm breeding centres. This was a blow from which the French silk industry never fully recovered. It also subsequently had to contend with strong foreign competition, the discovery of artificial fibres and mass industrialisation. Nonetheless, Lyon silk production has remained a standard of quality for the fashion world and among French luxury materials.

Sericulture, or the production of silk, involves raising silkworms in special silkworm farms (in French, *magnaneries*) from the egg to the cocoon stage. The silkworm chrysalids are suffocated in steam so that the cocoon can be unravelled as a single long filament of silk. The raw silk obtained at this stage is not strong enough to be woven and so undergoes a preparatory process – reeling, in which the silk fibres from several cocoons are wound together to form a single strand. Bobbins of this thread are arranged on a special frame, then unreeled in batches onto a warp frame. Next the warp is stretched on a draw loom to form parallel threads, across which the weft threads are drawn by a shuttle. To allow the shuttle to pass along with the weft, various mechanical systems for lifting the appropriate warp threads were developed, one of the most famous of which was Jacquard's (using punched cards). Various types of plain weave are possible using silk, to produce taffeta, silk serge and satin, for example. The manufacture of fancier, figured fabrics (with decorative motifs in coloured threads) requires a more complex system, however, using cords known – funnily enough – as simples. As for woven pile fabrics such as velvet, it is necessary to have a second set of warp threads which form the pile. Such fancy fabrics can be smooth (damask, lampas) or textured (brocade, brocatelle).

Silk can also be processed after it has been woven, for example in silkscreen-printing, or the manufacture of figured or watered silks.

The silk industry – It was silk which, in the 16C, made Lyon a major industrial city; until then most of the silk fabrics in France had been imported from Italy. Two main figures dominate the history of this new industry. In 1536, **Étienne Turquet**, a man from Piedmont in Italy, offered to bring to Lyon silk and velvet weavers from Genoa and set up a factory in Lyon. François I, who was anxious to stem the flow of money out of the country as a result of purchases of foreign silks, accepted his offer. In 1804 **Joseph-Marie Jacquard** invented a loom which, by using a system of punched cards, enabled a single worker to do the work of six. The Croix-Rousse district was filled with house-workshops – the upper storeys contained the looms on which the workers wove the silk provided by the manufacturer.

In 1875, a revolution occurred in the silk industry; the introduction of mechanical looms and the change in fashion away from figured fabrics and brocades quickly reduced the silk-workers to abject poverty. Only a few looms continued to exist in Lyon, capable of

Vieux Lyon by Montée du Gourguillon

producing special fabrics at exorbitant prices. Ordinary silks were made by workers in rural areas where labour was less expensive.

Today natural silk imported from Italy or Japan now represents only a minute proportion of the quantities of fabric processed here. It is subject to extremely meticulous care and attention in the silk-workers' centre (Maison des Canuts, *see below*). The so-called "silk-style" weaving, though, using all sorts of fibres (glass, carbon, borum and aramide) remains one of Lyon's specialities.

The traditional know-how of the silk weavers has found direct applications in the production of highly sophisticated parts for the aeronautics, space and electronics industries.

Lyon Fair – In the Middle Ages, Lyon was "one of the keys to the kingdom", situated as it was on the frontiers of Savoy, Dauphiné, Italy and Germany on one side, and Beaujolais, Burgundy, Languedoc, Forez and the Auvergne on the other. In 1419, the heir to the French throne, the future Charles VII, having realised the value of this geographical situation in commercial terms, ordered two fairs to be held here every year; he made Lyon one of the largest warehouses in the world. Traders and merchants flocked here from every direction.

From 1463 onwards, thanks to Louis XI, the fairs were held four times a year. Re-established in 1916 after a long break, the **Lyon International Fair** maintains the city's tradition as a major centre of international business.

A European crossroads – Lyon lies at the centre of a motorway network that links the city to northern and southern Europe in the north–south direction and to the Massif Central, Switzerland and Italy in the east–west direction, via St-Étienne, Clermont-Ferrand, Geneva, Annecy, Chambéry and Grenoble.

Since 1981, in addition to the many fast rail links with the rest of France, Lyon has enjoyed even more rapid communications due to the high-speed train (TGV) service. There is a busy international airport, **Lyon-St-Exupéry**, to the east of the town and the Édouard-Herriot harbour to the south of the Gerland district is full of heavy barges waiting to sail up to Auxonne on the Saône.

Lyon puts on a new face – There has been much development in Lyon since the "daring" tower blocks of the 1930s. In order to ensure its success in the future, Lyon is developing a number of science and technology parks, which bring together scientific research, higher education and industry. The **Cité Internationale** is the site of an International Conference Centre, the head offices of Interpol, a hotel complex and a Museum of Contemporary Art. To the east, around the university campus, there are major technical research offices and, further out of town, the St-Exupéry TGV station, designed by Spanish architect Calatrava to resemble a bird taking flight, which provides a TGV link to the local airport.

Vieux Lyon ★★★

Lyon old town, between Fourvière Hill and the Saône, includes the **St-Jean district** in the centre, the **St-Paul district** to the north and the **St-Georges district** to the south. This was once the town centre and the seat of all the corporations, in particular those representing silk-workers. Traders, bankers, clerks and royal dignitaries lived here, in magnificent townhouses. Almost 300 of these mansions still stand, forming quite an exceptional example of Renaissance housing.

> ▷ **Location:** Sandwiched between the Saône and Fourvière Hill.
> 👥 **Kids:** The Musée des Automates; the astronomical clock in the cathedral; one of the performances by Le Guignol (even if you don't understand it).
> ⊘ **Don't Miss:** The beautiful buildings of rue St-Jean and the neighbourhood; Galerie de Phillibert Delorme.

OLD TOWN

One of the main features of the old town is the numerous passages or alleyways known as **traboules** (from the Latin *trans ambulare* meaning "walking through") especially between rue St-Jean, rue des Trois-Maries and quai Romain-Rolland, rue St-Georges and quai Fulchiron. Since there was not enough space to build an extensive network of streets, these passageways, all perpendicular to the Saône, were built to link the buildings together; they are quite fascinating. The houses reflect their period of construction (15C–17C) and there are several architectural styles. The **Late Gothic houses** are distinguishable by the elegant decoration on the Flamboyant façades. The windows are often set asymmetrically into the walls. Most of the old houses, among them the most beautiful of all the mansions, are built in the **Renaissance style**. The basic structure remains unchanged, but the buildings are bigger and include new decorative features of Italian inspiration. The staircase turrets are beautiful; each courtyard has galleries, one above the other, each with surbased arches.

The **French Renaissance houses** are fewer in number. There is a noticeable return to Antiquity with the inclusion of architectural orders. The famous architect **Philibert Delorme** (1515–70), a native of Lyon, launched the new fashion with the gallery on squinches at No. 8 rue Juiverie. The main staircase, which was often rectangular, was set in the centre of the façade.

The **late-16C and pre-Classical houses** are distinguished by severe architectural lines. The decoration on the façade appears above the ground floor and includes triangular pediments with a central arch stone in relief, and rusticated bonding. The galleries overlooking the courtyard show Florentine influence with rounded arches supported by round columns.

🐾 WALKING TOURS

1 ST-JEAN AND ST-PAUL DISTRICTS

Place St-Jean

In the centre is a fountain with four basins topped by a small pavilion. To the east of the square is the cathedral of St-Jean and the choir school.

Manécanterie

To the right of the west front on place St-Jean is the 12C choir school. The front of the building, which lost 0.80m of its overall height when the ground level was raised, is decorated with a blind storey topped by red-brick encrustations, colonnettes and niches containing statues of human figures.

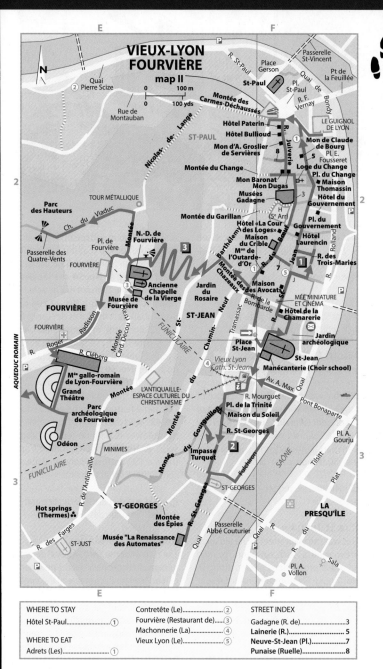

Primatiale St-Jean★

Dating originally from the 12C, St-Jean Cathedral is a Gothic building erected to complete a Romanesque apse. On the exterior the most notable features are the four towers, two on the west front and two over the arms of the transept. They are only slightly higher than the nave. In 1245 and 1274 the cathedral was the setting for the two Councils of Lyon.

Place St-Jean, Basilique Notre-Dame on the Fourvière Hill in the background

© Pierre Jacques/hemis.fr

In the following century it was chosen for the consecration of Pope John XXII. In 1600, Henri IV married Marie de' Medici here.

▶ Skirt the cathedral to the right on rue St-Étienne and go to the archaeological gardens.

Jardin Archéologique

In this archaeological park visitors can see the remains of several buildings that have occupied the former site of the church of St-Étienne to the north of the present cathedral, since the 4C. They include Gallo-Roman baths, a palaeo-Christian baptistery and an arch from the 15C church of Ste-Croix.

▶ The narrow rue Ste-Croix leads to rue St-Jean.

Rue St-Jean★★

This was the main street in the old town of Lyon and, as such, royal corteges and religious processions passed along it. **No. 7** has a Flamboyant Gothic façade. The old **Hôtel de la Chamarerie** at **No. 37** was built in the 16C for the cleric responsible for overseeing the cathedral cloisters, who was known as the chamarier.

The arcading in the galleries of the **Maison des Avocats★** (Barristers' House) is supported on massive columns and the outbuildings have pink roughcast. Seen from rue de la Bombarde, the house presents a fine example of 16C architecture in the Italian style. **No. 58** has an unu-

sual feature in the shape of a well with a tripartite roof so that it is accessible from the courtyard, the staircase and the workshop. At **No. 54**, the **longest traboule** in old Lyon crosses five courtyards before reaching **No. 27 rue du Bœuf**. Walk past the Palais de Justice to **No. 52**: the house of printer Guillaume Leroy (late 15C) has a spiral staircase in a round tower. The bays are supported on arches. **No. 50** is a fine example of a renovated courtyard enhanced by galleries and a spiral staircase.

The same features can be admired at **No. 42**, which has retained its corbelled passageway resting on sculpted consoles. At **No. 36**, a house dating from the late 15C, there is a polygonal tower containing a spiral staircase.

▶ Take rue du Palais-de-Justice and turn left onto rue des Trois-Maries.

Rue des Trois-Maries

The "Street of the Three Marys" derives its name from the niche on the pediment of **No. 7** containing a statue of the Virgin Mary flanked by two Holy Women. On the same side of the street, numerous traboules lead off downhill to the Saône. At **No. 3** a handsome example of French Renaissance has a staircase surmounted by a tower in the centre of its façade; this feature is repeated in the house at **No. 5 place du Gouvernement**. The façade of **No. 4** is adorned with a regular arrangement of fluted pilasters and, in the courtyard, a tower in which the spiral staircase is clearly visible.

▶ Retrace your steps to No. 6, and cross the traboule leading across two restored courtyards to No. 27 rue St-Jean.

The façade at **No. 27** has mullioned windows framed by fluted pilasters. **No. 28** conceals a magnificent **courtyard★★** with an imposing tower with a spiral staircase inside it. The **Hôtel Laurencin** at **No. 24** has a crenellated octagonal tower containing a spiral staircase.

▶ Cross place de la Baleine and go to place du Gouvernement.

Place du Gouvernement

The façade of **No. 5**, its doorways topped by wrought-iron imposts and a stone balcony, dates from the early 17C. **Hôtel du Gouvernement** (16C) stands at **No. 2**. The upper courtyard lies at the end of a long roofed passageway. All that remains of the well to the right is the shell-shaped top (note the *traboule* at No. 10 quai Romain-Rolland).

▶ Rejoin rue St-Jean and walk on until you reach place du Change.

Place du Change

This square, originally called place de la Draperie, was frequented by money-lenders in the 15C and 16C. The **Loge du Change** was designed mainly by Soufflot, the architect who altered the original design between 1747 and 1750. On the upper storey are engaged columns topped by Ionic capitals and carved entablatures. Opposite is the **Maison Thomassin** which has a 15C façade built in the 14C style. On the second floor the mullioned ogee bays rising to trefoiled arches are set into Gothic arches decorated with coats of arms.

▶ Continue along rue Lainerie.

Rue Lainerie

Note the vaulted corridor of **No. 18**. The **Maison de Claude de Bourg** at **No. 14** has a 15C flower-decked façade which is typical of Lyon, with ornate accolades.

▶ To the right is rue Louis-Garrand and the Guignol puppet theatre.

Rue Lainerie opens onto place St-Paul, where you can glimpse the train station and, further back, the **church**.

▶ Turn left onto rue Juiverie.

Rue Juiverie★

The Jews were expelled from this street in the late 14C and the Italian bankers who replaced them had luxurious mansions built. The **Hôtel Paterin**, also known as "Henri IV's House", at **No. 4** is an outstanding example of Renaissance architecture. The **staircase** in the courtyard, with its three tiers of arches, one above the other, supported on massive columns, is particularly impressive.

At **No. 8**, the second courtyard in the **Hôtel Bullioud** contains the famous **gallery★★** designed by **Philibert Delorme**, a gem of French Renaissance architecture in Lyon. Delorme built it in 1536 on his return from Rome. The Renaissance façade on the **Maison Antoine Groslier de Servières** (**No. 10**) has five arches on the ground floor topped by triangular or broken pediments of black marble. In the courtyard is a round tower with mullioned windows containing a spiral staircase. The corbels on the balcony on the first floor are carved with human figures. The house at **No. 21** has ogee windows with rounded frontons. There is a Gallo-Roman cellar in its basement.

Gallery, Hôtel Bulliou, no. 8 rue Juiverie

© M&G Therin-Weise/age fotostock

Le Guignol de Lyon – Compagnie des Zonzons

Guignol, the satirical puppet, is characterised by his black cap under which he has a short plait which he calls his *sarsifis*. His naïvety and waggish banter make him a perfect example of the "urchins" of Lyon. His wife, Madelon, with whom he has frequent arguments, is a model wife, if somewhat prone to grumbling. His inseparable friend is Gnafron whose most notable features are his tall stature and his ruddy nose, an

Guignol

© Tibor Bognar/Photononstop

indication of his marked liking for Beaujolais. If anybody asks him what he does for a living, he answers, "Educated people call us cobblers or botchers; the uneducated call us gowks" *("gnafres")*. Shows at the Guignol theatre are now a blend of tradition and modern innovation, influenced by contemporary authors and even films.

Between **Nos. 16** and **18** rises the picturesque, steep **ruelle Punaise**, which leads onto montée St-Barthélémy. In the Middle Ages it served as an open sewer. The mansion at **No. 20** was built by a wealthy 15C gentleman, E Grolier. The façade is decorated with mullioned windows flanked by colonnettes. At **No. 22** is the **Maison Baronat**, which has a corbelled corner turret overlooking montée du Change. At **No. 23**, at the corner of rue de la Loge, is the **Maison Dugas** whose long façade is decorated with bosses and lions' heads.

▷ Turn left onto rue de la Loge, then right into rue de Gadagne.

Musée Gadagne★

This mansion stretches from No. 10 to No. 14 rue de Gadagne and is the largest Renaissance building in the old town. In 1545, it was purchased by the **Gadagne Brothers**, bankers of Italian origin who had amassed a colossal fortune. Indeed, the expression "as rich as Gadagne" became a local figure of speech.

Musée Historique de Lyon★

In the Local History Museum the rooms on the ground floor have been laid out with **religious sculpture★**, including bas-relief sculptures from old churches or abbeys in Lyon, in particular from Ainay, St-Pierre and Île Barbe (Annunciation bas-relief, a mantelpiece known as "Charlemagne's Crown").

Musée International de la Marionnette★

The exhibits of this museum include not only Guignol and a number of glove puppets, but also an outstanding collection of string and rod puppets and shadow figures from France, England, Belgium, Holland, Venice, Turkey, Russia and the Far East.

▷ Walk across place du Petit-Collège and along rue du Bœuf.

Rue du Bœuf

This street owes its name to the statue of an ox (or more precisely a bull) at the corner of place Neuve-St-Jean.

The street contains some lovely examples of Renaissance architecture, some now occupied by luxury hotels. At **No. 6**, "La Cour des Loges" Hotel occupies a fine set of four restored houses. It is possible, with discretion or perhaps stopping for refreshment, to have a look at the beautiful courtyard with its U-shaped galleries on three floors.

No. 14 leads into a pretty courtyard with a polygonal tower and galleries supported on arches surmounted by a frieze of Greek motifs.

The **Maison du Crible★** at **No. 16** dates from the 17C. It has an ornate doorway with bosses and ringed columns topped by a pediment decorated with a small carving of the Adoration of the Magi said to have been the work of Giambologna. An alleyway leads to an inner courtyard in which the elegant round tower, with staggered openings, owes its name, **Tour Rose** (Pink Tower), to the colour of its famous roughcast. ☺*Do not go up to the terraced gardens.*

Place Neuve-St-Jean

This old street was transformed into a square under the Consulat. At **No. 4** is a vast building set slightly back from the others which features a superb staircase over arches corresponding to galleries with surbased arches.

▶ Return to rue du Bœuf.

The **Maison de l'Outarde d'Or** (House of the Golden Bustard) stands out at **No. 19** because of its carved stone sign. The courtyard is particularly interesting for its two turrets. One of them is round; the other, corbelled, turret is a rectangle built on an upturned pyramid.
Another building of interest can be seen at **No. 27** (the longest *traboule* in Lyon, leading to **No. 54** rue St-Jean) with an elegant 16C spiral staircase preceding three courtyards.
No. 36 opens onto a pretty courtyard decorated with restored galleries. It is interesting to compare these with those of **No. 38**, which are largely sealed up by additional structures. Most of the galleries were closed off when the district's fortunes sank to make more space and to keep in heat.

▶ No. 31 opens onto rue de la Bombarde (on the right). Almost opposite, take rue des Antonins, which leads back to place St-Jean.

From St-Jean métro station it is possible to take the funicular railway up to the top of Fourvière hill and come back down the same way after visiting the Basilica, Gallo-Roman Museum and Roman theatres.

② ST-GEORGES DISTRICT

▶ Walk from place St-Jean to place de la Trinité (follow rue Mourguet).

Place de la Trinité

The **Maison du Soleil**, which became famous after inspiring the backcloth for the Guignol puppet theatre, lends an old-fashioned touch to the square.

Montée du Gourguillon

Set on the hillside in the Fourvière district, this was the usual route taken by carriages heading for the Auvergne in the Middle Ages. It is difficult to imagine the heavy loads climbing such a steep slope. It was also the direct route between the cloisters of St-Jean belonging to the Canon-Counts, and St-Just, the fortified town of the Canon-Barons. At **No. 2** stands a Renaissance house. Slightly further up the hill is the **Impasse Turquet**, a picturesque passageway with old timber galleries.

Rue St-Georges

The ground floor of **No. 3** has basket-handled arches and the springer of the door is decorated with two rampant wrought-iron lions. At **No. 3 bis** the springer is decorated with a phoenix rising from the flames. At **No. 6**, the 16C house has a fine interior courtyard (art gallery). The spiral staircase is set in a round tower with sloping windows.

▶ Continue to no. 100 if you want to visit the Automata Museum.

👥 Musée des Automates
100 rue St-Georges.
&⏰*Daily 2–6pm.* ⏰*1 May, 3rd Mon in Sept, 25 Dec.* ⊛*€7 (child 3–17, €5).*
✆*04 72 77 75 28.*
www.museeautomates.com.
Seven rooms house 250 automata in perfect working order, displayed according to cultural, traditional and regional themes.

▶ Turn right at Église St-Georges and return via quai Fulchiron.

③ THE MONTÉES
👣*see FOURVIÈRE HILL*

Fourvière Hill★

The Fourvière district of Lyon stands on a hill of the same name; the term **Fourvière** is said to come from the Latin *forum vetus*, relating to the forum situated in the heart of the Roman colony established in 43 BCE; its theatre, odeon and aqueducts have survived to this day. The forum, which stood on the site now occupied by the esplanade in front of the basilica, is said to have collapsed in 840. In the 3C, people moved from the side of the hill and the stones were reused to rebuild the town at the bottom of the slope. In the Middle Ages the hill was largely given over to farming (in particular vineyards). In the 17C, numerous religious orders set up monasteries and convents here, which inspired the historian, Michelet, to make his famous comment about Fourvière, "the hill that prays" opposite La Croix-Rousse "the hill that works". Nowadays Fourvière, with its basilica, Roman monuments and museum is, with the old town below, one of the most popular tourist venues in Lyon.

▷ **Location:** Situated to the W of the Saône, dominating Vieux-Lyon.

Kids: The tree-climbing adventure (Go Ape in the UK).

Don't Miss: The spectacular view from the Fourvière Basilica.

WALKING TOUR

③ THE MONTÉES
see p307 for map.

The *montées,* or rises, consist of winding flights of steps or steeply sloping streets that climb the Fourvière hill, providing superb views down over the old town. Each of them has its own charm.

Montée des Chazeaux
With its 228 very steep steps, it leads onto montée St-Barthélémy.

Jardin du Rosaire★
Daily, 6.30am–9.30pm.
The **great rose gardens** are laid out between the lake and quai Achille-

---

Les Montées

Winding staircases or steep streets, "Les Montées" scale Fourvière Hill, offering dramatic views over the old town.

Montée des Carmes-Déchaussés – This derives its name (Rise of the Barefoot Carmelites) from the monastery founded in the early 17C which now houses the Regional Archives; it has 238 steps.

Montée du Change – This links rue de la Loge to montée St-Barthélémy. On the way down, there are interesting views of the spires on the church of St-Nizier which rises from the buildings on the banks of the Saône.

Montée du Garillan★ – This is a remarkable series of zigzag flights of steps (224 steps).

Montée du Chemin-Neuf and Montée St-Barthélémy – From these steps there is an extensive view over the rooftops of the old town and St-Jean Cathedral.

Montée du Gourguillon – See St-Georges district, p311.

Montée des Épies – This rise climbs up above the St-Georges district, high above the church dedicated to St George, a neo-Gothic building designed by Bossan, the architect also responsible for Fourvière Basilica.

Lignon, and boast 70 000 plants representing 350 varieties which are a stunning sight between June and October. The road, which climbs in zigzags (30min) is used each day by students attending a nearby school, by employees keen to find parking spaces close to Vieux Lyon and by pilgrims: note the numbered brass roses marking the route. The zigzags criss-cross woodland areas of maple, yew and boxwood. Owned by the church but managed by the city council, the garden is adorned with small flowery interludes. With its stunning vistas over the city and its welcome shade, the place is a popular location for picnics.

For a 360-degree **panoramic view★★** climb to the foot of the basilica's observatory; from there the hillsides of the Lyonnais area, Mont Pilat and Mont-d'Or are visible and, in good weather, also the Alps and Mont Blanc to the west and the Puy de Dôme to the east.

Basilique Notre-Dame★

The history of the religious buildings erected in honour of the Virgin Mary on the site of the Roman forum spans 800 years. The massive basilica standing today at the top of Fourvière hill is an integral part of the Lyon landscape. The basilica is a famous place of pilgrimage built to designs by an architect named Bossan after the Franco-Prussian War (1870) in fulfilment of a vow taken by Monsignor de Genouilhac, the Archbishop of Lyon, who undertook to build a church if the enemy did not approach the city.

Crenellated walls with machicolations, flanked by octagonal towers, form an odd blend of Byzantine and medieval features. The abundance of decoration inside (nave and crypt) is no less unusual.

Ancienne Chapelle de la Vierge

To the right of the basilica stands the real pilgrimage chapel dating from the 18C: the former Lady Chapel containing a statue of the Virgin Mary (16C).

Lyon viewed from Basilique Notre-Dame

Musée de Fourvière

🕐 *Mon–Thu noon–6pm, Fri–Sat 10am–7pm, Sun 2–5.30pm.*
🕐 *24–25 and 31 Dec.* 📞 *04 78 25 13 01. www.fourviere.org.*

This museum, housed in the chapel and buildings once belonging to the Jesuit Order, contains a collection of polychrome wooden statues (12C–19C), various projects designed for the basilica in the 19C, and votive offerings.

▷ Take the montée Nicolas-de-Lange to the right of the basilica.

Montée Nicolas-de-Lange

This has 560 steps which means that there is a total of 798 steps down to place St-Paul from the metal tower (Tour Métallique) on Fourvière.

Parc des Hauteurs

Follow a path to the left, just before the Tour Métallique.

This ambitious project was set up to enhance visitors' appreciation of Fourvière hill by laying out panoramic walks. The most original construction is that of the "Chemin du Viaduc", a footbridge that gives a breathtaking **view★** down onto Lyon and La Croix-Rousse.

Musée de Gallo-Romains de Lyon-Fourvière

Musée de Gallo-Romains de Lyon-Fourvière★★

⏱☉Tue–Sun 10am–6pm. ☉1 Jan,
1 May, 1 Nov, 25 Dec. ⊚€6, free 1st Sun
of the month. ☎04 72 38 49 30.
www.musee-site.rhone.fr.
This museum stands on the hill at Fourvière, at the heart of the district that was
once the plateau of the ancient town
of Lugdunum. The museum displays
thematic exhibitions of its mainly Gallo-
Roman collections.

Parc Archéologique de Fourvière★

☉Tue–Sun 10am–5.45pm (5pm Nov–
Jan). ☉1 Jan, 1 May, 1 Nov, 25 Dec.
☎04 72 38 49 30.
www.musee-site.rhone.fr.
Fourvière archaeological site, opened
in 1933, brought to light ancient and
medieval public buildings in the district:
Gallo-Roman baths in rue des Farges,
remains of early basilica in rue des Macchabées and quai Fulchiron.

Théâtres Romains

The group of buildings uncovered near
rue de l'Antiquaille includes a theatre
built during the reign of Caesar Augustus (1C BCE) and extended during the
reign of Hadrian (2C) and an odeum.

Grand Théâtre

This is the oldest theatre in France. It
is similar in size to those in Arles and
Orange (108m in diameter) but smaller
than the one in Vienne. The number
of tiers of seats was later increased by
building on top of the promenades.
The outer circular wall of the theatre
shows substructures in which archaeologists have noted the particular attention paid by the builders to exits via
underground corridors and to ground
drainage through a system of pipes and
sewers. The stage curtain machinery,
housed in the orchestra pit, is some
of the best preserved of its kind in the
world.

▷ Climb the staircase leading to the
top of the tiers of seats.

From here, the full size of the theatre
can be appreciated. It is possible to walk
round the upper section by following
the Roman road of large granite slabs.

▷ Walk down the Roman road to
the odeum.

Area Overlooking the Theatre

Beyond the paved road behind the theatre, recent excavations have revealed the
existence of an impressive residence and
not, as was thought at one time, a temple dedicated to Cybele. From the late
1C BCE there stood on this huge rectangular esplanade a vast and magnificent
house, bordered on one side by shops
sheltered by a portico.

Life at the Crossroads

As the "Gateway to the south of France", where the better qualities of the north of France can be found in a more Mediterranean context embodied not least by the red pantile roofs, Lyon enjoys not only the reputation of being a hard-working, major city, but also of having an outstanding standard of living in which good food plays a leading role. Life in Lyon is characterised above all by its lack of stress or complication. The Lyonnais are creatures of habit, and some of their favourite pastimes can be appreciated by visitors to the city as well, such as watching (perhaps even playing!) the odd game of boules, especially during the boules tournament at Whitsun, taking a quiet stroll along the banks of the Saône or Rhône, or a gentle wander around the sloping streets of La Croix-Rousse, or indulging in a little shopping spree on the peninsula or in the Part-Dieu district. Then there is the pleasure of drinking in the sumptuous Renaissance architecture in the old town, or the peacefulness of the Tête d'Or park early in the morning, not forgetting the rose garden which is an absolute must in June; lengthy conversations over a bottle of Beaujolais in one of Lyon's cafés, the somewhat noisier delights of local festivals, convivial lunches in a crowded Lyon bistro, or *bouchon*, surrounded by the delicious rich smell of Lyonnaise cuisine; and finally, for those who are young at heart, a Sunday afternoon spent watching the antics of the Guignol puppets.

Aqueducs Romains

On either side of the start of rue Roger-Radisson (once the road west to Aquitaine) are the interesting remains of one of the four aqueducts which provided the town's water supply.

SAINT-JUST QUARTER★

The long shopping street, rue de Trion, runs along the site of an ancient necropolis that flanked three Roman roads, hence its name.

▷ Turn right into rue St-Alexandre.

The square of the same name has a few low houses, one with a turret staircase.

▷ Take the charming rue des Macchabées, climbing between garden walls until you reach the church of St-Irénée.

The church and calvary of St-Irénée were rebuilt in the 19C, but the church occupies the site of an ancient 5C basilica, which houses the relics of St-Irénée, on of the founders of the Christian community in Lyon.

▷ Continue along the rue des Macchabées, then take the montée de Choulans.

Mausolées de Choulans

In the centre of place Wernert are three mausoleums that serve as reminders of the Gallo-Roman burial ground situated outside the town walls. The one in the centre, the oldest of the three (1C BCE), bears an inscription on one of the sides indicating that the monument was built by emancipated slaves once belonging to Calvius Turpion.

Rue des Macchabées

The street owes its name to the former cloister of the Maccabees. This important property was destroyed by Protestants in 1562, but a mural on the wall of no. 17 (as well as marks on the ground of the archaeological garden a little further to the right, revives the memory.

▷ Continue as far as rue de Trion and turn right towards rue des Farges.

Thermes Romains

Go under the porch of the residence that faces church of St-Just to discover the foundations of some of the municipal baths built around year 50; the visible part is the south side of the building.

▷ Retrace your steps to the funicular, by which you can return to the cathedral.

Place des Terreaux with the fountain by Bartholdi

La Presqu'île and its Squares★★

Lyon's main city centre districts lie around place Bellecour. "La Presqu'île" – the Peninsula – has long been the setting of the Lyon trading centre, and until the 19C commerce centred on rue Mercière. Two main pedestrian precincts run across it linking place des Terreaux to Perrache railway station. They are rue de la République to the north and rue Victor-Hugo to the south. La Presqu'île is the modern face of Lyon, and it was an important counterpoint to Vieux-Lyon during the Middle Ages and the Renaissance, and many picturesque streets still exist from this time. The Rue de la République in particular is bustling with department stores, shops, cinemas and bistros, and the street is lined with buildings typical of 19C Lyon. Their façades incorporate tall windows and lintels decorated with cut sheet-metal signs. The districts to the south of place Bellecour skirt the former Île des Canabae district, the site of Ainay Abbey.

▷ **Location:** A walking tour of La Presqu'île, sandwiched between the Rhône and the Saône, is the best way to get a feel for the city; this is where you'll find most of the shops and restaurants. The area is well served by the metro (A), and at the centre is the huge place Bellecour.

Don't Miss: The Musée des Beaux-Arts; the painted walls of the City of the Creation.

WALKING TOURS

1 PLACE DES TERREAUX TO SAINT-NIZIER

Place des Terreaux

This square is the hub of city life. It derives its name from the filling-in of a former bed of the Rhône by soil or leaf mould. The confluence of the rivers was situated nearby in Roman times. The famous monumental **lead fountain★** was made by the sculptor Bartholdi. Its four quivering horses symbolise the rivers running towards the ocean. The south side of the square is bordered by the 17C façade of the Palais St-Pierre. In

LYON
LA PRESQU'ÎLE
map III

0   200 m
0   200 yds

WHERE TO STAY

Artistes (Hôtel des) .... ①
Célestins (Hôtel) .... ②
Élysée (Hôtel) .... ③
Résidence (Hôtel La) .... ④
St-Vincent (Hôtel) .... ⑤

WHERE TO EAT

Brunet .... ①
Caro de Lyon .... ②
Étage (L') .... ③
Fédérations (Café des) .... ④

Jura (Le) .... ⑤
Mercière (Le) .... ⑥
203 (Café le) .... ⑦

1994, D Buren was entrusted with the restoration of the square. He added an area of granite paving slabs in a harmonious pattern, 14 pillars and 69 water jets, and the whole installation is illuminated to great effect at night.

Hôtel de Ville

This remarkable city hall, part Louis XIII in style, was designed by Simon Maupin. It consists of a large rectangle of buildings flanked by pavilions. Inside is the main courtyard, an unusual construction on two levels separated by a semicircular porch. The original façade of the Hôtel de Ville facing place des Terreaux was destroyed by fire in 1674. Jules Hardouin-Mansart and Robert de Cotte were commissioned to refurbish the building and they radically transformed the façade. The side pavilions and belfry were topped by a dome. In the centre, a large rounded tympanum supported by telamones is adorned with an equestrian statue of Henry IV.

Palais St-Pierre★

Pl. des Terreaux.

This 17C and 18C building was formerly the abbey of the Ladies of St Peter, one of the oldest Benedictine abbeys in Lyon, whose nuns were recruited among the highest ranks of French aristocracy. Inside, the buildings have retained part of their original Italianate decor, particularly in the refectory and main staircase. The building fell into disuse during the Revolution and was turned into a museum in the 19C. In 1884 the artist Puvis de Chavannes painted the "Sacred Wood" in the staircase at the entrance to the Fine Arts Gallery.

Ancienne Église St-Pierre

Next to No. 23 rue Paul-Chenavard.

Note the narrow 12C façade of the former church of St-Pierre and the austere Romanesque doorway flanking superb 18C wooden doors.

Musée des Beaux-Arts★★★

20 pl. des Terreaux. ⏱*Daily except Tue and public holidays 10am–6pm (Fri 10.30am–6pm).* ♿. ⊚*Museum €8; Exhibitions €9; Combined ticket €12.* ☎*04 72 10 17 40. www.mba-lyon.fr.* ✕ *At the heart of the museum, Les Terrasses Saint-Pierre café-restaurant offers light meals.*

From place des Terreaux, enter the gardens in the former cloisters, where the galleries are surmounted by terraces. Tall loggias crown the corner pavilions on the south side. The statues here include *The Shadow* by Rodin and *Carpeaux at Work* by Bourdelle. The Musée des Beaux-Arts ranks among the finest museums in France. Its splendid collections, carefully displayed, have been further enriched by the donation of 35

Courtyard, Musée des Beaux-Arts

famous Impressionist and modern paintings of Jacqueline Delubac's private collection. The Fine Arts Gallery presents an exceptional overview of art through the centuries, throughout the world. Its collections are organised into five separate departments: painting, sculpture, antiquities, objets d'art and medals.

Paintings

The rooms contain a selection of works from the great periods in European painting.

Sculpture

There are works from the Romanesque to the Gothic and Renaissance periods. Among the 17C to early-20C works, the most outstanding are busts by Coysevox and Lemoyne, and marble and bronze statues by Etex, Pradier, Bourdelle, Maillol and Rodin.

Antiquities

This department consists of three sections organised by theme. The **Egyptian** section contains the most extensive collections covering art from all the Ancient Egyptian periods.

In the **Near and Middle East section**, note the "priest's head" from Assyria, heads of statues from Cyprus and lead sarcophagi from Roman Syria (3C–6C). The final section covers art from **Ancient Greece and Rome**, and includes an exceptional Korah (statue of a young girl) from the Acropolis illustrating the degree of skill attained by the sculptors of Ancient Greece.

Objets d'Art

This section of the museum comprises a huge variety of exhibits from all ages and all continents.

Quai St-Vincent

From the quay there are views over the meander in the Saône overlooked by a row of buildings with Art Nouveau façades (caryatids, floral patterns).

Upriver is a vast architectural complex, known as Les Subsistances, consisting of an early-17C cloister, later turned into an army supply-storage space and extended by the addition of a large square building with two mills in the centre. The restored complex is now occupied by artists (visits: information available at the mill).

▶ Turn back along the quai St-Vincent.

Quai de la Pêcherie

Secondhand booksellers occupy the quai at weekends. The fresco of the city library opposite is dedicated to writers of the region (Rabelais, Stendhal, Clavel, Saint-Exupéry, Chevallier…).

▶ Follow the rue de la Platière as far as place Meissonier.

Quartier de Saint-Nizier

The central fountain (19C) is dedicated to Pleney, a benefactor of the city.

▶ Take rue Paul-Chenavart on the right to return to the place St-Nizier.

Église St-Nizier

Tradition has it that the present church of St-Nizier, much of which dates from the 15C, was built on the site of Lyon's very first church. On the outside, the nave is supported by double flying buttresses which can be seen clearly from rue de la Fromagerie. The spires on the bell-towers of the church of St-Nizier are one of the outstanding features of Lyon's urban landscape.

▷ The rue de la Fromagerie leads to rue Édouard-Herriot.

The ancient street of the Empress, displaying the influence of Haussmann, contains many banks and luxury shops. At the corner of rue de la Poulaillerie, the **clock** is driven by Guignol and his friends.

▷ Take the rue de la Poulaillerie. Go into No. 13 to admire the magnificent Renaissance courtyard, which houses the Printing Museum.

Musée de l'Imprimerie★★

13 rue de la Poulaillerie.
○*Daily except Mon and Tue 10.30am–6pm.* ○*1 Jan, 1 May, 1 Nov, 25 Dec.* ⊛€6. ℘*04 78 37 65 98. www.imprimerie.lyon.fr.*
The splendid late-15C Hôtel de la Couronne, once the property of a rich merchant, houses this printing museum. The collections retrace the glorious history of printing, from the invention of the printing press in the 15C.

Rue de la République

Many banks line the street leading to the **Stock Exchange★**. Renovated in 1994, the gardens around the Exchange have attractive displays of magnolia, rhododendron and azalea contained by box hedgerows. The façade of the **Palais du Commerce**, contemporary with the rue de la République, is decorated with allegories of trade, peace and abundance. The faces of the many buildings are typical of 19C Lyon, with high windows and decorative lintels, decorated with cut sheet-metal signs. The pedestrian precinct, Les Cordeliers, is very commercial and popular; this "street of the king" is bustling with department stores, shops, cinemas and brasseries.

▷ Turn right into the rue de l'Arbre-Sec, then turn into the rues du Garet and Pizay.

Rues de Bouchons

In Lyon, the colloquial term for bistro is *bouchon*. The lively streets close to Lyon Opera House are associated with local *bouchons* and in the evening this pedestrianised area comes alive with the chatter of diners. Tables spill out onto the street and the aroma of Lyon's finest food lingers in the air. The rue Pizay opens out onto the place de la Comédie where street dancers perform to hip-hop and rap. On the left stands the Opéra de Lyon, also known as the Grand Theatre.

Opéra de Lyon

&*See ADDRESSES for ticket information.*
On the south side of the square, opposite the Hôtel de Ville, stands the new Lyon opera house, the result of a successful modernisation scheme.
The façade of the old building has been preserved and the eight muses of the pediment appear to hold up the immense and splendid glass semi-cylindrical roof, the design of the architect **Jean Nouvel**. With a capacity of 1 300 seats, The Opéra includes an orchestra (60 musicians), a ballet (30 dancers), a choir (26 singers), a troupe and a solid expertise. With Ivan Fischer holding the baton, l'Opéra National de Lyon is an international-class company.
A 200-seat amphitheatre is the stage for a more varied programme, including classical, jazz and world music. The building takes on a particularly impressive appearance during the evening illuminations, which floodlight it in predominantly red tones, throwing its architectural contours into sharp relief.

Place Louis-Pradel

The square is decorated with a fountain and sculptures by Ipoustéguy, and is an aesthetic combination of old and modern forms.

② LES CORDELIERS TO BELLECOUR

Église St-Bonaventure

St Bonaventura's Church, which the people of Lyon cherish, has retained its original Franciscan layout. The bareness and simplicity of the architecture are a reminder of the Franciscans' respect for all forms of poverty.

Rue Grenette

This street was bustling with commerce at the time of the Renaissance, although you will no longer find any traces of that period; even the granary has disappeared. At the corner of rue Edouard Herriot stop to admire the symbolic mirrors and staffs in the secular café of the traders.

Rue Mercière★

Today pedestrianised, the rue Mercière was formerly one of the most important arteries of Lyon; the name itself, originally "Mercatoria", means "merchants". Today the street stands as a monument to those past times, and you will see many arches, and the remnants of old shops. Nos. 48, 50 and 52 in particular have beautiful Renaissance façades of red sandstone. No. 56 was where the first book in French was printed. This large mansion conceals a courtyard with galleries in the Italian style.

Place des Jacobins

The main feature of the square is the majestic Dominicans' fountain, erected in 1886 in memory of four local artists: Philibert Delorme, Hippolyte Flandrin, Guillaume Coustou and Gérard Audran.

Quartier des Célestins

Of pleasing dimensions and planted with magnolia the charming place des Célestins, which faces the 19C Italian theatre, is a delightful place to visit.

Yet it is beneath the square that you find the most amazing architectural achievement, of which a periscope in the middle of the square gives a general view.

To access the **underground Célestin-car park★**, take the elevator on the right. A spiral ramp loops around a central well, and the architectural lines are accentuated by alternating black and white paintings. At the bottom, a tilted circular mirror reflects the arches viewed through the periscope above. Titled "Sens dessus dessous" (Above and Below), the car park was designed by Daniel Buren and Michel Targe.

▶ Take the rue des Archers, then to the left the rue Émile-Zola. The high arcades of this little street host luxury shops.

Place Bellecour

This famous Lyon square, overlooked by the distinctive outline of Fourvière Basilica on its hill to the west, is one of the largest in France. The huge symmetrical Louis XVI façades lining the west and east sides of the square date from 1800.

The equestrian statue of Louis XIV is known to the locals as the "Bronze Horse". The pedestal is decorated with two bronzes by the Coustou brothers (17C–18C) representing the Rhône and the Saône, each facing in the direction of its respective river. On either side of the pedestal is the inscription: "Masterpiece by Lemot, Sculptor from Lyon." An earlier equestrian statue of the great King by Desjardins (1691) was erected on this spot in 1713. The symbol of royalty was overturned, smashed and melted down during the French Revolution. The present statue (1828) was itself threatened in 1848: it was about to be pulled down when the Commissary Extraordinary of the Republic saved it by suggesting that, if the pompous inscription in honour of Ludovicus Magnus were replaced by an homage to the talent of Lemot, this would constitute just as much of an attack on royalty.

To the south-east of the square, the bell-tower of the 17C former almshouse, the

19C Brocatelle by Maison Ronze et Vachon, Musée des Tissus

Hôpital de la Charité, stands on its own in front of the main post office.

To the north-east of the square, the Banque Nationale de Paris stands on the site of the cinema where the first films by the cinematographer **Lumière** were shown.

Hôtel-Dieu

Do not miss the ornate 18C **doorway★**; go through it to admire the pretty courtyards lined with arcades. The 17C chapel is in the style of Louis XIII, and while most of the buildings date from the 17C, the building itself dates from the 12C: Rabelais was a doctor here from 1532 to 1534. His achievements in helping the sick and the poor earned Lyon the epithet "City of Love".

Musée des Hospices Civils

1 place de l'Hôpital. ℘*04 72 40 75 74.* This museum is housed in the 17C building of the Hôtel-Dieu extended by Soufflot in the 18C. It contains an important collection of old ceramics used in pharmacies, a considerable amount of furniture including fine chests of drawers, objects made of pewter and objets d'art, in particular a bust by Coustou. Also on display are instrument cases once used by dentists, surgeons and doctors.

③ **FROM BELLECOUR TO CARNOT**

Place Bellecour

ⓒ*See Place Bellecour p321.*

Basilique St-Martin-d'Ainay

This church consecrated by Pope Pascal II in 1107 has undergone major alterations. The porch-belfry is topped by a pyramid roof, surrounded by unusual corner acroteria which give it its characteristic outline. Note the animal frieze beneath the cornice between the second and third levels, and the decoration of inlaid bricks.

Musée des Tissus★★★

34 rue de la Charité. ⓞ*Daily except Mon 10am–6pm.* ⓞ*Public holidays, Easter Sun.* ◎*€10 (combined ticket with the Musée des Arts Décoratifs).* ℘*04 78 38 42 00. www.mtmad.fr.*

The Textile Museum, founded by the Lyon Chamber of Commerce over a century ago and housed in the Hôtel de Villeroy (1730), former residence of the governor of the province, is the pride of the Lyon people, and a veritable "repository" of decorative fabrics. The prestigious collections come from the most influential Western and Eastern countries as regards fabric design and production.

Musée des Arts Décoratifs★★

34 rue de la Charité. ⓞ*Same as Musée des Tissus.* ◎*€10 (combined ticket).*

This museum is housed in a mansion built in 1739 and is mainly devoted to 18C furnishings. The collection includes pieces of furniture, objets d'art, musical instruments, tapestries, porcelain and faience. Among the sections devoted to Medieval and Renaissance art, the gallery containing over 200 examples of Italian majolica is of special interest.

Musée des Confluences

86 Quai Perrache. ⓞ*Tue–Wed and Fri 11am–7pm; Thu 11am–10pm; Sat–Sun and public holidays 10am–7pm.* ⓞ*1 Jan, 1 May, 25 Dec.* ◎*€9.* ℘*04 28 38 12 12. www.museedesconfluences.fr.*

Open in December 2014, the Musée des Confluences, at the very end of Presqu'île, is Lyon's most ambitious museum, seeking to tell the story of the world. This is an all-embracing museum that should not be missed.

La Croix-Rousse

La Croix-Rousse (literally "The Russet Cross") owes its name to a coloured stone cross which stood at one of the district's crossroads in the days before the French Revolution. The district still has all the character and flavour of a small village community and today remains the last bastion of true Lyon traditionalism. The most fiercely proud inhabitants of La Croix-Rousse are deeply attached to the "Plateau" and look down from a distance on the hustle and bustle below. They might even spend months on end without going down the hill.

A BIT OF HISTORY

The invention of new looms by **Joseph-Marie Jacquard** (1752–1834) led the "canuts" or silk-workers to abandon the low cottages in the St-Jean district and move to larger austere buildings with wide windows that let in the light. The *traboules* in La Croix-Rousse were used to move bolts of silk about the district without any risk of damage from inclement weather. In 1831, and again in 1834, they were the scene of bloody uprisings when the silk-workers waved black flags symbolising poverty and bearing the famous motto: "Life through work or death through conflict."

WALKING TOURS

1 HISTORIC TEXTILE WORKERS DISTRICT

Round tour starting at place des Terreaux.

Go to No. 6 (near the fountain), which communicates with rue Ste-Catherine. Turn right and walk down rue Romarin until you reach rue St-Polycarpe. Keep walking towards the church.

The **"Condition Publique des Soies"** at No. 7 has a porch in which the upper arch is decorated with a majestic lion's head and mulberry leaves. It was on

> **Location:** The Croix-Rousse hill dominates Presqu'île to the north. Park, for safety, in one of the car parks in Presqu'île not on the hill, as cars are sometimes vandalised.
>
> **Don't Miss:** The view from the rue Justin-Godart; the silk workshops; the gardens of the Grande-Côte.

these premises during the 19C that the hygrometric packing of silk cloth was monitored since, due to the fact that silk can absorb up to 15 percent of its weight in water, checks had to be made to ensure that the weight of the fabric actually complied with the official norms.

Walk up rue de l'Abbé-Rozier.

From No. 19 rue Leynaud (opposite No. 14), the passage Thiaffait (derelict) leads up a double flight of steps to rue Burdeau. Opposite No. 36 montée du Per-

Ateliers de Soierie Vivante★

This association was founded in 1993 to protect and promote the heritage of the Croix-Rousse silk working industry. It organises a number of tours of authentic family-run silk workshops, leaving from the Atelier Municipal de Passementerie, the municipal furniture trimmings workshop. Other workshops included in the tour are hand-loom weaving, machine-loom weaving, velvet weaving, making silk-wrapped thread and trimmings (gimping) and hand painting on silk. *(21 rue Richan; guided tours (30min) 2pm and 4pm Tue–Sat. €7. 04 78 27 17 13. www.soierie-vivante.asso.fr).*

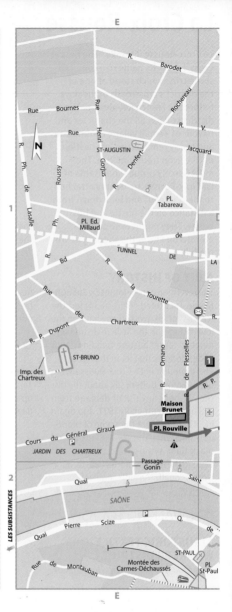

LYON
LA CROIX-ROUSSE
map IV

0   200 m
0   200 yds

N

WHERE TO EAT

Deux Places (Restaurant des).... ①
Maison Villemanzy........................ ②

ron climbs up to **place Chardonnet**, on which stands the monument erected in memory of Count Hilaire de Chardonnet (1839–1924), the inventor of artificial silk.

▶ Turn right onto rue des Tables-Claudiennes (steps).

Rue des Tables-Claudiennes (street of the Claudian Tablets) owes its name to the inscriptions on bronze discovered by the draper Gribaud in his vineyard.

▶ Take No. 29 opposite, which communicates with cour des Voraces

JARDIN ROSA MIR

ATELIER MUNICIPAL DE PASSEMENTERIE

MUR DES CANUTS

R. Pelletier

R. Calas

Pl. M. Bertone

d'Ivry

CANUTS

Maison des Canuts

LE PLATEAU

Godart

ATELIER DE TISSAGE

Couturier

Pl. des Tapis

Pl. de la Croix-Rousse

PDL.

Croix-Rousse

STATUE DE J.-M. JACQUARD

GROS CAILLOU

Pl. Bellevue

R. Philibert Delorme

Pl. L. Chazette

4

la

de

Crimée

R. CROIX-

ST-JOSEPH

ROUSSE

Pasteur

Bon

ST-BERNARD

R. des Pierres-Plantées

R. du Gén.-de-Sève

Pt de Lattre-de-Tassigny

Pl. Colbert

R. Diderot

Cour des Voraces

R. Pouteau

Colomes

Tables-Claudiennes

Imbert-

ÉCOLE NAT. DES BEAUX-ARTS

des

Blanc

Amphithéâtre des Trois-Gaules

Pl. Chardonnet

Burdeau

R. R. Violi

Croix Paquet

Jardin des Plantes

(1er Arr.)

Passage Thiaffait

Rue

ST-POLYCARPE

Leynaud

R. de l'A. Rozier

Capucins

Pl. du Griffon

Petite rue des Feuillants

R. de l'Annonciade

Pl. F. Rey

Pl. Sathonay

Pl. des Capucins

R. du Forez

«Condition publique des Soies»

R. du Griffon

Pl. Tolozan

Pt Morand

Fresque des Lyonnais

R. de la Martinière

LA MARTINIÈRE DES JEUNES FILLES

Vincent

R. Ste-Catherine

R. Romarin

R. Désirée

Pl. L. Pradel

Pl. Tobie-Robatel

d'Algérie

Pl. des Terreaux

Opéra

Quai

N.-D. ST-VINCENT

Pt de la Feuillée

R. de Constantine

Hôtel de Ville

Pl. de la Comédie

Bondy

FRESQUE BIBLIOTHÈQUE DE LA CITÉ

Palais St-Pierre

MUSÉE DES BEAUX-ARTS

St-Pierre

R. du Bât

R. de la République

d'Argent

RHÔNE

(steps and lane on the right, then turn left level with a street lamp).

Cour des Voraces with its imposing flight of steps is an impressive sight. In the 19C it was the meeting place of a silk workers' guild known as the *Voraces* or *Dévorants* ("The Ravenous").

Grande-Côte★

The Grande-Côte "montée" is well named; fortunately, you go down it. To compensate for the destruction of many old houses in its upper part, the Grande-Côte has benefited from much redevelopment.

Lyon, City of Light

Place des Terreaux

© Brice Robert www.b-rob.com/Lyon Tourisme et Congrès

With the famous Festival of Lights held here on 8 December, when the city twinkles with the light of thousands of candles, Lyon was already predisposed to investing generously in street-lighting, and it has done just that in the shape of a project called "Plan Lumière", which places the emphasis on public safety and the highlighting of the city's architectural heritage. Over 100 monuments and locations have been selected for inclusion in a comprehensive and homogenous system of illumination which gives them a whole new dimension. Fourvière Basilica stands out like a lighthouse on the top of its hill; the opera house takes on a futuristic appearance with its huge glass superstructure glowing red; squares such as place des Terreaux or place de la Bourse and the banks of the Saône and the Rhône are lit up by subtle lighting in a variety of colours in warm or cold tones depending on the location. The Part-Dieu district with the distinctive Crédit Lyonnais tower soaring up from it, the Port St-Jean, the Hôtel-Dieu and many more of the city's famous monuments feature in this huge light show which weaves an atmosphere of fairy-tale and magic. Along with the various events put on in the evenings, this invitation to explore "Lyon by night" proves irresistible.

Such is the drama and the skill of the artists, that many of the sites that feature in the Fêtes des Lumières need to be revisited to fully appreciate the magic of it all. During the four days, visitors are free to stroll around the "City of Light", appreciating a life-size art show at the cutting edge of technology. It is a breathtaking experience, and rightly praised and renowned.

A guide to the "Plan Lumière" is available from the tourist office. www.lyon.fr.

The Saône, Presqu'île and Part-Dieu viewed from Basilique Notre-Dame on Fourvière Hill

© Pierre Jacques/hemis.fr

The agreeable garden, planted in 2000, is oriented to best view the neighbourhoods of St-Paul, St-John and Fourvière.

▶ Go down as far as the rue des Tables-Claudiennes.

Amphithéâtre des Trois Gaules

According to the dedication discovered at the bottom of a well in 1958, this venerable spot was built in 19 BC by Rufus as a meeting place for delegates from the 60 Gallic tribes.

Jardin des Plantes

The garden remains virtually in name only. The Orangery developed in the late 18C was transplanted to the Tete d'Or in 1856.

▶ In the montée des Carmélites, take the rue Pierre-Blanc on the left, then the rue de Flesselles.

Place Rouville

From the square there is a fine **view**★ over Lyon. Jutting out from above the seemingly endless sea of red rooftops on the peninsula is the belfry of the Hôtel de Ville and the Part-Dieu district overlooked by the tower of the Crédit Lyonnais bank on the left. On the north side of the square, **Maison Brunet** is a typical silk-worker's dwelling.

Place Sathonay

On the north side of the square are the monumental steps of montée de l'Amphithéâtre, flanked by two lion-shaped fountains.

At the beginning of the street, on the right, there is a fine painted wall known as the **Fresque des Lyonnais**★.

▶ Turn into the rue Terme on the left, then take the rue des Capucins. At the place des Capucins, steps and the rue Ste-Marie lead to the place des Terreaux.

② LE PLATEAU★

▶ Begin on place de la Croix-Rousse, where there is a statue of Jacquard.

Place des Tapis

The square, shaded by a double line of plane trees, combines cinemas, terraces for a relaxing coffee, and daily market. A popular place with the Croix-Roussiens.

▶ Follow the rue Jacquard and the rue Villeneuve, to rejoin the boulevard des Canuts.

Quartier des Canuts★

At the junction of boulevard des Canuts, rue Denfert-Rochereau and rue Pelletier stands a tall **wall**★ adorned with a trompe-l'œil mural covering an area of 1 200sqm. Painted in December 1987 and updated in 1997, it serves as a picturesque reminder of life in one of the districts in La Croix-Rousse.

Note, in the windows, the puppet-theatre characters of Guignol, his wife Madelon and the Bailiff.

▶ Take the rue Pelletier, then the rue de Cuire et the little rue piétonne Victor-Fort.

A little market shelters each morning in place de la Croix-Rousse.

▶ Go down the narrow rue du Mail, a shopping street, then the rue d'Ivry on the right. The uniformity of the façades, enlivened by alternating shades of tan and pink, is typical of the silk-workers area.

Maison des Canuts

10 r. d'Ivry. 🔊*Guided tours (50min):* 🕐*Mon–Sat 11am and 3.30pm.* 🕐*Public holidays.* ♿. ⬤€7. ✆*04 78 28 62 04. www.maisondescanuts.com.*
At No. 10 and No. 12, craftsmen and women from the home-workers cooperative perpetuate the traditions of the Lyon silk-workers and promote the high-quality fabrics they produce.

Left Bank

The Left Bank of the Rhône has allowed the original 18C town to expand. From the Parc de la Tête d'Or to the very modern Gerland, passing buildings of glass and brick of the International City, the extension has brought together the most diverse areas and offers an ideal ecological lifestyle, combining water and green spaces.

> **Location:** This area is north-east of Lyon's old town, on the left bank of the Rhône.
> **Kids:** The open spaces and animals of the Parc de la Tête d'Or; the Gerland park.
> **Don't Miss:** The architecture of the Musée d'Art Contemporain, and of the Cité Internationale.

THE BANKS OF THE RHÔNE
Cité Internationale
This vast complex, comprising an imposing Conference Centre (Palais des Congrès), cinemas (14 screens), hotels and a Museum of Contemporary Art, was installed between the Tête d'Or Park and the Rhône.

Musée d'Art Contemporain★
Cité Internationale: 81 Quai Charles-de-Gaulle.
Tue–Fri 11am–6pm; Sat and Sun 11am–7pm. €16. 1 Jan, 25 Dec. 04 72 69 17 17. www.mac-lyon.com.
This new cultural focus is built around the atrium of the old market hall. Its modern structure allows for great flexibility of display and for works of art to be exhibited to their best advantage. The museum collection is very varied.

Parc de la Tête d'Or★
The name of the English-style gardens surrounding the Conference Centre derives from local folklore, which claims that a golden head of Christ is buried here. The entrance is marked by huge wrought-iron gates. The park is an ideal place to go walking and cycling and there is also a narrow-gauge railway.

Serres★ and Jardin Botanique
Alpine garden Apr–Sept 9–11.30am; Main garden Oct–Mar 9am–5.30pm; Apr–Sept 9am–6.30pm; Greenhouses Oct–Mar 9am–4.30pm; Apr–Sept 9am–5.30. 04 72 69 47 78. www.lyon.fr.

The **botanical gardens** are laid out to the south-east end of the park and consist of acres of outdoor plants, great glasshouses containing tropical vegetation including numerous palm trees, and an Alpine garden.

Jardin Zoologique
Nov–Mar 9am–5pm; Apr and Oct 9am–6pm; May–Sep 9am–6.30pm. 04 72 69 47 78. www.zoo.lyon.fr.
The **Zoological Gardens**, located north of the botanical gardens, are among the oldest in Europe (1858). They have 1 100 animals including numerous wild animals from outside Europe. West of the zoo lies the deer park.
Between the two, on place de Guignol, children's activities (merry-go-round, games) and Guignol shows are organised by the **Véritable Guignol du Vieux Lyon** team (*06 12 42 48 71. http://theatre-guignol-lyon.fr*).

Quaysides along the Rhône
Quai Augagneur, by the Hôtel-Dieu, is lined with imposing bourgeois houses built in the late 19C. This wonderful esplanade beneath the plane trees is enhanced by the lively atmosphere of an open-air market *(except Mondays)*, and is particularly attractive in misty weather, when the river is turbulent and fast-flowing. The district of Les Brotteaux, with its geometrically laid-out streets, stretches to the east; it lies on the site of sandbanks *(brotteaux)* once deposited by the Rhône, hence its name.

From Wilson bridge the **view**★ extends to the heights of La Croix-Rousse on the other bank, where the tall houses of the former silk-workers rise one above the other.

Centre d'Histoire de la Résistance et de la Déportation★

14 av. Berthelot. ◷*Wed–Sun 10am–6pm.* ◷*Public holidays except 8 May.* ◉€8. ℘*04 78 72 23 11.*

The museum is set up in part of buildings that from 1882 to the early 1970s were the Military Medical School and, from 1942 to 1944, housed the headquarters of the Gestapo in this region.

Halle Tony-Garnier

20 place des Docteurs . ✆*Guided visits by appointment.* ◉*No charge for admission during events.* ℘*04 72 76 85 85.* *www.halle-tony-garnier.com.*

The town planner, Tony Garnier created this massive symbol of construction in iron. It has been neglected for many years, but since its restoration in 2000, the hall hosts concerts, shows, exhibitions and other events.

Gerland District

This district sits opposite the confluence of the Rhône and the Saône and has a covered meat market at its centre. The area is one large "Science and Technology Park" and incorporates a high-level technical college, the Institut Pasteur, the Institut Mérieux and a sports centre. The International School is a glass construction overlooking the Parc Gerland.

THE PART-DIEU DISTRICT

A vast complex spread out over what was once Army land, it is built around a pedestrian precinct and consists of a large number of buildings and towers, including government offices, a shopping centre, the radio studios and the impressive library.

The **Crédit Lyonnais Tower** has now become the second most famous landmark in the city after the Fourvière Towers, and its brick-red colour blends in

well with the rooftops of the old urban districts.

Musée des Moulages

3 rue Rachais. ◷*Currently closed for renovation.* ℘*04 72 84 81 12.*

This fascinating museum, housed in a renovated ready-made clothes workshop, is devoted to the history of sculpture from Ancient Greece to the 19C.

Musée Africain

150 cours Gambetta. ◷*Wed–Sun 2–6pm.* ◷*Aug, 1 Jan, Easter, 1 May, 24–25 and 31 Dec.* ℘*04 78 61 60 98.* *www.musee-africain-lyon.org.*

This museum has three floors exhibiting over 2 500 objects from West Africa, particularly Benin and Côte d'Ivoire.

Musée Lumière

25 rue du Premier-Film, Lyon-Monplaisir. ◷*Daily except Mon 10am–6.30pm.* ◷*1 Jan, 1 May, 25 Dec.* ◉€7. ℘*04 78 78 18 95.* *www.institut-lumiere.org.*

Antoine Lumière, the father of Auguste and Louis who invented cinema, had this residence built between 1889 and 1901. The interior houses the **Institut Lumière** and hosts events based on still and moving pictures.

Musée Urbain Tony-Garnier

4 rue des Serpollières. ♿✆*Guided visits: Apartments (20min) Tue–Fri at 4.30pm, Sat 2.30pm and 4.30pm.* ◉€3; *Museum Sat 2.30pm.* ◉€8. ◷*Public holidays.* ℘*04 78 75 16 75.* *www.museeurbaintonygarnier.com.*

This group of buildings was built in the 1930s by the urban architect **Tony Garnier**. Since 1991 many of the blind walls of these large buildings have been decorated with murals painted by a group of artists calling themselves **"The City of Creation"**.

WHERE TO EAT

Brasserie Georges (La)	①	Orangerie de Sébastien (L')	⑤
Brunoise (La)	②	Petit Carron (Le)	⑥
Est (L')	③	St-Florent (Le)	⑦
Gones (Chez les)	④	Terrasse St-Clair (La)	⑧

Outskirts

"Grand-Lyon" unites 57 communes around the city. At the heart of this community of communes, Greater Lyon embraces 75 percent of the population of the Rhône. The contrast is therefore important, and to visit Greater Lyon quickly gives the impression of having escaped from the city.

VILLEURBANNE AND THE EAST

Adjacent to the Part-Dieu district, the municipality of Villeurbanne owes its name to the Villa Urbana, an important agricultural complex established by the Romans on the Cusset hill. The development of the town is relatively recent and it is interesting to note how it has always made a point of being independent from Lyon.

After the first wave of silk manufacturers at the end of the 19C, the expansion of the town increased during the 20C and in the 1930s Villeurbanne asserted its specificity by building the spectacular skyscraper district.

Today, the town is continuing to develop, concentrating its efforts on culture with a popular national theatre (TNP), an ultra-modern reference library, a museum of contemporary art and the antique-dealers' hall (boulevard de Stalingrad) where 150 antique shops can be found.

Skyscrapers

Around 1930, at the height of the economic crisis, the housing facilities in Villeurbanne were totally inadequate in view of the town's fast-growing population. The mayor, Lazare Goujon, launched his city into a daring development programme: the town centre, which was the first project to be completed, was soon nicknamed **"Skyscraper City"** as its unique architectural style was more reminiscent of North-American buildings than of French suburbia.

Avenue Barbusse ends with the imposing and austere **town hall** designed by

> ⊳ **Location:** Greater Lyon extends more than 20km/13mi from place Bellecour.
> 👥 **Kids:** Planetarium Vaulx-en-Velin; the aquarium of Lyon.
> 😋 **Don't Miss:** The automobile museum.

R Giroud: a belfry towers over the façade decorated with fluted columns.

⊳ Walk down cours de la République towards cours Tolstoï and cross over.

Nouveau Musée (Institut d'Art Contemporain)

11 rue du Docteur-Dolard. ♿🕐*Wed–Fri 2–6pm, Sat–Sun 1–7pm.* 🕐*1 Jan, 1 May, 25 Dec.* ♿€16. ☏*04 78 03 47 00. www.i-art-c.org.*
Created in 1978, the Association Nouveau Musée moved into this space a few years ago; there is an information section and an area presenting themed exhibitions on contemporary art.

Maison du Livre, de l'Image et du Son

247 cours Émile-Zola.
♿🕐*Mon 2–7pm, Tue–Fri 11am–7pm, Sat 10am–6pm.* 🕐*Sun and public holidays.* ☏*04 78 68 04 04. http://mediatheques.villeurbanne.fr.*
This reference library, designed in 1988 by the famous architect Mario Botta, is spread over five storeys round a central light shaft.

VAULX-EN-VELIN
👥 Planétarium de Vaulx-en-Velin

11km/7mi E of Villeurbanne. 🕐*Daily except Thu 9am–6pm, Sat–Sun 10.30am–6pm, but check website for seasonal variations.* ♿€9 (children under 12, €7). ☏04 78 79 50 13. www.planetariumvv.com.
As a prelude, a scientific display reveals the secrets of the heavens. The 15m hemispherical screen surrounds you, and captivates young and old alike.

MIRIBEL

Carillon

13km/8mi to the NE of Villeurbanne.
🕐*Open only during concerts.*
📞*04 78 55 61 16.*

Built between 1939 and 1947, this bell-tower is 30m high and overlooks a spectacular amusement park and the Miribel canal.

LA MULATIÈRE

Jardin de la Bonne Maison★

99 chemin de Fontanières.
Exit the A 7 for La Mulatière, then follow the directions for Oullins-Centre.
At the 2nd crossroads, turn right for Ste-Foy-lès-Lyon, then at the 1st set of traffic lights, turn right.
🕐*Daily Mar–Oct except Sun 9.30am–1pm.* 📞*04 78 37 38 37.*
www.labonnemaison.org.

Located in the residential part of Mulatière and surrounded by walls, this garden offers an exceptional display of shrubs, perennials and bulbs. There are also more than 750 varieties of rose.

🔱 Grand Aquarium de Lyon★

7 rue S.-Déchant (large car park).
🕐*Wed–Sun 11am–7pm (school holidays, daily).* 🕐*1 Jan, 25 Dec.* ⊗€15 *(child 5–10, €11).* 📞*04 72 66 65 66.*
www.aquariumlyon.fr.

This new, rather unobtrusive building on the banks of the Saône offers you a journey to the different rivers and oceans of the world: impressive fish reign supreme in rivers of temperate climates; nearby, sharks swim round a wreck inside a huge pool on two levels; a myriad of small brightly coloured fish of all shapes feel quite at home in tropical waters.

WEST OF LYON

LA DUCHÈRE

Musée des Sapeurs-Pompiers

358 av. de Champagne. 10km/6mi NW along the A 6 (direction Paris), then the D 342. 🕐*Wed–Fri 9am–noon, 2–5pm; 1st weekend of each month 2–5pm.*
⊗€6. 📞*04 72 17 54 54.*
www.museepompiers.com.

This museum presents an impressive collection of equipment from the 18C to present times including hand, steam and motorised pumps. A memorial hall housing helmets, flags and portraits is dedicated to the fire-fighters and recall two sad episodes in particular: St John (1930) and Feyzin (1966). There is a display of vehicles and rolling stock in the basement, but what is on view is only a small part of the total collection.

MARCY-L'ÉTOILE

Domaine de Lacroix-Laval

Rte de Sain-Bel. Leave Lyon heading NW (towards Mâcon), then follow the D 7 in the direction of Charbonnières.

Situated to the west of metropolitan Lyon, the Domaine de Lacroix-Laval (🕐*6am–10pm in summer, 7am–8pm in winter.* 📞*04 78 87 87 00*) serves as a welcome "green lung" for the city, and among the amenities in its 15ha/37 acre site is an interesting orienteering trail.

A small **tourist train** – Le Furet – serves to provide information about the castle and the park (🔵🕐*train rides from Mar–Nov, school holidays, Wed, Sat, Sun and public holidays; rest of the year by arrangement.* ⊗€3 single (children €2); €4 return (children €3). 📞*06 09 93 66 03*). At the edge of the park stands an elegant 16C **castle** where temporary exhibitions are presented.

While wandering around the garden, do not miss the history of the **vegetable garden**, where over 600 varieties of plant span four themes: Lyon horticulture; herbs and spices; a wild garden; and fruit and vegetable crops.

Charbonnières-les-Bains

10km/6mi (towards Mâcon), then D 307.
Set in woodland formerly worked by the charcoal burners, the Vale of Charbonnières is a traditional holiday resort popular with the people of Lyon. The ferruginous spring here was officially discovered by a priest in 1778. Pump rooms and a casino were soon opened. In 1900, people flocked to the spa, which quickly gained a reputation for excellence.

SOUTH OF LYON
Givors
20km/12.5mi S by the A 7, then the A 47.
The ruins of the castle of St-Gerald (accessed through Les Étoiles) overlook the city hall, two churches and the Rhône.

Ternay
18km/11.3mi S along the D 307 (direction Vienne by the N 7).
The 12C church perched on the edge of a hill overlooking the Rhône is an interesting legacy of the Romanesque school along the Rhône. Formerly dedicated to St-Mayol, the church belonged to a Cluniac priory. Inside, the most endearing aspect is the main apse, with its vaulted arches and pilasters. The remains of the cloister are to the south of the church.

🚗 DRIVING TOUR

BANKS OF THE SAÔNE★
38km/24mi round tour. Allow 3h.

From its source at Vioménil in the Vosges, the River Saône flows southwestward into Haute-Saône *département* near Corre, where it meets the Canal de l'Est. It then continues through Gray to Pontailler-sur-Saône and crosses Côte d'Or department to enter Saône-et-Loire, where it is joined by the Doubs River, its major tributary. The river then passes Chalon-sur-Saône, Tournus, Mâcon and Villefranche before eventually joining the Rhône in Lyon. The river banks are a favourite weekend destination with Lyon residents, who come to stroll along the towpath, or to indulge in a light lunch of fried fish washed down with a bottle of Beaujolais in one of the many riverside restaurants.

▷ Leave Lyon to the N, in the direction of Trévoux. The pleasant D 433 follows the east bank of the river, bordered by vegetation, as far as La Rochetaillée.

Musée de l'Automobile Henri-Malartre★★
🕐Daily except Mon (other than public holidays) 9am–6pm (Jul–Aug 10am–7pm). 🕐1 Jan, last week in Jan and 25 Dec. ✆€6 (free for visitors under 26). 𝄞04 78 22 18 80. www.musee-malartre.com.
This restored 15C castle, and its terraced grounds overlooking the Saône, contain remarkable collections of motorcars (1890–1986), cycles (1818–1960), motorcycles (1904–64) and public transport vehicles (1886–1935), all in full working order. Of the 150 cars on show, 50 date from before 1914, and 18 were built in Lyon, a reminder of the fact that there were once over 100 manufacturers in the region. Some of the exhibits are unique, such as the Rochet-Schneider (1895), the Gobron-Brillié (1898), the Luc Court (1901) and the Thieulin (1908). The collection of cycles ranges from the hobby horse to Anquetil's bicycle, not forgetting the amazing "Penny Farthings". Over 50 motorcycles are on show, including a Herdtlé-Bruneau (1904), the Koehler-Escoffier (1935) ridden by Georges Monneret, sidecars and a Zundapp (1937) used by the German Army in Africa and Russia.

▷ Drive on to D 433 and turn right.

Neuville-sur-Saône
The town lies in a picturesque setting on a bend of the Saône. The church, topped by twin bell-towers dating from the 17C, contains a set of wood panelling by Perrache, a sculptor from Lyon (18C).

Trévoux
🕮See VILLEFRANCHE-SUR-SAÔNE.

▷ Take D 933 and turn left onto D 504 towards Villefranche.

Villefranche-sur-Saône
🕮See VILLEFRANCHE-SUR-SAÔNE.

▷ Return to Lyon on the A 6 (30min).

ADDRESSES

🛏 STAY

VIEUX-LYON

🛏 **Hôtel St-Paul** – *6 r. Lainerie.* 📞*04 78 28 13 29. 20 rooms.* A small Renaissance hotel at the centre of the quarter. Rooms overlooking the street have been renovated.

FOURVIÈRE

🛏 **Chambre d'Hôte la Grange de Fourvière** – *89 quai Pierre Scize.* 📞*04 72 33 74 45. www.grangedefourviere.fr. 2 rooms.* A former 19C barn and stable completely renovated are the basis of this charming B&B in the centre of Old Lyon.

PRESQU'ÎLE

🛏 **Chambre d'Hôte Péniche "El Kantara"** – *Quai Rambaud.* 📞*04 78 42 02 75. 2 rooms.* What could be more romantic or unusual than this magnificently restored barge moored on the river?

🛏 **Hôtel St-Vincent** – *9 r. Pareille.* 📞*04 78 27 22 56. www.hotel-saintvincent.com. 32 rooms.* Located in a narrow street close to the Saône, this hotel, formerly cloisters, is very comfortable, with large rooms.

🛏 **Élysée Hôtel** – *92 r. du Prés.-Edouard -Herriot.* 📞*04 78 42 03 15. https://hotel-elysee-lyon.fr. 29 rooms.* A small family-run hotel where you can enjoy the vitality of the Presqu'île at affordable prices.

🛏 **Campanile Lyon Centre - Berges Du Rhone** – *4 r. du Mortier.* 📞*04 78 60 03 09. www.campanile.com. 134 rooms.* Just a five minute walk from place Bellecour, this modern hotel with a glass front is rather agreeable; all the rooms are identical; functional and well-equipped.

🛏 **Hôtel La Résidence** – *18 r. Victor-Hugo.* 📞*04 78 42 63 28. www.hotel-la-residence.com. 67 rooms.* Managed by the same family since 1954, this hotel borders on a pedestrian street quite near the place Bellecour.

🛏 **Hotel des Savoies** – *80 r. de la Charité.* 📞*04 78 37 66 94. www.hotel-des-savoies.fr. 44 rooms.* Look for a façade decorated with the Savoie coat of arms in the Perrache train station quarter. The cleanliness of the standard rooms, with their simple furniture and pastel carpets, the convenient garage and reasonable prices make this a popular address.

🛏 **Hotel Célestins** – *4 r. des Archers.* 📞*04 72 56 08 98. www.hotelcelestins.com. 25 rooms.* Charming hotel in the heart of the city between place Bellecour and place des Jacobins, and perfect for exploring the city on foot.

🛏 **Hotel des Artistes** – *8 r. G-André.* 📞*04 78 42 04 88. www.hotel-des-artistes.fr. 45 rooms.* Giving onto the adorable place des Célestins and the theatre, this hotel has lovely rooms and a theatrical ambiance.

RIVE GAUCHE

🛏 **Hôtel B&B** – *93 cours Gambetta.* 📞*08 92 70 75 34. www.hotel-bb.com. 114 rooms.* A chain hotel offering a central location near the railway station, and with spacious and comfortable rooms with king-size beds.

🛏 **Au Patio Morand** – *99 r. de Créqui.* 📞*04 78 52 62 62. www.hotel-morand.fr. 31 rooms.* This hotel has a patio where you can breakfast. The elegant rooms have large bed and plasma screen TV.

THE OUTSKIRTS OF LYON

🛏 **Hôtel la Chaumière** – *11 av. du Gén-de -Gaulle, 69410 Champagne-au-Mont-d'Or.* 📞*04 78 35 10 60.* This contemporary building has bright, very well maintained rooms. A delightful alternative to chain hotels.

🛏 **Hôtel Ariana** – *163 cours Émile-Zola, 69100 Villeurbanne.* 📞*04 78 85 32 33. www.ariana-hotel.fr. 102 rooms.* This is a practical address for those who wish to stay amid the 1930s high-rises of Villeurbanne. The hotel is modern; it has air-conditioned, soundproofed rooms with a sober interior.

🍴 EAT

VIEUX-LYON

🍴 **Le Vieux Lyon** – *44 r. St-Jean.* 📞*04 78 42 48 89. Closed Sun evening.* Local epicureans are all familiar with this tavern, in operation since 1947, where good humour and hospitality reign. Home-made Lyonnais cooking.

🍴 **Les Adrets** – *30 r. du Boeuf.* 📞*04 78 38 24 30. Closed Sat and Sun.* Exposed beams and tiled floor. Traditional dishes.

FOURVIÈRE

🍴 **Le Contretête** – *55 quai Pierre-Scize.* 📞*04 78 29 41 29. Closed Sat lunch and Sun.* This bistro cultivates authenticity and offers "grandmother's" slow-cooked recipes of yesteryear.

Restaurant de Fourvière –
9 pl. de Fourvière. ☎*04 78 25 21 15.*
www.restaurant-fourviere.fr. Perfectly
situated, this restaurant enjoys a superb
panorama and serves traditional cuisine.

PRESQU'ÎLE

Le Café 203 – *9 r. du Garet.* ☎*04 78
28 66 65. www.moncafe203.com.*
Customers come here for the fresh fare,
slate menu and bistro setting.

La Brasserie Georges – *30 cours de
Verdun.* ☎*04 72 56 54 54. www.brasserie
georges.com.* Open since 1836, this
brasserie near the Perrache train station
is still a favourite Lyon haunt.

Le Jura – *25 r. Tupin.* ☎*04 78 42 20
57. www.bouchonlejura.fr. Closed Mon from
Sept–Apr, Sat from May–Sept, and Sun.
Reservations requested.* Not far from the
Rue de la République, this eatery with
its 1920s decor and aproned matron
overseeing the stoves, it's as genuine as
they come.

Brunet – *23 r. Claudia.* ☎*04 78
37 44 31. Closed Sun–Mon and Tue lunch.
Reservations recommended.* An authentic
Lyon *bouchon* (tavern), Brunet has
elbow-to-elbow tables, Guignol-
marked tableware and tasty little dishes
enhanced by an enticing selection of
wines by the carafe.

Café des Fédérations – *8 r. Major-
Martin.* ☎*04 78 28 26 00. http://restaurant-
cafedesfederations-lyon.com. Closed Sun.*
Unrivalled guardian of the Lyonnais
culinary traditions, served in a perfect
setting and relaxing atmosphere.

Le Mercière – *56 r. Mercière.*
☎*04 78 37 67 35. www.le-merciere.com.
Reservations recommended.* Located in a
passageway giving onto one of the most
sought-after restaurant streets in town,
this old house serves traditional fare in a
classic Lyonnais setting.

Le Caro de Lyon – *25 r. du
Bât-d'Argent.* ☎*04 78 39 58 58. www.
lecarodelyon.fr. Closed Sun.* This restaurant
behind the Opera House, designed to
resemble a library, welcomes diners into
an intimate atmosphere comprised of
Murano chandeliers and antique knick-
knacks.

L'Étage – *4 pl. des Terreaux.* ☎*04
78 28 19 59. www.letage-restaurant.com.
Closed Sun and Mon.* The locals never
tire of climbing the stairs leading to the

humble silk workshop on the second
floor. Charming setting and seductive
and creative menus.

LA CROIX-ROUSSE

Restaurant des Deux Places –
5 pl. Fernand-Rey. ☎*04 78 28 95 10. Closed
Sat–Mon.* A few steps from the Place
Sathonay, this traditional little restaurant
boasts a convivial atmosphere, a décor
full of rural knick-knacks and time-
honoured cuisine.

Maison Villemanzy – *25 montée St-
Sébastien.* ☎*04 72 98 21 21. www.maison-
villemanzy.com. Closed Sun, and Mon lunch.*
Perched on the slopes of Croix-Rousse,
this restaurant offers a superb terrace
view over the city. Family recipes and
inventive cuisine.

RIVE GAUCHE

Le Petit Carron – *48 av. Félix-Faure.*
☎*04 78 60 00 57. www.lepetitcarron-
restaurant.com. Closed 3 wks in Aug,
Sat lunch and Sun. Reservations
recommended.* The little puppet who
inhabits the window of this tavern
beckons you into a muted dining room
featuring a slate *menu du jour*, composed
based on market availability.

Chez les Gones – *102 cours Lafayette.*
☎*04 78 60 91 61. www.chezlesgones.fr.
Closed Mon, and Sun evening Sept–May.*
This tavern set in the bosom of the
marketplace boasts typical Lyon dishes.

L'Est – *14 pl. J-Ferry.* ☎*04 37 24 25 26.
www.brasseries-bocuse.com.* The décor
is that of a big, old-fashioned brasserie
where electric trains circumnavigate the
dining room.

THE OUTSKIRTS OF LYON

La Brunoise – *4 r. A-Boutin, 69100
Villeurbanne.* ☎*04 78 52 07 77. www.
labrunoise.fr. Closed Sun and Mon evenings,
Tue and Wed.* The varied specialities are
displayed outside and invite you into this
bright restaurant.

La Terrasse St-Clair – *2 Grande Rue
St-Clair, 69300 Caluire-et-Cuire.* ☎*04 72 27
37 37. www.terrasse-saint-clair.com. Closed
Sat and Sun.* This tavern-like restaurant
has a terrace sheltered by plane trees
where you can dine on traditional
cuisine.

L'Orangerie de Sébastien –
*Domaine de Lacroix-Laval, 69280 Marcy-
l'Étoile.* ☎*04 78 87 45 95. www.orangerie
desebastien.fr. Closed Mon and Tue.* The

Marché de la Création

orangery is part of a 17C chateau, and serves dishes of the day on a beautiful terrace.

Daniel et Denise Créqui – *156 rue de Créqui . ☏04 78 60 66 53. www. danieletdenise.fr. Closed Sat and Sun.* The combination of checked tablecloths, and the simple, round wine glasses, copper pands and photographs leaves you with the impression that you have gone back in time at this traditional 'bouchon'. Not far from Part-Dieu railway station, and serving the finest of Lyon's bouchonnais cuisine. Reservations advised.

SHOPPING

Markets (*Marchés*) – The Marché de la Création, quai Romain-Rolland and the Marché de l'Artisanat, quai Fulchiron are held on Sunday mornings. These are no run-of-the-mill craft markets, as the workmanship is outstanding. Used-book sellers line the quai de la Pêcherie every afternoon. There are regional products and small taverns at the Halles de Lyon, 102 cours Lafayette.

For food, head for the quai Saint-Antoine, where food markets with producers from all over the region set up stall and sell their produce (*Tue–Sun, 7am–12.30pm*). There is also a Farmers' Market twice a week in the place Carnot (*Wed, 4–7pm; Sun, 5am–1.30pm*), in front of the Gare Perrache.

ON THE TOWN

Rue Ste-Catherine – A very lively street featuring many establishments open until the early hours of the morning. *The Albion Public House* is the most British pub in town, *The Shamrock* the most

Celtic. Rum fans convene at *La Taverne du Perroquet Bourré* (The Tavern of the Plastered Parrot), while *L'Abreuvoir* is highly recommended for those who fancy good French music.

THEATRE AND ENTERTAINMENT

Le Guignol de Lyon – *☏04 78 28 92 57. www.guignol-lyon.com. Wed and Sat: 3pm and 4.30pm, Sun 3pm; daily during school holidays.* The Théâtre Bazar stages children's performances that marry burlesque and fantasy. The shows for adults, inspired by aspects and events of life in Lyon, are more malicious.

Auditorium-Orchestre national de Lyon – *149 r. Garibaldi. ☏04 78 95 95 95. www.auditoriumlyon.com. Tickets: Mon–Fri 11am–6pm, concert Saturdays 2–6pm. Closed most of Aug.* The Auditorium Maurice Ravel regularly hosts l'Orchestre National de Lyon.

Maison de la Danse – *8 av. Jean-Mermoz. ☏04 72 78 18 10. www.maisondeladanse. com. Tickets: Mon–Fri 11.45am–6.45pm. Closed mid-Jul–mid-Aug.* From flamenco and tap dancing to ballet and the traditional dances of East and West, welcome to this, the citadel of the art.

Opéra National de Lyon – *1 pl. de la Comédie. ☏04 69 85 54 54. www.opera-lyon.com. Tickets: Mon–Sat 11am–7pm. Closed late Jul–end Aug.* See p320.

Halle Tony-Garnier – *20 pl. Antonin-Perrin. ☏04 72 76 85 85. www.halle-tony-garnier.com. Visits following schedule; phone ahead.* Since its restoration in 2000, this huge metallic structure presents a remarkable diversity of events from the Moscow State Circus to Lionel Richie and Johnny Hallyday.

BRESSE AND THE DOMBES

The area known as Bresse is endowed with many examples of fine architecture, not least Romanesque churches, farmhouses with clay walls, exposed beams and what are known as "Saracen" chimneys. The Dombes, to the south-west, is a major fish-farming area with more than 1 000 lakes dotted across the countryside. Farming fish has a long pedigree, dating at least to the 12C, and today more than 1 000 tonnes of fish are caught annually, most of which are bound for the markets of Germany.

Highlights

1 Tasting the local delicacy, **Poulet de Bresse** (see below)

2 Marvelling at the flamboyant **Royal Brou Monstery** (p340)

3 Touring the lakes of the **Dombes** plateau (p345)

4 The **Parc des Oiseaux** bird sanctuary, south of Villars-les-Dombes (p346)

5 Medieval architecture in **Pérouges** (p349)

Poulet de Bresse

Bresse chickens are treated like fine wine. They have an appellation, get to eat real food and walk around the countryside – all regulated by law.

The story of the poulet de Bresse, with its steel-blue feet and bright white plumage, begins in 1591 when the bird was first mentioned in the town registers of Bourg-en-Bresse. Henry IV, having stopped off at Bresse following an accident with his carriage, tasted the bird's meat and demanded its inclusion on his courtly menu.

Described by the French as "the fourth gastronomic wonder of the world", poulet de Bresse comes out on top because of its dense, flavoursome flesh. This is due to the strict government controls imposed on the region of Bourg-en-Bresse, where the chickens are given plenty of space to run around, producing a bird which is high in protein and low in fat. After an initial period of at least 35 days, the birds are raised on a grassy pasture of some 5 000 sq m (minimum), which provides their primary food, supplemented by local cereals (maize and wheat) and skimmed milk for a period of 9 weeks in the case of young chickens, 11 weeks for hens, and 23 weeks for capons. The chickens are intentionally given insufficient feed so that they have to supplement their diet by scratching for insects, worms or snails. Each chicken must have a minimum of 10 sq m of space and a single flock cannot exceed 500 birds. The final

Marshland, La Dombes

© Palaine/Dreamstime.com

BRESSE AND THE DOMBES

AUXERRE · A · B · DIJON

SAÔNE-ET-LOIRE

0   5 km

N

MONTLUÇON

Le Colombier
Vescours ▲
Ferme-musée de la Forêt
Grandval ▲   ▲ Bourbon
Pont-de-Vaux   D 2   St-Trivier-
de-Courtes
La Bresse bressane
D 58   Montrevel-
en-Bresse
D 975
St-André-de-Bâgé †
MÂCON   Musée de la Bresse
D 1079   St-Cyr-sur-
D 28   Menthon
Pont-   Vonnas   D 96   † Buellas   Bourg-
de-Veyle   Vandeins   en-Bresse
D 2   BROU
AIN   D 936

JURA

JURA

D 52
D 1083
D 39
D 3
D 936
D 52

GENÈVE

St-Paul-de-Varax
Châtillon-sur-   D 17   Lent
Chalaronne   La Dombes   Dompierre-
Sandrans   Beaumont   sur-Veyle
D 2   St-Nizier-le-Désert
Fléchères   Bouligneux   N.-D.-des-Dombes
Parc des Oiseaux   Tour du Plantay
VILLEFRANCHE-   Lapeyrouse   Villars-   Chalamont
SUR-SAÔNE   les-Dombes
Monthieux   Le Montellier
Trévoux   D 1083
Cordieux   Pérouges

CHAMBÉRY

RHÔNE

Montluel
A 42
St-Maurice-
de-Gourdans
D 65
ISÈRE

BROU   ★★★ Highly recommended
Pérouges   ★★   Recommended
La Dombes   ★   Interesting
Beaumont   Other sight described
⇐   Departure point for tour
→ La Bresse   → La Dombes

ST-ÉTIENNE   VALENCE · A · B

GRENOBLE

---

phase of the growing process is done in wooden coops in a dim, calm and well-ventilated structure. The chickens are cooped up for 8 to 15 days, and capons and poulards for 4 weeks. It is, for a while at least, a life of luxury.

Birdlife

With so much open space it is not surprising that the Dombes is important for birdlife. The area includes ponds, marshes, wet meadows, deciduous forests, moorlands and arable fields, and holds 20 000 or more waterbirds on passage and in winter, on a regular basis. As a result, the area is hugely popular with birdwatchers, and features such diverse species as black-winged stilt, squacco heron, marsh harrier, whiskered tern, red-crested pochard and purple heron. There are conservation issues, not least because 90 percent of the area is used for hunting, with 70 percent given to farming.

Bourg-en-Bresse★★

Bourg, a large market town in the fertile Bresse region, is famous for its poultry, as well as being a centre for furniture made from the wood of fruit trees. This and other industrial activities have endowed Bourg with the image of a lively and dynamic city. Bourg owes its architectural renown to the superb monastery commissioned by Marguerite of Austria to a master Flemish stonemason, Van Boghem.

▶ **Population:** 42 439.
⟳ **Michelin Map:** 328 E3.
🗊 **Info:** 6 av. Alsace-Lorraine, 01005 Bourg-en-Bresse. ℘04 74 22 49 40 www.bourgenbressetourisme.fr.
▶ **Location:** Bourg-en-Bresse is 62km/39mi NE of Lyon, via the D 1083.
👥 **Kids:** Farm-museum at St-Trivier-de-Courtes
🕐 **Timing:** Allow half a day to explore at a leisurely pace.

OLD HOUSES

A couple of half-timbered houses, dating from the 15C, are worth visiting: the **Maison Hugon**, on the corner of the rue Gambetta and the rue V-Basch, and the **Maison Gorrevod**, in the rue du Palais. Equally noteworthy is the beautiful 17C stone façade of the **Hotel de Bohan**, and, in rue Teynière, the **Hotel de Marron de Meillonnas**, which dates from the 18C and has impressive wrought-iron balconies.

MONASTÈRE ROYAL DE BROU★★★

Once a hamlet round a Benedictine priory outside Bourg, Brou is now in the town's south-eastern suburbs. Happily, the buildings survived the Wars of Religion and Revolution fairly unscathed.

Church★★

🕐*Daily: Jan–Mar and Oct–Dec 9am–noon, 2–5pm; Apr–Jun 9am–noon, 2–6pm; Jul–Sept 9am–6pm.* 🕐*1 Jan, 1 May, 1 and 11 Nov, 25 Dec.* ⊛*€8.* ℘*04 74 22 83 83.*
www.monastere-de-brou.fr.
The church is deconsecrated. The building, in which the Flamboyant Gothic style is influenced by the Renaissance, was built at the same time as the château of Chenonceau in the Loire valley.

Monastère Royal de Brou

© Franck Guiziou/hemis.fr

Exterior

The tympanum above the fine **Renaissance doorway**★ shows Philibert the Handsome and Margaret of Austria and their patron saints at the feet of Christ Bound. On the pier is St Nicolas of Tolentino, to whom the church is dedicated (his feast falls on the day of Philibert's death). Surmounting the ornamental doorway arch is a statue of St Andrew; St Peter and St Paul flank the doorway on the arch shafts.

The decorative sculpture includes a variety of Flamboyant Gothic floral motifs (leaves and fruit), some showing a decidedly Renaissance influence (laurel, vine and acanthus), intermingled with symbolic motifs such as palms interlaced with marguerites. Other motifs include the initials of Philibert and Margaret linked by love-knots intermingled with crossed batons, the arms of Burgundy. The simpler façade of the north transept has a pinnacled gable. The five-storey belfry is on the south side of the apse.

The roof had been modified significantly in 1759, so during restoration from 1996 to 1998 it was returned to its original design; Mansard frameworks were replaced by more steeply sloping forms. Flat roof tiles laid in a diamond pattern have been glazed in typical colours.

Interior

Nave – The pillars, formed by numerous little columns, thrust upwards in an un-broken line to the vaulting and open out into a network of ribs meeting at the carved keystones. A finely sculpted balustrade runs below the windows of the nave. The overall impression is one of elegance, magnificence and good taste. In the second bay of the nave (right) is a 16C black marble font bearing Margaret's motto.

The south transept is lit through a beautiful stained-glass window showing Susanna being accused by the Elders (above) and exonerated by Daniel (below).

To the right of the rood screen is the Montécuto Chapel which contains models explaining the construction of the church.

Rood screen★★ – The richly decorated screen, which separates the nave and transepts from the chancel, is composed of three basket-handled arches supporting seven religious statues.

Chancel – Margaret spared no expense to make this, the most important part of the church, as resplendent as possible. Taken as a whole, the sculpted decoration might border on the excessive, but the longer and closer one examines the ornamentation, the greater its charm, since the smallest detail is treated with quite extraordinary craftsmanship.

Choir stalls★★ – The 74 stalls, which line the first two bays of the choir, were carved from oak in just two years (1530–32). The master carpenter, Pierre Berchod, known as Terrasson, had to mobilise all the local wood craftsmen. They are carved in the same manner as the sculptures on the tombs, and the designs appear to be those of the same artist, **Jean de Bruxelles**. The stalls on the north side feature scenes from the New Testament and satirical characters, those on the south side show characters and scenes from the Old Testament.

The tombs★★★ – Many artists collaborated in the decoration of these three monuments, the high point of Flemish sculpture in the region. The designs were sketched by Jean de Bruxelles, who furnished the sculptors with life-size drawings. The ornamentation and the statuary, much admired by visitors, are attributed for the most part to a Flemish workshop which was set up in Brou, in collaboration with French, German and Italian sculptors. The statues of the three princely personages are the work of Conrad Meyt, born in Germany but trained in Flanders. The effigies of the prince and princess are carved in Carrara marble. Philibert and the two Margarets are represented, each lying on the tomb on a slab of black marble, their heads on embroidered cushions. A dog, emblem of fidelity, lies at the feet of the two princesses, and a lion, symbol of strength, at the feet of the prince. The tomb of Margaret of Bourbon occupies a recessed niche in the south wall of the choir.

The two other tombs differ in that they have two recumbent effigies: the first depicted alive and the second dead in a shroud. That of Philibert, the most sober in conception but also the most moving, is in the centre. The tomb of Margaret of Austria, with its huge canopy of chiselled stone, is north of the chancel. On the sole of her foot can be seen the wound which supposedly caused the princess' death by blood poisoning. Princess Margaret's motto is inscribed on the canopy: **Fortune in-fortune fort une** (Fate was very hard on one woman).

Stained-glass windows★★ – The windows in the centre of the apse show Christ appearing to Mary Magdalene (upper part) and visiting Mary (lower part), scenes taken from engravings by Albrecht Dürer. On the left and right, Philibert and Margaret kneel before their patron saints. The coats of arms of their families are above them: Savoy and Bourbon for the duke, and Imperial and Burgundian for the duchess.

Chapels and Oratories – The **chapel of Margaret**★★★ opens to the north of the choir. An altar screen and a stained-glass window, both fine works of art, deserve to be admired.

The **altar screen**★★★ depicts the Seven Joys of the Virgin Mary. This white marble masterpiece of delicate workmanship is exceptionally well preserved. A scene of the Seven Joys is set in each of the niches, designed for the purpose: on the left, below, is the Annunciation; on the right, the Visitation; above, the Nativity and the Adoration of the Magi; higher still are the Assumption, framed by Christ appearing to his mother, and Pentecost. The retable is crowned by three statues: the Virgin and Child flanked by Ste Mary Magdalene and Ste Margaret. On either side of the retable note St Philip and St Andrew.

The **stained-glass window**★★★ is inspired by an Albrecht Dürer engraving of the Assumption. The glass workers have added Philibert and Margaret kneeling near their patron saints.

The oratories of Margaret were arranged for her personal use. They are next to the Chapelle de Madame and are one

above the other, linked by a staircase. These two chambers were effectively little drawing rooms. An oblique window, below a highly original arch, allowed the princess to follow the religious services. The nearby chapel has a remarkable **stained-glass window**★★ and a triptych ordered by Cardinal de Granvelle.

Museum and Cloisters★

The museum is housed in the monastic buildings which are ranged around two-storey cloisters, unique in France.

Small cloisters – On the ground floor the sacristy and the chapter-house, now one room, are used for temporary exhibitions. From the galleries, now a stone depository with fragments of cornice and pinnacles, enjoy the view of the south transept gable and the spire.

Great cloisters – This leads to the second chapter-house, now the museum reception. A staircase leads up to the dormer where the old monks' cells now house collections of paintings and decorative art. On the landing and in the recess in the middle of the great corridor are some fine pieces of Bresse furniture and 18C Meillonnas earthenware.

The cells on the south side are devoted to 16C–18C art, among them a fine **portrait of Margaret of Austria**★ painted by B Van Orley c. 1518 and a triptych of the life of St Jerome (1518).

🚗 DRIVING TOUR

LA BRESSE★★
104km/65mi. Allow a whole day.

The Bresse, which lies to the south of Burgundy, is a captivating land renowned for its traditions and gastronomy. This is bocage country, with many waterways running across the area. The landscape is easily recognisable by its meadows populated by white poultry, corn dryers and pretty timber-framed farmhouses, some with peculiar chimney pots.

▷ Leave Bourg-en-Bresse to the west, taking the direction for

Villefranche-sur-Saône. At Corgenon, turn right on D 45 and follow this as far as Buellas.

Buellas

The **church** has a beautiful Romanesque choir.

▶ Continue on D 45 to Vandeins.

Vandeins

The **church** is adorned with a carved doorway dating from the 12C, and the tympanum is clearly Romanesque work.

▶ Continue on the D 96 which leads to Vonnas.

Vonnas

This small, peaceful, flower-decked town is a popular gastronomic stop on the border between Bresse and the Dombes. By all accounts, for the best chicken dish you are ever likely to taste, try "Poularde de Bresse aux gousses d'ail et foie gras" (Bresse chicken with garlic and foie gras).

▶ Return to D 96 and follow it in the direction of Biziat. Once there, join the D 2.

Pont-de-Veyle

Watered by the River Veyle and surrounded by drainage channels, the town has grown since the 13C, and served as a haven for Protestants until the Edict of Nantes (1685). There are some interesting architectural details, not least the doorway of the **clock tower** (16C), the **Maison de Savoie** (15C, 66 Grande Rue) and the Jesuit-style **church** (1752).

▶ Leave Pont-de-Veyle heading north along D 28. 3km/2mi further on, turn right onto D 1079 in the direction of Bourg-en-Bresse.

Saint-Cyr-sur-Menthon

The town includes several outstanding examples of rural architecture. North of the D 1079, you can still see one of the largest poypes (feudal mounds) in the area – 46m in diameter, and 9.5m high.

▶ After St-Cyr-sur-Menthon, you can join the A 40 in the direction of Mâcon, turning off at the aire de répos.

▲▲ Musée de la Bresse

⊙Mar–mid-Nov daily except Tue 10am–6pm. ⊚€4. ℘03 85 36 31 22. www.patrimoines.ain.fr.

This is a beautiful example of Bresse architecture, built during the summer of 2005 in a semi-subterranean, contemporary building. Undulating glass panels reflect the environment, and here you can discover Bresse through collections of costumes and jewellery, including exquisite Bresse enamels.

Following the plan of a farm courtyard, unusual in Bresse, the main area of the buildings is entered via a large porch, or "Passou". The house is remarkable for its Saracen chimney, and was built in 1490, and later restored using traditional techniques. From an inventory of 1784, found on the site it is possible to reconstruct the organisation and equipment of the farm at that time. Behind the house, the garden has been recreated with remarkable attention to detail. Other buildings portray the building of a farm, livestock and poultry from Bresse.

▶ Go back to St-Cyr-sur-Menthon, take the D 1079 to the junction with the D 28. Turn right towards Bâgé-le-Châtel.

Saint-André-de-Bâgé

The Romanesque church, isolated in the cemetery on the left before the village, was built in the 11C by the monks of Tournus. An elegant octagonal spire, topped by a stone steeple, dominates the apse and two chapels.

▶ On reaching Bâgé-le-Châtel, continue northwards on D 58 to Pont-de-Vaux.

Pont-de-Vaux

This small town is dedicated to the memory of General Joubert, commander of the Italian army, and companion of Napoleon Bonaparte, who died in 1799 and was buried in the church of

Pont-de-Vaux. Once a frontier town of Savoie, Pont-de-Vaux has developed in a meander of the Reyssouze, a tributary of the Saône. The river below the town has been channelled and allows navigation of the Saône as far as Pont-de-Vaux, with its half-timbered houses and 16C/17C façades. Each December, the town hosts one of the four annual *Glorieuses de Bresse*, the poultry competition.

Musée Chintreuil

🕐 *Apr–Nov daily except Tue 2–6pm.*
👝 €3.50. 📞 *03 85 51 45 65.*
www.musee-chintreuil.com.
The museum displays interesting paintings by Jules Migonney (Vieille Mauresque) and Antoine Chintreuil (pupil of Corot).

Église Notre-Dame

The church dates from the 15C; its façade in the Jesuit style is decorated with Baroque shells. Because of space constraints, the church was built long and narrow and ends with a Gothic choir illuminated by large windows. In addition to the woodwork, which came from the monastery at Montmerle following the Revolution, the church is decorated with 11 large paintings by a student of Boucher, Nicolas Brenet (18C).

▷ Leave to the NE on the D 2 in the direction of St-Trivier-de-Courtes.

Ferme-musée de la Forêt

© Christophe Boisvieux/age fotostock

Saint-Trivier-de-Courtes

Former strategic possession of the Lords of Bâgé, the town is famous for its many farms with Saracen chimneys, notably:
Ferme de Grandval – 1.5km/1mi to the west by the D 2.
Ferme de Vescours – 5km/3mi to the west; turn right at the entrance to the village.
Ferme du Colombier à Vernoux – 3km/2mi to the north-east.
Ferme de Bourbon à Saint-Nizier-le-Bouchoux – 6km/3.5mi to the east.

♿👤 Ferme-musée de la Forêt★

3km/2mi to the east.
🕐 *10.30am–12.30pm, 2.30–6pm: Apr–mid-Jun Sat–Sun and public holidays; mid-Jun–Sept daily except Mon; Oct Sat–Sun.* 👝 €3 *(children under 12, no charge).* 📞 *04 74 30 71 89.*
www.comcomsainttrivierdecourtes.fr.
♿ *(except the barn).*
This beautiful 16C–17C farm has been restored and converted into a typical farm of Bresse. Note the latticed wooden balconies and the Saracen chimney. The building has a traditional interior with a fireplace 4m from the side of the room supported by a beam. In an adjacent building you will find a collection of antique farm equipment.

▷ Back in St-Trivier, take the D 975 to the south in the direction of Bourg-en-Bresse.

Montrevel-en-Bresse

A former stronghold of the Montrevel family, the town is also the "home" of St Peter Chanel (1803-1841), a missionary martyred on the island of Futuna and who became the patron saint of Oceania. The village of Cuets, next to the town, commemorates the saint (Musée Océanie). The farmhouse has retained its beautiful 17C Sougey mitre square. Set in the gravel pits of the Reyssouze valley, the **Montrevel Leisure Centre** is an important tourist attraction.

▷ Continue along the D 975 to arrive back at Bourg-en-Bresse.

La Dombes★

The Dombes plateau owes its charm and rather unusual appearance to the presence of more than 1 000 lakes dotted across its entire area. Here and there are low hills, formed by moraines, which were transformed in the Middle Ages into veritable earth fortresses surrounded by moats. Rural housing in the Dombes region is built mainly of cob (pisé) whereas the castles and outer walls are built of rough red bricks known as carrons (terracotta).

The region's history, too, is somewhat out of the ordinary. Dombes was raised to the rank of a principality by François I following the confiscation of the property belonging to the Constable of Bourbon in 1523. A sovereign Parliament sat in Trévoux, its main town, and continued to sit until the mid-18C.

A BIT OF GEOGRAPHY

The impermeable soil encouraged local people very early on in their history to turn their fields into lakes enclosed by mud dikes. The **Grand Étang de Birieux**, one of the most extensive of the lakes, but now subdivided, dates from the 14C. In the 16C, Dombes boasted almost 2 000 lakes, many filled with stagnant water, which led to an unhealthy climate. Most of the lakes are intermittent, one being emptied to fill another: they are filled with water and stocked with fish for a period of six or seven years; then drained and for one year turned over to agriculture.

SIGHTS

Château de Fléchères★★

6km/3.5mi NE of Villefranche-sur-Saône via the D 933, in the commune of Fareins.

The early-17C château stands in a shaded 30ha park offering pleasant strolls. Built by a wealthy protestant from Lyon, the edifice included a temple (Protestant

---

⚙ **Michelin Map:** 328: C-4 to D-5.
ℹ **Info:** 3, Place de l'Hôtel de Ville 01330 Villars les Dombes. ✆04 74 98 06 29. www.villars-les-dombes.com.
▶ **Location:** The Dombes plateau is situated between Lyon and Bourg-en-Bresse and is bordered by the River Ain and the River Saône.
👁 **Don't Miss:** A grand tour of the lakes.
🕐 **Timing:** Allow a full day or two to explore the region.

church) on the third floor of the central building.

The huge hall beneath the church was used for gatherings of the local Protestant community. The owner's living quarters were confined to the wings, which were lower than the central building. The interior is decorated with superb Italian frescoes (1632) believed to be the work of Pietro Ricchi.

Châtillon-sur-Chalaronne

To the N of the Dombes, along the valley of the Chalaronne; 25km/15.5mi SW of Bourg-en-Bresse.

This pretty town in the shadow of its 11C castle on the border between the Bresse and Dombes areas spreads along the Chalaronne valley. Coming into Châtillon from the south-west on the road from Villefranche (D 936), there is a fine **view** over the town's red rooftops, dominated by the impressive bell-tower of the former almshouse. The half-timbered houses with cob or brick walls built in the style typical of the Dombes area are brightened up in summer with bunches of flowers arranged in wicker baskets called *nids-de-poule* (hens' nests).

Highlights include the **ramparts** of the Vieux Château (the remnants of one of the largest strongholds in Bresse) and the **Maison St-Vincent**, where St Vin-

Ruddy shelduck, Parc des Oiseaux

A Bird's Paradise

The **Parc des Oiseaux★** 🚶👤 bird sanctuary *(1km/0.6mi south of Villars-les-Dombes on N 83.* ♿🕐*Daily early Apr–mid-Nov.* 🍽*From €19 (child 3–12, €14).* 📞*04 74 98 05 54. www.parcdesoiseaux. com)*, close to the Dombes Nature Reserve, lies along one of the main migration routes in Europe. Over 2 000 birds from five continents live in the park.

At the entrance, the "Birds' House" provides a warm, humid atmosphere for a wonderful selection of brightly coloured exotic birds. Enjoy a walk round the park along the footpaths running round the lakes, which are the breeding ground for large birds such as common and night heron as well as rarer species in giant aviaries. Besides the spectacular Vallée des Rapaces, the Volière du Pantanal and the Cité des Perroquets are also fascinating. The park is engaged in several conservation programmes aimed at endangered species. These are explained to children through various activities in the Maison des Enfants.

cent de Paul was lodged by a Protestant, M Beynier, for five months while he was the incumbent of Châtillon. A municipal **museum** along the path leading up to the castle is devoted to rural life and ancient crafts, while the old **hospital**, commissioned by the Count of Châtelard in the 18C, now houses a regional arts centre.

Trévoux

Between Lyon and Villefranche-sur-Saône, its nearest neighbours.

This town is built on different levels along the steep bank of the Saône, its colourful façades and flower-filled gardens all facing southwards. Trévoux stands at the intersection of three Roman roads; it was once the capital of the Principality of Dombes, the seat of a sovereign Parliament, and was independent until 1762. After the Duke of Maine decreed that the town's magistrates and members of Parliament must also be residents here, a number of mansions were built in the 18C, along the alleyways of the old districts.

In the 17C and 18C the town was one of the most brilliant intellectual centres in France. Its printing house, founded in 1603, was famous. In 1704 the Jesuits published the first edition of the famous Trévoux Dictionary; under their supervision, the Trévoux Journal fought a relentless campaign against Voltaire and the "Encyclopædic" philosophers for 30 years.

Old Town Tour

▶ Park in boulevard des Combattants. Walk to place de la Terrasse which over-looks the Saône. The Palais du Parlement is on the other side of rue du Palais.

Palais du Parlement de Dombes

🎧*Guided visits 3pm from tourist office: Apr–Sept Sat–Sun and public holidays.* 🕐*Oct–Apr, 1 Jan and 25 Dec.* 🍽*€4 (under 18, free).* 📞*04 74 00 36 32. www.patrimoines.ain.fr*

Parliament House was built at the end of the 17C; the Dombes Parliament sat from 1697 to 1771.

The hall leads into the courtroom with its beautiful beamed ceiling with painted decorations.

Rue du Gouvernement

On either side of the street, just below the church, the Trévoux Dictionary and Journal were written and printed. The Jesuits who lived on the right, in the tall, spacious Maison des Pères, had only to cross the street to take their manuscripts to the printers opposite.

Further down are a number of old houses: the house of the Governor of Dombes, that of the Grande Mademoiselle and the Mint, their austere façades concealing terraces overlooking the Saône.

▷ Take Rue des Halles to the hospital.

Hôpital

Guided tours: same details as Parlement de Dombes.

The hospital was founded in 1686 by La Grande Mademoiselle; it still has the original wood-panelled pharmacy and a beautiful collection of pottery from Gien and Nevers.

▷ Return to rue des Halles and turn left onto rue du Port. Turn right onto rue de l'Herberie.

This street was once reserved for Jews. The intersection of rue de l'Herberie and Grande-Rue forms a triangle dominated by the square-shaped Arsenal Tower of 1405, later converted into a belfry.

▷ Walk up montée de l'Orme to the castle.

Château Féodal

Guided tours: same details as Parlement de Dombes.

Remains of the medieval castle (14C); from the top of the octagonal tower there is a view of the Saône.

▷ Walk down montée des Tours, then return along rue du Palais back to boulevard des Combattants.

🚗 DRIVING TOUR

TOUR OF THE LAKES★

Round trip of 99km/61mi from Villars-les-Dombes. Allow one day.

The region is well-known for its numerous lakes and the opportunities for fishing and bird watching.

Villars-les-Dombes

The unofficial capital of La Dombes, pleasant Villars is located on the right bank of the Chalaronne.

▷ Leave Villars on D 2 heading W.

Bouligneux

In a setting typical of this area stands a 14C brick-built castle that looks rather more like a fortress.

Sandrans

This village is known for its medieval fortress on which a large house was built in the 19C. Today a hillock remains, clearly visible, surrounded by a moat and crowned with a round tower.

Châtillon-sur-Chalaronne

See below.

▷ Leave Châtillon E on D 17 towards St-Paul-de-Varax.

St-Paul-de-Varax

The Romanesque church dates back to the 12C.

▷ Drive N along D 1083 then turn right onto D 64A.

Lent

The village still boasts fine 16C monuments: the church belfry (restored in the 18C) and some timber houses.

Dompierre-sur-Veyle

This village grouped around a Romanesque church is near the largest lake in the area (100ha/247 acres): **Le Grand Marais**.

▶ The D 70 road heading west to St-Nizier passes to the right of various stretches of water which are extensions of Le Grand Marais.

St-Nizier-le-Désert

This pleasant village offers facilities for fishing and gentle rambles.

▶ Follow D 90 which crosses D 1083 and leads to Marlieux. Drive through the village and join D 7. Just after a bend, take a small road towards Beaumont.

Beaumont

The **Chapelle Notre-Dame de Beaumont** stands on the lovely village square. This chapel was once a popular centre of pilgrimage, but subsequently fell into a state of disrepair. Restoration work has revealed 15C **frescoes★** which have been well preserved.

▶ Turn back along the small road on which you arrived to the first intersection. The road branching off to the right goes through the hamlet of Villardières, crosses D 1083 and leads to Le Plantay.

Le Plantay

The village is surrounded by the waters of the Grand Châtel. The **tower★** here (⊶ *not open to the public*), of large red bricks and decorated with white stone around the machicolations, is a symbol for the region.

Abbaye Notre-Dame-des-Dombes

Monks from this abbey, founded by Cistercians in the 19C, helped to drain the area and cultivated those sections of land which are fertile.

Chalamont

This is the highest point in La Dombes. Rue des Halles is lined with a few old houses (15C but restored) with overhanging storeys, and a wash-house.

▶ Take D 61 to Joyeux, where there is an attractive 19C house.

▶ The castle at Le Montellier comes into view on the right.

Le Montellier

The brick-built castle (⊶ *not open to the public*), the most impressive in La Dombes, is flanked at one end by a keep rising on its earth mound.

Cordieux

A handsome red-brick manor house stands here.

▶ Rejoin D 4 and turn left (W) to St-André-de-Corcy; take D 82 to Monthieux.

Monthieux

Breuil manor house (16C), just north of the village, has an interesting Saracen well.

▶ Head towards Ambérieux-en-Dombes and turn right onto D 6.

Lapeyrouse

From the war memorial there is a delightful view of the Alps and, in the foreground, the Grand Glareins lakes and the 15C Château de Glareins (⊶ *not open to the public*).

▶ Take D 904 back to Villars.

ADDRESSES

🖉 STAY AND 🍴 EAT

⊜⊜⊜ **Auberge des Bichonnières** – *545 Route du 3 Septembre 1944, Rte d'Ars, 01330 Ambérieux-en-Dombes. 11km/6.6mi W of Villars-les-Dombes via D 904. ℘04 74 00 82 07. www. aubergedesbichonnieres.com. Closed Sun. Reservations required.* An old smallholding characteristic of the farms of the Vallée de la Dombes offers regional specialities presented in fixed-price menus. Seating on the terrace in fine weather.

Pérouges★★

Pérouges is perched on a hilltop and surrounded by ramparts; it remains a model of medieval architecture, with narrow winding streets and ancient houses, making it very popular with visitors. Pérouges has such an authentic historical flavour that it is often used as the setting for period films by French directors.

A BIT OF HISTORY

During the Middle Ages and up to the French annexation (1601) the town was disputed many times by the sovereigns of Dauphiné and Savoy. In the rich and active town centre, hundreds of craftsmen wove fabric from hemp grown in the surrounding fields.

In the 19C the town's prosperity waned: Pérouges was too far from the railway line and local craftsmen could no longer compete with industry.

In 1909–10 the town nearly disappeared altogether: many of the owners turned to mass destruction and entire blocks of old houses were pulled down. Fortunately, a historical society from Lyon and a few artists from Pérouges stepped in, helped by the School of Arts. The most interesting houses were bought, restored, and classified as historical monuments.

- ▸ **Population:** 1 238.
- **Michelin Map:** 328: E-5.
- **Info:** Route de la Cité, 01800 PÉROUGES. ℰ04 74 46 70 84. www.perouges.org.
- **Location:** Pérouge lies 34km/21mi NE of Lyon, and 38km/23.5mi from Bourg-en-Bresse.
- **Don't miss:** The place de la Halle.
- **Parking:** There is limited parking, but you will find a car park near the church.
- **Timing:** Allow 2hrs to explore the town.

Most of the houses in Pérouges mark the transition between the Gothic and Renaissance styles. The houses of the gentry and richer townsfolk have large dimensions and luxurious interiors. Those of the merchants were more modest, with semicircular openings to light the workshop or serve as counters to display their goods. The streets have barely changed since the Middle Ages. Narrow and winding, they had double-sloping paving with a drainage channel in the middle.

Pérouges viewed from the watchtower of Musée du Vieux-Pérouges

© Franck Guiziou/hemis.fr

WALKING TOUR

OLD TOWN

Porte d'En-Haut★

This gateway, the main entrance to Pérouges, was also the most exposed. Its defence was reinforced by the fortress-church and a barbican.

Rue du Prince★

Butchers, basket-makers, drapers, the armourer and the apothecary held shop here. At one end stands the **Maison des Princes de Savoie**, which presently houses a museum.

Place de la Halle★★

This market square is one of the prettiest in France. It derives its name from the covered markets or **Halles**, which stood here and were razed in 1839.

Place du Tilleul★★★

Ostellerie – This inn has a sign bearing the town's coat of arms. The half-timbered east façade is 13C whereas the south front is Renaissance.

Musée du Vieux-Pérouges – (🕐10am –noon, 2–6pm: Jul–Aug daily; Apr–Jun and Sept–Oct Sat–Sun and public holidays; 🚫Nov–Mar. ⊛€4. ℘04 74 61 00 88). This museum is housed partly in the Maison des Princes de Savoie and in the Maison Heer which opens onto place de la Halle.

Maison du Vieux-St-Georges – A shell-shaped niche on the façade houses an unusual wooden 15C statue of St George, patron saint of Pérouges, mounted on a horse.

▶ Take the narrow street which goes downhill from the corner of the square.

Maison Herriot

This is a sumptuous-looking house with semicircular and mullioned windows.

▶ Return to the square and take rue de la Place, to the N.

Maison Cazin

This lovely house has projecting upper floors and half-timbering.

▶ Turn right onto rue des Rondes.

Rue des Rondes★

This street still has most of its ancient paving and central drainage channel. The old houses on either side are protected by wide eaves.

Porte d'En-Bas

The Lower Gateway is older than the Upper Gateway. On the outside there is an inscription referring to a siege in 1468, which can be translated as: "Pérouges of the Pérougians! Impregnable town! Those rascally Dauphinois wanted to take it but they could not.

So they went off with the doors, the hinges and the locks instead. May the devil take them!"

▶ Rue des Rondes leads round to place de l'Église.

Église Ste-Marie-Madeleine

This 15C church looks like a fortress with its north-western wall incorporating crenellations, arrow slits and very high, narrow openings.

▶ Rejoin rue des Rondes which leads to rue de la Tour.

Puits de la Tour

For a long time this well supplied water to the entire town. The tower built by the Romans was destroyed in 1749. A lantern in the upper part of the tower was used to send light signals to similar towers forming a relay right to Lyon.

The Two Curtain Walls

The path uphill from the Upper Gateway leads to **Promenade des Terreaux★** in the moat of the outer curtain wall of which only vestiges remains. The **Round Tower**, against which the house of the Sergeant of Justice is built, was formerly used as a prison.

EXCURSIONS

Montuel

Leave Pérouges on N 84 towards Lyon. Montuel has retained several interesting buildings worth admiring. Take a stroll through the flower-decked town starting from the collegiate church of Notre-Dame-du-Marais (16C–17C) past the chapel of the former Visitation Convent then the 12C St-Stephen's porch; note the carved wood decoration of the apothecary's shop (*guided visits May–Oct Wed and Sat 3–6pm; Nov–Apr Sat 3–6pm; public holidays; 04 78 06 06 23*).

St-Maurice-de-Gourdans

12km/6.6mi S on D 65B.
This village lies on the edge of a plateau dominating the confluence of the River Ain and the River Rhône. The 12C church

has been restored to reveal its original masonry: limestone and stone chippings with alternating layers of small bricks and flat pebbles.

ADDRESSES

🏨STAY

⌂ **Chambre d'Hôte M. et Mme Debeney-Truchon** – *01150 Chazey-sur-Ain. 04 74 61 95 87. 6 rooms.* The simplicity and welcoming atmosphere of this village farm is seductive. The owners are delighted to receive you and sad to see you go again so soon! If you have the time, the owner will show you how he makes his bread. Amateur *pétanque* players welcome.

⌂⌂ **Le Petit Casset** – *96 imp. du Petit-Casset, 01120 La Boisse – 9km/5.5mi SW of Montluel. 04 78 06 21 33. www.le petitcasset.fr. Closed Tue and Aug. 17 rooms.* Quiet, renovated hotel in a residential area. The atmosphere is friendly and the rooms, all individually decorated, overlook the garden. Swimming pool.

🍴EAT

⌂⌂ **Auberge du Coq** – *R. des Rondes. 04 74 61 05 47. Closed Sun evening, and all day Mon–Tue.* In a cobbled street, this restaurant evokes the essence of yesteryear.

⌂⌂ **Auberge de Campagne du Mollard** – *Le Mollard, 01320 Châtillon-la-Palud. 13.6km/8mi NE of Pérouges via D 984 and D 904, dir. Chalamont, and road on left. 04 74 35 66 09. www.auberge dumollard.com. Reservations required.* This farm settled amid the fields invites guests to stay over in its rooms furnished with attractive sculpted wood pieces.

⌂⌂⌂ **Hostellerie du Vieux Pérouges** – *pl du Tilleul, 01800 Pérouges. 04 74 61 00 88. www.hostelleriedeperouges.com.* The fame of this magnificent manor in the heart of the village has spread beyond national borders since Bill Clinton dined here in 1997. This is a beautiful place with a uniquely Bressan décor. Regional and traditional dishes.

Forever associated with the wines the region produces, Beaujolais can best be described as gently undulating rather than mountainous, and its distinguishing features are numerous mountain plateaux crisscrossed by narrow sinuous **valleys**. By contrast, the attractive Monts du Lyonnais southwest of Lyon have a gentle, pastoral countenance patterned by chestnut groves and oakwoods. Land in the low-lying valleys is used for market gardening, vineyards and orchards, although many pastures extend into the higher ground.

Highlights

The Father of Physiology

Born in the village of St-Julien, Claude Bernard (1813–78) moved to Paris in 1834. His study of liver glycogen make him the "creator" of physiology – a branch of biology that deals with the functions and activities of life or of living matter (as organs, tissues, or cells) and of the physical and chemical phenomena involved. His research has served as a foundation for modern medicine, and his methods, explained in the *Introduction à l'étude de la médecine expérimentale*, made him an expert in his field.

The "Beaujolais" grapes

In 1935, the Gamay grape variety was forbidden in Burgundy, so Beaujolais, to the south, decided to make the most of it, and grew the grape in abundance. Today, the region is planted with around 98 percent Gamay, with Pinot Noir and Chardonnay taking up the remaining 2 percent. Covering no less than 22 250ha, Beaujolais is larger than the three other Burgundy regions combined. The region is divided into two by the Nizerand river: to the north is Haut-Beaujolais, which has light soil, ideal for the Beaujolais-Villages wines and all ten crus. To the south are the Bas-Beaujolais, which produces around half of the total volume of wines at 10 percent alcohol, with a small amount of Beaujolais-Supérieur, which is a little stronger. Beaujolais Nouveau appears on the third Thursday of November.

Village and vineyards of Chénas

© Bernard Jaubert/age fotostock

BEAUJOLAIS AND THE MONTS DU LYONNAIS

Le Beaujolais	★★	Recommended
Corcelles	★	Interesting
Tarare		Other sight described
		Departure point for tour

0   10 km

SAÔNE-ET-LOIRE

MONTCEAU-LES-MINES

MÂCON

NANTUA

St-Amour-Bellevue

Juliénas

Chénas

La Terrasse

Avenas

Fleurie

Romanèche-Thorins

Les Écharmeaux

Chénelette

953

Mont Tourvéon

Beaujeu

Villié-Morgon

Corcelles

Col de Favardy

862

Claveisolles

Mont Brouilly
484

Belleville

St-Nizier-d'Azergues

Le Beaujolais

Vaux-en-Beaujolais

Arginy

Salles-Arbuissonnas-en-Beaujolais

AIN

Lac des Sapins

Signal de St-Bonnet
680

St-Julien

Chambost-Allières

Montmelas-St-Sorlin

Villefranche-sur-Saône

Chambost

St-Appolinaire

Jarnioux

Amplepuis

Ternand

Oingt

Theizé

Le Boitier

Marcy

Monts de Tarare

St-Laurent-d'Oingt

Bagnols

Charnay

Chazay-d'Azergues

Tarare

Chessy

Châtillon

St-Jean-des-Vignes

L'Arbresle

Éveux

ROANNE, MOULINS, VICHY

Savigny

RHÔNE

St-Pierre-la-Palud

Parc animalier de Courzieu

Col de la Luère
714

Grézieu-la-Varenne

LYON

LOIRE

Parc Salva Terra à Haute-Rivoire

Yzeron

CLERMONT-FERRAND

Aveize

N.-D.-de-la-Neylière

Signal de St-André
934

Chazelles-sur-Lyon

St-Symphorien-sur-Coise

Riverie

St-Galmier

CLERMONT-FERRAND

Monts du Lyonnais

St-Martin-la-Plaine

Parc naturel régional du Pilat

Veauche

VALENCE

RHÔNE

ST-ÉTIENNE, LE PUY-EN-VELAY

Villefranche-sur-Saône

This busy industrial and commercial city is the capital of the Beaujolais region. It was founded in 1140 by the Lords of Beaujeu, to match the Anse fortress belonging to the Archbishops of Lyon. The settlement sprang up quickly, and in 1260 Guichard IV de Beaujeu granted the town a charter, which earned it the name of *Ville Franche*, meaning free town. In addition to its historical role as a wine trading centre, Villefranche now earns its living from the manufacture of sports and work wear (Joannès Sabot founded an overalls factory here in 1887), shirts and hosiery. The metallurgy, mechanical and food-processing industries are also represented here.

SIGHTS
Old Houses

☞ *Guided tours (2h): check website for details.* ✆ *04 74 07 27 40. www.villefranche-beaujolais.fr.*

Most of the town's oldest houses built between the 15C and 18C are to be found along **rue Nationale**. They have relatively narrow façades, because of a tax imposed on the width of house façades in 1260, to make up for the exemption from taxes and the other privileges which had been granted to the town in its charter.

Odd-numbered side of the road

Note Nos. 375 (vaulted passageway), 401 (16C openwork spiral staircase in the courtyard) and, at No. 17 rue Grenette the turret staircase with skylights. In the courtyard of No. 507 the well is surmounted by a shell-shaped canopy in the courtyard.

At No. 523, the **Hôtel de Mignot de Bussy** is a lovely Renaissance building with a spiral staircase, mullion windows and shell-shaped niche containing an elegant statue. Behind the splendid

- ▶ **Population:** 37 084.
- ◔ **Michelin Map:** 327: H-4.
- 🛈 **Info:** 96 r. de la Sous-Préfecture, 69400 Villefranche-sur-Saône. ✆ 04 74 07 27 40. www.villefranche-beaujolais.fr.
- ◖ **Location:** The A 6 and D 306 link the town to Lyon, 34km/21mi to the south. The numbering of houses in Villefranche is based on a metric system, calculating the distance of each house from the beginning of the street. Street numbers run from rue Nationale east and west, and south from the north of town.
- 🅿 **Parking:** There are numerous spacious car parks in the centre of town.
- ⊛ **Don't Miss:** The lovely old houses along the rue Nationale.
- ◷ **Timing:** Normally allow 2 hours, but you can so easily be side-tracked.

1760 façade of No. 561, a vaulted passageway with sculpted supports leads to a 16C courtyard surrounded by pink-walled buildings. The **Maison Eymin** at No. 761 has an 18C façade with four levels of arches in the courtyard, hammer-wrought coats of arms (damaged) and an elegant turret housing a spiral staircase. No. 793, once the residence of the Roland de la Platière family, is indicated by a medallion and a commemorative plaque and features a monumental staircase with a wrought-iron bannister.

Even-numbered side of the road

From No. 400, there is a good view of the tower and stone balustrade of the Italian Renaissance house opposite. A 15C half-timbered house stands on the corner of rue du Faucon and rue Nationale (No. 476).

A 👑🚆 MÁCON ①
B 🚆 ①

VILLEFRANCHE-SUR-SAÔNE

0   200 m

1

THIZY

Av. Saint-Exupéry

R. du Faucon

Gambetta

Auberge de la Coupe d'Or ■ **Hôtel de Mignot de Bussy**

R. Grenette

Musée Paul-Dini

R. Etienne Poulet

R. Gantillon

Rue

Montplaisir

R. P. Bert

R. des Fayettes

R. Ph. Héron

la Paix

R. de la Sous-Préfecture

POL.

Pl. des Marais

■ **N.-D. des Marais**

Nationale

Blanc

NICHE DU PÉLICAN

Morgon

Rue

Jaurès

Rue de

Ancien hôtel de ville

Maison Eymin

R. L. Ampère

ROANNE, TARARE

D 504

D 338 Rte de Tarare

de

R.

A.

Aucour

Bd

Bernard

Giraud

R. P. Morin

de la République

Rue

R. Victor Hugo

R. Roland

R. P. Berthier

Louis

Pg

BOURG-EN-BRESSE

D 904, ARS-S-FORMANS

2

N

Thizy

Pl. Carnot

Pl. de la Libération

R. de Stalingrad

R. de la Gare

R. A. Arnaud

R. d'Anse

N 6

R. Grange-Blazet

R. J.-M. Savigny

A 6 🚗 LYON

WHERE TO STAY		WHERE TO EAT	
Émile Job (Hôtel) .... ①		Bicheronne (Ferme-auberge La) .... ①	
Plaisance (Hôtel) .... ②		Juliénas (Le) .... ②	

At No. 486, at the back of the alley on the right, a Renaissance bas-relief depicts two cherubs with chubby cheeks holding coats of arms with the date 1537.

The **Auberge de la Coupe d'Or** at No. 528 was the oldest inn in Villefranche (late 14C) before it was transformed in the 17C. On the corner of rue Paul-Bert, the façade on the right (No. 596) with

crocket gables dates from the late 15C, and that on the left with moulded mullioned windows and medallions is Renaissance. Note the Gothic corner niche at No. 706. A passage at No. 810 leads to a restored courtyard.

The **town hall** at No. 816 was completed in 1660. The façade is built of golden Jarnioux stone and has a solid

---

La Vague de l'Amitié

Every year, on the last Sunday in January, to mark the end of military service, local conscripts celebrate the **Fête des Conscrits**. Those eligible to take part are men between the ages of 20 and 80. Dress code for the occasion is a black suit and top hat, decorated with a coloured ribbon (different colour for each decade: 20s, 30s etc).

At 11am the participants form a procession, link arms and, clutching colourful bouquets of mimosa and carnations, make their way along rue Nationale close on each others' heels, in what is known as the Friendship Wave (*La Vague de l'Amitié*).

Aerial view of Villefranche-sur-Saône

oak door decorated with cast-iron nails. The house at No. 834 was built in the late 15C and has a charming courtyard with a staircase turret.

Musée Paul-Dini

2 pl. Faubert. &⊙*Wed 1.30–6pm; Thu–Fri 10am–12.30pm, 1.30–6pm; Sat–Sun 2.30–6pm.* ⊙*Mon–Tue, 1 Jan, 1 and 11 Nov, 23–24 and 31 Dec.* &€6. ℘*04 74 68 33 70. www.musee-paul-dini.com.* The former granary was converted in a museum by Paul Dini, director of Dauphiné Libéré; the museum houses a collection of regional paintings from 1875 to the present time.

Rue de la Paix

The façade of the building to the south of the post office features a "pelican niche", a Gothic sculpture decorated with finials and pinnacles. Next to it, set slightly further back, is a pretty Renaissance well.

Place des Marais

This pretty square to the north-east of the church contains a fountain and is enclosed by modern houses with arcades, painted in shades of pink and ochre. On the corner with rue Nationale, a ceramic plaque depicts Pierre II de Bourbon and Anne de Beaujeu in the same pose as that on the famous triptych by the Master of Moulins.

Notre-Dame-des-Marais

In the 13C, a chapel was built in honour of a statue of the Virgin Mary found in a nearby marsh *(marais)*; all that now remains of it is the small Romanesque tower above the chancel.

ADDRESSES

🛏STAY

⊜⊜ **Emile Job** – *12 rue du Pont, 01090 Montmerle-sur-Saône. 13km/8mi N of Villefranche. Take N 6 to St-Georges-de-Reneins, then D 20.* ℘*04 74 69 33 92. www. hotelemilejob.com. Restaurant* ⊜⊜ *(closed Sun evening from Oct–May, Tue lunch from Jun–Sept and Mon). 14 rooms.* Located just before the bridge crossing the Saône, here is a hotel-restaurant with a lovely terrace surrounded by linden trees. The rooms are bourgeois and clean, the renovated dining room is rather elegant, the menus are varied and the reception is hospitable: most enjoyable.

⊜⊜⊜ **Hôtel Plaisance** – *96 av. de la Libération.* ℘*04 74 65 33 52. www. hotel-plaisance.com. Closed 24 Dec–1 Jan. 68 rooms.* An impeccably managed hotel across from l'Esplanade de la Libération. The rooms, each with its own style, are clean and nicely furnished. Modern lounge bar to partake of Beaujolais.

⛽EAT

⊜ **Auberge La Bicheronne** – *977 Chemin du Bicheron, 01480 Fareins.* ℘*04 74 67 81 01. www.bicheronne.fr. 10km/6mi NE of Villefranche. Take D 44, then at Beauregard take dir. Château de Flécheres via D 933 and 2nd road on right towards "Le Bicheron". Closed Jan, Mon and Thu. Reservations recommended.* Wielding her saucepans and whisks, the owner of this farm has been delighting well-fed guests for over 20 years. Her farm chickens and guinea fowl, generally accompanied by a *gratin dauphinois*, are popular.

⊜⊜ **Le Juliénas** – *236 r. Anse.* ℘*04 74 09 16 55. www.restaurant-lejulienas.com. Closed Mon evening, Sat lunch and Sun.* In this bistro-style restaurant, Carine and Fabrice offer outstanding local wines and tasty seasonal dishes with a hint of the south, prepared and served with passion and conviviality in a charming dining room. There are four menus on offer plus the dish of the day and a children's menu. Colourful and imaginative cooking.

© Hervé Lenain / hemis.fr

Beaujolais★★

According to an old French saying, Lyon is fed by three rivers: the Rhône, the Saône and… the Beaujolais. It is true that the Beaujolais is renowned both within and beyond French borders largely as a wine-growing region, but although this industry makes a substantial contribution to local economy, it is by no means the region's only source of income.

- **Michelin Map:** 327: F-2/4/4, G-2/3/4, H-2/3/4.
- **Location:** The Beaujolais region lies north-west of Lyon and west of the Saône.
- **Don't Miss:** The 15C fortess: Château de Corcelles.
- **Timing:** Use Villefranche-sur-Saône as a base and allow two days to explore.

A BIT OF HISTORY

Beaujolais owes its name to the aristocratic Beaujeu family, at the height of their power from the 9C to the 11C. In 1400, Édouard de **Beaujeu** gave his estate to the House of Bourbon-Montpensier. The Beaujolais passed briefly into the hands of the Crown under François I, who confiscated it among other territories from the Connétable de Bourbon as punishment for his negative attitude towards his monarch, but by 1560, the Bourbon-Montpensiers had been reinstated as landlords. Anne-Marie-Louise d'Orléans, Duchesse de Montpensier, who was known as **"La Grande Mademoiselle"** (renowned for her love affairs and active support of the Roman Catholic Fronde movement), bequeathed the Beaujolais to the House of Orléans, who remained its owners until the Revolution.

A BIT OF GEOGRAPHY

The Beaujolais is a mountain range which stretches between the Loire and Rhône valleys, on the line where the Atlantic and Mediterranean watersheds meet. The Beaujolais is best described as hilly, rather than mountainous. Its distinguishing features are numerous mountain plateaux crisscrossed by narrow sinuous valleys. To the east the land drops sharply to the Saône, whereas to the west it slopes gently away. The cliffs formed by the subsidence of the Saône river bed are home to the vineyards of the "Côte Beaujolaise", whereas the rest of the region forms "La Montagne."

La Montagne – a region of picturesque hills, valleys and landscapes as varied as they are appealing. The upper slopes of the mountains are carpeted with broom and pines; lower down there are stands of oak separated by wide clearings.

BEAUJOLAIS WINE

Beaujolais vineyards and the wine they produce have secured the region's reputation far beyond the borders of France. Unlike most other red wines, Beaujolais is best drunk young, served slightly chilled.

The vine has been cultivated here since Roman times. Today, the vineyards stretch from Mâcon in the north to the Azergues valley in the south. A single grape variety – Gamay – is used to produce the light and fruity red Beaujolais wines with their characters determined by the soil in which the grapes were grown. Beaujolais vineyards are divided into two areas of production:

Coteaux de Beaujolais – North of Villefranche, the soil is granitic and perfect for the Gamay vine. This is the region of **Beaujolais-Villages**: Moulin-à-Vent, Fleurie, Morgon, Chiroubles, Juliénas, Chénas, Côte de Brouilly, Brouilly, St-Amour and Régnié.

Pays des Pierres Dorées – Between Villefranche and the Azergues valley the soil is composed more of sedimentary rocks which alter the flavour of the wine. The wines here are "Beaujolais" and "Beaujolais Supérieur".

🚗 DRIVING TOURS

On the map opposite, the wine-producing area is shown in green – Names of grands crus are underlined in red.

① BEAUJOLAIS VINEYARDS★

Villefranche-sur-Saône to St-Amour-Bellevue. 98km/61mi. Allow 5h.

The road winds its way through the vineyards, at first climbing the granite escarpments, then dropping down towards the Saône valley.

▶ Leave Villefranche on D 504, take D 19 on the right, then D 44 on the left.

Montmelas-St-Sorlin

Drive round to the north of the feudal castle, which was restored in the 19C by Dupasquier, a student of Viollet-le-Duc.

▶ Carry on from Montmelas as far as Col de St-Bonnet. From the pass, a track leads off to the right to the St-Bonnet beacon.

Signal de St-Bonnet

🚶 From the east end of the chapel there is a view of Montmelas in the foreground, set against the hills and vineyards of the Beaujolais and beyond them the Saône valley.

▶ From the pass, take D 20 on the right.

St-Julien

This pretty little wine-growing village is the birthplace of the doctor Claude Bernard (1813–78). The **Musée Claude-Bernard** (🕐Mar–Nov Wed–Sun 10am–12.30pm, 2–6pm. 🕐1 Jan 1 Mar. ⊛€5. 📞04 74 67 51 44) recalls his work in the field of physiology, in particular on the absorption of fats and sugars by the liver.

▶ Take D 19 as far as Salles.

Salles-Arbuissonnas-en-Beaujolais

The monks of Cluny founded a **priory** in the 10C. This was taken over by nuns of the Benedictine Order in the 14C, who ran it until they were replaced by "aristocratic" canonesses in the 18C.

▶ From Salles, take D 35, then eventually the D 49E to the right.

Vaux-en-Beaujolais

This wine-growing village and the ribaldry of its wine-tippling inhabitants in the 1920s inspired **Gabriel Chevallier** (1895–1969) to write his satirical novel *Clochemerle*.

▶ Carry on along D 49E through Le Perréon, then the D 133, and then D 62 towards Charentay.

The unusual shape of the Château d'Arginy comes into sight 1km/0.6mi east of Charentay.

BEAUJOLAIS

0 _____ 6 km

vineyards

The Great Growths (Grands crus)
are shown underlined in red

Château d'Arginy

All that remains of the castle is the great red-brick tower known as the Tour d'Alchimie: some say it was used by the Knights Templar to hide their treasure.

▶ Follow D 68, turn left onto D 19, then right onto D 37 to Belleville.

Belleville

This old fortified town at the crossroads of communications routes is now a centre of wine-production and industry (manufacture of agricultural machinery). The **Hôtel-Dieu** (&.⌂ *guided tours Wed–Fri 10am and 4pm, Sat–Sun 5pm (Jul–Aug, 10am, 4pm, 5pm);* ◷ *public holidays.* ⊚€5. ℘04 74 66 44 67), built in the 18C to replace the old hospital, was in use for the care of the sick until 1991.

▶ Beyond Cercié (carry on along D37), the road skirts Mont Brouilly.

▶ Those wishing to climb Mont Brouilly should take D 43, turn left onto D 43E, then 100m further on take the road signposted "La Côte de Brouilly" to the left.

Mont Brouilly

Côte de Brouilly, a fruity wine with a fragrant bouquet, comes from the grapes harvested on the sunny slopes of Mont Brouilly. From the esplanade, there is a marvellous **view★** of the vineyards, the Beaujolais hills, the Saône valley and the Dombes region.

▶ Return to Cercié. On leaving the village turn left onto D 68E towards the old village of Corcelles, then continue onto D 9 to the left.

Château de Corcelles★

&🕐Mon–Sat: Apr–Oct 10am–6.30pm; Nov–Mar 10am–12.30pm, 1.30–5.30pm. 🕐Sun, 1 Jan, 15 Aug, 1 and 11 Nov, 25 Dec. ⊚€5. ✆04 74 66 00 24. www.chateaudecorcelles.fr.
This fortress was built in the 15C to protect the border between Burgundy and Beaujolais. Above the entrance to the keep is the family coat of arms of Madeleine de Ragny. The inner courtyard is surrounded by Renaissance arcades and contains a fountain with an ornate piece of 15C wrought-iron work on top.

▶ Rejoin D 9 to the right.

The road goes through vineyards of famous *grands crus* of the Beaujolais.

Villié-Morgon

Unusually for Beaujolais wines, the wine produced in Villié-Morgon matures well. It has a particularly fruity taste because of the broken-up schist soil in which the vines are cultivated.

▶ Leave Villié-Morgon N on D 68.

Fleurie

Fleurie wines are best drunk young.

▶ In Fleurie take D 32 E; left on D 186.

Romanèche-Thorins

The famous Moulin-à-Vent wine is produced here and in the neighbouring village of Chénas. There is a wine museum located in the railway station – **Le Hameau en Beaujolais★** (🕐daily 10am–6pm; 🗓25 Dec. ⊚€20. ✆03 85 35 22 22; www.hameauduvin.com). The **Musée du Compagnonnage Guillon** (🕐Jan–May and Oct–mid-Dec 2–6pm; Jun–Sept 10am–6pm. 🕐1 May, mid-Dec–1 Jan. ⊚€4. ✆03 85 35 22 02. http://musee-compagnonnage. cg71.fr) displays exhibits from the days of itinerant craftsmen; there are particularly fine examples of their work.

▶ At the Maison-Blanche crossroads on N 6, take D 466B, leading to St-Romain-des-Îles.

🏊👪 Parc Zoologique et d'Attractions Touroparc★

&🕐Daily: Jul–Aug 9.30am–6.30pm; Sept–Nov 9.30am–6pm; Nov–Feb 10am–5.30pm. ⊚€20.50 (child 3–12, €16.90). ✆03 85 35 51 53. www.touroparc.com.
In a delightfully verdant setting dotted with ochre buildings, this zoo and breeding centre presents birds and animals from the five continents.

▶ Rejoin D 266, which goes through the hamlet of Le Moulin-à-Vent, to D 68.

Chénas

Home of robust, top-quality Moulin-à-Vent and the lighter Chénas.

Juliénas

The strong wines from this locality can still be tasted in the **Cellier de la Vieille Église** (&🕐May–Jun and Sept 10am–noon, 3–6pm; Jul–Aug 10am–12.30pm, 3–7pm; 🕐Tue from Oct–Apr. ✆04 74 04 42 98), tasting cellars in an old converted church.

▷ Drive on to St-Amour-Bellevue.

St-Amour-Bellevue
This village at the northerly tip of the Beaujolais produces full-bodied dark-red wines and high-quality white wines.

2 MOUNTAIN TOUR★
St-Amour-Bellevue to Villefranche sur-Saône. 134km/83mi. Allow 6h.

This pretty drive continues from **St-Amour-Bellevue**, through vine-clad hills to dark pine forests, then drops to the Azergues valley.

▷ From Juliénas, take D 26 uphill, going through two passes.

Beaujeu
The capital of the Beaujolais lies amid vine-covered hillsides.

La maison du terroir Beaujolais
&. ✪*Mar–Dec Mon–Sat 10am–12.30pm, 2–6pm, Sun and public holidays 10am–12.30pm, 3–6pm (7pm in Jul–Aug).* ✪*Jan–Feb.* ◉€6. ℘*04 74 69 20 56.* *www.lamaisonduterroirbeaujolais.com.* This wine centre is devoted to the development of the Beaujolais area.

Musée Marius Audin – Musée des Arts et des Traditions Populaires
✪*Mar–Apr and Oct–Nov Wed–Sun 10am–noon, 2–6pm; May daily 10am–noon, 2–6pm; Jun–Sept daily 10am–12.30pm, 2–7pm.* ✪*Dec–Feb.* ◉€2. ℘*04 74 04 87 75.* Audin (1872–1951) was a printer from Beaujeu who founded this museum of traditional folk art in 1942.

▷ Follow D 26 and D 18 to La Terrasse.

La Terrasse★★
The view from a bend in D 18 after Col du Fût d'Avenas covers the Saône valley, Bresse plateaux, Jura peaks and Alps.

Avenas
The Roman road from Lyon to Autun once passed through this village.

▷ Take D 18E, then D 32.

Shortly before the pass (Col de Crie), there is a beautiful view north down the Grosne Orientale valley. As the road carries on downhill, it passes Mont St-Rigaud, the highest peak in the region.

Chénelette
This small village lies in a charming wooded setting. The **Tourvéon** towers above it. This summit was once the site of the great fortress of Ganelon who betrayed Charlemagne's army, bringing about its defeat and the death of Roland at Roncevaux.

Les Écharmeaux
This summer resort is set against a backdrop of pine forests and meadows. From Les Écharmeaux, follow D 10 towards Ranchal. It crosses the Aillets pass and, after a stretch through forest, the Écorbans pass. Between Ranchal and St-Nizier-d'Azergues, D 54 affords **views★** of the Azergues valley.

St-Nizier-d'Azergues
This small town occupies a pleasant site above the Azergues valley. The pretty road carries on to Grandris.

▷ After Grandris, turn left onto D 504 as far as La Folletière, then left again on D 485 along the upper valley of the Azergues and through Lamure-sur-Azergues. In Le Gravier, turn right onto D 9.

Claveisolles
This little village is well known for its plantations of coniferous trees. In the 19C, the Comte du Sablon introduced Douglas firs from America.

▷ Drive back to D 485 and turn left to Chambost-Allières.

Chambost-Allières
This is an amalgamation of two very different villages: Allières in the valley, a busy place with lots of passing traffic; and Chambost, a rural hamlet above the valley.

The road from Chambost-Allières to Cogny via Le Saule-d'Oingt makes a **pretty drive★★**. It climbs to the Joncin pass and then runs along the ridge, offering a **view★** of the Alps.

▷ In Le Saule-d'Oingt, turn left onto D 31, then left again onto D 19.

As the road drops down to the valley, the view stretches over the Saône valley, the Bresse region and the Jura foothills.

▷ D 504 leads back to Villefranche.

③ LE PAYS DES PIERRES DORÉES★★

Round tour from Villefranche-sur-Saône. 59km/37mi. Allow 4h.

This region owes its name to the pretty ochre-coloured local stone used to build the farmsteads, castles and villages.

▷ From Villefranche, take the D 70 S.

Marcy

Outside this market town stands a **telegraph tower** (🕐*Mar–Nov Sun 2.30–6pm.* ✆*04 74 67 02 21 (town hall);* 🕐*Dec–Feb;* 🎫*€2)* built by Claude Chappe in 1799. The original semaphore mechanism was used to transmit messages until 1850.

Charnay

This small fortified town at the top of a hill still has the remains of its original citadel.

▷ Take a narrow road heading S from Charnay to St-Jean-des-Vignes.

St-Jean-des-Vignes

There is a good view of the countryside around Lyon from the small church perched on a hillside.

Espace Pierres Folles

🕐*Mar–Nov Tue, Thu and Fri 10am –12.30pm, 2–5pm, Wed, Sat–Sun and public holidays (except 1 May) 2–5pm.* 🎫*€6.* ✆*04 78 43 69 20.* *www.espace-pierres-folles.com.*

A museum founded to reflect the presence of a number of important geological sites in this area.

▷ Rejoin D 30 to reach Chazay-d'Azergues.

Chazay-d'Azergues

All that remains of the fortified town overlooking the Azergues is the belfry, a few 15C and 16C houses and a town gateway.

▷ Take D 30 as far as Lozanne, then D 385 to Châtillon.

Châtillon

A fortress built in the 12C and 13C to protect the mouth of the Azergues valley towers masterfully over this village. The **Chapelle St-Barthélemy**, originally part of the fortress itself, was extended in the 15C by Geoffroy de Balzac.

▷ Carry on along D 385.

Chessy

Near Chessy, a rich seam of copper which belonged to Jacques Cœur was once mined. The ore obtained was known as **chessylite** and was a variety of azurite with a beautiful blue glint to it, highly prized by collectors.

▷ Take D 19 to Bagnols.

Bagnols

In this village is a 15C castle converted into a hotel. There are pretty 15C–16C houses on the village square.

▷ Return to the D 19.

Le Boitier

As you leave this hamlet, the road takes you past Clos de la Platière, which belonged to the Rolands, who became famous during the Revolution. **Mme Roland de la Platière** stands out from her contemporaries as a cultured, well-educated woman. However, she made no secret of her antipathy towards Danton and Robespierre and paid for this in 1793 by being sent to the guillotine.

Theizé

This village, characteristic of the Pierres Dorées area, has two churches and two castles. The main attraction is the **Site de Rochebonne** in the upper part of the village, which includes the former chapel and the château.

Oingt★

All that remains of the once mighty fortress here is the Porte de Nizy, the gateway at the entrance to the village. Narrow streets lined with beautiful houses lead to the church, an old castle chapel dating from the 14C. From the top of the **tower** (◷*mid-Apr–Sept Sun and public holidays 2–7pm (Jul–Aug daily 3–7pm).* ◷*Oct–mid-Apr.* ✆*04 74 71 21 24. www.oingt.com)* there is a view of the Lyonnais and Beaujolais hills and the Azergues valley.

▶ Carry on along D 96.

In St-Laurent-d'Oingt, note the church with a porch.

▶ Turn right at the junction with D 485.

Ternand★

The town retains some early fortifications, such as the keep and the watchpath, which have a good view over the Tarare hills and the Azergues valley.

▶ Turn back through Les Planches and follow the D 31.

The pass **road★★** over **Col du Saule-d'Oingt** is very picturesque.

▶ At La Maladière turn right.

Jarnioux

The **castle** (☞❧*guided visits early Jul and mid-Aug–Sept, Mon, Wed, Fri 2–6pm, Tue and Thu 9am–noon;* ◷*rest of year, 14 Jul and 15 Aug.* ✆*04 74 03 80 85),* built between the 15C and 17C, has six towers and includes a particularly charming Renaissance section.

▶ D 116 and D 38 back to Villefranche.

ADDRESSES

Monts du Lyonnais★

This attractive mountainous region lying to the south-west of Lyon has a pastoral appearance with chestnut groves and oakwoods. Land in low-lying valleys is given over to market gardening, vineyards and orchards, whereas pastures extend over the higher ground. Traditional rural housing is still very prominent and adds to the charm of the region.

- **Michelin Map:** 327 F6, G5-6.
- **Info:** www.monts-du-lyonnais.fr.
- **Location:** Between St-Étienne and Lyon, above the Parc Naturel Régional du Pilat.
- **Kids:** Birds of prey at the Courzieu Animal Park.
- **Timing:** At least two days.

🚗 DRIVING TOUR

LYON ROUND TRIP
203km/126mi. Allow two days.

▶ Leave Lyon, heading west along the A 6. At the sortie for Tassin-la-Demi-Lune, take the N 7 to L'Arbresle.

L'Arbresle
At the confluence of the Brévenne and the Turdine, this industrial city, which spcialised in silk products, is dominated by the remains of the castle of the Abbots of Savigny, and by the pinnacles crowning the bell-tower (19C) of the church. L'Arbresle is the home town of Barthélemy Thimonnier, inventor of the sewing machine.

▶ Take the D 19 to the SE of L'Arbresle.

Couvent de la Tourette★
The convent of Sainte-Marie de la Tourette was built during the second half of the 1950s and is one of the most significant buildings of the work of Le Corbusier. *Guided visits: Apr–Jun Sun 2pm, 2.45pm; Jul–Aug Mon–Sat 10am, 2.30pm, 4pm, Sun 2.30pm, 4pm; check website for details of guided visits during the rest of the year.* 🕐*24–31 Dec.* 📞*04 72 19 10 90. www.couventdelatourette.fr.*

▶ Return to the D 389 and turn left.

Savigny
This town was built around a Benedictine abbey founded in the 8C.
In the centre of the town a little museum contains a number of sculptures dating from the 12C and 14C, from the abbey.

▶ Leave Savigny by the D 7, continue along this road to cross the D 389.

Musée de la Mine de Saint-Pierre-la-Palud
1 r. du Musée. *Guided visits: Mar–Nov Sat-Sun and public holidays 2–6pm; Jul–Aug additional visits Tue and Thu at 3pm.* ∞€5.50. 📞04 74 70 39 66.
The old mining site of this museum prospered from 1840 to 1972.

▶ Rejoin the D 389 towards St-Étienne. At Ste-Foy-l'Argentière, turn right onto the D 489, then take the D 81 to the left.

👥 Parc Salva Terra à Haute-Rivoire
🕐*Opening times are linked to school holidays: call or check website for details.* 🕐*Nov–Jan.* ∞€15.50 (children €4.50–€13.50). 📞04 74 26 35 92/06 10 65 09 33. www.salva-terra.com.
A journey through the 13C, with a walled city, and a chance to try your hand at fencing or throwing a javelin.

▶ Take the D 637 which leads to the D 389 and turn left onto it; turn right at the D 633 and follow the road to Aveize (where it becomes the D 4).

Aveize

At the entrance to the town, from the D 4, **view★** of Ste-Foy-l'Argentière in the valley of the Brévenne.

▶ Head for St-Symphorien-sur-Coise on the D 4, then turn right at the D 662.

Notre-Dame-de-la-Neylière

In addition to the **chapel** it is possible to visit the **Musées d'Océanie et de Jean-Claude Colin**, home of the Marist Fathers.

Saint-Symphorien-sur-Coise

A Gothic **church** dominates this ancient fortified town. Further on, **Chazelles-sur-Lyon** in the foothills of the Lyonnais area owes its fame to the production of high-quality felt hats, commemorated in the **Musée du Chapeau** (✆*04 77 94 23 29. www.museeduchapeau.com)*.
The village of **St-Galmier** may not be well known, but its product is: although it was only in the early 19C that its naturally sparkling water was marketed, thanks to the enterprising spirit of **Augustin Saturnin Badoit**.

Veauche

Veauche serves largely to manufacture the bottles needed for the water from St-Galmier. The church was originally a small priory dating from 970.

▶ Head in the direction of St-Martin-la-Plaine.

♣♦ Parc Zoologique de St-Martin-la-Plaine

🕐*Apr–Oct 9am–6pm; Nov–Mar 10am–6pm.* 🕐*25 Dec.* ⊛*€15 (child 3–9, €11).* ✆*04 77 75 22 93. www.espace-zoologique.com.*
This park specialises in breeding endangered species. From St Martin the route heads for the medieval market town of **Riverie**, before continuing to St-André-la-Côte, 800m to the north-west of which is a path leading to **Signal de St-André★★** (🏃*45min there and back on foot).* Continue to the relaxing, stone-built village of **Yzeron★**, famed for raising goats and beautiful landscapes. Follow the tortuous road to the **Parc Animalier de Courzieu** ♣♦ (🕐*mid Mar–Aug, 10am–7pm; Sept–mid Nov, Mon–Tue, Thu–Fri noon–6pm, Wed, Sat–Sun and public holidays 10am–6pm.* ⊛*€14.50, child 4–12, €10.50.* ✆*04 74 70 96 10)* where outdoor displays of birds of prey in flight will particularly delight children.

▶ Follow the D 24.

Grézieu-la-Varenne

This history of this town is closely linked to the activities of its laundry. It was here in the 17C that the clothes from religious communities were washed.

▶ Return to Lyon via the D 489.

ADDRESSES

ROANNAIS AND LE FOREZ

The Roannais is a splendid region with a sweeping countryside of lakes, forests and mountains, and with the river Loire lazily meandering through it. At the hub of several more well-known regions, the Roannais is within easy access of major cities (notably Lyon and St-Étienne), as well as towns and villages. The Forez is an ancient province of France, one that roughly equates with the central part of the Loire department. The inhabitants of the region are called Foréziens, and the dialect and language are unique, with subtle influences from the Auvergne. The celebrated Monts du Forez are a chain of mountains separating the valley of the Dore from the plain of Forez.

Highlights

1 The old medieval town of **Villerest** (p371)
2 The mountain village of **St-Germain-Laval** (p373)
3 The granite mountains of the **Forez** area (p377)
4 Winter sports at **Chalmazel** (p379)
5 The fascinating Ecomuseum of **Usson-en-Forez** (p385)

Roanne Excellence

Roanne is one of the most renowned centres in France for the production of industrial textiles, including rayon and other new fibres. Historically, the town was sited at a strategic point at the head of the navigable Loire, but its status declined with the collapse of long-distance trade. But from the 18C onwards, the rejuvenated navigation of the Loire was sympathetic to the export of local products, especially the Beaujolais wine which hitherto had to be transported overland, but also textiles and ceramics. In the 17C and 18C, almost half the population of Roanne was dependent in some way water-borne transportation of goods, including carriers, carpenters, merchants, coopers, boatmen, journeymen, oarsmen and river labourers.

Say Cheese!

The delicious *Fourme de Montbrison* is a cow's-milk cheese fabricated in the Rhône-Alpes and the Auvergne, and takes its name from the village of Montbrison in the Loire. It is one of a number of French cheeses awarded its own AOC (*Appellation d'Origine Contrôlée*), and has a fine blue mould, like Roquefort and the similar Fourme d'Ambert, but Fourme de Montbrison is one of the mildest blue cheeses. The rind is dry, and the cheese itself creamy and firm. Affinage is a minimum of 28 days, but is often more.

Pierre-sur-Haute, Parc Naturel Régional Livradois-Forez

© Christian Guy/hemis.fr

ROANNAIS AND LE FOREZ

0   10 km

A ◄ **MOULINS**

La Pacaudière

Le Crozet

La Bénisson-Dieu

Charlieu

St-Hilaire-sous-Charlieu

N

N 7

D 487

Ambierle

La Croix-du-Sud

La Tâche

D 8

St-Haon-le-Châtel

D 9

Renaison

D 482

D 49

Plateau de la Verrerie

D 47

Roanne

Montagny

D 504

ALLIER

Le Rouchain
Les Grands-Murcins

St-André-d'Apchon

D 51

RHÔNE

Rocher de Rochefort

D 51

Villerest

D 56

Belvédère de Commelle-Vernay

D 51

St-Maurice-sur-Loire

D 18

B⁹ᵉ de Villerest

D 203

N 82

N 7

LOIRE

D 53

D 56

D 38

Aubépin

La Roche

St-Marcel-de-Félines

Urfé

Grézolles

D 24

Pommiers

A 89

LYON

Cervières

D 53

D 89

D 26

735

D 38

Noirétable

D 1089

Belvᵉ de la Sauveté

D 21

St-Germain-Laval

Pouilly-lès-Feurs

La Vallette

Pierre branlante

D 21

L'Hôpital-sous-Rochefort

A 72

D 113

Col de la Loge
1253

St-Laurent-Rochefort

Boën

D 1089

Feurs

D 89

Sail-sous-Couzan

La Bastie-d'Urfé

D 1082

La Chambonie

D 101

Chât. de Couzan

Goutelas

D 37

1390

Chalmazel

D 110

Montverdun

Chambéon

Col du Béal

D 101

Sauvain

Chalain-d'Uzore

D 1089

1634

Monts du Forez

Champdieu

Montrond-les-Bains

Pierre-sur-Haute

Parc

Col des Supeyres
1366

D 44ᵃ

D 101

Essertines-en-Châtelneuf

Montbrison

D 496

naturel   *régional*

D 106

Jasserie du Coq-Noir

Moingt

D 8

Sury-le-Comtal

PUY-DE-DÔME

D 39

D 496

St-Romain-le-Puy

D 996

Livradois-   *Forez*

D 996

St-Anthème

D 5

D 498

D 498

ST-ÉTIENNE

St-Jean-Soleymieux

Marols

D 5

Luriecq

Montarcher

D 14

St-Bonnet-le-Château

Estivareilles

D 3

Usson-en-Forez

D 498

Apinac

D 104

St-Nizier-de-Fornas

D 104

D 109

Rozier-Côtes-d'Aurec

D 498

D 104

Saint-Hilaire-Cusson-la-Valmitte

Saint-Pal-de-Chalencon

A ━━━━━━━━━ B   **LE PUY-EN-VELAY** ►

CLERMONT-FERRAND

Monts du Forez	★★	Recommended
Pommiers	★	Interesting
Roanne		Other sight described
⊏⊐		Departure point for tour
━►		Côte Roannaise
━►		Gorges Roannaises de la Loire
━►		Vallées de l'Onzon et de l'Aix
━►		Via Col du Béal
━►		Via Col des Supeyres
━►		Les Belvédères
━►		Le Haut-Forez

367

Roanne

Rodumna, as the town was called in ancient times, dates to more than a century before the start of the Christian Era. Later, in the 11C, the lords of Roanne built a fortress. The Seignieury of Roanne belonged in turn to the counts of Forez, Jacques Cœur, the dukes of Bourbon and the dukes of Roanne. The inauguration of the Roanne–Digoin canal in 1838 brought intense activity to the port of Roanne, thereby determining the town's industrial vocation.

ROANNE TODAY

Roanne is one of the best-known French textile centres for ready-made garments, hosiery and knitted goods (second in France) and towelling.

Its other economic activities are highly diversified: food processing, metallurgy, armoured tanks, tools, boiler-making, tanning, dyes, paper mills, plastics and tyres. A Michelin tyre production unit has been operating in the north-east of the town since 1974.

The local gastronomy has earned a well-deserved reputation for excellence and the town boasts several fine restaurants, including one of the most famous establishments in France.

SIGHTS

Musée des Beaux-Arts et d'Archéologie Joseph-Déchelette

◐*Daily except Tue 10am–noon, 2–6pm (Sat 10am–6pm, Sun 2–6pm).* ≪€5, *no charge Wed afternoon.* ℘*04 77 23 68 77.* This eclectic museum, housed in an early-18C mansion, was founded by the archaeologist **Joseph Déchelette** (1862–1914), a native of the town. He gathered the rich **archaeological collections** which include many Gallo-Roman artefacts found during the course of excavations in the region. The museum is also known for its fine collections of faience including items of 16C and 17C Italian **majolica**.

> ▶ **Population:** 36 749.
> ⏱ **Michelin Map:** 327: D-3.
> 🛈 **Info:** 8 place Maréchal de Lattre de Tassigny, 42300 Roanne. ℘04 77 71 51 77. www.leroannais.com.
> ▶ **Location:** Roanne lies 85km/52mi north-west of Lyon, accessible by the A 72.
> 🅿 **Parking:** There are a number of car parks in the centre.
> ⊛ **Don't Miss:** You will be delighted by a visit to the Musée des Beaux-Arts.
> ◷ **Timing:** You should allow a full day to explore fully.
> 🚸 **Kids:** Visit to the Parc des Canaux.

Place de-Lattre-de-Tassigny

The site of the old castle (part of its keep still stands) is flanked by the church of St-Étienne with its 15C stained-glass window.

🚸 Muséo'Parc du Marinier

In Briennon. 🔄*Guided tours (45min) Apr–early Jul Sat–Sun 2.15–6pm; early Jul–Aug daily except Mon 2.15–6pm.* ≪€6 *(child 3–12, 3€).* ℘*04 77 60 12 42.*

This park, located along the canal between Roanne and Digoin, has a lot to offer children interested in inland navigation: a real barge turned into a museum and a hands-on system of miniature locks and barges.

Chapelle St-Nicolas-du-Port

The small chapel can be seen near the wharfs of the port. The date on the pediment – 1630 – marks the year the bargemen made a vow to erect a chapel to their patron saint if they were spared the death throes of the plague.

EXCURSIONS
Montagny
14km/8.7mi E along D 504.

▶ On leaving Montagny, follow the signpost indicating "La Roseraie".

Roseraie Dorieux
🕐 *Jul–mid-Sept, with free access to the rose garden; rest of the year, enquire for opening hours.* 📞 *04 77 66 11 46. www.dorieux.fr.*
This colourful and fragrant rose garden and nursery is freely accessible from July to September.

Plateau de la Verrerie
Leave Roanne W along D 9 to Renaison then follow D 47 to La Grand'Borne and turn right onto D 478 which leads to La Tourbière. To get back, follow D 39 from Col de la Rivière then D 9 to Roanne or D 4 if you fancy a detour via Briennon.
🚶 The solitary road climbs through the forest before reaching the Plateau de la Verrerie which offers a pleasant ramble and a view of the Roanne plain.

Le Crozet
25km/15.5km NW on N 7.
Leave the car at the entrance to Le Crozet.
The flower-decked houses of this small medieval town are spread out along the foothills of the Madeleine mountains. You enter the old main square by the Grand-Porte, flanked by two round towers that are truncated and partly concealed by houses.

Maison du Connétable
Fine front with wooden panels. The adjoining house with walled-in arcades used to be a cobbler's workshop (15C).

Maison Dauphin
A former meat market, a restored late-15C house with Renaissance windows.

Maison Papon★
Enter the courtyard to appreciate the Renaissance façade made with enamelled ceramics and with mullioned windows.

A Popular Marina
Traffic on the canal from Roanne to Digoin and in the port of Roanne, which was important until 1945, declined rapidly from 1970 onwards and came to a halt in 1992. This has been offset by an increase in pleasure boating with the opening of locks on Sundays during the summer months. **Barge trips** *(several options of trip are offered from or to Roanne aboard the barge* L'Infatigable; *groups take priority; Marins d'Eau Douce, Port de plaisance de Briennon;* 📞*04 77 69 92 92)* are also organised on the canal.

Tour de Guet
The 12C keep standing near the 19C church has lost its machicolated crown.

Museum of Popular Arts and Traditions
🕐 *Jun–Sept daily 3–7pm.* ✎€3.
📞 *04 77 63 00 87. www.leroannais.com.*
A peasant's interior has been carefully reconstructed in this 15C residence, alongside an old-fashioned smithy and a clog-maker's workshop.

🚗 DRIVING TOURS

CÔTE ROANNAISE★
Roanne to Ambierle. 100km/62mi.
Allow half a day.

A line of vineyard-covered slopes running north–south, known as the "Côte", dominates the Roanne basin to the west. Contrasting with the harshness of the Madeleine mountains, the Côte is gentle and colourful, with rectangular houses, often roughcast with green shutters and red-tiled double pitched roofs, reddish soil and vineyards that produce reputed AOC red wines, as well as rosés and whites.

▶ Leave Roanne on the D 9 W and turn left onto D 51 to St-André-d'Apchon.

St-André-d'Apchon

At the centre of the town, in a secluded setting, stands a 16C château built for the Marshal of St-André.

▶ From the War Memorial, walk up the street with the Lion d'Or Hotel on the corner, then along the covered passageway 30m on the right, next to a butcher's shop.

The church in Flamboyant Gothic style is decorated with 16C stained-glass windows.

▶ Continue along D 51 to Arcon.

The road twisting uphill above St-André offers vistas of the Roanne plain.

▶ Leave Arcon to the N, to Les Grands-Murcins and its arboretum.

Les Grands-Murcins

The arboretum, created in 1936–37 at the heart of a national forest, is particularly rich in coniferous trees, including Himalayan weeping pines.

▶ Return to Arcon and head S to La Croix-Trévingt. Turn right onto D 51 towards St-Priest.

Rocher de Rochefort★

The Rochefort Rock is equipped with a viewing table: **views** of the Roanne plain, the Beaujolais and Lyonnais hills.

▶ Return to La Croix-Trévingt. Turn left onto D 51 and left again onto D 41 along the Rouchain valley to the dam.

Barrage du Rouchain

Duplicating the Tache dam to supply Roanne with drinking water, this dam (1977), made of rockfill, is equipped with a spillway on the River Rouchain, and occupies three valleys.

Barrage de la Tache

This dam was built between 1888 and 1892. It is a gravity dam, that is, the sheer mass of the dam resists the pressure of the water.

Renaison

This is the economic heart of the Côte Roannaise. Its neo-Gothic church houses a Romantic organ by John Abbey.

▶ Turn back then follow D 9 to La Croix-du-Sud.

On the way, a **look-out rock★** on the left offers an attractive view of the Tache reservoir. The road up to the pass looks over the Madeleine mountain range.

La Croix-du-Sud

This pass is a major intersection on the rise separating the Madeleine mountain range from the Côte, and the valley of the Teyssonne from that of the Tache.

St-Haon-le-Châtel★

The **fortified village★** has preserved its medieval appearance and some of its ramparts. The restored **church** (12C–17C) is a modest building, with typical furniture from the Forez region.

▶ Take D 8 N to Ambierle.

Ambierle★

This pretty town, exposed to the morning sun, is set amid vineyards that yield a pleasant rosé wine. There is an old Cluniac priory in the upper part of the village.
The **Musée Alice-Taverne** (*Feb–Nov 10am–noon, 2–6pm.* €5. *04 77 65 60 99; www.museealicetaverne.fr*) focuses on traditional home life in the region – games, costumes, local superstitions – and has recreations of various interiors (workshop, inn etc).

▶ Take D 8 and D 9 back to Roanne.

On the left is an attractive view of the large round tower of the **Château de Boisy** (*not open to the public*). This castle (14C–16C) belonged successively to the Couzan family, Jacques Cœur and the Gouffier family, and occupies an important position in the history of Roanne.

GORGES ROANNAISES DE LA LOIRE★
Round trip of 139km/87mi.
Allow half a day.

▶ Leave Roanne to the S along avenue de la Libération. Turn right by the station onto D 43 and then right again onto D 56 to Commelle-Vernay viewpoint (signposted).

Construction of the Villerest dam upstream of Roanne created a new "Loire Lake", 33km/20.5mi long, which attracts sailing enthusiasts in the summer.

Belvédère de Commelle-Vernay★

The **view** encompasses Roanne and its outskirts and the Vernay bridge to the north, the town and dam of Villerest and the modern installations of the Villerest paper mills to the west.
A small **tourist train** 🚶‍♂️🚶 (*reservations required: Jul–Aug, daily at 3pm, 4.30pm and 6pm; Apr–Jun and Sept Sat–Sun and public holidays at 3pm and 4.30pm.* ♿. €6 (child 3–12, €3.50). *04 77 68 58 12*) offers a 7km/4.3mi ride along the shores of Lake Villerest.

Barrage de Villerest

Designed to combat low water levels and floods on the Loire, this is a solid concrete arch gravity dam with a crown length of 469m. Its curved shape reinforces its stability. The variable-level reservoir is 30km/19mi long and has an average width of 250m.

▶ Cross over the dam to Villerest.

Villerest

The old **medieval town★** is a pleasant place to visit; there are many houses with corbelled construction or timber-framed walls, and the remains of ramparts. The 13C **Porte de Bise** is the starting point for a tour on foot; points of particular interest are highlighted on information boards.
During the summer, crafts are sold from the traditional street stalls.

Musée de l'Heure et du Feu

Jun and 1st 2 wks of Sept Sat–Sun and public holidays 2–6pm; Jul–Aug daily except Tue 2–6pm. €5.
04 77 69 66 66.
www.museedelheureetdufeuvillerest.fr.
This unusual museum is divided into two parts; the **section on Fire★** traces the history of the creation and the upkeep of domestic fire since Antiquity and across different countries.

Leave to the W and head for St-Maurice-sur-Loire.

St-Maurice-sur-Loire★

This town occupies a **site★** overlooking the river. The old houses cling to a spur crowned by the ruins of a medieval castle.

Drive towards Bully, down the hill towards the Loire and over the bridge at Presle. Turn right onto D 56 and along the east bank of the river.

La-Roche
Château de la Roche

Guided visits. Mid-Apr–Jun and 1–mid-Sept daily except Mon 2–6pm; Jul–Aug daily 10am–noon, 2–7pm; mid-Sept–late Oct Sat–Sun 2–6pm. €5.50. *℘04 77 64 97 68. www.lechateaudelaroche.fr.*
This medieval manor presents the history of the Gorges de la Loire area in a refined 17C decor.

Shortly after the Chessieux viaduct the road meets N 82 near Balbigny; turn left towards Neulise. After 6km/4mi turn right onto D 5.

St-Marcel-de-Félines

This peaceful village facing the Forez mountains has a 12C fortified house altered in the 16C into a **château** (guided visits only: Easter–Oct Sun and public holidays. *℘04 77 63 54 98. www. chateaudesaintmarceldefelines.fr*). A bridge over the old moat leads to an inner courtyard of Italian inspiration. Inside, the decoration of the reception rooms is unified by the 17C wall and ceiling **paintings★**.

Rejoin N 82 and continue to Neulise; turn right onto D 38. At Croizet turn right, cross the River Gand and take the path to the right.

Château de l'Aubépin

Daily except Tue and Wed 10am–noon, 2–5pm.
This lovely old château (16C–18C), flanked by corner pavilions is topped

with a watch-turret set back from an avant-corps decorated with masks.

Return to Roanne on N 82.

ADDRESSES

⌂STAY

Grand Hôtel – *18 cours de la République (opposite the train station). ℘04 77 71 48 82. www.grand-hotel-roanne.fr. 31 rooms.* This well-maintained hotel dates from the early 20C.

Chambre d'Hôte Domaine de Champfleury – *Le Bourg, 42155 Lentigny (8km/4.8mi SW of Roanne via D 53). ℘04 77 63 31 43. Closed mid-Nov–mid-Mar. Reservations recommended in winter. 3 rooms.* A 19C bourgeois house surrounded by century-old trees in a handsome park. Perfect for a break.

♈/EAT

Le Central – *58 cours de la République (opposite the train station). ℘04 77 67 72 72. www.troisgros.fr. Closed Sun–Mon. Reservations requested.* In the sober but elegant setting of a 1920s hotel, this bistro-grocery belongs to the famous Troisgros family. Simple, light cuisine in seasonal menus.

Le Marcassin – *Rte de St-Alban-les-Eaux, 42153 Riorges (3km/1.8mi W of Roanne via D 31). ℘04 77 71 30 18. Closed Sun evening, Fri evening and all day Sat.* After visiting the Maille museum in Riorges, you might try this family restaurant offering modern fare from fixed-price menus and à la carte.

Troisgros – *728 Route de Villerest, 42155 Ouches. ℘04 77 71 66 97. www.troisgros.com. Closed Jan; Mon and Tue. Reservations essential.* With three Michelin stars, this is a veritable institution that sets the standard for French gastronomy. The Troisgros family receives its guests in a setting where modernism, quality, luxury and sobriety intermingle in perfect elegance.

© Cyrille Gibot/age fotostock

Pommiers Priory

St-Germain-Laval

This pretty mountain village is watered by the River Aix. The surrounding hills form a delightful natural setting, where the vegetation switches from golden brown to deep green, depending on the season.

▸ **Population:** 1 685.
⚲ **Michelin Map:** 327: D-5.
🛈 **Info:** 28 r. R.-Lugnier, 42260 St-Germain-Laval. ✆04 77 65 52 96.
▶ **Location:** The quickest approach is on the A 72, which passes 5km/3mi away. The town is 33km/20mi S of Roanne
◔ **Timing:** Allow 1–2 hours.

SIGHTS

The 18C **Église de la Madeleine**, crowned by a saucer dome, is used to host temporary art exhibitions in summer. The **parish church** at the far end of the village houses a stone statue of Moses (1065), on the right as you enter, and a small polychrome wooden Pietà in an alcove above the font.

On place de la Mairie, the **museum** (💬 *guided tours Mon–Fri 8.30am–noon, 2–5pm.* ✍ *no charge.* ✆*04 77 65 41 30)* installed in the former château displays tapestries, furniture and miniature objects from France and Oriental countries.

Note the two splendid Aubusson tapestries in the village hall. Place de la Mairie is lined with old houses, one of which has wooden panels: it is the birthplace of the explorer **Greyolon du Luth**.

EXCURSIONS

Chapelle Notre-Dame-de-Laval
1.3km/1mi via the D 38, W of St-Germain.
The Gothic chapel appears like a vision of grace at the edge of the Aix, which is spanned by a fine medieval bridge. The shrine attracted many pilgrims during the Middle Ages to the 17C, and was visited by Louis XI, returning from le Puy.

Pommiers★
3km/2mi to the E of St-Germain via D 21.
At the edge of Forez and Roanne, this lovely hilltop village will enchant you. The site was occupied from Roman times to the early Christian era, but mainly developed in the 9C around a Benedictine monastery attached to Nantua. In the 14C, as surrounding villages were becoming increasingly concerned about security, Pommiers saw the construction of strong defensive walls.
Church – The church is today a Benedictine parish. This 11C–12C building strikes you immediately with its austerity. In

places the vault is pierced with small holes, a technique used to improve the acoustics. The north apse has retained an interesting series of wall paintings from the 16C.

In the 16C, the prior built a façade before the main building where he held his court sessions. In the 17C–18C, the priory was completely rebuilt with a a majestic cloister overlooking the Romanesque church.

🚗 DRIVING TOURS

VALLÉE DE L'ONZON AND VALLÉE DE L'AIX
90km/56mi. Allow 5h.

▶ Leave St-Germain to the S on D 1. In Boën (see Monts du FOREZ), take D 21 on the right to L'Hôpital-sous-Rochefort.

L'Hôpital-sous-Rochefort
This village was fortified in the 15C and has retained two of its doorways. The 12C church has a narrow nave housing a superb **Virgin with Child★★** in polychrome wood dating from the late 15C. This life-size statue is a paragon of vivacity and grace.

▶ Leave L'Hôpital-sous-Rochefort to the W on D 21, heading for St-Didier-sous-Rochefort. This road gives onto the lane leading to Rochefort (old hill village). Rejoin D 21 and follow directions for St-Didier-sous-Rochefort.

St-Laurent-Rochefort
Note the fine 15C cross next to the church.

▶ Take D 21 to St-Didier-sur-Rochefort.

Between St-Didier-sous-Rochefort and St-Julien-la-Vêtre, a huge megalith, **La Pierre Branlante**, stands on the edge of the road (*D 73*).

▶ N 89 leads to Noirétable.

Noirétable
This pleasant mountain resort has retained its traditional economic activities (timber industry, cutlery). The 15C Flamboyant Gothic church has a remarkable porch, which used to be larger and served as a covered market. All the 17C statues carved out of black Volvic stone were brought here from the Hermitage monastery during the Revolution.

▶ Exit Noirétable W and take the D 24 N towards Cervières.

Cervières
Park the car on the esplanade at the entrance to the village.

The squat **Gothic church** has diagonal ribs resting on sculpted brackets depicting masks. Note the fine Renaissance house opposite the church. Walk through the vaulted passageway beneath the house and skirt the former fortifications on the left to a new granite arch; a steep street leads back to the church. The market ground beyond the town hall commands a lovely view of the surrounding countryside.

La Maison des Grenadières
Opposite the church. 🕐*Apr–Oct Thu–Sun 2.30–6pm, also Wed in Jul–Aug.* ⊜€5 (under 12s: no charge). ☏04 77 24 98 71. www.grenadieres.com. Housed in a picturesque Renaissance residence, this museum is devoted to gold-thread embroidery and the skilful workers who decorate civil and military ceremonial clothes (tools, drawings, costumes).

▶ Continue to les Salles on the D 24, then towards Champoly on D 53. Leaving Champoly (E), take the narrow signposted road leading to the site of Château d'Urfé.

Château d'Urfé
🚶 *45min on foot there and back.*
This 12C–15C stronghold was once home to the Urfé family, before they moved to Bastie-d'Urfé (📖*see Château de la BASTIE-d'URFÉ*). The castle is currently undergoing restoration. The **viewing**

table installed at the top of the keep affords a superb vista of the Monts du Lyonnais and the foothills of the Monts d'Auvergne.

▶ Drive back towards Champoly to take the D 24. After St-Marcel-d'Urfé, turn right onto the D 1.

Grézolles
Village dominated by the slate bell-tower of its 16C chapel.

▶ Go to St-Martin-la-Sauveté and, S of the village, turn left onto D 20, a path leading to the belvedere.

Belvédère de la Sauveté★
🚶 *15min on foot there and back.*
The path takes you to the foot of the watertower and a statue of the Virgin Mary, offering a sweeping **panorama** of the area.

▶ Return to St-Martin and take D 38 (on the right) to St-Germain-Laval.

Feurs

Owing to its strategic location in the Loire valley, this town was a thriving commercial centre back in the days of the Gauls. Trade remains an important activity today, as illustrated by the lively street markets. In fact, the name of the town is believed to be derived from the Latin word *forum*, symbolising a privileged place for communication and exchange.

SIGHTS
Musée de Feurs
3 rue Victor-de-Laprade. ⏱*Tue–Fri, 2–6pm; and one Sun of each month, 2–6pm (check website).* ⏱*1 Jan, 1 May, 25 Dec and public holidays.* ⊛€3.20. 🖉*04 77 26 24 48. www.feurs.org.*
The museum is devoted to Gaulish and Gallo-Roman archaeology as well as popular arts and crafts. The park is a delightful setting for the reconstructed villa displaying marble and stone exhibits, along with a pretty mosaic discovered in Feurs.

Église Notre-Dame
Flamboyant Gothic church with three naves. The heavily ornate bell-tower bearing a 15C clock was remodelled in

▶ **Population:** 8 134.
▶ **Michelin Map:** 327 E-5.
▶ **Info:** Place Drivet, 42110 Feurs. 🖉04 77 26 05 27. www.forez-est.com.
▶ **Location:** Between Roanne (41km/25.5mi to the N) and St-Étienne (50km/31mi to the S). At the centre of a plain, on the right bank of the Loire
▶ **Timing:** Allow 2 hours.

the 19C. Part of the 12C chancel is still standing. On the right, there is a Virgin with Child by J-M Bonnassieux. The wainscoting and stalls (18C) were taken from the priory in Pommiers.

EXCURSIONS
Plaine du Forez
As soon as you stray from the main roads and explore the more remote spots of the countryside, the Forez basin will delight you with its charming sights. The volcanic spurs dotted around the landscape are often the site of religious sanctuaries, namely St-Romain-le-Puy and Montverdun. Down below, in the

© Cyrille Gibot/age fotostock

plain, *bocage* meadows alternate with ponds and old farmhouses.

Pouilly-lès-Feurs

7km/4.3mi N of Feurs on N 82 and D 58.
Former fortified village where the unusual Romanesque church was once attached to a Cluniac priory. West of Pouilly, a small Renaissance pavilion has kept its sculpted pediment and an upstairs loggia.

La Valette

7km/4.3mi NE of Feurs on D 113. 2km/1.2mi E of Salvizinet. After the bridge spanning the Charpassonne, turn right onto the tarmacked lane that starts by the inn.
This modest country church nestled on a slope of the Charpassonne valley is a small Romanesque building with a single nave and a raised chancel. The somewhat crude furniture is peculiar to the Forez region.

Chambéon

Not far from St-Étienne airport and the River Loire, the **Écopole du Forez** *(6km/3.7mi S of Feurs via N 89 and D 107; signposted from Chambéon and Magneux-Haute-Rive; ⚹ guided tours 1.30–6pm (7pm in Jul–Aug); Nov–Mar Wed and Sat–Sun; Apr–Oct daily. ◷1 Jan and 24–25 and 31 Dec. €3. ℘04 77 27 86 40; www.ecopoleduforez.fr)* is a preserved park that has become an important centre for studying migratory birds and aquatic fauna. Nature

trails totalling 12km/7.5mi run along the banks of the Loire, enlightening visitors to the area's natural resources and riverside vegetation.

Château de la Bastie-d'Urfé★

19km N on D 8 and N 89. ⚹ Guided tours. ◷Apr–Sept 10am–7pm; Oct–Nov 10am–1pm, 2–5pm; Dec–Mar Sat–Sun 10am–1pm, 2–5pm. ◷1 Jan and 25 Dec. €5. ℘04 77 97 54 68.
In the 15C, the rough Lords of Urfé built a manor on the banks of the River Lignon. The family's rise to power was rapid. During the Italian Wars Claude d'Urfé spent several years in Rome as an ambassador, and on his return to France he converted Bastie Manor into a Renaissance château. **Honoré d'Urfé** (1567–1625), grandson of the ambassador and author of the first French novel, *L'Astrée*, grew up in these refined surroundings. The original manor (14C–15C) was enlarged in the 16C by Claude d'Urfé, who brought artists from Italy to help with the decoration.

Montverdun

18km/11.3mi W via the N 89 and D 42.
The "Peak" Montverdun is a geological curiosity rising between the Lignon valley and the Mont d'Uzore. It is a volcanic eminence, and during its history has been topped by a fortified priory below which the village developed. The church dates from the 12–15C, its severity enhanced by the use of black basalt in its construction.

Monts du Forez★★

The granite mountains in the Forez area, part of the **Parc Naturel Régional Livradois-Forez**, form a range some 45km/28mi long. Along the edge are parallel offshoots separating the picturesque valleys, some of which run down to the Dore whereas others head for the Loire. The eastern slopes stand high above the Forez plain; the slopes to the west, the only part of the range in the Auvergne, drop sharply down to the Dore basin and include some attractive beauty spots and magnificent views.

A BIT OF GEOGRAPHY

On the heights – Up to altitudes of 1 000m, the mountains are covered with fields (rye, potatoes) and meadows. The abundant supply of pure water rushing down all the slopes of the mountains is used to irrigate meadows where it is cool even in the height of the summer, and to turn the waterwheels in the mills, sawmills, and the last papermill in the Lagat valley; it also supplies the cutlery works in Thiers (*see p223*). At altitudes above 1 300m lie the summer pastures, called "Hautes-Chaumes", of the Forez.

🚗 DRIVING TOURS

1 VIA COL DE BÉAL★
84km/52mi. Allow one day.

Boën

Boën (pronounced "Bowen"), situated high above the left bank of the Lignon, specialises in metal-working and mechanical engineering. Boën was the birthplace of Father Terray (1715–78), Controller-General of Finances at the end of Louis XV's reign.

The unpopular measures he was forced to take in order to re-establish a balanced budget following the excessive spending of the royal court brought him the nickname "Emptier of Purses".

- ♿ **Michelin Map:** 327: B-5/6, C-5/6, D-5/6.
- ▶ **Location:** The Monts du Forez are part of the Parc Naturel Régional Livradois-Forez, so a good place to start is at the Maison du Parc in St-Gervais-sous-Meymont.
- 🅿 **Parking:** At the Maison du Parc.
- 👁 **Don't miss:** The panorama from the col du Bréal and from the balcon du Forez.
- 🕐 **Timing:** Allow at least a day-and-a-half to explore the region fully.

Musée des Vignerons du Forez★

♿🕐*Mar–Nov daily except Mon 2–6pm.* 🕐*Dec–Feb and 1 May.* ⊗€4.50. 📞*04 77 24 08 12.* *www.chateaumuseeboen.fr.*

The elegant 18C Château Chabert houses a Wine-making Museum established with a real concern for authenticity, both in its reconstructions of traditional interiors and in its technical presentations of wine-growing.

▶ Leave Boën on the D 1089. 2.5km/1.5mi on from Boën, turn left onto D 6 to Sail-sous-Couzan.

Sail-sous-Couzan

This peaceful village was the venue for the 1998 World Cup final between France and Brazil, won by the host country.

▶ Turn right off D 6 onto a very steep tarmacked road leading to the castle ruins.

Château de Couzan★

Park at the foot of the ruins; 15min on foot there and back. The ruins of this 11C fortress stand on a rocky promontory squeezed between the narrow valleys of the Lignon and Chagon. What remains of the curtain walls and towers

MONTS DU FOREZ

still suggests the strength of the Lords of Couzan, the oldest barons of the Forez. There is a good view of the castle walls from a rocky promontory behind the fort, and **panoramic views★** over the countryside from the ruins, which are being restored.

▷ Return to Sail-sous-Couzan and turn left onto D 97 towards St-Just-en-Bas.

Summer Pastures

The Monts du Forez feature a wide range of scenery, much of it covered by dark pine forests. Once above the tree line, the mountain summits, often shrouded in mist or cloud, are vast bleak stretches of moorland – the Hautes-Chaumes. This somewhat eerie landscape can look more like a moonscape in certain lights. The vast bare wastes are broken only by granite rocks, deep peat bogs or clumps of broom. Nonetheless, man – or rather, woman – has attempted to scratch a living from this unwelcoming environment. A matriarchal society evolved in the mountain farmsteads (*jasseries*) during the summer months; while the menfolk were down in the valley dealing with the harvesting, the women and children would be in charge of looking after the livestock in the summer pastures up in the mountains, where they would also make the famous local Fourme cheese and gather medicinal plants.

This harsh way of life gradually died out, and there are now no more working *jasseries*. However, some of them have been converted into open-air museums which inform visitors about the daily work and traditions of these "Amazons of the Mountains".

The road runs along the crest of the hill up above the upper Lignon valley overshadowed by Pierre sur Haute before reaching Jeansagnière. Continue on to the pass, **Col de la Loge**, where a curtain of pine trees opens onto a clearing carpeted with grass. Before La Chamba, the forest gives way to more pastoral scenery and the route, skirting a succession of corries filled with fine pastures, provides several outstanding views of the Dore basin and the Livradois area.

▶ Continue 2km/1.2mi beyond La Chamba and turn left towards Le Brugeron.

La Chambonie
A village nestling in a pastoral corrie.

▶ Immediately beyond a sawmill turn right onto D 37.

After a long climb up through the forest, there is a view over the Dômes mountain range. Beyond another stretch of road through the forest lie alpine pastures dotted with farmsteads (*jasseries*).

Col du Béal★
From this pass there is a wide **panoramic view** over the mountains of the Auvergne and the Lyonnais area. The pass forms a threshold between the two sides of the Forez mountains.

Pierre-sur-Haute★★
🚶 *2h30 on foot there and back; recommended in clear weather. Climb directly up to the summit across the alpine pastures and along the crest of the mountain, or take the chair-lift (*🕐*mid-Dec–Mar.* 𝒫*04 77 24 85 09. www.loire-chalmazel.fr).*
Pierre-sur-Haute, the highest peak in the Forez range (1 634m), is a dome-shaped granite mountain topped by military radar installations. The windswept moorland that carpets its slopes is gashed here and there by huge rockfalls. Small farmsteads dot the hillsides. From the summit to the right of the military installations, the **panorama** stretches right across the Forez, the

mountains in the Lyonnais area and Beaujolais, the Limagne, the Dômes and Dore mountain ranges, Cantal and the mountains in Velay and Vivarais.

▶ About 7km/4mi from Col du Béal, a road cuts off to the right; it leads to the ski slopes and the Pierre-sur-Haute cable-car.

Chalmazel✳
This mountain village, which clings to the hillside in the Lignon ravine, is a bustling place during the winter sports season. It is dominated by the old 13C **Château des Talaru-Marcilly**, a huge bastion flanked by corner towers which still has its parapet walkway. The chapel is decorated with 16C frescoes.

▶ Take D 101 to Sauvain.

Sauvain
The most notable feature of this village is the **Musée de la Fourme et des Traditions** (🕐🔓 *Jul–Aug, daily 10am–12.30pm, 2.30–6.30pm; May–Jun and Sept–Oct Sun and public holidays 2.30–6.30pm.* 👝€4. 𝒫*04 77 76 30 04. www.museedelafourme.com),* an old 17C farmhouse that belonged to the inventor **Louis Lépine**, who founded a famous competition for the most innovative device or technique.

▶ Continue on D 101 in the direction of Montbrison. Soon after crossing the Lignon at Pont-de-Pierre, turn left onto D 110, for Col de la Pelletière. Drive to Trelins via La Bruyère and Prélion (D 20) and take D 20A on the right.

Château de Goutelas
The château stands on a terrace high above the Forez plain; it is a late-16C residence which has been restored and is now used to host courses and seminars. The courtyard is open to visitors and it is possible to walk round the exterior.

▶ Turn back and take D 8 back to Boën.

② VIA COL DES SUPEYRES★
70km/44mi. Allow half a day.

Montbrison – *see MONTBRISON.*

▷ Leave Montbrison to the W along D 101 which climbs up the bare, rocky Vizery ravine. A short detour leads to the village of Essertines.

Essertines-en-Châtelneuf
From the village, with its small Gothic church with Flamboyant Gothic decoration, there is a view over the Forez plain from which emerges the rocky pinnacle of St-Romain-le-Puy.

▷ Rejoin D 101 and continue up the valley before turning left on D 44A. In Roche turn left onto D 44 and continue via D 113 to Col de Baracuchet.

From the road there are several glimpses of the Forez plain. The road continues to climb through valleys filled with farms and fields and dominated by wooded peaks. Near the pass, the trees become gnarled and twisted until eventually they give way to a vast clearing from which there is a view of the Ance valley *(left)* and, opposite the road, the crest of the Forez mountains. The road climbs to Col des Supeyres through alpine pastures, carpeted with heather and dotted with farmsteads.

Col des Supeyres
See AMBERT, Le Val Legat.
The route down from the pass towards St-Anthème passes the group of farmsteads known as **Les Jasseries du Grand Genévrier**, one of which is open to the public.

Jasserie du Coq Noir
See AMBERT, Le Val Legat.

▷ As the road runs down to St-Anthème there are views of the volcanic cones in the Velay area – Meygal, Lizieux, Mézenc and Gerbier-de-Jonc.

St-Anthème
The red-roofed village nestles in the depths of the Ance valley.

▷ Follow D 496 from St-Anthème to return to Montbrison.

ADDRESSES

⌂STAY
Les Genets – *63880 Le Brugeron.* ℰ*04 73 72 60 36. Closed end Nov–mid-Feb. 10 rooms.* Guests can unwind in a pretty park hidden behind this stone house in the heart of the village. The spotless bedrooms sport modern furnishings. Dining room where simplicity is the rule and traditional fare is served.

⊕/EAT
Auberge du Mazet – *42990 St-Georges-en-Couzan.* ℰ*04 77 24 80 95. Closed Sun evening.* If you've a taste for homemade delicatessen, you're bound to enjoy this farm-inn on the village heights. A convivial atmosphere reigns in the vast dining room where appetising farm-raised ham and pork dishes are served.

Auberge des Granges – *Les Granges, 42920 Chalmazel (5km/3mi SW of Chalmazel dir. Le Col du Béal).* ℰ*04 77 24 80 62. Closed Nov. Reservations recommended evenings.* This long chalet is a very convenient place to take it easy and re-energise after a hard day's skiing. The generous meals give healthy farm produce pride of place.

Gaudon – *63880 Le Brugeron (6km/3.6mi S of La Chambonie via D 101 and D 37).* ℰ*04 73 72 60 46. Closed Sun evening, Mon evening and Tue from mid-Sept–May.* In the bosom of the Monts du Forez, at the entrance of the village of Brugeron, this traditional house built in 1929 is a handy stopover.

Quai de l'Astrée along the Vizézy, Montbrison

Montbrison

The town is built around a volcanic mound and dominated by the 18C dome of the old Convent of the Visitation (today the law courts), and by the imposing belfry of its Gothic church, Notre-Dame-d'Espérance, which was founded in 1226 (restored 1970). The town was fortified following the attacks by the English army at the start of the Hundred Years War. During the Religious Wars, Montbrison was captured and pillaged by the Protestant forces in 1562, with the town's garrison thrown from the ramparts.

TOWN CENTRE

Opposite the church stands **La Diana** (◐*Wed and Sat 9am–noon, 2–5pm; Tue and Fri 2–5pm.* ℘*04 77 96 01 10. www. ladiana.com*), built in 1296 on the occasion of the marriage of the Count of Forez, Jean I, later served as a meeting place for priests; in Latin *Decanatus*, hence Diana.

The **Musée d'Allard** (◐*daily except Tue 2–6pm.* ◐*1 Jan and 25 Dec;* ◉*€4.* ℘*04 77 96 39 15*) contains a fine collection of minerals and stuffed birds. The town also features several splendid **hôtels particuliers**, notably on rue St-Pierre and rue Puy-de-la-Bâtie.

▶ **Population:** 16 339.
🜨 **Michelin Map:** 327: D-6.
🈁 **Info:** 1 Place Eugène Beaune, 42600 Montbrison. ℘04 77 96 08 69. www.loireforez.com.
◑ **Location:** 44km/27mi NW of St-Étienne, via the A 72.
◕ **Timing:** Allow half a day.

Old Houses

The town features several splendid **hôtels particuliers**, notably on rue St-Pierre (*Nos. 1, 7, 10, 11, 13 and 17*) and rue Puy-de-la-Bâtie (*Nos. 5, 9, 11, 14, 18, 19 and 20*).

EXCURSIONS
Moingt
3km/1.8mi. Leave Montbrison S on D 8.
This former Roman city has retained its medieval appearance and narrow winding streets.

Église de Champdieu
4.5km/2.8mi N on D 8.
Champdieu lies on the edge of the Forez plain and hills. It has a remarkable Romanesque **church** which was built for a Benedictine priory. In the 14C the church and priory buildings were

heavily fortified. The most surprising feature of this church is the extent of its system of defence. High arcading forms machicolations on the south side and the south arm of the transept. A similar system runs along the walls of the priory built in a quadrangle, with the church forming the south side. The church has two bell-towers, the more outstanding being the one over the transept, which dates from the Romanesque period. The second bell-tower, by the west front, dates from the 15C. Note, to the left of the west front's portal, the capital depicting a mermaid with two tails.

St-Romain-le-Puy
7km/4.3mi S of Montbrison.
The church of the former priory of St-Romain-le-Puy which, at the end of the 10C, belonged to the abbey of St-Martin-d'Ainay in Lyon rises on a volcanic peak emerging from the Forez plain, dominating a St-Gobain glass-works at the foot of the peak. Water is bottled from a mineral spring north-east of the village near D 8.

Église du Prieuré★
Jun–Sept daily except Tue 2–7pm; Apr–May Sat–Sun and public Holidays 2–6pm. 04 77 76 92 10.
From the plateau in front of the church, the panorama encompasses a vast circle of mountains: those of Forez to the west, the Monts d'Uzore to the north, the Tarare mountains and those of the Lyonnais from the north-east to the south-east.

Chalain-d'Uzore
7km/4.3mi N, off the D 8.
The 14C–16C **château** (*guided visits Jul–Aug on Fri at 5pm; €6. 04 77 97 13 12)* is notable for its former courtroom, converted into a village hall during the Renaissance (imposing fireplace) and for its gallery with sculpted doors.

Montrond-les-Bains
14km/8.7mi NE on D 496.
This spa resort, recommended for obesity and diabetes, has kept its **château** (*Jul–Aug daily except Tue 2.30–7pm; Apr–May Sat–Sun and public holidays 2.30–7pm; Jun and Sept Wed, Fri–Sun and public holidays 2.30–7pm. Oct–Mar. €4. 04 77 94 64 74. www.montrond-les-bains.com),* whose ruins stand proudly on top of a hill near the River Loire. Although the castle was damaged by fire in the 18C, the outer walls have survived. Beyond the vast porch, decorated with fluted pilasters and capitals, stand the remains of the 14C and 15C building where the lord of the castle lived with his family.

Sury-le-Comtal
13km/8mi SE on D 8.
This small town's 17C **château** features lavish **ornamentation★** consisting of sculpted ceilings and intricate wainscoting. There are also several fine fireplaces with carved panels.

ADDRESSES

STAY
Marytel – *95 rte de Lyon, 42600 Savigneux (1.5km/1mi E of Montbrison via D 496). 04 77 58 72 00. www.hotel-marytel.com. 33 rooms.* This modern edifice by the side of the road is protected from road noise by efficient double-glazed windows. The basic, functional rooms are neat and tidy. Above all, a convenient stopover.

EAT
Le Vieux Logis – *4 rte de Lyon, 42210 Montrond-les-Bains. 04 77 54 42 71. Closed Sun evening and all day Mon.* In the heart of this little spa town, a family restaurant in a modern building offering simple, generous cuisine. The "main dish and dessert" lunch menu and the basic fixed-price menu are reasonably priced. Terrace in summer.

St-Bonnet-le-Château★

St Bonnet is a village of considerable character, with its Gothic church and medieval streets climbing energetically towards the collegiate church. Today, St Bonnet is a small but active industrial centre, especially renowned for its *boules*.

OLD TOWN

On the road to the church stand two **Renaissance houses★★** at the entrance to the streets opening up onto place du Cdt-Marey. Further on, there are other houses dating from the 15C–16C which are particularly noteworthy. The **Chemin des Murailles★** follows the course of the ancient fortifications to reach the 14C **porte de la Châtelaine**, the name given to Notre-Dame-du-Bon-Secours. On the outbreak of the plague in the 18C, the Castel-Bonisontins was symbolically entrusted with the protection of the town by means of an oratory lodged in the gateway itself, which today lacks the original statue.

▶ Almost at the end of the road, cross the garden to the college.

▶ **Population:** 1 637.
- **Michelin Map:** 327 D-7.
- **Info:** 7 pl. de la République, 42380 St-Bonnet-le-Château. ℘04 77 50 52 48. www.pays-st-bonnet-le-chateau.fr.
- **Location:** 30km/19mi W of St-Étienne and 32km/20mi S of Montbrison.
- **Kids:** The Ecomuseum of Forez.
- **Timing:** Allow half a day to explore the Old Town, and another to tackle the Driving Tour.

From the terrace to the north of the Collegiale church, the **view★** extends across the Forez plain from which rises the prominent hill of St-Romain-le-Puy. The Gothic **collégiale**, from the beginning of the 15C, has two steeples.

The **crypt** situated at the heart of the building is covered with 15C murals, depicting scenes from the New Testament.

Murals in the crypt, Collégiale

© Mauritius/Photononstop

The **Chapelle de la Charité** dates from the 17C and is especially interesting for its decoration and its furniture.

🚗 DRIVING TOUR

LES BELVÉDÈRES
35km/22mi. Allow 1h30.

▷ Leave St-Bonnet on the D 498, to the N.

Luriecq
The simple **church** is a Gothic building with a Renaissance porch. Inside a **house** near the church is a modest collection of old artefacts from the Forez region.

▷ Do a U-turn and take the D 5 to the right.

Marols
The church was fortified in the 14C. Of the two towers, the slimmer is a true defensive structure.

▷ Follow the D 5.

Saint-Jean-Soleymieux
The **church** is interesting for its 12C crypt. The village is located near an ancient thoroughfare. Linking the future Lyon with Bordeaux, the great *Via Agrippa* has origins in antiquity.

▷ Follow the D 96, then the D 44.

Montarcher
From the terrace of the little **church** (12C–15C) there is a fine **view★** over Mont Pilat, the Mézenc, the Yssingeaux region and the mountains of Margeride. The water of Montarcher was first marketed in 1999.

▷ The D 14 and the D 498 lead to back to St-Bonnet.

LE HAUT-FOREZ
50km/31mi. Allow about 2h.

▷ Leave St-Bonnet on the D 3 to the SE, and take the D 109 to the right.

Saint-Nizier-de-Fornas
The lovely **church** retains significant Romanesque elements. Outwardly, the rectangular tower, adorned with pinnacles and large gargoyles, gives the southern aspect a distinctive silhouette. Inside there is a beautiful set of carved keystones.

▷ Continue on the D 109.

Rozier-Côtes-d'Aurec
The **church**, built in the 11C and 12C, is that of a Cluniac priory; the two-storey bell-tower has been rebuilt in its original form. The tympanum features a sculpted group representing the Adoration of the Magi and, in the long faces that are protrayed, shows a particular Spanish influence. Inside, the nave is supported with arches. Worthy of note is the apse decorated with a beautiful arch with fluted pilasters, characteristic of the Romanesque churches of the region.

▷ Turn round and take the D 104, to the left, then again turn left onto the D 42.

Saint-Hilaire-Cusson-la-Valmitte
Partially **Romanesque church** rebuilt in the 15C and 19C. Note the small ambulatory behind the arches of the original apse. Two statues in polychrome wood date from the 15C.

▷ Turn round, and immediately turn left onto the road that lead to the D 104, which you take to the left.

Apinac
The church, dating from the 19C, is noted for its colourful stained glass windows.

Moulin de Vignal

Guided visits (1h): Jul–Aug, 2.30–6.30pm; Mar–Jun and Sept–Oct, Sat–Sun and public holidays, 2.30-6.30pm. €4.50. 04 77 50 80 23. www.moulindevignal.fr.

Saved by a local association, this set of **18C mill buildings**, which includes four mills, has been carefully restored. Thanks to the restoration of the mill race, the wheels are turning once more and producing freshly ground flour, as well as canola oil. The mechanisms of the mill are ingenious and a pleasure to discover.

▶ Come back towards Apinac and turn left to take, the D 443 to the right. Continue on the D 24.

Saint-Pal-de-Chalencon

A fortified town of which several ancient gateways remain.

▶ The D 241 and D 91 lead to Usson.

Usson-en-Forez

The town, once fortified, is dominated by the 16C spire of its steeple. The nave of the church dates from the 15C.

Écomusée du Forez★

Quartier St-Joseph. *Daily 2–6pm.* *1 Jan, 25 Dec.* €4 (child 8–16, €1.50). 04 77 50 61 40. www.ecomusee-usson-en-forez.fr.

Created in 1993 from a private donation, the museum makes good use of former convent buildings, restoring and reviving the lifestyles, customs and crafts of the region. Step-by-step, from the comb to the washing machine and clothes made with lace, family life in a village house is carefully replicated.

The barn still houses the tools. Upstairs the focus of interest embraces the disappearing trades of clog-makers, carpenters, wheelwrights and the great tradition of lace-making. In the adjoining building, you can listen to stories passed down during the long winter evenings, and discover a collection of gleaming carriages. A pretty cottage garden, recreated from plans of Usson, completes the tour.

At the southerly exit from the town, 300m to the left of the D 498, the Romanesque apse of the **Chapelle de Notre-Dame-de-Chambriac** houses an ancient statue of the Virgin Mary.

▶ Take the D 498 towards Estivareilles.

Estivareilles

In August 1944, the regional *maquis* (the French Resistance force) hindered the withdrawal of German troops. As a result, the area saw fierce fighting during the liberation of Forez. The **Museum of 20C History** (*r. du Couvent.* *2–6pm: mid-Apr–Oct; rest of year daily except Sat and Mon.* *Sat and Mon, mid Nov–Mar, 1 Jan, 25 Dec.* 04 77 50 29 20) describes the various stages of the campaign, and the upheavals of this turbulent century.

▶ The D 498 leads to St-Bonnet.

ADDRESSES

🛏️STAY

Hotel-Restaurant le Béfranc – *7 rte d'Augel, 42380 St-Bonnet-le-Château.* 04 77 50 54 54. www.hotel-lebefranc.com. *Closed 1wk in Oct, Feb, Sun evening and Mon except July-Aug. 17 rooms.* Clean and comfortable; choice of traditional dishes in the restaurant.

Chambre d'Hôte la Campagnarde – *Rte d'Estivareilles, 42380 St-Nizier-de-Fornas.* 04 77 50 71 19. *5 rooms.* No frills, but a good atmosphere in this vast farm.

🍴EAT

La Calèche – *2 pl. du Cdt-Marey, 42380 St-Bonnet-le-Château.* 04 77 50 15 58. www.restaurantlacaleche.fr. *Closed Mon evening of Oct-Mar; Tue, Sun evening, Tue evening, and Wed.* The restaurant is furnished in the style of the 17C, and has three brightly coloured dining rooms. The chef produces choice dishes from personalised menus.

The influence of adjacent departments is particularly evident throughout this region. To the west lies the Loire and the Haute-Loire, closely linked with their rivers; to the north-east lies Isère, while to the south-east is the Ardèche. There is no doubting the importance of St Étienne and its many services and facilities to the region, but within the greater area lie many parochial cultures and loyalties. Consuming a huge swathe of land is the Parc Naturel Régional du Pilat, which alone embraces no less than 50 towns and villages, while preserving a beautiful countryside of beech and fir forests, pastureland, orchards and vineyards.

Highlights

1 Wandering the Old Town of **St Étienne** (p389)

2 20C art in the **Museum of Modern Art** in St Étienne (p392)

3 Gateway to the gorges of the Loire, **Monistrol-sur-Loire** (p396)

4 Nature trails through the **Pilat Regional Park** (p398)

5 The spectacular panorama from **Crêt de l'Œillon** (p399)

More About Le Pilat

Spread across a rural area in excess of 700sq km/270sq mi, Pilat Regional Park is especially rich and diverse in its natural and cultural heritage. Located in proximity to major urban centres, with a combined population of 50 000, it is a popular weekend getaway. Le Pilat's mountains, rising to 1 432m – higher than Ben Nevis, Britain's highest peak – lie where continental and oceanic influences collide. The result is an amazing and wide-ranging wealth of natural resources, and this is reflected in internal sub-divisions where a uniqueness of identity and culture linger on: Pilat du Gier, Piemont-Rhodanien, the valley of Déôme, les Crêts and Haut Pilat. The convergence of so many influences has made this a particularly rich area, and one that will gladden the hearts of botanists in particular, and nature lovers in general.

Regional Parks

Regional parks are different from national parks in their concept and purpose. They are inhabited areas selected for development of the local economy through specific activities (the creation of cooperatives, promotion of crafts), the preservation of the natural and cultural heritage (museums, architecture) and the appreciation of the distinctive character of the region.

Rhône valley viewed from St-Sabin Chapel, Parc Naturel Régional du Pilat

© Bertrand Rieger/hemis.fr

ST-ÉTIENNE AND LE PILAT

CRÊT DE L'ŒILLON	★★★	Highly recommended
Le Pilat	★★	Recommended
St-Étienne	★	Interesting
Le Bessat		Other sight described
		Departure point for tour

⇧ The Belvédères
⇧ Grangent Dam
⇧ St-Étienne to Condrieu
⇧ Vallée de l'Ance

0   5 km

387

St-Étienne★

St-Étienne lies in the Furan depression, close to the Massif du Pilat, Grangent lake and the Forez plain. The town is located at the centre of a coal basin which supplied over 500 million tonnes of coal until the mines were closed in the 1980s. Since then St-Étienne has adopted a new image: the façades of its buildings have been cleaned, its gardens and parks renovated. The busiest area lies along a north–south axis: place Jean-Jaurès to place de l'Hôtel-de-Ville. The 15C and 16C main church of St-Étienne, popularly known as the "Grand'Église", remains dear to the hearts of the local people. The hometown of the composer Jules Émile Frédéric Massenet (1842–1912), has an intellectual and artistic life which extends over the whole of Forez.

- ▶ **Population:** 174 985.
- ⚲ **Michelin Map:** 327: F-7 – Local map see Le PILAT.
- ℹ **Info:** 16 av. de la Libération. 42000 St-Étienne. ℘04 77 49 39 00. www.saint-etiennetourisme.com.
- ▶ **Location:** Close to the Massif du Pilat, south-west of Lyon.
- 🅿 **Parking:** The centre of St Etienne is a difficult place to drive and park, but there are parking areas at stages along the tram line.
- 👁 **Don't Miss:** The Museum of Modern Art and the Old Town.
- 🕐 **Timing:** You will need at least a whole day, maybe more.
- 👪 **Kids:** Go star-gazing at the Planetarium.

A BIT OF HISTORY

In the 12C, St-Étienne was a village on the banks of the Furan, bypassed by major communication routes. Local coal, and the enterprising spirit of the inhabitants, brought about an extraordinary development; the population shot up from 3 700 in 1515 to 45 000 in 1826, then 146 000 in 1901, while the industrial estate spread west, east and north.

Armeville – In 1296, the people of St-Étienne started working coal quarries for domestic needs, then to feed the forges which produced the first knives, followed by cutting and thrusting weapons, crossbows and finally, firearms – St-Étienne was quick to make this change in direction in the manufacture of arms. In 1570 the Arms Manufacturers' Lodge consisted of 40 trades. Mass production was already being practised. In 1746 the Royal Arms Factory was founded. During the Revolution this activity was to earn the town the name of Armeville.

GETTING AROUND

🚋 **TRAMWAY**

The tramway is the best way to get around town. You can buy a one-day pass and rent an audio tape to serve as a guide to help you discover St-Étienne. Information at the Tourist Office, ℘0810 342 342. www.reseau-stas.fr.

From St-Étienne to Andrézieux – In May 1827, the first French railway, built to plans by Beaunier, was inaugurated: it ran between St-Étienne and Andrézieux over a distance of 21km/13mi and was used to transport coal; the wagons were pulled by horses. This ancestor of modern means of transport, perfected in 1829 thanks to the tube boiler developed by Marc Seguin, led to a revolution in transport and a boom in industry.

The town that made everything – To the ribbon industry, imported from Italy, was added shirred fabric at the end of the 19C.

To escape the Depression, the region of St-Étienne had already specialised in quality steels, tools, hunting guns, bicycles and automobile parts.

Industrial redeployment – The mines saw their coal production decrease regularly between 1960 and 1980. This gradual closing was planned, allowing the metallurgical and textile industries time to restructure themselves; they now operate in conjunction with diversified activities such as precision mechanics, electronics, food processing, plastics and cardboard manufacturing.

 WALKING TOUR

OLD TOWN★

Start out from place du Peuple, which used to be the market square in the Middle Ages. On the corner of rue Mercière a 16C tower rises above an arcade; a timber-framed house stands opposite. Cross the avenue used by the trams to reach rue Denis-Escoffier, which marks the entrance to the old Outre-Furan district. At the junction of rue des Martyrs-de-Vingré is an unusual mid-18C house, adorned with a statue and eaves with four rows of tiles and large, visible beams, typical of the urban architecture to be found in Forez. On the left at no. 3 rue Georges-Dupré a massive façade includes imposing lintels in one piece. Turn back and follow rue des Martyrs-de-Vingré; nos 19 and 30 are examples of 18C houses incorporating weaving lofts or workshops.

▶ After reaching place Neuve, turn right onto rue Nautin, which leads to rue Michelet.

Rue Michelet

This artery, pierced along the north-south axis parallel to rue Gambetta, contains some examples of innovative architecture from the 1930s (Nos. 34, 36, 42 and in particular No. 44, an imposing building in reinforced concrete).

▶ Continue along rue Nautin and rejoin rue Gambetta.

Musée du Vieux St-Étienne

2.30–6pm. Check website for days; a temporary timetable is currently in operation. €3. ✆04 77 54 38 77. www.vieux-saint-etienne.com.
An 18C toll-marker from the old Outre-Furan district signals the entrance to the Hôtel de Villeneuve (18C). The City Museum inside is arranged on the first floor, in a series of rooms with fine moulded and coffered ceilings. The first charter mentioning St-Étienne (1258) is on display, together with maps and engravings illustrating the expansion of the city.

Place Boivin

This marks the site of the former 15C north rampart. Walk down rue Émile-Loubet; there is a fine façade adorned with five caryatids at no. 12, the 16C **Maison de "Marcellin-Allard"**.
Return to the square, one corner of which is occupied by the Grand'Église. To the right of the church, at the beginning of rue de la Ville, note the two handsome façades (15C and 16C): No 5, known as the **Maison François I** is decorated with five Renaissance medallions.

Grand' Église

The church of St-Étienne is the town's only example of Gothic architecture; its parish is the oldest in the city.

▶ On leaving the church, turn right and rejoin rue Ste-Catherine, leading down to rue du Général-Foy. Turn left towards place Jean-Jaurès.

Place de l'Hôtel-de-Ville, the main town square, and place Jean-Jaurès form the hub of city life in St-Étienne.

Place Jean-Jaurès

In the summer this square is a delight with its pretty bandstand and plane trees offering shade.

ST-ÉTIENNE

WHERE TO STAY

Bonnefond (Chambre d'hôte
  du domaine de)...................... ①
Carnot (Hôtel)............................ ②
Cèdres Bleus (Les)..................... ③
Midi (Hôtel du)......................... ④
Mme Grimand
  (Chambre d'hôte)................... ⑤

WHERE TO EAT

Corne d'Aurochs......................... ①
Evohé... ②
Insens (L')................................... ③
Presqu'Île (La)............................ ④

Musée d'Art et d'Industrie

© Christian Guy/hemis.fr

▶ Rue Gérentet leads to place Dorian, then rue Alsace-Lorraine will take you back to place du Peuple.

ADDITIONAL SIGHTS
Musée d'Art Moderne★★
4.5km/3mi from the city centre. Leave St-Étienne N via rue Bergson towards La Terrasse and follow signs to the Musée d'Art Moderne.
🅑🕐*Daily except Tue 10am–6pm.*
🕐*1 Jan, 1 May, 14 Jul, 15 Aug, 1 Nov, 25 Dec.* ✍€6 (guided visits €7); no charge 1st Sun of month. 𝒫04 77 79 52 52. www.mam-st-etienne.fr.

This vast art gallery located in the town of St-Priest-en-Jarez was designed by the architect D Guichard; it is devoted to 20C art, of which it provides an interesting retrospective owing to its policy of continual acquisition.

The sober, functional building looks like an industrial structure from the outside. Its walls, covered with black ceramic panels, are a reminder of the important role of coal.

Musée d'Art et d'Industrie★★
🅑🕐*Daily except Tue 10am–6pm.*
🕐*1 Jan, 1 May, 14 Jul, 15 Aug, 1 Nov and 25 Dec.* ✍€6 (guided visits €7).
𝒫04 77 49 73 00. www.musee-art-industrie.saint-etienne.fr.

This Art and Industry Museum located in the former Palais des Arts is a real reposi-

tory of local and regional know-how relating to tool-making and the evolution of equipment and machinery from the 16C up to the present day.

Puits Couriot, Musée de la Mine★
🕐*Jul–Aug daily 9.30am–12.30pm, 2–6.30pm (Mon 2–6.30pm); rest of year 9am–12.30pm, 2–6pm.* 🕐*1 Jan, 1 May, 14 Jul, 15 Aug, 1 Nov, 25 Dec.* ✍€6 (guided visits €7). 𝒫04 77 43 83 23. www.musee-mine.saint-etienne.fr.

The visit begins in the **Salle des Pendus★**, a vast locker room where, as space was limited, miners' clothes were hung from the ceiling to dry. The adjoining shower is evidence of the collective life they led. Visitors are taken to the lower galleries in the cages used by miners for accessing the mines, bringing up coal and sometimes the injured.

Site of the old Manufacture des Armes et Cycles de St-Étienne
Cours Fauriel.
Laid out under the Second Empire to be, together with Avenue de la Libération, one of the showcases of the industrial expansion in St-Étienne, cours Fauriel, was occupied by the buildings of the Arms Factory, which were built by Léon Lamaizière in 1893, and which were in use until 1985.

👤👤 L'Astronef, Planetarium★

*Espace Fauriel, 28 rue P.-et-
D.-Ponchardier.* 🔵🕐*Call or check website for times of shows and visits.* 🕐*Sept,
1 Jan, 1 May, 25 Dec.* ◉€10.30 (under
25, €8.20). 📞04 77 33 43 01. www.
planetarium-st-etienne.fr.

Crowned by a hemispherical dome, this
planetarium is fitted with highly sophisticated equipment which enhances the
appeal of its shows about the universe.
Most impressive is the astronomical
simulator, able to calculate and project
onto the screen the movements of the
planets and of some 3 000 stars.

EXCURSIONS
Firminy

11km/6.8mi. Leave S on the D 88.
Firminy lies in the Ondaine valley, halfway between the mountains and the
St-Étienne plain. The town is known for
its urban appearance stamped by the
famous architect **Le Corbusier** – housing complex, arts centre, stadium and
St-Peter's Church (unfinished) – making
it the second **"Le Corbusier site"**★ in
the world after Chandigarh in India.

👤👤 Écomusée des Bruneaux

🕐*Apr–early Nov daily except Mon
2–6pm; early Nov–Mar Wed–Sat
1.30–5.30pm, Sun and public holidays
2–6pm.* 🕐*1 Jan, 1 May, 1 Nov, 25 Dec.*
◉*Château €4 (children €2.50); château
and mine: €6 (child 6–15, €4.50).*
📞04 77 89 38 46.
www.chateaudesbruneaux.fr.

The castle features a nailer's workshop
and a collection of toys. The outbuildings house a reconstructed mine showing the types of support structures.

St-Chamond

7km/4.3mi W on the N 88.
This is the industrial cradle of the area,
bringing together a wide variety of factories (iron, steel, plastics, dyes, mechanics, synthetics etc.). It is also the birthplace of former racing driver Alain Prost,
affectionately nicknamed "Professor of
the Track", who became famous by winning the Formula 1 World Championship
four times (1985, 1986, 1989, 1993).

🚗 DRIVING TOURS

THE BELVEDERES

▶ Leave St-Étienne to the S along
Cours Fauriel (D 8). N 82 makes its way
along the Furet ravine, dotted with
schist outcrops.

Col du Grand-Bois
Charming forest site.

▶ Turn around and drive to Planfoy.
There, turn left and rejoin Guizay.

View from Guizay★★
From the foot of the Sacré-Cœur statue
there is a fine, extensive view over the
town. The village of **Rochetaillée** can
be seen, to the far right, perched on its
crest. To the left unfolds the Ondaine
corridor: Le Chambon-Feugerolles,
Firminy and the hills of Forez.

▶ The D 88 takes you back to
St-Étienne.

GRANGENT DAM★★
80km/50mi. Allow 4h.

▶ Leave St-Étienne SW on the D 3
then continue on the D 25.

Along the road, the Pertuiset bridge
marks the transition between the city
and the wild landscapes of the Loire.

Château de Cornillon
At St-Paul-en-Cornillon.
The castle, perched on a spur overlooking the Loire, was once the seat of the
most important baronies of Forez.

▶ Continue on D 108 for 10km/6mi.

The road runs along an escarpment
offering **views**★★ over the meanders
of the Loire.

Chambles
This site is one of the most beautiful
gorges of the Loire. Next to the squat
church, the tower of the old castle
stands on the edge of a cliff overlooking

Château de Cornillon

© Gérard Labriet/Photononstop

the meandering Grangent, characteristic of the defensive system of castles dating from the Middle Ages.

▶ 2km/1mi after Chambles, take the road on the right towards the Château d'Essalois.

Château d'Essalois

The silhouette of the castle stands above the gorge; from this beautiful sentinel there extends a fine **view★★** of the lake and the island of Grangent.

Close by the castle is a Celtic *oppidum* – a form of settlement – reflecting the strategic importance of the location. On the other side the plateau of the Danse (prehistoric site) and St-Victor-sur-Loire provide alternative points of view over the gorge. The history of these places is the stuff of legend, war and religious life, shrouding them, even today, in an air of mystery.

▶ Return to Chambles by the same route, then take the D 108 and the D 3².

Île de Grangent

This man-made lake has isolated a rocky spine bearing the remains of the 12C Château de Grangent.

▶ Take the D 108 heading north.

St-Just-St-Rambert

Located at the mouth of the gorges of the Loire, on the southern plains

of Forez, St-Rambert is a former Gallo-Roman town, clinging to the side of a hill. St-Just is the modern part of the town, extending along the right bank.

Musée des Civilisations

Pl. Madeleine-Rousseau. ◷*Wed–Sun 2–6pm.* ◷*1 Jan, 1 May and 24–25 and 31 Dec.* ⊚⊛€4. ℘*04 77 52 03 11. www.stjust-strambert.fr.*

Local history is represented by objects of art relating to St Rambert and the past life of the town. Other rooms house collections from other countries, in particular a collection of African art and Oceania: bronzes from Benin and an Egyptian mask.

▶ Take the D 8 towards St-Étienne, then turn onto the D 3 towards Roche-la-Molière where you rejoin the D 3² which leads to St-Victor-sur-Loire.

Plateau de la Danse

Leave the car in the car park and follow the path signposted "Point de Vue" that disappears into the woods.

🚶 This region, steeped in local history and legends, has a rocky belvedere commanding a lovely **view★** of Grangent dam and island, St-Victor promontory, Essalois Château, and the medieval tower in Chambles.

▶ Return to the car and drive to St-Victor.

St-Victor-sur-Loire

This pretty village adorned with roses overlooks the artificial lake formed by the Loire upstream of Grangent.

The **sailing base** is a popular meeting-place in summer and there are facilities for many other sports and leisure activities. The open-air theatre and the **castle** (www.chateau-saint-victor.com) sporting its 11C towers are perched on top of the hill.

ADDRESSES

🛏 STAY

☞ **Hôtel Carnot** – *11 bd Jules-Janin.* *℘04 77 74 27 16. www.hotel-lecarnot. fr. 24 rooms.* This hotel near the Carnot train station has a steady flow of regular customers who appreciate the warm reception and reasonable prices.

☞ **Chambre d'Hôte du Domaine de Bonnefond** – *42660 St-Romain-les-Atheux.* *℘06 71 10 57 04. www.chambres-hotes-equitation-pilat.fr. 3 rooms.* This former farmhouse is situated in beautiful countryside. The rooms are tastefully decorated. Heated indoor pool.

☞ **Chambre d'Hôte Mme Grimand** – *Pracoin – 42230 St-Victor-sur-Loire.* *℘04 77 90 37 95. www.chambre-hotes-loire.com. 3 rooms.* Close to the gorges of the Loire and of the medieval village of St-Victor, this house has three harmonious and comfortable rooms.

☞☞ **Hôtel du Midi** – *19 bd. Pasteur.* *℘04 77 57 32 55. www.hotelmidi.fr. 33 rooms.* Two buildings linked by a cosy lounge with an original fireplace. The rooms are a bit small, but practical and soundproofed.

☞☞☞ **Les Cèdres Bleus** – *Rte de Bas-en-Basset, 43110 Aurec-sur-Loire.* *℘04 77 35 48 48. www.lescedresbleus.com. Closed Jan. 15 rooms. Restaurant☞☞☞ (closed Sun evening, Mon and Tue lunches).* Between the gorges of the Loire and the Grangent lake, in a park, are three wooden chalets.

🍴 EAT

☞ **La Presqu'Île** – *Rte du Port, 42230 St-Victor-sur-Loire.* *℘04 77 53 70 08. Closed evenings.* Located just outside the medieval village with a beautiful view of the gorges of the Loire and the peninsula of the Chatelet.

☞ **Insens** – *10, rue de Lodi.* *℘04 77 32 34 34. www.insens-restaurant.fr. Closed Tue and Sat.* Following the modern trend this restaurant 'Bistronomique' echoes the fashions of Paris, and serves modern, inventive cuisine that won't break the bank.

☞☞ **Corne d'Aurochs** – *18 r. Michel-Servet.* *℘04 77 32 27 27. Closed all day Sat–Sun.* Just a short walk from the *hôtel de ville*, here's a bistro serving cuisine of the Lyon tavern genre.

☞☞ **Evohé** – *10 pl. Villebœuf.* *℘04 77 32 70 22. Closed Mon evening, Sat lunch, and all day Sun.* Opposite a green square, near the Maison de la Culture; the walls are decorated with colourful paintings (some for sale), and the table arrangement preserves privacy.

THEATRE AND ENTERTAINMENT

Comédie de St-Étienne, Centre Dramatique National – *7 av. du Prés.-Émile-Loubet.* *℘04 77 25 14 14. www. lacomedie.fr. Tickets: Mon–Fri 1–7pm. Closed Aug, Christmas and public holidays.* This centre was founded in 1947 in order to initiate and promote drama outside of the capital. Today it orchestrates a permanent troupe of actors, a stage set workshop and a costumes atelier, as well as four different performance halls.

Opéra Théâtre de St-Étienne – *Allée Shakespeare, Jardin des Plantes, BP 237.* *℘04 77 47 83 47. www.operatheatrede-saintetienne.fr. Tickets: Mon–Fri 2–7pm. Closed mid-Jul–Aug.* The focal point of cultural animation in St-Etienne offering theatre, ballet and operetta.

Le Triomphe – *4 sq. Violette.* *℘07 83 97 63 60 (reservations) Tue–Sun 2–8pm. Closed Jul–Aug.* This café-theatre in a converted cinema cultivates in its shows the spirit, the culture, the accents and the language of the region.

Nouvel Espace Culturel – *9 r. Claudius-Cottier, 42270 St-Priest-en-Jarez.* *℘04 77 74 41 81. Tickets: Mon–Fri 10am–4.30pm. Closed Aug and weekends.* The Nouvel Espace Culturel was created in 1991 in a suburb close to Saint-Étienne. Many professional and amateur theatre troupes from all over France appear here performing new works or repertory pieces.

Monistrol- sur-Loire

The town has a surprisingly Mediterranean feel about it, both in its appearance and its climate. Fortunately, the development of the city has spared this ancient town with its medieval streets.

THE OLD QUARTER
Château des Evêques

⏱*Check website for exhibition and openign dates.* ℰ*04 71 61 63 66. www.monistrol-lesamisduchateau.org.* An avenue of lime trees leads to the large round towers of the old Bishop's Palace (14C–18C), which now houses the tourist office and hosts temporary exhibitions.

▶ Follow path round château on right.

From the church, take rue du Commerce then the first street on the right. Take a stroll along the network of narrow alleyways and travel back in time, from the Middle Ages to the 17C (Classical façades of the Couvent des Ursulines and Couvent des Capucins).

EXCURSIONS
St-Didier-en-Velay

11km/7mi to the E via the D 12.
A small town in the heart of the Semène valley with an old quarter, Romanesque church and 19C corn exchange.

Pont-Salomon

9km/5½mi N via the N 88.
Nestled in the heart of the Semène valley, this factory-village began in the 19C. The **Musée de la Faulx★** is located in one of the original buildings, where time seems to stand still (⏱*visits can be arranged through the tourist office* ℰ*04 77 35 42 65, or direct with the museum.* ๛€4. ℰ*04 77 35 87 07. www.museedelafaulx.fr).*

Ste-Sigolène

9km/5.5mi SE via the D 44.
Four hundred years of weaving, 50 years of manufacturing plastics and a major

- ▶ **Population:** 9 266.
- ⌖ **Michelin Map:** 331: H-2.
- ℹ **Info:** 14 Faubourg Carnot, 43120 Monistrol-sur-Loire. ℰ04 71 66 03 14. www.tourisme-marches duvelayrochebaron.fr.
- ▶ **Location:** 45km/28mi north-east of Le Puy-en-Velay, and 30km/19mi south-west of St-Étienne.
- 🅿 **Parking:** Limited parking in the town centre.
- ⏱ **Timing:** Relax over a coffee and spend a few hours here.

industrial conversion is proof, if it were needed, of the determination and flexibility of the town's people.
The **Musée de la Fabrique** (⏱*3–6pm.* ๛€4. ℰ*04 71 75 01 55),* run by a team of former weavers, tells the story.

Château de Valprivas

In Valprivas, 16km/10mi W. ⏱*Call for details.* ℰ*04 71 66 73 52. www.chateaudevalprivas.com.*
In the court of honour, the round tower features an unusual spiral staircase entirely sculpted in oak and a porch framed by caryatids and crowned by a coat of arms.

🚗 DRIVING TOUR

VALLÉE DE L'ANCE

46km/29mi. Allow half a day.

▶ Leave Monistrol on D 12, heading for Bas-en-Basset.

Château de Rochebaron

in Bas-en-Basset (7km/4mi W): 330m above place des Marronniers, take the path running to the left of the rampart.

The ruins of this medieval castle (11C–13C), perched on a spur overlooking the Loire, are preceded by three rows of protective walls. The road follows the charming Ance valley and, after crossing Vert, develops into a **corniche★**. There are lovely views of the Loire basin, the Andrable valley and the Monts du Velay.

▷ In Tiranges, turn left onto D 24.

As you are descending towards the River Ance, the Tour de Chalencon looms into sight, perched on its promontory.

▷ Continue along D 24 until you reach the junction with D 9. Drive up D 9, then take D 29 on the right. Drive through St-André-de-Chalencon and take the road running along the cemetery. After 2km/1mi, park the car and continue on foot (15min there and back).

Château de Chalencon –
♿*See Gorges de la LOIRE.*

▷ Rejoin D 46 towards Beauzac.

Beauzac

The small 12C–17C **church** here has a Flamboyant portal and an elegant three-storey belfry; a Romanesque crypt lies under the apse. A few houses in the village, built within the old ramparts pierced by two gates, have unusual wooden galleries under the roof which rest on huge corbels.

▷ Return to Monistrol via Pont de Lignon on D 461 and then N 88.

Le Pilat★★

The influence of the Mediterranean to the east and the Atlantic to the west makes this massif something of a watershed, particularly at Chaubouret Pass; it also acts as a watertower for the St-Étienne region. The coolness of its fir plantations, swift streams and high pastures contrasts with the industrial aspect of the Ondaine, Janon and Gier valleys. Formation of the massif goes back to the Hercynian fold: it was then a high mountain with its folds lying in a south-west–north-east direction. During the Secondary Era, erosion reduced it to a plateau, sloping down towards the present-day Rhône valley; the plateau was then covered with water leaving several layers of sediment. During the Tertiary Era, the water withdrew. The Alpine fold then caused subsidence of the Rhône valley and tilting of the massif. Le Pilat, having been "rejuvenated", rose to an altitude of 1 500m while the rivers – the Gier

♿ **Michelin Map:**
327: F-7 to G-8.

ℹ **Info:** Maison du Tourisme du Pilat, Moulin de Virieu 42410 Pélussin.
℘04 74 87 52 00.
www.pilat-tourisme.fr.

▷ **Location:** The Massif du Pilat lies to the east of St-Étienne, between the Loire basin and the Rhône valley.

👁 **Don't Miss:** The panorama of the valley from the Crêt de l'Œillon.

🕐 **Timing:** Allow a whole day to explore; more if you can.

in the north and the Limony in the south – slid to the foot of the faults. During the Quaternary Era, erosion took its toll once again.

A BIT OF GEOGRAPHY

Grassy heights – Crêt de la Perdrix at 1 432m and Crêt de l'Œillon at 1 370m bristle with strange piles of granite blocks called **chirats**, resulting from complete erosion of the summits.

Many rivers rise near the summits and flow rapidly down towards the Gier, the Rhône or the Loire along steep-sided valleys. The Gier itself, close to its source, crosses a *chirat* at the **Saut du Gier** falls.

PARC NATUREL RÉGIONAL DU PILAT

Created in 1974, the park contains about 50 towns and villages in the Rhône and Loire *départements*. The countryside is diverse: forests of beech and fir at high altitude, pastureland on the plateaux, orchards and vineyards along the banks of the Rhône. Committed to preserving nature and the environment, Pilat Park promotes rural, craft, tourist and cultural activities.

🏛🎿 Maison du Parc – Moulin de Virieu à Pélussin

🛈*Reservation centre and tourist office, Moulin de Virieu, 42410 Pélussin. ℘04 74 87 52 00. www.parc-naturel-pilat.fr.*
The park's main information centre also organises exhibitions, special activities and walks. To facilitate an introduction to flora and fauna within the regional park there are 500km/310mi of marked footpaths (brown and white stripes), including sections of GR7 and GR42 (Grande Randonnée long-distance footpaths, marked with red and white stripes), three nature trails and eight special themed trails, each identified by a number.

The **Jean-Jacques Rousseau trail**, from Condrieu to La Jasserie is a reminder that the philosopher and writer came to Mont Pilat in 1769 for botanical reasons; the **flora trail** takes the rambler from the almost Mediterranean vegetation of the Malleval region to the sub-alpine formation of Perdrix ridge, from prickly pear to mountain tobacco. The **ornithological trail**, between St-Pierre-de-Bœuf and St-Sabin Chapel features up to 90 registered species of birds (particularly from mid-May–mid-June). To promote traditional activities and revive near-forgotten crafts, the park

has opened the **Maison de la Béate et de l'Allier à Marlhes** (🕐*Jul–Sept Sun and public holidays, 2–6.30pm. ℘04 77 51 24 70)* in Marlhes, the **Maison de la Passementerie** (🕐*early May–early Oct, Sun 2.30–6.30pm. ℘04 77 39 93 38. www.maison-passementerie.info)* in Jonzieux and the **Maison des Tresses et Lacets** (👁*Guided visits: Mar–Nov Wed–Sun 2.30pm and 4pm. ♿. ⊗€5. ℘04 77 20 91 06; www.tressesetlacets.com)* in La Terrasse-sur-Dorlay.

Tourist and sporting facilities include the St-Pierre-de-Bœuf Leisure Park which has an artificial river for canoeing and kayaking; the canoe base at Terrasse-sur-Dorlay; downhill skiing resorts at La Jasserie and Graix, and cross-country ski clubs at Le Bessat, Burdignes, St-Régis-du-Coin and St-Genest-Malifaux. Other sites are suitable for climbing, hang-gliding, cycling and orienteering.

Mountain-biking facilities are being developed, with numerous waymarked tracks categorised by degree of difficulty.

Festivals: Apple Day on 11 November at Pélussin, the Farm Produce Fair in Bourg-Argental in June, the Wine Fair in Chavanay (second weekend in December) and the Cheese and Wine Fair in Condrieu (1 May) provide an introduction to local produce.

Bourg-Argental

This small busy town lying at the foot of the Pilat massif has specialised in local craft and industrial activities.
The church, rebuilt in the Romanesque style in the 19C, presents a sculpted doorway (12C).

🚗 DRIVING TOUR

ST-ÉTIENNE TO CONDRIEU
89km/56mi. About 6hrs, not including St-Étienne.

▷ Leave St-Étienne on D 8 SE.

View from Crêt de l'Œillon

Rochetaillée

This is a small village perched on a narrow rocky channel between two ravines, below the ruins of a feudal castle.

Gouffre d'Enfer★★

🚶 *1h on foot there and back.*
To the right of the inn, Auberge de la Cascade, a path follows the bed of the old torrent to the foot of the dam.
The site is impressive: the heavily gouged walls of rock come together to form a dark, narrow gully, dramatically named "Chasm of Hell".
The dam was built in 1866 to supply water to St-Étienne; steps lead up to the top of it.

▶ To get back to the car, turn left and follow the path on the right running past the Maison des Ponts et Chaussées.

Beyond Rochetaillée, there are attractive views (right) over the dams of Gouffre d'Enfer and Pas-du-Riot.

Le Bessat

Small summer and winter resort.

▶ Beyond Le Bessat, take D 63 towards La Croix-de-Chaubouret.

Crêt de la Perdrix★

Just after La Croix-de-Chaubouret turn left onto D 8A towards La Jasserie.
The road winds past spruce, mountain pastures and heathland.

▶ After about 5km/3mi, at the top of the climb, park near the path leading to Perdrix ridge (15min on foot there and back) which is crowned with a chirat (granite rock).

The panorama from the viewing table takes in the peaks of Mézenc, Lizieux, Meygal and Gerbier-de-Jonc.

▶ Rejoin D 8 and follow D 63 to Crêt de l'Œillon.

The road meanders alternately through fir trees and moorland covered in broom.

Crêt de l'Œillon★★★

15min on foot there and back.
At the Croix de l'Œillon pass, take the road on the left leading to the turn-off to the private road ending at the television relay station.
🅿 *Park in the car park. At the top, walk to the left around the fence; the viewing table is on the eastern end of the promontory, at the foot of a monumental cross.*
🚶 The panorama is one of the most spectacular in the Rhône valley. In the foreground, beyond the rocks of the Pic des Trois Dents (Three Teeth Peak), there is a view of the Rhône valley.

▶ Continue to Pélussin.

Pélussin

Park on place Abbé-Vincent in front of the hospital. Walk down rue

Dr-Soubeyran and take rue de la Halle on the left.

The old covered market provides a view of the Rhône plain and the town of Pélussin. Go through a fortified gatehouse and turn left. Note the ancient chapel and castle.

▶ Turn back the way you came and take D 7 right to Pavezin Pass. Continue to Ste-Croix-en-Jarez.

Ste-Croix-en-Jarez

The Carthusian monastery of Ste-Croix (Holy Cross) was founded in 1280 by Béatrix Roussillon. During the Revolution the monks were forced to leave; the monastery was then split up, the cloisters demolished in 1840 and, in 1888, Ste-Croix became a municipality.

▶ Return to Pavezin Pass, turn left onto D 30 which, as it begins its descent, offers a beautiful view of the Rhône Valley. Continue to the D 28 for Condrieu.

Just before arriving, in a bend with a Calvary overlooking the town, there is a **panoramic view★** of the Condrieu basin and the bend in the Rhône below.

Condrieu

One of the largest markets in the region is held here, specialising in fruit and early vegetables.

The town is also famed for its excellent white wine, made from the viognier grape. The Maison de la Gabelle has an attractive 16C façade. The port – the town was once renowned for its sailors – is a pleasant place for a stroll, with its slightly Mediterranean feel.

ADDRESSES

🛏 STAY

🛏 **Chambre d'Hôte Le Moulin du Bost** – *42131 La Valla-en-Gier (13km/8mi N of Le Bessat).* ℘*04 77 20 06 62. Closed Nov–Easter. 3 rooms. Restaurant🍽.* An impassioned trekker and member of the *"relais randonneurs"* (lodgings for walkers), the owner of this house located in the Parc Naturel Régional du Pilat can recommend rambles adapted to your capacity and desires. Simple rooms and generous fare.

🛏 **Chambre d'hôte La Rivoire** – *42220 St-Julien-Molin-Molette (5km/3mi E of Bourg-Argental via N 82).* ℘*04 77 39 65 44. http://rivoire.webnode.fr. Reservations required in winter. 5 rooms. Restaurant🍽.* What a charming house, with its round tower and generous vegetable garden! It dominates the Vallée de la Déôme – an ideal vantage point with a splendid view that can be admired from all the bedrooms and the terrace.

🛏 **Castel-Guéret** – *42220 St-Julien-Molin-Molette (1km/0.6mi N of St-Julien).* ℘*04 77 51 56 04. Reservations required. 5 rooms. Restaurant🍽.* A noble 19C manor framed by a vast park. Carefully restored in the spirit of the era, the interior still has its original parquet floor. Bedrooms are furnished in Louis XV and Louis XVI styles.

🍽 EAT

🍽 **Auberge du Vernolon** – *42220 Colombier-sous-Pilat (8km/4.8mi E of Le Bessat).* ℘*04 77 51 50 07. www.aubergeduvernolon.fr. Closed Mon in summer and Mon–Fri lunch off-season. Reservations required.* The *patronne's* able cuisine is delectable – to be enjoyed under the magnificent woodframed ceiling in the barn or on the terrace with a panoramic view.

🍽 **Chanterelle** – *Sagnemorte, 42520 Roisey.* ℘*04 74 87 47 27. Closed Sun evening and Mon. Reservations required.* Located in a wooded, well-landscaped park, this stylish chalet looks out over a superb panorama of the Rhône valley and the peaks of the Pilat. Classic cuisine served in a contemporary setting.

THE UPPER VIVARAIS AND LE VELAY

The Haut-Vivarais stretches from Mont Pilat and Velay to the valley of the Rhône. The volcanic origins of the landscape is especially noticeable in Velay where there are many domes, known as "sucs", formed by lava flows. Velay is a region where the Occitan language and culture remain deeply rooted. The pride in their historic autonomy is a renowned feature of the people of Velay. In the 10C, Velay fell under the jurisdiction of the bishop of Puy, who at that time carried the title and distinction of "count". Le Puy-en-Velay has been the capital of the region ever since.

Orchards

Peach trees were first planted in 1880, on an experimental basis. The widespread cultivation of orchards is due to favourable natural conditions: light, warm soil which is easily drained; sites sheltered from the Mistral and the winds from the south; spring frosts which are rare; and summers which begin early. The success story of the orchards is also due to the determination of the local people. The D 120 is the best route to follow to admire the peach trees in blossom. The season lasts for some time, beginning in early spring with the orchards in the lower valley, and showcases an extraordinary array of colours ranging from pale pink, to carmine red, to purple.

The First Hot-Air Balloon

On 4 June 1783, the **Montgolfier brothers**, natives of Annonay, launched a balloon made of fabric and paper, held together by some 1 800 buttons. The balloon remained in the air for 30min and landed more than 2km/1mi from its launch site. This feat is commemorated by a plaque on place des Cordeliers, where the experiment was conducted.

Highlights

1 Taking the children to visit the safari park at **Peaugres** (p406)

2 Driving the **Corniche du Rhône** (p407)

3 The panorama from the **Château de Pierre-Gourde** (p411)

4 The hard climb to the summit of **Gerbier-de-Jonc** (p414)

5 The flora of the upper **Mézenc massif** (p415)

Beefing It Up

Rising to 1 753m, Mont Mézenc lies between the Ardèche and Haute-Loire, and is famous for its AOC beef, fed on the best hay in the mountain pastures.

Mont Mézenc

© Bios/Tips Images

PARC

NATUREL RÉGIONAL

DU

PILAT

Barrage du Ternay

Safari-parc de Peaugres

Bourg-Argental

Serrières

Champagne

Boulieu-lès-Annonay

Musée de l'Alambic

Albon

Annonay

Thorrenc

Cance

D 578

Quintenas-le-Peyron

St-Vallier

Défilé de St-Vallier

St-Uze

N.-D.-d'Ay

Ay

St-Jeure-d'Ay

Les Roches qui dansent

Lalouvesc

Vion

Belvédère de Pierre-Aiguille

Col du Buisson
920

Château de Rochebloîne

Devesset

Gorges du Doux

Doux

Tournon-sur-Rhône

Boucieu-le-Roi

CORNICHE DU RHÔNE

St-Agrève

Lamastre

Désaignes

ST-ROMAIN-DE-LERPS

Château de Rochebonne

ARDÈCHE

Boffres

Crussol

Vernoux-en-Vivarais

Château de la Tourrette

CORNICHE DE L'EYRIEUX

Château de Pierre-Gourde

RÉGIONAL

St-Sauveur-de-Montagut

St-Laurent-du-Pape

Beauchastel

DES MONTS D'ARDÈCHE

St-Pierreville

Le Fival

Vallée de l'Eyrieux

Eyrieux

La Voulte-s-Rhône

Le Bouschet

Le Mᵃⁿ-à-Vent

RHÔNE

Drôme

GAP

MT MÉZENC   ★★★ Highly recommended

Pic du Lizieux   ★★ Recommended

Désaignes   ★ Interesting

Chalencon   Other sight described

Driving Tour showing point of departure

Annonay

Annonay is located in a deep cleft of the Vivarais plateau, at the confluence of the River Deûme and River Cance. In the Middle Ages, the exceptional quality of the water here encouraged a leather and wool industry to be established, which then flourished. Being one of the first towns to uphold the principles of the Reformation, Annonay suffered greatly during the Wars of Religion. However, in the 17C, following the establishment in the town of the Johannot and Montgolfier families' paperworks, Annonay began to prosper again.

▶ **Population:** 16 720.
🕭 **Michelin Map:** 331: K-2.
ℹ **Info:** Pl. des Cordeliers, 07100 Annonay.
  📞04 75 33 24 51.
  www.ardechegrandair.com.
▷ **Location:** Almost directly south of Lyon.
🕭 **Don't Miss:** The Old Town.
🕘 **Timing:** At least half a day.

👣WALKING TOUR

OLD TOWN

The old quarter on the hills overlooking the two rivers is currently benefiting from a major restoration project.

▷ Begin from place de la Libération.

On this square stands a statue of the Montgolfier brothers, erected in 1883.

▷ Turn right onto rue Franki-Kramer.

Rue Franki-Kramer

Annonay's old high street, like the nearby place Grenette and place Mayol, is flanked by picturesque 16C–18C houses.

▷ Take rue de Trachin on the right, which opens out to the chapel.

Chapelle de Trachin

This Gothic chapel is all that remains of a priory founded in 1320 by Guy Trachin, a wealthy resident of Annonay.

Place de la Liberté

This square located in the centre of the old town becomes a bustling hub of trade on market days *(Wednesdays and Saturdays)*. The square is graced by a statue of Marc Seguin.

▷ From the bottom of place de la Liberté turn onto Montée du Château.

Fortified Gates

Montée du Château forms a steep incline up to the old machicolated gate; a second gate also survives, at the end of rue de Bourgville.

▷ Rue Montgolfier leads to the bridge.

Pont Montgolfier

Upstream, the view is of the humpback Valgelas bridge (14C) and the convent of Ste-Marie (16C). Downstream, the Deûme flows into the Défilé des Fouines, a dark, narrow rocky gorge.

▷ Walk to Valgelas bridge and follow Voûtes Soubise, a vaulted passageway, to the steps of rue Barville. Turn right onto rue de Deûme and continue to avenue de l'Europe.

Avenue de l'Europe partly covers the Deûme. From the intersection with rue de la Valette there is a view west over the Tour des Martyrs (12C–13C), the last remnant of the old ramparts.

Place des Cordeliers

The square owes its name to the former convent built on the site, where today there is a theatre. To the right, a plaque commemorates the first public enterprise of the Montgolfier brothers.

▷ Retrace your steps and then take the steps to Rue Grangeat. Turn left at rue Chalayer, then right.

Place Grenette

Built in 1585, this square retains the pillars and arcades of the ancient granary. At Nos. 1 and 3, notice the 16C doors.

▶ Turn right on rue Franki-Kramer, walk past the cathedral and turn right into rue Jean-Baptiste Bechetoille.

ADDITIONAL SIGHT

Musée des Papeteries Canson et Montgolfier

2.5km/1.5mi NE. Vidalon. ◔*Jul–Aug daily 2.15–6pm; rest of the year Wed and Sun 2.30–6pm.* ◔*24 Dec–1 Jan, Easter Sun.* ◉€5.50. ℘04 75 69 89 20. *www.musee-papeteries-canson-montgolfier.fr.*

This museum, in the house where the Montgolfier brothers were born, retraces the history of the local paperworks.

EXCURSIONS

Boulieu-lès-Annonay

5km/3mi to the N on avenue de l'Europe. Former fortified village with square ramparts flanking the main street.

Barrage du Ternay

10km/6mi via the D 206 to the N, then D 820 and D 306.

Constructed in 1867 to provide a water supply to Annonay; today it offers a lovely water space bordered by cedar.

Bourg-Argental

ᗱ*See Le PILAT.*

🚗 DRIVING TOURS

NORTH OF ANNONAY

39km/24mi. Allow half a day.

▶ Leave Annonay to the NW, along the boulevard de la République. Follow the D 121, then the D 519 and finally the D 820 in the direction of Serrières for a further 6km/3.5mi as far as a roundabout, where you take the first exit. About 300m further on, turn left.

🧍‍♂️ Safari-parc de Peaugres★

♿🕐*Check website, or call, for variable dates throughout the year.* 👓€24 *(child 3–12, €21).* 📞*04 75 33 00 32.* www.safari-peaugres.com.

Located at the foot of the Pilat massif, this nature reserve is home to 400 mammals, 300 birds and around 60 reptiles. There is an area exclusively for cars following the "safari" experience and a main zoo that can be explored on foot.

Serrières

This ancient city will remain forever associated with the epic tales of its boatmen on the Rhône. It is from this time that the celebrated annual nautical games animate the banks of the river.

Réserve Naturelle de la Platière

Access to the island is impossible during floods, and dangerous in strong winds. Come here early in the day, armed with a pair of binoculars to observe the waterfowl. Less easy to spot are beavers, which tend to be active at night.

▶ Go back over the Pont de Sablons and then head S on the D 86.

Champagne

In spite of its situation on the right bank of the Rhône, Champagne was a fiefdom of the powerful counts of Albon, whose castle rises on the opposite bank.

▶ Drive 2.5km/1.5mi further on the D 86 and turn right towards St-Désirat.

Musée de l'Alambic★

🕐*Mon–Fri 8am–noon, 2–6pm, Sat 10am–noon, 2–6.30pm, Sun and public holidays 2–6.30pm (Jul–Aug Mon–Fri 8am–noon, 2–6pm, Sat–Sun and public holidays 10am–noon, 2–6.30pm.* 🕐*1 Jan and 25 Dec.* 📞*04 75 34 23 11.* www.jeangauthier.com.

This museum within the Gauthier distillery, recalls the life of distillers and shows some interesting films.

▶ Follow the D 82 for Annonay. At St-Etienne-de-Valoux, turn left towards Thorrenc.

Château de Thorrenc

Recently restored, this 11C castle lies deep in the ravine of the Thorrençon.

▶ Beyond Ozas, you can return to Annonay by the D 370.

AY AND CANCE VALLEYS

Round tour of 48km/29mi. Allow 2h.

▶ Leave Annonay by rue de Tournon to the S heading for Lamastre.

Quintenas-le-Peyron

The village is dominated by the 14C belfry of its Romanesque church.

▶ In Quintenas, on the right, facing the church, follow directions for St-Romain-d'Ay.

The narrow road meanders through the countryside, affording pretty views of the Haut-Vivarais.

▶ Leave the church of St-Romain on your left and drive to D 6; turn left. After 90m, on the right, a steep road leads to Notre-Dame-d'Ay.

Notre-Dame-d'Ay

This modest sanctuary perched on top of a rocky outcrop is a popular place of pilgrimage.

ADDRESSES

🛏️ STAY

🛏️ **Chambre d'Hôte La Désirade** – *07340 St-Désirat.* 📞*04 75 34 21 88.* www.desirade-fr.com. *8 rooms.* Amid grapevines and trees, this renovated 19C house has pleasant rooms giving onto a courtyard, or park and vineyard.

🛏️ **Le Charmeyran** – *19 bd de la République.* 📞*06 03 32 24 27. 8 studios and 2 apartments.* 19C building transformed into studios and apartments.

⊜⊜ **Chambre d'Hôte La Palisse** – *804 Rte de Cheval, 07340 Peaugres.* ✆*04 75 67 08 37. www.lapalisse-peaugres. com. 3 rooms.* You can almost imagine you are in an African safari park.

⍟/ EAT

⊜⊜ **Restaurant La Moustache Gourmande** – *89 Rue de Bourbon, 07430 St-Clair (3.5km/2mi from Annonay).* ✆*04 75 67 01 81. Closed Feb school holidays, 15 days in Sept and Wed.* This restaurant in a charming village has a fine selection of seafood dishes.

⊜⊜ **L'Escabelle** – *1 av. de l'Europe.* ✆*04 75 67 64 09. Closed Wed and Sun.* Traditional cuisine served in an agreeable setting below a vaulted ceiling.

⊜⊜ **Restaurant du Parc** – *40 quai Jules-Roche, 07340 Serrières.* ✆*04 75 34 00 08. Closed Sun and Thu evenings, and Mon.* Delivering regional specialities like *raviola* and Ardèche sausages.

⊜⊜⊜ **Schaeffer** – *07340 Serrières.* ✆*04 75 34 00 07. www.hotel-schaeffer.com. Closed Sat lunch, Sun evening and Mon.* Cosy restaurant with rooms (⊜⊜⊜) extended over the Rhône river; classic cuisine.

Tournon-sur-Rhône★

This busy town on the Rhône overlooks Tain-l'Hermitage on the opposite bank, which is famed for its fine wines. Tournon is a lively shopping town. The shaded quayside and castle ruins on the hillside give the town a characteristic Rhodanien atmosphere.

TOWN

Tournon-sur-Rhône boasts a 15C–16C **château** containing a museum about bargemen on the Rhône, set in a charming **terraced garden★**.
The **Lycée Gabriel-Fauré** has an attractive Renaissance doorway, and a collection of busts and tapestries.

- ▸ **Population:** 11 171.
- ⚲ **Michelin Map:** 331: L-3.
- **Info:** 2 Place Saint-Julien, 07300 Tournon-sur-Rhône. ✆04 75 08 10 23. www.hermitage-tournonais-tourisme.com.
- ▸ **Location:** Not far from Romans-sur-Isère (20km/12.5 mi to the E) and Valence, to the S.
- **P Parking:** There are car parks on the left bank of the Rhône, and around the Place de la République.
- ◔ **Timing:** Allow half a day, at least. Arrive in time for lunch.

🚗 DRIVING TOURS

CORNICHE DU RHÔNE★★★
43km/26.5mi. Allow 2h.

▸ Leave Tournon-sur-Rhône to the S via rue du Dr-Cadet and rue Greffieux towards St-Romain-de-Lerps.

From Tournon to Valence the **panoramic road★★★** along the hillside offers magnificent views.

▸ In Plats turn left by the War Memorial onto GR 42.

St-Romain-de-Lerps★★★
This is one of the most impressive views along the Rhône: to the east, above the Valence plain, rises the Vercors bar, dominated by the Moucherolle needle and the dome of the Grand Veymont.

▸ Take the D 287 towards the S. At St-Péray, take the road in front of the Château de Beauregard. Park at the end of the road.

Tournon-sur-Rhône, the Rhône and the vineyards of Tain-l'Hermitage

© Didier Zylberyng/hemis.fr

Crussol★★

On the hillside above the plain lie the famous castle ruins. The white stone of Crussol was often used elsewhere because of its fine grain. The **site★★** is one of the finest in the Rhône valley
🚶 *You reach the ruins of the castle by a path (1h there and back).*

GORGES DU DOUX VIA THE CORNICHE ROAD★

50km/31mi. Allow 2h.

▷ Leave Tournon-sur-Rhône on the road to Lamastre.

The road runs along the pretty orchards of the Doux basin. The **corniche road★** dominates the Doux gorges.

Boucieu-le-Roi

This village was once the seat of a royal bailiwick in the upper Vivarais area.

▷ Return to Tournon-sur-Rhône via Colombier-le-Vieux and D 534, running on the opposite side of the gorges, through wild vegetation.

DÉFILÉ DE ST-VALLIER★

60km/37.5mi. Allow 2h.

▷ Leave Tournon-sur-Rhône to the N on D 86.

Vion

The church, partly Romanesque, has a transept crossing with capitals.

▷ In Vion, take the narrow road that leads to D 532. At Croix de Fraysse, head for St-Jeure-d'Ay, then turn right onto D 6. About 7km/4.3mi further on, take D 506 on the right, leading to Ozon.

The steep descent to Ozon offers **views★★** over **St-Vallier Gorges★** and the orchards and vineyards along the river.

▷ Cross the Rhône between Sarras and St-Vallier, then follow the N 7. As you leave St-Vallier, take the D 51 to the left in the direction of St-Uze.

Maison de la Céramique de St-Uze

🕐 *Mar–Dec Wed 2–6pm (school holidays Wed–Sun 2–6pm).* ✆€4. 📞04 75 03 98 01. www.territoire-ceramique.com.
At the beginning of the 19C, the discovery of kaolin clay in the region gave rise to a number of ceramic enterprises, and brought the town great renown.

▷ As you leave St-Uze, turn right towards St-Barthélemy-de-Vals. Go through the town and rejoin the D 500 towards Ponsas. After 1.5km/1mi, take a left into the forest.

Les Roches qui dansent

This section of the valley is evocative of the Rhône in medieval times: ruins of feudal strongholds and old defensive towers line the escarpments.

▷ Turn left towards Crozes-Hermitage. Go through the town and then follow signs for the Pierre-Aiguille.

Pierre-Aiguille Belvedere★

The far-reaching views from here encompass Tain-l'Hermitage and its vineyard; the town of Tournon across the river and the foothills of Vercors with the Alps in the background.

Vallée de l'Eyrieux★

The River Eyrieux rises to the north of St-Agrève then tumbles down from the high plateaux of the Vivarais area and flows into the Rhône after a distance of 70km/44mi. The upper valley has a mountainous appearance, with steep slopes covered with chestnut and spruce; this is the area known as Les Boutières. Downstream from Le Cheylard the torrent flows into gorges, then less rugged basins and rocky narrows alternate down to the final plain and the Rhône valley.

A BIT OF GEOGRAPHY

The Eyrieux flows swiftly. Because of the sloping ground on its upper course, autumn storms suddenly swell the main river and its tributaries.

Old, isolated hamlets cling to the hillsides marked into strips by the low walls surrounding terraced fields. Larger villages and small towns grew up in the small inner basins in the valley, or at the mouth of tributaries.

Some of them have industrial activity, but the dominant character of the valley derives from farming peaches. In the spring the peach trees turn this rugged valley into a carpet of pink-petalled blossom.

🚗 DRIVING TOURS

LA VOULTE-SUR-RHÔNE ROUND TOUR★
55km/34mi. Allow 3h.

La Voulte-sur-Rhône
Small town with an industrial past on the right bank of the Rhone, a place of narrow streets lined with old houses.

Beauchastel
Listed village at the foot of its castle ruins. A stroll through narrow alleys and streets takes you to the Maison du Patrimoine and the terrace offering a

---

Michelin Map:
331: J-4 to K-4/5.

Info: 8 rue Paul Montrochet, 69002 Lyon 04 72 59 21 59. http://en.auvergnerhonealpes-tourisme.com.

Timing: Allow a day for each of the Driving Tours.

---

pretty view of St-Laurent-du-Pape and the nearby valley.

▶ Rejoin D 21 and head towards St-Laurent-du-Pape.

St-Laurent-du-Pape
Attractive town at the valley entrance, enhanced by its bridge over the Eyrieux.

▶ Keep driving along the valley in the direction of Cheylard.

St-Sauveur-de-Montagut
Dominated by the ruins of Montagut Château *(access by D 244 and a forest lane)*, the village stands at the confluence of the Eyrieux and Gluyère.
The roads runs along the Gluyère valley, hugging the riverbanks almost up to St-Pierreville.

Temple du Fival
Open Jul–Aug, Tue, Thu and Fri, 3–7pm. 04 75 65 46 84.
This ancient temple has been converted into a **museum** dedicated to the history of the Huguenots.

▶ Continue along the D 8, which runs for 11km/7mi to St-Pierreville.

St-Pierreville
The **Maison du Châtaignier** (*11am–12.30pm. 2.30–6.30pm: Apr–Nov Wed, Sat–Sun and public holidays (Jul–Aug, daily). Dec–Mar. €4.50. 04 75 66 64 33. www.maisonduchataignier. fr)* presents an exhibition on chestnut production.
The **Musée Vivant de la Laine et du Mouton** (04 75 66 63 08. www.

CORNICHE DE L'EYRIEUX

ardelaine.fr) presents the different breeds of sheep and the types of wool produced on the plateaux flanking the Eyrieux.

▶ Follow the D 102 towards St-Saveur-de-Montagut and then the D 120 back to Voult-sur-Rhône.

CORNICHE DE L'EYRIEUX★★★
Round tour from St-Laurent-du-Pape. 90km/56mi. Allow 3hr30.

▶ Leave St-Laurent-du-Pape on D 120, then right onto D 21 for Vernoux.

As it winds up to Serre Mure pass, this road offers views of the Vivarois ridges, the upper basin of the Eyrieux and the Boutières region, as well as a view of the western slopes of the Pierre-Gourde peak.

▶ Turn left onto D 231, then D 331.

St-Julien-le-Roux
From the church, mountains can be seen along the **horizon**★, above the ruins of Château de la Tourette.

▶ Go back to the D 231, and take the D 233 towards Silhac. Park at the entrance to Charayre.

Écomusée des Terrasses
🕐 *Open Jul–Aug, Tue–Sun afternoons, Thu all day.* 📞*04 75 65 24 70. www. ecomuseedesterrass.wixsite.com*
Several houses boast ancient cultivation terraces, perfectly maintained and evidence of determined hard work; restoration continues at a gradual pace.

▶ Take the D 233. At Silhac, take the D 2 to the right.

Vernoux-en-Vivarais
Vernoux stands on the Vivarais plateau, between the Eyrieux and the River Doux, in the centre of a large hollow.

Château de la Tourette
The ruins of this stronghold, which once marked the gateway to the States of Languedoc, lie in an unspoilt **setting**★ and are among the most evocative in the Vivarais.

▶ Drive to Boffres situated 8.5km/5mi NE on D 14 and D 219.

Château de Pierre-Gourde

© S. Sauvignier/MICHELIN

Boffres

The village of Boffres is built on a projection in a semicircle at the foot of its simple church and the remains of a fortified castle. Just outside the village, a bronze bust has been erected to the memory of **Vincent d'Indy**, the French composer and teacher (1851–1931), born in Paris, but descended from a family in the region. It was at **Château des Faugs**, west of Boffres, that d'Indy came to seek inspiration. He composed his third melody without words from a shepherd's song heard near Les Estables, and his opera *Fervaal* one misty morning on the peaks of Mont Mézenc.

▶ Drive to the D 14, turn left onto D 232.

The road runs along the hillside, offering views of Vernoux-en-Vivarais in the centre of the basin. Beyond Croix-de-Nodon, there are generous glimpses of the Rhône valley and clear views of the deep wooded Embroye valley.

▶ At Le Moulin-à-Vent turn right onto D 266.

After a long wooded section, the road runs along a spectacular stretch of ledge, opposite Pierre-Gourde peak, in front of the mountain ridges enclosing the Eyrieux valley.

▶ A track, off D 286 to the right, leads to the Château de Pierre-Gourde. Park at a pass, in sight of the ruins.

Panorama from the Château de Pierre-Gourde★★

This medieval castle, now in ruins, occupies a magnificent **site★**. At the foot of the peak on which the keep was built lie the ruins of the main building, parts of the curtain wall and the feudal village.

▶ Walk left around the ruins to reach a rocky terrace.

The **panorama** encompasses the Rhône and Trois-Becs, between the Vercors bar, the Baronnies and Mont Ventoux. Opposite, the backbone of Croix de Bauzon overlooks the Haut-Eyrieux gap.
During the descent, two panoramic bends offer a view first of the Eyrieux valley, with its clearly delineated ridges, endlessly repeated, and then of the Rhône valley, on the left.

▶ About 5km/3mi from Pierre-Gourde, a sign on the right indicates the Serre de Pepeyrier ridge.

View from Serre de Pepeyrier★

There is a beautiful **view** from the ridge of the mouth of the Eyrieux valley with its vast peach orchards, the town of Beauchastel and the Rhône plain; in the background, Mont Ventoux.

▶ Rejoin the D 266 to return to St-Laurent-du-Pape.

St-Agrève

St-Agrève lies on the slopes of Mont Chiniac. There are few historic remains because the town suffered repeatedly during the Wars of Religion.

SIGHTS
Mont Chiniac★★
A road leads to the summit, crowned with fir trees. The view encompasses the Massif du Mézenc, the Massif du Meygal and the Monts de Lalouvesc.

Devesset
The nearby **Lac de Devesset** is a leisure centre providing facilities for many water sports (swimming, sailing etc).

EXCURSIONS
Lamastre
The ancient upper town is dominated by the Château de Peychelard, while the lower town, Savel, has developed along the banks of the Doux.

Désaignes★
The existence of this former Gallo-Roman settlement is evidenced by a great many ruins, including a Roman road. It was to become the most densely populated city in the Vivarais.
Of its past glory there remain large sections of the ramparts, a 14C **castle** (◷Apr–Jun and Oct Sat–Sun and public holidays 2–6pm; Jul–Aug daily 3–7pm. ☞€4.50. ℘04 75 06 66 21) housing the **Musée de la Vie Rurale**, and numerous Gothic houses.

🚗 DRIVING TOUR

LES BOUTIÈRES★★
80km/50mi round trip leaving from St-Agrève. Allow 4h.

▶ Leave St-Agrève to the S on D 120, heading towards Le Cheylard.

During the drive down, you will enjoy pretty views of the Mézenc, then the road enters the Eyrieux defile.

▶ **Population:** 2 579.
🚲 **Michelin Map:** 331 I-3.
🛈 **Info:** 35 Grande-Rue, 07320 St-Agrève. ℘04 75 30 15 06. www.ville-saintagreve.fr.
▶ **Location:** Midway between Puy-en-Velay and Valence.
🕐 **Timing:** Allow half a day.

▶ Take D 120 south. At the exit to St-Julien-Boutières, turn right on D 101.

Fay-sur-Lignon
This mountain-village (pronounced *fa-yee*) offers cross-country skiing facilities in winter. There is a good **view★** of the surrounding mountains from the graveyard next to the church.

▶ Take D 262 S and turn left to St-Clément.

St-Clément
Once past the town, there are attractive **views★★** of the Gerbier de Jonc, Suc de Sara and Mont Mézenc mountains, in line with the valley of the River Saliouse.

▶ Beyond Lachapelle-sous-Chanéac keep following the D 278.

▶ In Armanas turn left and then right onto D 478 to Le Bourget and Rochebonne.

This is a winding and attractive route with lovely views over the basin of the upper Eyrieux and of the confluence of the River Eysse and River Eyrieux.

Ruins of Rochebonne★
Park by the side of the road.
🚶 The magnificent **site★★** is the setting for the fissured, granitic ruins of the medieval castle, overlooked to the west by Mont Mézenc. Walk down to the ruins *(30min there and back).*

▶ Continue along D 478 towards Beauvert and down to D 21 which leads back to St-Agrève.

Yssingeaux

This is one of the largest communes in France, standing at the heart of a landscape of volcanic and wooded hills; a perfect base for walking.

🚗 DRIVING TOUR

MASSIF DU MEYGAL AND PAYS DES SUCS★
98km/61mi. Allow 3h30.

▶ Leave Yssingeaux to the S on D 7, then after 3km/2mi turn right onto D 42.

Forêt du Meygal
This forest, mainly conifers, was planted between 1865 and 1880.

▶ After the Araules crossroads, turn right onto D 18, towards Queyrières, then left onto the first forest lane, signposted in red and blue. At the next intersection, take the left-hand lane running along the east slope of the Grand Testavoyre.

Grand Testavoyre★★
🚶 A path through ferns and bilberry bushes leads to the summit from which there are splendid **panoramic views** over the volcanic landscape.

▶ Continue through the forest.

The west road goes past the **Maison des Copains,** which became famous after it was mentioned in a novel by the French writer **Jules Romains**.

▶ The left-hand forest lane leads to D 15. Turn left, then right onto the D 26, and again right onto the D 263.

Saint-Front
This village built on a large mound offers an excellent view towards the Mézenc.

▶ Take the D 39 to the west, then before Machabert, turn right towards Maziaux.

- ▶ **Population:** 7 568.
- 🕐 **Michelin Map:** 331 G-3.
- 🅸 **Info:** 16 Place Foch.
  𝄢04 71 59 10 76.
- ▶ **Location:** 28km/17.5mi NE of Puy-en-Velay.
- 🕐 **Timing:** Allow 2 hours to up to half a day.

Maziaux et Bigorre★
These hamlets have a number of buildings specific to the Mézenc, with slate or thatched roofs and small windows.

▶ Turn right onto the D 39, then the D 49 which you follow to St-Julien-Chapteuil.

St-Julien-Chapteuil
The village occupies an unusual **site★** in the middle of a leafy basin watered by the Sumène, bristling with volcanic peaks. The **Musée Jules-Romains** is devoted to the life and literary achievements of the author **Jules Romains** (1885–1972).

▶ Leave St-Julien to the N and take D 26 towards St-Pierre-Eynac.

St-Pierre-Eynac
Pretty country **church** with a Romanesque doorway underneath a Renaissance porch. During the drive to Aupinhac, note the **view** of Le Puy and the basin to the left: you can see the Corneille rock and St-Michel-d'Aiguilhe.

▶ Continue towards St-Étienne village on D 26 after crossing N 88. Take D 71 N towards Malrevers. After Rosières, turn right onto D 7. Take the first road on the right after the cemetery on the road to Mortesagne.

The route is dominated by the Suc d'Eyme. During the drive down towards **Glavenas,** enjoy the **view★** of the curious landscape.

▶ Return to Yssingeaux on D 431 and N 88.

Le Monastier-sur-Gazeille

This large village in Haute-Loire derives its name from the largest Benedictine monastery in the Velay area, founded in the late 7C. St Calmin, Count of Auvergne, founded the monastery and became its first abbot.

▶ **Population:** 1 806.
⚙ **Michelin Map:** 331: G-4.
▣ **Info:** Mairie, 43150 Le Monastier-sur-Gazeille. ✆04 71 08 37 76.
◗ **Location:** The village is 17km/11mi south-east of Le Puy-en-Velay.
◷ **Timing:** Allow one hour to visit the church.

SIGHTS

Abbey Church

The Romanesque church built in the 11C underwent extensive alterations in the 15C. The abbey's treasures include a stone Pietà dating from the 15C, and two lengths of Byzantine silk used to shroud the bodies of the founding saints.

Musée d'Art Populaire

♿◷May–Sept daily 9am–noon, 2–7pm; Jan–Apr and Oct–Dec Sat–Sun 9.30am–noon, 2.30–7pm.
✆04 71 03 81 31.
The local museum is housed in the vaulted chambers of the abbey castle. The collections illustrate the history of regional life (lace, traditional costumes), and the prehistoric period in the Upper Loire valley. One of the rooms deals solely with Robert Louis Stevenson.

🚗 DRIVING TOUR

LAUZE COUNTRY

125km/77.6mi. Allow 1 day.

Château de Vachères

(👁▬Not open to the public) A massive keep flanked by towers with pepper-pot roofs gives this 13C castle with its blocks of black basalt outlined in white mortar a typically Velay-style appearance.

Lac d'Issarlès★

Like a sapphire set in a deep crater, this pretty lake is breathtaking in spite of being used for hydroelectric purposes, which vary the levels of the water.

◗ Join the D 16 heading for Béage and follow directions for Ste-Eulalie.

Ste-Eulalie

This village belongs to the municipality of Gerbier-de-Jonc and lies at the source of the River Loire. On the way to the Mont Gerbier-de-Jonc, another traditional broom-covered farmhouse, **Ferme Philip**, can be visited.

◗ Continue along D 122, heading towards Lachamp-Raphaël until you reach the intersection with D 378.

Ferme de Bourlatier★

◷May–Jun Wed–Fri 2.30–5.30pm, Sat–Sun 10.30am–6pm; Jul–Aug daily 10.30am–6pm; Sept Wed 2.30–5.30pm, Sat–Sun 2–6pm; Oct Wed, Sat–Sun 2.30–5.30pm. ∞€4.50. ✆04 75 38 84 90. www.bourlatier.fr.
A fine example of regional rural architecture with its lauze roof tiling, this stately farmhouse has been extensively restored in local tradition. Its most salient feature is probably its superb framework, shaped like an inverted hull, able to support the 150-tonne roofwork!

◗ At the crossroads take D 378, for Les Estables and Gerbier-de-Jonc.

Gerbier-de-Jonc★★

The Gerbier-de-Jonc looks like a giant haystack or a huge heap of sheaves when seen from a distance.
The word "Gerbier" is a Latinisation of the Indo-European root gar meaning "rock". Similar names are found in

Stevenson's Travels

In front of the post office is a memorial commemorating the travels undertaken across the Cévennes, in the autumn of 1878, by the Scottish writer **Robert Louis Stevenson**, author of *Treasure Island*. As much to satisfy his wish to travel as to try and retrace the spirit that once fired the *Camisards*, or Protestant rebels, Stevenson, then aged 28, decided to cross the Cévennes on foot from Le Monastier to Alès, accompanied only by a somewhat capricious donkey. Sleeping outdoors or in any inns he happened to come across (with one menu for all, and all visitors sleeping in the one room), he took 12 days to reach Alès. His travel notebook is a mine of humorous and penetrating observations on the wonderful countryside he discovered and the people he met on his way.

His travels were full of comic incidents, which he recounts with glee. To carry the strange sleeping-bag that he had made, Stevenson acquired the donkey which he immediately christened Modestine. The conflict between the obstinacy of the Scottish novelist and the strong will of the donkey from the Velay lasted for the entire trip: "Modestine's pace is quite beyond description. It was something much slower than a stroll, when a stroll is much slower than a walk. She held back each hoof for an incredibly long time…"

other regions of France, in particular in the Pyrenees (Pic du Gar, Pic du Ger, Pic du Jer). The word *jonc* is derived from the Latin *jugum* meaning "mountain". Gerbier-de-Jonc therefore literally means "rocky mountain". The Gerbier de Jonc, which is part of the Mézenc range, consists of phonolithic rocks that have a tendency to flake, forming unstable scree slopes and clothing the mountainside in a scaly shell. At the foot of the south-western slope are several small streams; the sources of the Loire.

The Climb

From the top, though, there is an impressive **panoramic view★★**. On the north-east side the view extends over the dip formed by the Eysse, a tributary of the River Eyrieux. Mont Alambre, the Mézenc and the volcanic Sara close off the north horizon; Montfol obstructs the view to the west; the conical La Barre, recognisable by its tabular outline, lies in the foreground on the south side. A stretch of the Alps can be seen in clear weather.

▷ D 328 then D 36 to Les Estables.

Les Estables✳

This small mountain village lying in the foothills of the Mézenc massif is a popular winter resort offering a wide choice of pistes for both Alpine and cross-country skiing.

▷ Cross the village heading N and turn right for Mont Mézenc via the Peccata Cross.

Mont Mézenc★★★

The volcanic Mézenc range (the final "c" is not pronounced) forms a natural barrier that divides the rivers flowing to the Atlantic from those flowing to the Mediterranean. The Mézenc massif forms the centre of a volcanic trail that cuts across the axis of the Cévennes. It is flanked to the west by the granite mountains at La Margeride and to the east by the crystalline plateaux of the Upper Vivarais.

A vast tract of land called the **Zone Nordique du Mézenc** is popular in the winter months for the cross-country skiing it offers.

Access via the Boutières Cross

2.5km/almost 2mi from Les Estables via D 631 E. Park at the Boutières Cross (1 508m).

From the rock above the pass at the Boutières Cross, to the right, there is a superb **view★★** over Sara, Roche Borée and Les Boutières.

The Mézenc massif

Hillsides with contrasting appeal – On the Velay side of the Mézenc massif the range looks like a vast, bare plateau. In the summer months it resembles a windswept steppe dotted with low farmhouses crowned with thatched or stone-slabbed roofs. The Vivarais side of the range is rugged terrain, suddenly sweeping down towards the Rhône. The streams have worn the ground down to the granite rocks underneath.

Splendid basalt flows – On the hillsides flanking the valleys, erosion has revealed extensive basalt lava flows that are particularly impressive in the upper reaches of the River Ardèche and its tributaries (the Volane, Bourges, Fontaulière and Lignon). These flows, which now take the form of prismatic columnar basalt, have created famous beauty spots such as the Ray-Pic waterfall, the Thueyts causeway, Pourcheyrolles rock, Jaujac and Antraigues.

Flora in the peaks – The upper Mézenc massif has flora which will delight botanists, including a variety of groundsel which, in all the Massif Central, can only be found at the summit of the Mézenc massif: the famous "Mézenc grass" with silvery leaves and beautiful bright-yellow flower-heads. The great mountain violet, Alpine anemone, all sorts of gentians, globe flowers, arnica, willow-herb and saxifrages are the commonest of the plants but it is when the narcissi flower in June that the mountain acquires its finest appearance. A traditional market of medicinal herbs, known as the "Violet Fair", is held in Ste-Eulalie every year.

▶ Follow the footpath numbered GR7 (1h15 there and back) which climbs up to the left towards the summit.

🚶 Head for the south summit via the flat ground in between the two peaks.

Access via the Peccata Cross
3km/2mi NE from Les Estables. Park at the Peccata Cross then follow the path on the right (1hr on foot there and back).
🚶 This route climbs up through the woods then twists and turns amid the heather and juniper bushes.

▶ Bear left towards the north summit (1 749m) topped by a cross.

Panoramic View★★★
From the summit there is a sweeping **panorama**. To the north are the Meygal and Forez mountains; to the west, the Puy basin, the Velay area and the mountains of the Auvergne; to the south lie Lake Issarlès and a string of volcanic cones; and to the east the Saliouse and Eysse gorges, both of which cut into the Boutières area towards the Upper Eyrieux, where deep ravines are interspersed with ridges and peaks.

▶ Rejoin D 274 to the N.

Chaudeyrolles
Typical of the Mézenc, this village has a number of houses built from volcanic stone and roofed with *lauzes*. At the **Maison du Fin Gras du Mézenc**, there is an explanation of the methods of cattle rearing that produce the AOC beef of the region.

Moudeyres
The village still has several typical cottages, namely the **Ferme des Frères Perrel** (👁check website for details of guided visits. €5.80. 📞06 27 59 14 52). Apart from its basalt walls, its *lauze* tiles over the living quarters and its thatched roof crowning the outbuildings, it has kept its original furniture and farming tools.

▶ Turn back and rejoin D 500. Turn right towards Le Monastier-sur-Gazeille.

Freycenet-la-Tour
The tower has long since disappeared but the village is still worth a visit for its Romanesque church and its typical houses roofed with *lauze* tiles.

The Vivarais, as many still call the Ardèche, takes its name from the coat of arms of Viviers, and is an area inhabited since prehistoric times. This is a region of considerable contrast not least in elevation, which ranges from a mere 40m where the Ardèche flows into the Rhône, to more than 1 700m in Mont Mézenc; it is bordered to the east by the Rhône valley. The Bas-Vivarais, one of five distinct regions within the Ardèche, is a limestone region where streams flow through steep-sided valleys flanked by narrow ridges. This is a lovely countryside of wine, garrigue, cereals and orchards; a place of peaceful villages, caves and considerable antiquity.

Spring Time

About 145 springs rise around the town of Val-les-Bains, and many of these have been exploited since 1600, although the town only became popular as a spa resort in the mid 19C. The waters here are cold (13°C) and rich in sodium bicarbonate; the difference between the springs lies in their degree of mineralisation. The waters, which are mainly used for drinking (several million bottles are exported from Vals each year), have a settling effect on the stomach and at the same time a stimulating effect on the liver. They are recommended for treating diabetes and nutrient deficiencies, in which case the waters may be taken in showers, baths and massages as well as orally.

Candied Chestnuts

The practice of making sweets from chestnuts can be linked to the Crusaders who returned with sugar, and so started candying in the chestnut-growing areas in the south of France and in Italy. Sugar,

Highlights

1 Admiring the **Pont d'Arc** (p433)
2 A summer's day canoeing the **Ardèche Gorge** (p436)
3 The cave system of the **Aven d'Orgnac** (p438)
4 The scent of lavender on the **plateau de Gras** (p441)
5 Taking a stroll around the old town of **Viviers** (p442)

it seems, can do things that honey can't, and these moreish sweets are thought to have first been made in the 15C, although *marrons glacés* as such are believed not to have been produced until the 16C.

Like many of these lost-in-time factoids there is no certainty about who did what, and when, except that the first known records appear in the French language, and the sweet eventually gained royal approval at Versailles.

Architectural details of the old town, Viviers

© A. De Valroger/Michelin

Privas

Privas occupies an unusual **site★** in the Ouvèze basin, at the foot of Mont Toulon; a good example of relief inversion, the lava flow on which it stands was once at the bottom of the valley and is now in relief since the ancient unprotected calcareous heights have been eroded. Business in the town concentrates on small industry (milling, sprung bed bases) and the manufacture of *marrons glacés* (candied sweet chestnuts), of which it is the capital.

SIGHTS
Mont-Toulon
1h there and back – park near the museum and walk up boulevard du Montoulon.

🏃 A signpost marks the path to the right that goes to the hilltop, where there is a monumental **calvary** (three crosses) and a good **view★** over the town, the Ouvèze Valley, the Rhône and the Alps.

Pont Louis-XIII
South of the town centre. The bridge spanning the River Ouvèze has preserved its coping of rough-stone corbels and offers a good view of Privas.

EXCURSIONS
Le Bouschet de Pranles
15km/9.3mi N along D 2 and D 344.
A small **Protestant Museum** (🕐*May–Jun Sat–Sun and public holidays 2–6pm; Jul–Aug Mon–Sat 10am–6pm, Sun 2–6pm; Sept daily 2–6pm;* 🕐*Mon morning.* ⌨€5. 🖉04 75 64 22 74; www.musee-vivaraisprotestant.org) has been set up in the birthplace of Pierre Durand, one of the Desert Fathers in the 18C, and his sister Marie Durand. This 18C Huguenot heroine was locked up in the tower of Constance d'Aigues-Mortes for 38 years (1730–68).
Pranles has become the Mecca of Protestantism in the Vivarais region; a Protestant gathering is held here on Whit Monday every year.

▸ **Population:** 8 700.
⌀ **Michelin Map:** 331: J-5.
▣ **Info:** 3 Pl. du Gén.-de-Gaulle, 07000 Privas. 🖉04 75 20 81 81.
◗ **Location:** 30km/19mi from Aubenas (to the SW) and Montélimar (SE).
🕐 **Timing:** Allow half a day to get a feel for the place.

Mirabel★
Mirabel is a stronghold that once commanded the main road from the Rhône to the Cévennes, and played a strategic role during the Wars of Religion.

Grottes de Montbrun
🏃*45min there and back.*
To discover these mysterious caves, descend by a difficult path down the left flank of a ravine.

Sceautres
This miniscule vilage, nestled on a grassy terrace at the bottom of the valley, seems crammed against the black basalt rock that dominates it.

🚗 DRIVING TOUR

PLATEAU DU COIRON★★
74km/46mi from Privas.
Allow half a day.

▷ Head S from Privas along D 7, following signs to Villeneuve-de-Berg.

The deeply-eroded volcanic bar that forms the Coiron plateau marks, to the north, the limit of the Lower Vivarais area. Its black basalt rocks cut across the line of hills from the Escrinet pass to the River Rhône, creating the starkly contrasting Rochemaure dikes.
The upper part of the Coiron plateau takes the form of a vast, bare *planèze* with an average altitude of 800m rising from the banks of the Rhône in a north-westerly direction.

The road crosses the Ouvèze basin then enters the sun-baked Bayonne gorge. As the road climbs the hillside, there is a succession of superb views of Privas and the surrounding area. Suddenly, though, where the basalt has covered the base of the mountain, the scenery becomes darker and gloomier.

▶ At the junction with the road to Freyssenet, turn left towards Taverne.

The countryside stretches away as undulating moorland dotted with juniper bushes, box and broom, a landscape bereft of human habitation were it not for the hamlet of **Taverne**.

▶ In Taverne, take D 213.

Between the Col de Fontenelle) and Les Molières, a broad gap in the hills provides a view of the Rhône in the distance. In the foreground are basalt columns down which runs a thin stream of water. On one of the hillsides to the right, erosion has worn the rock down to the underlying limestone layer. The road then runs steeply down to Les Molières along the side of the ravine where the various strata in the rock are clearly visible.

▶ Beyond St-Martin-le-Supérieur turn right along the Lower Lavézon valley. The river bed is covered with large, rounded, black and white boulders.

Meysse
15min on foot there and back.
The old village can be discerned behind its façade of more modern housing. Around the old Romanesque church is a network of narrow streets and vaulted passages.

▶ Follow D 2 up the Lower Lavézon Valley; turn right towards St-Vincent-de-Barrès.

The road runs through the vast **Barrès** basin with its fertile farmland. It then follows a tributary valley of the River Rhône which separates the limestone uplands

of Cruas to the east from the volcanic Coiron plateau to the west.

St-Vincent-de-Barrès
This is a lovely village perched on a basalt neck jutting out from above the Barrès plain. It is dwarfed by the basalt towers of its old fortress. From the esplanade in front of the church there is a view over the Barrès area.

▶ Take the D 322 which winds to the east for 8.5km/5.2mi.

Cruas
Cruas pays a heavy price for its industrial development, but its unique heritage should not be overlooked. The town is dominated by an imposing tower and chapel.
In 804, Benedictine monks founded an abbey at Cruas, although the oldest part of the extant church dates from the 11C. To protect themselves from invasion and floods, the monks established themselves on a rocky ledge, and later integrated this into the town's defensive structure, earning it the name 'The Castle of the Monks'. In the 16C-17C, the abbey was attacked by the Huguenots.

Former abbey church★
Guided visits possible: ask at the tourist office.
This is a beautiful Romanesque building, dominated by a powerful lantern tower. The interior is sombre, with a vaulted ceiling. The earthen flooring was damaged from the 15C to the 18C by flooding.
There is an 11C **crypt**★ under the choir, with many examples of Romanesque bestiary sculpture.

Dungeon-chapel
Take rue Jean-Jaurès and after about 200m turn left onto an ascending lane. Leave the car on an esplanade and walk from there to the ruins (*visit organised by tourist office*).
Note the group of medieval houses lower down.

ADDRESSES

Vals-les-Bains

This spa resort lies in a surprising setting at the bottom of the deeply-encased Volane valley. The town has developed along the valley, resulting in a narrow urban corridor about 2km/1.3mi long but on average only 300m wide.

- ▶ **Population:** 3 522.
- **Michelin Map:** 331: I-6 Local map see Massif du TANARGUE.
- **Info:** 7 r. Jean-Jaurès, 07600 Vals-les-Bains. 📞04 75 89 14 97. www.aubenas-vals.com.
- **Location:** Just 5.5km/3.5mi N of Aubenas.
- **Timing:** Allow at least half a day to explore.

Intermittent Spring

East bank. This spring (discovered in 1865) gushes forth from the middle of the park at the southern end of town. It rises to a height of 8m every six hours *(11.30am and 5.30pm in summer, 10.30am and 4.30pm in winter).*

Rocher des Combes

2km/1.2mi E via a road alongside the hospital – 15min on foot there and back. This is one of many excursions starting from Vals.

🚶 From the viewing table there is a good view over the surrounding mountains.

🚗 DRIVING TOURS

VALLÉE DE LA VOLANE AND VALLÉE DE LA BOURGES★★
Round trip of 69km/43mi. Allow 4h.

▶ Leave Vals on D 578 N to Mézilhac.

The Volane valley is lined with terraced hamlets, dotted with boulders and darkened by ancient basalt flows. The site of Antraigues, perched on its rocky promontory, marks the end of the lava flows.

Antraigues-sur-Volane

This delightful hill village is clustered around a shaded square lined with attractive terraces and patronised by enthusiastic *boules* players in high season.

Mézilhac

The village stands on the sill between the Eyrieux and Ardèche valleys. From a basalt peak crowned by a cross there is a splendid **view★** north-west to the Gerbier-de-Jonc peak and the Mézenc range, north-east to the Boutières cirque and south down the Volane valley.

© Franck Guiziou/hemis.fr

Cascade du Ray-Pic

> Take D 122 along the crest to Lachamp-Raphaël then take D 215 down to Burzet.

Cascade du Ray-Pic★★

🚶 *45min on foot there and back.*

A path leads to the foot of these impressive falls, where the river gushes between two overhanging walls of basalt in an austere landscape at the bottom of a ravine.

Burzet

This village is renowned for its annual procession, commemorating Christ's Passion, up to a calvary overlooking the village and the River Bourges flowing beside it.

> Return to Vals via St-Pierre-de-Colombier, Juvinas and D 243. Or drive to Montpezat along D 26, then follow D 536 and join up with the tour described under AUBENAS.

COL DE L'ESCRINET★

85km/53mi. Allow 3h.

> Leave Vals S on D 578B.

Ucel

Ancient village built in a circle on a hilltop overlooking the River Ardèche.

> In St-Privat, turn left onto D 256, running along the Luol and Boulogne valleys.

It is a pleasure to drive through the pretty landscape of orchards and vineyards, alternating with pine and chestnut groves.

St-Julien-du-Serre

The village has an interesting 12C Romanesque **church** with an unusual silhouette, its apse supported by hefty flying buttresses.

> Drive through St-Michel-de-Boulogne to the ruins of the Château de Boulogne.

Château de Boulogne★

This was originally a fortress, built by the Poitiers family on a spur between two ravines. The castle was transformed over the centuries into a sumptuous residence which escaped the ravages of the Revolution, but was partly demolished in 1820.

The magnificent **gateway★★**, which René de Hautefort had built in the late 16C, incorporates twisted columns drawing on Renaissance tradition.

> Turn round and take D 256 on the right. Drive through Gourdon, then turn right onto D 122, skirting Roc de Gourdon. After 2km/1.2mi, turn left onto a narrow lane that leads to Pourchères.

Pourchères

The 12C church built on the nearby slopes features a single nave and a semicircular apse.

> Turn round and take D 122 on the left, then N 104, heading for Col de l'Escrinet.

Col de l'Escrinet

This pretty pass provides access to both the south of the Ardèche and the Plateau du Coiron. It offers a fine **panorama** encompassing the Plateau du Coiron, Privas valley, Tanargue massif and Mont Lozère.

> Before driving down towards Aubenas, turn left onto D 224, heading for Freyssenet.

Crête de Blandine

Park the car on the flat area and head for the television transmitter. This crest

MASSIF DU TANARGUE

Col de la Chavade △ 1266

Parc   naturel

D 536

VALS-LES-BAINS

N

Serre de la Croix de Bauzon

★ **Coulée basaltique**

Pont-de-Labeaume

D 239

★ **Col de la Croix de Bauzon**

Rocher d'Abraham

Bruget

Jaujac ★

D 19

△ 1538

△ 1498

△ 1308

Masméjean

D 19

Lignon

La Souche

des

D 5

ST-ÉTIENNE-DE-LUGDARÈS

D 301

★ **Borne**

Gorges de la Borne

Col de Meyrand ★★

√ 1370

△ 1448

régional

△ 572

Coupe de Jaujac

776

D 24

Le Tanargue ★★

Le Mas-de-Truc

Loubaresse

Valgorge

Col de la Croix de Millet

D 5

Monts

Beaume

D 24

d'Ardèche

Roche

is the highest summit of the plateau. The **view**★ extends over Privas to the east and Mirabel and Aubenas to the south.

▶ Return to Col de l'Escrinet, then drive back to Vals via St-Privat and Ucel.

THE MASSIF DU TANARGUE
80km/50mi round tour. Allow 3h.

The route passes the basalt flows of the Lignon valley; 2km/1.2mi beyond Pont-de-Labeaume, at a signpost, park and walk up to the edge of the volcanic platform on which the road runs; here and there the **basalt flow**★ takes on a striking appearance of perfectly vertical tube-like sections, some of a blue-grey colour.

Jaujac
This village has attractive 15C and 16C houses, especially in the Chastelas district on the west bank, and the ruins of its old fortified castle. To the southeast rises the "Jaujac dish", an ancient volcano from which the flows of the Lignon emerged, and where mineral springs emanate.

Col de la Croix de Bauzon★
From this pass the view extends over the valleys of the Borne and the Masméjean

to the mountains of the Margeride; to the east, the Lignon basin continues into the Aubenas depression.

A small ski resort has been created at the foot of the Tanargue slopes, between La Souche and St-Étienne-de-Ludgarès.

▶ Follow D 19 towards St-Étienne-de-Lugdarès and turn left on D 301 (narrow road).

Gorges de la Borne★
Beyond a stretch of route across broom-covered moorland, the descent to Borne offers plunging views over the gorge. To the west is the profile of Le Goulet mountain. **Borne**★ itself is a village in a secluded site, on a ledge above the deeply embanked torrent.

▶ Continue to Col de Meyrand, via Loubaresse. As far as the village the road is narrow and sometimes impassable due to rockfalls.

Col de Meyrand★★
From this pass a splendid ledge is suddenly revealed. An extensive panorama is visible, from left to right, over the summit of the Tanargue, the Valgorge valley, the Ardèche depression overlooked by the Dent de Rez, the Valgorge ridge opposite and, to the right, the back of Mont Lozère.

▷ Turn back.

Beyond Loubaresse there are views along the channel down to Valgorge, then of stretches shaded by chestnut trees. The road drops downhill, twisting along the upper valley of the Beaume.

Valgorge
This small village is situated within a lush setting of vineyards and orchards.

▷ Continue on D 24 until you reach Roche and take D 5 on the left.

The road follows the Ligne valley up to Col de la Croix-de-Millet.

▷ D 5 leads back to Jaujac and Pont-de-Labeaume. There, take N 102 on the right, heading for Vals.

MONTAGNE AND HAUTE VALLÉE DE L'ARDÈCHE★
Approx 82km/51mi. Allow half a day.

▷ Leave Vals-les-Bains heading S, and then take the N 102 on the right and follow the valley as far as Pont-de-Labeaume. The take the D 536 on the right – in the direction of Montpezat-sous-Bauzon.

The old town of Montpezat has given its name to a major hydroelectric project, commissioned in 1954. It is the first example in France of a group of reservoirs straddling the watershed, and several dams serve to collect water from the upper Loire and its tributaries.

Éperon de Pourcheyrolles★
800m before Montpezat turn right, and then 600m after the path to the power plant take a short paved road. Leave the car at the end of the road and walk from there (⚐ 15min there and back).
About 100m below the last pylon there is a great view of the outcrop on which rest the ruins of the feudal castle of Pourcheyrolles.

▷ After the bridge over the Fontaulière, take the narrow lane

to Chaudouards which branches on the right.

Église Notre-Dame-de-Prévenchère
The interior of this 12C–13C church is characterised by four short naves featuring Romanesque or Gothic vaulting. Driving back towards Montpezat, you encounter the **town** with its narrow main street flanked by old granite houses built in the mountain style: curved façades, with low porches resting on round arches.

Montpezat-sous-Bauzon
The old village has given its name to an electrical complex set up in 1954, consisting of several dams designed to collect the waters coming from the upper Loire valley and its tributaries.

▷ Take D 536 for Suc de Bauzon until you reach D 110. Turn left to go to St-Cirgues-en-Montagne.

Saint-Cirgues-en-Montagne
The church is Romanesque and typical of those found in the mountains with its squat appearance and bell-tower.

▷ Take D 239 S heading towards Mazan-l'Abbaye.

Mazan-l'Abbaye★
In a clearing of Mazan forest, this 12C abbey was the first Cistercian sanctuary built in the province of Languedoc.

Forêt de Mazan★
Small waterfalls, moss-covered rocks and wild blueberries and raspberries provide a charming backdrop to a walk through the lush undergrowth.

▷ Continue along D 239, which leads to Col de la Chavade and the start of the Ardèche valley.

Col de la Chavade
This pass marks the watershed between the Atlantic Ocean and the Mediterranean. N 102 between Le Puy and Viviers follows the traditional route from the

Velay area to the Rhône valley. Just over a mile beyond the pass, the road crosses the Ardèche. This hilly drive offers beautiful views down the valley.

Mayres
This hamlet is situated in a wooded gorge. From a footbridge on the river, about 1km/0.6mi above the hamlet, there is a lovely view of the upper valley.

Thueyts★
This small town surrounded by orchards lies on a basalt flow, the remains of an ancient volcanic eruption.
A **waymarked footpath★** (🏃1h30 return; follow the red arrows) leads along the edge of the lava flow. Just upstream from the Pont du Diable, the Ardèche flows through a narrow gorge, making an interesting **scene★** against the dark backdrop of the basalt cliffs. Steps lead up to the top of the basalt cliffs, affording pretty views of the valley.

Neyrac-les-Bains
This small spa town backs onto the slopes of the Soulhiol volcano. In the Middle Ages its bicarbonated hot springs were thought to cure leprosy.

▶ At the exit of Pont-de-Labeaume turn left following signs to Notre-Dame de Nièges; the road drops into a valley before reaching a plateau. Park the car down on the right.

Notre-Dame de Nièges
The church stands on a hill overlooking the river. Little remains of the original 10C building. The road back to Pont-de-Labeaume commands pleasant views of the medieval fortress of Ventadour.

Château de Ventadour
🚶Guided visits: Jul–Sept Mon–Fri 9am–noon, 2–7pm, Sat–Sun 3–7pm. ⊚€3. ℘04 75 38 00 92 (Jul–Oct), or ℘03 23 55 50 67 (Nov–Jun). http://chateau.ventadour.free.fr.
Partly demolished and abandoned, this imposing medieval fortress would have eventually disappeared without the valiant efforts of Pierre Pottier and his wife who, since 1969, have undertaken to restore it.

▶ N 102 and then D 104 lead back to Aubenas.

ADDRESSES

🛏STAY
⊝⊝⊝ **Grand Hôtel de Lyon** – 11, Avenue Paul Ribeyre. ℘04 75 37 43 70. www.grandhoteldelyon.com. 34 rooms. Restaurant⊝⊝. This hotel is centrally located, and has rooms that are spacious and well kept.

🍴EAT
⊝⊝ **Le Tanargue** – Au Village, 07110 Valgorge. ℘04 75 88 98 98. www.hotel-le-tanargue.com. Closed Sun evening and Mon except Apr–Sept and school holidays. 22 rooms. Inviting inn set in the Vivarois mountains; the restaurant serves a good selection of dishes every day.

ON THE TOWN
Casino – Av. Claude-Expilly. ℘04 75 88 77 77. www.casinodevals.fr. Located in a scenic, rather old-fashioned park also housing a theatre and a cinema, this casino is comprised of slot machines, a bar, and two restaurants.

Aux Chandelles – 4 av. Chabalier, a few miles from Aubenas near the casino. ℘04 75 37 46 83. Open daily (except Tue in Aug) from 6.30pm. This Mexican bar is warm and lively.

SHOPPING
Brasserie Bourganel – 7 av. Claude-Expilly. ℘04 75 94 03 16. www.bieres-bourganel.com. Set on the banks of the Volane, this brewery organises informative visits followed by tastings.

SPORTS AND LEISURE
🏞 Parc naturel regional des Monts d'Ardèche ℘04 75 94 35 20. www.maison.parc-monts-ardeche.fr. Founded on the initiative of local chestnut growers, this nature park comprises 132 municipalities committed to the protection of the natural and cultural heritage of the Monts d'Ardèche.

Aubenas

Aubenas stands in an impressive **setting★**, perched on a spur of rock overlooking the Ardèche. The roads hugging the Coiron cliffs to the east reveal a wonderful **view** of the valley below. Aubenas is known for its candied chestnuts and jam.

A BIT OF HISTORY

Following a bitter winter in 1669–70, which killed all the local olive trees, rumours of new taxes fuelled deep-seated dissatisfaction. On 30 April 1670 a farm inspector was stoned in Aubenas; the ringleader of the attackers was thrown into prison, but the rioters, led by a country squire from La Chapelle-sous-Aubenas, **Antoine du Roure**, effected his release the very next day. While the governor of Languedoc played for time by holding negotiations, Roure's men captured Aubenas.

Towards the end of July, the rebels fought the royal army at Lavilledieu. The peasants were massacred, and Roure was subsequently executed in Montpellier. Aubenas and La Chapelle were condemned to pay heavy fines as a reflection of royal wrath.

SIGHTS
Château
Guided tours (minimum 2 people). Tue–Sat 10.30am–2.30pm. Public holidays. €4.50. 04 75 87 81 11. www.aubenas.fr.
The oldest parts of this fine building date from the 12C. The castle was enlarged by a succession of families.

Dôme St-Benoît
Guided tours Jul–Aug at 5pm. 04 75 87 81 11.
This hexagonal building is the former Benedictine chapel of Aubenas (17C–18C).

Old Houses
The 16C "House of Gargoyles" stands opposite the château; its tall polygonal turret is decorated with magnificent

- **Population:** 12 563.
- **Michelin Map:** 331: I-6.
- **Info:** place de l'Airette, 07200. 04 75 89 02 03. www.aubenas-vals.com.
- **Location:** Aubenas is 40km/25mi W of Montélimar.
- **Parking:** There are numerous car parks in the centre of town.
- **Timing:** Allow half a day for a relaxed stroll around town.

Château d'Aubenas

© Franck Guizou/hemis.fr

gargoyles. There is a charming 16C staircase-turret in the courtyard of the "Maison de Castrevieille" on place Parmentier; handsome town houses line rue Jourdan.

EXCURSION
Jastres Panorama★
7.5km/4.5mi SE via N 102. 4km/2.5mi beyond the bridge spanning the Ardèche, turn left on the access road to an industrial estate. After 200m, turn right onto a tarred road. After 1km/0.5mi turn left on a rocky uphill road. Park at the top.
The edge of the plateau was the site of a prehistoric settlement. Where the road ends, the view embraces the entire Lower Ardèche, the Aubenas valley and the Coiron range to the north-east.

🚗 DRIVING TOUR

DÉFILÉS DE L'ARDÈCHE★
44km/27mi. Allow 2h.

▷ Take D 104 from Aubenas to St-Étienne-de-Fontbellon, then turn left onto D 579.

The light-filled Ardèche valley forms a wide dip stretching to the basin of the Lower Chassezac in the west. The river flows through fertile basins. Here the road runs close to the river, between orchards and vineyards.

Vogüé
The village of ancient, arch-spanned streets dominated by a castle is built against a cliff overlooking the Ardèche. The vast 16C **château** (◷*Apr–Jun and mid-Sept–early Nov Wed–Sun 10.30am–1pm, 2–6pm; early Jul–mid-Sept daily 10am–7pm.* ◷*1st wk in Jul.* ⬤€5. ✆*04 75 37 01 95. www.chateaudevogue.net*), which still belongs to the Vogüé family, replaced the original medieval fortress and now houses exhibitions on the Vivarais region.

▷ Head back S to D 1, then D 401 on the left to Rochecolombe.

Rochecolombe★
The medieval village of Rochecolombe occupies a secluded **site**★ overlooking a stream rising from a limestone corrie. There are in fact two villages of Roche-colombe: the upper one is the first, with houses clustered around a church.

▷ From the square in the upper village, turn left onto a road down to a bridge across the stream. Park a little further along, just before a bend, and follow the footpath down to the water's edge.

On the right stands the **medieval village**, at the foot of the ruins of a square tower and the bell-tower of a Romanesque chapel. At the bottom of the corrie, enclosed by limestone cliffs are two **Vauclusian springs.**

▷ Return towards Vogüé on D 401, turn left on D 114 after crossing the Ardèche.

In Lanas, the road crosses the river by a narrow bridge, offering a view of the Auzon confluence with the Ardèche.

▷ In St-Maurice-d'Ardèche turn right onto D 579, then right onto D 294 just after the station in Balazuc.

Balazuc★
This once-fortified village is perched above a secluded gorge. Cross the bridge to the opposite bank for a good view of the village.

▷ During the summer season, leave the car in the car park.

Like many villages in the Lower Vivarais area, Balazuc was founded by a Saracen colony in the 8C and 9C. It now makes a pleasant place for a stroll, particularly in the old streets up to the castle.

🚶 For a pleasant walk downstream along the banks of the Ardèche, take the dirt track to the left of the bridge at the foot of the village. Here the river flows through a narrow passage between walls of rock.

▷ Take D 104 to Uzer; on reaching Bellevue, follow D 4 to Ruoms.

The entrance to the Ligne gorge is marked by a narrow rocky passage. A beautiful **view** unfolds upstream of the Ardèche at the confluence of the two rivers. The Ligne gorge is followed by the **Défilé de Ruoms**★, alongside which the road passes through pictur-esque tunnels in the rock.

▷ Take the bridge on the left to Ruoms.

Ruoms
The walled centre of this town lies within a quadrilateral of ramparts flanked by seven round towers.

▷ Return to Aubenas on the D 4, D 294, D 114 and D 579.

Les Vans

In the heart of the Lower Vivarais, in the middle of a fertile basin watered by the River Chassezac and dominated to the west by the jagged spire of the Barre ridge lies the town of Les Vans (pronounce the "s" of Vans). The setting, for those arriving from the Cévennes, is a magnificent Mediterranean scene, with an austere landscape of schist ridges to the north giving way to the dazzling white limestone of the south.

> ▶ **Population:** 2 776.
> ◉ **Michelin Map:** 331: G-7.
> ▯ **Info:** Pl. Ollier, 07140 Les Vans. ℘04 75 37 24 48. www.cevennes-ardeche.com.
> ▶ **Location:** 38km/24mi SW of Aubenas.
> ▲▲ **Kids:** Go bathing at Mazet-Plage, or discover the rural life in Gravières.
> ◔ **Timing:** You should allow a full day to appreciate the town and its surroundings.

EXCURSIONS

Rocher de Sampzon
7km/4.2mi S of Ruoms.
🚶 *Leave the car in the car park down from the church of Sampzon and go to the summit on the tarmac road, then on the path level with the platform.*
From the top, the **panorama★★** encompasses the Vallon basin, the Orgnac plateau and the River Ardèche.

Labeaume
3.5km/2mi W of Ruoms. on the D 245.
At the edge of a gorge with arcaded streets and galleried houses.
🚶 The walk along the left bank of the river to the **Gorges de la Beaume★**, is most pleasant, offering pretty views of the shimmering waters and the sculpted limestone cliffs.

🚗 DRIVING TOURS

VILLAGES DU VIVARAIS CÉVENOL★
34km/21mi round trip. Allow 2h30.

▶ Leave Les Vans on D 10 N, turn right on D 250.

Chambonas
This is a village with a part-Romanesque church (12C–17C) with towers covered in glazed tiles, and formal gardens said to have been laid out by Le Nôtre.

▶ Follow D 250.

The road runs alongside the Chassezac, crosses the Sûre and climbs a sandstone slope between vineyards and stands of evergreens.

Payzac
There is a charming rural church (12C–15C) here.

▶ Take D 207 towards St-Jean-de-Pourcharesse.

The sandstone landscape modulates from grey to red tones. After the village of Brès the surrounding rock becomes schist and the road winds through chestnut groves.

St-Jean-de-Pourcharesse
A typical local church, built of schist with a roof covered in stone slabs *(lauzes)* stands in this village.

▶ Take the road to Lauriol village.

From here, the road passes more chestnut groves in a landscape slashed by ravines, to the edges of which cling tiny hamlets. Note the interesting stone-slabbed roofs.

St-Pierre-le-Déchausselat
This village is built on terraces. From the vineyards of the farm below the church there is an attractive view over the surrounding countryside.

Romanesque church, Thines

© Photoshot

▷ Return to Les Vans via Chambonas.

CORNICHE DU VIVARAIS CÉVENOL★

113km/70mi. Allow 5h.

▷ Leave Les Vans on D 901 towards Villefort and take D 113 right.

Gravières

The **church** (12C–15C) here has a sturdy belfry. Inside, in the wall of the chancel, there is a 14C Tree of Jesse of carved stone (*for visits call ☎04 75 37 31 07*).
👥 A round tour (6km/3.5mi) starting from **La Virade du Batistou** runs right around the village inviting children to discover the rural life of the early 20C.

▷ Continue along D 113 and, beyond the bridge on the River Chassezac, turn right on D 413.

Les Salelles

This village overlooks a meander in the Chassezac. The **church of St-Sauveur** is a Gothic edifice built of warm red sandstone. The fortified belfry, destroyed by lightning, was rebuilt in the early 20C.

▷ Follow the valley along D 113.

Usine de Pied-de-Borne

At the confluence of the Altier, the Chassezac and the Borne, the hydroelectric plant is powered by the Villefort and the Roujanel, producing more than half of the total energy output for the valley.

▷ Having crossed the Borne, turn right on the D 151 towards La Bastide-Puylaurent.

La Bastide-Puylaurent

The village was founded in the 19C during the construction of the Paris–Nîmes railway line; it is a pleasant, cool resort in the upper Allier valley.

▷ Leave La Bastide going E on the D 906, and turn left onto the D 4.

Trappe de Notre-Dame-des-Neiges

This Cistercian abbey was founded in 1850; it is isolated among woodlands of conifer and beech, and sheltered from the winds that sweep the Vivarais mountains.
On the descent to St-Laurent-les-Bains, a bend on the left offers a **view★★** at the entrance to the Borne valley.

Saint-Laurent-les-Bains

Confined in a narrow valley, this small spa resort treats different forms of rheumatism. From the main street, where there is a hot fountain (53°C/127°F), there is a nice view of an old tower on the ridge above.

◉ Continue on the D 4.

The road descends to cross the Borne and then climbs again passing through a beautiful pine forest that gives way to a more desolate landscape.

◉ Turn right towards Montselgues.

Montselgues

This tiny village in the middle of a vast undulating plateau, dotted with wild narcissi and broom in June, has a sturdy church with a lovely Romanesque doorway. The village is a cross-country skiing centre.

◉ Come back to the D 4, then take the D 513 on the right.

Thines★★

This small village sits on a spectacular site★★ perched above the Thines torrent and its ravine. It boasts old houses clinging to the rock, narrow alleyways and a fine Romanesque church. The east end★ is particularly attractive, with a cornice adorned with fanciful motifs below which is a blind arcade resting on carved consoles and engaged columns. The alternating colour of the stonework – pink sandstone, grey granite and white limestone – adds to the charm of the building.

◉ Go back as far as the crossroads with the D 4 and there turn right.

Shortly before Peyre, there is a good view★ to the right of Thines down below.

◉ Return to Le Vans via Pont de Chambonas.

ADDRESSES

⌂STAY

⊜ **Camping La Source** – *Chemin de la rouvière, 07460 Berrias-et-Casteljau (12km/7.2mi SE of Les Vans via D 901 and D 202). ℘04 75 39 39 13. Open Apr-Sept. Reservation recommended. 81 sites. Food*

service. This fairly new campground has been well planned: the clearly defined sites are already protected from the sun. The bar, pizzeria and grocery, located in the same building, provide on-site sustenance. Enticing pool.

⊜⊜ **Le Carmel** – *Montée du Carmel. ℘04 75 94 99 60. www.le-carmel.com. 26 rooms. Restaurant⊜⊜.* Dominating the medieval town, this former Carmelite convent has delightfull rooms, decorated with the fabrics and colours of Provence. Pretty garden, sunny breakfast room, shaded terrace and, at the table, dishes of the day.

⊜⊜ **Chambre d'Hôte l'Ensolleiade** – *07460 Casteljau (10km/6mi SE of Les Vans via D 901 and D 252). ℘06 95 56 15 80. www.ensolleiade.com. Closed Oct-Apr. 5 rooms.* The bedrooms of this peaceful low house in the middle of the countryside are simple, sunny and spacious. You will appreciate the beauty of nature walks and the freshness of a dip in the pool, unless you would rather catch forty winks under the cherry trees.

⊜⊜⊜ **La Santoline** – *07430 Beaulieu. 13km/8mi SE of Les Vans via D 901, D 202 and D 252. ℘04 75 39 01 91. www.la santoline.com. closed mid Sept-mid Apr. 8 rooms.* Isolated in the middle of the garrigue, this 16C edifice will delight those who yearn for peace and quiet. Colourful elegance prevails in the rooms, none of which is alike. Supper, for residents only, is served in a pretty, arched dining room. There is a pool and a garden for your pleasure.

ⵔ/EAT

⊜⊜⊜ **Chez Vincent et Michèle – Pizzeria le "C4"** – *07460 Berrias-et-Casteljau (10km/6mi E of Les Vans. Take D 901, D 252 and follow signs to VVF). ℘04 75 39 35 33. Closed mid-Sept-Apr. Reservation recommended.* Summertime, amid the rocky gorges, you can savour Le Lagon's fine cuisine by the waterfall pool or, more simply, have a pizza on the terrace next door. Off-season, take a seat at La Bastide d'Edouard.

Gorges de l'Ardèche★★★

The Ardèche gorge, overlooked by an audaciously engineered road, ranks among the most impressive sites of natural beauty in the south of France; a large part of the gorge is now a nature reserve. In 1993, this exceptional stretch of landscape was listed as a major national site (Grand Site d'Intérêt National).

A BIT OF HISTORY

Spates and droughts – In the upper valley, the Ardèche cuts a steep downhill course, but it is in the lower valley that the more interesting formations are to be seen. Here the river has carved a passage through the limestone of the plateau, already undermined by subterranean streams. The Ardèche's tributaries flowing down from the mountain accentuate its sporadic yet typically Mediterranean flow. During the autumn spates, when the river's volume can increase dramatically, there is a tremendous convergence of flood waters at Vallon-Pont-d'Arc.

The strength of these erratic floodwaters is such that the river pushes the flow of the Rhône eastwards and deposits alluvial debris in its river bed. In 1890, the force of the Ardèche spate was so strong that it cut right across the course of the Rhône and broke through the Lauzon dike on the opposite bank.

🚗 DRIVING TOURS

ROUTE PANORAMIQUE

38km/24mi starting from Vallon-Pont-d'Arc. Allow half a day.

The D 290 overlooks the gorge from the clifftops at the edge of the Gras plateau, giving views from the many look-out points *(belvédères)* along the way.

Vallon-Pont-d'Arc

This town is the departure point for boat trips down the gorge. Southeast of the town, on the slope of a hill, stand the

- ⚓ **Michelin Maps:** 331: I-7 to J-8.
- ▶ **Location:** It is difficult to get a complete overview of the gorges, but the view from the panoramic road is as good as any.
- 🏞 **Don't Miss:** The Pont d'Arc.
- 🕐 **Timing:** You should allow a whole day to do a complete circuit.
- 👪 **Kids:** If the water is calm, take a canoe trip on the river.

PRACTICAL INFO

A FRAGILE ENVIRONMENT

The **Ardèche Nature Reserve** is a conservation area, so every effort should be made to protect its ecosystem. In particular, visitors must not light a fire, leave behind rubbish, pick plants or stray from the signposted footpaths. Picnicking is possible all along the way. Camping or bivouacking is prohibited outside authorised camp sites (*see Where to Stay, p437*).

ruins of Vieux Vallon castle, a reminder of the old medieval village here.

Exposition Grotte Chauvet-Pont-d'Arc

At the end of 1994, a set of cave paintings was discovered on the site of the Combe-d'Arc in the Ardèche gorge. Part of a vast network of underground galleries, the cave (Grotte Chauvet) features numerous prehistoric red and black paintings of some 400 animals, including horse, mammoth, bear, woolly rhinoceros, cat and auroch; figures of a hyena and an owl are also portrayed, which is exceptionally rare. Initial studies of the art date them to about 30 000 years ago.

The number, quality and originality of the paintings place the cave on a par

Pont-d'Arc

with the Cosquer cave east of Marseille and the Lascaux cave in the Dordogne, in terms of the importance of its contribution to the study of prehistory worldwide.

▷ Head S for Pont-d'Arc on D 290.

The road skirts the ruins of Vieux Vallon castle and after crossing the Ibie, comes to the Ardèche. On the left is the Grotte des Tunnels, a cave through which an underground torrent once ran, and then **Grotte des Huguenots** (◐ *mid-Jun–Aug 10am–7pm. t04 75 88 06 71*), which houses an exhibition on speleology, prehistory and the history of the Huguenot population of the southern Vivarais region.

Pont-d'Arc★★

🏃 At one time the river skirted this promontory and the arch would have been just a gully through which underground waters drained. General erosion and the river wore away the land around the arch, and then the river itself, during some particularly large spate, abandoned its old meander to slip through the passage. Beyond Pont-d'Arc the landscape becomes more impressive. The river follows a series of gentle curves, interspersed with rapids, at the bottom of a deserted gorge. After Chames the road veers round to the left at the bottom of Tiourre valley which forms an impressive, rocky **cirque★** before reaching the edge of the plateau.

Belvédère du Serre de Tourre★★

Poised almost vertically above the Ardèche, this viewpoint offers a superb **view** of the meander known as the **Pas du Mousse**, with the ruins of the 16C Château d'Ebbo clearly visible on the rocky promontory.

Belvédère de Gaud★★

There is a fine view of the upstream sweep of the Gaud meander and the turrets of its small 19C castle.

Belvédères d'Autridge★

To reach the two viewpoints, take the panoramic curve. The needle of rock known as Aiguille de Morsanne soars up from the Ardèche like a ship's prow.

Belvédères de Gournier★★

These viewpoints are well situated, high above the Ardèche. Below, the Gournier farm lies in ruins in a meadow beside the river.

▷ Continue to the Marzal chasm along the road across the Gras plateau (D 590).

Aven de Marzal★

Interior temperature 14°C; 743 steps. The chasm is a natural well, and leads to caves rich in stalagmites, stalactites and other limestone formations.

You can also visit the **Musée du Monde Souterrain** (♿ ◐ *Apr–early Nov 10.30am–5.30pm (Jul Aug 9.30am–*

7pm). *04 75 04 12 45. www. aven-marzal.com*), a museum devoted to the history of speleology in France. The **Zoo Préhistorique** (♿⌚*mid-Feb–early Mar 2–4.30pm; Apr–early Nov 10.30am–5.30pm (Jul–Aug 9.30am–6.30pm).* ⛵€8.50. *04 75 55 14 82)* is laid out along a shaded route displaying life-size reproductions of extinct animals that lived from the Primary to the Quaternary Era.

▶ D 201 leads to Bidon.

Bidon

This is a tiny village of traditional houses built with drystone walls, where life has gone on peacably for centuries.

▶ Return to the La Madeleine junction.

This is the **Haute Corniche★★★**, the most outstanding section of the drive, offering views of the gorge from a series of viewpoints in quick succession.

Belvédère de la Madeleine★

From here there is an imposing view of the Madeleine "fortress", a rocky outcrop blocking the view of the rest of the gorge downstream. These are the highest cliffs of the entire gorge.
🚶 From the parking area, a stony footpath leads through dense vegetation to the Belvédère de la Cathédrale.

👥 Grotte de la Madeleine★

◀◀*Daily: Apr–Jun and Sept 10am–6pm; Jul–Aug 10am–7pm; Oct–Nov 10am–5pm.* ⛵€10.50 (child 6–15, €6). *04 75 04 22 20. www.grottemadeleine.com.*
This cave was carved by an underground river which once drained part of the Gras plateau.
Enter through the Grotte Obscure, then follow a tunnel hewn out of the rock

(⌚*steep stairway)* which leads to the Salle du Chaos, a vast chamber divided into two by columns coming down from the cave roof.

Belvédère de la Cathédrale★★

🚶 This look-out gives an unparalleled view of one of the most fascinating natural sights along the gorge: an immense jagged rock known as the "Cathedral" rising above the river.

Balcon des Templiers

From the "Templars' Balcony" there are striking views of a tight loop in the river,

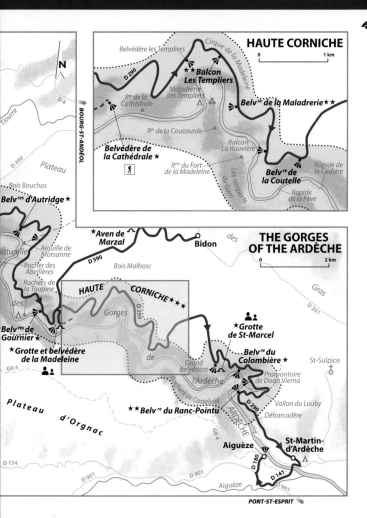

HAUTE CORNICHE

Belvédère les Templiers
Cirque de la Madeleine

★★**Balcon
Les Templiers**

D 290

R⁽ᵉ⁾ de la
Cathédrale

Maladrerie
des Templiers

Belvᵣₑ de la Maladrerie★★

Rᵉ de la Coucourde

**Belvédère de
la Cathédrale**★

Balcon
La Rouvière

Rᵉʳˢ du Fort
de la Madeleine

Les remparts
du Garn

**Belvᵣₑ de
la Coutelle**

Rapide de
la Cadière

Rapide
de la Fève

BOURG-ST-ANDÉOL

D 4

Tiourre

D 490

Plateau

Bois Bouchas

Belvᵣ d'Autridge★

N

★**Aven de
Marzal**

D 590

Bois Malbosc

Bidon

des

**THE GORGES
OF THE ARDÈCHE**

Gras

D 201

Aiguille de
Morsanne

Rocher des
Abeillères

Rochers de
la Toupine

HAUTE   **CORNICHE**★★★

Gorges

de

★**Grotte
de St-Marcel**

**Belvᵣₑ du
Colombière**★

St-Sulpice

Promontoire
de Dona Vierna

**Belvᵣₑˢ de
Gournier**★

★**Grotte et belvédère
de la Madeleine**

GR 4

Grand
Belvédère

l'Ardèche

Rochers de Castelviel

★★Belvᵣₑ du Ranc-Pointu

Vallon du Louby

Débarcadère

D 290

ARDÈCHE

Plateau   d'Orgnac

GR 4

Aiguèze

**St-Martin-
d'Ardèche**

D 174

D 901

D 180

D 901

Aiguèze

D 141

D 901

PONT-ST-ESPRIT

---

cut deep into the magnificent surrounding rock walls.

Belvédère de la Maladrerie
From here there is a good view of the "Cathedral" rock upstream.

Belvédère de la Coutelle
This viewpoint overlooks the Ardèche. To the right is the end of the Garn ramparts; to the left, along the axis of the gorge, are the Castelviel rocks.

Grotte de St-Marcel★
Guided tours: Apr–Jun and Sept 10am–6.30pm; Jul–Aug 10am–7.30pm;

Oct–early Nov 10am–5.30pm. €10.50 (child 6–15, €7). 04 75 04 38 07. www.grottesaintmarcel.com.
A tunnel dug through the rock leads into chambers and passageways lined with stalagmites and stalactites.

Belvédère du Colombier★
From here, there is a view over a meander enclosed by walls of rock. The road follows a loop along a dry valley, skirts the Dona Vierna promontory and makes a long detour along the Louby valley.

Following the Ardèche Gorge★★★

Downriver by boat or canoe

After a long, calm stretch, the river flows into a bend and enters the gorge. The impressive Rapide du Charlemagne comes just before the natural arch of Pont-d'Arc. After passing the Saleyron cliffs, the river forms rapids before reaching the Gaud meander and cirque. Rapids alternate with smooth-flowing stretches beneath impressive cliffs. After negotiating the boulders of the Toupine de Gournier, the Rocher de la Cathédrale looms into sight in the distance. Just before you actually pass this rock, the river takes you past a natural opening into La Madeleine cave.

Downriver from the Coucourde rock (Provençal for "crane") and the Castelvieil cliff, the opening of St-Marcel cave appears on the left and, as you round a bend, the Dona Vierna promontory and the Belvédère du Ranc-Pointu can be seen. The cliffs melt away as the valley finally widens out, overlooked by the tower of Aiguèze on the edge of the rocky outcrop to the right.

The whole trip covers a distance of 30km/18.6mi; however, it is possible to shorten this by starting from Chames. The river can be explored by canoe year-round, although the best times are in May, June and September.

Depending on the season and the water level, it is wise to allow six to nine hours to complete the trip (departures are not allowed after 6pm). There are a few difficult passages (rapids) which require a good canoeing technique; in addition, it is essential to be able to swim. Life jackets must be worn by participants and heavy fines are applied to those who do not comply with regulations.

Canoe hire – Some 50 hiring companies offer unaccompanied and guided trips lasting one or two days for an average price of €40 (one day) or €55 (two days without accommodation) per person (children under 7 years of age are not allowed on these trips). A list of hiring companies is available from tourist offices. For unaccompanied trips, it is necessary to book an overnight stop from central booking offices located in the above-mentioned tourist offices.

Overnight stops – Overnight stops along the gorge are allowed in two places only: Aire Naturelle de Gaud and Aire Naturelle de Gournier. Longer stays are possible at two campsites: Camping des Templiers (℘04 75 04 28 58; www.camping-templiers-ardeche.com) and Camping des Grottes de St-Marcel (℘04 75 04 14 65; www.campingdesgrottes.fr).

Following the gorge on foot

Two-day walking tour (21km/13mi) with an overnight stop at the Gournier bivouac (booking essential), or a one-day walk for strong walkers. A chance to spot the rare Bonelli's eagle that reigns supreme over the gorge.

A topoguide (French), *Les Gorges de l'Ardèche et leurs plateaux* (No. 2, Gilbert de Cochet) is published by the Syndicat Intercommunal des Gorges de l'Ardèche et de leur Région Naturelle (SIGARN ℘04 75 98 77 31).

Also available, and in part passing through the Ardèche, is *The Grand Traverse of the Massif Central* (in English) by Alan Castle (Cicerone Press, 2010: ISBN 978-1-85284-571-1. www.cicerone.co.uk), a guidebook to mountainbiking, cycling or walking the 700km GTMC, Grande Traversée du Massif Central, in southern France, from Clermont-Ferrand in the Auvergne to Montpellier and Sête on the Mediterranean. The long-distance route is described in stages for walkers, and mountain bikers, with on road alternatives for road cyclists.

Ardèche Gorges at St-Martin-d'Ardèche

© Bertrand Rieger/hemis.fr

Belvédère du Ranc-Pointu★★

This viewpoint at the mouth of the Louby valley overlooks the last meander of the Ardèche. From here the landscape changes dramatically on the way down to St-Martin: the bare defile gives way to a cultivated valley which opens out as it gets nearer the Rhône. On the opposite bank, the village of **Aiguèze** can be seen clinging to a rocky crest.

St-Martin-d'Ardèche

This is the first settlement since Vallon and a haunt of anglers, walkers and canoeists.

▶ Cross the river via the narrow suspension bridge then turn left onto D 901 and right again onto D 180.

Aiguèze

This medieval village crowns the last clifftops along the gorge. The 14C fort has a watch-path which offers **views★** of the mouth of the gorge, with Mont Ventoux in the distance and the suspension bridge linking Aiguèze to St-Martin-d'Ardèche in the foreground.

ADDRESSES

🛏 STAY

🍴🛏 **Hôtel-Restaurant Le Clos des Bruyères** – *Rte des Gorges, 07150 Vallon-Pont-d'Arc.* ✆*04 75 37 18 85.* *www.closdesbruyeres.fr. Closed Oct–Mar. 32 rooms.* The road through the gorges of the Ardèche is magnificent, but the curves can be awfully tiresome. Take a break in this regional-style house whose arcades open onto the summer pool. Rooms with a balcony or on the ground floor. Seafood served in the restaurant with a terrace.

🛏 **Camping Le Provençal** – *1.5km/1mi SE of Vallon-Pont-d'Arc.* ✆*04 75 88 00 48.* *www.camping-le-provencal.fr.* *Open mid Apr-mid Sept. Reservations recommended. 200 sites. Food service.* Beyond its pretty, flowery entrance, this elongated terrain stretches to the banks of the Ardèche. The sites are well defined and shaded. An agreeable place to stay, with its children's playground, attractive pool and tennis court.

🍴 EAT

🍴🛏 **L'Auberge Sarrasine** – *R. de la Fontaine, 30760 Aiguèze.* ✆*04 66 50 94 20.* *Closed Tue.* While meandering through the ancient village alleys, you'll come across this small restaurant taking up three vaulted rooms dating from the 11C. The chef does a fine job of marrying the flavours of Provence with different spices.

437

Aven d'Orgnac ★★★

Until 19August 1935 the people of Orgnac-l'Aven had paid little attention to the swallowhole known to them as "Le Bertras". Robert de Joly (1887–1968), President of the Speleology Society of France, who explored it at that time, then described its wealth of interesting features to them. He was an engineer with the College of Electricity in Paris and an enthusiastic potholer. He was also a daring explorer of this area of the Cévennes, where he lived, and he played a vital role in the development of equipment and techniques used in underground explorations. The huge chambers in the swallowhole were formed by the action of underground water from infiltrations in the cracked limestone rocks. The first concretions, some of which were 10m in diameter, were broken by an earthquake at the end of the Tertiary Era. These truncated or overturned columns then became the base for more recent stalagmites.

- **Michelin Map:** 331: I-8 – Local map see Gorges de l'Ardèche.
- **Info:** 1pl. de l'Ancienne-Gare, 07150 Vallon-Pont d'Arc. ✆04 75 88 0401. www.vallon-pont-darc.com.
- **Location:** Located 15km/10mi from Vallon-Pont d'Arc, the Aven d'Orgnac is at the southernmost edge of the Ardèche. The location is well signposted, 25km/16mi west of the Rhône valley.
- **Timing:** You will need at least half a day for the cave and area.

👥 UNDERGROUND MAZE

Temperature below earth 11°C. 👁700 steps, and return to the surface by lift. 👁Guided tours: Feb–Mar 10.30am, 11.30am 2.15pm, 3.30pm, 4.45pm; Apr–Jun every 30min from 10am–noon, 2–5.30pm; Jul–Aug all day; Oct–mid-Nov every 40min; Christmas holidays 2.15pm, 3pm, 3.45pm, 4.30pm. 👁"Pass Grand Site" (English tour of the Cave + guided or self-guided tour of the "Cité de la Préhistoire": €13 (child 6–14, €10.40) – payment by credit card only. ✆04 75 38 65 10. www.orgnac.com.

This fabulous cave system, discovered in 1935, is now a major tourist attraction and hugely popular. The development of the caves was a difficult task, and today the paths are at the bottom of the cave system up to 120m below the surface.

The system is entered through a long tunnel leading down to the entrance hall. The various tours descend by walking from chamber to chamber, which collectively cover 5km/3mi and over 30 000sq m. In June 2004, the cave system was listed as a Grand Site de France. Anyone contemplating touring the caves need to be tolerably fit and agile. The **Upper Chamber** (Salle Supérieure) is amazing for its sheer size (height: 17–40m; length: 250m; width: 125m) and the views in and around it. The dim light from the natural mouth of the swallowhole gives it a bluish tinge that appears somewhat unreal. It contains a number of magnificent stalagmites, in an incredible variety of shapes. The largest (in the centre) have the appearance of pinecones. For the most part, the height of the gallery roof has prevented stalagmites from joining up with the stalactites overhead to form columns; instead they have thickened at their base until some reach quite impressive dimensions. Other, more slender, stalagmites look like piles of plates, as a result of the slow oozing of water through the high, thin roof.

Beneath the lower sections of cave roof are slim **candle-like formations**, with straight or tapering sides. In the

© Christian Handl/imageBROKER/age fotostock

Cave of Aven d'Orgnac

niche of a huge formation of draperies and stalagmites like organ pipes is an urn containing the heart of Robert de Joly. In the **Rockfall Chamber** (Salle du Chaos), filled with concretions from the Upper Chamber, there are magnificent "drapes" of various colours – white, red and brown – hanging from a crack in the cave roof.

The **Red Chamber** (Salle Rouge) has a fantastic decor centred around colossal pillars of calcite. It owes its name to the layer of clay, the residue of the dissolving calcite, which covers floor, walls and concretions alike.

The climax of the tour is the **Grand Theatre** viewpoint overlooking a huge chamber which, at first, is in total darkness; however, music gradually fills the cave and, combined with light effects underlining details round the rock walls, creates a spellbinding atmosphere.

La Randonnée Souterraine

Cave enthusiasts may like to take part in this one-hour underground ramble, available to groups of restricted size only, through the red chambers, a magnificent part of the cavern that has been left as it was when discovered, apart from the electric lighting. This walk is an ideal compromise between standard guided tours of caves and full-blown potholing "in the raw", and is not unduly problematic or physi-cally taxing, although you will need to be reasonably agile.

Cité de la Prehistoire

The rooms, laid out around a patio, contain the finds from archaeological digs in Ardèche and the north of Gard. They date from the Lower Palaeolithic to the Iron Age (from 350 000 to 600 years BCE). Reconstructions, including an Acheulian hut from Orgnac 3, a flint workshop and a cave decorated with a Lion's Head provide an insight into the everyday life of prehistoric man.

🚗 DRIVING TOUR

PLATEAU D'ORGNAC
45km/28mi itinerary starting from Aven d'Orgnac; local map ⓒ see Gorges de l'ARDÈCHE.

Barjac

The narrow streets of the upper town, lined with fine 18C houses surround the castle now a cultural centre (cinema and multimedia library).

From the esplanade overlooking the valley, there is a fine view of the Cévennes mountains.

Twice a year (Easter weekend and around 15 August), Barjac holds an antique fair which attracts enthusiasts and specialists from all over the region.

▶ Follow D 979 N. In Vagnas, turn right onto D 355.

Labastide-de-Virac

This fortified village on the boundary between the Languedoc and Vivarais regions is an ideal departure point for outings to the Aveyron gorge or the Orgnac plateau.

Just north of the village stands a 15C castle, the **Château des Roure** (🕒*Jul–Aug daily 10am–7pm; Easter–Jun and Sept daily except Wed 2–6pm.* ⬗€7.20 (ticket including Musée de la Soie €9.20). 🔊04 75 38 61 13. www.chateaudesroure.com), which guarded the passage through the gorge at the Pont-d'Arc.

The two round towers were pulled down in 1629 during the Wars of Religion. Since 1825, the castle has belonged to the family of sculptor James Pradier (1795–1825) whose forebears were tenant farmers to the Counts of Roure; he carved the statues representing Lille and Strasbourg on place de la Concorde in Paris.

The tour takes in the Florentine courtyard, a spiral staircase and the great hall with its fine chimney-piece.

The castle watch-path overlooks the Ardèche and Gras plateaus, and in fine weather Mont Lozère and Mont Mézenc can be seen to the north.

The tour ends with an exhibition of handmade silk goods. A working silkworm farm illustrates traditional methods of silkworm breeding.

▶ Beyond Labastide, turn left off D 217.

The road runs through **Les Crottes**, a ruined village *(partly restored)* destroyed during World War II. A stele commemorates the inhabitants who were shot by the Nazis on 3 March 1944.

Continue to the **Belvédère du Méandre de Gaud**. This promontory commands an excellent **view**★★ of the Ardèche and the Gaud cirque.

▶ Drive back to D 217 and turn left. A minor road on the right leads to Aven de la Forestière.

Aven de la Forestière★

◆ Guided visits: Apr–Sept daily 12.30–5pm (Jul–Aug 10am–7pm). ⬗€8. 🔊04 75 38 63 08. www.avengrottelaforestiere.com.
This cavern, first explored by A Sonzogni in 1966, was opened to tourists in 1968. It is not far below ground and is easily accessible. The cleverly lit chambers contain a wealth of fine concretions in interesting shapes and subtle colours. A small underground zoo is home to a variety of fish, shellfish, frogs, toads and insects.

ADDRESSES

🛏STAY

⬗⬗ **Domain de la Sérénité** – Pl. de la Mairie, 30430 Barjac (6km/3.6mi W of the Aven d'Orgnac via D 317 and D 176). 🔊04 66 24 54 63. www.la-serenite.fr. Closed Dec–Easter. 3 rooms. Located in the heart of the village, a 17C residence sporting blue shutters and covered with Virginia creeper. Old furniture, odds and ends, ceramic wall tiles and earthen floor tiles give each room a personal touch.

🍴EAT

⬗ **Hotel-Restaurant les Stalagmites** – 07150 Orgnac-l'Aven. 🔊04 75 38 60 67. www.lesstalagmites.com. Closed mid Nov–Feb. A simple, very inexpensive family boarding-house with a warm welcome, located right in the village. In summer, the generous, traditional cuisine is served on the tree-shaded terrace.

⬗ **L'Esplanade** – Pl. de l'Église, 30430 Barjac. 🔊04 66 24 58 42. Closed Tue except during Jul–Aug. A small stone house dating from the 18C. The flowery terrace offers a lovely view of the countryside; the vaulted dining room is decorated with old farm tools.

Bourg-St-Andéol

A bas-relief of the god Mithras, aged by time, is all that remains of the cult that flourished here before the evangelisation of St Andéol.

SIGHTS

The Romanesque **Église Saint-Andéol** dates from the 11C–12C, and impresses with the simplicity of its interior design. The **Palais des Évêques**, the former palace of the bishops of Viviers, has "Sleeping Beauty" appeal with its monumental façade, huge chimneys and magnificent apartments.

At the entrance to the valley, between the sources of the **Tourne** a bas-relief of Gallo-Roman origin has been carved into the limestone rock; it represents the god Mithras, and in spite of its dull appearance you can still distinguish the god in the process of killing a bull.

🚗 DRIVING TOUR

PLATEAU DES GRAS★
51km/32mi. Allow about 3h.

The plateau des Gras, dominated by the Dent de Rez, lies between the Rhône to the east, the gorges of the Ardèche to the south, and the valleys of Ruoms and Balazuc to the west. Almond orchards, patches of lavender, gnarled mulberry trees and hedges border the roads.

▶ Leave Bourg-St-Andéol on the D 4, in the direction of St-Remèze.

Belvédère du Bois de Laoul★
A splendid view of the Rhône valley, the Pierrelatte plain and the hills of Mont Ventoux and Tricastin.

▶ Continue climbing and pass the foot of the relay tower. About 1km/0.5mi further on, a small road branches off, opposite the Auberge de la Belle Aurore, and leads to a chapel.

▶ **Population:** 7 462.
👤 **Michelin Map:** 331: J-7.
🚹 **Info:** Pl du Champ-de-Mars. ℘04 75 54 54 20. www.rhone-gorges-ardeche.com.
▶ **Location:** 28km/17.5mi S of Montélimar, via the D 86.
🕐 **Timing:** Allow half a day.

Musée-distillerie de la Lavande
Saint-Remèze. 👤🚶‍♂️*Guided visits: Apr–Sept daily 10am–7pm.* ☞€6.50. ℘04 75 04 37 26.
www.museedelalavandeardeche.com.
This distillery is set in a farmhouse on the plateau de Gras, surrounded by fields of lavender, and linked to a small museum.

▶ Retrace your steps and turn left onto the D 362. At the crossroads at Mas-du-Gras, turn left on the D 262.

Gras
A small hamlet of old houses. The vault of the church is decorated with curious medallions in bright colours.

Dent de Rez★
The curious profile of this rock, separated from the summit of Barres mountain by the col d'Eyrole, dominates the plateau.

▶ Return to Mas-du-Gras, and turn left onto the D 262, to Larnas.

Gorge de la Sainte-Baume★
After Larnas, the road plunges into a rocky gorge, where the heat of summer has earned it the name, **Val Chaud**.

Saint-Montan★
The ruins of the feudal castle that dominates the village is named after the hermit, Montanus. The village, with its arrangements of old houses, narrow streets, stairways and archways is especially engaging and pleasing.

▶ Return to Bourg-St-Andéol by the D 262 and the D 86.

Viviers ★

It was this episcopal town – created in the 5C – that gave its name to the province of Vivarais. Its location, boxed in between Jouannade hill and the rocky peak on which the upper town is built, meant that it remained almost untouched by the Industrial Revolution. Only the quarries, originally opened in about 1750 by the Pavin brothers in the hamlet of Lafarge north of the town to produce cement, are witness to the conversion of a small Ardèche business into a firm of international rank. The contrast between the cliffs on either side of the river, the isolated peaks in the middle of the gap and the stately flowing river upstream of Châteauneuf power plant form a picturesque sight.

▶ **Population:** 3 905.
⚕ **Michelin Map:** 331: K-7.
🄸 **Info:** 2 Avenue Mendès France, 07220 Viviers. ☎04 75 54 54 20. www.rhone-gorges-ardeche.com.
▶ **Location:** Viviers is easily reached from the A 7 and N 7; Montélimar is 17km/11mi to the N, Bourg-St-Andéol, 14km/9mi to the S.
🄿 **Parking:** Limited centre parking; park near the Hôtel de Ville (see local map).
☺ **Don't Miss:** Take a tour of the Old Town.
🕑 **Timing:** Allow 1–2 hours.

A BIT OF HISTORY

After Alba-la-Romaine, the Roman capital of the Helvia people, fell into ruins, Bishop Ausonne went to live in Vivarium, at the confluence of the Escoutay and the Rhône where the city had its port. In the 5C the upper town was fortified. Numerous donations and skilful politics gradually turned the Vivier bishops into overlords of an immense domain east of the Rhône – the Vivarais. They fiercely defended its independence against the Counts of Toulouse, sharing ownership with them of the Largentière mines and minting their own coins.

At the end of the 13C, the French monarchy wanted to expand its territory into the Rhône valley. The Bishop of Viviers finally recognised the suzerainty of the King of France in 1308; a large part of the Vivarais became "Crown" land, whereas the west bank of the Rhône remained "Empire" land, under the distant control of the Holy Roman Emperor.

Inside a second set of ramparts, a medieval city began to develop. All that remains of the defence towers and the main doors is a clock tower, the **Tour de l'Horloge**, extensively refurbished in the 19C. In 1498 Claude de Tournon, became Bishop of Viviers; he had the Romanesque cathedral destroyed and a Flamboyant Gothic chancel built.

Noël Albert, a nouveau-riche entrepreneur who had made his fortune in the salt trade and tax collection, had the Renaissance façade of the Maison des Chevaliers built. After becoming head of the Protestants, he captured the ecclesiastical city.

👣 WALKING TOUR

OLD TOWN ★

The ecclesiastical town is distinct from the lower town. They communicated via the Porte de la Gâche to the west and Porte de l'Abri to the south. The houses in the lower town, in a tight cluster, are roofed with Roman tiles. They generally consist of two upper storeys and a ground floor housing a high cellar or a shop. Most of them have kept their medieval appearance despite many alterations over the centuries. The houses in the ecclesiastical town hide their gardens and courtyards behind bare walls with semicircular openings, sometimes surmounted by a coat of arms.

▶ Park on place de la Roubine. Follow rue J.-B.-Serre and Grande-Rue as far as place de la République.

From the eastern corner of the square there is a view of the ruins of Château-vieux Tower.

Maison des Chevaliers

The "Knights' House", also called the House of Noël Albert, was built in 1546. The ornate window-frames on the first floor consist of columns and fluted pilasters with Ionic capitals; rams' heads and garlands of leaves have been carved on the lintels, between the modillions.

Grande-Rue

This street is lined with meticulously dressed façades, some with ornate portals surmounted by wrought-iron balconies such as **Hôtel de Tourville** and **Hôtel de Beaulieu** (18C). Grande-Rue leads to a series of little cross-streets, narrow, stepped and spanned by arches.

Place Prosper-Allignol

The square is flanked by two buildings erected between 1732 and 1738 by Franque. Their Classical symmetry and neat stonework makes them beautiful examples of 18C Viviers architecture.

▷ Walk up the steep montée de l'Abri, which passes under Porte de l'Abri and leads to place de l'Ormeau.

The street offers a fine view over the chapel of Notre-Dame du Rhône, rebuilt by Franque, and the mouth of the Donzère gorge.

Place de l'Ormeau

The square, lined with old canons' houses (17C) owes its name to a centuries-old elm tree *(ormeau)* which perished in 1976.

▷ Take the parapet walk (Chemin de Ronde) around the cathedral; from place de la Plaine, a passageway north leads to a vast terrace.

Belvédère de Châteauvieux

This belvedere, built on a natural acropolis at one time washed by the Rhône during floods, stands above place de la Roubine. The **view** embraces the old roofs of the city, the clock tower, the enormous cutting formed by the Lafarge quarries, the cooling towers of Cruas power station and the factory at Châteauneuf.

▶ Turn round and go downhill via rue de Châteauvieux (on the right) to Porte de la Gâche.

With its smooth cobblestones, covered passageways and arches, rue de Châteauvieux has a medieval air.

▶ Climb the steps to the tower.

Tower

In the 12C, this tower was the entrance to the upper town. Only the square part of the building existed at the time, with a Romanesque chapel dedicated to St Michael on the first floor.

Cathédrale St-Vincent

The only remains of the 12C Romanesque building are the porch, the west front and the lower part of the nave walls. The chancel is remarkable for its Flamboyant **ribbed vaulting★**.

EXCURSIONS
Chapelle Notre-Dame-de-Montcham Viewpoint★

The belvedere to the right of the chapel commands a lovely panorama of Mont Ventoux.

Défilé de Donzère★★

14km/9mi S on D 73 and D 144 to Donzère and then D 486 to the river.
This is a very picturesque canyon through which the Rhône flows. The vertical wall of the west bank contrasts with the isolated peaks lining the east bank. This point is traditionally considered to be the gateway into

Provence. The bridges upstream and downstream of the canyon offer attractive views of it.

▶ Park the car after crossing the first bridge, within sight of Viviers, and walk down to the Rhône along the path leading to the campsite.

Donzère

About 5km/3mi S on N 86 and D 486.
The terraced village is spread out over the slopes of a hill, at the foot of a 15C castle. Of the medieval fortifications, there remain several vaulted streets, ramparts pierced by gates and a 12C church built in the Provençal Romanesque style and remodelled in the 19C.

ADDRESSES

🛏 STAY

🛏🛏🛏 **Chambre d'Hôte Le Jeu du Mail** – *Alba-la-Romaine.* ☎04 75 52 41 59. *http://lejeudumail.free.fr. 5 rooms*. In the 1970s, the owners were among the first to receive guests in the Ardèche, and have continued to do so ever since, with evident pleasure. On the edge of town; swimming pool and garden.

🛏🛏🛏🛏 **Chambre d'Hôte Le Moulinage** – *Chemin des Carmes, 07220 St-Thomé.* ☎04 75 52 62 11. *www.le-moulinage.com. 2 rooms and a suite.* This old silk mill, in a "wild" setting has comfortable rooms and a delightful suite. *Table d'hôte* dinner with regional specialities and fresh, local produce of the season. Here you can swim all year; in winter in the original swimming pool on the mezzanine and in summer in the natural pools of the Carme.

☕/EAT

🛏🛏🛏 **Hotel-Restaurant le Relais du Vivarais** – *31 Faubourg des Sautelles.* ☎04 75 52 60 41. *www.relaisduvivarais.fr. Closed Sun evenings. 6 rooms (🛏🛏🛏)*. A warm welcome is assured in this family hotel-restaurant located in the lower town. Rustic dining room and pleasant summer terrace arranged under the willows. The kitchen specialises in local produce.

Château d'Alba-la-Romaine near Viviers
© Hervé Lenain/hemis.fr

With a clear affinity to the landscapes to the south, the borders of La Drôme Provençale are a bit hazy, and are not officially defined. The area lies between Dauphiné and Provence, and as such forms a gateway between North and South. Everything about La Drôme evokes the sights, sounds and smells of Provence, and although it is not part of Provence in an administrative sense, it certainly has all the hallmarks of a Provençal department. The landscape vibrates with luxurious lavender fields and olive groves, while gentle hills lead to "perched" villages, and then to mountains and forests, epitomising the many varied landscapes of this remarkable region.

Highlights

1 Exploring the medieval towns around **Montélimar** (p448)
2 Nougat from **Montélimar** (p448)
3 The elegant **Grignan castle** and its remarkable collection of funiture (p451)
4 The **crocodile farm** near Grignan (452)
5 Driving around the hills of the **Drôme** (p455)

A Little of What You Fancy

The wines of the Drôme have an excellent reputation, produced under the AOC "Côtes du Rhône" (Hermitage and Crozes-Hermitage) and "Côtes du Rhône Villages" from Rochegude, Vinsobres, Rousset and Saint Pantaléon. Here you will also find excellent black olives, truffles, goat's cheese (*picodon* and *foujou*) and, of course, nougat from Montélimar.

The Perfect Cliché

Café terraces clustered beneath the ubiquitous plane trees, pastis, olives, wine… and *pétanque*; all the clichéd icons of the villages of the Drôme. The climate is Mediterranean, the sky an endless cerulean blue, the light exceptional; lavender fields, vines and orchards stretch as far as you can see. Hectic weekly markets (see *www.jours-de-marche.fr*) are loud with farmer-speak and vibrant with the colours of Provence. It isn't Provence… and yet it is.

Pétanque… Or is it Boules?

Throughout the region, every town or village will have an area set aside for games of *pétanque*, a form of *boules* where the aim is, while standing with the feet together in a small circle, to throw metal balls as close as possible to a small wooden ball *(cochonnet)* or jack. The current form of the game is enjoyed by around 17 million people in France, and there are even 3 000 players registered in England!
For the record: in pétanque your feet must not move, and must remain within the throwing circle; in boules, it is permissible to take a stride before throwing.

Allées Provençales, Montélimar

© Camille Moirenc/hemis.fr

DRÔME PROVENÇALE AND THE PRÉALPES DRÔMOISES

Grignan ★ Interesting
Montélimar Other sight described
Departure point of tour
Medieval Towns
Les villages du Tricastin
L'Enclave des Papes
Les Préalpes drômoises

0   10 km

N

LYON

Jardin des oiseaux ▲

Allex

Réserve naturelle des Ramières

Crest
Aouste-
s-Sye

Chabrillan

GAP

Drôme

Mirmande
D 204

Forêt de Saoû ▲

Abbatiale
Ste-Marie
(Cruas)

St-Vincent-
de-Barrès

Saoû

Soyans

Marsanne

Le Poët-
Célard

Pic de
Chenavari

Meysse

507

Rochemaure

Montélimar

Puygiron

La Bégude-
de-Mazenc

Le Poët-Laval

Château de
Rochefort-
en-Valdaine

Dieulefit

Prieuré
d'Aleyrac

DRÔME

Viviers

Défilé de
Donzère

Notre-Dame
de Montcham

N.-D.-d'Aiguebelle

Taulignan

Donzère

Val-des-Nymphes

Grignan

La Garde-Adhémar

Chamaret

Grillon

Valréas

Nyons

Montségur-
sur-Lauzon

Richerenches

Ferme aux
Crocodiles

Clansayes

VAUCLUSE

St-Restitut

St-Paul-
Trois-Châteaux

Visan N.-D.-des-Vignes

Suze-la-Rousse

RHÔNE

NÎMES *MARSEILLE, ORANGE* *ORANGE*

A **B**

447

Montélimar

The name Montélimar derives from a feudal fortress, "Mont-Adhémar," built in the 12C by the powerful Adhémar family. The last member of the family was the Comte de Grignan who lived in the 17C and was the son-in-law of Madame de Sévigné, the lady of letters. Of the nine gates that were once part of the town walls, only the Porte St-Martin to the north of the town still stands. The diversion of the Rhône towards Montélimar feeds the Châteauneuf power plant.

▶ **Population:** 38 028.
Michelin Map: 332: B-6.
Info: Espace St Martin, 26200 Montélimar. ℘04 75 01 00 20. www.montelimar-tourisme.com.
▶ **Location:** On the banks of the Rhône, between Valence and Orange.
🅿 **Parking:** There are numerous car parks in and around the centre of town.
🕐 **Timing:** Take it easy and spend a whole day here.
Kids: The Château and the Musée de la Miniature.

SIGHTS

Old Town

In the centre, around the 15C **Collégiale Ste-Croix**, most of the streets have overhanging eaves. **Place du Marché**, lined with arcades surmounted by façades and wrought-iron balconies, has a southern feel about it. On place Émile-Loubet is **Diane de Poitiers' house** with its fine façade.

Château des Adhémar

🕐 10am–12.30pm, 2–6pm (Jul–Aug 10am–6pm). 🕐 1 Jan, 11 Nov, 25 Dec, and Tue from Nov–Mar. ≤€6 (under 18, free). ℘04 75 00 62 30.

The original fortress (12C) to the east of the town was extended in the 14C by order of the Pope. Only the *seigneur's* lodgings (main apartments) and the watch-path are open to the public.

Almonds and Honey

The nougat industry is fairly recent; originally the sweetmeat was made by artisans. In the 16C, almond trees were brought to France from Asia. The popularity of almond-growing across the Gras plateau, and the ready supply of honey from Provence and the Alps, were behind the growth of the nougat industry in Montélimar.

Allées Provençales★

The shaded pavements of these wide half-pedestrianised avenues are the hub of the town's activity and their boutiques offer a wide choice of regional products.

Musée de la Miniature★

🕐 Jul–Aug daily except Mon 11am–6pm; rest of year Wed–Sun 2–6pm. 🕐 Jan. ≤€5 (children €3.50). ℘04 75 53 79 24. www.ville-montelimar.com.

The success of the International Miniature Festival led to the exhibition housed inside the chapel of the Hôtel-Dieu (19C). The miniatures have to meet certain criteria, such as the use of the original material and a scale of 1:12.

DRIVING TOURS

OVERLOOKING THE RHÔNE

Tour begins 12km/7.5mi NW. Allow 2h.

▶ Leave Montélimar on the D 11.

Château de Rochemaure★

Near Rochemaure church (follow signs). Guided tours Jul–Aug at 3pm, 4pm, 5pm and 6pm. 🕐 Rest of year. ≤€3. ℘04 75 49 59 20.

The ruins of Rochemaure castle stand on an impressive **site★★** on the southern

Château de Rochemaure

edge of the Coiron plateau. The castle (12C–14C) was besieged by the Huguenots in the 16C and 17C and abandoned in the 18C.

▶ Turn left as you reach the plateau and park below the castle walls. A road veering to the left leads to the ruins.

The 12C square keep is surmounted by a pentagonal tower which enabled the archers to vary their angle of fire.

The Old Village
On your way back, take rue du Faubourg in front of the town hall (mairie), *then take rue de la Violle. The streets are lined with medieval houses.*

Pic de Chenavari★★
4.5km/2.8mi N of Rochemaure castle.
At the foot of the Chapelle St-Laurent, take the road on the right, heading for Les Videaux. Turn left onto Chemin des Freydières and keep on climbing. Ignore the right-hand lane to a farmhouse and take the dirt track to the plateau. From here you can easily reach the summit (45min on foot there and back).
From the top there is a **view** of Rochemaure castle, the Rhône, Vercors Barronies and the Lower Ardèche.

MEDIEVAL TOWNS★
87km/54mi. Allow approx 4h.

▶ Leave Montélimar on the D 540, then after passing beneath the autoroute, turn right towards Puygiron.

Notice along the Valdaine plain the small, rural homes built of limestone, a blank wall and curtain of cypress trees protecting them from the blasts of the Mistral.

Puygiron
Dominated by its ancient chateau (13C–16C), the village is worth visiting not least for its **view**★ of les Trois-Becs, Marsanne and the plateau du Coiron.

▶ Go back to the D 540 and turn right.

La Bégude-de-Mazenc★
At the crossroads in the centre of this modern town, turn left onto the D 9, then take the small paved road leading to the entrance of the old "perched" village; leave you car there.
You enter a wonderful maze of lanes by a fortified gate leaning against the church, which is partially Romanesque. A path climbs steeply to the top of a hill crowned by a beautiful pine forest.

▶ The D 540 climbs in the direction of Dieulefit, and the valley of the Jabron.

Le Poët-Laval★

This perched village, well restored and maintained, occupies a steep **site**★ and holds considerable medieval interest, not least a *commanderie de Malte*, a 12C dungeon, the remains of ramparts and of 15C houses.

Of the old church, only the tower and the Romanesque apse remain. The old temple, built in the 17C inside the house of a 15C knight at the centre of the village, houses historical documents on the region and a little museum dedicated to Protestantism in the area and the Dauphiné Reformation (*Apr–Jun and Sept–Oct 3–6.30pm (Jul–Aug 10am–noon, 3–6.30pm). Mon morning and Sun morning. €4. 04 75 46 46 33. www.museeduprotestantismedauphinois.com*).

▶ Return to the D 540.

Dieulefit

Beautifully situated at a point where the Jabron valley opens out, this small town with a strong Protestant tradition today survives on tourism and on visits by *"curistes"*, who visit the health centre; it is also renowned for its pottery; the Jabron valley is dotted with pottery workshops. In the centre of the town, a large house organises annual exhibitions of contemporary ceramics.

The D 538 descends through the Lez valley, dominated by the feudal remnants of Béconne and of Blacon (14C).

▶ Turn right onto the D 14, towards Taulignan.

Taulignan

On the boundary of Dauphiné and Provence, this ancient village has retained its medieval walls, circular and almost continuous, with 11 towers (nine round and two square) connected by curtain walls. To the north-east the Anguille gate is the only fortified gate to have survived. Wandering at random through the lanes you will discover ancient façades and houses with mullioned windows.

Atelier-musée de la Soie★

Daily except Tue 10am–12.30pm, 2–6pm (Jul–Aug daily 10am–6pm; guided tours Thu 11am and 3pm). 25 Dec, Jan–mid-Feb. €5.50. 04 75 53 12 96. www.musee-soie.com.

The museum houses an educational display about the plant and machinery needed to produce silk, and the manufacturing processes that prevailed in the region during the 19C.

Grignan★ (See GRIGNAN.)

▶ Leave to the N on the D 4, then turn left onto the D 56. After Réauville, turn right towards Notre-Dame-d'Aiguebelle.

Notre-Dame-d'Aiguebelle

The abbey was founded in 1137 at the instigation of St Bernard, Abbot of Clairvaux. Today the lives of the monks are governed by strict rules and they devote themselves to prayer, manual work and intellectual pursuits.

▶ Rejoin the D 4 heading N along the D 550 passing Montjoyer.

On the way you will notice the imposing ruins of the Château de Rochefort-en-Valdaine, dominating the wooded valley of the Citelles.

ADDRESSES

🛏STAY

⊖ **Provence** – *118 av. Jean-Jaurès. 04 75 01 11 67. Closed mid-Jan–mid-Feb and Sat from Nov–Feb. 16 rooms.* This hotel is modest but spick and span.

⊖⊖⊖ **Hôtel les Hospitaliers** – *26160 Poët-Laval. 04 75 46 22 32. www.hotel-les-hospitaliers.com. Closed 10 Nov-14 Mar. 20 rooms. Restaurant⊖⊖⊖.* Enjoying a select location in the village, this hotel occupies a cluster of stone houses with superb views of the valley and mountains.

⚕/ EAT

🍽 **Le Grillon** – *40 r. Cuiraterie.* ☎*04 75 01 79 02. Closed Sun evening and Mon.* Located on a little street in the old town, this restaurant has an inconspicuous façade that leads to a big dining room.

ON THE TOWN

Café Cantante – *18 r. Roger-Poyol.* ☎*04 75 00 01 30. Mon–Sat 6pm–2am.* This unusually alluring, original night-spot is in a class of its own.

SHOPPING

Nougat Chabert and Guillot – *9 r. Charles-Chabert.* ☎*04 75 92 20 20. www. nougat-chabert-guillot.com. Closed public holidays.* For nougat aficionados, pros and amateurs alike, this establishment founded in 1913 makes the definitive Montélimar nougat.

Au Rucher de Provence – *35 blvd Desmarais.* ☎*04 75 52 01 59. http://lartisan-nougatier.fr. Shop: daily 8am–7.30pm.* The Bonnieu family makes high-quality nougat under two brand names: Stoupany, the oldest (since 1787), and Le Rucher de Provence, launched in 1938.

Escobar Patissier-Confiseur-Chocolatier-Glacier – *2 pl. Léopold-Blanc.* ☎*04 75 01 25 53. www.nougats-escobar. com. There are 3 shops in Montélimar: Route de Marseille; Chemin de Gery, and Rue Pierre Julien. Closed Sun and public holidays Jun–Aug.* This chef belongs to the elite set of genuine Montélimar artisans.

Grignan★

The town became a hillside and fortified village in the 12C, developing around the base of its castle. The original town was protected behind 13C walls. Everywhere, changes in the population can be traced through the ornamental façades of the buildings, which date from the 15C to the 18C. Around the town, the countryside expands to embrace no less than 14 villages within the title "Pays de Grignan".

CHÂTEAU★★

🕐*Sept–Jun 10am–12.30pm, 2–6pm (Jul-Aug 10am–6pm).* 🕐*Tue from Nov–Mar, 1 Jan, 11 Nov and 25 Dec.* ✺€6. ☞*Guided tours* ✺€10). ☎*04 75 91 83 55.*

The castle was built in the 16C by Louis Adhemar, governor of Provence, and extended between 1668 and 1690 by the son of Madame de Sévigné, who then lived here. It was largely destroyed during the Revolution, but was restored and regained its style and elegance in the 20C under the new owner and later by the Conseil Général de la Drôme. Walking around the exterior you discover the great Renaissance façade, then the Cour du Puits with its pool opening

- ▶ **Population:** 1 634.
- ⚐ **Michelin Map:** 332: C-7.
- ▯ **Info:** Pl. du Jeu-de-Ballon, 26230 Grignan. ☎04 75 46 56 75. www.tourisme-paysdegrignan.com.
- ▶ **Location:** S of Montélimar, via the D 941 (Valréas).
- 👫 **Kids:** The Crocodile farm at Pierrelatte.
- 🕐 **Timing:** Allow 1–2 hours.

out onto a terrace framed to the left by a Gothic gallery, and then the main building itself.

From the terrace there is a vast **panorama★★** along the crest of the Montagne de la Lance to Mont Ventoux and the beautiful Dentelles de Montmirail, Comtadine plain and les Alpilles, the woodlands of Grignan and the mountains of Vivarais.

Inside the château there is a chance to see the grand staircase (17C), and visit the apartments of Madame de Sévigné and the Count of Grignan, the King's Hall and the oratory before descending by a Gothic staircase to the Great Gallery. There is a remarkable collection of furniture, including two magnificent cabinets, and Aubusson tapestries depicting scenes from mythology.

🚗 DRIVING TOUR

LES VILLAGES DU TRICASTIN
47km/29mi. Allow 3h.

▶ Leave Grignan west by the D 541, then take the D 472.

Chapelle du Val-des-Nymphes
In a valley kept cool by many waterfalls and which, as its name suggests, was once a place of pagan worship, stand the ruins of a 12C chapel. For a long while a ruin, this Romanesque chapel was restored from 1991, and an elegant timber ceiling now covers the nave.

La Garde-Adhémar
This old village is made visible from some distance away by its church, perched on a rise. It is an ideal spot for a stroll, with its picturesque limestone houses, its vaulted alleyways and its narrow, winding streets with their arches. In the Middle Ages this village was a major fortress belonging to the Adhémar family. In the 16C, a Renaissance château was built for **Antoine Escalin**, Baron de la Garde, who started life as a mere shepherd then became a soldier; he ended his career as one of François I's ambassadors and as General in charge of the French galleys. Old town walls can be seen on the north side; to the south of the village is a fortified gate and a few ruins, not far from the huge cross erected on a Roman base.

The Romanesque church is remarkable for its two apses and the attractive outline of its two-storey octagonal belfry topped by a stocky pyramid.

👥 La Ferme aux Crocodiles★
Pierrelatte. ♿ ⏰ Daily: Nov–Feb 10am– 5pm; Mar and Sept–Oct 10am–6pm; Apr–Aug 9.30am–7pm. 👓 €16 (child 3–12, €11). ☎ 04 75 96 09 37. www.lafermeauxcrocodiles.com.
This crocodile farm is stocked with a great many species from countries all over the world (Cuba, America, Egypt), installed in large basins. Further on, visitors can discover a vast hothouse containing tropical vegetation and superb exotic birds. From the many footbridges, visitors can watch some 300 crocodiles from the Nile region basking in the sun or swimming in dark waters.

▶ Go back along the D 59 and follow it SE after having re-crossed the autoroute.

St-Paul-Trois-Châteaux
The old town is surrounded by the remains of ramparts, but has never had the three castles that its name – St-Paul-Three-Castles – would suggest. It was appointed capital of the region during Roman times, under the name "Augusta Tricastinorum".

During the second half of the 4C, the first part of its Roman name was replaced by the name Paul, commemorating one of the town's first bishops. The name of the old capital of "Tricastini" may possibly have been Frenchified by a clerk in the 16C to "Trois Châteaux", though there is no evidence for this theory. The town was a bishopric until the Revolution. Modern St-Paul sits at the heart of the main truffle region of France.

Cathedral★
This imposing building, begun in the 11C and completed in the 12C, is a remarkable example of Provençal Romanesque architecture.

Most striking is the exceptional height of the transept walls and the powerful aspect of the nave.

Maison de la Truffe et du Tricastin
⏰ Open: Hours are variable according to the season; call for more information. 👓€4. ☎ 04 75 96 61 29. www.maisondelatruffe.com.
The Truffle Centre, located inside the tourist centre, houses an exhibition with posters, showcases and a video projection on the cultivation and marketing of what is known as the "black diamond" of the Tricastin region, and an ingredient in many tasty local dishes.

St-Restitut

The village **church★** in Provençal Romanesque style has fine **carved decoration★**.

Suze-la-Rousse

The principal Tricastin village during the Middle Ages, Suze developed along the left bank of the Lez. The town is enclosed within walls, and includes many fine Renaissance houses, a Romanesque church and a massive old city hall with a beautiful 15C–16C façade.

An imposing **castle** (🕐*daily Sept–Jun 10am–12.30pm, 2–6pm; Jul–Aug 10am–6pm;* 🕐*Tue from Nov–Mar, 1 Jan, 11 Nov and 25 Dec.* ✒*€6, guided tours €8.* 📞*04 75 04 81 44*) dominates a hill above the Garenne, embracing a park of 23ha. The main building (14C) is a beautiful example of medieval military architecture, and the interior was remodelled during the Renaissance as is reflected in the façades of the courtyard and the double staircase, which gives access to the first floor, where temporary exhibitions are arranged.

The Blue Room, decorated with stucco on the theme of the Four Seasons, and the octagonal room, which occupies a corner tower, are worthy of a visit, offering views of Mont Ventoux, the Lance mountains and the Dauphine alps.

In the other wing the guard room precedes the Salle des Armes, which boasts a magnificent ceiling.

▷ Take the D 117 to the N.

La Provence miniature villages

Rte de Visan, La Baume de Transit. ♿🕐*Jan–Mar Mon, Wed–Fri 2–6pm, Sat–Sun and public holidays 10.30am–noon, 2–6pm; Apr–Dec daily 10am–noon, 2–6.30pm (mid-Jul–Aug daily 10am–7pm).* ✒*€5.* 📞*04 75 46 91 68. www.village-miniature.fr.*

On this journey of discovery you can enjoy many beautiful villages built with the stones and tiles of the region. The six miniature villages, entirely imaginary, include a castle, a church, a belfry, farms typical of the Drôme Provençal bathed

in waterfalls, rivers and fountains, and mini-trains that the children can operate themselves.

▷ Follow the D 117 towards the N.

Montségur-sur-Lauzon

In front of the Mairie take the road to the left, then turn right and take a lane climbing to the summit of a hill on which the old village is built. A series of zigzag paths take you round the village and enable you to discover the ancient Romanesque chapel.

▷ Take the D 71 W, then the D 481.

Clansayes★

From here there is an extensive **view★★** over the Tricastin area and its peaks carved by erosion.

Chamaret

A beautiful belfry on a rock dominates the surrounding countryside, the view extending across the Tricastin area.

▷ Return to Grignan by the D 71.

ADDRESSES

🏨STAY AND ♟/EAT

🍽🍽**Tricastin** – *R. Caprais-Favier. 26700 Pierrelatte.* 📞*04 75 04 05 82. www.hoteldutricastin.com. 13 rooms.* A simple hotel in a calm street near the city centre.

🍽🍽**Gîte du Val des Nymphes** – *Val des Nymphes, 26700 La Garde-Adhémar.* 📞*04 75 04 44 54. 3 rooms. Restaurant🍽🍽.* Located on the hills of the Tricastin, in the midst of peach trees, this traditional house is absolutely delightful.

🍽🍽**Le Bistro** – *Hotel le Clair de la Plume, 2 pl. du Mail.* 📞*04 75 91 81 30. www.clairplume.com. Closed Thu lunch, Tue evening and Wed evening.* Traditional bistro cuisine in this appealing hotel-restaurant (which also includes the acclaimed Michelin-starred Le Clair de la Plume restaurant). A good range of Rhône valley wines.

Valréas

Besides its geographical oddity – a chunk of the Vaucluse enclosed by the Drôme – Valréas is a particularly agreeable old city founded originally on the manufacture of cardboard boxes, but now given to producing wine and truffles.

SIGHTS
Musée du Cartonnage and de l'Imprimerie

Apr–Oct daily except Tue 1–6pm. €3.50. 04 90 35 58 75.
This lovely museum is dedicated to the production of boxes and packaging.

DRIVING TOUR

L'ENCLAVE DES PAPES
22km/13.7mi. Allow 2h.

Leave Valréas on the D941, in the direction of Grillon (5km/13mi).

Grillon
Surrounded by vineyards, this peaceful village has two faces: lower down is the place de la Bourgade with its neo-Gothic clock tower, and the upper village, wherein lies its medieval heart.

Leave Grillon to the S and follow the D20 for 4km/2.5mi.

- **Population:** 9 798.
- **Michelin Map:** 332: C-7.
- **Info:** Av. Maréchal-Leclerc, 84600 Valréas. 04 90 35 04 71. www.ot-valreas.fr.
- **Location:** 10km/6.2mi to the E of Grignan.
- **Timing:** 2 hours to visit the town.

Richerenches
Founded in the 12C, this **commanderie de Templiers** was built to a rectangular plan, and has retained its walls flanked by four round corner towers.

Leave Richerenches heading SE, and follow the D 120.

Visan
This large village has many winding alleyways around its medieval castle. Located at the top of a hill, its caves serve each year to house 10 000 magnums of red wine.
Just outside the village (in the *direction of Vaison-la-Romaine*), a modern housing estate shelters the **chapelle Notre-Dame-des-Vignes**, which houses a 13C statue of the Virgin Mary.

Return to Valréas by the D 976.

Crest

The town of Crest (pronounced Crè), situated at the spot where the River Drôme flows into the Valence plain, is particularly proud of its castle keep. The town has grown up around it, with a dual role as market town and a community specialising in food processing. Among the many local gastronomic specialities are *défarde*, a stew made with lamb's feet and tripe, and *picodons*, small goat's cheeses.

- **Population:** 8 479.
- **Michelin Map:** 332: D-5.
- **Info:** Pl. du Dr-Maurice-Rozier, 26400 Crest. 04 75 25 11 38.
- **Location:** 28km/17.5mi SE of Valence.
- **Kids:** The bird sanctuary at Upie.
- **Timing:** Allow 1–2 hours to tour the keep.

SIGHTS
Keep★

184 steps to the upper terrace.
🕐*May–Sept daily 10am–7pm; Apr and Oct daily except Tue 2–6pm; rest of year, check website for times.* 🕐*1 Jan and 25 Dec.* ✆€6.50. ✆*04 75 25 32 53. www.tourdecrest.fr.*

The keep in Crest is all that remains of a fortress which was dismantled in 1633 on the orders of Louis XIII. The keep was erected over Roman foundations on a spur of rock, in various stages between the 11C and the 15C. The north wall, the tallest of the four, reaches a height of almost 52m; the base of the tower lies at an altitude of 263m.

From the upper terrace there is a view over the rooftops of Crest and beyond, in a superb **panoramic view★** to the north-east over Glandasse Mountain and the outcrops of the Vercors, and to the south over the Roche-Courbe range with the Trois-Becs, and Roche Colombe further in the distance. To the west the horizon is broken up by the long narrow ridge of the Vivarais area rising to the Gerbier-de-Jonc and Mézenc.

Old Houses

Along the main thoroughfare and the neighbouring streets are some of the vast mansions built for the wealthy bourgeoisie in Crest in the 16C and 17C.

👥 Jardin aux Oiseaux

In Upie, 11km/6.7mi N. Leave Crest on D 538 towards Chabeuil, then take D 142.
♿🕐*Jul–Aug 10am–7pm; Mar–Jun and Sept–early Nov 10am–6pm; early Nov–Feb 1.30–5.30pm.* 🕐*Jan.* ✆€11 (child 10–13, €9; 3–9 years, €8). ✆*04 75 84 45 90. www.jardin-aux-oiseaux.com.*

This superb Bird Sanctuary is home to over 200 different European and exotic species: hummingbirds, crested grebes, flamingoes, pelicans, ostriches, parrots etc.

🚗 DRIVING TOUR

THE HILLS OF DRÔME★
83km/52mi. Allow 3h.

▶ Leave Crest E on the D 93.

Head first for the **Forêt de Saoû**, planted with beech, oak and pine trees. **Saoû** itself is a small village famous for its AOC *picodon* goat's cheese.

▶ At Saoû, turn left onto D 538, then the D 328 on the right.

Le Poët-Célard – A town hall, a temple and a castle sum up this tiny village.

▶ Continue on the D 328, then the D 310 towards Pont-de-Barret. Cross the village and take the D 128.

The village of **Soyans** is dominated by the imposing ruins of its castle, burned during the French Revolution.

▶ Follow the D 57 to Mirmande.

The pretty houses of **Mirmande** spread out over the slopes of a hill. Towards 1930, the painter André Lhote (1885–1962) came to settle here and many contemporary artists followed.

▶ Go back to the N 7, and head N to Livron-sur-Drôme, then to Allex by the D 93A.

Allex is built on a limestone hill and dominated by a tower; all that remains of an 11C castle.

Réserve Naturelle des Ramières★ is a protected area extending for 10km/6mi along the Drôme; it owes its name to the vast forests that compose it.

▶ Cross the Drôme by the D 125.

Chabrillan is renowned among "perched" villages for its gardens and its castle.

▶ Go back to Crest on the D 104.

Le Valentinois is the small alluvial plain extending along the left bank of the Rhône, formed by the lower valleys of the two rivers flowing into it, the Isère to the north and the Drôme to the south. The region takes its name from the city of Valence, built on a terrace overlooking the Rhône. In 1349, the Dauphiné was attached to the kingdom of France, but retained a certain autonomy until 1457. Following the French Revolution, the region was divided into three departments: the Drôme, Hautes-Alpes and Isère.

Highlights

1 Strolling around **Parc Jouvet** in the city of Valence (p461)

2 The Old Town of **Romans-sur-Isère** (p462)

3 The unusual **Palais Idéal** in Hauterives (p465)

4 The emerald waters of **Lake Paladru** (p470)

5 The on-site museum at **St-Romain-en-Gal** (p477)

Hector Berlioz

Berlioz, the son of a wealthy local doctor, was born in La Côte-St-André in 1803. At the age of 17 he went to Paris to study medicine. He attended lectures but, at the same time, was a frequent visitor to the opera houses and the library in the Royal Music Academy where he later began learning composition. In 1830 he wrote his *Symphonie Fantastique* and won the Grand Prix de Rome.

Thereafter he worked as a music critic in order to earn a living, while at the same time continuing to compose works that brought him success and failure in turn. He seldom returned to La Côte-St-André. Having failed to win the fame he deserved during his lifetime, Berlioz died in Paris in 1869, but his genius earned him posthumous acclaim.

Pilate's Resting Place?

Not far from Vienne, La Pyramide, affectionately known as "L'Aiguille" (the Needle), is a fine white stone pyramid that rests on a small square plinth made from four columns and four arcatures, and which used to adorn the central forecourt of the vast Vienne amphitheatre in the 4C. It is a masterpiece of stonecutting, and is held together without the use of cement.

During the Middle Ages it was thought to be the tomb of Pontius Pilate; according to legend, after leaving Jerusalem for Vienne, the Roman procurator, struck with remorse, threw himself into the Rhône. The Pilat mountain range is said to be named after this event (there is a similar legend attached to Mount Pilate near Lucerne in Switzerland).

Postman Cheval's Palais Idéal, Hauterives

© Ludovic Maisant/hemis.fr

La Balme-les-Grottes
La Balme
AIN
Hières-s-Amby
Parc archéologique de Larina
St-Baudille-de-la-Tour
Chatelans
Gorges d'Amby
AIN
LYON-SAINT-EXUPÉRY
D 52
St-Julien
Crèmieu
Morestel

RHÔNE
Parc Walibi
Butte de Montceau
La Tour-du-Pin
CHAMBÉRY

Bourgoin-Jallieu

ST-ÉTIENNE
RHÔNE
Septème
Beauvoir-de-Marc
Virieu
Lac de Paladru
Pupetières
St-Romain-en-Gal
Vienne
Charavines
St-Mamert
ISÈRE
La Côte-Saint-André
Tour de Clermont

Roussillon
CHAMBÉRY
Beaurepaire
Bressieux
Tullins
GRENOBLE
Champagne
Marnans
Andance
Tour d'Albon
Hauterives
Mantaille
Labyrinthes
Roybon
N.-D.-de-l'Osier
Palais Idéal
Vinay
Ratières
Bathernay
St-Antoine-l'Abbaye
St-Andéol
St-Marcellin
Bren
St-Donat-sur-l'Herbasse
Chatte
Arthaudière
La Sône
Belvédère de Pierre-Aiguille 334
Chantemerle-les-Blés
Mours-St-Eusèbe
PARC NATUREL
RÉGIONAL
Tournon-s-Rhône
Curson
Romans-s-Isère
DU VERCORS
St-Romain-de-Lerps
Bourg-de-Péage
Hostun
N
Montélier
DRÔME
Valence
Château de Crussol

VALENTINOIS AND THE LOWER DAUPHINÉ

0   8 km

Vienne	★★	Recommended
Crèmieu	★	Interesting
Romans-s-Isère		If you have time
⇨		Driving Tour showing point of departure

Valence ★

This ancient Gaulish city, named Colonia Julia Valentia by the Romans at the beginning of the 2C BCE, owes its development to its location on the Rhône, near the meeting of the tributary valleys of the Doux, Eyrieux, Isère and Drôme which mark out a vast internal basin and where the flora and fauna of Mediterranean France begin. The city, dominated by St-Apollinaire cathedral, is built on a series of terraces going down to the river. Old Valence, surrounded by boulevards built in the 19C on the site of the old ramparts, has a network of shopping streets and picturesque sloping lanes, animated in season by the "Summer Festivals".

▶ **Population:** 63 258.
⬡ **Michelin Map:** 332: C-4.
▯ **Info:** 11 boulevard Bancel, 26000 Valence 𝒫 04 75 44 90 40. www.valence-romans-tourisme.com.
◐ **Location:** Valence is 103km/64mi south of Lyon, and accessible from the A 7.
▣ **Parking:** Parking is difficult in the centre, but there are ample car parks within walking distance.
◉ **Don't Miss:** Try to be there for either sunset or sunrise from the Esplanade.
◕ **Timing:** Half a day is probably enough, but you can easily be distracted.

A BIT OF HISTORY

A regional hub – The city, which is served by a large network of communications (A 7 motorway, N 7 national highway, River Rhône, airport), is the true centre of the middle Rhône valley and a focal point for entertainment and other attractions within the Drôme and Ardèche *départements*.

The population of Greater Valence, including the outlying suburbs spread out on either side of the Rhône – Bourg-lès-Valence, St-Péray, Portes-lès-Valence, Granges – is over 100 000, including numerous students enrolled at the Law Faculty and engineering schools.

Rabelaisian studies – In 1452 the dauphin Louis, who was to begin his reign a few years later under the name of Louis XI and who, at the time, was preparing for his kingly role in his princedom of Dauphiné, founded a university in Valence consisting of five faculties, including an Arts Faculty. Among the students was **François Rabelais**. He was to recall his student days here in his tales of the adventures of Pantagruel. Courses were given by reputed masters, including the lawyer Cujas. Besides studying under this strict academic taskmaster, Rabelais is said to have had a love affair with his daughter.

Bonaparte in Valence – In 1785 Napoleon Bonaparte, a 16-year-old military cadet, arrived in Valence to improve his knowledge of warfare at the School of Artillery. Every morning, he went to the Polygon to direct his bombardiers' tactical exercises.

He lived almost directly opposite the Maison des Têtes (◐ *see Old Town Walking Tour*) which was occupied by a bookseller named Marc Aurel. Bonaparte soon befriended him, and in less than a year had read his entire stock. The future emperor had already embarked on a voyage of self-discovery. In a letter to a friend, he used a striking image to describe himself: "the southern blood which runs through my veins flows with the rapidity of the Rhône…"

Aurel's son was to publish the famous *Souper de Beaucaire*, in which Bonaparte set forth his ideas about the Revolution, a few years later in Avignon.

🐾 WALKING TOUR

OLD TOWN

◐ Leave from Peynet kiosk.

WHERE TO STAY		WHERE TO EAT	
France (Hôtel de)......................①	Négociants (Les)........................③	Clercs (Le Bistrot des)..............①
Mare (Chambre d'hôte La)......②		7 (Le)..②

Kiosque Peynet

This structure, built in 1880, owes its name to the artist **Raymond Peynet** (1908–99) who once drew a sketch of a pair of lovers seated beside it.

Champ-de-Mars

This vast esplanade, built on a hillside opposite the Rhône, overlooks Jouvet park. From the belvedere there is a beautiful **view★** of the Crussol mountains. The sunsets visible from here are famous; they throw the mountain range into relief. However, it is at sunrise that the view of Crussol is the most striking.

▸ Take the staircase below the belvedere and cross avenue Gambetta. The narrow rue des Repenties and côte St-Estève lead round the cathedral and onto place du Pendentif.

Pendentif

This small monument was built in 1548, in the Antique style. The structure is completely open with a semicircular arch on each side, and has lovely proportions. It draws its name from the shape of its vault, reminiscent of the pendentives of a dome.

Cathédrale St-Apollinaire

This vast Romanesque construction was largely rebuilt during the 17C in the primitive style.

▶ Enter the cathedral through the north door.

Under the porch, on the left, notice the lintel from the original portal; its carved compartments represent the Annunciation, the Nativity, the Adoration of the Magi and the Magi before Herod.

Interior★

The influence of Auvergne Romanesque architecture is evident; the nave, with its barrel vaulting and transverse arches, is lit by the aisle windows.

An arcade separates the chancel from the ambulatory. Note the depth of the transept arms, unusual in Rhône buildings. Behind the chancel stalls is a cenotaph-bust of Pope Pius VI, who died in Valence in 1799.

▶ Leave through the south door.

Under the porch *(left)*, on the carved tympanum of the original portal, is Christ Giving Benediction, and on the lintel Christ Multiplying the Loaves.

▶ Walk around the east end.

Note the elegant billet-moulding above the arcades of the apse and the transept arms.

Musée de Valence, Art et Archéologie

◷ Tue 2–6pm, Wed–Sun 10am–6pm; 9pm on 3rd Thu of each month.
☞ €5.10. ✆ 04 75 79 20 80.
www.museedevalence.fr.
The Fine Arts Museum, located in the former bishop's palace, also provides dance and theatre performances, along with storytelling, lectures and readings to establish closer links between the art and arcaeology collections.

▶ Take rue du Lieutenant-Bonaparte, then rue Pérollerie to reach the Maison Dupré-Latour.

Maison Dupré-Latour

The interior courtyard of No. 7 has a Renaissance staircase turret with a door surrounded by a remarkable carved frame.

▶ From place de la Pierre, take rue St-James on the left then follow rue Sabaterie and rue Malizard.

On the left stands the former St-Ruf temple. As you reach the public gardens, you will get a view of Crussol in the distance.

▶ Head for place St-Jean via côte des Chapeliers.

Église St-Jean

This church was rebuilt in the 19C. The porch features some interesting original Romanesque capitals.

▶ Walk along Grande-Rue.

Maison des Têtes★

The "House of Heads" at No. 57 is recognisable by the abundance and originality of the sculptures on its façade. Note two standing figures (Eve is on the left) and, under the roof, the four enormous haut-relief heads symbolising the winds, after which this Renaissance house (1532) was named.

▶ Grand-Rue, then rue Saunière, lead back to place du Champ-de-Mars.

Centre du Patrimoine Arménien★

14 r. Louis-Gallet.
◷ Currently closed for development; check website for latest update.
✆ 04 75 80 13 00.
www.patrimoinearmenien.org.
Why go to Valence rather than elsewhere? The Armenian Centre, located in a formar law school provides the answer. The story is one of genocide and exile, and poignant in the extreme.

Detail on the façade of Maison des Têtes

Take the rue du Jeu-de-Paume into the boulevard Bancel. Admire the beautiful façades by Haussmann along the Champ-de-Mars.

👥 Parc Jouvet

This verdant setting in the heart of the city owes its existence to the generosity of a great vintner, Jouvet Theodor (1837–1905). You will find more than 700 species of trees here. Children will love the deer and the aviary.

EXCURSIONS

Châteaux d'eau de Philolaos

Take the autoroute towards Valence, leaving it at junction 32. Then head for Fontbarlette, Valence-le-Haut and parc Jean-Perdrix.
These water towers are the work of a sculptor, Philolaos, who frequently collaborates with architects and is responsible for works in Lyon, Évry, Créteil and La Défense.

Montélier

15km/9mi E via the D 68, then the D 538.
Montélier has made a speciality of its decorative trees and shrubs with nearly 300 varieties. You should take time to walk through the historical centre of the village, dominated by its 19C church. On some of the street corners you will see works by contemporary artists, notably Christian Maas and Philippe Jamet-Fournie.

Jardin Sémaphore

Chemin de Loches.
🕐*Daily 9am–7pm.* 📞*04 75 59 93 93.*
At the entrance to the gardens, the pavilion exhibition invites you to test your knowledge of natural sciences and communication by attempting fun experiments. Outside, the Wall of Generations traces, in the form of a mural 40m long, the history of the village from the time of Clovis (c. 466–511) to World War II.

Musée de Madagascar

Av. de Provence.
♿🕐*Mon–Sat 10am–noon 2–7pm, Sun 2–7pm (Jan–Feb 2–6pm).* 🕐*1–4 Jan, 25–27 Dec.* 🎫*€6 (child 7-16, €5).* 📞*04 75 59 97 61.*
www.museedemadagascar.com.
Created by a Franco-Madagascaran love of the country, this vast space portrays the island off the coast of Africa, an island with an area greater than the whole of France (Madagascar, 587 036sq km/226 656sq mi; France, 551 667sq km/213 000sq mi). Through photographs, formal staged settings, scenes of life recreated in miniature, tools and many artefacts, the exhibition conveys the culture, natural wealth and way of life.

ADDRESSES

⌂STAY

⊖**Hôtel Les Négociants** – *27 av. Pierre-Sémard.* ☏*04 75 44 01 86. www.hotel valence.com. 36 rooms.* A friendly, air-conditioned hotel close to the station.

⊖**Chambre d'Hôte La Mare** – *Rte de Montmeyran, 26800 Étoile-sur-Rhône.* ☏*04 75 59 33 79. http://la.mare.free. fr. 4 rooms.* This family farm is the right place to become acquainted with the local *savoir-vivre* and the charm of the Drômois.

⊖⊜⊜**Hôtel de France** – *16 blvd du Gén.-de-Gaulle.* ☏*04 75 43 00 87. www.hotel-valence.com. 46 rooms.* A modernised hotel that is elegant, sober and in tune with the times.

⌢/EAT

⊖⊜**Le Bistrot des Clercs** – *48 Grande Rue.* ☏*04 75 55 55 15. www.michel-chabran.com. Closed Sat.* Bistro in the Parisian style, serving hearty food.

⊖⊜**Le 7** – *285 av. Victor-Hugo.* ☏*04 75 44 15 32. www.anne-sophie-pic.com.* Modern cuisine based on classic styles and recipes.

ON THE TOWN

Le Djam – *11 Grand-Rue.* ☏*04 75 43 32 32.* An original decoration scheme reigns in this small neighbourhood bar reminiscent of Alice in Wonderland. .

Café Victor-Hugo – *30 av. Victor-Hugo.* ☏*04 75 40 18 11. www.restaurant-victor-hugo.fr. Open 6.30am–11pm.* Valence's chic literary café – chic but vivacious! Lunchtime, it is a noisy brasserie.

Le Malvern – *27 r. Denis-Papin.* ☏*04 75 44 10 07.* Rather rustic decor of the Irish pub ilk.

RECREATION

Marina – *Chemin de l'Épervière.* ☏*04 75 81 18 93. Apr–Oct daily 9am–noon, 2–8pm; Nov–Mar Mon–Sat 8am–noon, 2–6pm. Closed public holidays.* The Port de l'Épervière is the Rhône river's number one harbour. Several clubs organise sports activities here, including windsurfing, water skiing, para-skiing. There is also a bowling lane, a tennis facility, a pool, a campground, a hotel and several restaurants.

Romans-sur-Isère

The town is built on a hillside opposite Bourg-de-Péage, whose name is a reminder of the toll once collected by the Chapter of St Barnard to cross the bridge linking the two towns. Romans, a flourishing trade centre in the Middle Ages, was once the capital of footwear. Lovers of good food will appreciate the local *pogne*, which is a type of *brioche* or sweet bread flavoured with orange blossom, *saint-genis* (praline *pogne*) and goat's cheese, *Tomme*, which is also used to make the local dish, *ravioles*).

- ▶ **Population:** 34 525.
- ⚏ **Michelin Map:** 332: D-3.
- ▯ **Info:** Bd Gambetta, 26100 Romans-sur-Isère. ☏04 75 02 28 72. www.ville-romans.fr.
- ▷ **Location:** 17km/10mi E of Tournon, 13km/8mi NE of Valence.
- ▣ **Parking:** There are central parking areas.
- ◉ **Don't Miss:** It's all about shoes; visit the shoe museum.
- ◴ **Timing:** Allow at least half a day.
- ᪲ **Kids:** Goblins and trolls at Le Monde Merveilleux des Lutins.

A BIT OF HISTORY

Dauphiné joins France – From the 11C on, the counts of Albon, natives of Vienne, gradually took over the region from the Rhône valley to the Alps that eventually formed Dauphiné. The origin of the name "Dauphin", given to members of the dynasty which then reigned over Dauphiné, remains uncertain.

The last of the Vienne *dauphins*, Humbert II, lived mostly at Beauvoir Castle, opposite St-Marcellin. After the death of his son, which left him without an heir, he sold Dauphiné to the French crown. It was in St-Barnard Collegiate Church that the treaty unifying the Dauphiné region, formerly part of the Holy Roman Empire, to France, was solemnly signed on 30 March 1349. This province was to become the attribute of the oldest sons of the kings of France, who subsequently bore the title of Dauphin.

WALKING TOUR

OLD TOWN

▷ Start from place du Pont.

A maze of picturesque streets surrounds St-Barnard Collegiate Church and, half way down the hill from the church, place de la Presle and place Jacquemart.

Collégiale St-Barnard

Quai U.-Chevalier. ℘04 75 72 25 87.
In the 9C, St Barnard, Archbishop of Vienne, founded a monastery here. It was destroyed in the 12C and replaced by a Romanesque church of which the western porch, the northern portal and lower parts of the nave still remain. Towards the middle of the 13C the chancel and transept were rebuilt in Gothic style. Largely destroyed by the Protestants in the 16C, the church was completely restored in the 18C.

▷ Take rue Pêcherie, opposite the west end of the church.

Escalier Josaphat

These **steps** go down from rue Pêcherie towards the houses with their wooden balconies on place de la Presle. The stairway is part of the "Great Journey" or Way of the Cross which attracts a large crowd of people on Good Friday.

▷ Rue du Fuseau runs straight onto rue de l'Armillerie.

At No. 15 rue du Mouton, off to the right, the Gothic windows on the first floor are now mullioned windows; above, the outline of a sheep's head carved in a projecting stone can just be made out.

▷ Continue towards place Fontaine-Couverte.

Place Fontaine-Couverte

This square in the heart of the old town is decorated with a modern fountain representing a flautist.

Côte Jacquemart

The hill is lined with 13C and 14C houses.

Le Jacquemart

This is an old square tower from the outer curtain wall of Romans, converted into a belfry in the 15C and given a Jack-o'-the-clock, which since 1830 has proudly sported the costume of a 1792 volunteer.

▷ Facing towards the river, turn left to côte des Cordeliers; walk down to rue Fontaine-des-Cordeliers and rue St-Nicolas.

Hôtel Thomé

This fine townhouse presents a Renaissance façade with beautiful mullioned windows on the upper floors.

▷ Continue towards the river via rue Sabaton and turn right onto rue des Clercs.

Rue des Clercs

The street is very picturesque with rounded cobblestones. Notice, opposite the town's archives, the portal decorated with fine chiselling.

Rue des Trois-Carreaux

This is an extension of rue des Clercs. At its intersection with place aux Herbes there is a monumental door, surmounted by an unusual corbelled construction with machicolations.

WHERE TO STAY	WHERE TO EAT
Chez M. et Mme Imbert (Chambre d'hôte)............①	Mandrin...①

Place Maurice-Faure

Beside St-Barnard, to the right of the St-Jean door on the north side of the church, is a beautiful house with a corner tower.

SIGHTS
Musée International de la Chaussure★

Jan–Apr and Oct–Dec Tue–Sat 10am–5pm; May–Jun and Sept Tue–Sat 10am–6pm; Jul–Aug Mon–Sat 10am–6pm; Sun and public holidays all year 2.30–6pm. 1 Jan, 1 May, 1 Nov, 25 Dec, and 15 days following Christmas holidays. €6. 04 75 05 51 81. www.ville-romans.fr.

The Shoe Museum is located to the east of town and reached through the gateway in rue Bistour, across terraced gardens in front of the building, which is adorned with an elegant colonnade. The museum aims to present the technical, ethnographic and aesthetic aspects of footwear. Numerous documents and other material trace the evolution of the shoe-maker's craft and associated activities in the town.

In the old nuns' cells, the collections of footwear are displayed in chronological and thematic order from Antiquity to 1900. Some of them are extremely comprehensive, such as that of Paris designer Victor Guillen.

These sumptuous, amusing and enigmatic shoes reveal the ingenuity of their creators and evoke the customs of their country of origin and fashion throughout the ages: Roman sandals, cracowes whose length varied with social rank, patterns inlaid with tortoiseshell and pearl from Mauritania, Indian moccasins from North America, shoes from Ardèche used to open chestnuts and ankle boots from the Belle Epoque.

The 18C and 19C paintings on the theme of shoes and shoe-making add another angle of interest to the museum visit.

EXCURSIONS
Bourg-de-Péage

1.8km/1mi S along the D 2092.
Located by the old bridge, Bourg-de-Péage gets its name from the toll that used to be charged here.

Mours-St-Eusèbe

4km/2.5mi N. Leave Romans on D 538 then turn right onto D 608.
The village church has kept only its belltower, at the west end, and the south wall of the nave from the 11C. It houses

an interesting **Musée Diocésain d'Art Sacré★** (🕐Sun mid-Jun–mid-Sept 2.30–6.30pm. ⌨€4. 𝄢04 75 02 36 16. http://museeartsacre.free.fr) with rich sacred art (15C–20C) arranged according to a new theme each year.

Hostun

Leave Romans E towards St-Nazaire-en-Royans. Shortly beyond L'Écancière, turn right onto D 125C to Hostun.

An old farm (at Les Guerbys) has been turned into ♿ **Le Monde Merveilleux des Lutins** (the Wonderful World of Elves – 🕐Jul–Aug 10am–6.30pm; Apr and Dec Wed, Sat–Sun 2–6pm; May daily except Mon 2–6pm; Jun daily except Mon 2–6pm, Sat–Sun 11am–6pm 🕐1 Jan, 25 Dec. ⌨€7 (children €6). 𝄢04 75 48 89 79. www.mondedeslutins.com), a fantasy realm where children can meet trolls, gnomes, sprites, gremlins and other goblins.

Hauterives★

25km/15.5mi N of Romans on the D 358.
The village of Hauterives, situated at the foot of a hillock bearing the ruins of the medieval castle, which once belonged to the lords of Clermont, has an unusual tourist attraction – the "Ideal Palace".

♿ Palais Idéal★★

♿🕐Jul–Aug 9.30am–7pm; Apr–Jun and Sept 9.30am–6.30pm; Feb–Mar and Oct–Nov 9.30am–5.30pm; Dec–Jan 9.30am–4.30pm. 🕐25 and 31 Dec, 1 Jan and mid-end Jan. ⌨€6.50 (children €5). 𝄢04 75 68 81 19. www.facteurcheval.com.
In the late 19C Ferdinand Cheval, the local postman, began bringing home strangely shaped stones that he picked up during his round. Each evening he would add them to an unusual construction he was building in his garden, based on books and dreams, and possibly also inspired by the remains of petrified springs that were common in this area. Cheval continued his work when he retired, bringing sand and stones back to his home in a wheelbarrow. After 33 years of relentless labour, he finished his weird and wonderful "palace". He then spent the last 10 years of his life building his own grave in the cemetery, in the same style. He died in 1924.

♿ Les Labyrinthes

3.5km/2.2mi from Hauterives. Follow D 51 towards Le Grand-Serre and turn left in St-Germain. ♿🕐Mid-Apr–Aug and Sat–Sun in Sept 11am–7pm. 🕐Oct–mid-Apr. ⌨€11 (child 3–14, €9.50). 𝄢04 75 68 96 27. www.labyrinthes-hauterives.com.
Four large mazes, occupying the top of a hill, combine their network of paths and hedges to offer young visitors a thrilling treasure hunt. The Maison des Enfants, located in a shaded position, organises activities involving mosaics.

Albon

17km/10.5mi to the W of Hauterives by the D 51 and D 132.
Albon owes its existence to its counts who progressively extended their domain from the 11C onwards, and so created Dauphiné. The Tour d'Albon is a link with the past and offers a lovely **panorama★** over the Rhône valley.

Château de Mantaille

11km/7mi W of Hauterives by the D 147 and the D 132.
The ruins of the château stand on the side of the Bancel; it was here that Boso was crowned King of Burgundy in 879.

🚗 DRIVING TOUR

LES COLLINES
44km/27mi. Allow 3h.

▶ Leave Romans to the NW by D 53.

St-Donat-sur-l'Herbasse

This old Drôme village is a popular haunt among music lovers. The 12C–16C **collegiate church** houses modern organs designed after plans made by the famous Silbermann Brothers (three keyboards, three sets of pipes).
Every year the church hosts a prestigious **Johann Sebastian Bach Festival** (𝄢04 75 45 10 29).

▶ Leave St-Donat on D 584 and head N for Bathernay.

Bathernay

This pretty village enjoys a charming setting in the midst of the lush countryside. West of Bathernay a narrow road leads to the octagonal tower of **Ratières**.

▶ Take D 207 to the S, then D 53 for 1.3km/0.9mi; a path to the right will take you to the Chapelle St-Andéol.

Chapelle St-Andéol

The small chapel commands a superb **panorama** over the Isère valley, the Galaure Basin and Mont Pilat.

▶ A short, picturesque road to the S leads to Bren, where you turn right to join the D 112. Turn left at the D 109.

Chantmerle-les-Blés

Leave the car in the square behind the post office. The footpath begins at the war memorial by the church.

🔜 The highlight of this small town is the view of the surrounding hills *(15mins walk from the church)*.

ADDRESSES

🛏 STAY

🛏 **Chambre d'hôte Chez M. et Mme Imbert** – *"Les Marais", Hameau de St-Didier, 26300 St-Didier-de-Charpey (9km/5.4mi S of Romans. Take D 538 to Alixan, then left onto road to St-Didier).* ✆ *04 75 47 03 50.* **3 rooms.** The former stables of this farm are now pleasant, simple bedrooms with. Meals, with an accent on regional cookery, are served with the family.

🍴 EAT

🍴 **Mandrin** – *70 r. St-Nicolas.* ✆ *04 75 02 93 55. www.lemandrin.com. Closed Sun eve, all day Mon, and Wed eve.* Mandrin, the famous smuggler, found refuge in this house, dating from 1754. The tiled floor, wooden beams, timber-framing, studs and rounded stones give the restaurant a medieval atmosphere; it serves traditional cuisine.

St-Antoine-l'Abbaye★

Nestling in an undulation of the Chambaran plateau north of the River Isère is the old village of St-Antoine-l'Abbaye, dominated by an imposing Gothic abbey church.

THE ABBEY CHURCH

St Anthony's fire – In the 11C a nobleman from Vienne, Jocelyn de Châteauneuf, made a pilgrimage to the Holy Land. On his return he brought back from Constantinople the bones of Anthony the Great, the original "desert father", who lived in the Upper Nile valley. In the Middle Ages this saint

▶ **Population:** 1 072.
🚗 **Michelin Map:** 333: E-2.
ℹ **Info:** Pl. Ferdinand-Gilibert, 38160 St-Antoine-l'Abbaye. ✆ 04 76 38 53 85. www.saint-antoine-labbaye.fr.
▶ **Location:** 24km/15mi NE of Romans-sur-Isère.
🕐 **Timing:** Allow a day to visit the abbey and the village.

owed his popularity as much to the pig who was the daily companion of his hermetic life as to his battles with the devil.

Saint-Antoine-l'Abbaye

The relics in the church of La Motte-St-Didier, which took the name of St-Antoine, were entrusted by the Bishop of Vienne to Benedictines from Montmajour Abbey. A first monastery was built. Not long after, in 1089, a dreadful epidemic broke out in Dauphiné – St Anthony's fire. It was a sort of gangrene which burnt away the limbs. The saint's relics drew a large crowd of sick and poor people; to help and care for them, a group of young nobles created the Brotherhood of Charity.

A powerful order – In the 13C the brothers managed to supplant the Benedictines. In 1297 the brotherhood became the Hospital Brothers of St Anthony; the Antonine monks founded hospices all over Europe.

The great abbey church of St-Antoine, which took from the 13C to the 15C to build, was visited by popes, emperors from Germany, and kings of France who came to kneel before the relics.

Abbey

♿ 🔊 *Guided visits Apr–Oct daily except Mon and Tue.* 🕐 *Nov–Mar, although the church is open all year.* 📞 *04 76 36 44 46.*
www.saint-antoine-labbaye.fr.
The entrance to the abbey church is at the top of the village, through the

17C **main entrance gate** (Entrée d'Honneur), now the town hall (Hôtel de Ville), with its glazed mosaic tiles.

Musée de Saint-Antoine-l'Abbaye

♿ 🕐 *Early Mar–Apr and Sept–mid-Nov daily except Tue 2–6pm; May–Jun Mon, Wed–Fri 2–6pm, Sat–Sun 10.30am–12.30pm, 2–6pm; Jul–Aug daily except Tue 10.30am–12.30pm, 2–6pm.* 🕐 *1 May.* 📞 *04 76 36 40 68.*
www.musee-saint-antoine.fr.
This museum, located in the monastery's old novitiate, contains works by Jean Vinay (1907-78), a landscape artist from Dauphiné, and thematic exhibitions by his friends from the Paris School, and exhibitions on the Middle Ages or the Antonine Order.

EXCURSIONS
Château de l'Arthaudière
7km/4.3mi to the S by the D 27B.
🕐 *Jul–Aug daily except Tue and Fri 3–7pm; Jun and Sept Sat–Sun 3–7pm.* 📞 *04 76 38 63 88.*
Built on the site of 13C house, the castle (16C–19C) has been altered many times. The stables are 18C, and now house a permanent exhibition on local architecture. Note the covered wells (18C) and the elegant lantern in the barn.

© Franck Guiziou/hemis.fr

St-Marcellin

10km/6.2mi to the E on D 27, then D 20 on the right.

This town, where the last Viennese dauphin Humbert II set up his Parliament in the 14C, was badly hit by the Wars of Religion: besieged twice by the Baron des Adrets, it was subsequently recovered by the Catholics in 1568.

The colourful Saturday market and annual fairs attract a great many locals from Bas-Grésivaudan; the area is known for Saint-Marcellin, a small, round cheese made with cow's milk that has a soft and moulded rind. The **Promenade de Joud** affords pretty views of the Isère valley and the Royans, overlooked by the Vercors ramparts.

Chatte

8km/5mi to the SE on D 27.

The most interesting sight in this small village is its **Jardin Ferroviaire**👥 (♿🕐*Apr–Jun Mon–Fri 2–7pm, Sat–Sun 10.30am–7pm; Jul–Aug daily 10am–7pm; Sept Mon–Fri 2–6pm, Sat–Sun 10.30am–7pm; Oct Sat–Sun 10.30am–6.30pm.* 👓*€9.50 (child 3–12, P6).* 📞*04 76 38 54 55. www.jardin-ferroviaire.com)* a miniature park complete with paths and 200 plant varieties, cut across by 1km/0.6mi of tiny tracks served by 30 trains. A charming outing for children and parents alike.

La Sône

6km/3.7mi to the S on D 20, then on the D 71.

This village stands in a lush, peaceful setting along the banks of the Isère.

Do not miss the **Jardin des Fontaines-Pétrifiantes** (🕐*May–mid-Oct: call for information.* 👓*€9.50.* 📞*04 76 64 43 42. www.jardin-des-fontaines.com)*, set up in a niche where petrified water concretions have coated the surrounding relief and objects with glittering crystals. The leafy grounds, featuring around 15 000 plant species, are enhanced by a series of basins and small waterfalls.

The most picturesque way to visit the region is to take a 👥**boat ride** (♿🕐*cruise with commentaries Apr–mid-Oct, check website for times and tariffs.* 📞*04 76 64 43 42. www.bateau-a-roue.com)* on board the Royans-Vercors paddle-boat, which will enlighten you on the local fauna and flora lying at the foot of the Vercors.

Le Grand Séchoir★

Vinay: 26km/16.3mi E via the D 27 then the D1 092. ♿🕐*Apr–Oct Tue–Sun 10am–6pm; Nov–Mar daily except Mon 2–5.30pm.* 🕐*Jan, 1 May, 25 Dec.* 👓*€4.50.* 📞*04 76 36 36 10. www.legrandsechoir.fr.*

This great "drying" farm is dedicated to walnuts, the story of which is told from different angles: mythical and traditional, with a fine collection of nuts of the world, and explanations of harvesting techniques.

Notre-Dame-de-l'Osier

26km/16.3mi E via the D 27, then the D 1092. Cross Vinay on the D 22, then turn right onto the D 201.

The present church, built in 1873, incorporates a mosaic of the 1649 miracle: Peter Port-Combet, peasant and Protestant, made the mosaic bleed before witnesses.

ADDRESSES

La Côte-St-André

This small town, a liqueur-producing centre built in a semicircle on a hillside above the Bièvre plain, is the birthplace of *Hector Berlioz* (1803–69) (♿*see Introduction above*). The Berlioz Festival is held every year during the second fortnight in August in the covered market and parish church of La Côte-St-André.

▶ **Population:** 5 118.
♿ **Michelin Map:** 333: E-5.
🪧 **Info:** 5 Place Hector Berlioz. ✆04 74 20 61 43. www.tourisme-bievre-liers.fr.
⊳ **Location:** NW of Grenoble via A 48.
🅿 **Parking:** There are parking places in the centre.
😊 **Don't Miss:** The Château Louis XI and the Berlioz Museum.
🕐 **Timing:** Allow 3hrs to walk around town and visit the museum.

SIGHTS

Musée Hector-Berlioz
Rue de la République.
🕐*10am–12.30pm, 1.30–6pm: Jul–Aug daily; rest of year daily except Tue.*
🕐*1 Jan, 1 May and 25 Dec.* ✆*04 74 20 24 88. www.musee-hector-berlioz.fr.*
This museum is housed in the composer's birthplace, a handsome residence built in the late 17C and restored in 1969.

Château Louis XI
Built in the 13C for Philip of Savoy on a fine defensive site, this castle was designed as both fortress and residence; it suffered extensive damage during the wars in the 16C but was rebuilt thereafter.

Musée des Liqueurs
♿🕐*Mid-Jul–Sept daily except Mon 3–6pm; rest of year Sun and public holidays 3–6pm.* 🕐*Jan–Feb, 14 Jul, 15 Aug, 25 Dec.* ✆*04 74 93 38 10. www.cherryrocher.com.*
The Cherry Rocher company, which was set up in 1705 in a neo-Classical mansion, offers tours of its plant.
The museum contains a collection of old machinery (fruit press, stills, infusers).

EXCURSIONS

Château de Bressieux
8km/3mi S on D 71, then a narrow road to the left when you leave St-Siméon-de-Bressieux. In the centre of the village, when the road takes a bend, turn left into the small lane (15min on foot return).

Perched high on a promontory overlooking Bressieux village, the castle ruins make an attractive, picturesque sight.a

Marnans
18km/11.3mi to the S via the D 71, then the D 130, Viriville, and the D 156C.
Out in the wilds of the plateau of Chambaran, this humble village has a beautiful Romanesque church of considerable architectural merit.

Roybon
17km/10.6mi S on D 71.
This small town boasts a charming group of buildings with traditional façades characteristic of the area: carved clay and wood decorated with pebbles. This architectural heritage is enhanced by the remains of a medieval rampart.

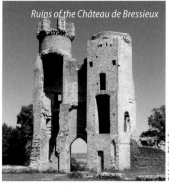
Ruins of the Château de Bressieux
© L. Lainey/Michelin

Lac de Paladru

© Lionel Montico/hemis.fr

Lac de Paladru★

Lake Paladru lies in a depression originally formed by a glacier. The lake, mainly supplied by rain and snow, has a tributary at its southern end; the Fure, which flows down to the River Isère. Its beautiful emerald waters form a lovely stretch 6km/4mi long which, during summer months, attracts many watersports enthusiasts and ramblers from Lyon and the Dauphiné region. Anglers will find a wide variety of fish to test their skills, including char and freshwater crayfish. The hillside farms overlooking the lake and Upper Bourbre valley will appeal to those interested in traditional rural architecture: these houses are remarkable for their imposing eaves, sometimes reaching over the barn almost right down to the ground. The walls are made of mud, sometimes combined with shingle.

A BIT OF HISTORY

The discovery of a large number of piles emerging at low water level proves the existence of houses built directly on chalk shoals. The variety and abundance of the remains discovered as well as an analysis of pollen contained in the sediment have helped define the nature of the surrounding forest mantle and the

- ⚲ **Michelin Map:** 333: G-5.
- **Info:** 230 rue des Bains, 38850 Charavines. ☏ 04 76 93 17 60. www.paysvoironnais.info.
- ▶ **Location:** Just over 20km/ 12.5mi to the E of Côte-St-André.
- **Don't Miss:** Take a walk around the lake.
- ⌚ **Timing:** Allow around 2 hours.

daily activities of the inhabitants, who were mostly woodlanders.

"Les Baigneurs"

This farming village underwent two successive phases of occupation around 4 700 years ago, both connected with the Saône-Rhône civilisation. Axe handles, wooden spoons, flint stones, spindle-whorls and charred debris indicate the practice of several crafts as well as burn-beating after deforestation in preparation for cropping.

Colletière

This site to the south reveals a fortified village set up towards the end of the 10C, following a considerable drop in the level of the lake as a result of the climate warming up. The inhabitants were farmers, stock-breeders and fishermen. The discovery of riding equipment, lances and heavier weapons would indicate that there were knights with regular military duties whose task was to protect the community. This pre-feudal society was governed by laws concerning work and seems to have been more than able to provide for all its needs. The good condition of the dwellings has enabled specialists to reconstruct the original dwellings with accuracy, using a model to represent the three buildings identified.

The lakeside environment has preserved numerous everyday objects, such as leather shoes, textiles, rare wooden musical instruments, games (a complete chess set) and even toy weapons.

AROUND THE LAKE
Musée Archéologique du Lac de Paladru

🕐 *May–Sept daily 2–6pm; Oct–Apr Sun and school holidays 2–5pm.* 🗫€4 *(under 26 years, free).* 🖉*04 76 55 77 47. www.museelacdepaladru.fr.*
This museum displays the finds of underwater archaeological excavations of the drowned Neolithic and medieval villages.

Tour of the Lake★

It is possible to walk all round the lake *(for details ask at the tourist office in Paladru).* The Maison du Pays d'Art et d'Histoire de Paladru organises **heritage trails (visites-découvertes du patrimoine** – *information at the Musée du lac de Paladru in Charavines).* Two scenic roads – D 50 and D 50^D *(which become D 90)* – encircle the lake (15km/9.5mi). They connect the lively resort of **Charavines** on the southern point of the lake to the village of **Paladru** at the other end.

Tour de Clermont

🚶 *From Charavines, take the footpath along the Fure as far as the D 50 bridge, then the trail waymarked in yellow which goes uphill through fields. After the hamlet of La Grangière, take the path on the left up to the Tour de Clermont.*

This 13C pentagonal keep is all that remains of the powerful stronghold of Clermont. The top of the tower has disappeared, and the doorway was knocked out after the original date of construction. This was the residence of one of the oldest families of the Dauphiné, which married into Burgundy to give rise to the Clermont-Tonnerre branch of the family.

EXCURSIONS
Château de Virieu★

7.5km/5mi NW on D 17. ♿🕐*2–6pm: Easter–Jun and Sept–Oct Sat–Sun and public holidays; Jul–Aug Tue–Sun.* 🗫€8. 🖉*04 74 88 27 32. www.chateau-de-virieu.com.*
The castle overlooking the Upper Bourbre valley dates from the 11C to 18C, and was restored at the beginning of the 20C; it still looks like a fortress.

Château de Pupetières

South of Virieu.
It was in the rustic setting of the Bourbre valley, at the Château de Pupetières, that Burgundy-born Alphonse de Lamartine (1790–1869), poet and statesman, composed, in 1819, his celebrated poem, *Le Vallon*, published the following year with his *Méditations poétiques*.

ADDRESSES

🛏STAY

🍽 **Chambre d'Hôte Mme Ferrard** – *145 chemin de Béluran, lieu-dit Vers-Ars, 38730 Le Pin (1km/0.6mi SW of the Lac de Paladru via D 50).* 🖉*04 76 06 68 82. 5 rooms.* This old farm looks out over the Lac de Paladru. Nearly all of the bedrooms enjoy a view of the lake.

🍽EAT

🍽 **Hôtel les Bains** – *345 r. Principale, 38850 Charavines (1km/0.6mi S of Lac de Paladru via D 50).* 🖉*04 76 06 60 20. www.hoteldesbains-charavines.com.* This restaurant's appealing, old-fashioned decor – parquet, bistro furnishings, flowered plates – is most enjoyable. Traditional cuisine with one speciality: *la friture*, tiny fish fried whole.

Crémieu★

Crémieu sits in a narrow valley between fairly rugged hillsides and was once a fortress standing guard over one of the gateways into the Dauphiné region; it was also a busy trading centre. Among the local gastronomic specialities are *sabodets* (a variety of sausage) and *foyesse* (a type of cake).

✦ WALKING TOUR

OLD QUARTER

▶ Start from Porte de la Loi, which was part of the 14C town walls. Go through Porte des Augustins.

Place de la Nation
The name of this square dates back to the French Revolution. In the NE corner is a lever-operated well built in 1823.

Hôtel de Ville
The town hall stands on place de la Nation and is housed in part of what was once an Augustinian friary founded in the 14C.
The former **cloisters** (*cloîtres*) are entered from place de la Nation through a beautiful 18C wrought-iron gate.

Église
This monastery chapel has undergone many changes between 1318 and 1791 and remains of architectural interest.

▶ Take rue Porcherie to the market.

Halles★
The covered market was built in the 15C. The roof covered in *lauzes* is supported at each end by a thick wall comprising three arches. At the end on the right are the stone troughs over which corn measures were fitted.

▶ Take rue Mulet then turn right onto rue du Four-Banal to Porte Neuve.

▶ **Population:** 3 408.
▶ **Michelin Map:** 333: E-3.
▶ **Info:** 9 Pl. de la Nation, Crémieu. ✆04 74 90 45 13. www.tourisme-cremieu.fr.
▶ **Location:** E of Lyon, and midway between the A 42 and A 43.
▶ **Parking:** There are a number of car parks around the edge of town, along the Cours Baron Raverat, for example, but limited parking in the centre.
▶ **Timing:** Half a day is sufficient; more if you take the tour.

Fortified Gateways
Porte Neuve was built in the 16C; **Porte de Quirieu**, which has steps and a central gutter, dates from the 14C.

▶ Head along rue du Marché-Vieux.

On the right, at No. 14, note the 14C Window of the Three Hanged Men (Fenêtre des Trois Pendus).

▶ Carry on up montée St-Laurent.

Château Delphinal
This fortress on St-Laurent hill dates back to the 12C. On St-Hippolyte hill to the left are the remains of a 16C fortified Benedictine priory, including the old clock tower (*a footpath on the left leads to a viewing table*).

▶ Return down montée St-Laurent; turn right at bottom; left on côte Faulchet.

At the crossroads with rue du Four-Banal is a 16C house with mullioned windows, the **Maison du Colombier**.

▶ Go down rue St-Jean, rue du Lieutenant-Colonel-Bel and, after skirting the south-west corner of the covered market, rue des Adobeurs.

CRÉMIEU

0   100 m

AMBÉRIEU-EN-BUGEY ①② ② ISLE-CRÉMIEU

D 65

D 52

Chemin   du   Luminaire

Côte

Porte de Quirieu

Fenêtre
des Trois-Pendus

Bd de la
Porte-Neuve

Château
delphinal

Montée
St-Laurent

R. du Marché Vieux

R. St-
Antoine

◆ Porte Neuve

Chausson

Banal

R. Juiverie

Côte
Faulchet

Frandin

Maison du
Colombier

Cloître

Four-
du

R. St-
Jean

R. Mulet

LYON, VIENNE

PTE DES
AUGUSTINS

R. de la Loi

Pl. de
la Nation

H

Église

R. du Colonel

R. Porcherie

Bel

Halles

PORTE DE LA LOI

Cours

Pass.
Humbert

Baron

R. des
Adobeurs

Raverat

ST-HIPPOLYTE
TOUR DE
L'HORLOGE

Fg des Moulins

D 517

N

BOURGOIN-JALLIEU

WHERE TO STAY	WHERE TO EAT
Basses Portes (Chambre d'hôte Les)........①	Chaite (Auberge de la)........①
Maison de la Noisette (Chambre d'hôte La).........②	Val d'Amby (Le).........②

This street is lined with tiny low houses that used to contain craft workshops, including those of the town's tanners.

▶ Passage Humbert on the left leads to cours Baron-Ravenat.

🚗 DRIVING TOUR

ISLE CRÉMIEU: LAND OF STONE ROOFS
70km/44mi. Allow 5h.

With its cliffs, lakes, roofs covered in heavy stone slabs known as lauzes, fields bordered by standing stones, and country houses, the Île Crémieu region is quite unlike elsewhere in this area.

▶ Leave Crémieu on D 52 NE and follow signs to Optevoz.

As the road runs up the hill there is a view of Lake Ry and, further up the slope, of the large, modern **Château de St-Julien**.

▶ Beyond the cool Optevoz basin, follow D 52 as far as Surbaix then turn left on a pleasant little road (D 52B) which runs through a valley full of trees and meadows.

St-Baudille-de-la-Tour
This charming village contains an attractive 15C fortified house, known as the **Maison des Dames**, with a tower covered in *lauzes* and a porch decorated with a coat of arms; it is the headquarters of Roulottes Dauphiné *(see above)*.

▶ Drive through Torjonas to D 65; turn right towards La Balme-les-Grottes.

La Balme-les-Grottes
Pleasant village especially known for its grottoes lying at the foot of a cliff marking the edge of the Île Crémieu plateau. The **Grottes de la Balme**★ (◐*Apr–Jun Mon–Fri 2–6pm, Sat–Sun and public holidays 11am–6pm; Jul–Aug daily 11am–7pm; Sept daily 2–6pm. ⊸€10 (child 4–11, €6.50) – prices reduced outside Jul–Aug.*

04 74 90 63 76. www.grotteslabalme. com) were discovered during the Middle Ages, visited by François I, described as one of the "seven Wonders of Dauphiné", and are said to have been used in the 18C by the infamous brigand Louis Mandrin.

The Lake Gallery skirts a series of small **pools ★★** forming terraces of waterfalls before reaching the underground torrent.

◗ Turn back along D 65 then take the first road on the left, to Hières-sur-Amby.

Hières-sur-Amby

This tiny village stands at the end of the Amby valley, at the foot of the Larina plateau. The former rectory is now the **Maison du Patrimoine** (🕐2–6pm: Oct–Mar Mon–Fri; Apr–Sept daily. *04 74 95 19 10).* This modern museum houses objects

discovered during archaeological digs at Larina *(see below)* including bones, tools, coins and jewellery, and includes a model of a Merovingian farm. Models, videos and a display retrace the origins of the people living in Île Crémieu, with popular arts, crafts and traditions.

◗ Drive through Hières-sur-Amby, turn left onto D 52A.

Gorges d'Amby

The river twists and turns between rocks covered with scrubby vegetation. There is a view of the 15C Brotel fortified house on the cliff.

◗ A narrow road (right), opposite an old cement works, crosses the River Amby and runs up a hill to Chatelans.

Chatelans

At the centre of the village is the **Musée de la Lauze** (&⊙daily except Mon–Tue 9am–3pm) which explains the traditional techniques in this region for cutting and fitting the stone slabs.

▶ In the centre of the village, turn right onto a narrow road that runs for 2.5km/1.5mi to the tip of the plateau.

Parc Archéologique de Larina★

The Larina site is bordered by the cliffs overlooking the Rhône plain and Amby valley. The existence of human settlements on this site has been evidenced by objects dating from 5000 BCE. At the end of the Roman era and in the early days of the Dark Ages, two large farms existed in succession on this spot. The earlier one (4C and 5C) had a villa at its centre and included a number of farm buildings with stone foundations that are still clearly visible. From the 6C to 8C a second farm developed around a large stonehouse.

EXCURSIONS

Morestel

21.8km/13.6mi E.

The lovely setting and exceptional luminosity here have attracted countless artists since the mid-19C, namely Corot, Daubigny and Turner; this has earned Morestel the nickname of "Painters' Town." **Auguste Ravier** (1814–95) spent the latter part of his life in Morestel.

The D 517 road from Crémieu gives a delightful **view** of the village of Morestel, dominated by its Gothic church and the remains of a 12C square tower.

Maison Ravier

⊙Mar–Nov daily except Tue 2.30–6.30pm. ⊙1 May. ⊛€5. ℘04 74 80 06 80. www.maisonravier.fr.

This handsome residence was home to Auguste Ravier between 1867 and 1895. The house has been bought by the municipality and hosts art exhibitions.

Tour Médiévale

This former keep is all that remains of the 11C citadel overlooking the town. It offers lovely views of the region.

♟♟ Parc d'Attractions Walibi Rhône-Alpes★

15km/9.5 mi S. Leave Morestel on N 75 towards Grenoble and in Veyrins turn left towards Les Avenières; D 40 on the right leads to the park (signposted).
⊙Jul–Aug daily 10am–6pm/7pm; early Apr–Jun, Sat–Sun and public holidays 10am–5pm/6pm. ⊛€31 (child 3–11, €25). ℘04 74 33 71 80. www.walibi-rhone-alpes.fr.

This is one of nine Walibi parks in Europe, found in Belgium, France and the Netherlands. The Avenières Park is surrounded by lakes; with countless thrill rides, attractions and two shows.

ADDRESSES

⌂STAY

⊜**Chambre d'Hôte La Maison de la Noisette** – *La Prairie, 38460 Annoisin-Chatelans.* ℘04 74 83 86 09. www.maison-noisette.com. 4 rooms. A warm welcome awaits at this country house; rooms are cheerful, and in summer you might enjoy a barbecue.

⊜⊜**Les Basses Portes** – *23 rue des Russes, Torjonas, 38118 St-Baudille-de-la-Tour.* ℘06 03 57 00 61. www.basses-portes.com. This old farm has been extensively remodelled without detracting from its pastoral charm.

ⵌ EAT

⊜⊜**Auberge de la Chaite** – *Pl. des Tilleuls, Crémieu.* ℘04 74 90 76 63. Closed Sun evening, Wed lunch, and all day Mon. This country house serves up traditional dishes in a rustic room or on a shaded terrace. Also has rooms (⊜⊜) available.

⊜⊜**Le Val d'Amby** – *Pl. de la République, 38118 Hières-sur-Amby.* ℘04 74 82 42 67. www.hotel-levaldamby.com. Closed Sun evening and all day Wed. This beautiful stone country house is on the village square. Café area and more comfortable, less noisy, dining room.

Vienne★★

Vienne, "perched like an altar on the buttresses of the noble Dauphiné", to quote a local poet, is a town of exceptional interest. In a delightful setting★ basking in sunlight reflected from the Rhône, a Gothic cathedral stands next to a Roman temple, while Romanesque cloisters and several ancient churches rub shoulders with an Antique theatre. The charm of "Vienne the Beautiful" of Roman times is enhanced by the charm of "Vienne the Holy", the Christian city. The flower-filled pedestrian precinct, along cours Brillier and around the Hôtel de Ville, is a popular place for a leisurely stroll. Two bridges connect Vienne to the west bank of the Rhône. The old suspension bridge is now used as a footbridge; the modern bridge (1949) has a remarkable central arch. A 15C humpbacked bridge spans the Gère.

▶ **Population:** 30 122.
◉ **Michelin Map:** 333: C-4.
▯ **Info:** 14 Cours Brillier, 38200 VIENNE. ℘04 74 53 80 30. www.vienne-tourisme.com.
◗ **Location:** Situated 38km/24ml to the S of Lyon, and 52km/32mi E of St Étienne.
▣ **Parking:** There are ample parking areas to the south of the town.
⊘ **Don't Miss:** The important Gallo-Roman city of St-Romain-en-Gal; the cathedral of St Maurice, and the Temple of Augustus ad Livia.
◷ **Timing:** Allow half a day to explore Vienne; maybe an hour to visit St Romain.

A BIT OF HISTORY

Vienne the Beautiful – More than 50 years before Julius Caesar conquered Gaul, the stomping ground of the Allobroges tribe – of which Vienne became the capital in the 1C BCE – was subjugated by the Roman legions. In the absence of a more open site, the town was chosen for its geographical location which was easier to manage than that of Lyon as there was only one river to cross. Public monuments were erected at the foot of Mont Pipet, with private residences and trade and craft establishments on both banks. Vienne soon extended its suburbs beyond the Rhône to the present-day villages of Ste-Colombe and St-Romain-en-Gal. Drapers, leather workers and potters had flourishing businesses and the poet Martial described the town as "Vienne the Beautiful".

Joys and sorrows of "Greater Burgundy" – After the Western Roman Empire was dissolved in 476 and despite political confusion, Vienne remained a centre of artistic achievement: the construction of the church and necropolis of St-Pierre was continued; the foundations were laid for the abbey of St-André-le-Bas. The incessant in-fighting between the Carolingians for Charlemagne's heritage enabled Boson, Count of Vienne, Arles and Provence to proclaim himself "King of Burgundy" at Mantaille Castle in 879.

Vienne, the Holy City – As the distant Holy Roman Emperor only exercised nominal suzerainty, the temporal authority of the bishops, who were also the Counts of Viennois, held sway over the city and over an area of land on the east bank of the Rhône.

Around the abbey of St-André-le-Bas, which was at the height of its power, a large Jewish community plied a thriving trade. Two famous prelates sat on the throne of the "primate of the primates of the Gauls" – **Gui de Bourgogne** (1088–1119), crowned Pope in his own cathedral under the name of Calixtus II, and Jean de Bernin (1218–66), who directed the extensions to the cathedral of St-Maurice based on Gothic principles, ordered restoration of the Roman bridge over the Rhône, and built a hospital and the Château de la Bâtie.

Modern times – During the centuries of the Renaissance and the absolute monarchy, Vienne's decline offers a painful contrast with the prosperity of Lyon – commercial activity collapsed and the population dropped by one-fifth between 1650 and the beginning of the 18C. Even the bridge over the Rhône, swept away by flooding in 1651, was not rebuilt until the 19C. A certain industrial rebirth occurred once the Revolution had swept away the Ancien Régime.

ST-ROMAIN-EN-GAL

St-Romain-en-Gal and Ste-Colombe, on the west bank of the Rhône, are located in the Rhône administrative *département* whereas Vienne, opposite, is in the Isère *département*. In Ancient times, these three towns formed a single urban centre.

Gallo-Roman City of St-Romain-en-Gal★★

Excavations of the site since 1967 have unearthed an urban district including not only sumptuous villas but also businesses, workshops and *thermae* (hot baths).

© Franck Guiziou/hemis.fr

Mosaics in the museum, St-Romain-en-Gal

Museum★

&⊙*Daily except Mon 10am–6pm (5pm Nov–Jan).* ⊙*1 Jan, 1 May, 1 Nov, 25 Dec.* ⊛€*6 (no charge on 1st Sun of month).* ℘*04 74 53 74 01.*
www.musees-gallo-romains.com.

This on-site museum was designed as a showcase which presents the archaeological site on the one hand and the Rhône and Vienne of today on the other. A staircase, situated just before the entrance, leads to a terrace offering a panoramic view of the town, the river and the excavations. The site includes a wealth of workshops and sumptuous

ST-ROMAIN-EN-GAL

Great storehouse

Maison des Dieux Océan

Thermal baths

R. Commerce

3

2

House of the Five Mosaics

des Thermes

N

Wrestler's Baths

5

4

R. du

R. du Portique

Palais du Miroir

GIVORS

D 502

1 ★★MUSEUM

Entrance

P

0   100 m

RHÔNE

VIENNE

Pont de-Lattre-de-Tassigny

Dwelling

Workshops, shops and strorehouses

residences, the most splendid of all being the **Maison des Dieux Océan** (House of the Ocean Gods).

The **Dieux Océan mosaic★** invites visitors to discover works of art of the Gallo-Roman period. Vienne was a thriving city under Roman occupation; the Rhône, which played a key role in the town's prosperity, separated the city itself from the more residential district of St-Romain-en-Gal. The main assets of the site are the magnificent floor mosaics which are as beautiful as the *opus sectile* pavings, made with much larger marble slabs.

Archaeological Site★

The remains found in the area so far indicate occupation from the end of the 1C BCE to the 3C, though the structure of the area does not correspond to the grid layout usually adopted by the Romans. A portico runs along the side of **rue du Portique**, from east to west. **Rue du Commerce** and **rue des Thermes**, which run approximately north–south, converge in the northern part of the site.

Dwellings

At the entrance to the site is a vast residence, the **House of the Ocean Gods**; its southern entrance is its only connection with the outside. The vestibule had a mosaic floor depicting ocean gods with bearded heads and long flowing hair, and marine motifs. To the north of the House of the Ocean Gods is the **House of the Five Mosaics**, named after the different mosaic floors discovered mainly in the peristyle, the *triclinium* and the reception room.

Northeast of the site, on the other side of rue des Thermes, is another residential area with **houses**, and **baths** that follow a typically Roman arrangement: *hypocaust, caldarium* (hot room), *tepidarium* (warm room) and *frigidarium* (cold room).

SAINTE-COLOMBE

During Roman times this suburb was filled with luxurious residences decorated with works of art and mosaics.

Tour Philippe-de-Valois

The tower was built next to the Rhône by Philippe de Valois in 1343, after Ste-Colombe became part of the royal domain.

WALKING TOUR

ROMAN AND CHRISTIAN VIENNE★★

▷ Leave from place St-Maurice.

Cathédrale St-Maurice★★

Built from the 12C to 16C, the cathedral combines both Romanesque and Gothic. The patronage of St Maurice is a reminder of the veneration given to martyrs of the Theban Legion in the Burgundian kingdoms.

Doorways

The west front with its three doorways is adorned with fine Flamboyant ornamentation. Although the Wars of Religion deprived it of the statues decorating the niches of the engaged piers and tympana, the delightful decoration of the covings has fortunately remained intact.

The late-14C **south doorway** has two covings: the inner row depicts the prophets seated under canopies; the outer row has pairs of musician angels. The **central doorway**, with its cut-off gable, dates from the late 15C. It has three covings with sculptures which are to be read horizontally. The **north doorway**, from the second half of the 15C, is devoted to the Virgin.

Interior

The vast nave, with no transept, reflects a surprising harmony despite its construction over a period of four centuries. The far seven bays enclosing the Gothic nave are Romanesque. Reminiscent of Roman times, the piers are flanked with antique-style pilasters and fluted half-columns; this stage of construction, from the early 12C, is contemporary with or slightly later than the pontificate of Gui

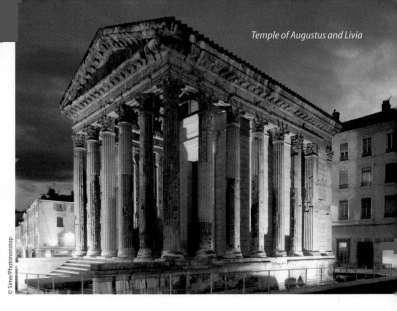

Temple of Augustus and Livia

de Bourgogne. The four bays of the nave nearest the west front were built in the 15C in pure Gothic style, their engaged columns rising in an unbroken line to the base of the ribbing.

The **Romanesque capitals** form a decorative whole, closely inspired by Antiquity. They feature narrative scenes (right aisle) or whimsical subjects.

In the apse, on the right of the High Altar, stands the **mausoleum** of archbishops Arnaud de Montmorin and Henri-Oswald de La Tour d'Auvergne (1747), by **Michel-Ange Slodtz**; it is one of the finest 18C works in Dauphiné. A splendid Renaissance stained-glass window, the Adoration of the Magi, throws light from the east into the chancel from the right aisle. The stained-glass clerestory windows in the chancel date from the 16C; the central window depicts St Maurice, in armour, with St Peter.

The north aisle has interesting sculptures: between the sixth and seventh chapel a large 13C bas-relief depicting the meeting of Herod and the Magi is striking for the very noble poses; an amusing detail is the two grotesque heads on either side of Herod, symbolizing his two-facedness – one, turned towards the kings, appears to listen to them attentively while the other, unseen by them, is laughing maliciously.

A covered passageway (north aisle) once connected the cathedral to the ancient cloisters, which no longer exist.

▶ Leave the cathedral along the covered passageway (north aisle).

Outside, the decoration on the door of the north wall combines Romanesque and Gothic elements with Roman fragments. Beneath the pointed arch, delicate griffons and leaves decorate the lintel.

▶ Walk to place du Palais.

You will be taken aback by the beauty of the Roman temple standing in the centre of the square, pleasantly contrasting with the 18C façades of the houses framing place du Palais.

Temple of Augustus and Livia★★

This is a rectangular building of agreeable proportions. Its dimensions are approximately the same as those of the Maison Carrée, the well-known Roman temple in Nîmes. A row of six Corinthian columns supports the entablature on the façade and the sides; the carved ornamentation is better preserved on the north side. The rear part, which is the oldest, probably dates from the end of the 1C BCE.

VIENNE

WHERE TO STAY

Bontemps (Camping)	①
Central (Hôtel)	②
Gabetière (La)	③
Pré Neuf (Chambre d'hôte Le)	④

WHERE TO EAT

Chamade (La)	①
Estancot (L')	②
Medina (La)	③

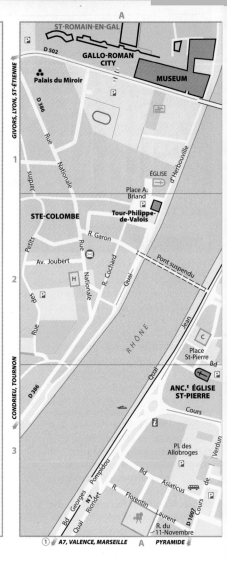

The façade, facing east, overlooked the forum. It was rebuilt under the reign of Augustus. Its triangular pediment bore a bronze inscription to the glory of Augustus and Livia, his wife.

▷ Rue des Clercs leads to the church.

Église St-André-le-Bas★

Apart from the lower parts of the east end, the apse, a large part of the southern wall and a few later additions, the church is mainly 12C. The large freestone gable wall provides an unusual decorative effect. The whole of the decoration is remarkable: piers and colonnettes on the twin openings, small festooned arches ending in consoles bearing expressive masks.

The Salle du Patrimoine (Heritage Gallery) hosts a **standing exhibition** on the theme "The Many Faces of Vienne".

▷ Walk into the southern courtyard flanked by the base of the bell-tower.

The first mask to be seen is poking out an enormous tongue. The nave was originally covered with timber framing; the restoration in 1152 consisted of raising and vaulting it, which required the construction of outside flying buttresses and reinforcement of the walls by arches and piers.

The decoration of the fluted pilasters is attributed to Guillaume Martin who signed and dated his work (1152) on the base of the second pier from the right; the most beautiful capitals depict Samson overwhelming the Lion (second pier from the left).

▶ Leave the church through the north door.

Cloître St-André-le-Bas★

🕐 *Daily except Mon.* 🕐 *1 Jan, 1 May and 11 Nov, 25 Dec.* ✆ *04 74 85 50 42.*

These small, trapezoidal cloisters date from the 12C. They have a series of blind arcades, resting alternately on twinned colonnettes and the piers marking the bays. The colonnettes in the south gallery show an element of fantasy: spiral or zigzag fluting, strings of beads or palm leaves with knotted stems.

▶ Take rue de la Table-Ronde to rue Marchande.

At No. 32, there is a beautiful portal with coving and a carved arch stone.

▶ Continue to rue des Orfèvres.

No. 11 has a 15C–16C inner courtyard whereas No. 9 has a beautiful Renaissance façade.

▶ Turn around and take rue du Collège on the right.

Église St-André-le-Haut
This church was once a Jesuit College chapel but was consecrated to St Louis in 1725.

Théâtre Romain★
The Roman theatre had been abandoned since the time of Emperor Constantine, in the early 4C, and was one of the largest theatres in Roman Gaul; its diameter is greater than that of the Roman theatre at Orange in Provence and is only 1m less than that of the great theatre of Marcellus in Rome.

▶ Take rue des Célestes, then walk down montée St-Marcel to rue Victor-Hugo and the archaeological gardens.

Jardin Archéologique
A white-stone double archway is the only remaining part of a **portico**, thought in the past to be part of some Roman baths; note the fine decorative frieze on the inside.
On the right of the portico is a wall which formed the northern side of a **theatre**.

▶ Take rue Chantelouve, then rue Ponsard to the Musée des Beaux-Arts.

Musée des Beaux-Arts et d'Archéologie
Daily except Mon. 1 Jan, 1 May, 11 Nov, 25 Dec. €3. 04 74 78 71 04.
The Fine Arts and Archaeology Museum is housed in a 19C covered market and comprises several collections: prehistoric and Gallo-Roman antiquities; 18C French earthenware; paintings from the 17C and 18C European Schools and the Lyon, Vienne and Dauphiné Schools; and works by the Vienne sculptor, J Bernard (1866–1931).

▶ Cours Romestang, then boulevard de la République, lead to place St-Pierre.

ADDITIONAL SIGHTS
Ancienne Église St-Pierre★
The church of St-Pierre is the oldest building of Christian Vienne, dating to the 5C. The church was the burial place of the bishops of Vienne. St-Pierre, built "outside the walls", was to suffer from the devastations of the Saracens in about 725, followed by those of the Carolingian princes in 882.

EXCURSIONS
Beauvoir-de-Marc
19km/12mi E. Leave Vienne on D 502. At La Détourbe turn left onto D 53B.
The small 11C–14C **church** with its painted ceiling stands on a hillside from the top of which there is a **panorama★** of the Viennois hills, dominated by the sombre mass of Mont Pilat.

St-Mamert
13km/8mi S. Leave Vienne on N 7 S and turn left onto D 131A.
The **Chapel of St-Mamert**, with its 11C belfry-wall and 17C restored interior, is built on a terrace of pebbles which offers a view of the Pilat mountain range.

Château de Septème
12km/7.5mi E on D 502 and D 75.
The 14C–16C castle is not far from Septème village. Overlooking the inner courtyard are Renaissance loggias on two storeys and a colonnaded gallery.

The castle is surrounded by curtain walls that have kept many of their loopholes, and part of the watch-path.

ADDRESSES

🛏 STAY

Camping Bontemps – *38150 Vernioz (19km/12mi S of Vienne via N 7, D 131 and D 37).* ℘*04 74 57 83 52. www.camping-lebontemps.com. Open mid-Apr-Sept. Reservations recommended. 100 sites. Food service.* Tourism and sports are on this campground's programme. Set off walking or sightseeing to discover the region – unless you'd rather stay put and take advantage of the on-site sports facilities to go horseback riding, mountain biking or swimming.

Hôtel Central – *7 r. de l'Archevêché.* ℘*04 74 85 18 38. 25 rooms.* In the heart of the city, as its name implies, this simple hotel's best feature is its central location.

Chambre d'Hôte Le Pré Neuf – *9 r. des Guillemottes.* ℘*04 74 31 70 11. http://aupreneuf.e-monsite.com. 3 rooms.* On the edge of town, this 19C house has a nice garden; the rooms are furnished with homely items.

La Gabetière – *269 Le Logis-Neuf, 38780 Estrablin.* ℘*04 74 58 01 31. www.la-gabetiere.com. 12 rooms.* A beautiful 16C mansion surrounded by a park. Swimming pool.

🍴 EAT

La Chamade – *24 r. Juiverie.* ℘*04 74 85 30 34.* The decor of white walls, yellow tablecloths and indirect lighting is simple, the service efficient and the prices quite affordable.

L'Estancot – *4 r. de la Table-Ronde.* ℘*04 74 85 12 09. Closed Sun–Mon and public holidays.* Interested in trying some *criques*, the delicious Ardéchois potato-pancake dish? Then take a seat in this restaurant. Featured for dinner daily, they can be ordered with vegetables, foie gras or prawns.

La Medina – *71 r. de Bourgogne.* ℘*04 74 53 51 35. www.restaurantmarocain-lamedina.fr.* Here the emphasis is on Morocco; cuisine, decor and furnishings. The perfect place to try a tagine and couscous.

ON THE TOWN

Canicule – *5 r. Cornemuse.* ℘*04 74 59 71 40.* "La canicule" means "the dog days" - will this new cocktail bar succeed in turning up the heat in the rather complacent city of Vienne? In a pretty, exotic setting, you can order sizeable cocktails spiked with varying quantities of alcohol.

Bar du Temple – *5 pl. du Gén.-de-Gaulle.* ℘*04 74 31 94 19. Daily except Sun and public holidays 7am–1am.* This is THE café that everyone who's anyone in Vienne knows about. Its best feature is the superb terrace at the foot of the Temple d'Auguste and de Livie.

O'Donoghue's Pub – *45 r. Francisque-Bonnier.* ℘*04 74 53 67 08. 4pm–3am.* All year round, this Little Brittany in Vienne holds Celtic music concerts attended by a cluster of Breton "ex-pats". If you've never tasted a Coreff, typical Breton beer, this is your chance.

SHOPPING

Markets – On Saturday mornings, the streets of the city centre, from the banks of the Rhône to the Jardin de Cybèle, overflow with market stalls. This is the perfect time to shop for a few bottles of Côte-Rôtie, a delicious Côtes-du-Rhône wine made in the region.

Ets Patissier Jean-Guy – *16 pl. de Miremont.* ℘*04 74 85 08 77. Tue–Sun 8am–7.30pm.* Founded in the 1970s and remodelled in 2000, this pastry shop/tearoom's fine reputation has spread throughout the province. Its chocolate, (made with the finest cocoa beans), pastries (made with grade AA butter), ice cream and cakes are delicious.

THEATRE

Théâtre de Vienne – *4 r. Chantelouve.* ℘*04 74 85 00 05. http://theatredevienne.com.* Built in the early 18C, when Marivaux, Goldoni and Beaumarchais prevailed, this theatre exudes history and charm. Events of all genres are staged here, including drama, classical and pop music, dance, opera and children's shows.

INDEX

INDEX

INDEX

489

INDEX

INDEX

INDEX

INDEX

MAPS AND PLANS

MAP LEGEND

★★★ **Highly recommended**

★★ **Recommended**

★ **Interesting**

Tourism

◉ ⟶	Sightseeing route with departure point indicated	AZ **B**		Map co-ordinates locating sights
🏛 ⚥ 🏛 🏛	Ecclesiastical building	🛈		Tourist information
⬚ 🕌	Synagogue – Mosque	⤚ ⁘		Historic house, castle – Ruins
⬛	Building (with main entrance)	⌣ ☼		Dam – Factory or power station
▪	Statue, small building	☆ ⌓		Fort – Cave
⊥	Wayside cross	🕎		Prehistoric site
◎	Fountain	▼ ♈		Viewing table – View
⟞●⟝▪	Fortified walls – Tower – Gate	▲		Miscellaneous sight

Recreation

🏇	Racecourse	🚶	Waymarked footpath
⛸	Skating rink	◆	Outdoor leisure park/centre
≋ 🖼	Outdoor, indoor swimming pool	🎢	Theme/Amusement park
⬓	Marina, moorings	⋎	Wildlife/Safari park, zoo
⬡	Mountain refuge hut	❀	Gardens, park, arboretum
⬝▪◼▪⬝	Overhead cable-car	◐	Aviary, bird sanctuary
🚂	Tourist or steam railway		

Additional symbols

═ ═	Motorway (unclassified)	✉ ◉	Post office – Telephone centre
❶ ❶	Junction: complete, limited	✉	Covered market
⟞═⟝ ═	Pedestrian street	⁖✕⁖	Barracks
⊥≡≡≡⊥	Unsuitable for traffic, street subject to restrictions	△	Swing bridge
▦ ----	Steps – Footpath	⌣ ✕	Quarry – Mine
🚊 🚌	Railway – Coach station	▣ 🄵	Ferry (river and lake crossings)
□┼┼┼┼□	Funicular – Rack-railway	⛴	Ferry services: Passengers and cars
⟶ ◉	Tram – Metro, underground	⛴	Foot passengers only
Bert (R.)...	Main shopping street	③	Access route number common to MICHELIN maps and town plans

Abbreviations and special symbols

A	Agricultural office (Chambre d'agriculture)		**P**	Local authority offices (Préfecture, sous-préfecture)
C	Chamber of commerce (Chambre de commerce)		**POL.**	Police station (Police)
H	Town hall (Hôtel de ville)		🛡	Police station (Gendarmerie)
J	Law courts (Palais de justice)		**T**	Theatre (Théâtre)
M	Museum (Musée)		**U**	University (Université)
			🅗	Hotel
			🅟	Park and Ride

Some town plans are extracts from plans used in the Green Guides to the regions of France.

travelguide.michelin.com
www.viamichelin.com

MAPS

Regional and local Maps

Motorists who plan ahead will always have the appropriate maps at hand. Michelin products complement each of the sites listed in *The Green Guide*; map references are given to help you find your location on our range of maps.

♦ The regional maps at a scale of 1 : 200 000 **nos 519, 522, 523 and 526**, which cover the main roads and secondary roads, include useful indications for finding tourist attractions. In addition to identifying the nature of the road ways, the maps show castles, churches and other religious edifices, scenic view points, megalithic monuments, swimming beaches on lakes and rivers, swimming pools, golf courses, race-courses, air fields, and more.

♦ The local maps maps at a scale of 1:150 000 and 1:175 000 are the latest maps in our collection. They include useful symbols for identifying tourist attractions, town plans and an index. The map diagram below indicates which maps you need to travel in Auvergne and the Rhône Valley.

Road Map

Remember to travel with the latest edition of the **map of France no 721** (1 : 1 000 000), which gives an overall view of the region, and the main access roads that connect it to the rest of France. Convenient Atlas formats (spiral, hard cover and "mini") are also available.

INTERNET

Michelin offers travellers a route-planning service on the internet: **travelguide.michelin.com www.viamichelin.com**

Choose the shortest route, a route without tolls, or the Michelin recommended route to your destination; you can also access information about hotels and restaurants from the *Michelin Guide France*.

LYON METRO MAP

Caluire Place
Square É. Vignal
Montessuy Fleming
Montessuy Calmette
Mon des S
Cité Interna Centre de C
C1
CUIRE
Impasse Mathieu
Musée d'Art Contempo Centre de Cong
C
Henon
Parc Tête d'Or Pt Churchill
GARE DE VAISE
D
Museum
Croix-Rousse
Parc Tête d'Or Duques
SAÔNE
GARE SAINT-PAUL
Croix-Paquet
Vitton-B
Masséna
La Feuillée
Foch
BROT
Valmy
C3
HÔTEL DE VILLE Louis Pradel
Garibaldi Lafayette
Par Jules
FOURVIÈRE
2
Terreaux
Halles Paul Bocuse
Gorge de Loup
Bât d'Argent
Saxe Lafayette
Part-Dieu Servient
GAR
VIEUX LYON Cath. St-Jean
C
P. de Justice Mairie du 3e
Minimes Théâtres Romains
CORDELIERS
Molière
Viv
FUNICULAIRE
Saxe Préfecture
Place Guichard Bourse du Travail
C
1
BELLECOUR
Liberté
Dépa
SAINT-JUST
GUILLOTIÈRE Gabriel Péri
SAXE GAMBETTA
Ampère Victor Hugo
Saint-André
A
Rue de l'Université
Garibaldi
Ma
PERRACHE
Quai Claude Bernard
Lycée Colbert
T1
Suchet
T2
Centre Berthelot
Garibaldi Berthelot
M
Sainte-Blandine
JEAN MACÉ
Route de Vienne
Hôtel de Région Montrochet
Musée des Confluences
Place Jean Jaurès
JET D'EAU Mendès France
ENS Lyon
Lycée Lumière
Halle Tony Garnier
DEBOURG
Prof Beauvi
T1
Stade de Gerland
B
GARE D'OULLINS
Saint-Fons
Lénine-Corsière
Mau Tho
Darnaise
Vé
Pierre-Bénite
HÔPITAL FEYZIN VÉNISSIEUX
T4
Herric
RHÔNE

B Ligne de métro   T2 C3 Ligne de tramway - Trolleybus Cristalis

Place Foch
C2 RILLIEUX SEMAILLES
RHÔNE
IUT-FEYSSINE
T1
VAULX-EN-VELIN
La Grappinière
C3

Montée
des Soldats
St-Clair-
Square Brosset
Vaulx les Grolières

Internationale
re de Congrès
Cité Internationale
Transbordeur
Croix-Luizet
Mas du Taureau

temporain
e Congrès
Parc Tête d'Or
Stalingrad
INSA-Einstein
LA DOUA GASTON BERGER

Or
rill
Interpol
Université Lyon 1
T4
Lesire

um
Rosselini
Condorcet
Grand Vire

uquesne
Tonkin
Le Tonkin
Hôtel de Ville
Campus

tton-Belges
B
République Villeurbanne
Cuzin Stalingrad

éna
Gratte-Ciel
Flachet
Alain Gilles
Lefèvre

BROTTEAUX
CHARPENNES
Charles Hernu
Cusset
Pont des
Planches

Part-Dieu
Jules Favre
Collège Bellecombe
L. BONNEVAY
Astroballe
VAULX-EN-VELIN
La Soie

THIERS-LAFAYETTE
Ste-Geneviève
Léon
Blum
Décines
Centre

GARE PART-DIEU
T3
Alsace
Cyprian
Léon Blum
Bon Coin
A

u
Vivier Merle
Institut d'Art
Contemporain
Bernaix
Bel Air-
Les Brosses
Décines
Grand Large

t
C1 **C2**
Villette
Poizat
Meyzieu
Gare

ard
ravail
Part-Dieu
Villette Sud
Verlaine
Grandclément
MEYZIEU Z. I.

Archives
Départementales
L. Braille-
Montaland
Blanqui Centre
Mémoires et Société
Gare de
Villeurbanne
MEYZIEU LES PANETTES
T3

Dauphiné
Lacassagne
Reconnaissance Balzac
De Tassigny
Curial
AÉROPORT LYON
SAINT-EXUPÉRY

TA
Boutasse-
Camille Rousset
Les Alizés
PARC
DU CHÊNE

Manufacture-
Montluc
Ambroise
Paré
Essarts-Iris
Lycée
Jean-Paul
Sartre
T5

Sans Souci
T5
Vinatier
Hôtel
de Ville-Bron
Rebufer
EUREXPO

Monplaisir
Lumière
GRANGE BLANCHE
Parilly-Université
Hippodrome

Jean XXIII-
Maryse Bastié
Laënnec
Europe-Université
Parc
Technologique

Villon
Bachut-Mairie du 8e
Mermoz-Pinel
Porte des Alpes

ce
mière
États-Unis
Musée Tony Garnier
Hauts de Feuilly

Professeur
Beauvisage CISL
États-Unis
Viviani
Salvador Allende

Joliot-Curie
Marcel Sembat
Parilly
Alfred de Vigny

Maurice
Thorez
La Borelle
St-Priest Hôtel de Ville

Division Leclerc
GARE DE
VÉNISSIEUX
Esplanade des Arts

Vénissy
D
Jules Ferry

Herriot-Cagne
Croizat-Paul Bert
Cordière

Lycée Jacques Brel
Marcel Houël Hôtel de Ville
T2
ST-PRIEST
BEL AIR

Terminus/correspondance - Station
Tram aéroport "rhônexpress"

Ligne SNCF - Gare
Gare routière - Parking Relais

MICHELIN IS CONTINUALLY INNOVATING FOR SAFER, CLEANER, MORE ECONOMICAL, MORE CONNECTED... BETTER ALL-ROUND MOBILITY.

Tyres wear more quickly on short urban journeys.

?

TRUE!

You tend to accelerate and brake more often when driving around town so your tyres work harder!
If you are stuck in traffic, keep calm and drive slowly.

Tyre pressure only affects your car's safety.

?

FALSE!

Driving with underinflated tyres (0.5 bar below recommended pressure) doesn't just impact handling and fuel consumption, it will shave 8,000 km off tyre lifespan.
Make sure you check tyre pressure about once a month and before you go on holiday or a long journey.

Fitting **2 winter tyres** on my car *guarantees maximum safety.*

?

FALSE!

In the winter, especially when temperatures drop below 7°C, to ensure better road holding, all four tyres should be identical and fitted at the same time.

2 WINTER TYRES ONLY =
risk of compromised road holding.

4 WINTER TYRES =
safer handling when cornering, driving downhill and braking.

If you regularly encounter rain, snow or black ice, choose a **MICHELIN Alpin tyre**. This range offers you sharp handling plus a comfortable ride to safely face the challenge of winter driving.

MICHELIN

MICHELIN IS COMMITTED

▶ MICHELIN IS **GLOBAL LEADER IN FUEL-EFFICIENT TYRES** FOR LIGHT VEHICLES.

▶ *EDUCATING OF YOUNGSTERS IN ROAD SAFETY,* NOT FORGETTING TWO-WHEELERS. LOCAL ROAD SAFETY CAMPAIGNS WERE RUN IN **16 COUNTRIES** IN 2015.

QUIZ

1 TYRES ARE BLACK SO WHY IS THE MICHELIN MAN WHITE?

Back in 1898 when the Michelin Man was first created from a stack of tyres, they were made of natural rubber, cotton and sulphur and were therefore light-coloured. The composition of tyres did not change until after the First World War when carbon black was introduced. But the Michelin Man kept his colour!

2 FOR HOW LONG HAS MICHELIN BEEN GUIDING TRAVELLERS?

Since 1900. When the MICHELIN guide was published at the turn of the century, it was claimed that it would last for a hundred years. It's still around today and remains a reference with new editions and online restaurant listings in a number of countries.

3 WHEN WAS THE "BIB GOURMAND" INTRODUCED IN THE MICHELIN GUIDE?

The symbol was created in 1997 but as early as 1954 the MICHELIN guide was recommending "exceptional good food at moderate prices". Today, it features on the MICHELIN Restaurants website and app.

If you want to enjoy a fun day out and find out more about Michelin, why not visit the l'Aventure Michelin museum and shop in Clermont-Ferrand, France:

www.laventuremichelin.com